Genealogical Events
from
Newspapers for Crawford, Vernon and Grant Counties, Wisconsin
1870-1901

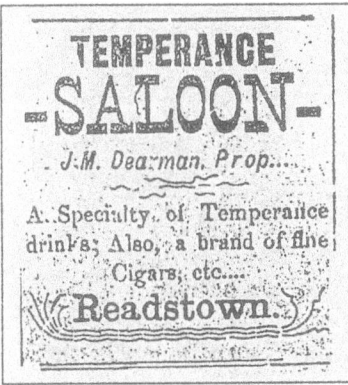

Compiled by
Vernon D. Erickson

HERITAGE BOOKS
2008

HERITAGE BOOKS
AN IMPRINT OF HERITAGE BOOKS, INC.

Books, CDs, and more—Worldwide

For our listing of thousands of titles see our website
at
www.HeritageBooks.com

Published 2008 by
HERITAGE BOOKS, INC.
Publishing Division
100 Railroad Ave. #104
Westminster, Maryland 21157

Copyright © Vernon D. Erickson

Other books by the author:
Genealogical Gleanings From Early Newspapers For Residents In and Near Crawford Co Wisconsin , 1897-1902
Births, Deaths, Marriages and Other Genealogical Gleanings From Newspapers for Crawford, Vernon and Richland Counties, Wisconsin, 1873-1910

All rights reserved. No part of this book may be reproduced or transmitted in any form or by any means, electronic or mechanical, including photocopying, recording or by any information storage and retrieval system without written permission from the author, except for the inclusion of brief quotations in a review.

International Standard Book Numbers
Paperbound: 978-0-7884-1938-6
Clothbound: 978-0-7884-7033-2

Dedicated to my brothers and sister,

Alan Scott Erickson,

Jeffery Brian Erickson

and

Barbara Marie Erickson Zembles

Table of Contents

Dedication	iii
Introduction	vii
Genealogical and Historical Abstracts from Newspapers	1
Newspaper Articles of Genealogical and Historical Interest	199
Organization of a Voluntary Military Company in Boscobel, WI	201
Civil War Soldiers Residing in the Boscobel Area	203
The Reunion, What Boscobel Did to Entertain the Soldier Visitors	205
Boscobel Area Civil War Pensioners	214
List of Members Belonging to James Mason Post No. 106, G.A.R., De Soto, WI	217
Vernon County Teachers	218
The Live Teachers	221
List of Voters of the Town of Wheatland, Vernon County	223
People's County Convention	225
De Soto Plum History	226
Christian Temperance Union	227
National Christian Temperance Union Activity in the Boscobel, Wisconsin Area	230
Appendix 1 – Maps	233
Appendix 2 – Gazetteer	235
Appendix 3 – Newspapers Researched for this Project	239
Appendix 4 – Southwestern Wisconsin Ministers Mentioned in Local Newspapers, 1870 – 1910	241
Index	247

Genealogical Events from Newspapers for Crawford, Vernon and Grant Counties, Wisconsin, 1870-1901

Introduction

Despite the flood of interest on the Internet by people researching their family history, there are few primary and secondary sources available to individuals exploring their roots in southwestern Wisconsin. Foremost, this book was prepared to help fill that void. Outside of a few local history books, which are difficult to access in most parts of the country, little of genealogical significance has been published for people investigating their ties to the early settlers of this region. While the Internet has made a lot of vital records and genealogies available to the public, the accuracy of that information is often doubtful. A lot of undocumented data is being downloaded and people are not able to substantiate the names they claim on their family tree. Second, the information is meant to tell us about our ancestor's interests and activities and give us a sense for the personalities of these people. Family history is more than names and dates on a series of charts. And last, the book is meant to help family historians get past "dead ends" in their research by uncovering clues for new avenues to investigate.

This volume is the third in a series of books on genealogical data abstracted from early newspapers published in Vernon, Crawford and Grant Counties, Wisconsin. After making slight modifications to the format used in the earlier books, I was able to get more citations and names on each page. This book contains over 7,300 citations. They have been culled from area newspapers that were published between 1870 and 1901. These newspapers were especially rich in local news. Over 13,500 people are mentioned in the entries. Of course, some people are mentioned several times in the book. The citations give information on people throughout southwestern Wisconsin, especially western and southern Vernon County, northern and southern Crawford County and northern Grant County. There are also a sizeable number of citations for people in the Lansing, Iowa area. The newspapers abstracted for this book were published in De Soto (on the Vernon/Crawford County border), Readstown (southern Vernon County), Boscobel (northern Grant County and Wauzeka (southern Crawford County). The use of correspondents from neighboring small towns assured considerable coverage of local news. My first book of newspaper abstracts (*Births, Deaths, Marriages and Other Genealogical Gleanings From Newspapers for Crawford, Vernon and Richland Counties, Wisconsin, 1873-1910*) had extensive coverage of northern parts of Crawford County. The second book (*Genealogical Gleanings From Early Newspapers for Residents In and Near Crawford County, Wisconsin, 1897-1902*) is especially useful to people researching ancestors in central and southern Crawford County.

A wide variety of data has been included in this book. As expected, I have abstracted birth, death and marriage announcements. Since vital records were not consistently recorded in Wisconsin until 1907, these citations supplement the official records. A great deal of the local news items in early, small-town newspapers recorded who was sick and who visited whom. This can be useful information, as it may help establish family ties between people. Some of this data has been included in this book. I have also culled out data on:

- pensions
- teachers
- adoptions
- family reunions
- immigrants/emigrants
- crime
- military service
- military campaigns (e.g. Black Hawk War)
- probate hearings
- auctions
- real estate sales
- election results
- schools
- churches
- desertions by spouses
- recipients of county aid
- quarantines
- funerals
- sanity hearings
- anniversaries
- civic organizations
- divorces
- fires
- accidents

Genealogical Events from Newspapers for Crawford, Vernon and Grant Counties, Wisconsin, 1870-1901

- patents
- settlement and village history
- occupations
- business ownership
- social movements (e.g. temperance)
- transportation (e.g. steamboats)
- relations with Native Americans

The citations are organized by surname, given name, source code (a newspaper abbreviation followed by page number, column number and date of publication) and the event. The surnames are alphabetized according to the primary individual mentioned in each citation. Spouses for marriage announcements are cross-indexed. Many citations reference additional people, so an everyname surname index has been prepared. Please take the time to use this index as many citations include lists of people and it was not practical to give each person a separate entry in the book. Also, please notice that information surrounded by brackets in the event column contains notes provided by the author. The abbreviation, Supp., has been used to indicate that information was abstracted from a newspapers' supplement. The second section of the book contains several newspaper articles that were copied in whole or in part. In some cases, this will help researchers discover kinship or other relationships among the people mentioned in the articles. The appendix contains maps, a gazetteer, a list of the newspapers used in this book and a list of ministers and their religious affiliations.

Researchers should be creative when trying to find a surname in the book. The spelling of many surnames changed over time and in earlier years many educated people, including newspaper editors, were not concerned about the use of accurate, standard spelling. I have attempted to abstract data I thought would be of genealogical significance, but I am sure I missed many items that would be useful. It may be worthwhile for others to review the newspapers, too. Also, be aware that the newspaper may have printed inaccurate or misleading news (and I may have made an error when compiling or typing the information). For example, there are numerous entries in the book that tell the readers about people who went west. "Going west" could have meant an individual: 1) relocated for seasonal or temporary work (harvesting crops in the Dakotas or laying track for the railroad); 2) went on vacation; 3) searched for cheap, fertile farm land; or 4) sold his possessions in Wisconsin and emigrated to another state or territory. Many family trees contain a few sinners among the saints. Nonetheless, keep in mind that not all people who were charged with a crime were guilty, nor were all individuals found insane by the courts mentally disturbed. Please consider researching newspapers in nearby towns and even adjacent counties when looking for data on your ancestors. Many genealogists have found useful information in unexpected places, so do not limit your search efforts to newspapers published in the immediate area of your ancestors residence. Finally, keep in mind that this data comes from secondary sources. In the absence of primary sources, it is important to base research conclusions on the preponderance of evidence. Do not accept a single newspaper citation as authoritative. When possible, find other secondary sources to establish a research conclusion.

Researchers may want to contact the Lower Wisconsin River Genealogical and Historical Research Center at P.O. Box 202, Wauzeka, Wisconsin 53826. Their website can be found at www.mwt.net/~bcobe/genealogy.html. The group (usually called the LWR) has a growing collection of genealogy reference materials. Many of their resources are one-of-a-kind or difficult to access. The LWR started a newspaper abstraction program several years ago that focuses on vital records from early newspapers published in Prairie du Chien, Wauzeka and Boscobel. They also have microfilmed copies of old *Kickapoo Chief*, *Kickapoo Papoose*, *Wauzeka Chief* and *Wauzeka Kickapoo Chief* newspapers. As a service to the genealogy public, the LWR will make copies of newspaper articles for a $3.00 fee. The LWR also has several publications for sale, including *Index to Crawford County Marriages, 1816-1866*, compiled by Carol Higgins, and *Crawford County, Wisconsin Birth Records – Earliest to 1907*, compiled by David W. Taft.

Newspaper research is cumbersome and time-consuming; however, it can be very rewarding. The news and town gossip sections may yield valuable information. The newspapers also help the readers appreciate the world their ancestors lived in. It is my hope that this compilation of data will encourage many people to read the original articles abstracted for this book to validate information and peer into that world from which we came.

Vern Erickson
Bellbrook, Ohio

Genealogical Events from Newspapers for Crawford, Vernon and Grant Counties, Wisconsin, 1870-1901

LAST NAME	FIRST NAME	NEWSPAPER, PAGE/COLUMN MONTH/DAY/YEAR	GENEALOGICAL DATA
Ableiter	Albert	BD, p3c1, 9/26/1879	Albert Ableiter married Lizetta Brechler on Sept. 23, 1879 at the German Lutheran Church. Bride and groom from Boscobel.
Ableiter	M.	BD, p3c6, 2/4/1881	Proprietor of the Boscobel Plow Factory.
Ableiter	M.	BD, p3c3, 9/18/1883	In the money demand case M. Ableiter vs Anton Kieren, there was a verdict in favor of the plaintiff in Grant County Circuit Court.
Ableiter	M.	BD, p3c4, 7/27/1877	Offered a reward for a cow that strayed or was stolen. Resided in Boscobel area.
Ableiter	Mr.	BD, p2c6, 10/22/1880	Operated a blacksmith business in Boscobel for the last 15 years. Had 30 years of experience in the business. Mr. Ableiter was one of the pioneer citizens of Boscobel.
Abrams	Delos	BD, p3c2, 5/28/1880	Appointed to be a census enumerator in Little Grant, Grant Co.
Adair	S., Mr.	DC, p1c1, 7/12/1889	Nephew of Rev. Haughton. Visited Retreat on his way to St. Paul. He was a native of Owen's Sound, Ontario.
Adams	Belle	BD, p3c3, 12/14/1877	Belle Adams married Andrew Amos on Nov. 29, 1877 at the home of the bride's father in Algona, IA. Bride formerly lived in Boscobel. She was the sister of Charles Adams of Boscobel. Groom was the son of Dr. Amos of Oshkosh.
Adams	Benjamin	RH, p6c5, 9/2/1897	Benjamin Adams married Rosey Glass at Manning on Aug. 14, 1897. John Benson, J. P. officiated.
Adams	C.	DC, p1c6, 10/29/1887	Recently qualified for a pension for his military service. Resided in Bridgeport.
Adams	Charles	BD, p3c1, 10/6/1882	Resided in Boscobel. Called to Wesley, IA to attend the funeral of his sister, Hattie R. Adams, daughter of G. J. Adams [of Wesley, IA]. Died Sept. 25, 1882 of consumption when she was 18 years, 6 months and 9 days old. She was born in Grant Co. and moved to Algona in 1876.
Adams	Clark	BD, p3c3, 8/11/1882	Lived in Clayton, Crawford Co. Entertained Mrs. Clark Hill of Rock Island, IL, Mrs. Mary McDaniel and Miss Jennie McDaniel of Ohio.
Adams	Cyrus	RH, p5c3, 10/17/1901	From the Readstown Village Proceedings, "On motion and by vote, the name of Cyrus Adams was ordered stricken from the black list."
Adams	D. C.	DC, p3c5, 8/14/1886	Proprietor of a restaurant in Ferryville.
Adams	D. C.	DC, p2c2, 3/19/1887	According to the Ferryville news column, he keeps a supply of ground feed and flour.
Adams	D. D.	DC, p1c2, 6/14/1889	Died June 6, 1889 in Ferryville after an illness that lasted over 2 years.
Adams	David	RH, p5c3, 4/20/1899	David Adams married Miss Amaun on April 11, 1899 at the Methodist Episcopal Church in De Soto, per De Soto news column. Rev. James Jefferson officiated.
Adams	Frank	BD, p2c1, 10/5/1877	Taken to Waupon for a 6-month sentence by Sheriff Birchard. His crime was burglary.
Adams	girl	DC, p3c4, 11/6/1886	A daughter was recently born to Jesse Adams of Retreat.
Adams	girl	RH, p4c2, 11/22/1900	A daughter was recently born to Will Adams of Readstown.
Adams	H. E.	BD, p3c1, 11/27/1883	H. E. Adams recentlly married Frances A. Perrigo. Bride and groom lived in Genoa, NB. Both formerly resided in Boscobel. Groom worked as a bank cashier [in Boscobel or Nebraska].
Adams	Howard	RH, p4c3, 11/14/1901	Howard Adams married May Frazier last week, per the Pleasant Valley news column.
Adams	Josiah	DR, p3c3, 10/26/1871	Killed 2 bears and 10 racoons last week in the De Soto area.
Adams	Milo	DC, p3c5, 9/18/1886	Died Sept. 10, 1886 in Retreat from consumption.
Adams	Minnie	DC, p2c3, 8/27/1887	George Dederick recently married Minnie Adams, per rumor. Groom was the station agent in Ferryville.
Adams	Minnie E.	DC, p1c1, 7/12/1889	W. T. Robertson married Minnie E. Adams on June 30, 1889. Bride and groom from Ferryville. The Rev. C. B. Gordon of Freeman officiated.
Adams	Mr.	BD, p3c3, 9/13/1878	Former proprietor of the Adam's House in Chicago. Visited Dr. Cannon in Boscobel. He was the father-in-law of Will Cannon.
Adams	Mrs.	DC, p2c2, 5/28/1887	Ran a boarding house in Ferryville.
Adams	Mrs.	DC, p1c2, 8/9/1889	Traveled from her home in Ferryville to Dawson, MN to visit her sister.
Adams	Sadie	DC, p3c2, 9/3/1887	Sadie Adams married G. L. Dederick on Aug. 18, 1887 in Ferryville. Bride from Ferryville. Groom was the Ferryville [railroad] station agent. Esquire Davis officiated.

Genealogical Events from Newspapers for Crawford, Vernon and Grant Counties, Wisconsin, 1870-1901

LAST NAME	FIRST NAME	NEWSPAPER, PAGE/COLUMN MONTH/DAY/YEAR	GENEALOGICAL DATA
Adams	W. C. T.	RH, p4c1, 7/15/1897	Became the sole proprietor of *The* [Readstown] *Herald*.
Adams	W. C. T.	RH, p4c2, 7/21/1898	Sold *The* [Readstown] *Herald* to M. A. Andrews and W. H. Maiben.
Adams	W. C. T.	RH, p5c2, 12/1/1898	Hired to take charge of the West Lima schools.
Adams	W. C. T.	RH, p5c2, 12/8/1898	Former principal in Readstown. Hired to teach this winter in West Lima. Will take his degree, B. Ped. [Bachelor of Pedagogy], in Fenton [Michigan] College this winter.
Adams	W. C. T.	RH, p4c2, 9/6/1900	Left Readstown. Accepted a position in Minneapolis at the Archibald Commercial College where he will be Professor of English and Commercial Law. His salary will be $1000 a year.
Adams	W. C. T.	RH, p5c3, 9/20/1900	Wrote a letter describing the business college and his responsibilities at his new position in Minneapolis. It was published in the newspaper.
Adams	W. C. T.	RH, p5c3, 4/11/1901	Newspaper published a letter he wrote in Hunter, ND. He mentioned several Vernon Co. people. Miss Hubbell and Miss Hunter of Viroqua taught school in Hunter. John McAuley buys grain there. Brother, Ray McAuley, lived there.
Adams	William	DR, p1c3, 12/7/1871	"William Adams furnished proof of the loss of tax receipts on SW1/4 of SW1/4 of section 31, town 13, range 6 west, for the year 1857. On motion, the clerk was ordered to cancel the certificate of sale." [Taken from minutes of Vernon County Board of Supervisors.]
Adams	William	DC, p2c2, 9/24/1887	Died Sept. 18, 1887 in Genoa. He was the father of Alfred Adams of Wyoming, IL.
Adams & Hurlbut		RH, p2c1, 7/1/1897	Published the first issue of the *Readstown Herald*.
Adkins	Clara	BD, p3c1, 3/3/1880	John Faris married Clara R. Adkins on Feb. 23, 1880 in Fennimore. Groom from Dakota. Bride from Mount Ida. Otho Shrader officiated.
Adkins	Dinah	BD, p2c2, 3/22/1878	Dinah Adkins and "the Russell girl" were paupers chargeable to the Town of Mount Ida.
Adkins	Levi	RH, p4c2, 5/25/1899	Gertrude McDowell married Levi Adkins on May 22, 1899 at the home of the bride's parents, Mr. and Mrs. M. McDowell of Readstown. Groom from Werley, Grant Co. C. H. Davenport, Justice of the Peace, officiated.
Adson	W. H.	BD, p2c3, 3/31/1882	Lived in Akan. Arrrested in Richland Center on a charge of seduction by Marshall George Spangler.
Aduddell	G. W.	BD, p2c2, 9/26/1879	Advertised an auction sale of farm, tools and stock in Woodman.
Aiken	L. A.	DC, p3c4, 5/7/1887	Owned a mill in Newton.
Aiken	L. A.	DC, p3c3, 11/12/1887	Operated a flouring mill in Newton. Set up bunks in a building for farmers who needed to spend the night. Gave farmers free stable room for their teams
Aiken	V. E.	DC, p3c2, 11/12/1887	V. E. Aiken of Retreat, G. W. Furman and W. S. Cushing of De Soto and A. B. C. Vaughn of Mt. Sterling received increases in their military pension.
Aikens	Al	RH, p5c2, 7/8/1897	Moved his house. It was on the right-of-way of the KV & N Railroad.
Aikens	boy	RH, p4c2, 1/25/1900	A 9½ pound son was recently born to Frank Aikens of Brookville.
Aikens	Dan.	RH, p5c3, 7/29/1897	Planned to return to Oklahoma after an extended visit in Readstown.
Aikens	Elva, Miss	RH, p7c2, 7/1/1897	Left home in Readstown to visit sister, Mrs. Frank Cook of the Viroqua area.
Aikens	Frank, Mrs.	RH, p5c2, 4/21/1898	Resided in Brookville. Visited parents, Mr. and Mrs. Ben Salmon of Readstown.
Aikens	Minnie	RH, p5c3, 6/2/1898	Returned to Readstown from Viroqua where she was learning the millinery trade.
Aikens	Mrs.	RH, p5c3, 1/13/1898	Resided in Readstown. She hosted a visit by her brother-in-law, John Lawrence and Mr. and Mrs. John Ackelberry of Kokomo, IN. They had not seen each other for over 40 years.
Aikins	Charles	RH, p4c2, 10/3/1901	Recently sold his property near Readstown to Taylor Fowell of Sylvan.
Aikins	Dan	RH, p4c2, 8/10/1899	Sold property in Oklahoma so he could move back to Readstown.
Aikins	Frank, Mr. and Mrs.	RH, p4c2, 5/10/1900	Live in Crawfordsville, OR. Visited friends in the Kickapoo Valley, their former home. Since leaving the area, they have lived in several states and territories.
Aikins	G. W.	RH, p4c2, 1/24/1901	G. W. Aikins and wife of Brookville took the train to Grand Junction to help their son-in-law, George Maiben, manage a fruit farm. If they like the area, they may remain there.

Genealogical Events from Newspapers for Crawford, Vernon and Grant Counties, Wisconsin, 1870-1901

LAST NAME	FIRST NAME	NEWSPAPER, PAGE/COLUMN MONTH/DAY/YEAR	GENEALOGICAL DATA
Aikins	George	RH, p5c2, 10/6/1898	He was an old [former?] Readstown boy who had been traveling in the South and West. He and his brother, Will, planned to operate a barbershop in Sparta.
Aikins	Herman	RH, p4c4, 9/15/1898	Wrote a letter describing the Red River Valley of Minnesota. It was published in the newspaper. He was working 18 hours a day helping with the harvest. Wages were $2 a day. Firemen earned $2.50 a day. Engineers received $3 a day.
Aikins	Herman	RH, p4c2, 4/12/1900	Herman Aikins of Brookville married Leota Rogers on April 4, 1900. Groom from Brookville. Bride from Readstown. Rev. Peckham of Springville officiated.
Aikins	Mary, Mrs.	RH, p5c3, 10/13/1898	Visited Readstown and then returned to her home in Greenwood, Clark Co., WI.
Aikins	Minnie	RH, p4c1, 4/27/1899	Minnie Aikins announced the opening of a new millinery shop in Readstown.
Aikins	Minnie	RH, p4c2, 9/6/1900	Minnie Aikins married E. T. Van Winter on Sept. 2, 1900. Bride was the daughter of W. H. Aikins of Kickapoo. Rev. Bell officiated.
Akey	Mattie	BD, p2c3, 2/9/1883	Nellie Akey married L. C. McCollum last Sunday at the home of the bride's parents, Mr. and Mrs. Lemuel Akey of Buena Vista, Richland Co. Groom from Fifield, Price Co., WI. This was a double wedding with Mattie Akey and N. H. Burgor. Groom from Viola. The Rev. Pearce of Richland Center officiated.
Akey	Nellie	BD, p2c3, 2/9/1883	Nellie Akey married L. C. McCollum last Sunday at the home of the bride's parents, Mr. and Mrs. Lemuel Akey of Buena Vista, Richland Co. Groom from Fifield, Price Co., WI. This was a double wedding with Mattie Akey and N. H. Burgor. Groom from Viola. The Rev. Pearce of Richland Center officiated.
Albee	Horace	BD, p3c2, 2/8/1878	Recently died of suicide by cutting his throat. No one knows what drove him to take his life. Lived in Lancaster Township. Lost a son a year ago. Last fall sold his farm to John Zens, intending to move to Michigan. Body found by a neighbor, Alvin Cook. Survived by wife and several small children.
Alcheon	Thomas	BD, p3c3, 8/17/1877	Recently died of consumption. Lived many years in Fennimore [where he was born], but lived in Iowa for the last 4-5 years. He was about 50 years old at death.
Alcorn	George	DC, p3c3, 9/11/1886	Opened a saloon in De Soto.
Alcorn	George	DC, p3c4, 5/7/1887	Received a liquor license in De Soto.
Alcorn	John	DC, p3c2, 11/12/1887	Obtained 600 pounds of honey from 11 bee trees on the islands near De Soto.
Alden	Eliza, Mrs.	BD, p3c3, 9/17/1880	Died Saturday evening. Wife of A. Alden of Boscobel. They moved to Boscobel about 10 years ago. She was born in Freetown, MA in 1811 and married A. Alden in 1826. She was a Baptist. Services were held by Rev. J. C. Kermott. Survived by husband and two sons, Mr. A. H. Alden of Boscobel and another son in Canada.
Alderman		BD, p3c1, 10/8/1880	The 12-year-old daughter of Mr. Alderman was gored in the neck by a cow horn. She was recovering. Family lived on the Kickapoo River at the mouth of Bear Hollow.
Alexander	boy	RH, p4c4, 2/2/1899	A boy was recently born to James and Enia Alexander of Sugar Grove.
Alexander	boy	RH, p4c4, 2/2/1899	A boy was recently born to Grant Alexander of Sugar Grove.
Alexander	boy	RH, p4c4, 2/9/1899	A son of Mr. and Mrs. Grant Alexander of Sugar Grove recently died.
Alexander	Elmer E.	DC, p3c3, 3/5/1887	Arrived from Spokane Falls, Washington Terr. Planned to visit the editor, Fred Z. Alexander.
Alexander	Elmer E.	DC, p3c3, 3/10/1888	Elmer E. Alexander married Bertie Lewis in Spokane Falls on Feb. 22, 1888 at the home of the bride's mother on Third Street. Groom was a miner and former owner of the "Old Dominion." The Rev. W. C. Gray officiated. [per news clip originally published in a Spokane newspaper]
Alexander	F. W.	DC, p3c3, 9/17/1887	Sold a farm near Viroqua to Elihu Cass for $1,100. Will probably go to Nebraska.
Alexander	F. W.	DC, p2c2, 10/22/1887	Planned to have an auction to sell his possessions and then move from Viroqua to Spokane Falls, Washington Territory.
Alexander	F. W.	DC, p2c1, 3/10/1888	Left Spokane. He was discouraged. Currently in Britt, IA.
Alexander	F. W.	DC, p3c4, 7/31/1886	The La Belle Lodge, No. 84, F. & A. M. met at the Masonic Lodge in Viroqua. F. W. Alexander was Secretary. F. W. Van Wagner was W. M.
Alexander	F. Z.	DC, p2c2, 6/26/1886	Prepared a report on the De Soto Union School.
Alexander	Felecia	RH, p5c4, 4/28/1898	Hired to teach at Trout Creek.

Genealogical Events from Newspapers for Crawford, Vernon and Grant Counties, Wisconsin, 1870-1901

LAST NAME	FIRST NAME	NEWSPAPER, PAGE/COLUMN MONTH/DAY/YEAR	GENEALOGICAL DATA
Alexander	Forest	DC, p3c3, 10/2/1888	Returned from the west and rented Rev. William Haughton's farm.
Alexander	Forest W., Mr. and Mrs.	DC, p3c4, 10/29/1887	Mr. and Mrs. Forest W. Alexander, Mrs. E. M. Alexander and Miss Maggie Wolford departed for Spokane Falls, Washington Territory. They were the brother, mother and niece of the F. Z. Alexander, the editor of the *De Soto Chronicle*.
Alexander	Forrest	DC, p2c1, 2/11/1888	Wrote a letter regarding the Spokane, Washington Territory. Published in newspaper.
Alexander	Frank Z.	DC, p3c4, 7/17/1886	Bought the *De Soto Chronicle* from Clemence Comstock.
Alexander	Fred Z.	DC, p3c4, 1/15/1887	Editor of the *De Soto Chronicle*. Acquired a relic of the Black Hawk War from the Battle of the Bad Axe. It was a solid ball of buckshot, about 1 inch in diameter. It was picked it up on the bluff at Battle Creek by Albert Protsman, who gave it to LeGrand Hickok, who used it as a plumb bob.
Alexander	Fred Z.	DC, p3c4, 3/3/1888	Publisher of the *De Soto Chronicle*. Purchased the *News of North La Crosse* with D. O. and P. W. Mahoney. Planned to serve both newspapers from office at 802 Rose Street, North La Crosse.
Alexander	Fred Z.	DC, p2c1, 7/31/1886	Has served as principal of the De Soto schools for the last several years.
Alexander	General	DC, p2c1, 2/5/1887	Participated in the Black Hawk War. He was a progenitor of the Fred Z. Alexander, editor of the *De Soto Chronicle*.
Alexander	Grant	RH, p5c4, 4/28/1898	Grant Alexander married Nettie Hazeltine on April 17, 1898, per Sugar Grove news column.
Alexander	Kittie	RH, p5c4, 11/30/1899	Alex McEathron planned to marry Kittie Alexander tomorrow [Thursday] per the Sugar Grove news column.
Alexander	Kittie, Miss	RH, p5c3, 8/12/1897	Hired to teach in Rusk Creek, Crawford Co. Attended school in Readstown last year.
Alexander	Nettie	RH, p5c4, 4/28/1898	Hired to teach at Rush Creek.
Alexander	Reuben, Mrs.	RH, p4c3, 6/27/1901	Died Monday of heart failure in Sugar Grove. Buried in Sugar Grove Cemetery.
Alexander	Reuben, Mrs.	RH, p4c3, 7/4/1901	Died June 24, 1901 at Sugar Grove. She was born as Hannah Jane Churchill in Knox Co., OH on Nov. 28, 1828. As a child she moved to Indiana, where she later married Reuben Alexander. Moved to Wisconsin in 1856 and settled on a farm 3 miles east of Readstown. Survived by her husband and 4 children -- William, James, Grant [of Sugar Grove] and Mrs. Pettit [of Valley Junction, WI]. Buried in Sugar Grove Cemetery.
Alexander	Spencer L.	DC, p3c3, 5/8/1888	Spencer L. Alexander planned to marry Ella G. Patrick [niece of W. S. Salyer] on May 16, 1888 in Spokane Falls, Washington Territory.
Alford	Lew	BD, p3c1, 11/17/1882	Lew Alford married Esther Graham on Nov. 11, 1882 at the residence of Mr. A. McKinney in Boscobel. Groom from Madison. Bride from Boscobel. J. McLaughlin, Justice of the Peace, officiated.
Allen	Anna C.	BD, p3c4, 12/28/1877	Allan Bell married Anna C. Allen on Tuesday. Groom was from Franklin, PA. Bride was the daughter of J. G. Allen. The Rev. G. W. Nuzum officiated.
Allen	Annie B., Mrs.	DC, p1c2, 4/12/1889	Resigned by letter from the church in Cooley Valley. She lived in La Crosse.
Allen	Dexter E.	DR, p3c3, 12/14/1871	He was a blacksmith in Newton, WI. He had been a blacksmith in western New York for the last 15 years. Wrote a letter to the editor commenting on an earlier article on horseshoeing.
Allen	E., Mrs.	DC, p3c3, 12/24/1887	Buried Saturday in De Soto. Died of lung fever. She was the mother of Mr. I. Sheets.
Allen	George	DC, p2c2, 5/28/1887	George Allen married Miss Kimball on May 8, 1887, per Lynxville news column.
Allen	Hartwell	DC, p3c5, 8/28/1886	He was the former Supt. Of Schools in Vernon Co. He is expected to teach in Mt. Sterling next year.
Allen	J. F.	DC, p3c3, 8/14/1888	Received a $1500 pension [probably backpay] for his military service. Resided in the De Soto area.
Allen	J. Matt	RH, p5c4, 11/11/1897	Lost his barn and granary to fire. Lived in Readstown area.
Allen	Mr.	BD, p3c2, 12/22/1882	Mr. Allen's mill burned down. It was located 3 miles from Boscobel on Richland Creek. Building was insured for $700. Loses estimated at $4000.
Allen	Mrs.	DC, p3c3, 12/18/1886	Visited friends in La Crosse [per Victory news column]. Nee Annie Bean.
Allen	T.	DC, p3c2, 9/11/1886	Returned to De Soto after spending the last year in California.

Genealogical Events from Newspapers for Crawford, Vernon and Grant Counties, Wisconsin, 1870-1901

LAST NAME	FIRST NAME	NEWSPAPER, PAGE/COLUMN MONTH/DAY/YEAR	GENEALOGICAL DATA
Allen	Theo	BD, p3c2, 5/31/1878	Theo Allen recently married Annetta J. Rounds in Gays Mills. The Rev. George Nuzum officiated.
Allison	J., Rev.	BD, p3c3, 10/1/1880	Gave his farewell sermon at Boscobel.
Allison	John, Mrs.	BD, p3c2, 3/31/1882	Died a few weeks ago in Jessup, IA. Originally from Boscobel. [Denied by Prof. John Allison in BD, p3c1, 4/7/1882.]
Allison	John, Rev.	BD, p3c1, 2/14/1879	Named to the pastorship of the Methodist Episcopal Church in Boscobel.
Alsop	Thomas	BD, p3c3, 3/1/1878	Buried in a mine for 46 hours. Recovering with the help of physicians in Dubuque.
Altizer	Raymond	BD, p3c1, 1/19/1883	Died Jan. 8, 1883 in Boscobel. He was 3 years, 19 days old. His parents were Eli and Jane Altizer.
Amaun	Miss	RH, p5c3, 4/20/1899	David Adams married Miss Amaun on April 11, 1899 at the Methodist Episcopal Church in De Soto, per De Soto news column. Rev. James Jefferson officiated.
Ames	A.	DC, p3c4, 10/30/1886	Lived in Fowler's, NB. New subscriber to the *De Soto Chronicle*.
Ames	A. C.	DC, p2c2, 9/3/1887	Left the Cooley Valley for his home in Nebraska where his brother was lying at the point of death.
Ames	A. H.	DC, p2c2, 5/28/1887	"A. H. Ames intends to return home shortly and travel with his invalid brother," per Freeman news column.
Ames	Abe	DC, p3c2, 12/31/1887	Returned to his home in Freeman. Came from Nebraska.
Ames	C. M. and Abb	DC, p3c5, 9/25/1886	Departed Freeman for new homes in Nebraska.
Ames	Mary S.	DC, p3c2, 1/14/1888	Mary S. Ames married Jacob Stussy on Dec. 29, 1887. Bride from Freeman. Groom from Seneca.
Ames	Mr.	DC, p3c4, 5/1/1888	Visited De Soto for the first time in 1852. Recently returned to visit friends in De Soto. Currently resides in Keokuk Co., IA.
Amos	Andrew	BD, p3c3, 12/14/1877	Belle Adams married Andrew Amos on Nov. 29, 1877 at the home of the bride's father in Algona, IA. Bride formerly lived in Boscobel. She was the sister of Charles Adams of Boscobel. Groom was the son of Dr. Amos of Oshkosh.
Amos	Belle	BD, p3c3, 4/19/1878	Died April 6, 1878 of consumption in Algona, IA at the age of 22 years, 9 months and 22 days. She was the wife of Andrew Amos and daughter of George J. and Ellen Adams. Born in June 1855 in Monroe, WI. Moved with parents to Algona in the summer of 1876. Taught school for awhile. Married on Nov. 29, 1877. Andrew Amos was also a teacher.
Amphlett	William	BD, p2c3, 9/16/1881	According to the *Grant County Witness* of Sept. 3rd, "William Amphlett, brother to Mrs. George Potter, of this city, was robbed while on his way from California of $440 in gold. He had carried the money in a belt around his body from the time he left California until he reached Kansas, where, on account of the extreme heat, and intending to stop during the day to visit a relative, he took off the belt and put it in his pocket. Being tired and sleepy he dozed for a few moments, and when he got awake he missed his belt and has not heard from it since. The money represented the savings of a number of years, and the loss falls quite heavily on him."
Amundson	Hans	RH, p5c4, 7/29/1897	Hans Amundson and his cousin, Mr. Grosven, formerly of Vernon Co., departed for Klondyke, Alaska to seek their fortunes.
Ancheutz	Leo, Mr. and Mrs.	BD, p3c3, 6/22/1883	Mr. and Mrs. Kramer of Reading, PA visited with Mr. and Mrs. Leo Ancheutz of Boscobel.
Ancient Order of United Workmen		BD, p3c2, 8/2/1878	The officers of the Boscobel chapter of the Ancient Order of United Workmen were Lou P. Lesler, R. J. Arthur, N. J. Francisco, Henry Walters, R. R. Lesler, H. W. Favor, J. D. Wilson, L. G. Armstrong, Ed Bowers and A. Kieren.
Anderson	Andrew	RH, p4c1, 8/2/1900	Resided in Brookville. Lost his barn and 3 horses to a lightening strike.
Anderson	Annie	BD, p2c5, 9/11/1883	Advertised the sale of the home formerly owned by Martin Anderson on Oak Street in Boscobel.
Anderson	Bessie	BD, p3c3, 6/22/1883	Bessie Anderson and Herbert Henderson returned [to Boscobel?] for the summer break from the Deaf and Dumb Institute.
Anderson	Bessie	RH, p4c4, 6/2/1898	Bessie Anderson, Rosa Crook, Helen Carter, Frank Randall and Arthur Ward graduated from school in Readstown.
Anderson	Chris	DR, p2c3, 5/11/1871	Proprietor of a boot and shoe shop in De Soto.
Anderson	Cora	BD, p3c1, 10/22/1880	Dwight T. Parker, Jr. married Cora Anderson on Oct. 13, 1880 at the home of the bride's father in Ripon. Groom and bride were "well known" in Boscobel.

Genealogical Events from Newspapers for Crawford, Vernon and Grant Counties, Wisconsin, 1870-1901

LAST NAME	FIRST NAME	NEWSPAPER, PAGE/COLUMN MONTH/DAY/YEAR	GENEALOGICAL DATA
Anderson	Dite	BD, p3c1, 12/23/1881	Once again charged with bastardy.
Anderson	Dite	BD, p3c4, 12/30/1881	On trail for bastary. Couldn't make bail, so placed in jail until next term of the court. Town will pay for the care of his children.
Anderson	Dyke	BD, p3c3, 6/10/1881	Resident of Boscobel. Arrested on a charge of bastardy. He was a widower, over 40 years of age and had children. Cora Butler, a 16 year old girl who had been adopted by the Ostranders of Boscobel, claimed Anderson was the only person with whom she had been intimate. She was later seen with two young men at the same time.
Anderson	Emil	DC, p3c3, 8/20/1887	Returned to De Soto after spending the last year in Minneapolis where he attended school and clerked in a grocery.
Anderson	Emil	DC, p3c3, 10/1/1887	Left De Soto. Returned to his studies at Augsburg Seminary in Minnesota.
Anderson	Henry	BD, p3c1, 5/20/1881	Now a merchant in Minnesota. Visited with friends in Boscobel, his former home.
Anderson	Henry, Mrs.	BD, p3c3, 9/4/1883	Mrs. Henry Anderson of Montevido, MN arrived in Boscobel with her three children to visit her father, Mr. A. Palmer.
Anderson	Magnus	DR, p3c4, 4/20/1871	Magnus Anderson married Annette L. Baker on April 13, 1871. Bride and groom from De Soto. Groom may have served in the 27th Iowa Regt. P. A. Steele, J.P., officiated.
Anderson	Martin	BD, p3c2, 9/9/1881	Preparing to move his family from Boscobel to a farm 4 miles from Pochahontas Center, IA.
Anderson	Mary	DC, p2c2, 7/24/1886	Widow of Richard Anderson. Denied a pension by the veto of Pres. Grover Cleveland. Her husband suffered from chronic diarrhea that he picked up in the army. She lived in a log house in the Kickapoo Valley [near Viroqua?]. She was very poor, with 8 children between the ages of 3 and 16 years of age.. Anderson may have committed suicide when he placed his body on a railroad track. He enlised in the army in 1856. Served army in Utah in 1857. Went to New Mexico. In 1861 he went to Texas. Discharged at the close of the war.
Anderson	Mary Elizabeth	BD, p3c2, 2/2/1883	Henry Leoby married Mary Elizabeth Anderson on Dec. 16, 1882. Groom from Prairie du Chien. Bride from Boscobel. The Rev. Charles Schroudenback officiated.
Anderson	Mr.	BD, p2c3, 7/1/1881	Formerly of Boscobel. Died June 25, 1881 in Ripon, WI at age 87. Father of Robert Anderson. Served in the War of 1812. Built ships for Perry's fleet on Lake Erie. Moved to Boscobel in 1867 and to Ripon 3 years ago.
Anderson	Ole	RH, p4c2, 9/13/1900	Helen Perham married Ole Anderson on Sept. 9, 1900. Bride and groom from Readstown. Rev. G. W. Nuzum of Viroqua officiated.
Anderson	Olof	BD, p3c1, 3/3/1882	Died Feb. 20, 1882 at age 9 of billious fever. He was the son of Mr. S. Anderson of Boscobel.
Anderson	Oscar	RH, p4c1, 5/9/1901	Resided in Liberty Pole. Opened a furniture store in Readstown. He was the brother of George Anderson of Towerville. Oscar has been in Chicago for the last few years, per RH, p4c2, 5/16/1901.
Anderson	Robert	BD, p2c3, 11/12/1880	Petitioned the Grant County Courts to be named administrator of the Thomas J. Anderson estate.
Anderson	Robert	BD, p2c3, 12/9/1881	Anderson was 11 or 12 years old. He saved the lives of Joseph Lawler and 2 other boys who fell through the ice near the mouth of the St. Feriole in Prairie du Chien on Thanksgiving Day. Joseph was the son of John Lawler.
Anderson	S.	BD, p2c5, 10/22/1880	Manufactured boots and shoes in Boscobel. Opened his business 5 years ago. Had 15 years experience in the business.
Anderson	S.	BD, p2c8, 1/5/1877	S. Anderson & Co. was a boot and shoe store in Boscobel.
Anderson	Sever	BD, p3c1, 5/4/1883	Left Boscobel on a trip to Dakota to look after his interests there. He planned to return to Boscobel to attend to his shoemaking business.
Anderson	T. J., Major	BD, p3c2, 11/29/1878	Committed suicide Monday night and died Tuesday morning. Mrs. Anderson died Sunday. He was inconsolable. Monday evening's watchers were John Brindley, Arthur Nixon and Mattie Barnett. They sat in the kitchen and decided to go upstairs to the room that contained the body of Mrs. Anderson. Mrs. Delany, daughter of Mrs. Anderson, joined them. At that time they heard a noise downstairs and then groans in the locked storeroom. Noise came from two balls from a revolver.
Andrew	George	RH, p5c4, 11/3/1898	Father of Dr. and Miss Fannie Andrew. Returned home from Jacksonville, FL after spending the summer in the South, per De Soto news column.
Andrews	Ben	RH, p5c2, 11/11/1897	Moved from Kickapoo Center to the Bliss Building in Readstown.
Andrews	Ben, Mrs.	RH, p4c3, 4/14/1898	Tom Sandmire of Corwin was in Readstown to visit his daughter, Mrs. Ben Andrews.

Genealogical Events from Newspapers for Crawford, Vernon and Grant Counties, Wisconsin, 1870-1901

LAST NAME	FIRST NAME	NEWSPAPER, PAGE/COLUMN MONTH/DAY/YEAR	GENEALOGICAL DATA
Andrews	boy	RH, p4c1, 7/25/1901	A son was born last Friday to Ben Andrews of Readstown.
Andrews	H. C.	RH, p5c4, 1/20/1898	"Mr. H. C. Andrews was called to Viola on account of the illness of her father Mr. H. B. Hopkins." [This probably refers to Mrs. Andrews. Taken from the Kickapoo Center news column.]
Andrews	H. C., Mrs.	RH, p5c4, 1/20/1898	Called to Readstown because of the illness of Ben Andrew's child who was sick with lung fever, per Kickapoo Center news column.
Andrews	Keith	RH, p4c1, 11/23/1899	Resided in Kickapoo. Serving as an apprentice with the tin shop of Davenport Bros.
Andrews	M. A.	RH, p4c1, 3/23/1899	M. A. Andrews and William Crook of Readstown lost 40 ponies during the flood.
Andrews	M. A.	RH, p4c2, 1/4/1900	M. A. Andrews married Miss C. E. Mackie on Dec. 25, 1899 at the home of the bride's mother. Groom was the Town Treasurer in Readstown for many years. He was also the depot agent, Secretary and Treasurer for Readstown Broom Company and President of Readstown Telephone Company. Bride lived at 37 Elm Street, Toronto, Canada.
Andrews	M. A., Mrs.	RH, p4c2, 12/20/1900	Returned to Readstown from Toronto, Canada, where she has been the last 6 weeks during her mother's sickness.
Andrews	Morley	RH, p5c2, 10/7/1897	Resident of Kickapoo. Worked as the railroad stationmaster in Readstown.
Andrews	Morley	RH, p5c2, 12/16/1897	Wanted to buy all kinds of poultry at the highest market price in cash in Readstown.
Andrews	Sabra	RH, p5c3, 3/22/1900	Paul Lange married Sabra Andrews on March 18, 1900. Bride and groom were from Kickapoo.
Andrews	Sabra	RH, p5c4, 3/22/1900	Paul Lange married Sabra Andrews on March 11, 1900. C. H. Davenport officiated at the ceremony.
Andrews	Thomas, Captain	BD, p2c4, 4/9/1880	Born April 23, 1822 in Adams Co., IL. Emigrated with widowed mother to Iowa Co., WI in 1834. Moved to Richland Co. in 1843. Settled at Port Andrew. Died about March 27, 1880. Leaves a wife and two daughters, Mrs. Ransom Powers of Port Andrew and Mrs. T. P. Logan of Excelsior. Andrews first worked as a farmer. He brought the first span of horses into the county and raised the first corn. Soon became a river pilot. Bought the steamer, *Wisconsin*, in 1860. Sold it and built the *Zouave*. Sold it. Engaged in railroad tie trade until last fall.
Andrews	William	BD, p3c2, 5/11/1877	The William Andrews home in Mt. Ida was destroyed by fire on April 21, 1877.
Angell	Allen	DC, p1c4, 5/3/1889	Resided in Stoddard. Called home last week. His father died.
Angell	Charles	RH, p5c2, 8/5/1897	Left Readstown for Dakota to help with the harvest.
Angell	Charles	RH, p5c4, 6/9/1898	Planned to build a blacksmith shop on a lot in Readstown purchased from Duncan Cade.
Angell	Charles	RH, p4c1, 6/15/1899	Charles Angell and Frank Rowe received saloon licenses in Readstown.
Angell	Charles	RH, p4c2, 1/3/1901	Sold his saloon in Readstown to George Dowse [also spelled Douse].
Angell	Ed	DC, p3c2, 12/11/1888	Maggie Joseph married Ed Angell on Nov. 29, 1888 at home of the bride's brother, William Joseph of Cooley Valley. Groom son of Robert Angell. Planned to live in Michigan. [and p3c4, 12/18/1888] Rev. William Haughton officiated.
Angell	Ellis	RH, p5c2, 1/20/1898	Ellis Angell and family of Harpers Ferry, IA spent New Years with Mr. Angell's brother in Readstown.
Angell	Frank	DC, p1c2, 5/31/1889	Frank Angell and his bride left the Cooley Valley for a new home in St. Charles, IL.
Angell	George and Ed.	DC, p2c3, 10/29/1887	Returned to De Soto after "a summer's campaign in the north."
Angell	George N.	DC, p3c2, 11/19/1887	Eliza M. Foster married Willie Haverley on Nov. 25, 1887 at the residence of William Haverley of Red Mound. It was a double ceremony. Francis Haverley married George N. Angell, too.
Angell	George T.	RH, p4c3, 4/11/1901	Newspaper published his essay that advocated the establishment of mortuarires to prevent premature burials. "My own father barely escaped such burial, being declared by his physician dead."
Angell	George, Mr. and Mrs.	DC, p3c2, 12/10/1887	Left for Waucedah, MI.
Angell	Mr. and Mrs.	DC, p2c2, 5/21/1887	Celebrated their silver wedding on May 11, 1887 at their home in the Cooley Valley.

Genealogical Events from Newspapers for Crawford, Vernon and Grant Counties, Wisconsin, 1870-1901

LAST NAME	FIRST NAME	NEWSPAPER, PAGE/COLUMN MONTH/DAY/YEAR	GENEALOGICAL DATA
Angell	Nellie	DC, p2c2, 2/11/1888	Resided in Cooley Valley. Planned to partner with Mrs. Maggie Joseph in De Soto to make dresses.
Ankeny		DC, p2c1, 11/26/1887	In 1856 or 1857 the De Soto firm of Ankeny & Townsend was dissolved and replaced by Ankeny & Ochiltree.
Ankeny	Emma	DR, p3c2, 12/7/1871	George D. McDill married Emma Ankeny on Nov. 25, 1871 at the parsonage by Rev. J. M. Mitchell. Bride and groom were from De Soto.
Ankeny	T. C.	DR, p1c1, 12/15/1870	Advertised his services as an attorney in De Soto.
Ankeny	T. C.	DR, p1c3, 12/29/1870	Resided in De Soto. Wrote a letter that was published in newspaper advising farmers to open new farms on cheaper land in Vernon County or northern Crawford County rather than move to Iowa or Kansas.
Ankeny	T. C.	DR, p3c2, 12/29/1870	Operated a law office and collection agency in De Soto. Mr. Ankeny is so busy he scarely has time to take his meals. George McDill assists him.
Ankeny	T. C.	DR, p2c2, 11/2/1871	Resided in De Soto. He was an independent candidate for senator from his district.
Ankeny	T. C.	DC, p2c1, 1/21/1888	Lived in Dickson, TN. Wrote a letter that was published in the newspaper expressing his appreciation for the series written by C. B. Whitting on the early settlers of De Soto.
Ankeny & Co.		DR, p3c3, 9/21/1871	Carlyle, Douse & Co. and Ankeny & Co. were the only merchants in De Soto in 1856.
Ankeny & Townsend		DC, p2c2, 10/29/1887	In 1856 they operated a store half-way up the hill in De Soto.
Anschuetz	Leo.	BD, p2c7, 10/22/1880	Operated a photography studio in Boscobel for the last 19 years.
Anthwerp	Van, Mrs.	BD, p3c2, 5/27/1881	Arrived from out-of-town to visit her daughter, Mrs. George C. Hazelton of Boscobel.
Appleby	Mrs.	DC, p1c1, 5/31/1889	Mrs. Appleby of Sparta visited her sister, Mrs. Latimer of Genoa.
Arenndo	Jane Roena	DR, p3c2, 9/21/1871	Died Aug. 19, 1871 in the Town of Genoa when she was 2 months and 18 days old. Daughter of George and Mrs. Arenndo.
Arms	J. R., Mrs.	DC, p1c6, 10/8/1887	Resided in Boscobel. Qualified for a pension for deceased husband's military service.
Armstrong	"Uncle Sam"	DC, p3c4, 8/21/1886	Operated a hotel in Lynxville.
Armstrong	Charles	BD, p3c1, 9/10/1880	Left Boscobel to attend the State University in Madison.
Armstrong	Charles	BD, p3c2, 12/9/1881	Attended college in Milton. Returned to Boscobel.
Armstrong	L. G., Dr.	BD, p3c2, 5/28/1880	Dr. L. G. Armstrong and his brother-in-law, Mr. Ames of Brodhead [formerly of Boscobel], visited their farming interests in Iowa.
Armstrong	S., Mrs.	DC, p2c2, 5/28/1887	Mrs. Crolmbeck of Winona, MN spent a few days with her aunt, Mrs. S. Armstrong, per Lynxville news column.
Armstrong	Samuel	DC, p2c1, 8/21/1888	Resided in Lynxville. Received a pension for his military service.
Arneson	Martha	DC, p3c2, 6/19/1886	Martha Arneson married George Golden on June 15, 1886. Bride from Sterling. Groom from Baraboo. Justice M. Loftus officiated.
Arneson	Mr.	DC, p3c2, 12/3/1887	Miss Lund married Mr. Arneson on Thanksgiving Day at Purdy. "Miss Lund's mother was present from Chicago where she lives in affluence."
Arnold	Harry	DC, p3c3, 11/12/1887	Left Cooley Valley on Tuesday for Crystal Falls, MI.
Arnold	Henry	DC, p3c3, 9/17/1887	Left Viola with his family by steamboat for Arkansas.
Arnold	O. J.	BD, p3c2, 5/28/1880	Appointed to be a census enumerator in Mt. Ida, Grant Co.
Arnold	Samuel, Jr.	DC, p1c2, 4/12/1889	Joined the church in Cooley Valley.
Arnold	Sarah	DC, p1c2, 4/12/1889	Miss Sarah Arnold returned to the Cooley Valley after a 2-year absence in St. Charles.
Arthur	Robert	BD, p3c2, 7/15/1881	Lived in Boscobel. Mother, Mrs. Robert Arthur of Ishpeming, MI, and sister, Mrs. M. M. Bacon of Milwaukee, arrived for a visit.
Arthur	Robert J., Mr. and Mrs.	BD, p3c1, 3/28/1879	An infant daughter of Mr. and Mrs. Robert Arthur of the Boscobel area died Monday.

Genealogical Events from Newspapers for Crawford, Vernon and Grant Counties, Wisconsin, 1870-1901

LAST NAME	FIRST NAME	NEWSPAPER, PAGE/COLUMN MONTH/DAY/YEAR	GENEALOGICAL DATA
Asbury	Isaac, Mr. and Mrs.	DC, p3c3, 9/4/1888	Arrived from their home in Martinsburg, NB to visit Mrs. Asbury's parents, Mr. and Mrs. William Stevenson of the De Soto area.
Asbury	Mrs.	RH, p4c1, 9/20/1900	Mrs. Asbury of Pleasant Ridge was in Readstown to see her brother, Alfred Davenport, who is recovering from typhoid fever. She was also a sister of A. S. and C. H. Davenport.
Asbury	Richard	DR, p3c1, 3/23/1871	Resided near Victory, WI. Planned to hold a public sale of his stock and farm implements.
Asbury	Thomas	DC, p3c3, 1/7/1888	Pension [for military service] application increase was approved. Lived in Victory.
Asbury	Vina, Miss	DC, p8c2, 6/21/1889	Visited sister, Mrs. C. B. Upham of De Soto.
Asheley	Mary R.	BD, p3c1, 12/26/1879	Zack Barnard recently married Mary R. Asheley at the residence of the bride's father in Avoca. Groom from Arena. The Rev. William Stoddart officiated.
Ashmore	James	BD, p2c4, 5/18/1883	Published a notice that the public should not trust his wife, Louisa, or any of his family without a written order from him as he will not pay their bills.
Ashmore	Jeff	BD, p3c4, 2/22/1878	Pleaded guilty to horse stealing in Grant Co. Circuit Court.
Ashmore	Jerry, Mrs.	BD, p3c2, 7/20/1883	Filed suit against her husband for assault and battery. Suit was dismissed due to the conflicting testimony of witnesses. A divorce was pending.
Auel	Mr.	BD, p2c2, 7/13/1877	Mr. Auel was recently shot by Mr. Meyers at Highland. He was expected to recover.
Austin	Ed	BD, p2c3, 5/26/1882	Served in Co. H., 5th WI Regt. during the Civil War. Killed early in the war. From Richland Co.
Austin	Edward A.	BD, p3c1, 1/16/1880	Married Nellie Smith on Dec. 25, 1879 in Boscobel. Bride and groom from Town of Marion. J. McLaughlin, Esq. officiated.
Avery	Mr.	BD, p3c3, 9/19/1879	On Friday evening, after the funeral of Mr. Avery, 3 persons entered the Excelsior home of Avery to take his valuables. Frank Avery, son of the deceased, was upstairs with a revolver when the intruders arrived. Three beehives were taken from the yard.
Babcock	John D.	DC, p2c3, 2/19/1889	Had charge of Fred Eckhard's grain and stock business in De Soto.
Babcock	Liberty, Mrs.	DC, p3c2, 1/22/1889	Found dead Thursday at home of her daughter, Mrs. William Green. Survived by 3 children. She was 74 years old. Remains taken to the cemetery on Lawrence Ridge.
Bachman	August	DR, p3c4, 9/21/1871	Held for a bond of $4000 for the murder of Jerry Black at Bachman's saloon in Chaseburg.
Bachman	Augusta	DR, p3c4, 9/21/1871	Wife of August Bachman. Held for $4000 bail [with her husband] for the death of Jerry Black.
Bagley	D. L.	BD, p2c4, 11/26/1880	Grant County paid him a bounty for scalps turned into the county.
Bailey	E.	DC, p1c3, 5/3/1889	E. Bailey married Jane Riley on April 26, 1889. Groom worked at C. M. & St. Paul Railroad. He was from Minneapolis. Bride from Genoa. Planned to live in Minneapolis. M. Monti, Esquire officiated.
Bailey	E.	BD, p3c3, 1/3/1879	Killed by a bull in Platteville on Christmas morning. Mrs. Bailey was in New York.
Bailey	Ella	BD, p3c3, 12/3/1880	Ed R. Bishop married Ella Bailey on Oct. 24, 1880 in Lena, OR. Groom from Pendleton, Umatilla Co., OR. Bride from Batter Creek, formerly from Boscobel. She was daughter of James Bailey.
Bailey	Emma	BD, p3c1, 6/24/1881	The Boscobel High School Class of 1881 graduates were Emma Bailey, Minnie Walker, Anna Anderson, Mina Brekke, Nettie Van Buren and C. F. Menkhausen.
Bailey	H. T.	BD, p2c3, 12/30/1881	The H. T. Baileystore in Richland Center was ransacked Monday night.
Bailey	James	BD, p3c2, 7/29/1881	James Bailey and son purchased the woolen mills in Boscobel from Mr. Muffley for a little less than $2400.
Bailey	James	BD, p3c3, 10/23/1883	Returned to Boscobel. Spent the last 3 months driving cattle from Ellendale, Dakota to Northwestern British Possessions in Canada.
Bailey	James	BD, p3c2, 5/11/1877	Left Boscobel for the Black Hills.
Bailey	James	BD, p3c4, 8/29/1879	James Bailey married Lucretia Folyer last Friday and then deserted her upon the advice of Lucretia's doctor. [Implied that Lucretia was pregnant.] Bride and groom from Hickery Grove.
Bailey	Jim	BD, p3c3, 6/10/1881	Jim Bailey and Mr. Starr of Boscobel were recently trapped on an island in the Wisconsin River after the water rapidly rose. [Interesting story.]
Bailey	Mark	BD, p3c3, 3/23/1877	Former resident of Boscobel. Now a member of the Dakota legislature where he represented Lincoln Co. Educated as an attorney.

Genealogical Events from Newspapers for Crawford, Vernon and Grant Counties, Wisconsin, 1870-1901

LAST NAME	FIRST NAME	NEWSPAPER, PAGE/COLUMN MONTH/DAY/YEAR	GENEALOGICAL DATA
Bailey	Mark W.	BD, p3c4, 11/22/1878	Died Nov. 15, 1878 at the home of his father in Fennimore as he was surrounded by his family. Reared in the Boscobel area. Most recently, resident of Canton, Dakota. Aged 30 years. Taught school for awhile. Became an attorney. Left Wisconsin 7 years ago for Dakota. Died of consumption. Elected to Dakota Territorial Senate in 1876.
Bailey	Thomas	BD, p3c1, 12/4/1883	Thomas Bailey married Emma Mann on Dec. 2, 1883 in Prairie du Chien. Groom from Boscobel. Bride from Prairie du Chien.
Bailey	Tom	BD, p3c2, 11/14/1879	Lost a toe while working in a cooper shop. He dropped an adz on his foot. Resided in Boscobel.
Bailey	Walter W.	BD, p2c3, 7/8/1881	Died Saturday night in Richland Center. Brother of H. T. Bailey.
Baker	Amanda	BD, p2c5, 1/17/1879	The Grant County Circuit Court published a Summons for Relief in the case, Amanda Baker, plaintiff, vs. George Baker, defendant.
Baker	Annette L.	DR, p3c4, 4/20/1871	Magnus Anderson married Annette L. Baker on April 13, 1871. Bride and groom from De Soto. Groom may have served in the 27th Iowa Regt. P. A. Steele, J.P., officiated.
Baker	C. J., Mrs.	RH, p5c3, 9/30/1897	Returned from Minneapolis to visit parents, Mr. and Mrs. Craigo of Readstown.
Baker	C. M.	DC, p2c1, 1/22/1887	During the Black Hawk War, the Gen. Atkinson's troops trailed Black Hawk to the Kickapoo River. They passed through C. M. Baker's property in Soldiers Grove where they found a body of pine timber.
Baker	Charles, Mrs.	RH, p4c2, 7/5/1900	Arrived in Readstown from Harmony, SD. Visited parents, Mr. and Mrs. J. M. Craigo.
Baker	Jesse	BD, p2c3, 7/21/1882	Lived in Readstown. Accidently shot last Sunday by his brother-in-law while hunting in the woods. He died [per *Crawford Co. Journal*, 7/12/1882]. He was a businessman. Remains buried in Viola.
Baker	Joe, Mrs.	DC, p3c3, 3/19/1887	Arrived from Mayville, Dakota to visit friends in De Soto.
Baker	John	BD, p3c3, 9/20/1878	John Baker married Mary M. Robinson on Sept. 11, 1878 in Boscobel. Groom from Pleasant Hill, Richland Co. The Rev. Dr. Stoddart officiated.
Baker	Orrin	DR, p3c2, 12/29/1870	Operated a grocery store in De Soto.
Baker	Orrin, Jr.	DR, p3c3, 5/4/1871	Recently deceased. Notice published by Mrs. Rosie L. Baker. Persons owing debts to the estate were asked to settle their accounts. Past due accounts were going to be given to T. C. Ankeny to collect.
Baker	Will	DC, p8c2, 6/21/1889	Replaced Will Kalhar as clerk in the W. F. Davidson store in De Soto.
Balch	M. B., Mrs.	DC, p3c3, 6/19/1888	Miss Millie Monroe of Green Co., sister of Mrs. M. B. Balch, organized an auxillary to the Christian Woman's Board of Mission at Viroqua.
Balch	Mr.	DC, p3c4, 11/13/1886	Served as librarian for the De Soto Literary and Library Association. The library was located at the residence of Rev. Balch. Joseph Freehoff was the acting librarian.
Balch	Mrs.	DC, p3c4, 8/13/1887	Received a visit from a 12-year-old girl from the State Dependent School of Sparta. She may adopt the girl. A 4-year-old boy visited J. Babcock.
Baldrick	David	BD, p3c5, 7/27/1877	David Baldrick married Ellen Homer on July 16, 1877 at Caseville. Bride and groom from Iowa. Henry Burgen officiated.
Baldwin	Arthur B.	DC, p3c3, 11/20/1888	Mary Gross recently married Arthur B. Baldwin. Bride and groom from Dubuque. Bride was a former resident of De Soto. Groom was freight conductor for the C. M. & St. Paul Railroad.
Baldwin	Net	RH, p5c4, 1/13/1898	Worked as a dressmaker in Kickapoo Center.
Ball	Phebe, Mrs.	BD, p3c3, 4/13/1877	Celebrated her 90th birthday at a party held on April 7, 1877 in Lone Rock. She was the mother of G. O. Ball and grandmother of J. C. Bancroft of Lone Rock.
Ballon	L. A.	BD, p3c3, 8/5/1881	Arrived in Boscobel from Bristol, NH to visit Hiram Favor.
Bancroft	Dexter	BD, p2c1, 6/10/1881	Drowned in the Wisconsin River on Thursday evening. Aged 14 years. He was the son of George Bancroft of Lone Rock.
Bancroft	L. H.	RH, p5c2, 11/11/1897	Appointed as a Richland County judge to succeed Judge Downs, who died several weeks ago.
Bangs	Mattie S.	BD, p3c2, 1/24/1879	Frank P. Simkins married Mattie S. Bangs on Jan. 1, 1879. Bride from Woodman. Groom from Minnesota. The Rev. W. Stoddart officiated at the ceremony in Boscobel.
Banker	Charley, Mrs.	RH, p5c4, 1/20/1898	Resided in Richland Center. Visited her brother, L. S. Kellogg of Kickapoo Center.
Banks	girl	DC, p8c1, 8/9/1889	A daughter was born Tuesday, July 22, 1889 to William Banks of De Soto.

Genealogical Events from Newspapers for Crawford, Vernon and Grant Counties, Wisconsin, 1870-1901

LAST NAME	FIRST NAME	NEWSPAPER, PAGE/COLUMN MONTH/DAY/YEAR	GENEALOGICAL DATA
Banks	William, Mrs.	DC, p3c2, 7/17/1886	Returned to De Soto after visiting her parents in Harpers Ferry, IA.
Bannon		BD, p3c3, 4/5/1878	The 5-year-old son of Patrick Bannon died March 19, 1878 in the Town of Scott, Crawford Co. The boy was burning out a stump and fell. His clothes caught on fire.
Barabeaux	John	BD, p3c1, 10/23/1883	Managed work on a bridge abuttment in Boscobel.
Baraboo	John	BD, p3c2, 4/12/1878	Resident of Boscobel. Departed Monday in his wagon for the West.
Barber	Lafe	RH, p5c3, 7/8/1897	He was a liveryman in Viola.
Barber	Nellie	BD, p3c2, 11/23/1877	Fred Durand married Nellie Barber at the residence of the bride's parents in Boscobel. Groom from Osage, IA. Bride daughter of Jay Barber, Esq.
Barham	N.	DC, p2c2, 9/17/1887	Left Ferryville for Kansas this week.
Barker	F.	DR, p3c1, 11/30/1871	F. Barker married Amelia Seaman on Nov. 21, 1871 by D. A. Steele, J.P., of De Soto. Bride and groom were from Lansing, IA.
Barlett	Frank	BD, p3c1, 8/25/1882	Sheriff Lane departed for Detroit to arrest Frank Bartlett, alias Haines, for horse stealing in Platteville.
Barnard	Zack	BD, p3c1, 12/26/1879	Zack Barnard recently married Mary R. Asheley at the residence of the bride's father in Avoca. Groom from Arena. The Rev. William Stoddart officiated.
Barnes	Dexter S.	BD, p3c1, 9/2/1881	Dexter S. Barnes married Helen L. Davis on Aug. 25, 1881 in Boscobel. Groom from Harved, IL. Bride from Wyalusing, WI. The Rev. T. M. Evans officiated.
Barnett	Chad [Crad?]	BD, p3c2, 9/6/1878	Arrived in Boscobel from Independence, IA for a visit.
Barnett	Charles	BD, p3c3, 7/20/1877	Returned to Boscobel for a vacation after an absence of 4 years.
Barnett	Crad	BD, p3c2, 11/14/1879	Crad Barnett recently married Miss Luckey. Bride from Independence, IA. Groom was a former resident of Boscobel but now lived in Independence, IA. Planned to live in Williamsport, PA, the groom's native state.
Barnett	Daniel	BD, p3c1, 3/16/1883	Daniel Barnett married Ida Virginia Wicks on Mar. 12, 1883 in Boscobel. Bride from Boscobel. Groom from Wauzeka.
Barnett	Frank	BD, p3c2, 5/5/1882	Youngest brother of Boscobel's former mayor. He was dying of consumption at the home of his sister in Janesville. Taken their last week from Cedar Rapids, IA.
Barnett	Frank	BD, p3c1, 1/12/1883	Died last Friday in Janesville. He was the youngest of 9 children and brother of Mrs. John Pepper of Boscobel. Funeral held in Janesville.
Barnett	George	BD, p2c3, 9/8/1882	Navy midshipman. Portions of his log book were published in the newspaper.
Barnett	George	BD, p3c3, 5/4/1877	Scheduled to leave June 15th for the Naval Academy in Annapolis, MD.
Barnett	James	BD, p3c1, 1/5/1877	Proprietor of the Central House in Boscobel.
Barnett	James	BD, p3c4, 5/3/1878	Sold the Central House in Boscobel to Frank Muffley.
Barnett	James, Mrs.	BD, p3c3, 8/14/1883	Left Boscobel for Beetown to attend the funeral of her mother, Mrs. Callis.
Barnett	James, Mrs.	BD, p2c1, 12/23/1881	Gen. J. B. Callis of Lancaster visited his sister, Mrs. James Barnett of Boscobel.
Barnett	John	BD, p3c3, 9/20/1878	Eunice Tabor will marry John Barnett at the home of the bride's parents in Independence, IA on Sept. 25, 1878. Bride daughter of Mr. and Mrs. S. J. W. Tabor. Groom from Independence, IA.
Barnett	John	BD, p3c2, 1/10/1879	Clerked at Meyer Bros. in Boscobel. Planned to depart for Chicago.
Barnett	Mattie	BD, p3c2, 5/11/1877	Celebrated her 20th birthday last Saturday. She was the daughter of James Barnett of Boscobel.
Barnett	Thomas	BD, p3c2, 9/30/1881	Lt. Thomas Barnett and Capt. R. J. Whittleton attended a reunion of the 25th WI Volunteers at the Central House in Boscobel. The officers had not seen each other since 1864.
Barnett	William	BD, p3c2, 3/12/1880	Boscobel Post Officer published a list of owners of uncalled letters. List included: William Barnett, Helger Larson, Mrs. Rebecca Lewis, William Bennington, Edward O. Williams and Miss Tuelly Walker.
Barney	Ed	RH, p5c4, 10/13/1898	Ed Barney recently married Mrs. Estella Barney [nee Drake].
Barney	Estella, Mrs.	RH, p5c4, 10/13/1898	Ed Barney recently married Mrs. Estella Barney [nee Drake].

Genealogical Events from Newspapers for Crawford, Vernon and Grant Counties, Wisconsin, 1870-1901

LAST NAME	FIRST NAME	NEWSPAPER, PAGE/COLUMN MONTH/DAY/YEAR	GENEALOGICAL DATA
Barney	Mrs.	DR, p3c3, 5/4/1871	Recently lost a log stable, straw stack and 40 bushels of wheat to a fire.
Barque	Margarette, Mrs.	BD, p3c1, 7/4/1879	George Smith married Mrs. Margarett Barque on June 28, 1879 in Montfort. Bride and groom from Wingville. The Rev. D. L. Hubbard officiated.
Barr	Nettie	DC, p3c4, 11/13/1886	Departed Freeman for her home in Merrill.
Barrett	Eli	DC, p3c3, 3/10/1888	Squire McMichael recently sentence 4 young men [aged 16-18] from Genoa for carrying concealed weapons. Abram Morr was sentenced to 30 days of hard labor. Harry Spauling sentenced to 20 days of hard labor. Eli Barrett sentenced to the Industrial School at Waukesha. Emil Gunderson paid a fine.
Barrie	David B.	RH, p4c3, 3/9/1899	David B. Barrie married Mary Guist on Feb. 23, 1899 at the residence of John Tate, Esquire. Bride and groom from Kickapoo.
Barron	W. C. S., Capt.	BD, p3c1, 5/21/1880	Resided in Richland Center. Visited friends in Boscobel while selling insurance.
Barron	W. C. S., Col.	BD, p3c1, 3/10/1882	New sheriff in Richland Co. Has held post before.
Bartels	B.	BD, p3c1, 3/16/1883	Bartels' funeral was held Tuesday afternoon at the Methodist Episcopal Church in Boscobel. Funeral was conducted by the Odd Fellows.
Bartels	B.	BD, p3c3, 3/23/1883	The International Order of Odd Fellows published a resolution of respect upon the death of B. Bartels.
Bartels	B.	BD, P3c7, 1/5/1877	Advertised his cigar and tobacco store in Boscobel.
Barth	Charles	BD, p3c4, 10/12/1877	Recently died in Boscobel. He was a former wagon maker. No relatives lived in the area. A brother and sister lived in Leavenworth, KS. He lived on the interest of his investments. Left an estate valued at $20,000. Lived very frugally. Born in Germany.
Barth	Charles	BD, p2c4, 10/11/1878	Grant County published a probate notice for Charles Barth, deceased. Melchoir Ableiter to be executor.
Bartholemew	Ara, Miss	DC, p3c2, 7/3/1886	Returned to De Soto after teaching in Retreat.
Bartholemew	Pete	DC, p3c1, 6/12/1886	Proprietor of a livery and sale stable in De Soto.
Bartholomew	Ara	DC, p3c2, 12/11/1886	Taught school in the Howarth District.
Bartholomew	Ara	DC, p3c4, 4/2/1887	Planned to teach at Stevenson's this summer.
Bartholomew	J. C.	DC, p2c1, 11/27/1888	J. C. Bartholomew, Charles Lawrence and L. W. Clark opened a hoop factory in Victory.
Bartholomew	Louisa	DC, p3c3, 11/20/1886	Taught school in Victory.
Bartholomew	Louisa	DC, p3c4, 4/2/1887	Planned to teach at Victory this summer.
Bartholomew	Mary	BD, p3c1, 8/4/1882	Albert Beam married Mary Bartholomew on July 30, 1882 at the residence of Morris Thorp in Watterstown. Groom from Watterstown. Bride from Livingston. A. F. Henerson, J.P. officiated.
Bartholomew	P. D.	RH, p5c4, 11/10/1898	Suffered a stroke while climbing down stairs in De Soto. He fell and was badly bruised. One side of his body is paralyzed.
Bartholomew	Peter	DC, p2c2, 2/26/1889	Proprietor of a livery stable in De Soto.
Bartholomew	Robert	DC, p3c3, 10/16/1888	Robert Bartholomew and Ed Dyer started a meat market in De Soto. Jim Van Zant went out of business.
Bartlett	Frank	BD, p3c2, 9/26/1879	Sheriff Streeter took him to Waupon to serve a 2-year sentence for horse stealing.
Barton	Deett	BD, p3c2, 10/3/1879	Stuart E. Reid married Deett Barton on Sept. 25, 1879. Bride and groom from Hickory Grove. T. J. Jones, Esquire officiated at the ceremony in Hickory Grove.
Bartow	Nathan	BD, p3c4, 8/21/1883	Resided in Hickory Grove. Published a notice that he had given time to his son, Elijah Bartow. [He made him an emancipated minor.]
Bash	Mrs.	BD, p3c2, 10/12/1877	The Boscobel home of Mrs. Bash was damaged by fire. She a widowed German woman.
Bass	Helen	RH, p5c3, 11/25/1897	Taught at Viola High School.
Bassett	E. N., Mr. and Mrs.	DC, p3c4, 7/31/1888	The Bassetts visited Mrs. Bassett's parents, the Steels.

Genealogical Events from Newspapers for Crawford, Vernon and Grant Counties, Wisconsin, 1870-1901

LAST NAME	FIRST NAME	NEWSPAPER, PAGE/COLUMN MONTH/DAY/YEAR	GENEALOGICAL DATA
Baswortz	Millie, Mrs.	BD, p3c3, 9/15/1882	Mrs. Baswortz and her sister, Clara Finn, arrived from Omaha to visit friends in Boscobel.
Bates		DC, p2c1, 2/5/1887	During the Black Hawk War, Black Hawk camped on the pond at the old Bates farm, Sec. 11, T. 11, R. 6, in Vernon Co., just across from Crawford Co.
Bates	A., Mr. and Mrs.	DC, p3c4, 7/24/1886	Resided in Retreat. They were recently given a surprise party to honor their 20th wedding anniversary.
Bates	Benjamin	DR, p3c1, 7/20/1871	Died July 17, 1871 in the Town of Sterling, Vernon Co. at the age of 73.
Bates	Bill	DC, p3c2, 9/11/1888	Taken before Judge Loftus in De Soto and fined $50.
Bates	Ida	DC, p3c2, 12/11/1888	Ida Bates married John Pennell on Nov. 30, 1888 at home of bride's parents in De Soto. Martin Loftus officiated.
Bates	Mary	DC, p3c4, 9/25/1886	Traveled from home in Victory to visit her ill mother in Horicon.
Bates	Mary, Mrs.	DC, p3c3, 2/19/1887	Hosted a meeting of the Women's Christian Temperance Union at her home in Retreat.
Bates	Walter	DC, p2c1, 3/10/1888	Commencement exercises were held for the Retreat and Bishop schools. The graduates were Walter Bates, Emma Sallander, Robert English, Annie Bates, Alice Minor and Abram Bates. The teachers were Misses M. Hinkst and M. A. Loftus.
Bates	Walter	DC, p3c2, 5/22/1888	Taught school in Northville, Dakota. Resident of Retreat.
Battles	George	DR, p3c2, 3/30/1871	Town Treasurer for the Town of Wheatland.
Baty	Jennie	DC, p2c3, 7/9/1887	Jennie Baty married Charles Poehler on July 4, 1887. Bride and groom from Lansing, IA. Police Justice Ingersoll officiated.
Baumgartner	Amelia	BD, p3c3, 4/16/1880	Valentine Stuka recently married Amelia Baumgartner at the Jacob Baumgartner residence in Fennimore. Planned to live in Plainville, Rock Co., KS.
Baumgartner	Laura I.	BD, p3c1, 10/1/1880	George Christ, Jr. married Laura I. Baumgartner on Sept. 23, 1880 at the Horstman House in Lancaster. Groom from Marietta. Bride from Hickory Grove. Groom's mother departed for a visit with relatives in Illinois after the wedding.
Baxter	Ezra	DR, p3c1, 7/13/1871	Died June 29, 1871 at the age of 72 in Pawtucket, R.I. "The deceased has a number of friends in this vincinity [De Soto] who are pained to hear of his death."
Bayse	Elizabeth L., Mrs.	BD, p3c3, 3/16/1883	Died Feb. 2, 1883 from heart disease at Swan Lake, Dakota. Moved from Boscobel to Dakota in 1871.
Beabel	Peter	BD, p3c4, 1/26/1883	Resided 3½ miles west of Boscobel. Placed an advertisement in paper. Asked for return of stray sheep.
Beach	Sallie	BD, p2c3, 11/24/1882	A. K. Graves married Sallie Beach on Nov. 16, 1882. Bride and groom were from Prairie du Chien. Bride was the daughter of the Hon. H. Beach. Rev. A. McMaster officiated.
Beam	Albert	BD, p3c1, 8/4/1882	Albert Beam married Mary Bartholomew on July 30, 1882 at the residence of Morris Thorp in Watterstown. Groom from Watterstown. Bride from Livingston. A. F. Henerson, J.P. officiated.
Beam	Nellie, Mrs.	BD, p3c1, 3/21/1879	Died Mar. 14, 1879 at the residence of J. O. Beals in Sioux Co., IA. She was 76 years, 6 months and 13 days old. She was the wife of J. M. Beam, formerly of Boscobel.
Bean	Alice, Miss	DC, p1c2, 4/12/1889	Miss Alice Bean of Cooley Valley visited her sister, Mrs. Allen of La Crosse.
Bean	Allie	DC, p3c2, 7/24/1888	Allie Bean and Lucinda Ames were baptized in a Cooley Valley creek by Rev. William Haughton.
Bean	C.	DC, p3c3, 6/18/1887	C. Bean of Tacoma, Washington Terr. Surprised his parents when he appeared for a visit. Mr. Bean has been city engineer for 5 years. He was on a trip to all the large cities inspecting systems of electric and gas lighting machinery.
Bean	C.	DC, p3c3, 11/12/1887	Messrs. C. Bean and S. Arnold left Cooley Valley for Merrill, WI. Mr. Bean's wife plans to join him in a few weeks.
Bean	Catherine	BD, p3c1, 5/26/1882	Ed Dennison married Catherine Bean [Beam?] on May 15, 1882 at the residence of J. M. Riggs in the Town of Watterstown. A. F. Henderson officiated.
Bean	Clarence	DC, p3c4, 7/17/1886	Visited friends in Cooley Valley and left for Dakota to join his parents.
Bean	Clarence E.	DC, p3c1, 6/11/1887	Anna Haverly married Clarence E. Bean on June 1, 1887. Bride was the daughter of William Haverly of Red Mount. The Rev. William Haughton officiated. Couple moved to De Soto.
Bean	Dr.	DC, p3c3, 5/8/1888	Left home in Retreat to visit his son, Theron, a lawyer in Michigan City, Dakota.

Genealogical Events from Newspapers for Crawford, Vernon and Grant Counties, Wisconsin, 1870-1901

LAST NAME	FIRST NAME	NEWSPAPER, PAGE/COLUMN MONTH/DAY/YEAR	GENEALOGICAL DATA
Bean	Dr.	DC, p2c1, 2/5/1887	"The trail [used by Black Hawk during the Black Hawk War] passed north of Brodhead's and it is claimed along the ridge directly over where Dr. Bean's house stands; a little north of the Red Schoolhouse, and followed not far from the present highway, past the Law house, over the site of Central church, and along the ridge past the forks toward Victory."
Bean	Dr. and Mrs.	DC, p2c2, 6/18/1887	Resided in Retreat. Enjoyed a visit from their son, Clarence, of Washington Territory.
Bean	Dr. and Mrs.	DC, p2c2, 6/18/1887	Celebrated their 37th wedding anniversary last Friday at their home in Retreat.
Bean	E., Mrs.	DC, p3c3, 12/25/1886	Resided in Victory. Traveled to Merrill after receiving a telegram saying her mother was dying.
Bean	Fred	DC, p3c4, 11/27/1886	Taught school at Genoa.
Bean	Fred	DC, p1c2, 6/14/1889	Fred Bean married Louise Slater on June 5, 1889 at the residence of the bride's father in Retreat. Rev. Haughton officiated.
Bean	Mr.	DC, p3c5, 8/14/1886	Served as agent and operator of the railroad depot in Ferryville.
Bean	Sarah, Mrs.	DC, p2c2, 12/11/1886	Arrived from Dakota to visit her parents, Mr. and Mrs. J. Eckhardt of Retreat.
Beardsley	Frank	BD, p3c1, 9/10/1880	Left Boscobel to attend the State University in Madison.
Beardsley	Lester	RH, p5c4, 2/23/1899	Left De Soto to resume his work as a telegraph operator in Breckenridge, MN.
Beaumont	Charles Wesley	BD, p3c2, 12/9/1881	Charles Wesley Beaumont married Olive Elender Lucis on Dec. 8, 1881. Groom from Boaz, Richland Co. Bride from Boscobel. The Rev. T. M. Evans officiated.
Beck	A. N., Mrs.	DR, p3c2, 2/2/1871	Ran the hotel in Victory, WI.
Beck	David	DR, p3c3, 11/9/1871	A summons for relief from the Vernon Co. Circuit Court was published in the case, R. P. Spencer and Frank H. Spencer, Partners in the firm named R. P. Spencer & Son, plaintiffs, vs. David Beck, Anna Beck and George H. Battles, defendants.
Beck	H. A.	DR, p1c1, 12/15/1870	Proprietor of the Vernon House in Victory, WI.
Beck	J. D.	RH, p5c4, 7/29/1897	Elected principal in Westby school.
Beck	S.	BD, p3c2, 12/18/1883	Operated a gun shop in Boscobel. Sold revolvers to the 12-year-old sons of W. T. Scott and A. B. Alden. City Marshall Woodward retrieved the guns and made Beck refund the money.
Beckwar	Anthony	BD, p3c2, 8/17/1877	Anthony Beckwar married Maggie Stark on Aug. 10, 1877 in Boscobel. Groom from Crawford Co. Bride from Moscoda.
Beckwith	A.	RH, p5c4, 11/3/1898	Mr. A. Beckwith of Richland City visited his sister, Mrs. W. N. Miller, per Mound Park news column.
Beebe	Mrs.	BD, p3c2, 9/9/1881	Resided in Boscobel. Fractured her ankle after dropping a buggy whip while traveling with Mrs. DeWitt to the dedication of the new Mt. Zion Methodist Church at Rolling Ground.
Beeley	Lieutenant	BD, p3c5, 3/15/1878	Beeley resided in Bloomington. Shot in the shoulder at Gettysburg during the Civil War. The ball gradually moved down and can now be felt in the crook of the elbow.
Beffa	D.	DC, p2c3, 7/3/1888	D. Beffa and Louis Gussetti returned to Genoa from Washington Territory. They liked the area and will probably move there.
Beffa	Daniel	DC, p3c3, 4/17/1888	Daniel Beffa and Louis Gussetti left Genoa for Washinton Territory. B. Gadola and family plan to leave soon, too.
Beffa/Buffa	Daniel	DC, p1c1, 6/14/1889	Died June 3, 1889 of consumption in Genoa. Mrs. Philip Franzeni of St. Louis, a daughter, attended the funeral. Buried in the Catholic Cemetery.
Bell	Allan	BD, p3c4, 12/28/1877	Allan Bell married Anna C. Allen on Tuesday. Groom was from Franklin, PA. Bride was the daughter of J. G. Allen. The Rev. G. W. Nuzum officiated.
Bell	Edward	BD, p3c2, 3/9/1883	Owned a store building in Montfort that was recently destroyed by fire.
Bell	Frank, Rev.	RH, p4c1, 9/21/1899	Preached his farewell sermon in Readstown.
Bell	Rev.	RH, p4c2, 12/29/1898	Scheduled to hold revival meetings in North Clayton this week.
Bell	Rev.	RH, p4c2, 9/20/1900	Rev. Bell of the Methodist Episcopal Church has been transferred to Montfort. Replaced by Rev. J. A. Neill of Tunnel City.
Bell	Thomas A.	DC, p3c2, 10/2/1888	Former resident of Waukon, IA. He is now 93. Voted for Andrew Jackson in 1828.

Genealogical Events from Newspapers for Crawford, Vernon and Grant Counties, Wisconsin, 1870-1901

LAST NAME	FIRST NAME	NEWSPAPER, PAGE/COLUMN MONTH/DAY/YEAR	GENEALOGICAL DATA
Bell	W. E.	BD, p3c1, 12/29/1882	W. E. Bell married Nettie Van Buren on Sunday at the residence of Mrs. Beebe. Bride was a teacher and native of Boscobel. Groom was a member of the Grant Co. Bar and resided in Montfort.
Bembrick	John	DC, p2c3, 7/3/1886	Resided in Brownsville. He was robbed of $150 that was taken from a trunk.
Bemis	E.	DC, p3c2, 7/16/1887	Resided in Harmony. Knocked down and robbed of $4.50.
Bender	Christ	BD, p2c2, 9/11/1883	Published a notice that he will not be responsible for the debts of his son, Fred Bender.
Bender	Dan	RH, p5c4, 10/27/1898	Dan Bender's funeral was held Sunday at Hopewell.
Bender	E. P. and E.	DC, p3c3, 11/20/1886	Resided in Viola. Came to De Soto looking for a young man who was supposed to have crossed the river in De Soto last April. Nothing has been heard of him. The remains of a body found last summer and buried on Woodbury's island were disinterred. The identity was inconclusive.
Benedict	George L.	DR, p3c2, 8/3/1871	George L. Benedict married Minnie A. Anderson on July 30, 1871 at the home of the bridegroom. Bride and groom were from the Town of Wheatland. The Rev. D. L. Hubbard officiated.
Benedict	Le Roy	DC, p2c3, 7/24/1888	Resided in De Soto and volunteered for Civil War service. "Some smiled when he enlisted – first on account of his youth and second because they did not believe he had in him the stuff from which soldiers are made. . . . His companions soon learned to appreciate him for no braver soldier ever shouldered a musket . . ." He died of fever and was buried in Virginia.
Benn		RH, p5c3, 12/29/1898	The Benn Brothers of Kickapoo were "putting up ice."
Benn	Dora	RH, p4c2, 10/25/1900	Dora Benn married Wesley Fishel on Oct. 16, 1900 at the home of the bride. Bride and groom from Viola. The Rev. A. C. Vaughan officiated.
Benn	George A.	RH, p5c4, 3/16/1899	George A. Benn married Myrtle M. Kanable last Sunday per the Sugar Grove news column.
Benn	Susan, Mrs.	RH, p5c4, 12/8/1898	Enjoyed a visit from Charley Eales and George Hollinger, her nephews from Jefferson Co., per Kickapoo news column.
Bennett	Carrie	DC, p3c4, 3/10/1888	Edgar Ely married Carrie Bennett on Wednesday evening at Col. May's home near Viroqua. The Rev. S. S. Hebbard officiated.
Bennett	Charles	BD, p3c3, 8/7/1883	Charles, Henry and Frank Bennett of near Muscoda were charged with disorderly conduct in Boscobel.
Bennett	Charles, Frank and Harrison	BD, p3c1, 10/23/1883	The court case involving the Bennetts was finally started. It involved a fight at Mike Meger's saloon in Muscoda on July 20, 1883. Constable Joseph Stork tried to break up a fight and was assaulted.
Bennett	Dick	DC, p3c3, 9/18/1886	Former resident of Caledonia Junction. Recently married in De Soto under the name Richard Folie. Bennett has a wife and children in Genoa. He was not divorced prior to the De Soto marriage.
Bennett	E. M.	DC, p2c2, 11/5/1887	Crushed his leg at Oregon, IL. An amputation may be necessary. Later news indicated that he died and his body was brought back to Crawford Co. for burial.
Bennett	Elva	BD, p3c1, 11/21/1879	Charles W. Burrows married Elva Bennett on Nov. 4, 1870 at the residence of James Henderson in Hickory Grove. Bride and groom from Watterstown.
Bennett	Emma	DC, p3c4, 1/15/1887	R. W. Marin recently married Emma Bennett per the Seneca news column.
Bennett	H. E.	RH, p5c2, 10/7/1897	Left Readstown for La Farge to run the railroad depot.
Bennett	James	BD, p3c3, 9/1/1882	Candidate for Grant Co. Sheriff. Settled in Grant Co. in 1847. Republican. Kept a tavern.
Bennett	William Edwin	BD, p3c2, 10/18/1878	William Edwin Bennett married Hermana M. Brekke on Oct. 14, 1878 at the home of the bride's father in Boscobel. Groom from Chicago. Rev. Dr. Stoddart officiated.
Bennish	Frank	BD, p3c3, 10/26/1877	Frank Bennish and C. Yusaw were crushed by rock while digging a hole to get a rabbit they were hunting near Castle Rock last Thursday.
Benoy	James	BD, p3c3, 2/27/1880	Employed as foreman of the wood department at the Ruka Bros' Wagon Manufactory in Boscobel.
Benoy	John	BD, p3c1, 5/5/1882	Left Boscobel for Fairmont, MN where he had leased a blacksmith shop.
Benoy	John	BD, p3c1, 11/3/1882	Resided in Boscobel. Opened a blacksmith shop in Excelsior.
Benoy	John	BD, p3c2, 5/18/1883	Departed Boscobel for Blunt, Dakota to open a blacksmithing business.

Genealogical Events from Newspapers for Crawford, Vernon and Grant Counties, Wisconsin, 1870-1901

LAST NAME	FIRST NAME	NEWSPAPER, PAGE/COLUMN MONTH/DAY/YEAR	GENEALOGICAL DATA
Benoy	John	BD, p3c3, 9/20/1878	Planned to hold an auction on the Joe Button farm. Will sell wagons, animals and farm utensils on Oct. 1, 1878.
Benson	Charles	BD, p2c2, 6/10/1881	Arrested in Wauzeka for stealing a coat and vest filled with money.
Benton	Robert R.	BD, p2c3, 5/12/1882	Resided in Town of Marshall, Richland Co. After a 2 month tour of IA, MN, Dakota, NB, TX, MO, OH and IL he decided Richland Co. was "not the worst place in Christendom."
Berg	Betsy	RH, p5c4, 11/4/1897	Edward Halverson married Betsy Berg on Oct. 14, 1897 in Viroqua. Bride from Viroqua. Groom from Ferryville.
Bergh		DC, p3c3, 12/25/1888	Sheriff-elect Bergh announced appointments of undersheriff Peter Hanson of Bloomington and the following men as deputies: Frank Minshall of Viroqua, Clarence Culver of Ontario, Elias Fox of Hillsborough, J. M. Brown of Chaseburgh and Byron Lane of De Soto.
Bergh	Wayne	DC, p3c2, 7/30/1887	Died July 22, 1887 in Viroqua. He was the 8-month-old son of M. C. Bergh. The funeral was attended by Mrs. A. N. Miller, Mrs. E. Cooper and Lyman Smith [Mrs. Bergh's mother, sister and brother]. They were all from De Soto.
Bernier	Anna	DC, p2c2, 5/7/1887	Hired to teach school in the Stony Point District per the Seneca news column.
Berry	Fred	BD, p2c4, 11/26/1880	Grant County paid him a bounty for scalps turned into the county.
Berry	John C.	DC, p2c2, 3/20/1888	Berry was the "oracle and chief man" of [Victory] and was married to the daughter of George G. Van Wagoner. Owned a store in Victory.
Betts	J. A., Mrs.	BD, p3c1, 7/30/1880	Resided in Glenwood, IA. Bought the Carrier House in Boscobel. Planned to renovate it.
Betts	Lillian Myrtle	BD, p3c3, 12/23/1881	Lillian Myrtle Betts married Seymour M. Chase on Dec. 15, 1881. Bride was the leassee and proprietor of the Betts House in Boscobel. Groom was formerly from Cazanovia, NY. The Rev. E. L. Morse of the Congregational Church officiated. Extensive article.
Betts House		BD, p2c3, 10/22/1880	Mrs. J. A. Betts is the proprietor of this Boscobel hotel formerly known as the Carrier House. Operated by Mr. M. DeWitt, an old resident of Boscobel. Location convenient to both cars and business houses. Recently thoroughly overhauled and refurbished.
Bevan	Emma	DC, p3c3, 1/7/1888	Wedding invitation were sent our for the Jan. 11, 1888 wedding of Emma Bevan and A. J. Smith.
Bevan	Emma	DC, p2c4, 1/14/1888	Emma Bevan married A. J. Smith on January 11, 1888. The groomsmen were the bride's brothers, Thomas, Reese and John, and the bridesmaids were "Misses Mary Cushing Smith and Maggie Joseph". The newly weds left for a new home in Dubuque where Mr. Smith is employed by the C. M. & St. P. Railway. Rev. Counch officiated.
Bevan	Thomas	DC, p3c1, 12/10/1887	Returned to Wisconsin after spending the summer in the Black Hills.
Bever	William	DR, p3c4, 1/5/1871	Former resident of Vernon Co. Injured by a falling tree at Tom Price's lumber camp. Broke a leg. It can probably be saved, per the *Tomah Journal*.
Bigelow	J. S.	DC, p3c5, 8/7/1886	J. S. Bigelow of Seneca and Clark Mettick of Utica lost horses on Saturday and Sunday, probably from driving during the extreme heat.
Billiard	J. M.	DC, p2c2, 6/18/1887	Operated a grocery in Victory.
Billiard	James	DC, p3c3, 5/7/1887	Postmaster in Victory.
Billiard	Mr.	DC, p3c3, 7/17/1886	He was a harness maker in Victory.
Bills	A. G.	DC, p3c2, 5/7/1887	Resided in Buena Vista, Richland Co. Lost a hand while splitting a post.
Bills	J. H.	BD, p2c4, 1/20/1882	Resided on a farm in Buena Vista that had many Indian mounds. He plowed them up and collected many relics from them. Some are supposed to be over 1000 years old. Relics were at the office of the *Republican and Observer* newspaper in Richland Center.
Bird	Eleanor	BD, p3c3, 6/14/1878	Delos G. Davis married Eleanor Bird on June 2, 1878. Bride and groom from Boscobel. Justice Jacob McLaughlin officiated.
Bird	James	BD, p2c8, 12/10/1880	A summons was issued in the Grant Co. courts in the case, Jane A. Bird, plaintiff vs. James Bird, defendant.
Bird	Mrs.	DC, p2c2, 6/18/1887	Mrs. Bird visited her mother, Mrs. H. J. Phelps, per Ontario news column.
Birk	Mary	BD, p3c1, 10/30/1883	Edward Swingle married Mary Birk on Oct. 23, 1883 at Muscoda. The Rev. John Schoeberle officiated.
Bishop	Earl	RH, p4c2, 2/28/1901	"... The tinner is the most industrious young man in our town [Readstown]. He is not content with 10 hours work in the tinshop but has accepted a position as night man. He will not even let anyone go after a doctor for his patient but will go himself for fear they will loiter on the way."

Genealogical Events from Newspapers for Crawford, Vernon and Grant Counties, Wisconsin, 1870-1901

LAST NAME	FIRST NAME	NEWSPAPER, PAGE/COLUMN MONTH/DAY/YEAR	GENEALOGICAL DATA
Bishop	Ed R.	BD, p3c3, 12/3/1880	Ed R. Bishop married Ella Bailey on Oct. 24, 1880 in Lena, OR. Groom from Pendleton, Umatilla Co., OR. Bride from Batter Creek, formerly from Boscobel. She was daughter of James Bailey.
Bishop	Eliad Taylor, Deacon	DC, p3c3, 2/18/1888	Resided in Retreat. He was a second cousin of P. T. Barnum, the great showman. Spent his early life in Bethel, CT.
Bishop	Eliza	DC, p3c3, 5/29/1888	Died May 24, 1888 of apoplexy. She was the wife of E. T. Bishop of near Retreat. Born in County Sligo, West Ireland in 1825. Converted to the Baptist faith 40 years ago. Baptized in County Down, North Ireland. Moved to Port Washington, Wisconsin in 1850. To De Soto in 1857. Married Dr. G. S. Sperry in 1867. He died in 1874. Married E. T. Bishop of Retreat in Mary 1876. She was a sister of Mrs. M. Kahlar of De Soto.
Bishop	Emmanuel	BD, p2c2, 11/13/1883	Died Nov. 3, 1883 of heart disease in Beetown. He was one of the area's earliest settlers. Born in Pike Co., PA in 1826 to Moses Bishop. Moved to Luzerne Co., PA in 1833. Moved to Susquehanna Co., PA in 1836. Married the daughter of Elipahlet Stevens in 1852. Moved to Cassville, Grant Co., WI in 1853. Moved to Beetown in 1855.
Bishop	Thomas W.	BD, p3c2, 9/18/1883	Former editor of the *Boscobel Journal*. He now publishes a weekly in Iowa called the *Cedar Falls Journal*.
Black	Jerry	DR, p3c2, 9/14/1871	Murdered by a saloonkeeper in Chaseburg after he refused to pay for sour beer. He was a cattle dealer in Vernon Co.
Black Hawk War		DC, p2c1, 1/8/1887	C. V. Porter, M. D. wrote a series of articles on the Black Hawk War. He interviewed many people in the area who had first-hand accounts of the events. The installments were published in the *De Soto Chronicle* on 1/8/1887, 1/15/1887, 1/22/1887, 1/29/1887, 2/5/1887 and 2/12/1887.
Blackburn	George R.	BD, p2c4, 11/26/1880	Grant County paid him a bounty for scalps turned into the county.
Blair	Jane L.	DR, p3c2, 1/4/1872	Michael Eckhart married Jane L. Blair on Dec. 27, 1871 at the home of John Blair in the Town of Sterling. Bride and groom were from Town of Sterling. The Rev. D. L. Hubbard officiated.
Blair	John	DR, p2c3, 9/21/1871	Announced candidacy for Vernon County treasurer.
Blair	John	DR, p3c1, 10/5/1871	Resided in the Town of Sterling. Sold farm to Robert Johnson. Bought a lot in De Soto where he planned to erect a warehouse.
Blake		DR, p3c2, 12/29/1870	Operated a flouring mill on Front Street in De Soto.
Blake	boy	DR, p3c1, 11/2/1871	A son was born last Tuesday night to I. W. Blake of De Soto.
Blake	I. W.	DR, p3c5, 12/29/1870	Proprietor of the De Soto Mills.
Blake	I. W.	DR, p3c5, 3/23/1871	Advertised the sale of the De Soto Grist Mill in De Soto.
Blake	J. W.	DR, p3c5, 12/15/1870	He was a constable [in De Soto?]. Took a prisoner to Prairie du Chien.
Blake	Mr.	DR, p3c2, 6/29/1871	Sold the De Soto steam flouring mill to H. F. Blodgett. Blake planned to go into the carpentry business.
Blakely	Mrs.	RH, p4c2, 2/7/1901	Died Monday in Viola. She was the mother of Flem. and John Blakely and Mrs. J. C. Hall [all of Viola].
Blanchard	Lydia A.	BD, p3c2, 1/24/1879	Walter A. Clark married Lydia A. Blanchard at the Muffley House in Boscobel on Jan. 14, 1879. Bride from Marion. Groom from Fennimore. The Rev. W. Stoddart officiated.
Bliss	A. P.	BD, p3c1, 6/6/1879	A. P. Bliss [also known as Parker] recently died at his home in Readstown. He was a well-known businessman.
Bliss	Allen	RH, p5c3, 8/26/1897	Allen Bliss married Bertha Simmons at the residence of the bride's brother, Dolph Simmons, last Sunday afternoon. Groom from South Dakota. Bride from Viola and was a former teacher in Readstown.
Bliss	Allen, Mr. and Mrs.	RH, p4c1, 9/13/1900	Arrived in Readstown from Lake Preston, MN to visit at the Patterson home.
Bliss	Bertha, Mrs.	RH, p4c2, 9/21/1899	Former teacher in Readstown. Came from Lake Preston, SD to visit with relatives and friends in the Readstown area.
Bliss	D. G.	BD, p3c1, 3/21/1879	Scheduled to address the Temple of Honor in Wauzeka.
Bliss	John and Edith	DC, p3c2, 10/8/1887	Boarded a train for Arlington, KS.
Bliss	Mr.	DR, p2c4, 8/24/1871	Operated a store in Readstown.

Genealogical Events from Newspapers for Crawford, Vernon and Grant Counties, Wisconsin, 1870-1901

LAST NAME	FIRST NAME	NEWSPAPER, PAGE/COLUMN MONTH/DAY/YEAR	GENEALOGICAL DATA
Bliss	Nellie	BD, p2c2, 3/9/1883	Nellie Bliss married J. O. Davidson last Wednesday [per *Crawford County Journal* of 2/28/1883] at the residence of the bride's mother. Bride was from Readstown. Groom was from Soldiers Grove. The Rev William Haughton of Viroqua officiated.
Bliss	Will A.	RH, p5c4, 7/8/1897	Funeral held July 4, 1897. He was born in Readstown in 1866. Worked in the mercantile business. Appointed postmaster. Married Viola Meachem of Vernon Co. in 1893. Moved to Grand Junction, CO two years ago for a healthier climate. Died in Colorado.
Bliss	William N.	BD, p3c2, 5/21/1880	William Bliss married Belle McCarthy on Saturday in Boscobel at the Muffley House. Bride from Bell Center, Crawford Co. Prof. J. Allison officiated.
Bloss	James	DC, p3c4, 3/5/1887	James Bloss and family visited with the J. S. Haines family and then moved to Mason City, IA, per the Seneca news column.
Blossingham	Ed	BD, p3c3, 7/20/1883	Worked as a tailor in Eagle. His home was hit by lightening. Wife was injured.
Bloyer	Benjamin	BD, p3c1, 2/20/1880	Benjamin Bloyer married Annie C. Searles on Jan. 15, 1880 at Watterstown. Bride, daughter of Gideon Searles, Esq., from Watterstown. Groom from Muscoda. The Rev. J. Allison officiated.
Bloyer	Robert	BD, p3c1, 1/2/1880	Married Miss M. Whitts on Dec. 28, 1879 in Boscobel. Bride from Watterstown. Groom from Muscoda. Prof. J. Allison officiated.
Bobel	Adam	BD, p3c1, 3/16/1883	Planned to auction off his entire livery stock in Boscobel.
Bobel	Adam	BD, p3c4, 4/13/1877	In the case Adam Bobel vs. Fred Fritz, the arbitration award was confirmed at the Iowa term of the Circuit Court held in Dodgeville. This was a case from Grant Co.
Bobel	Mr.	BD, p3c1, 1/21/1881	Rebuilding the Central House in Boscobel. The hotel was destroyed in a fire.
Bock	Charles	DR, p3c4, 2/9/1871	Charles Bock married Anna Nilson on Feb. 8, 1871. Bride and groom were from Lansing. J. H. Hinds, J.P., officiated.
Bock	Walter	DC, p3c2, 9/24/1887	Lou Speery married Walter Bock on Sept. 9, 1887 at her home in Bowville, MI. Groom was Chief Clerk of the Michigan Central Railroad. Bride was a steno for Detroit Stove Co. She was the sister of E. B. Speery of De Soto.
Bodendine	Joseph	BD, p2c3, 11/24/1882	Bodendine's saw mill and stable in Bear Valley, Richland Co. were torn apart by a storm.
Boenner	John A.	BD, p3c2, 5/28/1880	Appointed to be a census enumerator in Liberty, Grant Co.
Bohland	Mrs.	DC, p2c2, 9/18/1888	Suffered a stroke and lies near death at her home in Retreat.
Bolden	Daniel	DR, p1c1, 12/15/1870	Proprietor of the Grant Hotel [formerly the North Star] in Viroqua.
Bolster	Chris	DC, p2c1, 4/9/1887	Miss Elsie Olstead of Chicago visited her cousin, Chris Bolster, per Cooley Valley news column.
Bolster	girl	DC, p3c3, 1/28/1888	A daughter was born Jan. 12, 1888 to Mr. C. Bolster of Cooley Valley.
Bolster	Widow	DC, p1c3, 8/9/1889	Lived in Cooley Valley. Her condition was better after an attack of cholera morbus.
Booth	Dick	BD, p3c1, 1/5/1883	Recent victim of an accidental shooting in Richland Center. His condition was improving.
Booth	Dick	BD, p3c1, 3/28/1879	Dick Booth and Henry McReynolds were new members of the band in Boscobel.
Booth	Richard	BD, p3c2, 12/29/1882	His face was injured at a "pleasure party" in Richland Center. Miss Carrie Fuller picked up a revolver and playfully pointed at Booth, discharging a blank into his face. Skin over the eye was wounded and powder was blown into the eye. Booth's sister, Mrs. Henry McReynolds of Boscobel, was caring for him.
Boothby	Mr.	DR, p3c3, 9/21/1871	Ran a blacksmith shop in De Soto in 1856.
Borgen	William	BD, p3c2, 5/12/1882	Editor of the *Crawford County Journal* in Soldiers Grove. Sold newspaper to Hon. Atley Peterson, Messrs Sime and Dinsdale.
Borgen	William	BD, p3c1, 1/13/1882	Published the first issue of The *Crawford County Journal* in Soldiers Grove on Jan. 1, 1882.
Borrman	Joseph	BD, p2c4, 11/26/1880	Grant County paid him a bounty for scalps turned into the county.
Borst	Prof.	DC, p3c5, 7/24/1886	Lead a singing school at the Central Church in Red Mound.
Borst	Prof.	DC, p3c3, 11/20/1886	Prof. Borst and Prof. Thayer were scheduled to discuss the vexatious Mormon question at the newly organized Literary Society in Liberty Pole.

Genealogical Events from Newspapers for Crawford, Vernon and Grant Counties, Wisconsin, 1870-1901

LAST NAME	FIRST NAME	NEWSPAPER, PAGE/COLUMN MONTH/DAY/YEAR	GENEALOGICAL DATA
Bort	A. K.	DC, p3c3, 2/18/1888	A. K. Bort recently married Mrs. Nancy Thompson at Viroqua, per De Soto news column.
Bort	Elizabeth, Mrs.	DC, p3c3 7/30/1887	Died Monday [per *Viroqua Censor*] She spent her girlhood in the De Soto area, where her brother, George Mosholder, still lives.
Boscobel Baseball Team		BD, p3c4, 8/30/1878	Boscobel's baseball team lost to Lancaster. The team members were G. Goodenow, George Wheeler, H. W. Hubbell, William Allen, David Shipley, Harry Stoddart, John Stoddart, Louis Ruka and John Barnett.
Boscobel Congregational Church		BD, p3c4, 10/6/1882	Celebrated their 25th anniversary. Church was established in 1857 with nine members: Mr. and Mrs. Moors [Morris?] Rice and their two daughters [Myra A. and Lucy M.]; John Tyler; Addison D. Allen; William Beals; Betsy Kellogg and her daughter, Maria [Mrs. Carley]. The four surviving members are Mrs. Rice of Boscobel, Myra Rice [Mrs. Ricks of Boscobel], Lucy M. Rice [now of Meriden, IA] and Mrs. Kellogg of Boscobel.
Boscobel Fire Department		BD, p3c2, 1/12/1877	The officers of the Boscobel Fire Department were T. N. Hubbell, S. F. Watkins, Henry Nelson, H. W. Favor, G. F. Hildebrand, Jacob Creager and T. J. Anderson.
Boscobel High School		BD, p3c2, 6/29/1883	The graduates of the Boscobel High School Class of 1883 were Albert Muffley, Augusta Brindley, R. D. Blanchard, Ida Kistler and August Deringsfeld.
Boscobel High School		BD, p3c2, 6/15/1877	The first graduates of the Boscobel High School were Alice Carrier, Fred Carley, Jennie Chandler, Lillie Limbocker, Laura Pepper, Katie Sarles, Herbert Partridge and Alice Simpkins.
Boscobel I.O.O.F.		BD, p3c2, 1/5/1877	Installed as officers in the Boscobel I.O.O.F. Lodge No. 122: S. R. Willoughby, C. F. Adams, Frank Rowe, H. W. Favor, William M. Rese, W. DeLap, M. DeLap, B. Hopkins, W. Young, Morris Wells, James McKinney, John Benoy, W. W. Hurd, Andrew Oleson and G. W. Nuzum.
Boscobel Mills		BD, p3c2, 7/24/1883	Established in 1867. Being upgraded by the Sylvester Co.
Boscobel Pauper Fund		BD, p3c5, 4/12/1878	The Boscobel Pauper Fund provided money between April 1877 and April 1878 to Joseph Evans, Mrs. Barr, Leroy Rogers, Mrs. Closson, Mrs. Benson, Mrs. Shippley, Mrs. Rose, Mrs. Schwauber, Mrs. Shorty, Mrs. Dolan, Mrs. Anderson, Mrs. Hughey, Mrs. Eggleston, J. Clark and B. Cheaver.
Boscobel Protection Fire Co.		BD, p3c2, 1/12/1877	The officers of the Boscobel Protection Fire Co., No. 1 officers were Morris Wells, William Bose, Frank Rowe, Hiram Favor, William Cook and Gottleib Christ.
Boscobel Teachers		BD, p3c3, 8/23/1878	The Boscobel school teachers were S. R. Willoughby, Principle; Carrie Sylvester, Asst.; Nettie Brainerd, Grammer School; Mattie Barnett; Ella Ford; Annie Proudfit Addie Willis and Laura Peppers.
Boscobel Teachers		BD, p3c1, 9/4/1883	The Boscobel schools open on Sept. 10th with the following teachers: S. R. Willoughby, Principal; Carrie Sylvester, Assistant; Ettie Lane, Grammer Dept.; Texanna Cobb, 2d Intermediate; Martha Fox, 1st Intermediate; Emma Bailey, 3d Primary; Emma Stahel, 2nd Primary; Mary Bartley, 1st Prinary; Mrs. O. P. Knowlton, 4th Ward Primary. Miss Mary Bartley, who succeeded Miss Sarles, is a sister of Mr. P. Bartley [former Principal of the Bloomington schools].
Bosh	W. S.	BD, p2c4, 7/21/1882	Recently died near Lone Rock after being run over by a train. Death was ruled an accident. Bosh was intoxicated. Aged about 50 years. No relations were known. On his person were found a tax receipt for property he owned in the Town of Richland and a deed for land in Ohio.
Boss	May, Mrs.	RH, p4c4, 2/2/1899	Eli Willison married Mrs. May Boss on Jan. 22, 1899, per Sugar Grove news column. Justice Benson officiated at the ceremony.
Bosworth	C., Mrs.	RH, p5c2, 10/20/1898	Arrived in Readstown to visit relatives. Resided in Spooner.
Bottom	boy	DC, p3c3, 7/31/1886	A son was born on July 23, 1886 to Charles Bottom of De Soto.
Bottom	C. F.	DC, p3c3, 4/9/1887	Served as the acting engineer for the ferry, Mertie. Returned home after spending the winter in Providence, MS.
Bottom	Edward	BD, XXXX, 1/18/1878	Died Tuesday in Waseca, MN when he fell between the cars. He was a railroad brakeman. Brother of Mrs. Spencer [of Boscobel?].
Bovee	Marcus	BD, p3c2, 7/20/1883	Bovee of Eagle hired to hang wallpaper in the Matt Pittman home in Boscobel.
Bowell	George Edwin	BD, p3c1, 12/26/1879	George Edwin Bowell married Julia Annie Cowell on Nov. 21, 1879 in Boscobel. Bride and groom from Avoca. Rev. William Stoddart officiated.
Bowen		BD, p2c3, 1/6/1882	A seven-month-old child of Mr. Bowen was severely scalded by the upsetting of a teakettle of hot water. The child's back was scalded the entire length of the spine. Dr. Samuels was called. Bowen was an employee at the Railway House in Soldiers Grove.
Bower	Julia	BD, p3c1, 4/14/1882	Henry Reichman married Julia Bower in Boscobel on April 6, 1882. Groom from Wauzeka. Bride was the daughter of George Bower of Marietta. Justice of the Peace Jacob McLaughlin officiated.

Genealogical Events from Newspapers for Crawford, Vernon and Grant Counties, Wisconsin, 1870-1901

LAST NAME	FIRST NAME	NEWSPAPER, PAGE/COLUMN MONTH/DAY/YEAR	GENEALOGICAL DATA
Bowers	Dwight	BD, p3c2, 7/9/1880	Resident of Blanchard, IA. Former resident of Boscobel.
Bowers	Dwight	BD, p3c2, 7/9/1880	Arrived in Boscobel from Blanchard, IA. He will be home in Boscobel for the next two weeks. He reported that the former Boscobellians in Blanchard were doing well.
Bowers	Dwite	BD, p3c1, 9/1/1882	Arrived from Blanchardville, IA to visit friends and relatives in Boscobel area.
Bowers	Ed	BD, p3c2, 9/16/1881	Arrived in Boscobel from Lathrop, CA to visit with friends and relatives.
Bowers	Will	RH, p5c3, 8/18/1898	Private Will Bowers of Camp Douglas visited people in Readstown.
Bowles	Adam	BD, p3c2, 1/19/1877	Opened a hotel of Boscobel.
Bowling	William	RH, p5c3, 6/16/1898	William Bowling married Minnie Stout at home of the bride in Ross on June 1, 1898. They were both graduates of the deaf and dumb schools in Delavan.
Bowman	Frank M.	BD, p3c2, 2/23/1877	Former publisher of the *Prairie du Chien Union*. Died Jan. 31, 1877 in Gilroy, CA.
Bown	William	DC, p3c3, 8/7/1888	Injured his hand while loading a rifle. Lived with Eli Shisler.
Boyd	David	BD, p3c3, 8/10/1877	Died from suicide last Friday. Hung himself. Resided in Ellenboro. Lived in Grant County for the last 20 years.
Boylan	M. J.	BD, p3c3, 3/21/1879	Resided in Crawford Co. Tried to cheat Sam Long, liveryman, out of his fee for driving him home.
Boyle	John	RH, p5c3, 2/7/1901	Resided on Oak Ridge. Purchased a violin from Lewis Larson. Now gives music lessons.
Boyle	John	RH, p4c3, 9/19/1901	Traveled from his home at Oak Ridge to visit his sister, Mrs. Nels Helgerson of Viroqua.
Boyle	William, Mrs.	RH, p4c5, 11/14/1901	Left her home at Oak Ridge for Chicago to care for her sick mother, Mrs. Gibbert.
Bradley	J. C.	BD, p3c2, 5/28/1880	Appointed to be a census enumerator in Ellenboro, Grant Co.
Bradley	Rev.	RH, p5c2, 8/5/1897	Lived in Excelsior. Visited sister, Mrs. Goyer of Readstown.
Bradley	Will	RH, p4c1, 9/6/1900	Served as a minister in Custer, SD at a Methodist Episcopal Church. He was a former resident of Readstown. Visited at Dr. Goyer's Readstown home.
Brainard	Nettie	BD, p3c1, 9/10/1880	Left Boscobel for a teaching position in Milwaukee.
Brainerd	Alvin	BD, p3c2, 9/15/1882	Departed from Boscobel to study at Oberlin College in Ohio.
Brainerd	Nattie	BD, p3c1, 7/5/1878	Graduated with honors from Platteville State Normal School and returned to her home in Boscobel. Applied to teach in Boscobel.
Brainerd	Nora	BD, p3c5, 3/8/1878	Mr. Dennis married Nora Brainerd on Monday evening in Boscobel. Bride from Boscobel and groom from Minnesota. They departed by train for their future home.
Brake	B. M.	BD, p3c1, 4/21/1882	Former resident of Boscobel. Now resident of Kansas City. Married April 4, 1882 to Fannie Smiley at the bride's home in Wabash, IN.
Brake	B. M.	BD, p2c4, 8/3/1877	Attorney in Boscobel. Advertised to help process pension claims.
Brake	B. M.	BD, p3c5, 8/17/1877	Resided in Boscobel. He was a railroad agent for farm land in Kansas.
Brake	B. M.	BD, p2c2, 6/6/1879	Wrote a letter to *The Dial* describing Kansas settlement and farms and attractions.
Brandenburg	Jacob	RH, p5c3, 10/13/1898	Died Oct. 5, 1898 in De Soto at the age of 80 years. Funeral held at the Catholic Church in Genoa. Buried in Genoa.
Brandes	George	RH, p5c3, 11/24/1898	Opened a harness shop in the Fish Building in Readstown.
Brandes	George	RH, p4c2, 3/22/1900	Returned to Readstown from Minneapolis to set up a harness shop.
Brandon	Robert	BD, p3c1, 11/26/1880	Robert Brandon married Alameda McLiman on Nov. 18, 1880 in Boscobel. Bride and groom were from Grant Co. Peter Rae, Esquire officiated.
Brandt	Fred	BD, p3c?, 12/24/1880	Fred Brandt of Brandtville, Grant Co. married Judy Brandt of Mt. Hope on Dec. 19, 1880.
Brandt	Judy	BD, p3c?, 12/24/1880	Fred Brandt of Brandtville, Grant Co. married Judy Brandt of Mt. Hope on Dec. 19, 1880.

Genealogical Events from Newspapers for Crawford, Vernon and Grant Counties, Wisconsin, 1870-1901

LAST NAME	FIRST NAME	NEWSPAPER, PAGE/COLUMN MONTH/DAY/YEAR	GENEALOGICAL DATA
Brannon	Anna	RH, p5c4, 4/14/1898	Anna Brannon and Joseph Monti sent out invitations to their wedding, per De Soto news column.
Brar	Ammon, Mr.	DC, p3c5, 7/24/1886	Arrived from Merrill to visit relatives in Retreat.
Brechler	Lizetta	BD, p3c1, 9/26/1879	Albert Ableiter married Lizetta Brechler on Sept. 23, 1879 at the German Lutheran Church. Bride and groom from Boscobel.
Breckler	Mr.	BD, p3c3, 9/21/1877	He was in a farm accident south of town [Wauzeka]. His "lower area" was amputated.
Breed	Elder	DC, p4c4, 5/21/1887	Baptized 8 converts in Victory for the Seventh Day Adventists Church.
Brekke	Charles	BD, p3c1, 6/25/1880	Charles Brekke married Delia Smith on June 21, 1880 at Brekke's Hotel. Groom from Soldiers Grove. Bride from Viroqua. Prof. J. Allison of Boscobel officiated.
Brekke	Charles	BD, p3c2, 2/17/1882	Died of consumption on Monday at home of father, Martin Brekke, in Boscobel. Aged about 27 years. Survived by wife of 18 months. He was a partner in Brekke and Davidson of Soldiers Grove.
Brekke	Cornelius	BD, p3c2, 11/19/1880	Died Monday in Boscobel from a hemorrhage caused by consumption.
Brekke	Hermana M.	BD, p3c2, 10/18/1878	William Edwin Bennett married Hermana M. Brekke on Oct. 14, 1878 at the home of the bride's father in Boscobel. Groom from Chicago. Rev. Dr. Stoddart officiated.
Brekke	M. O.	BD, p3c1, 2/4/1881	M. O. Brekke's father died Saturday in Boscobel at 80 years of age.
Brekke	M. O.	BD, p3c1, 4/28/1882	Left Boscobel for a wheat farm he purchased in Jamestown, Dakota.
Brekke	Mina	BD, p3c1, 4/7/1882	Mina Brekke and Sylvia Kelty left Boscobel for new homes in Dakota.
Brekke	O. G.	BD, p3c2, 5/2/1879	Departed Boscobel for Christiana, Dane Co. to operate a drug store.
Brekler	Christ	BD, p3c2, 2/24/1882	Christ Bekler married Hannah Kreul on Feb. 16, 1882 at the home of the bride's parents in Fennimore. Rev. Mutchman officiated.
Bremmer	Margaret, Mrs.	BD, p2c3, 1/13/1882	Died Jan. 1, 1882 in Muscoda at the residence of her son. Born Dec. 27, 1799 in Enskirchen, Prussia. [See Mrs. Regina Schneider obituary. She was also from Enskirchen. Related?] Married J. B. Bremmer when she was 26. Emigrated in 1847 to Milwaukee. Lived there for a short time and then moved to Mineral Point. Moved to Muscoda in 1854. Husband died Dec. 2, 1862. After his death she sold the farm and lived with her children, usually Jacob [who lived in town] or with Adolph [who lived on a farm]. Her two oldest daughters, Mrs. Schaefer and Mrs. Dieter, lived in Castle Rock. The youngest daughter, Mrs. W. F. Wicker [Wicken?], lived in Muscoda.
Brennan	Thomas	DR, p3c2, 1/4/1872	Died Dec. 23, 1871. Lived about 5 miles from De Soto. Came into town to fill his jug with whiskey. Started for home in the late afternoon, walking through deep snow in a storm. He took frequent draughts from the jug. His body was found a half-mile from home where he laid down in the snow and died. He was survived by a wife and 4 children. [Per p3c1, 1/11/1872, this was an error. Mike Brennan died, not his brother, Thomas. Family claimed he died of heart disease.]
Brenneman	Belle, Mrs.	RH, p4c2, 12/13/1900	Arrived in Readstown from Delmont, SD to visit relatives.
Brewer	Peter	BD, p2c3, 12/22/1882	His overcoat was stolen, recovered and returned. Resided in Excelsior.
Brice	Mr.	DC, p3c2, 7/24/1886	Mr. Brice of Onalaska visited his son, Harvey, in De Soto.
Brickler	Mr.	BD, p3c2, 2/21/1879	Susan Grazer married Mr. Brickler Thursday morning. Bride from Town of Fennimore. She was the daughter of Karel Grazer. Groom from Town of Marion.
Brickner	Emily	BD, p3c1, 6/11/1880	J. N. Kast married Emily Brickner last Monday in Boscobel. Justice DeWitt officiated.
Brienig	Dr.	DR, p1c1, 12/15/1870	Physician in Lansing, IA.
Briggs	Fay P.	RH, p7c4, 7/1/1897	President of the Readstown Improvement Co.
Briggs	Frank and Arthur	RH, p4c1, 9/20/1900	Resided in Viroqua. Purchased the *Tomah Herald*.
Briggson	Ingvald	RH, p5c3, 5/3/1900	Briggson was "insane." He was a ward of L. O. Thompson of Vernon Co. Thompson petitioned the court for approval to sell Briggson's real estate.

Genealogical Events from Newspapers for Crawford, Vernon and Grant Counties, Wisconsin, 1870-1901

LAST NAME	FIRST NAME	NEWSPAPER, PAGE/COLUMN MONTH/DAY/YEAR	GENEALOGICAL DATA
Brigham	N. W.	RH, p4c2, 3/29/1900	Owned a Bible published in Edinburgh, Scotland in 1676. It was originally owned by Guy Edson. Edson served in the Revolutionary War and was the footman for John Quincy Adams. Brigham also has an old almanac from 1852.
Brigham	W.	DR, p1c2, 12/7/1871	Vernon Co. Board of Supervisors allowed payment to W. Brigham and Seth Edson for care of the insane.
Bright	J. L., Rev.	DC, p1c1, 8/9/1889	Served as pastor of the Congregational Church in Lynxville.
Bright	T. C.	DC, p3c4, 8/21/1886	Operated a general store in Lynxville.
Bright	T. C.	DC, p3c3, 2/19/1887	The T. C. Bright & Co. store in Lynxville was robbed. Lost items were found in the possession of a man named Comstock, "a worthless character who has managed to live quite well since he has been there, a year past, without any visible means of support." This man claimed to be a nephew of the original owner of the great Comstock silver mine in Nevada.
Bright	T. C.	DC, p1c1, 8/9/1889	The T. C. Bright & Co. of Lynxville finds "the coal trade very profitable this season."
Brightman	F. C.	RH, p4c2, 2/7/1901	Planned to leave Bell Center on Monday for Oklahoma. Wanted to take up timberland.
Brightman	Mrs.	DR, p1c5, 2/23/1871	Operated a boarding school for the young ladies attending the Mt. Sterling Academy.
Brindler	Josephine	BD, p3c1, 12/10/1880	Casper Maeliotka married Josephine Brindler on Dec. 8, 1880 in Boscobel. Bride from Hickory Grove. Groom from Muscoda.
Brindley	boy	BD, p3c1, 12/16/1881	A son was born on Sunday to John Brindley of Boscobel. Weighed 10 pounds.
Brindley	John	BD, p3c2, 6/4/1880	Left Boscobel for a new home in La Crosse. Formed a law partnership there.
Brindley	John, Jr.	BD, p3c3, 12/10/1880	John Brindley, Jr. married Addie Willis on Thursday at the Congregational Church in Boscobel. Mrs. Stickel played the organ. The bride and groom were from Boscobel. Their new home will be in La Crosse. An extensive guest list was published.
Brindley	Martha	BD, p3c2, 7/8/1881	Daughter of Hon. John Brindley. Plans to teach in the La Crosse schools for $40 a month.
Brindley	W. A.	RH, p4c1, 9/13/1900	W. A. Brindley, Elma Wilson and Gertrude Ewers taught in the Readstown schools.
Brisbane	William, Dr.	BD, p1c6, 4/19/1878	Died last week at his home in Arena, Iowa Co. at the age of 75. Born in South Carolina. When young, he took 30 slaves to Ohio, freed them and gave them land. Active in abolition causes. Came to Wisconsin in 1857.
Broadhead	Edna	DC, p3c4, 11/27/1886	Taught school in the Morgan neighborhood according to the Retreat news column.
Broadhead	Edna, Miss	DC, p2c1, 7/9/1887	Died July 5, 1887 from consumption at her home near Retreat. Funeral was the largest ever witnessed in Retreat. There were 50 teams.
Broadhead	Stella	DC, p3c4, 3/27/1888	Lived in Retreat. Visited sister, Mrs. Dach near Liberty Pole.
Brooks		BD, p3c1, 6/20/1879	A 13-pound boy was born on Wednesday to T. J. Brooks of Boscobel.
Brooks	girl	BD, p3c1, 10/2/1883	A daughter was recently born to T. J. Brooks of Grant Co.
Brooks	Jesse	BD, p3c2, 5/28/1880	Appointed to be a census enumerator in Bloomington, Grant Co.
Brooks	Mr.	RH, p4c4, 8/1/1901	Flora Chambers recently married Mr. Brooks. Bride from De Soto. Groom was a hardware dealer in Iowa.
Brooks	T. J.	BD, p3c1, 1/5/1877	Attorney in Boscobel.
Brooks	Thomas J.	BD, p3c4, 1/9/1880	A notice was published that Brooks was the administrator for the Nathaniel Wilmarth estate. Wilmarth was late of Hickory Grove.
Brown		DR, p3c1, 1/11/1872	A child was born on Jan. 3, 1872 to Charles Brown of De Soto.
Brown	Americus	BD, p3c1, 5/23/1879	Americus Brown and Frank Tice were arrested in Boscobel for stealing and placed in jail. Deputy Sheriff James Bailey made the arrest.
Brown	Belle L., Mrs.	DC, p3c3, 5/8/1888	Taught school in Victory.
Brown	C. D.	BD, p3c1, 10/24/1879	Died Oct. 9, 1879 in Watterstown of billous fever when he was 59.

Genealogical Events from Newspapers for Crawford, Vernon and Grant Counties, Wisconsin, 1870-1901

LAST NAME	FIRST NAME	NEWSPAPER, PAGE/COLUMN MONTH/DAY/YEAR	GENEALOGICAL DATA
Brown	C. K.	DC, p2c1, 4/30/1887	Served in Co. A, 7th Regt. WI Vol. Wrote a letter criticizing Gen. Bragg of the Iron Brigade for speaking against the Dependent Pension Bill in Congress.
Brown	C., Mr. and Mrs.	BD, p3c3, 7/22/1881	Arrived in Boscobel from Jackson, MI to visit cousins, Mr. and Mrs. M. A. Sawyer.
Brown	Charles	DC, p3c4, 4/2/1887	Returned to Red Mound after spending the winter in Chippewa Falls.
Brown	Columbus	DC, p2c2, 2/3/1888	Shopkeepers in De Soto in the early years remember Columbus Brown. He always bought on credit. Though the shopkeepers declared they would not extend further credit, he always obtained what he wanted as he was "simply irresistible." One day Brown gave Whiting & Carr an old cow and insisted upon taking it for $30 towards his account. Whiting gladly did so and then sold the cow to William Heal for $10. Brown and his large family ultimately left the area.
Brown	E. A., Miss	BD, p3c2, 9/19/1879	E. F. Markum married Miss E. A. Brown last Sunday at Muscoda. Bride from Watterstown. Groom from Boscobel. The Rev. George Haigh officiated.
Brown	F. J., Rev.	DC, p3c3, 12/18/1886	Held services in Victory.
Brown	F. P.	DC, p3c2, 4/2/1887	Departed Victory for Iowa.
Brown	Fanny	BD, p3c2, 6/13/1879	Fanny Brown married Raymond S. Olmstead last Sunday at the Brown home. Bride daughter of George Brown of Woodman. Groom from Cherokee, IA. Planned to live in Cherokee. The Rev. William Cook officiated.
Brown	George	BD, p3c1, 6/2/1882	Resided in Woodman. Traveled for a visit to England, his homeland. Left on Thursday, 30 years to the day since he landed in New York. He was accompanied by Charles Robinson, Robinson's children [George and Anna] and Miss Maria Collier of Patch Grove.
Brown	George	BD, p3c2, 5/28/1880	Appointed to be a census enumerator in Woodman, Grant Co.
Brown	H. R., Mr.	BD, p3c4, 8/3/1877	Mr. H. R. Brown and his wife, Sarah Warren, of Belmont and Miss Ella Ford of Boscobel arrived from St. Paul on Tuesday. Mr. Brown and his family were the guests of O. E. Comstock.
Brown	Hank	RH, p4c1, 5/31/1900	Worked as an apprentice at Davenport Bros.
Brown	Henry	RH, p4c1, 3/14/1901	Planned to leave Readstown for Janesville, MN this week.
Brown	Leb, Mrs.	BD, p3c3, 9/16/1881	Departed Marietta for a visit in Philadelphia.
Brown	Levi	DC, p3c3, 8/21/1886	House in Harmony was damaged [destroyed?] by fire.
Brown	Lou, Mrs.	RH, p4c1, 10/24/1901	Arrived from Yuba, AZ to visit with mother, Mrs. Susan Angell of Readstown.
Brown	M. E., Mrs.	BD, p2c5, 1/5/1877	Resided in Boscobel. Advertised services as an organ teacher.
Brown	Mary E., Mrs.	BD, p3c2, 3/9/1877	William Partridge married Mrs. Mary E. Brown on Mar. 7, 1877. Bride and groom from Boscobel. The Rev. George Nuzum officiated.
Brown	Mattie	BD, p3c2, 10/30/1883	From Woodman. Taught grammer school in Werley.
Brown	Minnie	BD, p3c1, 2/16/1883	George Wicken married Minnie Brown on Feb. 6, 1883 in Excelsior.
Brown	Mr.	RH, p5c3, 12/28/1899	Owner of the Brown Broom patent. The newly formed Readstown Broom Company manufactured the brooms. The company of 6 workers can not keep up with demand. They want to employ 50 people.
Brown	Mrs.	DC, p2c2, 6/18/1887	Mrs. Brown of Bad Axe visited her brother, Mr. Campbell of Freeman.
Brown	Nellie	BD, p3c1, 4/15/1881	Charles H. Keyes married Nellie E. Brown at the home of the bride's father in the Town of Scott on April 12, 1881. Rev. W. Stoddart officiated. Groom from Excelsior.
Brown	Ole	BD, p3c1, 3/19/1880	The Ole Brown family of Hickory Grove loaded their goods and chattles on the cars for a new home on the Red River of the north on Tuesday.
Brown	Ole S.	BD, p3c1, 2/27/1880	Resided in Hickory Grove. Will auction off stock and household goods on March 5, 1880.
Brown	Paulina	BD, p2c5, 12/11/1883	Andre J. Linderlin applied to the Probate Court to administer the estate of Paulina Brown, late of Hickory Grove.
Brown	Robert W.	BD, p3c1, 6/2/1882	Robert W. Brown married Minnie C. Long on May 28, 1882 at Boscobel. J. McLaughlin, J.P. officiated.
Brown	Volney A.	BD, p3c1, 12/25/1883	Died of consumption Saturday in Boscobel. He was 25. Returned to Boscobel from Kansas City to die. He was gone for 3 years. He was the son of Mrs. Abrams of Boscobel.

Genealogical Events from Newspapers for Crawford, Vernon and Grant Counties, Wisconsin, 1870-1901

LAST NAME	FIRST NAME	NEWSPAPER, PAGE/COLUMN MONTH/DAY/YEAR	GENEALOGICAL DATA
Brown	W. P.	RH, p5c3, 1/13/1898	Died Jan. 3, 1898 at his home in Avalanche. Buried in Salem Cemetery by the GAR Post of Viroqua.
Brudas	Tom, Mrs.	DC, p3c3, 4/17/1888	Arrested for not paying her tab at Davidson's store in De Soto. She had boarded a train for Dakota when she was arrested. Planned to meet her husband, who had already departed.
Bruhn	L. E.	BD, p2c4, 11/26/1880	Grant County paid him a bounty for scalps turned into the county.
Bruland	Louis A.	RH, p4c2, 7/25/1901	Died Friday evening, July 19, 1901 of heart failure at the home of his son, Mons Bruland. Mons lived about 2 miles northwest of Readstown. Louis was 79 years old. He looked well Friday afternoon during a trip to Readstown. Mrs. J. T. Dregne asked him to spend the night, but he was fine and walked home. Louis' wife died about 2 weeks ago.
Brunson	Alfred	BD, p2c2, 8/11/1882	Died Aug. 3, 1882 in Prairie du Chien. Born Feb 9, 1793 in Danbury, CT. Educated in the common school and at Sing Sing Academy in New York, where the family moved in 1800. Father died in 1806. Mother returned to Danbury with 7 children, Alfred being the oldest. He was put to a trade as a shoemaker. Decided to study law, but in 1808 experienced religion and felt a call to the ministry. Married in 1812 and moved to Trumbull Co., OH. In 1813 served under Gen. Harrison at the Battle of the Thames. Licensed to preach in 1815. In 1818 preached on his first circuit in Huron Co., OH. Went on missionary work with Sioux and Chippewa Indians in 1835. He and 3 families came to Prairie du Chien in 1836. Had a section of his house prepared in advance and towed by boat and then constructed in Lowertown [Prairie du Chien]. Lived in that house until his death. Admitted to the bar, served as a J.P. and as a Supreme Court commissioner. Member of Legislature. Indian agent. Survived by wife and 6 children.
Brunson	Ira B.	BD, p3c2, 9/4/1883	Ira B. Brunson died in Prairie du Chien on Aug. 21, 1883. He was born in Fowler, OH on Nov. 5, 1815 and came to Prairie du Chien in 1836 in company with his father, Alfred Brunson. He served in the territorial legislature in 1837-1840. Served as a postmaster, register of deeds, county surveyor, sheriff and clerk of circuit court. In 1853 he was made a county judge, a position he held for 30 years. He was the father of Theophilus, Arthur and Mrs. Dr. Eddy by his first wife and 3 daughters by his second wife. A brother and 2 sisters remain to mourn his loss. Services conducted by Rev. A. McMaster at the Congregational Church. Buried in Lowertown Cemetery.
Bryson	John C.	BD, p3c2, 5/31/1878	John C. Bryson married Elizabeth J. Tennant in Mt. Ida on May 7, 1878. R. Buggins, Esquire officiated.
Buchanan	Frankie	DC, p2c2, 3/10/1888	Died Mar. 7, 1888 of lung fever in Victory. His brother, Willie, also ill with the disease.
Buchanan	Robert	BD, p3c1, 12/25/1883	Died Sunday near Excelsior. He was 74.
Buchanan	Samuel	BD, p3c1, 11/3/1882	Samuel Buchanan married Rebecca Nobel on Oct. 28, 1882 at the Central House in Boscobel. Bride and groom from Excelsior. The Rev. E. L. Morse officiated.
Buckmaster	Jesse	BD, p3c4, 9/21/1877	Published a notice that he found a stray horse in Haney Township.
Bugbee	Henry	BD, p3c3, 5/28/1880	Resided in Mt. Ida. Published a notice in the newspaper that his wife, Mary Jane Bugbee, and children had left him and that he would not be responsible for their debts.
Bugbee	Henry	BD, p3c2, 2/9/1877	At the Supreme Court in Madison, the appeal in the case of City of Boscobel vs. Henry Bugbee, was dismissed with costs.
Bugbee	Henry	BD, p3c3, 2/22/1878	Received Boscobel city funds for boarding Mrs. Shorty.
Bugbee	Henry	BD, p3c2, 1/17/1879	Bugbee residence in Rogers Hollow was destroyed by fire.
Bull	John	BD, p3c2, 6/4/1880	John Bull's barn in Lower Town [Prairie du Chien] was struck by lightening on Sunday.
Bullock	Lucetta	BD, p3c3, 5/24/1878	Gardner A. Hurd married Lucetta B. Bullock on May 20, 1878 at the residence of Philip Kelts of Lancaster. Groom from Boscobel. The Rev. W. L. Brown officiated.
Bunnell	Dr.	DC, p3c2, 6/19/1888	An elaborately carved olive wood snuffbox was discovered near Esofea, Vernon Co. in an old grave around an old camping site. The box had the inscription "I. H. S." and the date 1790 on the cover. Dr. Bunnell, "the well known writer on local historical subjects" suggested it was once the property of a Jesuit missionary who died while exploring or converting the Indians.
Burchard	George W., Mrs.	BD, p3c2, 8/24/1877	Mrs. George W. Burchard of Kankakee, IL [and an unnamed daughter of Kankakee] visited her daughter, Mrs. M. D. Tillotson in Boscobel. Mr. Miles D. Tillotson was the cashier at the First National Bank. Mrs. Cropsey, wife of the private secretary for the Governor of Nebraska, was also a guest..
Burchard	Mat., Capt.	BD, p3c2, 1/5/1877	New sheriff in Grant Co. Mr. McCoy retired as sheriff.

Genealogical Events from Newspapers for Crawford, Vernon and Grant Counties, Wisconsin, 1870-1901

LAST NAME	FIRST NAME	NEWSPAPER, PAGE/COLUMN MONTH/DAY/YEAR	GENEALOGICAL DATA
Burchardt	Jacob	BD, p3c3, 12/6/1878	Resided in the Boscobel area. He was tarred and feathered Monday evening. It is believed to be related to some family troubles. Warrants were issued.
Burchardt	Jacob	BD, p3c2, 12/20/1878	Peter Babel, John Babel, David Freymiller and Daniel Trum, Jr. were arrested for tarring and feathering Jacob Buchardt.
Burchill	Samuel	DC, p3c3, 10/23/1886	Died Oct. 4, 1886 at Hillsboro at the age of 112. He was born on the day of the Battle of Bunker Hill [June 17, 1775]. Until recently, he was able to work.
Burdick	B. S.	BD, p3c1, 12/3/1880	Returned from Mitchell, Dakota where he secured a position in the railroad office.
Burdick	B. S.	BD, p3c1, 12/17/1880	A son was born to B. S. Burdick on Friday night.
Burdick	B. S.	BD, p3c2, 8/14/1883	Brainerd ["Bain"] S. Burdick was arrested in Memphis, TN for bigamy. His first wife lived in Boscobel. He recently married Miss Mattie Thomas in Memphis. He lived under several alias names. Arrested for robbery of a gold watch, too. [Memphis papers called him J. B. Burdick.]
Burdick	B. S., Mrs.	BD, p3c1, 8/28/1883	Planned to travel to Memphis to testify against her husband in a bigamy case in Memphis, TN.
Burdick	Bain	BD, p2c2, 10/16/1883	Acquitted in Memphis due to the failure of witnesses from Wisconsin to appear.
Burdick	Bain	BD, p2c2, 7/20/1877	A letter written by Bain Burdick was published that described his travel in the eastern United States. He visited relatives in Fulton, NY.
Burdick	Bain	BD, p3c2, 1/17/1879	Misses Ella and Clara Gillett of Hastings, MN visited their cousin, Mr. Bain Burdick of Boscobel.
Burdick	Bain and Carlos	BD, p3c2, 5/31/1878	Planned to leave Boscobel next Monday for Iowa in a prairie schooner.
Burdick	Brainard S.	BD, p3c2, 9/19/1879	Brainard S. Burdick planned to marry Emma Stoddart next Wednesday at the Congregational Church in Boscobel.
Burdick	Brainard S.	BD, p2c2, 10/3/1879	Brainard S. Burdick married Emma Stoddart on Sept. 24, 1879 at the Congregational Church in Boscobel. There was extensive coverage of the guests.
Burdick	Brainerd S.	BD, p2c1, 8/21/1883	A complete account of the Burdick bigamy case was abstracted from a Memphis, TN newspaper. Burdick, alias Bennett, was being held in jail. On Aug. 9, 1883 J. B. Bennett [Bain Burdick] sent a telegram to a Boscobel attorney asking if the Emma Burdick/B. S. Burdick divorce had been granted. Burdick married Mattie Thomas of Galloway, Fayette Co., TN. Burdick had been involved in a robbery in Crookston, MN. He pawned a musical instrument he stole. It was found in Memphis. Emma Burdick was the daughter of the Congregational minister in Boscobel. Bain's father was a former railroad agent in Boscobel and got a job for his son as a day operator at the Boscobel station. Burdick was suspected of "crookedness" at the station. He departed for Mitchell, Dakota, where he was later jailed for stealing, forgery and perjury. Emma was unaware of his crimes until his arrest in Mitchell, at which time she left him and returned to her father's home in Boscobel.
Burdick	Emma	BD, p3c1, 9/4/1883	Emma Burdick and her father, Dr. William Stoddart, planned to leave on Sept. 6, 1883 for Memphis.
Burdick	F. B., Capt.	BD, p3c3, 3/1/1878	Capt. F. B. Burdick and his wife planned to celebrate their 25th wedding anniversary on Mar. 4, 1878. [Burdick's of Boscobel area?]
Burdick	F. B., Capt.	BD, p3c1, 7/18/1879	Retired after 20 years of service in the railroad depot at Boscobel. Planned to build up his farm. He was succeeded by Dr. T. D. Wadsworth, formerly of South Evanston.
Burdick	George C.	DC, p3c3, 2/11/1888	Died on a street in Waseca, MN last week at the age of about 26. Former editor of a newspaper in De Soto. Probably committed suicide by taking "choral hydrate."
Burgbur	John	DC, p2c1, 12/18/1886	Son of Jerry, an old time Retreat resident. Visited his grandfather, Leo Bishop in Retreat.
Burger	John	DC, p3c2, 3/12/1887	From Huron, Dakota. Spent the winter in Retreat.
Burger	L., Mr.	DC, p2c3, 11/26/1887	Lived in Dakota. He was the guest of his grandfather, Deacon Bishop of Retreat.
Burger	N. H.	RH, p5c3, 12/8/1898	N. H. Burger and Frank Austin of Viola did business in Readstown. Burger insured the Herald building and H. M. Pond's merchandise and residence.
Burgess	J. F.	DC, p3c4, 10/23/1886	Taught school in Wauzeka for the last 5 years. He was the Republican candidate for Superintendent of Schools.
Burgh	George	BD, p3c2, 9/26/1879	Sheriff Streeter took him to Waupon to serve a 1-year sentence for burglary.
Burgor	N. H.	BD, p2c3, 2/9/1883	Nellie Akey married L. C. McCollum last Sunday at the home of the bride's parents, Mr. and Mrs. Lemuel Akey of Buena Vista, Richland Co. Groom from Fifield, Price Co., WI. This was a double wedding with Mattie Akey and N. H. Burgor. Groom from Viola. The Rev. Pearce of Richland Center officiated.

Genealogical Events from Newspapers for Crawford, Vernon and Grant Counties, Wisconsin, 1870-1901

LAST NAME	FIRST NAME	NEWSPAPER, PAGE/COLUMN MONTH/DAY/YEAR	GENEALOGICAL DATA
Burke	Charles	DC, p3c2, 11/12/1887	The Charles Burke funeral was held Wednesday at Harper's Ferry. Killed from a fall off the C.B. & N. bridge. Miss Nellie McEvoy and A. B. Downey, his cousins from De Soto, attended the funeral.
Burke	Charles	DC, p3c1, 12/3/1887	The relatives of Charles Burke have sued the county for $10,000. Burke was recently killed on the C. B. & N. bridge the crossed the Wisconsin River.
Burke	Mr.	DC, p3c4, 7/16/1887	Resided in Omaha, NB. He was a cousin of the Downey and Banks families in De Soto. Arrived for a visit with his relatives.
Burke	Patrick	BD, p3c2, 7/16/1880	Died about July 1, 1880 in Rolling Ground, Crawford Co. Bachelor. Recently received a $1100 pension. Lived by himself in a shanty on his farm. No foul play suspected.
Burn		RH, p5c3, 11/18/1897	A daughter was recently born to Prof. Robbie Burn of Viola.
Burnard		RH, p6c5, 9/2/1897	The infant child of George Burnard of Ross died last night of cholera.
Burnn	John	BD, p2c4, 11/26/1880	Grant County paid him a bounty for scalps turned into the county.
Burns	A., Mrs. Dr.	BD, p3c2, 4/27/1877	Planned to see patients this summer at the Carriage House in Boscobel.
Buroker	Milton	RH, p5c3, 7/8/1897	Milton Buroker married Bessie Randall last Thursday at the home of Dr. Randall, the bride's parents. Bride and groom from Sugar Grove.
Buroker	Milton	RH, p4c3, 3/17/1898	Moved to Sugar Grove and opened a blacksmith shop. Frank Middleton is helping him.
Burr	Addison, Esq.	BD, p3c3, 5/17/1878	Recently died in Lancaster.
Burrison	John	DC, p8c1, 6/7/1889	Lived in Town of Webster. His 5 and 7-year-old children recently drowned in the Kickapoo River. Their mother was unable to save them. The younger child "raised the alarm."
Burrows	Charles W.	BD, p3c1, 11/21/1879	Charles W. Burrows married Elva Bennett on Nov. 4, 1870 at the residence of James Henderson in Hickory Grove. Bride and groom from Watterstown.
Burton	C.	BD, p3c2, 1/31/1879	Mr. C. Burton, former proprietor of the *Boscobel Dial*, now lives in Granite Falls, MN.
Busby	Harry	BD, p2c3, 3/3/1882	Served as Richland Co. Sheriff. Died Monday of heart disease while watching a play at Kroushop Hall in Richland Center [per Feb. 23rd issue of *Republican and Observer*]. Remains were taken to the home of his sister, Mrs. F. P. Brown. He was born in New York and had New England heritage. Moved here 12 years ago. Survived by wife and 2 children. They were in Chicago when he died.
Buschhausen	Mrs.	BD, p3c1, 3/28/1879	Resided in the Boscobel area. Buried Wednesday.
Bush	H. H., Dr.	DC, p3c4, 9/4/1886	Resided in Victory. Attended his daughter's funeral in Pepin.
Bush	H. H., Dr.	DC, p3c4, 12/4/1886	Physician in Victory.
Butcher	W. M.	BD, p3c1, 1/5/1877	Attorney in Boscobel.
Butler	J. L.	RH, p5c4, 11/25/1897	J. L. Butler and Charles Benton of Elkhorn plead guilty to burglary. They were sentenced to 3 years in Waupon.
Butler	James	DR, p3c2, 10/12/1871	Escaped after his trial for burglarizing Bartholomew's saloon in De Soto. He was last seen at Mr. J. S. Gibb's where he took supper after the escape. He was also known as Jeems Butler.
Butler	James	DR, p3c1, 10/26/1871	Burglerized Bartholomew's saloon. Sent to Waupon Prison for 1 year.
Butler	Jeems	DR, p3c3, 10/5/1871	Resided in Prairie du Chien. Arrested for robbing the saloon of Pete Bartholomew in De Soto. Caught in the act by "Deacon" Woodbury and James Loftus.
Butler	R.	DC, p2c2, 3/12/1887	Conducted a cooper store in Ontario, WI.
Butler	R.	DC, p3c5, 2/3/1888	Returned to Ontario from California. Decided to stay here for awhile longer.
Butler	W. W.	DC, p2c2, 12/11/1886	Opened a feed and gristmill in Retreat.
Butler	W. W.	DC, p3c3, 4/3/1888	Died March 28, 1888 in De Soto from a self-inflicted gunshot wound. Gave up his business 2 years ago to care for his wife who was stricken with paralysis. He was 52 years old and had no children. [More details provided.]
Butler	W. W., Mrs.	DC, p3c4, 7/24/1886	Resided in Retreat. Stricken with apoplexy.

Genealogical Events from Newspapers for Crawford, Vernon and Grant Counties, Wisconsin, 1870-1901

LAST NAME	FIRST NAME	NEWSPAPER, PAGE/COLUMN MONTH/DAY/YEAR	GENEALOGICAL DATA
Butler	W. W., Mrs.	DC, p3c3, 12/4/1888	Died last Wednesday. Born in Retreat. Died in Berlin, WI.
Butler	W. W., Mrs.	DC, p3c3, 12/11/1888	Died Nov. 28,1888 at the residence of Dr. J. S. Walbridge in Berlin, WI. She was 45 years old and had suffered a stroke 2 years ago. After her husband's death last spring she moved to Berlin. Remains were brought to Retreat by her aunt, Mrs. Cone. She was laid by her husband and mother.
Butt	C. M.	DR, p2c3, 12/15/1870	Attorney and real estate agent in Viroqua.
Buxton	Charles	RH, p4c1, 4/11/1901	Offered a reward for his pocket book that was lost between his place and Readstown. Pocket book had $55 in it.
Byer	Zelma, Miss	RH, p7c2, 7/1/1897	Came from Wauzeka to visit her brother, Max, in Readstown.
Byerly	J.	BD, p3c1, 6/22/1883	Resided in Wauzeka. Brought his 8-year-old boy to Boscobel for medical treatment. The boy fell off a railroad car.
Byerly	Lebius	BD, p3c2, 12/7/1877	Died Nov. 25, 1877 in Fennimore. Aged 17 years and 6 months.
Byerly	Tressie	BD, p2c3, 6/22/1883	Ferrin Shuttleworth and Tressie Byerly were the first graduates of the Fennimore High School.
C. M. A. Lodge of Kickapoo		RH, p5c4, 4/13/1899	The newly organized C. M. A., Kickapoo Valley Lodge officers are Owen Kellogg, Keith Andrews, Guy Hopkins, Eugene Lange, Curtis Smith and Gene Heal.
Cabinas	G. E.	BD, p3c2, 5/28/1880	Appointed to be a census enumerator in Smelser, Grant Co.
Cade	J. A.	DC, p3c1, 1/21/1888	Resided in West Prairie. Published a notice that he had taken up a lost steer.
Cade	Wesley	DC, p3c4, 8/7/1886	Held a Honey Festival at his Retreat residence to benefit Rev. J. T. Morgans. Ice cream was also served.
Cain	G. W., Mrs.	BD, p2c6, 10/22/1880	Established a millinery and fancy goods store in Boscobel 3 1/2 years ago. Mrs. Cain has 26 years of experience in the millinery trade. For many years she ran her business in Dubuque, Iowa.
Cain	G. W., Mrs.	BD, p3c2, 4/4/1879	Returned to Boscobel from Chicago with new stock for her millinery store.
Cain	George W.	BD, p3c2, 12/18/1883	Died on his farm near Remington, Wood Co., WI. Born April 17, 1811 in Shenandoah Co., VA. Moved to Ohio in 1831. Married Priscilla Morris on Oct. 6, 1831 in Ohio. Five of their 6 children survive. Moved to Dubuque, IA where Priscilla died. On Jan. 18, 1850 he married Mrs. C. H. Messmore. She survives him. Moved to Boscobel "some years ago." Moved to Wood Co. two years ago.
Cain	Henry	DC, p3c1, 6/11/1887	Died June 5, 1887 in De Soto. Born 69 years ago in Ireland. Moved to Canada in 1844 and to the U.S. in 1846. Naturalized a citizen in 1853. Buried in the Genoa Catholic Cemetery. During his last illness Charles Smith, his faithful friend, cared for him.
Caitlin	Horace	BD, p2c3, 3/31/1882	He was an old settler in the Town of Willow, Richland Co. Lived alone. Considered to be insane. Twenty men searched the surrounding woods for him after he vanished. Complained that 100 men were after him.
Calbert	Henry	BD, p3c3, 5/18/1877	Died Tuesday in Richwood Township, Richland Co. Aged 88 years. Lived apart from his wife for about a year. Calbert was believed to have been murdered.
Caldwell	Charles	DR, p3c2, 5/25/1871	Native of De Soto. Home on furlough from the Nineth Infantry. Stationed in Omaha.
Caldwell	Charles	DR, p3c1, 6/8/1871	Returned to his regiment in Omaha last week after a visit in the De Soto area.
Caldwell	Charley	DR, p3c1, 12/7/1871	Native of De Soto. Promoted to Sergeant in the [U. S. Army?].
Caldwell	Will	RH, p5c5, 7/15/1897	Resided in the Ross area. Planned to "start west" soon. Per the 8/5/1897 issue of the paper, Caldwell went to Minnesota and returned when he was unable to find work.
Calkins	Levi	RH, p5c5, 9/30/1897	Died Sept. 21, 1897 in Brush Hollow, Liberty Township, Vernon Co. Buried in Brush Hollow. Rev. Smith conducted the funeral service.
Calkins	Levi, Mrs.	RH, p5c3, 12/8/1898	Enjoyed a visit from her mother, Mrs. Sands of Viroqua, per Mound Park news column.
Callahan	Daniel	BD, p3c1, 10/29/1880	Died Saturday. Aged 73 years. Resided in Blue River. Buried at Muscoda. Survived by wife, 3 sons and 3 daughters.
Calloway	J. D.	BD, p3c1, 4/30/1880	Resided in Crawford Co. Sold his farm to Anson Fish. Planned to go west and farm.
Calloway	J. V.	DC, p3c3, 9/18/1886	Resided in Millett. Planned to run for Register of Deeds in Crawford Co.

Genealogical Events from Newspapers for Crawford, Vernon and Grant Counties, Wisconsin, 1870-1901

LAST NAME	FIRST NAME	NEWSPAPER, PAGE/COLUMN MONTH/DAY/YEAR	GENEALOGICAL DATA
Calloway	Jennie	BD, p3c4, 12/28/1877	James A. Dull married Jennie Calloway on Christmas Day, 1877. Bride from Marietta, Crawford Co. Groom from Waterloo, Grant Co. Rev. Dr. Stoddart officiated.
Caloway	J. W.	RH, p4c2, 11/22/1900	Resided in La Farge. Worked as a traveling salesman for the La Crosse Cracker Co.
Camp	George W.	DR, p3c1, 7/13/1871	Worked for the law firm of Camp & Watts in Lansing, IA. Planned to open a branch office in De Soto.
Camp & Watts		DR, p1c1, 12/15/1870	Attorneys and collection agents in Lansing, IA.
Campbell	Ellen H., Mrs.	BD, p3c1, 2/27/1880	Died Feb. 13, 1880 in Waco, TX. She was an old resident of Traverse City, MI, but recently lived in Boscobel. Departed Boscobel on Dec. 13th for Waco, where her daughter resides.
Campbell	girl	RH, p4c2, 11/7/1901	A daughter was born Nov. 4, 1901 to H. Campbell of the Readstown area.
Campbell	Peter	BD, p3c1, 8/13/1880	Peter Campbell of Marietta, Crawford Co., supplied Boscobel people with some of the choicest Red Astrican apples ever brought to market.
Campbell	Peter	BD, p3c4, 12/9/1881	Published notice that he taken up stray sheep in section 17, town 8, range 3W in Crawford Co.
Campbell	Peter	BD, p3c2, 1/27/1882	Hosted a party for about 40 people at his home in Marietta, Crawford Co. The Scott Cornet Band provided music. People stayed from tea until breakfast the next morning.
Campbell	Will	BD, p3c1, 10/20/1882	Selected by fellow Democrats to be their candidate for clerk of Circuit Court in Crawford Co. Resided in Marietta. He was the son of Peter Campbell of Marietta.
Canfield	Al, Mrs.	RH, p5c4, 11/3/1898	Mrs. Canfield was very ill at the home of her parents, Mr. and Mrs. Legrand Hickok, per De Soto news column.
Canfield	Al, Mrs.	RH, p4c3, 5/9/1901	Arrived in De Soto from Ripon to visit parents, Mr. and Mrs. Hickok.
Cannon	C. D.	BD, p3c2, 5/9/1879	The steamboat, *Emma*, left Boscobel for Dubuque with 3 barges in tow. They were loaded with oak and were owned by C. D. Cannon. The wood was produced by Cannon's mill on Richland Creek.
Cannon	George, Dr.	BD, p3c2, 6/27/1879	Died last Sunday in Boscobel. Funeral conducted under rituals of the Episcopal Church. Born March 18, 1817 in Wilton, CT. Studied at Yale College. Married Martha Taylor in July 1837 at LeRoy, Genessee Co., NY. Settled in Logansport, IN. Moved to Wisconsin in 1858. Moved to Boscobel in 1860. Divided time between medical practice and a sawmill he operated about 8 miles from the city in Crawford Co. Survived by a large family.
Capron	Franklin P., MD	BD, p3c1, 6/25/1880	The wedding of H. Maria Comstock to Franklin P. Capron, MD, was announced. Wedding was scheduled to take place June 23, 1880 in Phenix, RI.
Carley	D. W.	BD, p3c4, 7/23/1880	Resident of Boscobel. Published a notice that he will no longer be responsible for the debts of his son, Ed. P. Carley.
Carley	D. W.	BD, p3c1, 1/5/1877	Physician in Boscobel.
Carley	Mrs.	BD, p3c4, 3/19/1880	Resident of Boscobel. Won a lawsuit against Sylvester Bros. who had dug a ditch through her land to carry water away from their mill. Case was taken to the Supreme Court.
Carley	Russell	BD, p2c4, 11/26/1880	Grant County paid him a bounty for scalps turned into the county.
Carlin	John	BD, p3c2, 4/22/1881	John Carlin of Crawford Co. died Saturday in the Wisconsin River. After shopping in town he had some drinks. He and Daniel McSweeney crossed the bridge to go home. Unsure how he ended up in the river. Aged about 55 years.
Carlin	Morris [or Miles]	BD, p3c2, 8/29/1879	Morris [or Miles] Carlin of Crawford Co. was robbed of $700 in cash and $200 in notes and mortgages. [See also p3c3, 9/12/1879]
Carlson	Mrs.	DC, p3c2, 7/24/1886	Mrs. Carlson and her 2 children, from the De Soto area, were taken to the poor farm. Her husband deserted her last winter.
Carlyl	Annie	DC, p3c3, 3/27/1888	Hired to teach in Inland, NB. Resided in De Soto.
Carlyle	A.	DC, p2c1, 7/9/1887	The officers of the De Soto School District were A. Carlyle, C. H. Upham and R. M. McAuley.
Carlyle	A.	DC, p3c2, 12/10/1887	Called to La Crosse for the funeral of his 2-year-old daughter. W. J. Carlyle has 3 of his remaining children sick with diphtheria.

Genealogical Events from Newspapers for Crawford, Vernon and Grant Counties, Wisconsin, 1870-1901

LAST NAME	FIRST NAME	NEWSPAPER, PAGE/COLUMN MONTH/DAY/YEAR	GENEALOGICAL DATA
Carlyle	Adam	DC, p3c3, 12/4/1886	His homestead was destroyed by fire. Built in 1860 in De Soto. The fire was found in the south parlor by Miss Annie Carlyle. Most items of value were saved. The building cost $2700. Had insurance of $600 on the building and $400 on the furniture. The barn was saved by Harry Dyer and D. A. Steele.
Carlyle	Adam	DC, p2c2, 2/3/1888	Joined N. S. Cate in De Soto to operate a store about 1859.
Carlyle	Adam	DC, p2c1, 3/20/1888	The 1860 Town of Wheatland candidates on the "regular" ticket were Adam Carlyle, Chairman of the Board of Supervisors; James McCormick and Peter N. Shumway, Supervisors; George G. Van Wagoner, Town Clerk; John C. Kurtz, Superintendent of Schools; Richard Asbury and Peter N. Shumway, Assessors; William Ferguson, Treasurer; James D. Conway, David Waller, Henry W. McAuley and Hiram H. Ferguson, Justices; and, Darius Loper, William Burlock, Richard Asbury and George G. Waller, Constables. This core of individuals served in their offices for many years in the 1850s. An opposition ticket was comprised of John W. White for Chairman, Addison R. Worth for Town Clerk, Samuel Morgan for Superintendent of Schools and Peter Bouley, Justice of the Peace. [Article documents an interesting account of an early town election.]
Carlyle	Annie	DC, p3c3, 7/17/1888	Returned to De Soto with her niece, Miss Nellie Spangler of Inland, NB. Miss Carlyle taught school for several months.
Carlyle	George	DC, p3c3, 10/1/1887	Died Sept. 27, 1887 in De Soto. Born Jan. 27, 1870 at De Soto. Funeral held at the Congregational Church.
Carlyle	John	DR, p3c2, 4/6/1871	Appointed clerk of the steamboat *John C Gault* of the Diamond Jo line.
Carlyle	John	DR, p3c2, 11/30/1871	John Carlyle of De Soto was expected to marry soon to a Chicago girl. [Per p3c2, 12/14/1871 this rumor was untrue.]
Carlyle	Pearl Augusta	DC, p3c3, 10/1/1887	Died Sept. 25, 1887 at Savannah, IL. Buried in De Soto. She was 3 years, 10 months and 11 days old. Daughter of Mr. and Mrs. T. D. Carlyle.
Carlyle	T. D., Mrs.	DC, p3c3, 1/7/1888	Visited her mother, Mrs. Pape [Pope?] of Lansing.
Carlyle & Dowse		DC, p2c2, 10/29/1887	In 1856 they operated a store at the foot of Main Street in De Soto.
Carlyle & Dowse		DC, p2c1, 2/3/1888	In 1857 Caryle & Dowse of De Soto sold out to Tilford & Co., the goods going to Lansing. Ankeny & Ochiltre retired about this time.
Carlyle, Douse & Co.		DR, p3c3, 9/21/1871	Carlyle, Douse & Co. and Ankeny & Co. were the only merchants in De Soto in 1856.
Carmody	Johanna	BD, p3c1, 4/13/1883	Nicholas Tormey married Johanna Carmody on April 3, 1883 at Mt. Hope. Bride from Mt. Hope. Groom from Fennimore.
Carpenter	Charles O.	DC, p3c3, 11/12/1887	Emma B. Moore married Charles O. Carpenter on Nov. 5, 1887 in De Soto. Bride and groom from Lansing, IA. The Rev. Thomas Crouch officiated.
Carpenter	George C.	DC, p2c2, 10/22/1887	Moving to Grand Rapids, MI [from De Soto] where he will be a salesman. He has been on the road for Thompson and McClay of Dubuque for several years [per p3c2, 12/3/1887]. His wife is visiting her mother, Mrs. E. K. Miller of Netherwood, NJ, for the winter.
Carpenter	H., Mrs.	DC, p3c4, 6/4/1887	Arrived in De Soto from Redfield, Dakota to attend to her property.
Carpenter	Jack	RH, p4c2, 5/30/1901	Resided in Genoa. Received a bounty for killing 73 rattlesnakes.
Carpenter	Lee, Miss	DC, p3c3, 3/19/1887	Miss Lee Carpenter and mother moved their millinery shop from Pierre to Redfield, Dakota.
Carpenter	Newton F.	DC, p2c2, 7/3/1888	Moved to De Soto about 1860. Ran as a Republican for the Wisconsin Assembly. He was opposed by George D. McDill, who had just returned from the war. Carpenter won, as the district was largely Republican.
Carr	Fred	DC, p2c2, 10/29/1887	In 1856, Fred Carr operated a small lumberyard in De Soto.
Carr	Frederick	DC, p3c2, 12/17/1887	Carr and two or three other De Soto residents organized a movement [in the 1850s?] to build a Congregational Church in De Soto after a Baptist society faded away. Elder Radcliff was the first preacher. He came from Prairie du Chien. "Sunday after Sunday he dwelt upon the wrath of God toward the sinner." Due to his gloomy sermons, there were no conversions under Radcliff's leadership. Rev. Alexander Parker succeeded Radcliff and occupied the pulpit in 1865.
Carr	Frederick	DC, p2c1, 5/29/1888	Lived in De Soto. He was born in New Hampshire and when a child moved to Massachusetts.

Genealogical Events from Newspapers for Crawford, Vernon and Grant Counties, Wisconsin, 1870-1901

LAST NAME	FIRST NAME	NEWSPAPER, PAGE/COLUMN MONTH/DAY/YEAR	GENEALOGICAL DATA
Carrell	Abraham	BD, p3c1, 12/1/1882	"The death of another centinarian is announced, that of Mr. Abraham Carroll [Carrell/Correll], of Clayton, Crawford County, who died on Thursday evening last at the age of 106 years, leaving quite a large family of children and grandchildren, all in comfortable circumstances. It will be remembered by quite a large number of residents of this city that the old gentleman was in Boscobel during the Centennial year and quite anxious to visit Philadelphia, but not having the means was obligated to forego that pleasure. Mr. Carroll served in the War of 1812 and had seen General Washington. [Note: This an ancestor of the compiler of this book. Abraham's true age is difficult to ascertain as his birthdate varied from census to census. He was probably 90 years old when he died.]
Carrell	Abraham	BD, p3c2, 6/14/1878	"Mr. Edward Carrell [should say Abraham Carrell], born in the Town of Hancock, Hancock County [should say Washington County], Maryland on 3d day of August in the year 1776 [probably born about 1792], now residing in the town of Rolling Ground, Crawford County, Wis., is the oldest man that we have heard of in this State. He frequently visits Boscobel, riding from place to place in a farm wagon a distance of twelve miles, returning the same day. The last time he was in Boscobel, [one day last week] thinking his son-in-law had gone home and left him, he started from Ritter & Hubbell's store in this city about 4 p.m., to make the trip on foot." [Abraham Carrell is an ancestor of the author of this book.]
Carrell	Abram	BD, p3c1, 12/17/1880	"Crawford County has a centennarian in the person of Mr. Abram Correll of Clayton township. At the recent election Mr. Correll voted for Garfield and Arthur and the entire Republican ticket." [Surname usually spelled Carrell.]
Carrier	Alice	BD, p3c2, 5/13/1881	Fred Mortimer married Alice Carrier at the home of the bride's father on May 9, 1881. Bride from Boscobel. Took train to Milwaukee after the ceremony. Rev. William Stoddart officiated.
Carrier	Allie, Miss	BD, p3c2, 8/10/1877	Departed Boscobel to visit sister, Mrs. W. E. Howe of La Crosse.
Carrier	T.	BD, p2c5, 1/5/1877	Handled the lease/sale of property in Boscobel.
Carrier	T.	BD, p3c4, 2/9/1877	The Grant Co. Circuit Court issued a warrant of attachment in the case T. Carrier & Co. [of Boscobel] vs. A. L. Holin.
Carrier	T.	BD, p3c2, 4/6/1877	Returned to Boscobel after visiting his 80-year-old father in Watertown.
Carrier	T.	BD, p3c4, 4/13/1877	In the case T. Carrier, et al vs. A. McFall and wife, judgement was found for the plaintiff at the Iowa term of the Circuit Court held in Dodgeville. This was a case from Grant Co.
Carrier	T.	BD, p3c3, 5/30/1879	The T. Carrier [of Boscobel] property was heavily damaged by flooding.
Carrier	T.	BD, p2c4, 10/22/1880	T. Carrier & Co. was a dealer in hardware, stoves and agricultural machinery in Boscobel. Mr. Carrier and M. McSpaden operated the business that was opened 5 years ago. Mr. Carrier was one of Boscobel's pioneer citizens. He moved there 22 years. For many years he ran the Carrier House [now the Betts House]. The store was housed in a large two-story building with basement. Offered shelf and heavy hardware, stoves, tin and sheet-iron ware, agricultural machinery and builders and carriage-makers' hardware. Prof. Cliff was the supervisor of the tin department.
Carrigan	Tim	BD, p3c5, 4/14/1882	Lived near Boscobel. Lost a pocketbook containing $58.
Carroll [Carrell]	Abraham	BD, p3c1, 8/8/1879	Abraham Carroll [Carrell] married Mary J. Dean on August 2, 1879 in Boscobel. Bride and groom from Clayton, Crawford Co. Justice McLaughlin officiated.
Carry	Mrs.	DC, p3c3, 1/28/1888	Miss Maggie Eck of New Albion visited her sister, Mrs. Carry of Genoa.
Carson	Olonzo	BD, p3c5, 8/17/1877	Grant Co. published an Administrator's Notice in the case of Olonzo Carson, deceased. Mrs. Eliza Carson, the widow, took over as executrix when T. J. Brooks resigned.
Carson	Sarah C.	BD, p3c4, 1/11/1878	John S. Stoddart married Sarah C. Carson on Jan. 8, 1878 at the home of the bride's mother. Groom from Boscobel. Bride from Richwood, Richland Co. The Rev. William Stoddart officiated.
Carswell	George J.	BD, p2c4, 7/22/1881	Lived at Bear Creek [Richland Co.?]. Reported that the four cheese factories on Bear Creek, Beckwith's, Eaton's, Martain's and Carswell's, sold four carloads of cheese made in the last three weeks.
Carter		RH, p6c5, 9/2/1897	A boy was recently born to Readstown Town Clerk, Clarence Carter.
Carter	C. H.	RH, p4c1, 7/20/1899	A house is being built for Carter in Readstown. The cellar is being built by Albert Hebbard and Dan Austin. N. D. Hale is constructing the house.
Carter	Helen	RH, p4c2, 3/29/1900	Left Readstown for Viroqua to work with Ella Lake in the millinery business.

Genealogical Events from Newspapers for Crawford, Vernon and Grant Counties, Wisconsin, 1870-1901

LAST NAME	FIRST NAME	NEWSPAPER, PAGE/COLUMN MONTH/DAY/YEAR	GENEALOGICAL DATA
Carter	Helen	RH, p4c1, 2/14/1901	Left Readstown for Mandon, ND to teach school.
Carter	Helen, Miss	RH, p4c3, 1/17/1901	Resigned her teaching position in Readstown. Hired to teach in Little Heart, ND where she will earn $30 a month.
Carter	Minnie, Mrs.	RH, p4c2, 5/31/1900	Lived in Readstown. Mrs. Carter's father, Mr. Truax [of Muscoda], visited relatives in Readstown.
Carter	Minnie, Mrs.	RH, p4c1, 6/21/1900	Called from Readstown to go to the bedside of father, Mr. Treuax of Muscoda. He suffered a stroke.
Carter	William	DC, p2c1, 3/27/1888	Served as postmaster in Viroqua. He was one of the youngest soldiers in the Civil War. Enlisted Nov. 22, 1861 at the age of 16 years, 6 months and 25 days.
Carter	William, Mrs.	RH, p5c4, 4/27/1899	Mrs. William Carter and daughter, Velma, of Boaz visited Mrs. Carter's parents, Mr. and Mrs. A. H. Hopkins, in Viola, and sister, Mrs. Myrta Townsend, of Readstown.
Carver	George	BD, p3c4, 4/5/1878	Resided in Avoca. Shot a gun several months ago at Mr. Wilkie, the principal of Avoca High School. Shot intended to "scare him." Wilkie had "severely beaten" Carver's 14 year old daughter with a stick for misbehavior. Carver was arrested and found not guilty.
Carver	George	BD, p3c4, 4/12/1878	Last May, C. A. Wilkin, principal of Avoca, punished the 12 year old daughter of George Carver. Carver was arrested, broke jail and left the country. Returned on his own several months later and went to jail. Jury couldn't agree on his guilt and they were discharged. Carver left "for parts unknown." Author of this news item noted there were numerous falsehoods in the prior news account on the incident.
Carver	Henry	BD, p3c2, 9/25/1883	Moved to Muscoda from Ohio in 1848. He brought white polled oxen with him. The history of his oxen herd was described. In 1853, A. Palmer of Boscobel bought one of Carver's white heifers.
Carver	John	BD, p3c1, 12/2/1881	Appointed Postmaster at Port Andrew in place of his father who has passed away.
Cary		RH, p5c4, 7/29/1897	A son of Mrs. Al Cary died Monday in the Ross area. He was blind.
Case	Alanson	BD, p3c3, 6/1/1883	Butcher in Boscobel. Deserted his wife of nearly 40 years and their children when he eloped with Miss Anna Ferrel. She was a family domestic. It was assumed that he went to Dakota to open up a farm.
Case	Effie	BD, p2c4, 1/27/1882	Byron Poole recently married Effie Case. Bride was from Richland Co. "Uncle Freeman" gave the bride an Estey organ.
Case	Orin	BD, p3c1, 1/16/1880	Married Alice A. Sherrard on Dec. 31, 1879 at home of bride's father in Boscobel. Groom from Crawford Co. The Rev. William Stoddart officiated.
Case	Seymore	BD, p3c1, 11/21/1879	Case's fingers were badly crushed at Seaton's hoop and strap factory in the Boscobel area.
Case	Seymour	BD, p3c1, 6/10/1881	Served as the managing clerk at the Betts House in Boscobel.
Casler	Johnson and P. N.	BD, p5c5, 11/25/1881	Newspaper printed a Dissolution Notice of Partnership between Johnson Casler and P. N. Casler of Mt. Hope.
Caspers	Frank	BD, p2c4, 11/26/1880	Grant County paid him a bounty for scalps turned into the county.
Cass	A. C.	DC, p4c2, 5/17/1889	House destroyed by fire. The loss was $1200 and was insured for $500. Resided in the Town of Franklin, 2 miles south of Liberty Pole.
Cass	Emeline, Mrs.	DC, p3c2, 1/7/1888	Died Dec. 26, 1887 at her home in Liberty Pole. She was 63.
Cass	Emma	DC, p3c2, 1/7/1888	Miss Emma Cass and her brother left De Soto for their home in Oxford, NB.
Cass	Queen	RH, p4c2, 5/23/1901	Herman Layer recently married Queen Cass. Bride and groom from Viroqua. Ceremony was held at the home of the bride's parents, Mr. and Mrs. James Cass of Sumner, IA. Groom was a partner with Mr. Mellum in a clothing business.
Casseboom	Emily B.	BD, p3c4, 8/9/1878	Will T. Hurd married Emily B. Casseboom on Aug. 6, 1878 at the Congregational Church in Boscobel. Rev. William Stoddart officiated.
Casson	John R.	DC, p3c2, 4/17/1888	Resided in Viroqua. Qualified for a pension for his military service.
Castle	Bryan J., Mrs.	DC, p3c2, 7/10/1886	Arrived in De Soto from Black River Falls to visit her father and relatives. She was a former teacher in the area.
Castley	Mr.	BD, p3c2, 9/26/1879	Resided near Blue River. His flouring mills recently burned to the ground. Most of the family was gone, except an infirm old couple who couldn't save anything, when the fire erupted.
Caswell	Hiram	DR, p3c1, 9/7/1871	Hiram Caswell married Margaret Riley on Aug. 26, 1871. Bride and groom were from Genoa. Thomas D. Wallar, Esq. officiated.

Genealogical Events from Newspapers for Crawford, Vernon and Grant Counties, Wisconsin, 1870-1901

LAST NAME	FIRST NAME	NEWSPAPER, PAGE/COLUMN MONTH/DAY/YEAR	GENEALOGICAL DATA
Caswell	Rose	DC, p2c1, 4/30/1887	Albert Halderson married Rose Caswell last Sunday in Genoa.
Caswell	William	RH, p4c2, 5/30/1901	Resided in Hillsboro. Former resident of Richland Center. Convicted of holding himself out to the public as a physician.
Cate	Norman S.	DC, p2c1, 2/3/1888	A wealthy New England company headed by Norman S. Cate established a sawmill in De Soto in 1858/9. H. M. Chamberlain was his partner. Although the mill was busy, it was harder than expected to get lumber to market. After a few years, the property was abandoned and sold for almost nothing.
Cawley	J. G.	BD, p3c3, 8/16/1878	J. G. Cawley, of the firm Butler & Cawley of Platteville, was arrested for forgery. He jumped bail.
Chadeayne	Hiram E.	RH, p5c4, 4/27/1899	Hiram E. Chadeayne married Amy Felton on April 22, 1899, per Sugar Grove news column. Groom was a Crawford County farmer.
Chambers	Flora	RH, p4c4, 8/1/1901	Flora Chambers recently married Mr. Brooks. Bride from De Soto. Groom was a hardware dealer in Iowa.
Chambers	Jane	RH, p4c4, 8/1/1901	Jane Chambers recently married Mr. Day. Bride from De Soto. Groom was a pearl buyer in Lynxville.
Chambers	William	DC, p3c4, 6/18/1887	Granted a pension and arrearages of $550. Resided in the De Soto area.
Chambers	William	DC, p2c2, 11/27/1888	William Chambers and Joseph Halpin were found guilty of attempted robbery in De Soto.
Chambers	William S.	DR, p3c2, 12/7/1871	William S. Chambers married Aurora Belle Sperbeck on Dec. 3, 1871 by D. A. Steele, J.P., at the residence of the bride's father. Bride and groom were from Dec. 3, 1871.
Chandler	Alice Jane	BD, p2c3, 12/8/1882	W. F. Collins recently married Alice Jane Chandler at the Methodist Church in Richland Center. The Rev. J. D. Tull officiated.
Chandler	Alonzo	DC, p2c1, 9/18/1886	The "... botton bones and clay from the funeral pile of Alonzo Chandler of Chandler Hollow, just north of Lynxville, who disappeared in 1869" were displayed at the Crawford Co. Fair.
Chandler	George	BD, p3c2, 12/18/1883	Returned to Boscobel after spending a year prospecting in Dakota.
Chandler	Jennie	BD, p3c3, 10/26/1877	Hired to teach school in the Red Schoolhouse near Fennimore.
Chandler	Lell E.	BD, p3c4, 8/9/1878	William Snow married Lell E. Chandler on Aug. 6, 1878 at the home of the bride's mother in Boscobel. Groom from Richland Center. Rev. Dr. Stoddart officiated. The wedding was attended by Mr. And Mrs. H. C. Snow of Milwaukee, Mrs. Williard Snow [mother of groom], Mr. and Mrs. N. H. Snow of Avoca and Miss Ida Snow of Worchester, MA.
Chandler	Mr.	DC, p2c3 8/20/1887	Mr. Chandler sold his Brush Creek farm to Mr. Lee of Tomah. Planned to move to Nebraska, per Ontario news column.
Chapel	Elmer Octavius, Rev.	RH, p4c3, 11/8/1900	Hettie Olivia Levergreen married the Rev. Elmer Octavius Chapel at the home of the bride's parents on Wednesday evening. Bride was the daughter of Isaac Levergreen and was employed as a milliner. Groom was the Congregational minister in Readstown. C. Melbourne Chapel of Chicago was the groom's brother. Couple planned to live in Readstown. The Rev. C. A. Randolph of Schickley, NB officiated. Reprinted from an article in the *Aurora Beacon*.
Chapman	Charles H.	DC, p3c2, 3/3/1888	Former De Soto teacher. Recently received a B.S. at Johns Hopkins University.
Chapman	H. H.	DR, p1c2, 12/7/1871	Vernon Co. Board of Supervisors allowed payment to H. H. Chapman for the care of an infant.
Chase		DC, p2c1, 2/5/1887	Mr. Chase, father of Arvin and A. D. Chase, who settled on Sec. 3 [in Vernon Co.] found the barrel of a pistol lost by a soldier on the camping ground used by Black Hawk during the Black Hawk War.
Chase	A. D.	DC, p3c2, 6/19/1888	Returned from Dakota for a visit in Retreat.
Chase	Capt.	DR, p3c1, 12/15/1870	Prominent Madison lawyer. Visited in De Soto, his former home.
Chase	Charles	DC, p2c2, 4/2/1887	Resident of Horicon, WI. Visited his sisters, Mrs. John and Aaron Bates of Retreat.
Chase	Effie Augusta	DR, p3c1, 10/19/1871	Died Oct. 12, 1871 in Madison at the age of 2 years and 23 days. She was the daughter of R. J. and M. M. Chase.
Chase	H. A.	DC, p3c2, 2/25/1888	Received pension for military service. Resided in Viroqua.
Chase	Mr.	DC, p1c1, 6/7/1889	Lived in Horicon. Planned to build a house on the farm of his son-in-law, Aaron Bates of Retreat.
Chase	Paulina, Mrs.	DC, p3c2, 11/12/1887	Joseph Pulver married Mrs. Paulina Chase on Nov. 2, 1887 in Viroqua.

Genealogical Events from Newspapers for Crawford, Vernon and Grant Counties, Wisconsin, 1870-1901

LAST NAME	FIRST NAME	NEWSPAPER, PAGE/COLUMN MONTH/DAY/YEAR	GENEALOGICAL DATA
Chase	Seymour M.	BD, p3c3, 12/23/1881	Lillian Myrtle Betts married Seymour M. Chase on Dec. 15, 1881. Bride was the leassee and proprietor of the Betts House in Boscobel. Groom was formerly from Cazanovia, NY. The Rev. E. L. Morse of the Congregational Church officiated. Extensive article.
Chenoweth	C., Mrs. Dr.	BD, p3c3, 7/22/1881	Arrived in Boscobel from Decatur, IL to visit her mother, Mrs. Hon and sister, Mrs. Freely.
Chenvert	Nicholas	BD, p2c3, 1/27/1882	Died Jan. 20, 1882 in Frenchtown, Prairie du Chien. Aged about 70 years. Born and raised "on the prairie."
Cherrier	Paul	DC, p3c3, 2/26/1887	Former sheriff in Crawford County. Completed the Merchants Hotel in Lynxville.
Cherry	John	DC, p2c2, 2/3/1888	In 1859 John Cherry came from West Prairie to open a shoe shop in De Soto. This lasted a short time. Patrick De Lacy succeeded him.
Chesebro	girl	BD, p3c3, 4/5/1878	A daughter was born on March 28, 1878 to Frank Chesebro of the Muscoda area.
Chester	C. H.	BD, p3c2, 4/27/1877	Arrived from Boston to set up a tailoring shop in Boscobel.
Chester	C. H., Mrs.	BD, p3c4, 11/23/1877	Advertised his desire to organize a juvenile singing class in Boscobel.
Chitwood	boy	RH, p4c1, 6/22/1899	A son was recently born to J. R. Chitwood of Readstown.
Chitwood	J. R.	RH, p5c3, 8/18/1898	Advertised services as a contractor and builder in Readstown.
Chitwood	J. R.	RH, p3c2, 2/15/1900	Lived in Readstown and worked as a traveling salesman for the Readstown Broom Company.
Chitwood	J. R.	RH, p4c2, 10/10/1901	Left his home in Readstown for a job in Ladysmith. Hired to build Charles Aikins [of Readstown] a house in Ladysmith.
Chitwood	Jake	RH, p5c3, 4/7/1898	Jake Chitwood and Frank McMillen of the Readstown area were hired to build a house for Leonard Bankus in Soldiers Grove.
Chitwood	Jake, Mrs.	RH, p5c3, 12/9/1897	Visited with her sister, Mrs. Groves, at Ross.
Chizek	Jacob	BD, p3c2, 9/24/1880	Bohemian native. He was injured while returning from a trip to Muscoda. A foot was caught in a stirrup. Horse became frightened while he tried to mount. He was dragged until foot came out of boot. Doctors were hopeful for his recovery.
Cholerton	Fannie	BD, p3c2, 12/9/1881	George M. Francisco married Fannie Cholerton at the home of the bride's father on Dec. 4, 1881. Groom from Boscobel. Bride from Richland Center.
Christ	George	BD, p3c3, 1/30/1880	Recently died in the Boscobel area. Buried Sunday at the Methodist Episcopal Church. Member of the German Lutheran Church. The Rev. Mr. Mutschman officiated in German and Prof. J. Allison later spoke in English. Born in Hausen, Kingdom of Wirtenberg on May 4, 1816. Married to Johanna Frederika Keller in Kauglen on the Neck on Nov. 24, 1842. Survived by wife and 7 or his 10 children. Moved to Buffalo, NY in 1853 where one of his brothers had a successful business. Moved west, first to Ohio, and then to Galena. In March 1854 moved to Town of Marietta, Crawford Co.
Christ	George	BD, p3c2, 7/13/1883	A five-year-old horse was stolen from his pasture in the Town of Marietta.
Christ	George, Jr.	BD, p3c1, 10/1/1880	George Christ, Jr. married Laura I. Baumgartner on Sept. 23, 1880 at the Horstman House in Lancaster. Groom from Marietta. Bride from Hickory Grove. Groom's mother departed for a visit with relatives in Illinois after the wedding.
Christ	Gotlieb	BD, p3c3, 5/30/1879	The Gotlieb Christ home in Boscobel was recently flooded with 7 inches of water.
Christ	Gotlieb	BD, p3c4, 5/30/1879	The funeral for an infant child of Gotlieb Christ was held Wednesday at the Methodist Episcopal Church.
Christ	Gottleib	BD, p3c2, 4/6/1877	Gottleib Christ married Lottie Eldon on Wednesday. Groom from Boscobel where he worked as a deliveryman for Meyer Bros. Store. Dr. Stoddart officiated.
Christ	J., Mrs.	BD, p3c1, 3/16/1883	J. Jetter married Mrs. J. Christ on Mar. 10, 1883 in Prairie du Chien. Bride from Marietta. Groom from Wauzeka. Major L. F. S. Viele officiated.
Christ	May	BD, p3c4, 4/19/1878	Died April 12, 1878 in Boscobel at the age of 9 months and 4 days. She was the only child of Charles and Jennie Christ.
Christianson	Martin	DC, p3c3, 11/12/1887	Worked as a shoemaker in Genoa.
Christie	J. C.	DC, p3c3, 3/5/1887	Lillie Elger married J. C. Christie on Feb. 17, 1887 per an item originally printed in the Prairie du Chien Union.
Churchill	G. W., Mrs.	RH, p5c3, 8/5/1897	Died at home in Clay Center, NB on July 20, 1897. She was well-known around Sugar Grove.

Genealogical Events from Newspapers for Crawford, Vernon and Grant Counties, Wisconsin, 1870-1901

LAST NAME	FIRST NAME	NEWSPAPER, PAGE/COLUMN MONTH/DAY/YEAR	GENEALOGICAL DATA
Churchill	George W.	RH, p4c2, 1/18/1900	Churchill and Sam Wallace of Manning went to Chippewa County to block out new homes and prepare to move their families in the spring.
Churchill	Mary, Mrs.	RH, p5c4, 10/13/1898	Came from Valley Junction, CO to visit her brother, William Cox of Kickapoo, and Mrs. Jane Harris, per Kickapoo news column.
Chynoweth	Mrs.	BD, p3c3, 8/1/1879	Mrs. Chynoweth of Decatur, IL and sister, Mrs. Freely, arrived in Boscobel to visit their sister, Mrs. Ed Meyer. Mrs. Freely planned to move to Boscobel.
Cilley	A. D.	DC, p3c3, 1/28/1888	Mr. and Mrs. A. D. Cilly and child arrived from Ashton, Dakota to visit E. Cilley of Red Mound.
Cilley	E.	DC, p3c2, 9/4/1886	Planned to move to De Soto to work in the stock business with F. Eckhardt.
Cilley	E.	DC, p2c3, 3/19/1887	Left De Soto for Dakota with a car of horses.
Cilley	Erastus	DR, p3c1, 8/31/1871	Harvested 12 bushels of wheat per acre.
Cilley	Erastus, Jr.	DC, p3c2, 12/11/1886	Returned to De Soto from Ashton, Dakota.
Cilley	William W.	BD, p2c2, 11/13/1883	Died of heart disease on Oct. 29, 1883 in Bloomington. Born in Williamstown, VT on Sept. 20, 1801, the eldest son of William and Abigail Cilley. His grandfather was born in England and settled in Massachusetts. His father moved to Vermont and served in the War of 1812. Spent his early life in Poultney, VT where he learned the carpenter trade. Joined the Baptist Church when he was 17. Married Roxana Castle at Essex, VT in 1829. Moved to Lancaster, WI in 1845 and to Blake's Prairie in 1852. His wife died in 1851. He married two more times. Those wives were also dead.
Clancy	E. L., Mrs.	BD, p3c3, 8/11/1882	Mrs. E. L. Clancy and Miss Julia Bennett of Chicago visited with Mr. and Mrs. William Tate of Bell Center.
Clancy	James	RH, p4c1, 9/13/1900	Mr. Clancy's funeral was held last Sunday in Rising Sun. J. T. Dregne of Readstown attended the service.
Clancy	James	RH, p5c3, 9/13/1900	Died last Friday at his home from an illness caused by a tumor. He was 47 years old last week. Funeral took place at the Catholic Church in Rising Sun.
Clancy	James	RH, p5c3, 2/21/1901	James Clancy and Charles Hall, both of Spring Valley, plan to sell farms, implements and household goods and then move south in the spring.
Clancy	William, Mrs.	RH, p4c2, 10/12/1899	Died Oct. 8, 1899 of consumption at her home near Readstown. Funeral held at St. Phillips Catholic Church in the Town of Clayton. Buried in Rolling Ground Cemetery.
Clapp	A. B.	DC, p2c2, 10/29/1887	In 1856, A. B. Clapp and George Meade ran a sawmill about a quarter mile up the river from De Soto. Clapp had also erected a small warehouse on the levee.
Clapp & Howard		DR, p3c3, 9/21/1871	Ran a mill in De Soto in 1856.
Clark		DC, p3c4, 3/5/1887	Grandmother Clark, 83, of Victory, fell and has internal injuries that may prevent her recovery.
Clark	Abner	BD, p3c2, 12/18/1883	Returned from the western country to visit parents in Boscobel area. He left home 6 years ago.
Clark	boy	DR, p3c2, 1/12/1871	A son was born Jan. 9, 1871 to Z. T. Clark of De Soto.
Clark	Braman	BD, p3c1, 5/9/1879	Relocated from Woodman for a new home in Pattersonville, IA.
Clark	Charles	DC, p2c1, 5/7/1887	Charles Clark married Emma Hayden on May 1, 1887. Bride and groom from Town of Wheatland. Alex. Latshaw, J.P., of Victory officiated at the ceremony.
Clark	Cora	BD, p3c3, 10/26/1877	Hired to teach school in the Bowers District near Fennimore.
Clark	Cora J.	BD, p3c2, 11/7/1879	M. Leavitt Parker married Cora J. Clark on Wednesday at the home of the bride's parents. Bride from Boscobel. Took a train to their future home in Sheldon, IA.
Clark	Coral	RH, p4c3, 6/2/1898	Coral Clark and Frank Brown of De Soto departed for Dakota.
Clark	Effie	DC, p2c3, 7/3/1886	Resided in Victory. Taught school in Genoa.
Clark	Effie B.	DC, p2c2, 7/2/1887	Effie B. Clark married H. D. Forey on Wednesday in Victory. Alex Latshaw officiated. Their new home will be in Minneapolis per the 7/9/1887 issue of the newspaper.
Clark	Etta	DC, p4c1, 3/12/1889	Left De Soto to work as a clerk in the store of her cousin, E. Helpman in Shreveport, LA.
Clark	G. C.	DR, p2c3, 5/18/1871	Lived in Town of Sterling. Offered a reward for the return of a 5-year-old cow stolen from him.

Genealogical Events from Newspapers for Crawford, Vernon and Grant Counties, Wisconsin, 1870-1901

LAST NAME	FIRST NAME	NEWSPAPER, PAGE/COLUMN MONTH/DAY/YEAR	GENEALOGICAL DATA
Clark	G. C.	DC, p3c3, 11/20/1886	Returned to Victory from a trip up the Wisconsin River where he was searching for horses to buy.
Clark	G. C.	DC, p3c4, 11/27/1886	Left Victory for Chippewa Falls to sell horses.
Clark	G. C., Mrs.	DC, p3c2, 4/2/1887	Went to La Crosse for medical treatment. May lose sight in her eyes. Resided in Victory.
Clark	George D.	DR, p1c6, 8/24/1871	The 3 and 5 year old daughters of the late George D. Clark died Monday in the Town of Seneca when their clothes caught on fire while a brother was lighting a stove.
Clark	George W.	RH, p4c3, 9/28/1899	The Vernon County Circuit Court published a summons for, George W. Clark, plaintiff, vs. Mary R. Clark, defendant. J. N. Kast of Bell Center was the attorney for the plaintiff.
Clark	girl	DC, p3c3, 6/5/1888	A daughter was recently born to Charlie Clark of Victory.
Clark	Harvey	BD, P3c2, 4/23/1880	Sworn in as an alderman of Boscobel.
Clark	Harvey	BD, p3c1, 4/21/1882	Rented his store in Boscobel to Jacob Sablotzky of Chicago.
Clark	Harvey	BD, p3c1, 6/16/1882	Departed Boscobel for Huron, Dakota with his carpenter tools. Planned to work there until the fall.
Clark	Harvey	BD, p2c4, 10/22/1880	Opened a grocery store in Boscobel last February. Mr. Clark has been a businessman in Boscobel for the last 20 years.
Clark	Harvey, Mrs.	BD, p3c3, 6/10/1881	Mr. and Mrs. Rochester Rapalee and Mr. and Mrs. Meyer Longcore, all of Starkey, NY, arrived in Boscobel to visit with the ladies' sister, Mrs. Harvey Clark.
Clark	J. M., Mr. and Mrs.	RH, p5c3, 12/8/1898	Visited their daughter, Mrs. Mills Griffin, near Bloom City, per Mound Park news column.
Clark	Joseph	BD, p3c1, 9/4/1883	Joseph Clark married Emma L. Kelsey on Aug. 31, 1883. Bride from Rock Co., WI. Groom from Crawford Co. J. McLaughlin, J.P., officiated at the wedding in Boscobel.
Clark	L. L.	DC, p2c3, 9/11/1888	Miss L. L. Clark married W. B. Storm on Aug. 22, 1888 at the home of G. C. Clark in Victory. Groom from Hector, MN. Took the train to Minneapolis to visit the bride's sister, Mrs. _. D. Forey. Planned to live in Hector where Storm was a druggist and grocer.
Clark	L. W.	DC, p3c4, 11/27/1886	Prepared upper floor of G. C. Clarks store for a photo gallery in Victory.
Clark	Lolo	DC, p3c4, 11/27/1886	Taught school in the Brown District per Victory news column.
Clark	M. B. [M. C.?]	BD, p2c2, 2/15/1878	Fire destroyed Clark's residence and shop in Woodman. Arson suspected.
Clark	Matilda, Mrs.	DC, p2c2, 11/19/1887	Buried at the Retreat Cemetery on Monday. Lived in Victory.
Clark	Matilda, Mrs.	DC, p3c2, 11/19/1887	Died Nov. 13, 1887 at Victory at the age of 83 years, 9 months and 2 days. Born in Woodford Co., KY in 1804. Married William Clark and moved to Knox Co., IN. He died in 1838. In the Spring of 1847 she moved to Retreat with her children – James, William, George, Caroline, Frank, Elizabeth, Martha, Jane and her daughter, Mrs. Alex Latshaw. Moved here with John Tewalt, Louis Trainer and their families – all of whom settled in Vernon Co. Survived by 2 sisters, 3 brothers, 4 sons, 3 daughters, 37 grandchildren and 21 great-grandchildren. Funeral held at Retreat.
Clark	Matt	DC, p3c3, 2/25/1888	The Matt Clark Transportation Company went out of business. Sold the steamboat, *Isaac Staples*, to Isaac Staples; *Menomonee*, to Knapp, Stout & Co.; *Evansville*, to John Robson; and *Ben Hershey*, to Durant & Wheeler. The *Brunson* and the *J. K. Graves* will be sold later.
Clark	Minnie	DC, p4c2, 3/19/1889	Closed her school in Seneca a few days early and returned to De Soto. She lost most of her personal effects when the home of Mr. Ingham was destroyed by fire. She boarded with Mr. Ingham.
Clark	Mr.	BD, p3c1, 5/5/1882	Clark was a crippled violinist who played music on the Boscobel streets for change thrown in a hat. Had a small boy with him. Jailed in Lancaster for polygamy. His latest wife was a Miss Davenport who lived across the river.
Clark	Mr.	DC, p2c3, 7/3/1886	Re-erecting his store in Victory.
Clark	O., Rev.	DR, p3c2, 12/22/1870	Lived in Lansing, IA. Scheduled to speak on temperance at the Congregational Church in De Soto.
Clark	S., Mrs.	RH, p5c4, 11/10/1898	Died Nov. 6, 1898 at the home of her daughter, Mrs. Wash Wilson of [on?] Kickapoo. Resided in Viola. Buried in the Viola Cemetery.
Clark	Seth	RH, p4c2, 9/20/1900	Died Tuesday on the John Flanagan farm, 1 mile west of Readstown. Clark worked for Flanagan. He was found dead in the hog lot. Aged about 60 years. Death caused by apoplexy. Survived by wife and several children.

Genealogical Events from Newspapers for Crawford, Vernon and Grant Counties, Wisconsin, 1870-1901

LAST NAME	FIRST NAME	NEWSPAPER, PAGE/COLUMN MONTH/DAY/YEAR	GENEALOGICAL DATA
Clark	Seth, Mrs.	RH, p5c2, 11/29/1900	Died Thursday in Spring Valley. Funeral held at the Methodist Episcopal Church in Liberty Pole.
Clark	W. B.	BD, p3c1, 1/26/1883	Resident of Bloomington for the last 17 years. Planned to move to Minneapolis.
Clark	Walter A.	BD, p3c2, 1/24/1879	Walter A. Clark married Lydia A. Blanchard at the Muffley House in Boscobel on Jan. 14, 1879. Bride from Marion. Groom from Fennimore. The Rev. W. Stoddart officiated.
Clark	Z. T.	DR, p4c6, 12/15/1870	Advertised his services as a plasterer and stonemason in De Soto.
Clark	Z. T.	DC, p3c2, 11/13/1886	Installed as C. T. at the I.O.G.T. in De Soto.
Clark & Brekke		BD, P3c7, 1/5/1877	Advertised their drug and grocery store in Boscobel.
Clarke	W. P.	DC, p2c2, 7/9/1887	Resided in Victory. Visited friends in Tomah, his old hometown.
Claus	William	BD, p2c4, 11/26/1880	Grant County paid him a bounty for scalps turned into the county.
Clawater	Jennie	DC, p2c1, 11/20/1886	Jennie Clawater married Fred Free on Nov. 14, 1886 at the residence of C. L. Ingersoll. Bride was the daughter of Hon. Wm. Clawater of Liberty Pole. Groom from Cobb, WI. The Rev. Thomas Crouch officiated.
Clawater	William	DC, p3c3, 5/21/1887	While working in a field he became overheated and suffered a partial sunstroke. Since then he has been insane. Resided in Liberty Pole.
Clawfot	Mrs.	RH, p4c3, 4/5/1900	Mrs. Clawfot moved her family from the farm to De Soto so her children could go to school.
Clayton	Robert Casper	BD, p3c2, 2/16/1877	Died Feb. 7, 1877. He was the son of A. P. and Josephine Clayton of Spring Green, Sauk Co. Robert was 2 years, 7 months and 15 days old.
Clement	M. C.	BD, p3c1, 2/11/1881	M. C. Clement, eldest of Clement Bros., died Jan. 27, 1881 at his home in Beloit.
Clementson	Joseph, Mrs.	BD, p3c1, 3/14/1879	Died March 3, 1879 at the age of 70 in Hazel Green. She was the mother of George Clementson of Lancaster.
Cliff	Thomas	BD, p3c1, 9/11/1883	The officers of the Boscobel Rough and Ready Fire Company were Thomas Cliff, James Rose, Frank Kumreen, Com. Rogers and R. J. Stephens.
Cliffton	Bell	BD, p3c2, 7/6/1877	Albert Hoppin married Bell Cliffton on June 25, 1877 in Muscoda. Bride from Washburn. Groom from La Crosse. Rev. Bishop Lench of Avoca officiated.
Clise	Will	BD, p3c3, 7/25/1879	Arrived from California to visit his aunt, Mrs. John Barnett in Boscobel. Clise was the son of Frank Clise, deceased.
Clise	William	BD, p3c1, 5/30/1879	Ex-sheriff William Clise and Arthur Moulton sent newspapers from Colorado to *The Dial*.
Clossen	Mary	BD, p2c4, 4/13/1877	An execution sale ordered in Grant Co. courts in the case J. S. and J. R. Shipley, plaintiffs vs. Mary Clossen, defendant. Property in Boscobel scheduled to be sold at public auction to satisfy debts.
Clyde	Robert P., Capt.	BD, p3c1, 7/11/1879	Died July 1, 1879 at Valley Springs, Dakota Territory where he kept a hotel. He was a former livery stable owner in Boscobel and the brother of Mrs. Davy of Boscobel. Clyde chased his son with a gun after an altercation. Son claimed he shot father in self-defense. No verdict available at this time.
Co. I, 6th WI Regt.		DC, p2c1, 9/11/1888	Served in the Civil War. Composed almost exclusively of Vernon Co. men. The De Soto soldiers were Andy Miller, Billie Lawrence, George McDill, Fred Page, Shep Cushing, A. Sears, N. Smith, Dick Wareham, Frank Waller, Sam Waller, Henry Fosdick, Albert Fosdick, John White, and Leroy Benedict. First battle was at Gainsville, VA, a battle preliminary to Bull Run. Fred Page and Dick Wareham were wounded at Gainsville. Shep Cushing and Sam Waller wounded at Bull Run. Billie Lawrence died at South Mountain. Gabriel Ruby wounded at Antietam. Ruby later killed at Fitzhugh Crossing. A. Sears died in the hospital. Albert and Henry Fosdick were wounded and went to the hospital. Cushing received a second wound in another battle. John White was wounded in the leg. Leroy Benedict, was a new recruit who came to the company in the spring of 1864. He was killed in Spotsylvania, 10 days after joining his unit. At Petersburg, Sam Waller volunteered for an assignment and was captured and sent to Andersonville, where he died. Cushing received his third wound at Hatches Run. Frank Waller was the received a medal of honor. In April 1864 George McDill was commissioned a Lieutenant in the 38th Regt. He was wounded in the charge at Crater. N. Smith was the drummer boy and served 4 years.
Coalburn	C. F., Mr. and Mrs.	RH, p4c2, 5/2/1901	Celebrated their golden wedding anniversary on Apri 27, 1901 in the Town of Scott. As a reminder of the day, he gave each of 13 grandchildren a $5 gold piece. He was the uncle of W. S. Hurlbut and wife.

Genealogical Events from Newspapers for Crawford, Vernon and Grant Counties, Wisconsin, 1870-1901

LAST NAME	FIRST NAME	NEWSPAPER, PAGE/COLUMN MONTH/DAY/YEAR	GENEALOGICAL DATA
Coalburn	Charles F.	DC, p2c2, 1/29/1887	C. V. Porter interviewed Charles F. Coalburn for a serires of articles on the Black Hawk War. Coalburn stated that the Gen. Atkinson's army passed through "Scott township and down Crow Hollow to where Bell Center now stands. Messrs Fisher and Sterling claim that the trail spoken of by Mr. Coalburn was the Indian trail followed by the different tribes that traded at Fort Winnebago and at Fort Crawford and traveled between the two forts; also the trail of the Indians between the lead mines and the Indian villages at Haney Valley and at the forks of the Kickapoo above Readstown."
Coates	B. M., Mrs.	BD, p3c1, 12/9/1881	Left Boscobel on Wednesday. Planned to settle in Barron Co. and live with her daughter, Mrs. Thomas Parr.
Coates	Benjamin M.	BD, p3c3, 9/10/1880	Resided in Boscobel. Recently died. A resolution of respect was published on behalf of the Hall of Grand Lodge, No. 169.
Coates	Jefferson	BD, p3c4, 1/30/1880	Died Tuesday evening in Dorchester, Saline Co., NB of intermittant fever from a wound received at Gettysburg during the Civil War. He was a member of the 7th WI Infantry. Went west 7 years ago. Operated a 1000-acre farm and raised stock. Blinded by wounds received in army. Aged 37 years. Survived by wife and 4 children. Son of William Coates.
Coates	Lill L.	BD, p3c1, 10/22/1880	Thomas W. Parr married Lill L. Coates on Oct. 15, 1880 at the home of the bride's mother. Bride from Boscobel. Groom from Madison. The Rev. W. Stoddart officiated.
Coates	Lillie	BD, p3c2, 12/21/1877	Returned to her home in Boscobel for a vacation from State University in Madison.
Coffin	George	DC, p3c2, 7/16/1887	Left the area for his farm near Ashton, Dakota.
Coffin	George	DC, p3c3, 12/25/1888	Mrs. Hannah Trott married George Coffin on Dec. 20, 1888 at the residence of J. H. Rogers in De Soto. Bride from De Soto. Groom from Ashton, Dakota.
Coffin	George, Mr. and Mrs.	DC, p3c4, 1/8/1889	Planned to live in the J. H. Rogers building in De Soto until next August when they will go to Dakota for awhile.
Coffin	Peleg	DC, p2c1, 4/30/1887	House in Lynxville has now been completed. Planned to put in a stock of goods on the first floor.
Coffin	W. H.	DC, p3c3, 11/27/1886	Partner in the grocery firm of Parks & Coffin of Lincoln, NB. Coffin learned his trade from J. H. Rogers of De Soto.
Coher	Christopher	RH, p5c4, 4/28/1898	Died at the home of his son at the age of 87, per Sugar Grove news column. He was a former soldier.
Coker	John	BD, p3c2, 8/3/1877	The 4-year-old son of John Coker of Wingville injured his arm in a farm accident. He may lose it.
Colburn	Eliza E.	BD, p3c2, 1/24/1879	Robert C. Jones married Eliza E. Colburn at the residence of the bride's father on Jan. 15, 1879. Bride from Crawford Co. Groom from Mt. Ida. The Rev. W. Stoddart officiated.
Cole	boy	DC, p3c2, 8/28/1888	A son was born Aug. 20, 1888 to Teller Cole of the De Soto area.
Cole	Charles	DC, p3c2, 9/25/1888	Left Red Mound for an extended visit in Raymondsville, NY.
Cole	Charles, Mrs.	DC, p3c4, 6/26/1886	Died at the age of 59 on June 22, 1886 in the Town of Wheatland from an inflamation of the bowels. She was one of the first settlers in Vernon Co. Survived by husband and 11 children.
Cole	Edward	BD, p2c2, 3/15/1878	Lyman Bangs was shot Tuesday night by Edward Cole. Bangs and Elliot Brandon are accused of stealing money from Cole. Dr. Armstrong was unable to retrieve the ball.
Cole	Mrs.	DC, p1c6, 10/8/1887	Resided in Watertown. Arrived in Retreat to make her home with daughter, Mrs. S. J. Duston.
Cole	Sam B., Mrs.	BD, p3c1, 10/22/1880	Formerly of Boscobel, but lately of Ottawa, IL. Died Saturday during a storm on Lake Michigan when the steamboat *Alpena* was wrecked.
Cole	T. W.	BD, p3c1, 10/23/1883	Named the new pastor at the Congregational Church in Boscobel.
Cole	Thomas	BD, p3c2, 6/3/1881	Mr. and Mrs. Thomas Cole and their son, Earnest, all of Jonesville, OH, visited friends in Boscobel, their former home. They were the guests of John Benoy.
Coleman	Alice	BD, p2c2, 4/4/1879	Frank Payne married Alice Coleman at Rolling Ground on March 31, 1879.
Coleman	Annie	BD, p3c1, 10/15/1880	George W. Philips married Annie Coleman on Oct. 7, 1880 in Boscobel. Bride and groom from Town of Scott, Crawford Co.
Coleman	C.	DC, p3c3, 11/27/1886	C. Coleman and wife of Fruitport[?], MI and Mrs. Joe Lamb of Waterford, Dakota visited friends in De Soto.
Coleman	C.	RH, p4c1, 7/20/1899	Resided in Bell Center. Looked around in Readstown for a building site.
Coleman	Emma, Mrs.	DC, p3c4, 11/27/1886	Returned to her home in Fruitport, MI after visiting relatives in Victory. Nee Wilcox.

Genealogical Events from Newspapers for Crawford, Vernon and Grant Counties, Wisconsin, 1870-1901

LAST NAME	FIRST NAME	NEWSPAPER, PAGE/COLUMN MONTH/DAY/YEAR	GENEALOGICAL DATA
Coleman	John T.	BD, p3c2, 3/2/1883	Died last Thursday at his home in the Town of Scott from an accident while chopping timber.
Coleman	John, Jr.	BD, p3c4, 8/7/1883	Promoted to section boss in the Prairie du Chien division of the Chicago, Milwaukee & St. Paul Railroad.
Coleman	Martin	BD, p3c1, 8/18/1882	Examined in Richland Center for the death of his mother. There may be insufficient proof.
Coleman	Martin	BD, p3c1, 8/25/1882	Bound over for $1000 in Richland Center on a charge of murder.
Coleman	Martin	BD, p3c1, 10/27/1882	Released from jail in Richland Center by Judge Cothren for insufficient evidence to hold on a charge of murder.
Coleman	Mrs.	BD, p3c2, 8/4/1882	Lived in Knapps Creek area of Richland Co. Buried on July 23, 1882. Evidence has surfaced that her son, Mathew Coleman, murdered her. Deputy Sheriff Spangler was ordered to arrest Coleman, but he had already departed from the area. It is believed Coleman is in Minnesota where he has relatives. Evidence and motives are described in the article. Mathew was about 21 years old, slender and 5' 6" tall. Coleman recently proposed marriage to Miss Groom, a nearby neighbor, who rejected him.
Coleman	Mrs.	BD, p3c1, 8/11/1882	Martin Coleman was arrested for Mrs. Coleman's murder.
Coleman	Otto	RH, p4c1, 2/28/1901	Died Feb. 24, 1901 of penumonia at the age of 9 months, 10 days. He was the son of Scott Coleman of Readstown. Funeral handled by Rev. Gander at the Methodist Episcopal Church. Buried in Readstown Cemetery.
Coleman	Scott	RH, p4c2, 10/25/1900	Purchased the dray line from M. A. Andrews in Readstown.
Coleman	Scott	RH, p4c1, 4/4/1901	Sold his dray line in Readstown to McDowel Bros.
Coleman	Scott	RH, p4c2, 10/3/1901	Recently sold his farm near Readstown to A. B. Ewers.
Coleman	Scott	RH, p4c1, 10/24/1901	Departed Readstown by team with his family for Ladysmith.
Collard	Charles	BD, p2c8, 1/5/1877	Advertised the sale of sheep in Lindeau, Iowa Co.
Collens	S. J.	BD, p3c2, 7/9/1880	Employed as the Assistant Superintendent of the Prairie du Chien division of the Chicago, Milwaukee and St. Paul railroad.
Collins	Charley	RH, p4c3, 9/26/1901	Charley Collins married Maud Lytle last week in La Crosse. Bride and groom from De Soto.
Collins	Clara	DC, p2c2, 6/4/1887	Clara Collins married Alex Tulloch on May 25, 1887 at the home of the bride. Bride from Purdy. The Rev. William Haughton officiated.
Collins	Margaret	BD, p3c1, 9/15/1882	James Kerr married Margaret Collins on Sept. 10, 1882 in Muscoda. Bride and groom from Boscobel. The Rev. I.[J.?] J. Wright officiated.
Collins	W. F.	BD, p2c3, 12/8/1882	W. F. Collins recently married Alice Jane Chandler at the Methodist Church in Richland Center. The Rev. J. D. Tull officiated.
Combe	John	BD, p2c4, 9/9/1881	Moved to Port Andrew, Richland Co. in 1841. He was the oldest living settler in Richland Co.
Combes	John	BD, p3c2, 5/5/1882	Recently died in Town of Richwood, Richland Co. at 75 years of age. He was the oldest settler in the county. Moved there in 1839. His wife is the sister of the Hon. J. T. Mills of Lancaster. Fathered 7 children. Wife, 3 sons and 3 daughters survive.
Compton	Mrs.	RH, p5c4, 4/27/1899	Recently buried at West Lima Cemetery. Member of Disciple Church. Sister of Mrs. D. Smith, who lived on the old Wamberg farm in Sugar Grove.
Comstock	C. A.	DC, p2c1, 6/12/1886	C. A. Comstock and Elmer Dunlap started publication of the *De Soto Chronicle* in the the upstairs rooms of the Ingersoll Building in De Soto. It was to be a Republican paper.
Comstock	C. A.	DC, p3c5, 6/19/1886	A Dissolution Notice was published noting the demise of the partnership between C. A. Comstock and E. E. Dunlap. Clemence A. Comstock will continue the newspaper operation by himself.
Comstock	Emma	BD, p3c2, 9/21/1877	Taught school in Pascoag, RI.
Comstock	Emma J.	BD, p3c3, 10/24/1879	Fred E. Newbury married Emma J. Comstock on Wednesday evening at the Congregational Church. Bride from Boscobel. Groom from Southbridge, MA. Extensive coverage of wedding and guests.
Comstock	H. Maria	BD, p3c1, 6/25/1880	The wedding of H. Maria Comstock to Franklin P. Capron, MD, was announced. Wedding was scheduled to take place June 23, 1880 in Phenix, RI.
Comstock	Hiram	BD, p2c4, 4/19/1878	Placed a legal notice in the newspaper warning that trespassing livestock would be pastured at 25 cents per head per week.

Genealogical Events from Newspapers for Crawford, Vernon and Grant Counties, Wisconsin, 1870-1901

LAST NAME	FIRST NAME	NEWSPAPER, PAGE/COLUMN MONTH/DAY/YEAR	GENEALOGICAL DATA
Comstock	Jesse	BD, P3c7, 1/5/1877	Advertised his grocery store in Boscobel.
Comstock	John N.	BD, p3c3, 6/8/1877	Returned to Boscobel after visiting in Deadwood City. He was looking at investing opportunities. He had mining experience in California and Australia. He concluded there was no gold in the Deadwood area.
Comstock	William	BD, p3c3, 6/22/1883	Arrived from Massachusetts to visit brothers, John and Jesse Comstock of Boscobel.
Coney	Andrew	BD, p3c1, 4/4/1879	Found money in Boscobel and offered to return it to the rightful owner. Resided in Sand Prairie, Richland Co.
Congregational Church Sunday School		DC, p3c3, 10/16/1886	The officers of the Congregational Church Sunday School in De Soto were D. A. Steele [his 24th year], Superintendent; Z. T. Clark, Assistant; Nellie Green, Treasurer; and Minnie Clark, Secretary.
Congregational Convention		DC, p3c4, 11/12/1887	De Soto hosted a convention of the Congregational Church. Those attending from the area were: Rev. Wm. Haughton, D. A. Steele, De Soto; J. T. Shaw, E. T. Bishop and wife, D. A. Bean and wife, Mrs. A. Chase, Sterling; Rev. S. S. Hebbard, H. Trowbridge; Wm. Crawford, Miss Anna E. Herbst, Sparta; Rev. E. W. Jenney, West Salem; Miss Mary Kingsland, Lynxville; Mesdames H. M. Nichols, L. A. Casson, M. E. Ely, W. Haughton, Viroqua. The Lynxville church was admitted to the convention, Rev. R. L. Cheney gave its organizational history.
Conklin	Hattie, Mrs.	DC, p2c2 8/20/1887	Left Cooley Valley for her old home in St. Charles, IL. Lived in Cooley Valley for several years. Taught school.
Conklin	Henry	DC, p3c3, 4/24/1888	Carrie I. Rose married Henry Conklin on April 18, 1888 at the home of the bride's father, W. R. Rose of Cooley Valley. Rev. Houghton officiated.
Conklin	J. N., Mrs.	DC, p3c4, 11/27/1886	Taught school in Cooley Valley.
Conklin	James	DC, p2c2, 12/25/1886	Worked at the Goodhue Wind Engine Co. in St. Charles, IL. Home for the holidays [in Cooley Valley].
Conklin	W. G.	DC, p3c3, 2/26/1887	Lived in Diamond Mills. Served in the Mexican War.
Conklin	W. G.	DC, p3c2, 3/3/1888	Received a pension for military service. Resided in De Soto.
Conklin	William G., Mr. and Mrs.	DC, p2c3, 2/12/1887	Celebrated their 50th wedding anniversary on Feb. 8, 1887 [date provided in 2/19/1887 issue] in Cooley Valley. About 120 guests attended the party. Five of 10 families who emigrated to the west together in 1833 from Buffalo, NY have celebrated their 50th wedding anniversaries. All were cousins. D. A. Ingersol, a cousin, came from Ft. Dodge, IA. Charles Morse, grandson, came from Huron, Dakota. They received many gifts. Some of the gifts came from Marion, a daughter, of Elgin, WI [IL?]; Charles Morse; 4 unnamed sons; Mrs. M. Fulton of St. Charles, IL; Mr. and Mrs. Charles Conklin of Elgin, IL; Mrs. M. Webster of Elgin, IL; Mr.and Mrs. J. V. Darret of St. Charles, IL; Mr. and Mrs. C. W. Conklin; L. P. Howard of Aurora, IL; Mrs. S. L. Pratt of Elgin, IL; Mr. and Mrs. Thomas Delacy; Mr. and Mrs. Samuel Arnold; Mr. and Mrs. Charles Cooley; Mr. and Mrs. Charles Lawrence; Mr. and Mrs. Angell; Mr. and Mrs. Chris Bolster; Mr.and Mrs. William Rose and Mr.and Mrs. C. L. Ingersol.
Conley	Con	DC, p2c1, 8/21/1888	Moved to La Crosse.
Conley	Mattie, Mrs.	DC, p3c3, 5/14/1887	Mrs. Conley, of De Soto, visited her brother, Thomas Carlyle, of Savannah.
Connelly	James	BD, p3c1, 7/20/1883	Lost his finger to amputation in Boscobel.
Connor	J., Capt.	BD, p3c3, 8/30/1878	Father-in-law of H. Keene of Boscobel. Arrived from Philadelphia to visit.
Connor	John	BD, p3c2, 3/8/1878	The Connor residence was destroyed by fire on Feb. 18, 1878. It was located about 4 miles west of Highland. Insured by P. A. Daggett's agency in Muscoda.
Conrad	Andrew	DC, p2c2 11/20/1888	Killed Nov. 14, 1888 by a train. He was about 39 years old. The C. B. & N. Railroad bought the coffin. Conrad was born in Pennsylvania and moved to Victory with his parents about 30 years ago. Married Melinda Stoda about 12 years ago. Survived by wife, 3 sons, 1 daughter, mother, 3 sisters. One son predeceased him. Buried in Retreat. [p2c2] His remains were taken to the home of his mother after the funeral sermon, as she was too feeble to go out. The funeral sermon was given by Rev. J. Schneller of Prairie du Chien. [p3c3]
Conrad	boy	DC, p2c2, 9/17/1887	A son was recently born to A. Conrad of Victory.
Conti	Mathew and Lewis	RH, p6c2, 7/25/1901	Lived in Genoa. Found what they believe to be a gold mine on the west branch of the Kickapoo River in Vernon Co.

Genealogical Events from Newspapers for Crawford, Vernon and Grant Counties, Wisconsin, 1870-1901

LAST NAME	FIRST NAME	NEWSPAPER, PAGE/COLUMN MONTH/DAY/YEAR	GENEALOGICAL DATA
Contoit	James B.	BD, p3c1, 10/16/1883	Died Oct. 4, 1883 of congestive fever at Tyler, TX. Death was "brought on by overwork, exposure, irregular times for meals and business for which he had no constitution." He was born in Boscobel on Nov. 24, 1865. Left on Oct. 22, 1882 for Texas, where he worked as a brakeman on the railroad. His father was summoned when he fell ill. The son died 25 minutes after his father's arrival at his sickbed.
Contoit	Jennie A.	BD, p3c2, 11/1/1878	Thomas Crinklaw married Jennie A. Contoit on Oct. 30, 1878 at the residence of the bride's parents in Boscobel. The Rev. William Stoddart officiated.
Cook	Arthur	RH, p4c2, 5/23/1901	Died May 15, 1901 at the home of his son, Thomas, in the Town of Eagle. Mr. Cook lived in the Town of Marshall, Richland Co. for more than 50 years.
Cook	Charles	BD, p3c1, 5/18/1883	Charles Cook, Harvey Clark and J. W. Nice returned to Boscobel after exploring for new homes in Dakota. Clark and Nice returned to Dakota.
Cook	Grace Bell	BD, p3c1, 8/19/1881	Died Sunday, Aug. 14, 1881 at age 2 years, 4 months. Daughter of Mr. and Mrs. A. N. Cook of Boscobel.
Cook	H. A.	DR, p3c3, 6/22/1871	Resided in Mt. Sterling. Suddenly died last Friday at the Sherman House in Viroqua per the *Viroqua Censor*. "He probably had been drinking liquor too freely."
Cook	Marah, Mrs.	BD, p3c2, 1/13/1882	Died Jan. 4, 1882 in Platteville. Aged 81 years and 10 months. Moved to Grant Co. in 1844. Survived by four children: Mrs. J. L. Taylor of Boscobel, William Cook of Boscobel, Mrs. Susan Grindell of Platteville and Webster Cook of Algona, IA. Died of pneumonia.
Cook	Minnie	BD, p3c2, 12/2/1881	Fell through the mill pond while skating. Got out without trouble because she fell in a shallow spot.
Cook	Mr.	DR, p1c4, 12/22/1870	Resided in Prairie du Chien. Elected principal of the Mt. Sterling Academy in 1869.
Cook	Will	DC, p2c4, 1/14/1888	Confined to his home in Seneca all winter with rheumatism.
Cooley		DC, p2c2 8/27/1887	Two infant daughters of Sylvester Cooley were recently buried in Retreat Cemetery.
Cooley	Aaron	DC, p2c3, 7/24/1888	He was a quiet, mild mannered farmer who gave his name to Cooley Valley [its first inhabitant]. At the outbreak of the Civil War he was 50 or 55 years old, too old to enlist. He "resorted to various devices to look young" and was accepted into the army. He went to the front, but caught malaria in the swamps, rendering him unfit for services. He eventually went home and died a few days after his return. "It may be said he ought never to have gone. Perhaps this was so, but what an example of patriotism this old man set for future generations."
Cooley	Alice	DC, p2c2, 7/2/1887	Recently baptized at the Methodist Episcopal Church in Retreat.
Cooley	C. H.	DC, p2c3, 8/28/1888	C. H. Cooley was elected Superintendent and Nellie R. Green Treasurer of the Sunday school [in De Soto] in place of D. A. Steele and Myra Steele, who resigned after 25 years of service.
Cooley	C., Mr. and Mrs.	DC, p2c2, 12/25/1886	They celebrated their 10th wedding anniverary on Dec. 21, 1886 [per the Cooley Valley news column].
Cooley	Charles	DR, p3c2, 5/18/1871	Cooley and his family left De Soto for their new home in Lincoln, NB.
Cooley	Charles, Mrs.	DC, p4c2, 5/24/1889	Resided in Stoddard. Visited parents, Mr. and Mrs. W. K. Lowrie of De Soto.
Cooley	Ella	DC, p2c2, 4/2/1887	Native of Retreat. Hired to teach school in the Brown District.
Cooley	Ella	DC, p2c2, 7/9/1887	Left her home in Cooley Valley for Waukon, IA. Returned with her brother, Orrin, and cousin, Ethel Cowen.
Cooley	F., Mrs.	DC, p2c2 7/30/1887	She was a Christian Science Doctor. Cared for the ill in Victory.
Cooley	F., Mrs.	DC, p2c3 8/6/1887	Departed Victory for her home in Clear Lake, IA to attend her son's marriage.
Cooley	F., Mrs.	DC, p2c2, 7/10/1888	Departed home in Clear Lake, IA for a new home in Tennessee, per the Victory news column.
Cooley	Maria	DC, p2c4, 1/15/1887	Maria Cooley [Conley?] recently married William La____ [Lawrence?]. Bride from De Soto. Groom from Boscobel. Married in Boscobel.
Cooley Valley School Board		DC, p2c3, 7/10/1886	The 1886 Cooley Valley School Board consisted of R. Angell, H. Kloak, A. Hanson and R. Ostinan.
Cooly	Mrs.	DC, p2c2, 1/1/1889	Mrs. Cooly [Cooley?] was in Victory. Planned to go to Chicago and join a party of 20 relocating to Tennessee.
Coomes	F. E.	BD, p3c1, 12/31/1880	Dentist. Announced that he had appointments available during his next visit to Boscobel.
Coomes	F. E.	BD, p3c1, 1/5/1877	Dentist in Boscobel.

Genealogical Events from Newspapers for Crawford, Vernon and Grant Counties, Wisconsin, 1870-1901

LAST NAME	FIRST NAME	NEWSPAPER, PAGE/COLUMN MONTH/DAY/YEAR	GENEALOGICAL DATA
Coon	L. E.	BD, p2c4, 11/26/1880	Grant County paid him a bounty for scalps turned into the county.
Cooper		DC, p3c4, 1/21/1888	The McGinnis and Cooper families were quarantined in De Soto. Seymour Marker submitted a bill to the village Board for attending them.
Cooper	Alice	DC, p1c1, 7/26/1889	H. C. Grass married Alice Cooper on Wednesday, July 24, 1889 at the residence of the bride's mother in De Soto. Groom was a lawyer in Curry, MN. Bride taught school. The Rev. William Haughton officiated.
Cooper	Alice	DC, p3c3, 7/3/1888	Returned to De Soto after teaching in Currie, MN
Cooper	Alice M.	DC, p3c3, 3/5/1887	Attended the Winona Normal School. Native of De Soto.
Cooper	Bessie	DC, p8c2, 6/21/1889	Celebrated her 6th birthday on June 14, 1889 in De Soto.
Cooper	J. A.	DC, p3c3 8/13/1887	Worked as a traveling salesman in Nebraska for the Humphrey Soap Co. of Prairie du Chien. Resided in [De Soto?].
Cooper	J. A.	DC, p2c4, 6/12/1886	Proprietor of a general store in De Soto.
Cooper	J. A., Mrs.	DC, p3c2, 11/13/1886	Left De Soto to visit her daughter, Alice of Winona, MN.
Cooper	Jane, Mrs.	DC, p3c2, 7/3/1886	Announced the next meeting of the Good Templars in De Soto.
Cooper	Julia, Mrs.	RH, p5c2, 7/29/1897	Arrived in Readstown from Idaho to visit with parents, Mr. and Mrs. Dr. Goyer.
Cooper	Uriah	DC, p2c2, 3/19/1887	Hosted his brother from New York at his home in Lynxville.
Cooper	W. A.	DC, p3c3, 9/11/1888	Arrived from Blanding, IL to attend the wedding of his aunt, Addie Coy, in De Soto.
Copsey	Fred	DC, p2c2, 5/7/1887	Resided in Seneca. Lost a thumb from an accident while chopping a tree.
Copsey	Jennie	DC, p2c2, 3/12/1887	Planned to leave next week from Seneca for Nebraska.
Corcoran	Thomas	BD, p2c4, 11/26/1880	Grant County paid him a bounty for scalps turned into the county.
Cordry	J. E.	DC, p3c3, 9/4/1888	Addie Coy married J. E. Cordry on Sept. 4, 1888 at the residence of J. A. Cooper in De Soto. Groom from Janesville, MN.
Corell	John	DR, p3c2, 3/30/1871	Worked as a furniture maker in Lansing.
Cornet Band Assoc.		BD, p3c3, 8/23/1878	The officers of the new Cornet Band Association in Boscobel were Thomas Crinklaw, H. W. Hubbell and R. J. Arthur. Other members were Will DeLapp, B. F. Burdick, Frank Rowe, Henry Bennis, W. T. Hurrd, Arthur Nixon, Myron DeLapp and Wesley Nice.
Cornwall	Horace	BD, p2c4, 12/18/1883	Died Dec. 6, 1883 in the Town of Eagle, Richland Co. at 74. He was the father of 11 children, 8 of whom were present for the funeral. Born near Syracuse, NY. Moved to Cleveland, OH when young. Moved to Eagle in 1883 [probably a typo]. Buried in the Basswood Cemetery. He was one of the old settlers.
Correll	Ed	BD, p3c2, 6/22/1877	Mr. and Mrs. Ed Correll of Madison visited friends in Boscobel.
Cory	James	DC, p2c1, 4/16/1887	Died April 5, 1887 at the home of E. Shesler of Victory. The only living relative is a baby grandchild to carry on the name. Buried in Victory Cemtery. [First name given in the 4/13/1887 issue.]
Cory	Minnie	DC, p2c3, 3/19/1887	Native of Viola. She was the sister of Dr. Cory of Chaseburgh. Planned to open a dress making shop in Mrs. Heald's building.
Cothren	C., Mrs.	BD, p3c1, 8/6/1880	Resided in Mineral Point. Died July 27, 1880 at 83 years of age. She was the mother of the Hon. M. M. Cothren.
Cothren	M. M.	BD, p3c1, 1/5/1877	Attorney in Boscobel.
Cottrell	Julia N.	BD, p3c2, 9/13/1878	Sidney Hauxshurst recently married Julia N. Cottrell in Milwaukee. Groom lived in Boscobel during the war. Bride from Milwaukee.
Couillard	boy	BD, p3c1, 10/23/1883	A son was recently born to Mart Couillard, the popular conductor on the way-freight.
Coult	B. W.	BD, p3c1, 2/11/1881	Bookkeeper at Ruka Brothers in Boscobel. Planned to move west in the spring.

Genealogical Events from Newspapers for Crawford, Vernon and Grant Counties, Wisconsin, 1870-1901

LAST NAME	FIRST NAME	NEWSPAPER, PAGE/COLUMN MONTH/DAY/YEAR	GENEALOGICAL DATA
Coult	B. W.	BD, p3c2, 2/25/1881	Planned to leave Boscobel for Swan Lake, IA to operate a hardware business.
Coult	B. W., Mrs.	BD, p3c1, 6/23/1882	Mrs. Coult of Swan Lake, IA and her "Mormon sister", Mrs. Mason of Salt Lake City, UT, visited old acquaintances in Boscobel.
Coult	N. M., Miss	BD, p3c3, 7/25/1879	Arrived from Litchfield, IL to visit brother, B. W. Coult of Boscobel.
County Board		DR, p3c3, 4/13/1871	Those chosen to the Vernon County Board during the last election were: Bergen, Levi Shorey; Christiana, John Michelet; Coon, Hans Nelson; Clinton, E. S. Alderman; Forest, W. C. Stelting; Franklin, F. K. Van Wagoner; Genoa, John W. Greenman; Greenwood, Martin Rogers; Harmony, A. J. Wiard; Hambury, J. W. Hoyt; Hillsborough, J. Manhart; Jefferson, D. H. Pulver; Kickapoo, Joseph Harris; Liberty, Allen Rusk; Stark, J. O. Parker; Sterling, R. W. Jordan; Union, T. S. Jordan; Viroqua, Ralph Hall; Webster, Simcon Adams; Wheatland, A. Glodery and Whitestown, G. White.
Court Cases		DR, p3c3, 6/8/1871	Messrs. Ankeny and McDill [of De Soto] are engaged in the following cases this week in Prairie du Chien: Mary Jane Mulick vs. D. R. Lawrence; Mary Jane Mulick vs. Lawrence Bird; Town of Freeman against Crawford County; L. O. Place against Thomas Shannon; William Zeiprecht vs. Mary J. Mulick; D. R. Lawrence vs. Adam Heiss; John Rutter vs. G. L. Sperry; N. W. Wells vs. Ole T. Nash; George Crum vs. Thomas Joseph; J. H. Jewell vs. A. C. Anderson and Ankeny vs. Morse et al.
Court Cases		DR, p3c3, 6/8/1871	Messrs. Ankeny and McDill [of De Soto] are engaged in the following cases next week in Viroqua: Ellen H. Knowlton, Administratrix, vs. Town of Freeman; T. C. Ankeny vs. Town of Freeman; T. C. Ankeny vs. Daniel Hill; T. C. Ankeny vs. U. C. Barnes; C. L. Ingersoll vs. Charles Brown; F. Jaeger and Adam Jaeger vs. William Campbell et al.; Ed. Lankford vs. George P. Griffin et al.; William Waldron vs. D. J. Spear; State of Wisconsin vs. James Loftus; State of Wisconsin vs. Edward Sweeney; H. M. Chamberlain vs. Isaac Corbet et al.; James Whitney vs. F. A. Waller et al.; Lucinda Freeman vs. Joseph Freeman; Sarah Ann Troop vs. Lester P. Miller et al.; George S. Sperry vs. W. E. Heald; Franklin J. Tenney vs. Lester P. Miller et al.; Town of Viroqua vs. A. J. Miles and C. L. Ingersoll vs. E. Ellefson.
Cover	Joe	BD, p3c2, 7/6/1877	Joe Cover married Miss Walworth on Thursday at the home of the bride in Richland Center. Groom from Lancaster.
Cover	Joseph	BD, p3c2, 8/10/1877	Joseph Cover married Della G. Walworth on July 29, 1877. Bride from Richland Center. Groom from Lancaster. Rev. J. Walworth of Richland Center officiated.
Cowan	Albert	DC, p2c3, 10/29/1887	"Albert Cowan came all the way from Star, to try the Burlington route to Estill Springs, Tenn. Albert is one of the good boys of Seeleyburg -- he is an old schoolmate of 'ye scribe' [Fred Z. Alexander]."
Cowan	George C.	BD, p3c3, 8/17/1877	Blinded by a 4th of July accident. Resided in Boscobel.
Cowan	George W., Mrs.	BD, p3c2, 1/12/1877	Died Jan. 10, 1877 at 49 years, 3 months and 10 days of age. She was one of Boscobel's "oldest" inhabitants.
Cowan	Isabella	BD, p3c2, 9/7/1877	James Gupth married Isabella Cowan last Thursday in Boscobel. Bride was the daughter of George W. Cowan. The Rev. Dr. Stoddart officiated.
Cowden	Bessie	RH, p4c4, 12/7/1899	Hired to teach in the Day District per Readstown news column.
Cowden	Lafe	RH, p4c2, 9/20/1900	Arrived in Readstown from Angus, MN to visit relatives.
Cowdrey	Joseph	DC, p3c2, 9/11/1888	Addie Coy married Joseph Cowdrey on Tuesday. Bride from De Soto. Plan to live in Janesville, MN. Rev. Haughton officiated.
Cowdry	Mrs.	DC, p8c2, 7/26/1889	Daughter of Mrs. J. A. Cooper. Arrived in De Soto with her 2 little stepsons last Friday and attended the wedding of her niece, Alice Cooper.
Cowell	Julia Annie	BD, p3c1, 12/26/1879	George Edwin Bowell married Julia Annie Cowell on Nov. 21, 1879 in Boscobel. Bride and groom from Avoca. Rev. William Stoddart officiated.
Cowen	Dick	DC, p2c3, 1/22/1887	Dick Cowen and his sister, Mrs. Belle Guptil [or Guptill], of Boscobel, visited friends in Seneca.
Cox		RH, p4c1, 4/12/1900	The infant child of James Cox of Readstown recently died. Funeral held on April 8, 1900.
Cox	boy	RH, p6c3, 5/25/1899	A son was recently born to Will Cox of Kickapoo.
Cox	William, Mrs.	RH, p5c4, 8/5/1897	Died July 24, 1897 in Viroqua. Survived by husband, 3 sons and 1 daughter. She was one of the county's oldest settlers.
Coy	Addie	DC, p3c3, 7/9/1887	Completed a year of school at Janesville, Minnesota and is spending her vacation with sister, Mrs. J. A. Cooper of De Soto.

Genealogical Events from Newspapers for Crawford, Vernon and Grant Counties, Wisconsin, 1870-1901

LAST NAME	FIRST NAME	NEWSPAPER, PAGE/COLUMN MONTH/DAY/YEAR	GENEALOGICAL DATA
Coy	Addie	DC, p3c3, 9/4/1888	Addie Coy married J. E. Cordry on Sept. 4, 1888 at the residence of J. A. Cooper in De Soto. Groom from Janesville, MN.
Coy	Addie	DC, p3c2, 9/11/1888	Addie Coy married Joseph Cowdrey on Tuesday. Bride from De Soto. Plan to live in Janesville, MN. Rev. Haughton officiated.
Coy	Addie, Miss	DC, p3c2, 6/19/1886	Taught school in Janesville, MN. Spent vacation with her sister, Mrs. J. A. Cooper.
Coy	Edward, Mrs.	DC, p3c2, 10/2/1886	Arrived from Lansing, IA to visit Mrs. J. A. Cooper of De Soto, her husband's sister.
Coyne	Patsy	BD, p3c2, 3/10/1882	Crawford Co. resident. Fined $3 for being drunk and disorderly in Boscobel.
Cragan	Mike	DC, p1c1, 5/31/1889	Left home in Ferryville for St. Paul to get the body of his recently deceased sister. Sister went to St. Paul to have cancer removed from her lip.
Craigo	George	RH, p4c1, 3/22/1900	Arrived from Oakland, CA. Visited brother, J. M. Craigo of Readstown.
Craigo	J. M.	RH, p7c1, 7/1/1897	Proprietor of the Readstown Roller Mills.
Craigo	J. M.	RH, p5c4, 4/28/1898	Delivered a speech at the Methodist Episcopal Church in Readstown on "Popular Representative Government."
Craine	E. A.	DC, Supp, 10/23/1886	E. A. Craine married Sadie Stewart on Sept. 7, 1886 in La Grace, Dakota Territory.
Cramer	Elizabeth Allison, Mrs.	BD, p3c2, 8/21/1883	Mrs. Cramer's funeral was held Monday at the Methodist Episcopal Church. She was born 54 years ago in Bath Co., KY. Moved to Boscobel 20 years ago with her husband, Joel Cramer.
Cramer	George	BD, p2c4, 11/26/1880	Grant County paid him a bounty for scalps turned into the county.
Cramer	Joel	BD; p3c1, 7/21/1882	Worked as a wheelright at Ableiter plow works in Boscobel.
Cramer	Milton	BD, p3c2, 1/10/1879	Recently died of consumption in Boscobel.
Crane	Estella	DR, p3c3, 1/4/1872	Recently badly burned by the explosion of a kerosene lamp. Former resident of West Prairie [now Lansing, IA?]. Daughter of L. P. Crane.
Crawford	Luella, Mrs.	RH, p4c2, 9/14/1899	Came from Iowa to visit relatives in the Town of Kickapoo. She was the daughter of H. C. Andrews of Kickapoo the sister of M. A. Andrews and Mrs. C. H. Davenport of Readstown.
Crawford County Board		DC, p3c3, 4/24/1888	The following men were elected to the 1888 Crawford County Board: A. F. Jones, Bridgeport; Wallace Bennett, Clayton; William Gleason, Eastman; J. N. Kast, Haney; James Patten, Marrietta; James Norris, Prairie du Chien; John Bull, M Menges, James McCabe, C. Nugent, all of City of Prairie du Chien; Bow Cron, Seneca; George Churchill, Scott; P. N. Peterson, Utica; and Fred Stuckey, Wauzeka.
Crawford County Election Results		DC, p2c1, 11/6/1886	Crawford Co. went Republican for the first time in years. Winners were: Gov. Rusk, Atley Peterson, O. B. Thomas, Hon. Hugh Porter of Seneca to the Assembly, T. N. Sime-Sheriff, C. E. Alder-County Clerk, J. D. Stuart-Register of Deeds, G. L. Miller-Dist. Atty., J. I. Thomas-Clerk of Court, Prof. J. F. Burgess- County Supt., J. J. Hurlbut-Surveyor, Chauncy Blancher-Coroner, and Henry Otto-Treasurer [the only Democrat elected].
Crawford County Republicans		DC, p2c1, 10/9/1886	The Crawford County Republican ticket was: Assembly, Hugh Porter of Seneca; Sheriff, T. N. Sime of Clayton; District Attorney, G. L. Miller of Freeman; Treasurer, Ole Holverson of Utica; County Clerk, C. E. Alder of Eastman; Register of Deeds, Joseph Stuart of Prairie du Chien; Clerk of Court, J. I. Thomas of Seneca; and County Supt., J. F. Burgess of Wauzeka.
Crawley	John	BD, p3c3, 1/5/1883	Suffered a big loss from fire at the Boscobel House. The building and most of its contents were destroyed at the hotel that was built in 1856. The first landlords were Messrs. Hall and Cole. They ran it for a short time. The senior partner ran off with the wife of the junior partner. Succeeding owners were: Messrs. Shearer [now of Muscoda] and Wood [now of Boscobel]; Joseph Walker [uncle of Lew Wayne]; C. D. Smith [now of Fennimore]; Mart Bartholomew; C. Chandler of Wingville [who died. in the hotel office]; Joseph Button [who departed for Missouri where he was killed]; M. O. Brekke; and John Crawley.
Creager	Jacob	BD, p2c3, 4/20/1877	Jacob Creager and W. F. Thompson of Boscobel, WI announced the dissolution of their partnership.
Crinklaw	Thomas	BD, p3c1, 4/8/1881	Son born on Saturday to Thomas Crinklaw of Boscobel.
Crinklaw	Thomas	BD, p3c1, 10/13/1882	Crinklaw and George Cowan plan to leave Boscobel for Soldiers Grove to open up a business.
Crinklaw	Thomas	BD, p3c2, 11/1/1878	Thomas Crinklaw married Jennie A. Contoit on Oct. 30, 1878 at the residence of the bride's parents in Boscobel. The Rev. William Stoddart officiated.

Genealogical Events from Newspapers for Crawford, Vernon and Grant Counties, Wisconsin, 1870-1901

LAST NAME	FIRST NAME	NEWSPAPER, PAGE/COLUMN MONTH/DAY/YEAR	GENEALOGICAL DATA
Crinklaw	Thomas M.	BD, p2c8, 1/5/1877	Operated a blacksmith shop in Boscobel.
Crinklaw & Parnell		BD, p2c4, 4/13/1877	T. M. Crinklaw and William H. Parnell formed Crinklaw & Parnell to provide carriage, wagon and blacksmith services in Boscobel.
Cron	Hiram	DC, p2c2, 4/2/1887	Departed Seneca for the West with 5 span of horses. Planned to be gone for "some time."
Crook	Frank	RH, p5c2, 7/8/1897	Mr. and Mrs. Frank Crook of Readstown visited Mrs. Crook's parents, Mr. and Mrs. Charles Aikens.
Crook	Lily, Mrs.	RH, p5c3, 1/20/1898	Died Tuesday at home in Brookville. Funeral at Brookville Church and burial at Brookville Cemetery. She was the daughter of Charles Aikens of Readstown. Born 27 years ago in Readstown. Married Frank Crook a few years ago. Survived by husband, a 3-year-old daughter, a 5-week-old son and a sister, Mrs. W. C. T. Adams of Readstown.
Crook	Rose	RH, p4c2, 12/27/1900	William Hutchison, Jr. married Rose Crook on Dec. 23, 1900 at the home of the groom's parents, Mr. and Mrs. William Hutchison. Bride and groom from Readstown.
Crook	William	RH, p7c2, 7/1/1897	Constructed a new store building in Readstown.
Crook	William	RH, p5c5, 9/16/1897	William Crook and Thomas Flanagan of Readstown published a notice of dissolution of partnership.
Crook	William	RH, p5c5, 10/28/1897	Proprietor of a general store in Readstown.
Crouch	Flora, Mrs.	BD, p2c3, 10/11/1878	Died of consumption on Oct. 3, 1878 in Boscobel. She was the wife of James and daughter of R. S. and Martha Lathrop. Aged 17 years and 8 months.
Crouch	James	BD, p3c2, 6/7/1878	James Crouch married Flora Lathrop last Tuesday. Bride was from Boscobel. The Rev. G. W. Nuzum officiated.
Crouch	M. F.	BD, p3c2, 9/6/1878	Departed Boscobel for a new home in Lemars, IA.
Crouch	Minnie Bell	BD, p3c2, 5/31/1878	Died May 24, 1878 in Mt. Ida at the age of 8 months. She was the daughter of Phillip and Melissa Crouch.
Crouch	Orrin G.	BD, p3c2, 4/5/1878	Died March 25, 1878 in the Town of Fennimore. Aged 32 years. Survived by wife and 3 small children.
Crouch	Thomas, Rev.	DC, p3c2, 10/9/1886	Replaced Rev. J. T. Morgans who left for Onalaska, WI.
Crow	Henry	BD, p3c1, 8/28/1883	Died Aug. 21, 1883 at his residence in Crawford County. Aged 74 years.
Crow	Wesley	BD, p2c2, 10/30/1883	Resolution of respect was published by the Lincoln Lodge, No. 176, I.O.O.F., upon the death of Wesley Crow.
Crowell	Seth	DR, p3c3, 9/21/1871	He was the proprietor of the only hotel in De Soto in 1856. The lower part of the building was a barn for horses and cattle and the upper part was used for lodging and dining rooms. In 1871 the hotel building was used as a barn by Benj. Trott.
Crowell	Seth	DC, p2c1, 10/29/1887	In 1856 he was the proprietor of a barn that served as one of De Soto's two hotels. Mr. Crowell's daughter was married to Byron Townsend, of the firm Ankeny and Townsend, one of the leading business houses in early De Soto.
Crowfoot	F.	RH, p6c3, 1/5/1899	Recently died at his home near Victory.
Crowley	John	BD, p3c4, 5/20/1881	Proprietor of the Boscobel Hotel.
Crum	boy	DC, p3c3, 7/31/1886	A son was born on July 23, 1886 to G. A. Crum of De Soto.
Crumerine	A. D.	RH, p5c2, 12/8/1898	Purchased a pair of bob sleighs in Readstown. Lived in Sugar Grove.
Cull	Ellen	BD, p3c2, 1/10/1879	Bernard McGuigan married Ellen Cull on Jan. 1, 1879. Bride and groom from Woodman. The Rev. Charles Schraudenbach, a Catholic priest in Boscobel, officiated.
Cull	J.	BD, p3c3, 1/5/1883	Insurance covered $90 worth of damage caused by a fire at his saloon and rsidence in Boscobel.
Cull	Mamie	BD, p2c2, 6/10/1881	Died recently at age 14 at home in Mt. Hope. Daughter of John Cull. Funeral held on May 28, 1881.
Cull	Mary	BD, p3c1, 6/17/1881	Daughter of John and Ann Cull of Mt. Hope. Died May 28, 1881 of cerebro spinal menengities.
Cull	Michael	BD, p3c1, 3/4/1881	Lived in Mt. Hope. Planned to auction off livestock and grain.
Culver	C. W.	BD, p3c1, 2/10/1882	Station agent at Woodman and Wauzeka. Given a new position in [Fona?].

Genealogical Events from Newspapers for Crawford, Vernon and Grant Counties, Wisconsin, 1870-1901

LAST NAME	FIRST NAME	NEWSPAPER, PAGE/COLUMN MONTH/DAY/YEAR	GENEALOGICAL DATA
Culver	Charles	DC, p3c3, 3/26/1887	Resided in Ontario. Found not guilty by a jury of selling liquor without a license.
Culver	Charles, Mrs.	DC, p3c3, 10/15/1887	Lived in Ontario. Went to Mauston to see sister. The sister died.
Culver	L. M.	BD, p3c4, 9/14/1877	Post master and depot agent in Wauzeka.
Culver	N.	DC, p1c6, 10/29/1887	Recently qualified for a pension for his military service. Resided in Ontario.
Cumerine	Dora	RH, p4c4, 12/29/1898	From Sugar Grove. Taught school in Fort Atkinson.
Cumings	J. A.	DR, p2c4, 8/24/1871	Made wagons in Viola.
Cummens	A. R.	BD, p3c1, 10/8/1880	Shot an owl that measured over 5 feet from wingtip to wingtip. It was one of the hooling [howling?] varieties and a great source of annoyance. Lived in Marietta.
Cummings	John	BD, p2c2, 2/9/1883	John Cummings, James and John McCormick, and Jeremiah Flynn were pardonned by the Governor for manslaugher of a neighbor in Crawford County.
Cummings Schoolhouse		BD, p3c1, 2/21/1879	The Cummings Schoolhouse in Rolling Ground, Crawford Co. burned last week.
Curley	Lizzie	DC, p4c2, 3/29/1889	Taught school in Ferryville.
Curley	Thomas	BD, p2c3, 2/23/1883	Thomas Curley of Utica had his foot amputated by Dr. J. Conant in Prairie du Chien.
Curley	Thomas, Colonel	BD, p3c1, 316/1883	The Curley residence in the Town of Haney was destroyed by fire at a loss of between $2500 and $3000. He lost a sword valued at $1000 that was presented to him by the citizens of St. Louis in 1865. Served as Lt. Colonel in the 27th MO Infantry during the Civil War. Recently involved in passage of a railroad bill in Madison.
Currie	Guy	RH, p5c3, 3/24/1898	Attended the teacher examination at Readstown. Lived in Viola.
Curry	boy	BD, p3c1, 1/16/1880	Son recently born to Seth Curry of the Boscobel area.
Curry	Charles	RH, p4c2, 9/13/1900	Owned and operated a cheese factory in Manning. Moved into the Crook residence in Readstown.
Curry	Elija	RH, p4c3, 5/30/1901	Lived in Spring Valley. He was improving after being kicked by a horse.
Curry	girl	RH, p5c3, 1/31/1901	A daughter was born on Jan. 28, 1901 to Charles Curry of Readstown.
Curry	Seth	BD, p3c2, 9/2/1881	Fire destroyed building and hay on a farm co-owned by Seth D. and Hansey Curry [brothers] in Barnes Co., Dakota. Seth was at his Boscobel home when he heard the news.
Curry	Steve, Mrs.	BD, p3c5, 10/12/1877	Died last Tuesday when a tree cut by her husband fell sooner than expected and caught her as she ran away. Lived near Wauzeka.
Curtis	Emma	DR, p1c4, 12/22/1870	Elected the first teacher of the Mt. Sterling Academy in 1867. From Fond du Lac. Left the school after the spring 1869 term when the majority of the students left to teach in the common schools.
Curtis	John Lyman	BD, p3c2, 9/27/1878	Mary Jane Groom married John Lyman Curtis on Sept. 25, 1878 at the home of the bride's parents in Marion. Groom from Fond du Lac Co. Rev. Dr. William Stoddart officiated.
Curtis	Perry	DR, p1c1, 12/15/1870	Proprietor of the De Soto Livery Stable.
Curtis	William	BD, p3c2, 5/28/1880	Appointed to be a census enumerator in Glen Haven, Grant Co.
Cushing		DC, p2c2, 10/29/1887	Occupied the old Winnesheik Hotel building in 1856. Cushing made tin ware and repaired leaky vessels.
Cushing		DC, p2c2, 2/3/1888	Cushing, the tin-man in De Soto, departed sometime before 1859. C. B. Stevens opened a shop.
Cushman	A. C.	DR, p2c4, 8/24/1871	Operated a saw mill and flouring mill in Viola.
Custin	Albert Eugene	RH, p5c4, 10/26/1899	Died Oct. 22, 1899 in Cashton. He was a former resident of Readstown. Born in Geneva, OH in 1850. Moved to Wisconsin when he was a young man. Lost his mother when he was a boy. "He was cast on the world at the mercy of strangers. He was given to despondency." Funeral held by Rev. Bell at the Methodist Episcopal Church and buried in the Readstown Cemetery.
Dailey	Mr.	DC, p3c4, 10/23/1888	Left De Soto to live with his daughter, Mrs. Parker of Chicago.

Genealogical Events from Newspapers for Crawford, Vernon and Grant Counties, Wisconsin, 1870-1901

LAST NAME	FIRST NAME	NEWSPAPER, PAGE/COLUMN MONTH/DAY/YEAR	GENEALOGICAL DATA
Dalton	Clara A.	DC, p3c2, 9/18/1886	Elmer E. Dunlap recently married Clara A. Dalton. Groom former owner of the *De Soto Chronicle*. Bride from La Crosse.
Dalton	John	BD, p2c1, 10/5/1877	Taken to Waupon for a 6-month sentence by Sheriff Birchard. His crime was housebreaking.
Danils	C., Mrs.	DC, p3c3, 1/21/1888	Per Ontario news column, departed for Aberdeen, Dakota.
Darnell	R. J.	BD, p3c2, 5/21/1880	R. J. Darnell married Mrs. Hannah Hinders on May 9, 1880 at the Forest House in the Town of Forest, Richland Co. This was Darnell's third marriage and Hinder's fourth marriage. They are both blind.
Davenport	A. N.	RH, p4c1, 2/14/1901	Traveled from Readstown to the county seat.
Davenport	A. N. and George	RH, p4c1, 5/16/1901	Constructed a windmill for Charles Crook.
Davenport	A. S.	RH, p5c2, 4/12/1900	Resided in Readstown. Davenport has been sick, but is now able to get out again.
Davenport	A. S.	RH, p5c3, 8/30/1900	Slowly recovering from typhoid fever in Readstown.
Davenport	Alfred	RH, p4c1, 9/21/1899	Planned to move to Readstown. He was the brother of C. H. Davenport.
Davenport	Alfred	RH, p4c1, 10/4/1900	From Readstown. Had been low with typhoid fever. Able to get out again.
Davenport	Anna	BD, p3c1, 8/8/1879	Cecil H. Stowell married Anna Davenport on August 3, 1879. Bride and groom from Clayton, Crawford Co. Justice J. McLaughlin officiated.
Davenport	Benoni	RH, p5c4, 2/22/1900	Resident of Soldiers Grove. Purchased lots from J. D. Cade in Readstown. Planned to build a house in the spring.
Davenport	Bertie	RH, p4c2, 1/19/1899	C. H. Davenport of Readstown gave a party for his sister, Bertie Davenport. Otis Wilson was the "Hobson of the evening."
Davenport	C. H.	RH, p4c1, 7/21/1898	Advertised services as Justice of the Peace in Readstown.
Davenport	C. H.	RH, p4c5, 12/29/1898	Served as an agent for the Challenge Wind-Mill and Feed-Mill Co. of Batavia, IL. Lived in Readstown.
Davenport	C. H.	RH, p4c3, 8/10/1899	Came down the railroad from Viroqua. Herman had a position there as a tinner working for Martin and Kueubler's Hardware Store.
Davenport	C. H.	RH, p4c2, 9/13/1900	C. H. Davenport and Earl Bishop did tin work in the new parsonage for the St. Phillips Church in Rolling Ground. John Ward did the architectural work. George Ward of Readstown was the lead carpenter.
Davenport	C. Herm	RH, p5c2, 12/1/1898	Father of a son named Danny who was born on Nov. 28, 1898 in Readstown. The newspaper printed the words of a song about the boy.
Davenport	Claude	DC, p3c4, 5/14/1887	The officers of the Methodist Episcopal Church in Retreat were Mary Bates, Claude Davenport and Hattie Allen.
Davenport	Claude	DC, p3c3, 9/4/1888	Went to Janesville to learn telegraphy. Resided in Retreat.
Davenport	F.	DC, p3c4, 1/8/1889	Installed as Sargeant of the Guard for the John M. White Camp 20 Sons of Veterans.
Davenport	F. E.	DC, xxxx, 7/19/1889	Sold horses to C. L. Woodbury of De Soto.
Davenport	Fannie, Mrs.	RH, p5c3, 7/22/1897	Lived in the Readstown area. Visited her parents, Mr. and Mrs. Andrews at Kickapoo.
Davenport	Fannie, Mrs.	RH, p4c4, 3/24/1898	Resided in Readstown. Visited her parents, Mr. and Mrs. H. C. Andrews of Kickapoo Center.
Davenport	Fanny, Miss	RH, p5c4, 1/13/1898	Resided in Readstown. Attended the Ladies Aid Society at the home of her sister, Mrs. C. B. Holcomb of Kickapoo Center.
Davenport	George	RH, p5c3, 11/3/1898	He was the brother of C. H. Davenport. Wrote a letter from "Porto Rico" that was published in the newspaper. Served in Co. I, 3rd Regiment Wisconsin Volunteers during Spanish American War. Planned to visit his relations in New York while on furlough.
Davenport	George	RH, p5c2, 11/17/1898	George Davenport and his wife, of Sparta, visited brother, C. H. Davenport of Readstown. Recently returned from the war.
Davenport	George	RH, p5c3, 6/8/1899	George Davenport of Sparta and Walter Ramsey of Milwaukee visited H. C. Andrews in Readstown.
Davenport	George	RH, p4c2, 11/8/1900	George Davenport of Sparta planned to move to Readstown and join his brother, C. H. Davenport, in the tinshop.

Genealogical Events from Newspapers for Crawford, Vernon and Grant Counties, Wisconsin, 1870-1901

LAST NAME	FIRST NAME	NEWSPAPER, PAGE/COLUMN MONTH/DAY/YEAR	GENEALOGICAL DATA
Davenport	George	RH, p4c1, 12/13/1900	Davenport and his family were expected to return to Sparta this week. They had been in Readstown.
Davenport	girl	RH, p4c2, 8/1/1901	A daughter was born Monday night to C. H. Davenport of Readstown.
Davenport	H.	RH, p5c2, 7/22/1897	Attended the soldiers reunion in Steuben.
Davenport	H.	RH, p4c4, 6/16/1898	Brother was serving in Co. L, camped at Chickamauga Park, GA.
Davenport	Herman	RH, p5c2, 7/8/1897	Worked as a barber in Readstown.
Davenport	Herman	RH, p5c3, 7/8/1897	Attended the M. W. A. picnic in Viroqua.
Davenport	Herman	RH, p5c3, 1/13/1898	Installed a telephone in his tinshop. It will be for private use.
Davenport	Leonard	RH, p4c2, 6/14/1900	Lived in Readstown. A large darning needle was accidently run into his hand.
Davenport	Mr.	DC, p3c3, 2/19/1887	Mr. Davenport married Miss Eitzert Monday at Mt. Sterling.
Davenport	N.	RH, p5c2, 8/18/1898	N[elson] Davenport of Sparta and his daughter, Mrs. Asbury of Viroqua, visited with L. H. Davenport in Readstown.
Davenport	Nelson	RH, p5c4, 7/15/1897	Resided in Viroqua. Visited his son, Herman of Readstown.
Davenport	Nelson	RH, p4c1, 11/23/1899	Nelson Davenport and his daughter, Bertie, visited Viroqua.
Davenport	Nelson	RH, p4c2, 1/18/1900	Recently moved into the Thomas Davenport residence.
Davenport	Nelson	RH, p5c2, 4/12/1900	The Readstown Village Board approved a bill for 25 cents submitted by Nelson Davenport for manure.
Davenport	Nelson	RH, p4c3, 5/2/1901	Presented a bill for $1.37 to Readstown Village Board for 11 hours of work on the highway.
Davenport	Thomas	RH, p4c2, 11/15/1900	George Sutherland purchased the Readstown residence of Thomas Davenport.
Davenport	Tom A.	RH, p5c5, 10/28/1897	Proprietor of a restaurant in Readstown.
Davenport	W. A., Mrs.	BD, p3c4, 7/13/1883	Mrs. W. A. Davenport of Le Claire, IA, but formerly of Boscobel, visited her friend, Miss Eva Seeds of Boscobel.
Davenport & Maiben		RH, p5c2, 7/29/1897	Completed the iron roof on the Crook building in Readstown.
Davenport Bros.		RH, p4c1, 2/28/1901	Plan to add a building to the side of their tinshop for farm machinery. Will handle a full line of Plano harvesting machinery this season.
Davey	Mamie	BD, p3c1, 4/27/1883	Mamie Davey and Alice McReynolds left Boscobel to engage in dressmaking in Montfort.
Davey	Will	RH, p5c4, 11/17/1898	Departed De Soto for a railroad job in Eagen, SD to work as a day operator.
David	Frank	BD, p2c3, 8/24/1877	Frank David and R. Woodward operated a drug store in Muscoda.
David	Frank	BD, p3c2, 2/8/1878	Served as postmaster in Muscoda.
David	J. W.	BD, p3c1, 1/5/1877	Physician in Muscoda.
David	Lester	BD, p3c3, 7/20/1877	Drowned June 14, 1877 at Muscoda. He was the 17-year-old brother of Dr. J. W. David and Frank David of Boscobel. Frank Bennett, age 16, tried to help. The body was found 4 miles downstream by Wenzel Morevitch.
David	Oscar	BD, p3c1, 10/30/1883	Oscar David married Maria Noble on Oct. 24, 1883 at the Central House in Boscobel. The bride and groom were from Excelsior. The Rev. W. Fletcher DeLap officiated.
David	Warren	DC, p2c2, 12/24/1887	Arrived from La Crosse to visit his sister, Mrs. D. P. Smith of Retreat.
Davidson		BD, p3c1, 7/22/1881	A young man who recently arrived from Norway was quarantined for small pox in Soldiers Grove. Proved to either be a very mild case or a false rumor.
Davidson		BD, p3c2, 7/29/1881	Recently emigrated to America. Came down with "ships fever," not small pox as previously reported. Lived in Soldiers Grove.

Genealogical Events from Newspapers for Crawford, Vernon and Grant Counties, Wisconsin, 1870-1901

LAST NAME	FIRST NAME	NEWSPAPER, PAGE/COLUMN MONTH/DAY/YEAR	GENEALOGICAL DATA
Davidson	Ingeborg, Mrs.	BD, p3c1, 5/12/1882	Died April 27, 1882 at 64 years of age. She was the mother of J. D. Davidson of Soldiers Grove and Mrs. Sever Anderson of Boscobel.
Davidson	J. O.	BD, p3c1, 10/13/1882	J. O. Davidson of Soldiers Grove sold his mercantile business to Mrs. Mary Tate of Bell Center.
Davidson	J. O.	BD, p2c2, 3/9/1883	Nellie Bliss married J. O. Davidson last Wednesday [per *Crawford County Journal* of 2/28/1883] at the residence of the bride's mother. Bride was from Readstown. Groom was from Soldiers Grove. The Rev William Haughton of Viroqua officiated.
Davidson	J. O.	DC, p2c2, 8/7/1886	Resided in Soldiers Grove. Expected to run for Assembly.
Davidson	James	DC, p2c1, 4/2/1887	Departed Eastman for Dakota with lumber and household goods in 2 railroad cars.
Davidson	Ole	BD, p2c2, 2/24/1882	Appealed to Boscobel City Council to have a fine remitted. He cut down a tree in the Boscobel City Park.
Davidson	P. S.	DC, p3c3, 4/10/1888	Disposed of his De Soto real estate and mercantile interests to his son, William F. Davidson.
Davis		DC, p1c2, 6/21/1889	A child of Langdon Davis died of scarlett fever in Retreat on Sunday.
Davis	Cora	DC, p4c2, 3/12/1889	Will Sargent married Cora Davis on Mar. 7, 1889 in La Crosse. Bride and groom grew up in De Soto.
Davis	Delos G.	BD, p3c3, 6/14/1878	Delos G. Davis married Eleanor Bird on June 2, 1878. Bride and groom from Boscobel. Justice Jacob McLaughlin officiated.
Davis	Elvin	RH, p5c3, 11/30/1899	Lived in Sugar Grove and attended school in Readstown.
Davis	Helen L.	BD, p3c1, 9/2/1881	Dexter S. Barnes married Helen L. Davis on Aug. 25, 1881 in Boscobel. Groom from Harved, IL. Bride from Wyalusing, WI. The Rev. T. M. Evans officiated.
Davis	J. A.	DR, p2c2, 5/18/1871	Authored a letter published in paper describing his trip to Oregon.
Davis	J. A.	DR, p3c4, 6/15/1871	Authored a letter published in paper describing Oregon. Former resident of De Soto.
Davis	J. B., Sheriff	BD, p2c3, 3/17/1882	Davis and his son, John, of Prairie du Chien bought a 1000 acre farm near Mitchell, Dakota. They have sold their house. Family will move when the Dakota house is ready. He still owns a farm near Bridgeport.
Davis	J. W., Dr.	DR, p1c1, 12/15/1870	Physician in Lansing, IA. Advertised services in the *De Soto Republican*. Saw patients in Crawford and Vernon Counties.
Davis	John	DR, p3c1, 12/15/1870	Advertised a going-out-of-business sale in De Soto. Selling his entire stock of merchandise.
Davis	John	DR, p3c2, 12/15/1870	Surveying new roads for the county.
Davis	John and Nellie	DC, p3c4, 3/26/1887	Returned to Retreat after spending the last year in Henry, Dakota. John planned to return to Henry. Nellie planned to stay in Retreat.
Davis	John C.	DR, p3c2, 12/29/1870	Operated a store on the corner of Main and Front streets in De Soto. Sold a large, general assortment of merchandise that he was offering at cost as he wanted to look after his farm and dispose of his stock.
Davis	John C.	DC, p2c2, 3/20/1888	John C. Davis, Doctor Sperry and Charles B. Whiting coordinated an opposition ticket for the 1860 Town of Wheatland elections because they thought the "democratic doctrine of rotation in office ought to be observed." [Election strategy makes for interesting reading.]
Davis	John C.	DR, p3c1, 9/7/1871	Advertised desire to trade a 3 year old mare for a good yoke of oxen.
Davis	John C.	DC, p2c1, 2/18/1888	H. M. Chamberlain brought John C. Davis from Boston to work at the Cate sawmill in De Soto about 1858/9. "He was an indefatigable worker, and when he participated in any movement he did so with all his might." When the lumber company failed he stayed to close out the business. He then rented the building in De Soto formerly occupied by Carlyle & Dowse and operated a store for several years. He also purchased a farm on the ridge and later died there. He was full of humor, quick at repartee.
Davis	John L.	DC, p2c3, 5/1/1888	Resided in Retreat. Went to Dubuque to visit his son.
Davis	John, Dr.	DC, p3c3, 11/13/1886	Arrived in Retreat to visit parents. From Dubuque.
Davis	Kelly	BD, p3c2, 1/26/1877	Shot in a Moline, IL saloon on Jan. 12, 1877. He was "well known in Boscobel."

Genealogical Events from Newspapers for Crawford, Vernon and Grant Counties, Wisconsin, 1870-1901

LAST NAME	FIRST NAME	NEWSPAPER, PAGE/COLUMN MONTH/DAY/YEAR	GENEALOGICAL DATA
Davis	L. L.	DC, p2c3, 8/28/1888	Died in Retreat on Aug. 21, 1888 of apoplexy. Funeral held in the Methodist Episcopal Church. Grieved for his daugher, Mrs. McKay, who died a few days ago. Resided in Retreat since its founding.
Davis	Laura M.	BD, p3c5, 7/27/1877	O. Parker married Laura M. Davis on July 4, 1877 at Patch Grove. Bride and groom from Patch Grove. J. A. Davis, Esq. officiated.
Davis	Martha, Mrs.	RH, p4c2, 7/26/1900	Resided in Readstown. She was over 80 years old and quite low with complication of diseases. Recovery feared to be impossible.
Davis	Martha, Mrs.	RH, p4c3, 6/27/1901	Died June 16, 1901 in Readstown. Born Nov. 1827 in Ispwich, MA. Moved to Readstown about 50 years ago. Lived with her son, Parker, for the last few years. Funeral held at the Methodist Episcopal Church. Buried in Readstown Cemetery.
Davis	Maud	DC, p2c2, 4/2/1887	Native of Retreat. Hired to teach school at Mound Ridge.
Davis	Phebe	DR, p3c3, 10/26/1871	A summons for relief was published in the case, Phebe Davis, plaintiff, vs. John A. Davis, defendant, in the Vernon Co. Circuit Court.
Davis	Richard	BD, p2c3, 12/23/1881	Grew tobacco on his Richland Center area farm last season. Tobacco buyers from Stoughton, WI called it good quality tobacco. [Tobacco became a popular cash crop in later years in Richland/Crawford Counties.]
Davis	Richard	BD, p2c5, 2/3/1882	From Richland Center. Sold 1500 pounds of tobacco for 12½ cents/pound to a Reedsburg dealer. Planned to devote more of his effort to raising tobacco.
Davis	S. H.	DR, p2c5, 12/15/1870	Proprietor of the Allamakee Co. Marble Works in Lansing, IA.
Davis	S., Mr.	BD, p3c1, 9/8/1882	"Mr. S. Davis, a colored gentleman, living across the river [from Boscobel], was so unfortunate as to have a horse and fourteen hogs die in his hands a few days ago. He can ill afford the loss and a subscription has been started. Those who feel like helping a worthy man can find the list with T. Carrier & Co."
Davis	Thomas	DC, p3c4, 11/27/1886	Recently married in Dakota. Former resident of Retreat.
Davis	W. G.	DC, p3c4, 9/25/1886	Lived in Retreat. Celebrated his 25th wedding anniversary on Aug. 15th.
Davis	Warren	DC, p1c2, 8/2/1889	Lived in North La Crosse. Visited sister, Mrs. Smith of Retreat.
Davis	William	DC, p3c5, 8/14/1886	Served as postmaster in Ferryville.
Davis	William	DC, p2c2, 5/28/1887	Postmaster and grocery store owner in Ferryville.
Davis	William	DC, p4c3, 4/19/1889	Served as postmaster in Ferryville. He was 6' 6" tall.
Davis Bros.		DR, p2c2, 4/13/1871	Wrote a letter of farewell. Published in newspaper. Planned to head for Oregon and Washington Territory. Moved to Crawford Co. in 1855, when they were boys.
Davisson	Samuel	RH, p5c4, 11/3/1898	Recently stricken with a stroke of paralysis. He was slowly improving, per Mound Park news column.
Day	Charles	BD, p2c4, 11/26/1880	Grant County paid him a bounty for scalps turned into the county.
Day	Hattie	BD, p3c4, 6/21/1878	C. L. Young married Hattie Day on June 18, 1878 in Boscobel. Bride from Cresco, IA. Groom from Chicago. The Rev. George W. Nuzum officiated.
Day	James	BD, p2c4, 11/26/1880	Grant County paid him a bounty for scalps turned into the county.
Day	Jehru	DC, p1c5 8/13/1887	Resided in Hurlbut. Granted a pension [for military service].
Day	John	BD, p3c2, 3/19/1880	John Day and Henry Mindham, both of Crawford County, ran into each other at Gorman's Store at the north end of the bridge. A feud has existed between the two since Day assessed Mindham's property. "Mindham informed Day it was a good time to settle their differences. After exchanging words, Day started to club Mindham with a wagon stake. Mindham was severely beaten. Two days later he was still bleeding from the mouth, nose and ears." There were slim chances of recovery. Day believes he will be arrested for the assault.
Day	Josh	RH, p4c2, 7/18/1901	Day was an old time resident of Readstown who now lives in Steuben. He has not been in Readstown for over 20 years but was "up the line the first of the week." Those who he once knew are either dead or have moved away.
Day	Linda	BD, p3c1, 10/15/1880	John Harris married Linda Day on Oct. 7, 1880. Bride and groom from Wauzeka.
Day	Mr.	RH, p4c4, 8/1/1901	Jane Chambers recently married Mr. Day. Bride from De Soto. Groom was a pearl buyer in Lynxville.

Genealogical Events from Newspapers for Crawford, Vernon and Grant Counties, Wisconsin, 1870-1901

LAST NAME	FIRST NAME	NEWSPAPER, PAGE/COLUMN MONTH/DAY/YEAR	GENEALOGICAL DATA
Day	N., Mrs.	DC, p2c2 8/13/1887	Departed Lynxville to visit her mother at Osage, IA.
Day	Rufus M.	BD, p3c2, 5/28/1880	Appointed to be a census enumerator in Mt. Hope, Grant Co.
De Hart	Alice	DC, p2c3 8/20/1887	Paul W. Mahoney married Alice De Hart on Aug. 17, 1887. Bride from West Lima. Groom was a lawyer in North La Crosse.
De Lacy	John	RH, p4c2, 6/6/1901	Resided in Springville. Hired to teach in the Readstown schools next season.
De Lacy	Johnnie	DC, p1c2, 8/2/1889	Baptized in Cooley Creek by Mr. William Haughton.
De Lacy	Thomas	DC, p8c2, 7/19/1889	Sold F. E. Davenport his imported Clydsdale stallion.
De Lap	Robert H., Jr., Mrs.	RH, p4c2, 6/13/1901	Died Saturday at the home of her parents, Mr. and Mrs. D. G. James. Beulah James was born July 2, 1873 in Richland Center and graduated from school in 1896. Studied music in Milwaukee and at the Conservatory of Music in Boston.
De Rhine	Orilla L.	DC, p2c2, 11/26/1887	Arrived in De Soto in 1857 and taught school. "She was bright and vivacious and created quite a little stir."
De Soto		RH, p5c4, 12/8/1898	An article was published describing De Soto's geography, scenery, business establishments, churches and civic organizations.
De Soto Baseball		DC, p4c2, 4/12/1889	De Soto fielded the following baseball players to represent the De Soto Club this season: W. H. Lewis, J. Dunlevy, H. T. Hare, B. Hemenway, E. Dyer, M. Hurley, F. Angell, W. Marker, C. Clark, F. A. Carr and E. Marker.
De Soto Cemetery Assoc.		DC, p8c3, 8/9/1889	The trustees of the newly formed De Soto Cemetery Association were C. L. Ingersoll, A. Carlyle and N. E. French.
De Soto Chronicle Subscribers		DC, p3c5, 1/15/1887	The following are new newspaper subscribers: James Voysey, William P. Daly, Miss S. Hinds, George W. Eckhardt, C. C. Colwell, Milo Whitney, P. Ostman. They were all from De Soto. New Retreat subscribers: M. Host, William Morton, Dr. S. A. Mellen and V. E. Aiken. New Viroqua subscribers: F. Eckhardt, W. F. Lindemann, George Michaelsohn and George K. Hazen.
De Soto Chronicle Subscribers		DC, p3c5, 1/15/1887	The following are new newspaper subscribers: W. R. Mansfield, Lynxville; O. Slade, Lynxville; Barnet Latshaw, Oaktown, IN; Albert Shaw, Marshall, IL; G. I. Spear, Geneva, NB; M. A. Welsh, Ontario; George M. Foster, Greene, IA; William P. Clark, Victory; W. A. Hodge, Victory; E. Wise, Victory; M. W. Parker, Fargo, Dakota; Ed Zitzner, Rising Sun; Charles Cole, Red Mound; S. Cole, Waddington, NY; George O. Chapman, Merrimac; R. C. Turner, Cornelious, OR; W. S. Milliken, IA; and Mary McKay, Richland Center.
De Soto I.O.O.F.		DC, p2c1, 2/19/1887	Officers of the "nearly extinct" De Soto I.O.O.F. were Thomas Lawrence, J. A. Cooper, J. W. Caldwell, J. H. Rogers, N. E. French and C. E. Reiter.
De Soto Lumber Co.		DC, p2c2, 2/19/1889	Lately organized by P. S. Davidson, W. F. Davidson and Lafe Holmes. They succeeded C. Lyttle & Co. Business conducted by Charles Lind. Adam Carlyle keeps the books.
De Soto M. E. Church		DC, p4c2, 4/5/1889	The De Soto Methodist Episcopal Church baptized the following persons: Thomas N. Lawrence, William James Lawrence, Matthew Lawrence, Alice Z. Lawrence, Minnie French and Aggie R. Owens.
De Soto Officers		DC, p2c3, 8/14/1886	At the first annual election of the Village of De Soto, the following officers were elected: President, Adam Carlyle; Trustees -- Charles Lyttle, N. E. French, James Thompson, Martin Loftus, John Devlin and Orlando Ewers; Clerk, Alfred McDowell; Treasurer, C. H. Upham; Marshall, William Waldron; Constable, James Thompson; Justice of the Peace, C. E. Woodbury; Police Justice, C. L. Ingersoll; Supervisor for Crawford Co., A. Carlyle and Supervisor for Vernon Co., C. L. Ingersoll.
De Soto Plum		DC, p3c4, 9/25/1886	About 1 mile below De Soto is a small plum orchard first seen by early settlers in 1854/5. The origin is unknown, but Chief Winneshiek's oldest son, John Waukon, who died 15 years ago said some Indians came from the setting sun away beyond the mountains, or in other words the Pacific slope and brought the plums with them. Mr. Godfrey, an old Indian trader under Col. Dousman, who originally owned the Cheney addition to the village, told the same story. It can be reasonably asserted these delicious plums, that have no equal in size, taste, abundance or surety of a crop and which trees are now sold at every nursery in the country originally came from California.
De Soto Settlers		DC, p2c2, 10/29/1887	The first settlers in De Soto were two Frenchmen. In 1856 they lived in a log house across the creek in the Crawford County side of the village. It was the only local source of milk during the winter. The milk sold for 10 cents per quart.
De Soto Teachers		RH, p4c3, 1/13/1898	The De Soto teachers were: W. A. Thomas, Principal; Laura Gander, Assistant Teacher and Louisa Bartholemew, Assistant Teacher.

Genealogical Events from Newspapers for Crawford, Vernon and Grant Counties, Wisconsin, 1870-1901

LAST NAME	FIRST NAME	NEWSPAPER, PAGE/COLUMN MONTH/DAY/YEAR	GENEALOGICAL DATA
De Soto Union School		DC, p3c4, 11/13/1886	The newspaper published the De Soto Union School Honor Roll [for punctuality, deportment and attendance]. The honorees were Minnie Rogers, Lizzie French, Blanche Rice, Yvonne Whitney, Jane Chambers, Mary Davy, May McGinnis, Minnie Chambers, Bennie Warne, Cassius Cushing, James Rogers, Harry Lawrence and Bertie Lane. The teacher was Ellen J. Lawrence.
De Soto W.C.T.U.		DC, p3c2, 10/29/1887	The officers of the De Soto Womens Christian Temperance Union were Miss S. Hinds, Mrs. C. F. Page, Mrs. M. Kalhar, Mrs. R. J. Kalhar and Mrs. J. W. White.
Dean	Bruce	BD, p3c4, 5/10/1878	He was 19 years old. Arrested for stealing from Anton Keiren, Dr. Hewitt, M. B. Pittman, Enos Bros. Store and others. He camped in the bluffs outside Boscobel. To avoid arrest, he hopped a train and went west to various parts of California. His tracks were well documented. He got tired of the traveling and returned to Wisconsin and was arrested.
Dean	J. L.	BD, P3c6, 1/5/1877	Advertised sale of candy and oysters in Boscobel.
Dean	Mary J.	BD, p3c1, 8/8/1879	Abraham Carroll [Carrell] married Mary J. Dean on August 2, 1879 in Boscobel. Bride and groom from Clayton, Crawford Co. Justice McLaughlin officiated.
Dearman	J. M.	RH, p4c2, 10/28/1897	Proprietor of the Temperance Saloon in Readstown.
Dearman	J. P.	RH, p5c5, 10/7/1897	J. P. Dearman married Mrs. Mary Mayhan on Oct. 3, 1897. Bride and groom from Arbor, Vernon Co. Charles W. Reeve, J. P. officiated.
Dearman	John	RH, p4c2, 10/11/1900	Granted a pardon by Gov. Schofield. He served 3 of a 7-year sentence in Waupon. Returned to Readstown.
Dearman	Maude	RH, p4c1, 9/20/1900	Richard Goode married Maude Dearman on Sept. 18, 1900. Groom from Manning. Bride from Readstown. Justice Benson officiated.
Dearman	William	RH, p5c2, 8/12/1897	Lost his home to fire in Ottervale.
Dearman	William	RH, p5c2, 9/9/1897	Departed Readstown to visit son-in-law, George Harris of Ottervale.
Dearman	William	RH, p4c1, 1/18/1900	Victim of a holdup in Readstown.
Dearman	William	RH, p4c1, 9/13/1900	He was in Milwaukee at the Soldiers Home. Planned to testify in a lawsuit against 2 men who robbed him of $60 last winter in Milwaukee. They were sentenced to 5 years in Waupon, per RH, p4c2, 9/13/1900.
Dearman	William	RH, p4c1, 10/31/1901	Dearman and wife departed for La Crosse. After visiting relatives in different parts of the State, they will take up residence at the Veteran's Home in Waupaca.
Deaver	Bertha	RH, p4c3, 12/9/1897	Lived in Ross. Planned to spend the winter with her sister, Mrs. Groves.
Deaver	Will	RH, p4c3, 12/9/1897	Returned to his home in Ross with a new wife from Minnesota. The area young people held a charivari for the couple.
Decker	boy	DC, p4c1, 3/19/1889	The infant son of Dr. F. E. Decker recently died in Seneca.
Decker	Dr.	DC, p2c4, 1/14/1888	The parents of Dr. Decker are staying with their son in Seneca this winter. Dr. Decker's father is in poor health. He is unable to sit up.
Decorah	Spoon	DC, p3c2, 11/19/1887	Died Oct. 13, 1887 at Necedah at the age of 85. He was the son of old Gray-headed Decorah, who was chief of the Wisconsin River Winnebagos during the first third of the present century. He was a nephew of One-eyed Decorah, or Big Canoe, to whom belongs the honor of capturing the fugitive Sac tribe chief, Black Hawk, in 1832, soon after the slaughter of the Sacs at Bad Axe.
Dederick	G. L.	DC, p3c2 9/3/1887	Sadie Adams married G. L. Dederick on Aug. 18, 1887 in Ferryville. Bride from Ferryville. Groom was the Ferryville [railroad] station agent. Esquire Davis officiated.
Dederick	George	DC, p2c3 8/27/1887	George Dederick recently married Minnie Adams, per rumor. Groom was the station agent in Ferryville.
Dederick	George	DC, p3c4, 2/25/1888	Resided in Ferryville. Appointed the new station agent in De Soto for the C. B. and N.
Deertz	Lizzie, Mrs.	DC, p3c4, 9/25/1886	Mrs. Deertz [Durtz?] of Watertown, Dakota visited relatives in De Soto.
DeGrote	John, Mrs.	BD, p3c1, 5/12/1882	Mrs. DeGrote and her daughter arrived in Boscobel from their home in Hillsboro, Dakota. Visited her sister, Mrs. John H. Sarles.
DeHart	J. L.	BD, p2c4, 3/3/1882	J. L. DeHart, D. V. DeHart, Henry Ladd, J. W. Gross, W. A. Gross, B. J. Drake, Gbe [Abe?] Driskill, R. Parker, C. Lawton and S. Krauss left area to see land in Dakota, Nebraska and Kansas. They were from the Fancy Creek and West Lima area.
DeHaven	Prof.	BD, p3c1, 1/12/1883	He was the orchestra leader at a dance being held at Ruka's Hall in Boscobel.

Genealogical Events from Newspapers for Crawford, Vernon and Grant Counties, Wisconsin, 1870-1901

LAST NAME	FIRST NAME	NEWSPAPER, PAGE/COLUMN MONTH/DAY/YEAR	GENEALOGICAL DATA
DeHeus	Nellie	BD, p3c2, 8/2/1878	Arrived from Grand Rapids, MI to visit cousins and other relatives in Boscobel. She visited Mrs. John Barnett, per p3c2, 8/16/1878.
DeLacy	Henry	DC, p3c2, 12/24/1887	Left Retreat to seek his fortune in the vicinity of Merrill, WI.
DeLacy	J. S.	DC, p2c4, 6/12/1886	Proprietor of a boot and shoe shop in De Soto.
DeLacy	T.	DC, p1c3, 5/3/1889	Lost a fine Clydesdale colt. This is the seventh horse he has lost in last 2 years. Lived in Cooley Valley.
DeLacy	Thomas	DC, p3c3, 7/24/1886	Owned one of the area's finest horses. Had a half-mile track on his farm at Retreat.
DeLacy	Thomas	DC, p3c2, 12/10/1887	Recently lost a valuable Clydesdale stallion. It was worth $3,000.
DeLap	girl	BD, p3c3, 4/29/1881	A daughter was born to William DeLap of Boscobel on April 23, 1881.
DeLap	John, Mrs.	BD, p3c1, 5/11/1883	Resided in Boscobel. Mrs. DeLap's funeral was held Wednesday at the Methodist Church. She was about 56 years old. Survived by husband, Postmaster W. E. DeLap, and four sons, W. E., M. W., Fletcher and Charles.
DeLap	John, Rev.	DC, p2c2, 7/9/1887	Preached at the church in Ontario and visited his brother, George.
DeLap	Olive	BD, p3c1, 7/11/1879	George Walker married Olive DeLap on July 4, 1879 in Boscobel. The Rev. G. W. Nuzum of Viroqua officiated.
DeLap	Thomas	DC, p3c3, 7/3/1888	Thomas DeLap and family returned to Ontario after spending a year in California.
DeLap	Thomas L.	DC, p3c3, 2/5/1887	The Thomas L. DeLap family, formerly of Ontario, arrived at a new home in Colton, CA.
DeLap	W. E.	BD, p3c2, 1/2/1880	A petition was circulated to make W. E. DeLap the Boscobel postmaster.
DeLapp	Mr.	RH, p5c3, 1/20/1898	Recently died in Readstown. Buried in the Readstown Cemetery.
DeLapp Bros.		BD, p3c2, 1/5/1883	Purchased the insurance business of P. A. Daggett and Son of Muscoda.
Delvin	Mr.	BD, p3c2, 7/20/1877	Mr. Delvin of De Soto captured Mr. Ryan, a horsethief, and received a $100 reward.
Dempsey	Philo A.	BD, p3c4, 3/24/1882	Located in Fennimore in 1844. He was chairman of the town board in 1852.
Dempsey	Samuel	BD, p3c2, 2/9/1883	Died Feb. 3, 1883 in Prairie du Chien when he was 60 years old. Worked as a newspaper compositor and pressman.
Dennis	Mr.	BD, p3c5, 3/8/1878	Mr. Dennis married Nora Brainerd on Monday evening in Boscobel. Bride from Boscobel and groom from Minnesota. They departed by train for their future home.
Dennison	Ed	BD, p3c1, 5/26/1882	Ed Dennison married Catherine Bean [Beam?] on May 15, 1882 at the residence of J. M. Riggs in the Town of Watterstown. A. F. Henderson officiated.
Dennison	Henry	DC, p2c2, 9/25/1888	A warrant was issued for the arrest of Henry Dennison and Henry Schlong of Bergen. They were charged with assaulting a mail carrier.
Densmore	Mrs.	RH, p5c2, 4/7/1898	Left Readstown with her son for Grant Co. to stay with her parents. She was recovering from the effects of an explosion.
Denson	Edward	BD, p2c5, 12/17/1880	"The public is cautioned against buying or trafficking for two promisory notes, one drawn for Forty Dollars by John Foner, payable to Edward Denson in September 1880. The other note was drawn for Fifteen Dollars by Thomas Beam with Morris Thorpe as security, payable to Edward Denson in November 1880. The above notes have been lost and payment has been ordered stopped if presented by other than the loser." Edward Denson, Hickory Grove, WI, Dec. 7, 1880
Dent	Mrs.	DC, p3c3, 9/18/1888	Arrived in De Soto from Portage, WI to visit brother, Fred Fowler.
Dermody	Annie	DC, p3c4, 12/31/1887	Annie Dermody married Daniel O'Riley on Dec. 27, 1887 at Genoa. Bride from De Soto. Groom from National, IA. Father Wirtz officiated. A present list was published.
Devaney	P.	DC, p3c3, 3/12/1887	He engineers the limited express between Norwalk and Ontario.
Devenport	Mr.	DC, p1c3, 4/26/1889	Returned to Mt. Sterling from La Crosse where his wife was being treated by Dr. Powel.
Devlin	John	DC, p3c1, 6/12/1886	Proprietor the City Meat Market in De Soto.

Genealogical Events from Newspapers for Crawford, Vernon and Grant Counties, Wisconsin, 1870-1901

LAST NAME	FIRST NAME	NEWSPAPER, PAGE/COLUMN MONTH/DAY/YEAR	GENEALOGICAL DATA
Devlin	John	DC, p3c3, 8/28/1886	Arrived from Guttenberg, IA to visit his son, John of De Soto.
Devlin	John	RH, p5c3, 1/27/1898	Ran a butcher shop in Viroqua.
Devlin	John, Mr. and Mrs.	DC, p3c3, 11/27/1886	Celebrated their 17th wedding anniversary at their home in De Soto.
Devlin	Willie	DC, p3c3, 7/3/1886	Willie and Frankie Devlin of De Soto visited their grandparents, Mr. and Mrs. Fleming of Lansing.
Devoe	A.	BD, p2c4, 11/26/1880	Grant County paid him a bounty for scalps turned into the county.
DeVoe	Amos	BD, p3c1, 4/7/1882	Delivered in Boscobel a large quantity of flour, barrel hoops and straps.
DeVoe	Amos	BD, p3c1, 1/5/1883	Called a "boss deer-slayer" for bringing down 12 deer since the snow started to fall. Resided in Boscobel area.
DeVoe	Amos	BD, p3c2, 3/9/1883	The Wisconsin Legislature passed a bill granting DeVoe $138 for killing wolves outside of the county in which he resided.
DeVoe	Amos	BD, p3c1, 4/29/1881	Newly appointed to office of constable in Boscobel.
Devorce	May	DC, p2c2, 6/11/1887	May Devorce, Anna Schubert and Lizzie Gould graduated from Mound Ridge school this spring and passed the teacher examination.
Dewey	H. B.	BD, p3c1, 11/21/1879	Dewey's store in Spring Green was destroyed by fire.
Dewey	Lucian	BD, p3c1, 12/16/1881	Received $324 in bounty money in Grant Co.
Dewey	Lucian	BD, p2c4, 11/26/1880	Grant County paid him a bounty for scalps turned into the county.
DeWitt	J. L., Dr.	DC, p3c3, 10/9/1886	Resided in Newton. Owned a large collection of Indian relics.
DeWitt	M.	BD, p3c1, 8/20/1880	The Betts House in Boscobel was refurnished and opened for business under the management of M. DeWitt. Formerly called the Carrier House.
DeWitt	M., Mrs.	BD, p3c1, 6/4/1880	Mrs. M. DeWitt was host to a visit by Mrs. Betts and Mrs. Persing of Glenwood, IA. Mrs. Persing was Mrs. DeWitt's sister.
DeWitt	M., Mrs.	BD, p3c1, 12/16/1881	Hosted a visit by her sister, Mrs. L. Persing of Glenwood, IA, at her Boscobel home.
Dexter	John	BD, p3c1, 7/14/1882	Worked for the railroad in Portage City. Visited his parents in Boscobel.
Dickerson	C. J.	BD, p2c6, 10/22/1880	Dealer in books and stationary, toys, gancy goods, fruits, oysters, etc. in Boscobel. Business opened by Mr. Dickerson's father 19 years ago. The father was Boscobel's postmaster for many years. He died about 5 years ago. C. J. succeeded as postmaster and managed the store. Also ran a restaurant in the store.
Dickerson	C. J.	BD, p3c1, 1/5/1877	Worked as an assistant postmaster in Boscobel.
Dickerson	Charles J.	BD, p3c1, 3/19/1880	Charles J. Dickerson married Anna L. Stahel on March. 11, 1880 in Muscoda. Bride and groom from Boscobel. The Rev. George Haigh officiated.
Dickerson	James M.	BD, p2c4, 1/26/1877	The Commissioners of Grant Co. published a notice seeking claimants to the estate of James M. Dickerson, recently deceased, late of Boscobel.
Dickerson & Messersmith		BD, P3c7, 1/5/1877	Advertised their toy, book and stationary store in Boscobel.
Dickinson	Lizzie	BD, p2c3, 3/31/1882	Ten-year-old daughter of Mr. and Mrs. Dickinson of Muscoda area recently assaulted/raped by Dr. H. F. McNelly. This was confirmed by an examination performed by Dr. Geyer. Miss Josephine Ballard mentioned in this item. [See BD, p2c4, 4/7/1882, too.]
Dike	Pearl	RH, p5c4, 11/3/1898	Seriously ill with lung fever, per Mound Park news column.
Diley	Walter	BD, p3c4, 5/30/1879	A freight train jumped the tracks at a wash out near Haggarty cut, 3 miles west of Boscobel. H. B. Mills, conductor; William Newell, engineer; and Walter Diley, fireman, were injured. Newell was severely burned. His left hand was also crushed.
Dilger	M.	BD, P3c6, 1/5/1877	Proprietor of the City Bakery in Boscobel.
Dilger	M.	BD, p3c3, 1/3/1879	A fire in Boscobel burned buildings/homes of Thompson Brothers, Bartells Brothers, P. Ryan [household goods lost], M. Dilger [household goods], N. McGraw [butcher, lost stock and tools] and James Barnett [lost furniture].

Genealogical Events from Newspapers for Crawford, Vernon and Grant Counties, Wisconsin, 1870-1901

LAST NAME	FIRST NAME	NEWSPAPER, PAGE/COLUMN MONTH/DAY/YEAR	GENEALOGICAL DATA
Dillon		BD, p2c3, 2/24/1882	The youngest daughter in the Dillon family died of small pox on Friday per the Feb. 16, 1882 issue of the Richland Center *Republican and Observer*. This was the fourth family member to die of the illness.
Dillon	Capt.	BD, p3c1, 3/3/1882	The Wisconsin Assembly promptly passed an appropriation for the benefit of Dillon's family.
Dillon	D. C.	RH, p5c4, 1/24/1901	Discovered a vein of copper in the Town of Webster on the J. P. Allen farm.
Dillon	Henry, Capt.	BD, p3c3, 1/13/1882	Died Tuesday night at Lone Rock, WI. His daughter, Miss Adie Dillon, was telegraphed the news.
Dillon	Henry, Capt.	BD, p2c3, 1/20/1882	Died last Tuesday. He was the second cousin of the famous Irish land-leaguer, John Dillon. Born 52 years ago in Niagara Co., NY. Served in Sherman battery during the Mexican War. Moved to Richland City, WI in 1852. Civil War activities were described.
Dillon	Riley	BD, p3c4, 3/24/1882	Riley Dillon's hat was used as a ballot box at Fennimore's first town meeting. The meeting was held in 1849. Fourteen of the original 66 voters are still present: C. W. Loney, Wm. R. Dixon, Robert Munns, Philo Dempsey, W. R. Dillon, Philander Wright, John Smith, H. A. W. McNair, James McNair, C. D. Smith [all of present-day Fennimore], Samuel Borah, John A. Shearer, Sigmund Steuert, John Nauert [in that part of the town that has become Mt. Ida].
Dinsdale	Isabelle M.	BD, p3c1, 9/9/1881	Ross L. Smith married Isabelle M. Dinsdale on Aug. 11, 1881 in Boscobel. Bride and groom from Soldiers Grove. The Rev. T. M. Evans officiated.
Dixon	Fred	RH, p4c2, 11/29/1900	Resided in Richland Center. Pleaded guilty in Prairie du Chien to a charge of stealing a watch from James Rowe of Soldiers Grove.
Dixon	William, Mrs.	DC, p2c2, 3/19/1887	Mrs. William Dixon and daughter, Mrs. A. Peterson, visited with relatives and friends in Tennessee, IL, per the Lynxville news column.
Dodge	E. R., Mrs.	DC, p3c3, 8/13/1887	Mrs. E. R. Dodge recently married French B. White. Bride, a teacher, was the daugher of Mrs. Marshall of Red Mound, WI. Groom was a farmer in Sterling. The Rev. Thomas Crouch officiated.
Dodge	General	BD, p2c1, 2/15/1878	Congress passed a law giving pensions to soldiers under the command of General Dodge during the Black Hawk War. Among the veterans receiving pensions were Gen. Charles Bracken, Col. Dan W. Parkinson, John Mepesmith, Col. Abe Nichols, Henry I. Dodge and Paschal Bequith [Beckwith? Becwith?].
Dodge	Mrs.	DC, p3c4, 4/2/1887	Planned to teach at Sunnyside this summer.
Doe	D. D.	DR, p3c2, 3/30/1871	Opened a new general store in Lansing, IA.
Dolan	James	BD, p3c3, 1/4/1878	James Dolan installed a steam sawmill in Yankeetown to make railroad ties and hardwood lumber. There are now 2 mills on a 40-acre tract.
Dolan	Maggie, Miss	DC, p1c2, 6/14/1889	Arrived in Ferryville from Kansas City for her father's funeral.
Dolan	Patrick	BD, p2c3, 1/20/1882	The case, State vs. Patrick Dolan, Peter Dolan and Michael Dolan, Jr., was heard in Prairie du Chien. They were acquitted in an assault case resulting from a feud. Patrick badly whipped Mr. Burns of Rising Sun on Jan. 3, 1882. Fight started when Mr. Bang and Mr. Burns went to the home of Michael Dolan, Sr. and abused the old gentleman. Patrick was remanded to jail for 60 days for not paying cost of the suit.
Dolan	William, Mrs.	DC, p2c4, 1/14/1888	Doctors Gott, Dinsdale and Porter attended the wife of William Dolan in Rising Sun on Dec. 25, 1887. A craniotomy was performed. Mrs. Dolan is in very serious condition.
Dolan	Winefred, Miss	DC, p1c2, 6/14/1889	Resided in Prairie du Chien. Called to Ferryville to attend the funeral of her father. He died Sunday while reading the newspaper.
Dolan	Winefred, Miss	DC, p1c1, 6/21/1889	From Rising Sun. Returned to school in Prairie du Chien, per Ferryville news column.
Dolly	William	BD, p3c3, 5/31/1878	William Dolly died Tuesday while digging a well for Mr. Gibbs. The earth caved in on him. Tom Patten was also buried during a rescue attempt. Patten was saved.
Dolphin	John	BD, p2c4, 11/26/1880	Grant County paid him a bounty for scalps turned into the county.
Don	S., Mrs.	RH, p5c4, 1/27/1898	Resided in Scotland. She was spending the winter with her sister, Mrs. A. Sanford of Viola. Presently visiting a cousin, David Barrie, per Kickapoo Center news column.
Donahue	John	DC, p2c2, 3/12/1887	New postmaster in Ontario, WI.
Donaldson	May	BD, p2c1, 11/20/1883	A. H. Rogers married May Donaldson on Nov. 11, 1883 at the residence of the bride's parents in DeSmet, Kingsbury Co., Dakota. Groom from Dakota, but formerly from Boscobel.
Donavan	Dennis	BD, p3c1, 7/6/1883	Came to Boscobel to shop. He was 96 years old and lived in Excelsior. He has lived in Wisconsin for the last 23 years.

Genealogical Events from Newspapers for Crawford, Vernon and Grant Counties, Wisconsin, 1870-1901

LAST NAME	FIRST NAME	NEWSPAPER, PAGE/COLUMN MONTH/DAY/YEAR	GENEALOGICAL DATA
Doose	Henry	DC, p2c1, 12/18/1886	Opened a boot and shoe repair shop in Stoddard.
Dosch	John	BD, p3c2, 1/26/1883	Lost 40 sheep to the extremely cold weather at his farm in Excelsior.
Dosch	John	RH, p5c4, 7/29/1897	Found the bones of a large pre-historic animal on his farm near Boaz. Believed to be the bones of a mastadon.
Douse	George, Mrs.	RH, p4c1, 11/7/1901	Returned to Readstown from Steuben after spending last month attending her father during his sickness and death.
Dousman	Jane, Mrs.	BD, p2c3, 1/20/1882	Died Jan. 13, 1882 at 77 years 8 months from pneumonia. Born April 12, 1804 in Prairie du Chien. Married Col. Hercules L. Dousman in 1844.
Dowlen School		BD, p3c2, 11/15/1878	The Dowlen School House in the Town of Haney, Crawford Co. was destroyed by fire on Oct. 28, 1878. The building was insured by J. McLaughlin, agent in Boscobel.
Dowling	Orwin	BD, p3c1, 8/29/1879	Lost his crop after it was burned by incendiaries. He lived 8 miles north of Boscobel in Crawford County.
Dowling	William R.	BD, p3c3, 3/16/1883	Planned to sell farm stock and implements at his farm in the Town of Haney.
Dowling	William R.	BD, p3c1, 10/2/1883	The Supreme Court reversed the ruling of the Circuit Court in the case, William R. Dowling vs D. R. Lawrence.
Downey	A. B.	DC, p3c1, 6/12/1886	Harness maker in De Soto.
Downey	A. B.	DC, p3c2, 12/3/1887	Accepted a position as operator at Hager.
Downey	A. B.	DC, p3c2, 1/14/1888	Leaving the harness making business.
Downey	A. B.	DC, p2c3, 3/20/1888	Accepted a position in Graf, IA as operator for the M. N. and N.W.
Downey	Abe B.	DC, p3c3, 11/26/1887	Passed the exam of the C. B. & N. telegraph department.
Downey	girl	DC, p3c2, 1/1/1887	A daughter was recently born to A. B. Downey of De Soto.
Downey	girl	DC, p3c4, 12/25/1888	A daughter was born on Thursday to William Downey of Ferryville.
Downey	John	RH, p5c4, 1/20/1898	Repaired shoes for a living in Kickapoo Center.
Downey	John	RH, p5c4, 12/1/1898	John Downey and John Smith were hired to build a bridge near Mr. Griffin's in the Kickapoo area.
Downey	John, Mrs.	RH, p5c3, 7/27/1899	Died Sunday at Kickapoo. She was the mother of Eva Downey. Miss Downey was called from her work in Iowa to see mother before the death.
Downey	John, Mrs.	RH, p5c3, 8/3/1899	Died July 23, 1899 after a short illness. Survived by husband and 13 children.
Downey	William	DC, p2c4, 2/19/1887	Annie Kenefic married William Downey last Thursday. Father Wurtz of Genoa officiated.
Downey	William	DC, p3c2, 3/12/1887	Departed De Soto for Hermansville, MI to work for C. Lyttle.
Downs	Hubert	BD, p3c2, 5/2/1879	Lightning struck his barn near Richland Center and destroyed the structure and many animals.
Downs	Katie	BD, p3c3, 2/15/1878	Eugene Wolfing married Katie Downs on Feb. 4, 1878. Bride and groom from Richland Center. Rev. Sturges of Richland Center officiated. Bride's parents recently died.
Doyle	James	BD, p3c3, 7/1/1881	Fell under the [train] cars and died on Saturday morning.
Drake	boy	RH, p4c4, 2/2/1899	A boy was recently born to Elmer and Dora Drake of Sugar Grove.
Drake	John	RH, p4c1, 11/29/1900	John Drake married Grace Midthum on Nov. 28, 1900. Bride and groom were from Spring Valley. The Rev. G. W. Nuzum officiated.
Drake	R. H., Mr. and Mrs.	RH, p5c4, 8/29/1901	Planned to go to the Pan American Exposition in Buffalo, NY. Lived in Sugar Grove.
Drake	R. H., Mrs.	RH, p5c3, 11/1/1900	"Mrs. R. H. Drake and Mrs. A. Eathron of Sugar Grove departed Dr. Chase's office in Viroqua leaving 27 teeth in the Doctor's care."
Drake	Reuben	DC, p3c3, 5/29/1888	Reuben Drake, his wife and 2 grandchildren [aged 4 and 5] were murdered by robbers at the Drake home in the Town of Kickapoo. Drake recently received pension money and Mrs. Drake received a $1400 legacy. Gov. Rusk offered a $500 reward to help solve the crime.

Genealogical Events from Newspapers for Crawford, Vernon and Grant Counties, Wisconsin, 1870-1901

LAST NAME	FIRST NAME	NEWSPAPER, PAGE/COLUMN MONTH/DAY/YEAR	GENEALOGICAL DATA
Dregne		RH, p7c1, 7/1/1897	Sold groceries in Readstown.
Dregne	J. S.	RH, p4c1, 3/23/1899	J. S. Dregne of the firm, J. T. and J. S. Dregne is retiring.
Dregne	J. S. and J. L.	RH, p7c2, 7/1/1897	Advertised the sale of grocery items in Readstown.
Dregne	J. T.	RH, p4c3, 6/15/1899	J. T. Dregne recentlly married Elizabeth Sovede. Groom from Readstown. Bride from Town of Franklin.
Dregne	John T.	RH, p4c1, 8/1/1901	Died July 29, 1901 of appendicitis. An operation was performed the day before the death. John was the brother of Solfest T. Dregne.
Dregne	John T.	RH, p4c3, 8/8/1901	Died July 29, 1901 of appendicitis. Dr. Gunderson of La Crosse, Dr. Lerche of Soldiers Grove and Dr. Henika of Readstown performed an operation on him on July 28, 1901. He was a member of the U. B. Church. Born May 26, 1865 in Skjolden, Norway. Came to America 16 years ago and moved to Readstown 5 years ago. Married Susan Sovde on June 24, 1899. He was "engaged in the merchantile business" and "possessed a goodly share of this world's wealth." Buried in Folsom Cemetery.
Dregne	Solfest, Mr.	RH, p4c1, 2/7/1901	Resided in Readstown. He was taking lessons in English from Mrs. J. O. Anderson. Rapidly learning.
Drew	Sweetie Pearl	BD, p3c4, 2/23/1877	Died Feb. 12, 1877 of diptheria in Muscoda. She was 3 years, 8 months and 10 days old. Only daughter of F. M. and J. A. Drew. Freda Angelo Drew died Feb. 17, 1877. He was 7 years, 3 months and 15 days old. Wilbur Jacob Drew, the last child, died Feb. 17, 1877. He was 10 years, 2 months and 8 days old.
Drinkwater	Annie	BD, p3c1, 1/2/1880	Married Frank A. Statzer on Dec. 24, 1879 in Fennimore at the residence of John Smith. Bride from Lancaster. Groom from Mt. Ida. Otho Shrader, Esq. officiated.
Driscoll	Mrs.	BD, p3c3, 7/28/1882	Murdered on July 19, 1882. Tragedy occurred in Richland Co., near Brady's Post Office, which is near Mike Hernan's place. Hernan was a brother of Mrs. Driscoll. Mrs. Driscoll was first married to a Coleman. Her second husband was never seen by the neighbors. She lived alone with a 19-year-old son on what was known as the McDermont farm. She owned property 3 miles from her residence. Body was found by a search party in the woods. She was a well-to-do lady, aged about 60 years. She parted from her second husband in New York and brought 3 or 4 children with her when she moved to Wisconsin. Only the 19-year old remained with her. This son was suspected of the crime. Henry Puckett, Justice of the Peace, empaneled a jury who found Mrs. Driscoll was murdered by person[s] unknown.
Dubois	Augustus	DR, p3c2, 12/22/1870	Died Dec. 8, 1870 of typhoid fever in Lansing, IA. He was the eldest son of William Dubois.
Duke	Alva	RH, p4c2, 10/24/1901	Returned to Readstown after working for the last 3 months in North Dakota.
Duke	Rob	RH, p4c1, 9/14/1899	Came from Bell Center to Readstown to take charge of the stave sawing at the Huffman & Lewis stave mill.
Duke	Rob	RH, p4c1, 10/31/1901	Bought stave bolts in Readstown for $2.75/cord.
Dull	James	BD, p3c4, 12/28/1877	James A. Dull married Jennie Calloway on Christmas Day, 1877. Bride from Marietta, Crawford Co. Groom from Waterloo, Grant Co. Rev. Dr. Stoddart officiated.
Duncan	Cora Emma	BD, p3c2, 1/10/1879	Died Jan. 1, 1879 in Boscobel. Aged 10 years, 10 months and 21 days. She was the only child of John E. and Emma A. Duncan.
Duncan	Emma A., Mrs.	BD, p3c2, 7/20/1883	Resided in Decorah, IA. Buried last Wednesday in Boscobel. Aged 35 years, 9 months and 17 days. Wife of John E. Duncan.
Duncan	H.	BD, p3c4, 5/11/1877	H. Duncan & Co. advertised the services of the Boscobel Carding Mills.
Duncan	H. E.	BD, p3c1, 5/30/1879	Started up a woollen mill in Boscobel.
Duncan	John	BD, p3c1, 9/10/1880	Deputy Sheriff James Bailey returned from West Virginia where he arrested John Duncan.
Duncan	John	BD, p3c1, 10/1/1880	Brought to Wisconsin from West Virginia on a charge of forgery. Acquitted and returned "from whence he came."
Duncan	John E.	BD, p3c1, 4/28/1882	Former Boscobel resident. Has a five-year lease for the woolen mills in Decorah, IA.
Duncan	John E.	BD, p2c4, 1/19/1877	Grant County Circuit Court published a summons for the case John R. Muffley of Boscobel, plaintiff vs. John E. Duncan, Emma A. Duncan [his wife], Eleanor J. Duncan, Robert E. Duncan, James Bridger and Beekman & Co., defendents. The complaint was filed in Lancaster.
Duncan	John E.	BD, p3c3, 2/23/1877	The saloons and drugists in Boscobel were ordered by the City Council to not sell alcohol to John E. Duncan.

Genealogical Events from Newspapers for Crawford, Vernon and Grant Counties, Wisconsin, 1870-1901

LAST NAME	FIRST NAME	NEWSPAPER, PAGE/COLUMN MONTH/DAY/YEAR	GENEALOGICAL DATA
Duncan	John E.	BD, p3c1, 2/28/1879	John E. Duncan and A. B. Alden, both of Boscobel, received a patent for a new kind of combination lock.
Dunlap	Elmer	DC, p2c1, 6/12/1886	C. A. Comstock and Elmer Dunlap started publication of the *De Soto Chronicle* in the the upstairs rooms of the Ingersoll Building in De Soto. It was to be a Republican paper.
Dunlap	Elmer E.	DC, p3c2, 9/18/1886	Elmer E. Dunlap recently married Clara A. Dalton. Groom former owner of the *De Soto Chronicle*. Bride from La Crosse.
Dunlap	W. W.	DC, p3c4, 5/28/1887	Given the contract for the mail route between Viroqua and De Soto.
Dunlap	W. W.	DC, p3c2, 12/3/1887	"He is the only one of the first two families who settled and is yet living at Viroqua."
Dunlevy	J. M.	DC, p3c2, 2/5/1887	Took a portrait of Lizzie Waukon, aged 103, widow of Chief Waukon. Sold copies of it for 25 cents to the public.
Dunlevy	Jerrie	DC, p2c3, 2/19/1889	Ran a phtography business in De Soto. Also sold furniture.
Dunlevy	Mr.	DC, p3c3, 6/12/1886	Photographer in De Soto.
Dunn		BD, p2c4, 4/21/1882	A family named Dunn recently arrived in Richland Center after loosing everything they owned in a flood in Mississippi. They came to start over. Dunn lived in the area 25 or 30 years ago and has a distant relative here. For now, the wife [who was blind] and 4 or 5 children were taken to the poor farm.
Dunn	Mary E., Mrs.	BD, p3c2, 5/31/1878	Died by suicide in Muscoda. Drowned in the Wisconsin River. She was the 73-year-old relict of Judge Dunn of Belmont and mother of Mrs. Governor Dewey. Mrs. Dunn was shattered by the death of her son, Tarlton, in Colorado. She was buried with Episcopal rites in Platteville. Mrs. Mary E. Parker of Boscobel was her niece.
Dunston	Antoine L.	BD, p3c1, 11/21/1879	Antoine L. Dunston married Ella E. Heberling on Nov. 18, 1879 in Boscobel. Peter Rae, Esquire officiated.
Durand	Fred	BD, p3c2, 11/23/1877	Fred Durand married Nellie Barber at the residence of the bride's parents in Boscobel. Groom from Osage, IA. Bride daughter of Jay Barber, Esq.
Durrie	Daniel L.	DC, p2c1, 1/21/1888	Served as Librarian at the State Historical Society. Asked for copies of the De Soto history series written by C. B. Whiting.
Durstin	L. B.	BD, p3c1, 2/17/1882	Departed Boscobel for the Red River country. Seeking suitable place for a lumber business.
Durstin	L. B.	BD, p3c1, 3/10/1882	Resident of Boscobel. Entertained his uncle, Rev. John Hartman of Boston.
Durstin	L. B.	BD, p3c1, 3/10/1882	Durstin, wife, child and uncle departed Boscobel for their new home in Jamestown, Dakota where Durstin and his uncle planned to start a lumber business.
Durstin	L. B.	BD, p3c2, 8/21/1883	Resided in Jamestown, Dakota. He was the son-in-law of J. H. Sarles of Boscobel. Durstin, Sarles and T. Weston of Neceda, WI took a pleasure/business trip to the Black Hills from Jamestown by prairie schooner.
Durstine	Lee B.	BD, p3c2, 12/27/1878	Lee B. Durstine married Kate M. Sarles on Wednesday, Dec. 25, 1878 at the home of Mayor Sarles in Boscobel. Bride only daughter of John H. and M. B. Sarles of Boscobel. Groom resided in Wooster, OH. Their future home will be in Conneaut, OH. Elder J. D. Sarles officiated.
Duston	Frank	DC, p2c2, 2/11/1888	Recently died while working in the woods near Bloomer, WI. Son of J. S. Duston of Retreat. Grandfather will bring home the body.
Duston	Frank	DC, p3c4, 2/18/1888	Died Feb. 6, 1888 near Bloomer. He would have been 19 years old in April.
Dutcher	Rodney	BD, p3c2, 6/1/1883	Died Sunday of heart disease in Omaha, NB. He was the eldest son of the Hon. William Dutcher of Boscobel. Rodney lived in Omaha for the last 25 years where he was a prominent lawyer. He was a government employee for the last 10 years.
Dutcher	Thomas R.	BD, p3c2, 4/6/1877	Died Mar. 28, 1877 in Phoenix, NY at 69 years of age. He was born in Litchfield, Herkimer Co., NY. Moved to Phoenix 47 years ago. He first settled at Gilbert's Mills and later moved to Phoenix. Thomas was the brother of William Dutcher of Boscobel.
Dutcher	William	BD, p3c2, 6/29/1883	William Dutcher and his wife and child arrived from Boston, MA to visit with his parents in Boscobel.
Dyer	Abner	BD, p3c5, 2/4/1881	Died Jan. 26, 1881 at age 64. Resided in North Lancaster. Born Jan. 28, 1817 in Danville, KY. When 3 years old moved to Texetteville, TN. When 14 moved to Alabama. When 17 moved to Illinois. In 1837 moved to Grant Co., WI. Married Rebecca Walker on Nov. 24, 1840. Survived by 8 of his 8 children.
Dyer	E. H.	DC, p1c2, 8/2/1889	E. H. Dyer married Mary Smith on July 17, 1889 in Cassville at the Denniston House. Bride and groom from De Soto. The Rev. G. D. Stevens officiated.

Genealogical Events from Newspapers for Crawford, Vernon and Grant Counties, Wisconsin, 1870-1901

LAST NAME	FIRST NAME	NEWSPAPER, PAGE/COLUMN MONTH/DAY/YEAR	GENEALOGICAL DATA
Dyer	Ed	DC, p3c2, 11/5/1887	Quit steamboating for the season.
Dyer	Ed	DC, p4c3, 5/10/1889	Worked on the boat, *Sam Atley*. Resided in De Soto.
Dyer	Ed	DC, p3c3, 1/8/1889	Sold his share of the meat market in De Soto to Robert Bartholomew.
Dyer	Ernest	DC, p2c1, 12/18/1888	Former resident of De Soto. Currently employed as a telegraph operator in St. Paul Park, MN.
Dyer	Fin, Mrs.	RH, p5c2, 9/8/1898	Mr. and Mrs. Houston of Webster visited their daughter, Mrs. Fin Dyer of Readstown.
Dyer	Harry	DC, p3c2, 1/1/1887	Left De Soto for Iowa to join Till's surveying party.
Dyer	Harry G.	DC, p3c3, 6/26/1886	Left De Soto for a position on the steamboat, *Lily Turner*.
Dyer	Nellie, Mrs.	DC, p3c2, 11/20/1886	Returned to De Soto after spending 4 weeks with a cousin, Mrs. Dr. Foster of Chicago.
Dyer	W.	DC, p3c2, 7/2/1887	S. T. Ferguson came to De Soto from Minneapolis to visit Dyer. They were schoolmates 30 years ago, "away down in Maine and along in the 50's they worked together at Minneapolis."
Dyer	William	BD, p3c3, 1/30/1880	Died Jan. 22, 1880 in Boscobel. Born Aug. 4, 1800 in Boston, MA. Moved to Boscobel in 1863 and established a drug business. Retired in 1876. Buried in the family vault in Potosi.
Dyer	William	BD, p2c6, 3/19/1880	Probate notice published for the William Dyer estate. Cornelia Dyer petitioned to administer estate.
Dyer	William, Mrs.	BD, p3c1, 12/9/1881	Departed Boscobel to spend the winter with her sister, Mrs. Block of St. Louis.
Earl	Olive L.	BD, p3c3, 11/30/1877	H. Burt Lewis married Olive L. Earl on Thursday last week at the house of the bride's father, Rev. H. H. Earl. Bride and groom from Fennimore. The Rev. D. L. Hubbard officiated.
Eastman	Henry	BD, p3c2, 3/9/1883	Owned the bank building in Montfort. It was destroyed by fire.
Eastman	Mr.	BD, p3c1, 1/23/1880	Mr. Eastman of Richland Center scheduled to speak in Excelsior at a celebration of the birth of Tom Paine on Jan. 29, 1880.
Eaton		BD, p2c3, 8/5/1881	The 10-year-old son of Peter Eaton of Richwood died July 13, 1881 from the effects [tetanus] of a wound caused by a toy pistol on the fourth of July.
Eaton	James	BD, p3c1, 6/29/1883	Died Wednesday in the Town of Richwood, Richland Co. He was an old resident. Found dead in his bed by his aged wife. He was 68 years old. His death may be related to injury suffered from a wagon fall. He was the father of 8 children. Moved to Richland Co. 16 years ago from Madison Co., IN. Eaton was the third man to settle in Madison Co.
Eaton	S. W., Mrs.	BD, p3c2, 6/22/1877	Mrs. S. W. Eaton of Lancaster departed to see the graduation of her son, Louis Eaton, at Yale College.
Eberly	Lou	BD, p3c3, 12/1/1882	Lou Eberly married Anna Menkhauser at the Catholic Church on Tuesday. Bride was the daughter of Mr. and Mrs. Charles Minkhausen of Boscobel. Groom was from Montfort. [more details in BD, p3c2, 12/8/1882]
Eck	Maggie, Miss	DC, p2c3, 5/1/1888	Miss Maggie Eck of New Albin visited her sister, Mrs. F. Cary of Genoa.
Eck	Maggie, Miss	DC, p1c2, 4/19/1889	Lived in New Albin. Visited sister, Mrs. Eugene Carey of Genoa.
Eckhard	L.	RH, p5c3, 11/25/1897	Operated a successful country store in Sylvan.
Eckhardt	George	DR, p1c1, 12/15/1870	Proprietor of the De Soto Brewery in De Soto, WI.
Eckhardt	Jacob	DC, p2c2, 4/16/1887	Died April 12, 1887 at home near Retreat. He was born 79 or 80 years ago in Alsace, France [now Germany]. Moved to Washington Co., WI in 1854/5 and to Vernon Co. in 1860. He was the father of 8 boys and 2 girls. All children survived Jacob, except Jacob, Jr. and Martha. Jacob, Jr. served in the Wisconsin Assembly in 1879 and 1880. Barney A. is a State Senator in Illinois from a Chicago District. All surviving children were present for the funeral, except Michael, who arrived from Dakota as the funeral cortege left the church. Buried in the Retreat Cemetery. The surviving children were George of Milwaukee; Fred of Viroqua; Michael of Green, IA; B. A. of Chicago; John of Chicago; Adam of Ashton, Dakota and Mrs. Theron Bean.
Eckhardt	Levi	RH, p4c2, 10/3/1901	Resided in Sylvan. Exhibited his draft horses at the Vernon Co. Fair. They were the "finest ever witnessed in this part of the State." The horses were full-blooded Percherons.
Eckhart	B. A.	DR, p3c3, 10/26/1871	Former resident of Vernon Co. Recently escaped with his life and a few possessions kept in his safe during the great fire of Chicago. He was a temporary office at 192 West Lake Street in Chicago.

Genealogical Events from Newspapers for Crawford, Vernon and Grant Counties, Wisconsin, 1870-1901

LAST NAME	FIRST NAME	NEWSPAPER, PAGE/COLUMN MONTH/DAY/YEAR	GENEALOGICAL DATA
Eckhart	Fred	DR, p3c1, 9/14/1871	Home in De Soto was burglerized by two youths, Fred Wilcox and ____ Burrell. They stole a silver watch valued at $25 and all the "cooked victuals."
Eckhart	Jacob, Sr.	DR, p3c3, 9/14/1871	He was quite an old man. Recently came into De Soto with a load of wheat. On the way home the team became frightened in the dark. The wagon went over a log and Eckhart was thrown out. He broke his leg.
Eckhart	Michael	DR, p3c2, 1/4/1872	Michael Eckhart married Jane L. Blair on Dec. 27, 1871 at the home of John Blair in the Town of Sterling. Bride and groom were from Town of Sterling. The Rev. D. L. Hubbard officiated.
Eckleberry	Viola	RH, p5c4, 11/4/1897	Viola Eckleberry recently married Albert Shaper at Bloom City.
Edison	Sam	RH, p5c2, 12/16/1897	Departed Readstown for Floyd, IA.
Edson	Mr.	BD, p2c3, 2/17/1882	Fell from a wagonload of ties being driven by his son. Presumably fell because of heart disease. Lived in Wheat Hollow, near Neptune. [Notes unclear -- may have died.]
Edson	Seth	RH, p4c1, 9/20/1900	Returned to Readstown area after visiting with relatives and friends in Iowa for the last month.
Eggleston	John B.	BD, p3c4, 1/16/1880	Died Jan 6, 1880 at home in Boscobel. Aged 48 years. Moved from Connecticut to Madison, WI, where he stayed with a relative, W. H. Main. Later moved to Watterstown. Joined army when war broke out. In 1863 he was discharged with disabilities and moved to Boscobel. Worked as a painter. Married two times. Had 3 children by first wife and 6 children by second wife.
Eike		DC, p3c5, 9/25/1886	A child was recently born to Ole Eike of Freeman. This was his first child.
Eisfelder		BD, p3c3, 10/25/1878	The daughter of Louis Ruka and the son of F. G. Eisfelder [both of Boscobel] were taken to the deaf and dumb asylum in Milwaukee.
Eisfelder	Amelia, Miss	BD, p3c1, 3/3/1882	Departed Boscobel for Green, IA to visit her grandmother.
Eisfelder	F. G.	BD, p3c4, 6/17/1881	Published a notice that he would prosecute people who fished in Seeley Creek, Boydtown, Crawford Co. where he had contracted for exclusive fishing rights from the landowner. Resident of Boscobel.
Eisfelder	F. G.	BD, p2c7, 10/22/1880	Leading retailer of watches, clocks and jewelry in Boscobel. Also sold silverware, toys, revolvers and musical instruments. Opened the business 13 years ago, though he has 30 years of practical experience. Did a lot of repair work. His early career was launched in Germany.
Eisfelder	F. G.	BD, p3c1, 1/5/1877	Jeweler in Boscobel.
Eisfelter	girl	BD, p3c2, 1/12/1877	Daughter born last Saturday to Fred Eisfelter of [Boscobel area?].
Eitzert	Miss	DC, p3c3, 2/19/1887	Mr. Davenport married Miss Eitzert Monday at Mt. Sterling.
Elder	Emma	DR, p3c1, 5/11/1871	Thomas Peacock married Emma Elder last Sunday. Bride and groom were from Lansing. D. A. Steele, J.P., officiated.
Elder	girl	RH, p4c1, 8/30/1900	A daughter was recently born to D. Elder in Readstown.
Elder	Walter	RH, p5c3, 1/10/1901	Chloe Van Fleet married Walter Elder on Christmas Day. Justice Ward of Sugar Grove officiated.
Eldon	Lottie	BD, p3c2, 4/6/1877	Gottlieb Christ married Lottie Eldon on Wednesday. Groom from Boscobel where he worked as a deliveryman for Meyer Bros. Store. Dr. Stoddart officiated.
Election Results		DR, p3c2, 4/6/1871	In the Town of Wheatland, William P. Lyon will fill vacancy and full term as Judge. Lyon's opponent was D. J. Pulling. A. Glodery was elected Chairman. His competitors were J. B. Wilcox, C. L. Ingersoll and D. W. Joseph. The vote for Supervisor [from highest number of votes to lowest number] went as follows: L. J. Miller, A. Latshaw, J. B. Wilcox, J. W. White, J. T. Shaw, J. C. Davis, G. H. Battles and George Foster.
Election Results		DR, p3c2, 4/6/1871	W. H. Coffin defeated R. H. Rice and L. W. Tenney for Town Clerk in the Town of Wheatland election. Edmund Houghton defeated J. H. Rogers and S. E. Phillips for Treasurer. R. F. Lemen defeated J. D. Davis, W. P. Dailey and J. H. Rogers for Assessor.
Election Results		DR, p3c2, 4/6/1871	Justices of the Peace results in the Town of Woodland were L. P. Miller, 147 votes; C. E. Woodbury, 77 votes; and J.H. Hinds, 69 votes. The Constable results were: J. M. Bailey, 144 votes; C. G. Caldwell, 136 votes; N. E. French, 67 votes; Joseph Freeman, 45 votes; and O. D. Wilson, 34 votes. G. S. Sperry defeated T. C. Ankeny to be Sealer.
Election Results		DR, p3c2, 4/6/1871	In the Town of Franklin the following ticket was elected: for Supervisors -- F. K. Van Wagner, Ira Wilcox, Arthur Conley; for Town Clerk -- H. D. Williams; for Assessor -- Christian Ellefson; for Treasurer -- Samuel Henry; for Justices -- Andrew Henry, Thomas Cade; for Constables -- Oscar Henry, William O. Johnston, A. A. Henry; and for Sealer -- Thomas Cade.

Genealogical Events from Newspapers for Crawford, Vernon and Grant Counties, Wisconsin, 1870-1901

LAST NAME	FIRST NAME	NEWSPAPER, PAGE/COLUMN MONTH/DAY/YEAR	GENEALOGICAL DATA
Election Results		DR, p3c2, 4/6/1871	In the Town of Sterling the following ticket was elected: for Associate Justice – William P. Lyon; for Supervisors – R. W. Jordan, John M. Vance, Peter Jerman; for Town Clerk – John Blair; for Assessor – C. C. Oleson; for Treasurer – William Davis; for Justices – John Blair, A. M. Hayden; for Constables – Charles Lind, Simcon Gibbs and Isaac C. Peaslee.
Election Results		DC, p2c1, 4/9/1887	Town of Wheatland officers will be: Chairman, R. McAuley; Supervisors, Alex. Latshaw, George. W. Eckhardt; Clerk, J. H. Rogers; Treasurer, C. H. Upham; Assessor, W. Dyer; Justices, C. Tenney, C. G. Caldwell; and Constables, D. B. Collins, R. Ferguson, J. W. VanZant. Town of Franklin officers will be: Chairman, Chris Ellefson; Clerk, L. L. Thayer; Assessor, T. O. Torger; and Treasurer, Torger Berg.
Election Results		DC, p2c1, 4/9/1887	Town of Clayton officers will be: Chairman, T. B. Ward; Supervisors, James Davis, Ole Johnson; Clerk, N. O. Peterson; Treasurer, S. Lawson; Assessor, William Barney; Justices, J. H. Brightman, J. L. Stowel; and Constables, R. Banta, Joseph Briggs, R. W. Abbey. Town of Seneca officers will be: Chairman, Bow Cron; Supervisors, Lot Gay, N. Benhart; Clerk, A. B. Withey; Treasurer, Daniel Smethurst, Sr.; and Assessor, Jono. Lynch; Justices, A. B. Withey, Ed. McNamara, Thomas Clary.
Election Results		DC, p2c1, 4/9/1887	Town of Christiana officers will be: Chairman, E. C. Bratlie; Supervisors, J. P. Flugstad, A. J. Moen; Clerk, Ole Juston; Assessor, Hans Sjerve; Justices, A. J. Moen, S. Severson; and Constables, C. H. Johnson, Paul Steenson, H. Hermanson. Town of Sterling officers will be: Chairman, Peter Jerman; Supervisors, S. Ottoson, G. H. Battles; Clerk, P. F. Molland; Treasurer, J. C. Johnson; Assessor, Sylvester Cooley; Justices, E. Lund, S. A. Mellen; and Constables, Jessie Adams, Tom Everson, Ed. Tewalt.
Election Results		DC, p2c1, 4/9/1887	Town of Genoa officers will be: Chairman, William Riley; Supervisors, John Fopper, August Vaghlan; Clerk, Matthew Monti; Treasurer, Albert Zobolla; Justices, William Riley, William Hall; and Constables, Albert Hall, Sidney Gillette, Oswald Bobst.
Election Results		DC, p3c4, 4/16/1887	The Town of Freeman officers will be: Chairman, Thomas Lawrence; Supervisors, A. J. Runice, L. Christianson; Clerk, C. H. Conklin; Treasurer, H. Helgerson; Assessor, A. T. Lysne; Justices, Martin Loftus, A. T. Sandy; and Constables, W. W. Miller, O. B. Copper. The Town of Harmony officers will be: Chairman, John Stevenson; Supervisors, Albert Haldorson, William Oldenberg; Clerk, H. P. Buswell; Treasurer, O. F. Patterson; Assessor, O. Runnigen; Justices, Jessie Cowen, Thomas Torger; and Constables, J. De Witt, C. Farr, Frank Esler.
Election Results		DC, p3c4, 4/16/1887	The Town of Utica officers will be: Chairman, P. W. Peterson; Supervisors, E. G. Briggs, J. S. Oleson; Clerk, G. W. Davis; Treasurer, Erick Johnson; Assessor, Ole Severson; Justices, John Burns, Sam Turner; and Constables, Ralph Copper, Reed Peck, A. E. Spencer.
Election Results		DC, p4c2, 5/10/1889	The following officials were elected by the voters of De Soto: Chairman, A. Carlyle; Trustees, R. J. Kalhar, A. McDowell, William Green, Willis Owens, C. H. Uphan, Dr. O. Ewers; Clerk, H. T. Hare; Treasurer, C. B. Upham; Police Justice, Martin Loftus; Constable, W. K. Lowrie; Supervisor of Vernon Co., C. L. Ingersoll; and Supervisor of Crawford Co., Martin Loftus.
Election Results		BD, p3c4, 4/6/1877	The Town of Boscobel announced election results. The winners were: L. J. Woollery, N. Brainard - Supervisors; Martin DeWitt - Town Clerk; Theo. Kronshage - Treasurer; J. P. Willis - Assessor; G. W. Limbocker, O. E. Comstock - Justices of the Peace; C. Parce, John Kelty, Isaac Woodard - Contables; and John Pepper - Sealer of Weights and Measurers.
Elger	Lillie	DC, p3c3, 3/5/1887	Lillie Elger married J. C. Christie on Feb. 17, 1887 per an item originally printed in the Prairie du Chien Union.
Ellefson	Eric	DR, p3c2, 1/12/1871	Resided in Lansing. His team broke through the ice. One horse was drowned. A load of pork was saved.
Ellefson	Jens	BD, p3c4, 6/4/1880	Notice was published that the estate of Jens Ellefson, formerly of Hickory Grove, was in Probate Court.
Ellifson	John, Mrs.	BD, p3c1, 3/3/1880	Died Monday. Left 7 children. The oldest child was 16 years old. She was sister of Mr. G. Gunderson. Many people from Boscobel attended the funeral.
Elliott	T. B., Mrs.	RH, p5c5, 7/8/1897	Nee Thomas. Visited friends in Viola, where she once taught school.
Ellis	Ed	DC, p3c2, 4/16/1887	Planned to open a photo gallery in Lynxville this week.
Ellis	Edwin H.	DC, p3c3, 10/1/1887	Died Sept. 26, 1887 from a farm accident at Wilmer, MN. Brother, John, lived in Minneapolis. Aged 34 years. Survived by wife, 1 child, 2 brothers and his mother. Buried in De Soto Cemetery.
Ellis	John	RH, p5c4, 11/25/1897	Ellis' son was stabbed at a dance in Eastman by a man named Atkinson. Ellis "may recover."
Ellis	John, Rev.	RH, p5c3, 1/13/1898	The Rev. John Ellis married Minnie Wilson at the residence of the bride's parents near Webster. Rev. Ellis is pastor of the Kickapoo Congregational churches.
Ellis	Vet	RH, p5c4, 11/18/1897	Stabbed last Monday at a wedding dance in Eastman.

Genealogical Events from Newspapers for Crawford, Vernon and Grant Counties, Wisconsin, 1870-1901

LAST NAME	FIRST NAME	NEWSPAPER, PAGE/COLUMN MONTH/DAY/YEAR	GENEALOGICAL DATA
Elmandorf	L. M.	DR, p4c4, 12/15/1870	Sold watches, clocks, jewelery, silverware, glassware and musical instruments in Lansing, IA.
Elston	S. B.	BD, p3c2, 11/22/1878	Died Monday from internal injuries in the Town of Eagle, Richland Co. Received injuries while training a horse.
Ely	Arilla M.	RH, p5c4, 11/4/1897	Frank E. Gay married Arilla M. Ely on Oct. 27, 1897 at Avalanch. Bride and groom from La Farge. Joseph Peacock officiated.
Ely	Edgar	DC, p3c4, 3/10/1888	Edgar Ely married Carrie Bennett on Wednesday evening at Col. May's home near Viroqua. The Rev. S. S. Hebbard officiated.
Emberson	Ida, Mrs.	DC, p2c2, 7/2/1887	Arrived from her home in La Crosse to visit parents, Mr. and Mrs. Ira Stevens of Victory.
Emberson	J., Mr. and Mrs.	DC, p2c3, 11/26/1887	Spent the week with her parents, Mr. and Mrs. Ira Stevens of Victory.
Emendorf	M. T.	RH, p4c2, 10/19/1899	Sold his Manning farm to Frank Chase of Viroqua and then moved to Chippewa Co.
Emery	John DeLos	BD, p3c1, 7/11/1879	John DeLos Emery married Annie B. Newlin on July 4, 1879. Bride and groom from Wauzeka. Justice J. McLaughlin officiated.
Endfield	Mr.	RH, p5c2, 7/8/1897	Lived in Crawford Co. Visited his sister, Mrs. Hurlbut of Readstown.
Eng	Mr.	DC, p3c2, 7/31/1886	Worked as a letter carrier in La Crosse. Planned to open a general store in Stoddard.
Engle	Thomas E.	DC, p3c1, 11/26/1887	Greeted old friend in De Soto. He was a former resident of the area. Now lived in Minnesota.
Enright	P. H.	BD, p3c2, 5/30/1879	A Brussels carpet stolen a year ago from Mr. F. C. Jenkins was found at the home of a neighbor, P. H. Enright. Enright was arraigned, found guilty and fined $5 and costs.
Enright	P. H.	BD, p3c4, 6/27/1879	The Boscobel Town Council approved the bond of P. H. Enright and Joseph Roscinp to sell alcohol.
Enright	P. H.	BD, p3c2, 3/18/1881	P. H. Enright funeral held Saturday. Two brothers from "abroad" attended.
Enright	Patrick W.	BD, p3c3, 3/11/1881	Landlord of the Shamrock House in Boscobel. Found dead on Wednesday. Complained of domestic troubles earlier. Tried to commit suicide last year. Died Mar. 9, 1881 from excessive use of alcohol.
Enyart	Sarah Ann	BD, p2c3, 3/18/1881	Town of Clayton and Town of Scott squabbled over support for Sarah Ann Enyart. In Jan. 1875 Mrs. Enyart and her "2" children moved from the Town of Clayton to the Town of Scott. In Aug. 1875 they were declared to be paupers and in need of township support. The Town of Scott supervisors [Squire Toney and Isaac Brown] advised Town of Clayton to take charge of the family and pay for their support. The Town of Clayton agreed to pay Mrs. Enyart's father to care for them. She refused to move back to Clayton to live with him. In 1878 Scott supervisors [G. W. Churchill, David Quick and Wm. Mindham] advised Clayton to take charge of Enyart and her "3" children. Clayton ignored the request. The Wisconsin Supreme Court ruled on the responsiblities of the township to care for her.
Enyart	Sarah Ann	BD, p2c3, 3/18/1881	The Town of Clayton and Town of Scott argued in the Supreme Court of Wisconsin over which town was responsible to pay for the support of Sarah Ann Enyart, a pauper. In January 1875 she lived in Clayton and then moved to Scott. Sarah Enyart made application to Scott for assistance for herself and her two children. Clayton arranged to pay Sarah's father two dollars per week to provide for her needs. In Oct. 1877 Clayton requested the mother to move back to Clayton and receive support in that town. She refused to move. They gave her a clothing allowance and notified her there would be no additional assistance. On Sept. 20, 1878 the supervisors of Scott [G. W. Churchill, David Quick, William Mindham] sent the following to the Clayton supervisors, " You are hereby notified that Sarah Enyart and her three children, paupers, who have gained a settlement in your town, to which they belong, are in the town of Scott, for which the undersigned are supervisors. You are therefore notified and required, forthwith, to take charge of and provide for said paupers."
Erickson	John	DC, p3c3, 1/29/1889	Fell through ice on a return trip from Lansing, IA. His companions were too drunk to help him. Assistance came an hour later. Doing well. Resident of Sterling.
Ericson	Edward	RH, p5c4, 7/15/1897	Served as Undersheriff of Vernon Co. Arrived in Readstown to search for a thief.
Estes	boy	RH, p5c4, 11/17/1898	The infant son of Samuel Estes recently died of pneumonia at the home of his grandparents, Mr. and Mrs. George Kendall. Buried at Kickapoo on Nov. 15, 1898.
Estes	Sam	RH, p4c4, 3/24/1898	Recently moved from Kickapoo Center to Viola.
Evans	Charles	BD, p3c1, 4/9/1880	Recently sold his farm. Planned to move next week to Blakely, NB. Purchased 160 acres in Nebraska.

Genealogical Events from Newspapers for Crawford, Vernon and Grant Counties, Wisconsin, 1870-1901

LAST NAME	FIRST NAME	NEWSPAPER, PAGE/COLUMN MONTH/DAY/YEAR	GENEALOGICAL DATA
Evans	H.	BD, p3c3, 6/21/1878	Evans resided in Wauzeka. He has killed 91 wolves since April 7. "He is the boss wolf hunter in Wisconsin."
Evans	Henry	BD, p3c2, 1/31/1879	Resided in Wauzeka. He was a "wolf-scalper." Planned to depart for Olmstead and Fillmore Counties, MN to hunt wolves. Crawford Co. has discontinued wolf bounties.
Evans	Joe	BD, p3c2, 12/9/1881	Joe Evans, oldest resident of Boscobel, died on Monday.
Evans	Julia	BD, p3c5, 7/27/1877	Ira H. Stevens married Julia Evans on July 13, 1877 at Jamestown. Groom from Liberty. Bride from Jamestown.
Evans	Minnie	BD, p3c2, 8/19/1881	Funeral held Tuesday at home of Mr. and Mrs. Frank Lewis of Boscobel, her grandparents. Died at her parent's home in Stephenson, MI. Born in Boscobel to William and Stella Evans. Aged 8 years and 8 months.
Evans	William H.	BD, p3c2, 2/2/1877	Recently moved to Prairie du Chien from Yankeetown, Crawford Co. to fulfill the term as District Attorney.
Everson	boy	DC, p3c2, 10/15/1887	A son was born Sept. 16, 1887 to Mr. and Mrs. T. Everson of West Prairie.
Everson	Gutram	BD, p3c5, 1/5/1883	Published a notice that he had taken up calves in the Town of Hickory Grove, Grant Co.
Ewers	Achilles	RH, p5c2, 8/31/1899	Advertised the services of the new Bank of Readstown.
Ewers	Al, Mrs.	RH, p4c1, 2/7/1901	Left home in Readstown to visit her parents, Mr. and Mrs. William Fowell of Sylvan.
Ewers	Ben	RH, p5c2, 1/20/1898	Resided in Sylvan. Visited his nephew, G. A. Ewers of Readstown.
Ewers	boy	RH, p4c1, 8/10/1899	A son was born on Saturday to Gip Ewers of Readstown.
Ewers	boy	RH, p4c3, 9/13/1900	A son was recently born to Edgar Ewers. He weighed 10 pounds.
Ewers	Chill	RH, p6c4, 6/22/1899	Chill Ewers and son, Edgar, of Richland Center, and nephew, Al Ewers of Mill Creek, went to Readstown seeking a business location. They want to establish a bank, buy live stock and buy grain. Al Ewers purchased the Bliss farm. He plans to plat it and offer lots for sale.
Ewers	Edgar	RH, p4c2, 5/23/1901	Opened a real estate company in Readstown [Edgar Ewers & Co. Real Estate Agency].
Ewers	Edgar	RH, p5c3, 10/17/1901	Submitted a bill of $2 to the Village of Readstown for his attorney fees in the case of Ole Larsen vs. Village of Readstown.
Ewers	Floyd	RH, p4c2, 1/18/1900	Ewers' funeral held at Mill Creek last Saturday.
Ewers	Floyd L.	RH, p5c4, 1/18/1900	Died Jan. 12, 1900 of haemopelia at Mill Creek at the age of 17. He was the youngest son of Achilles Ewers and brother of Edgar Ewers.
Ewers	G. A.	RH, p4c2, 5/9/1901	Ewer's steam saw mill in Sugar Grove caught on fire, but was saved. In addition to damage done to the equipment, fire destroyed lumber stored in the area.
Ewers	girl	RH, p4c1, 7/25/1901	A daughter of G. A. Ewers died July 20, 1901. She was 6 months and 9 days old.
Ewers	Gladney	RH, p5c5, 10/28/1897	He was a hardwood lumber dealer in Readstown.
Ewers	Hollis Edgar	RH, p4c1, 10/10/1901	Died Oct. 6, 1901 of membraneous croup. He was the son of Edgar Ewers. Aged 12 months 24 days old. Buried in Readstown Cemetery.
Ewers	Inscoe	RH, p4c2, 1/18/1900	Worked as the assistant cashier at the bank in Readstown.
Ewers	Isaac	RH, p5c3, 7/15/1897	Departed Readstown for Chicago where he was employed as a recorder of freight bills at the railway office at $30 per month.
Ewers	Isaac	RH, p4c2, 11/11/1897	Employed by M. and St. P. Railroad. Worked in Chicago. Visited father, Jesse Ewers of Readstown.
Ewers	Isaac	RH, p5c3, 12/16/1897	Has been employed in a Milwaukee railroad office in Chicago during the fall. Secured a position as Transfer Agent from the same company in Omaha and Nebraska at an increased salary.
Ewers	Isaac	RH, p4c4, 6/23/1898	Isaac Ewers, Lester Hale, Ob Sutherland, Bird Rossin, Guy Fish, Charley Carter, Fay Johnstone and Elmer Sime, all of Readstown, volunteered for the army so they could fight in the Spanish American War. They prepared to leave for training at Camp Douglas.
Ewers	Isaac	RH, p5c6, 8/11/1898	Wrote a letter from Camp Douglas that was published in the newspaper that outlined camp life. He was in Co. M, 4th Regt. WI Vol.
Ewers	Isaac	RH, p4c4, 11/17/1898	Authored a letter describing soldier life. Published in the newspaper.

Genealogical Events from Newspapers for Crawford, Vernon and Grant Counties, Wisconsin, 1870-1901

LAST NAME	FIRST NAME	NEWSPAPER, PAGE/COLUMN MONTH/DAY/YEAR	GENEALOGICAL DATA
Ewers	Isaac	RH, p4c4, 4/6/1899	Opened a law office in the Peterson Building in Readstown. Planned to do a "general business in the line of law, loans, insurance and collections."
Ewers	Isaac	RH, p4c2, 8/17/1899	Lived in Readstown. Visited relatives in Springfield, IL.
Ewers	Isaac	RH, p5c1, 8/31/1899	Served as Justice of the Peace in Readstown.
Ewers	Isaac	RH, p4c1, 2/22/1900	Departed Readstown for Springfield, IL where he worked in Uncle Sam's secret service.
Ewers	Isaac	RH, p4c2, 9/20/1900	Isaac Ewers planned to marry Anna Wendle. Bride from Springfield, IL. Groom is a U. S. detective and former resident of Readstown.
Ewers	Isaac, Sgt.	RH, p4c4, 12/1/1898	Wrote a letter from Anniston, AL describing riots between white and black soldiers. Published in the newspaper.
Ewers	Isaac, Sgt.	RH, p5c4, 12/15/1898	Letter written by Ewers from Anniston, AL was published.
Ewers	Isaac, Sgt.	RH, p4c3, 2/2/1899	A letter written by Ewers from Anniston, AL was published. The 4th WI Regiment is to be mustered out.
Ewers	Jesse	RH, p7c2, 7/1/1897	Returned to Readstown after a trip to Illinois, Indiana and Tennessee. Visited his son, Rev. M. H. Ewers, the owner of 2000 acres in Tennessee.
Ewers	Jesse	RH, p4c3, 3/23/1899	Jesse Ewers married Mattie McCarty on March 17, 1899. Bride and groom from Readstown. The Rev. George Nuzum of Viroqua officiated.
Ewers	Jesse	RH, p6c4, 6/22/1899	Civil War veteran. Lived in Readstown. His pension [for military service] was increased by $2 per month.
Ewers	Jesse	RH, p4c2, 5/23/1901	Died Monday of heart failure. Embalmed by Joseph Pulver of Viroqua. Buried at Mill Creek.
Ewers	Jessie	RH, p5c2, 7/21/1898	Worked as a carpenter in Readstown.
Ewers	M. H., Rev.	RH, p4c1, 5/30/1901	Resided in Springfield, IL. Delivered the funeral sermon for his father, Jesse Ewers, last Sunday evening in the Readstown Methodist Episcopal Church.
Ewers	Maude	RH, p4c3, 7/18/1901	Maude Ewers married Loyd Taylor on July 4, 1901. Bride was daughter of G. A. Ewers of Readstown. Groom lived in Shortville, Clark Co., WI, the couple's future home. Justice C. H. Davenport officiated.
Ewers	Nellie	RH, p4c1, 1/4/1900	Left home in Readstown to attend college in Appleton, WI.
Ewers	O., Dr.	DC, p2c3, 2/19/1889	Sold drugs and medicines in De Soto.
Ewers	Romeo	RH, p4c2, 9/6/1900	Died Saturday morning in Sylvan. Recently had an operation for an appendicitis attack.
Ewers	William	RH, p5c2, 11/24/1898	Recently died in Mill Creek at the age of 80. He was the brother of Jesse Ewers of Readstown.
Eyers	Henry	BD, p3c2, 4/27/1883	Henry Eyers married Emma F. Green on April 18, 1883. Bride was the daughter of Thompson Green of the Town of Scott. Groom was also from Scott.
Fairchild	L.	DC, p5c1, 7/19/1889	The officers of the Bank of Prairie du Chien were L. Fairchild, President; A. Peterson, Vice President and E. I. Kidd, Cashier.
Fanny	Mrs.	DC, p2c2, 9/3/1887	Mrs. Fanny and Mrs Mary Bates of Retreat entertained their father, Mr. Chase of Horicon, WI.
Faris	David	BD, p3c1, 4/4/1879	Died of croup on April 5, 1879 when he was 4 years old. He was the son of Mr. and Mrs. James Faris of Woodman.
Faris	James	BD, p3c4, 8/13/1881	Grant Co. Circuit Court published a summons for the case, James Faris, plaintiff, vs. J. D. Bowles, defendant.
Faris	John	BD, p3c1, 3/3/1880	John Faris married Clara R. Adkins on Feb. 23, 1880 in Fennimore. Groom from Dakota. Bride from Mount Ida. Otho Shrader officiated.
Farmer	girl	RH, p4c2, 2/21/1901	A daughter was born on Tuesday to P. N. Farmer of Readstown.
Farmer	Henry	BD, p3c2, 4/12/1878	Died of consumption last Friday night at the home of Mr. Walbridge of Avoca. Resident of Marengo, IL. Body returned to Marengo for burial.
Farquharson	H. D.	BD, p2c1, 1/6/1882	Purchased the *Boscobel Dial* in September 1875 and sold it to Lou P. Lesler on Jan. 1, 1882.
Farquharson	H. D.	BD, p1c1, 1/19/1877	Published the *Boscobel Dial*.
Farquharson	H. D.	BD, p3c3, 8/30/1878	Departed Boscobel for Chicago to visit friends and relatives.

Genealogical Events from Newspapers for Crawford, Vernon and Grant Counties, Wisconsin, 1870-1901

LAST NAME	FIRST NAME	NEWSPAPER, PAGE/COLUMN MONTH/DAY/YEAR	GENEALOGICAL DATA
Farrell	James D., Mr. and Mrs.	DC, p3c3, 6/4/1887	Mrs. Farrell, of Chamberlain, Dakota, visited her mother, Mrs. A. N. Miller of De Soto. Miss Mary Smith went with the Farrells on their return trip to Dakota.
Farrell	James, Mr. and Mrs.	DC, p3c3, 5/8/1888	Recently departed the area for a new home in Chamberlain, Dakota.
Farrell	Jane	BD, p3c1, 6/17/1881	Deputy Sheriff Ora Richards and Mrs. Farrell took Mrs. Farrell's daughter, Jane Farrell, to the State Hospital for the Insane. She had previously been arrested on suspicion of arson to the Bailie property.
Farrin	Frank	BD, p3c1, 9/1/1882	Lived in Darlington. Visited sister, Mrs. Will Osborn of Boscobel.
Faust	Jack	BD, p3c2, 7/4/1879	Jack Faust and William McDaniel were severely injured while fighting each other. Dispute arose at a baseball game played in Boydtown, Crawford Co. The two have been feuding for a long time.
Favor	E. W., Mrs.	BD, p3c2, 8/31/1877	Aged 65 years. Died last Saturday at home in Bristol, NH. She was the mother of Hiram Favor of Boscobel.
Favor	H. W.	BD, P3c2, 4/23/1880	Sworn in as clerk of Boscobel.
Favor	H. W.	BD, p3c2, 6/3/1881	Published a notice that the Boscobel Light Guard Band was available to furnish music for the Fourth of July. Favor was the band's secretary.
Favor	Hiram W.	BD, p2c4, 5/27/1881	Petitioned the court to be named administrator of the Juliett Nelson estate, late of Boscobel.
Favor	Hiram, Mrs.	BD, p3c2, 2/21/1879	Returned from a trip to Vermont, New Hampshire and Massachusetts. Her mother, Mrs. Gage, returned with her.
Fawcett	Mahlan	BD, p3c3, 2/3/1882	From Livingston. Died Jan. 31, 1882 at the home of his nephew, Abe Howell, from billious fever. Aged 80 years.
Fay & Bisbee		BD, p3c4, 9/14/1877	Operated a stave factory in Wauzeka.
Felton	Amy	RH, p5c4, 4/27/1899	Hiram E. Chadeayne married Amy Felton on April 22, 1899, per Sugar Grove news column. Groom was a Crawford County farmer.
Felty	Sheridan	RH, p4c4, 10/31/1901	Slowly recovering from typhoid pneumonia at his home in Sugar Grove. Neighbors husked corn for him.
Fennimore		BD, p3c4, 3/24/1882	The village of Fennimore was named after a man of that name who settled in the grove a few miles from the present village at an early day, but on the breaking out of the Black Hawk War suddenly left, never to be heard from again. To designate the village from the town, the people called the place "The Center," afterwards "Fennimore Center," and finally Fennimore.
Fennimore Businessmen		BD, p3c6, 3/24/1882	The following ran businesses in Fennimore: Dry goods and groceries - Oswald & Hinn, Craven Shuttleworth; Druggists - J. A Farnham & Co., Leavitt & Brown; Hardware - Otho Shrader, Roach & Perkins; Grocer - C. W. Looney; Hotels - Varrell House, Geo. Smith, Jr., proprietor, Central House, H. C. Wenzel, proprietor; Blacksmithing - Fisher Brothers, John Griffith, Wm. Linton; Shoemakers - Wm. Weaver, Wm. Burns; [cont.]
Fennimore Businessmen		BD, p3c6, 3/24/1882	Additional Fennimore businesses: Photographer - George Perry; Saloons - M. Montz, John Phillips, H. C. Wentzel, Worden Stephens; Billards - Milton Green; Grain and Stock - Thompson Bros., T. C. Hawley, Leroy Booher; Lumber - J. H. Sarles; Tailor - A. Govier; Butchers - T. Popejoy, A. Belling; Harness Makers - W. H. Peddicorn, John Doan; Milliners and Dressmakers - Della Wannamaker, Emma Owen; Physicians - D. O. Pickard, J. Wolf, Leavitt & Brown; Livery - Geo. Smith, Jr., John Moore; Restaurant - George Graves; Furniture - G. P. Goble, John Allen; Wagonmakers - Fisher Brothers, Benjamin Niehause; Carpenters - John Allen, Smith Graham, Jeff Varnell, John Curtis; Painter - Frank Perry; Masons - Moody & Monroe, John Scanlan.
Ferguson	Florence	DC, p2c1, 5/7/1887	Claud Griffin married Florence Ferguson on May 1, 1887. Bride and groom from Victory. Alex. Latshaw, J.P., of Victory officiated at the ceremony.
Ferrell	Annie, Mrs.	DC, p2c2, 4/16/1887	Arrived from Chamberlain, Dakota to visit her mother, Mrs. A. N. Miller of the De Soto area.
Ferris	James A.	BD, p3c1, 1/5/1877	Proprietor of the American House in Woodman.
Ferris	James A.	BD, p2c2, 2/15/1878	Fire destroyed Ferris' warehouse in Woodman. Arson suspected.
Ferris	M. L., Mrs.	BD, p2c5, 10/22/1880	Opened a millinery and fancy goods trade in Boscobel two years ago, although she has been 11 years in the county. Stock comprised of hats, flowers, ribbons, laces, gloves, yarn, zephyrs and paper patterns.
Fetterhoff	J.	BD, p3c2, 12/16/1881	Advertised painting and graining services.

Genealogical Events from Newspapers for Crawford, Vernon and Grant Counties, Wisconsin, 1870-1901

LAST NAME	FIRST NAME	NEWSPAPER, PAGE/COLUMN MONTH/DAY/YEAR	GENEALOGICAL DATA
Fettie	Willie	BD, p3c2, 12/21/1877	Died in Milwaukee on Tuesday at the age of 21. He was ths son of William F. Fettie, a former Boscobel resident.
Fetty	Sheridan	RH, p4c3, 10/17/1901	Fetty was dangerously ill with typhoid pneumonia at his home in Sugar Grove.
Field	W. W.	BD, p3c1, 1/5/1883	Owned a farm in Iowa. Visited friends in Boscobel, his former home.
Filkins	Fannie	BD, p3c1, 1/7/1881	Charles D. Vine married Fannie Filkins on Dec. 30, 1880 at the home of Charles Cook of Boscobel. Bride and groom from Marquette, WI.
Finkle	Therresa	DC, p3c4, 12/4/1886	Taught school in the Dach District per Liberty Pole news column.
Finney	Jennie	DC, p3c4, 4/2/1887	Planned to teach at Fosdick this summer.
Fish	Albert	RH, p5c2, 6/9/1898	Returned to Readstown. Spent the last year working in St. Paul.
Fish	boy	RH, p4c1, 8/10/1899	A son was recently born to J. Fish of Readstown.
Fish	C. W.	RH, p4c2, 10/11/1900	C. W. Fish, William Hutchison and Achilles Ewers were trustees for the Readstown Methodist Episcopal Church.
Fish	Charles	RH, p4c3, 3/16/1899	Charles Fish of Readstown and Will Hebard of La Farge formed a partnership to open a blacksmith shop in Readstown.
Fish	Charles	RH, p4c1, 6/15/1899	Resigned as Readstown Village Marshall. Replaced by A. S. Aikens.
Fish	Frank	BD, p3c1, 1/12/1883	Died in Decorah, IA from "pneumonia consumption." He was born in Boscobel. He was a brother of Mrs. D. G. Bliss, who recently died in Boscobel.
Fish	Frank O.	BD, p3c2, 3/28/1879	Sent a letter to the *Boscobel Dial* from Denver, CO about Boscobel people in Colorado. Fish saw George Collins who worked in Boulder City. He saw Mr. Josephson, who planned to start an auction clothing house at Silver Cliff. Fish planned to stay in Colorado as there was plenty of work.
Fish	Guy	RH, p4c1, 8/17/1899	Guy Fish and Otis Wilson departed Readstown to work in the western harvest fields.
Fish	J.	RH, p4c1, 7/21/1898	Advertised services as an optician in Readstown.
Fish	Jerome	RH, p7c2, 7/1/1897	Lived in Readstown. Purchased a new bicycle.
Fish	Jerome	RH, p5c4, 6/15/1899	Wrote a series of letters describing the country as he traveled back and forth to the Gulf of Mexico on a sales trip. Letters were published.
Fish	Jerome	RH, p4c1, 6/22/1899	Returned to Readstown from a trip to Galveston, TX.
Fish	Jerome	RH, p4c2, 7/13/1899	Replaced N. D. Hale on the Readstown Village Council.
Fish	Jerome	RH, p4c1, 4/5/1900	Purchased a saloon from Frank Rowe in Readstown.
Fish	Jerome	RH, p4c2, 5/10/1900	Lost a finger while working in a stave mill in Readstown.
Fish	Jerome	RH, p4c2, 6/13/1901	The "Minneapolis photographer" planned to open a gallery in Readstown.
Fish	Lizzie	DR, p3c4, 2/9/1871	Thaddeus Hopkins married Lizzie Fish in De Soto on Feb. 6, 1871. Bride and groom were from Lansing. The Rev. Mr. Hubbard of the Methodist Episcopal Church officiated.
Fish	Mason	BD, p2c1, 2/22/1878	Former resident of Boscobel. Lived in Clay Township, Shelby Co., IA. Wrote letter to *Boscobel Dial* stating that contrary to earlier reports, Slippery Jim Parish [formerly of Boscobel area] was not dead. Fish saw Parish Feb. 6, 1878 in Walnut, Pottawatonie Co., IA. Parish told Fish he had been in Utah. Parish was also seen by William Brindley of Sanders Creek, Grant Co. when Parish visited his brother.
Fishel	Wesley	RH, p4c2, 10/25/1900	Dora Benn married Wesley Fishel on Oct. 16, 1900 at the home of the bride. Bride and groom from Viola. The Rev. A. C. Vaughan officiated.
Fisher	Henry	BD, p3c2, 3/8/1878	Taken from Fennimore to the asylum in Madison by Thomas Tormey, Chairman of the Town of Fennimore.

Genealogical Events from Newspapers for Crawford, Vernon and Grant Counties, Wisconsin, 1870-1901

LAST NAME	FIRST NAME	NEWSPAPER, PAGE/COLUMN MONTH/DAY/YEAR	GENEALOGICAL DATA
Fitch	Frederick E.	BD, p3c3, 9/24/1880	Died of billious fever last Wednesday at his home in Woodman. Born Aug. 2, 1836 in Boardman, OH. Moved to Patch Grove, WI in 1855. Married July 2, 1859 to Sarah A. Dodge in Beetown. He was the father of one son and one daughter. Moved to Boscobel in 1864 and to Woodman in 1869. Worked for Weston, Miner & Co., lumber dealers in Woodman. The funeral was held at the Congregational Church in Boscobel. [Joined the Congregational Church in Boscobel in 1866 and served as a deacon. Organized a Sabbath school in Woodman. From Oct. 1, 1880 issue, page 3c3.]
Fitch	Johnny	BD, p3c2, 12/13/1878	He was the stepson of Marti Rowen of Scott Township. Broke both bones of his right arm while playing at school.
Fitzgibbons	Mike	BD, p2c2, 10/11/1878	Lived in Seneca, Crawford Co. Fitzgibbon's "horse lost 80 lights of glass during a severe hail storm."
Flagg	Sut, Mr.	BD, p3c1, 2/27/1880	Departed Boscobel for a mercantile position in Edgerton.
Flanagan	James	BD, p3c2, 8/19/1881	Murdered Aug. 16, 1881. Lived in the first house beyond the Wheatville post office in Crawford Co. He was hit by a rock after yelling several times at revellers. He was the brother-in-law of Dist. Attorney Evans of Crawford Co.
Flanagan	Nellie	RH, p4c2, 10/31/1901	Nellie Flanagan married Sherman McVey on Oct. 19, 1901. Bride lived in Estherville, IA; however, she was a former resident of Readstown. Groom from Rockton, WI. Planned to live in La Crosse.
Flanagan	Thomas	RH, p4c2, 10/25/1900	Arrived in Readstown from Esterville, IA to visit relatives and friends.
Flanagan	W. H., Mrs.	RH, p4c2, 6/1/1899	Mrs. Flanagan's household items were shipped from Readstown to Brainard, MN. She joined her husband who was a timber inspector for Northern Pacific Railroad.
Flannagon	J. C.	RH, p5c4, 1/11/1900	Purchased his partner's ownership interest in a warehouse co-owned by Flannagon and William Crook.
Flannigan	James	BD, p3c2, 8/26/1881	An inquest was held by John Tate, J.P., regarding the death of James Flannigan, late of Crawford Co. Flannigan was hit by stones thrown by Jerry Flynn [also called Jeremiah Flinn], James Conley [also called James Connelly, Jr.], John McCormick, Jr. and James McCormick. John Cummins was with the defendants, but did not throw any stones. No one was sure who threw the fatal stone. All taken to jail in Prairie du Chien, except Flynn who posted a $1000 bail bond. Per Nov. 18, 1881 issue, defendants found guilty of manslaughter in third degree. Case to be taken to Supreme Court. Per Dec. 2, 1881 issue, defendants sentenced to 2 years at Waupon. Judge Cothren's remarks were published.
Fleming	Mary, Miss	DC, p2c4, 1/29/1887	Resided in Lansing. Visited sister, Mrs. Devlin of De Soto.
Flinn	Charles	BD, p2c2, 3/7/1879	Charles Flinn [Flynn?] planned to marry Mary Conley on Feb. 24, 1879. Groom from Rolling Ground.
Flint	J.	BD, p2c4, 10/22/1880	Moved to Boscobel 14 years ago. Opened a bakery and restaurant in town 5 years ago.
Flint	J., Mrs.	RH, p4c1, 7/11/1901	Mrs. Flint and her children arrived in Readstown from Wellsville, KS to visit at the home of William Hall.
Flint	John, Mr. and Mrs.	BD, p3c1, 6/1/1883	Left Boscobel area for a three-week visit in Ohio. In their absence, their business will be conducted by their grandson, Arthur David.
Flynn		BD, p3c2, 1/5/1877	Fight took place at Flynn's saloon in Boscobel.
Flynn	O. W.	BD, p3c3, 4/27/1877	The wedding party of O. W. Flynn and Catharine Moran was held at the Central House in Boscobel on Tuesday. Bride from Wauzeka. Groom was the brother of P. Flynn of "narrow gauge railroad fame."
Flynn	P., Mrs.	BD, p3c2, 7/12/1878	Recently died at her home in Boscobel. Survived by husband and 5 children. Buried in Iowa.
Flynn	William	BD, p3c4, 2/3/1882	Applied in the Grant Co. probate court to administer the estate of William D. Flynn.
Foley	Mart	RH, p5c4, 9/9/1897	Resided in Readstown. Put up a cross on the St. Phillips' Church in Rolling Ground.
Folie	Richard	DC, p3c4, 8/28/1886	Richard Folie married Emma E. Green on Aug. 23, 1886 at the residence of the bride's parents in De Soto. Charles E. Woodbury, J.P., officiated. [See p3c3, 9/18/1886. Folie's real name was Dick Bennett. He was a married man from Genoa.]
Folks	W. F.	RH, p5c4, 2/15/1900	Resided in Milroy, IN. Offered the pastorate at the Christian Church in Sugar Grove.
Folsom		DC, p3c3, 6/11/1887	A new post office was established in the O'Leary neighborhood in the Town of Franklin. Given the name Folsom.

Genealogical Events from Newspapers for Crawford, Vernon and Grant Counties, Wisconsin, 1870-1901

LAST NAME	FIRST NAME	NEWSPAPER, PAGE/COLUMN MONTH/DAY/YEAR	GENEALOGICAL DATA
Folyer	Lucretia	BD, p3c4, 8/29/1879	James Bailey married Lucretia Folyer last Friday and then deserted her upon the advise of Lucretia's doctor. [Implied that Lucretia was pregnant.] Bride and groom from Hickery Grove.
Foner	John	BD, p2c7, 10/22/1880	Advertised that he had taken up a colt on his land in the Town of Watterstown.
Fopper		DC, p3c3, 3/5/1887	The 16-year-old daughter of Mrs. Micheal Fopper of Victory recently died of consumption. She was the fourth member of the family to die in the last 2 years.
Fopper	Mrs.	DC, p2c3, 11/26/1887	Lived at Bad Axe. Her funeral was held last Sunday at the Congregational Church in Retreat.
Ford	Ella, Miss	BD, p3c1, 3/26/1880	Teacher in Boscobel. Resigned position. Planned to go west.
Ford	Thomas, Mrs.	BD, p3c2, 10/30/1883	Moved to Blanchardville, IA from Boscobel three years ago. Came back to visit.
Foreman	Rudolph	RH, p4c3, 1/25/1900	Born April 18, 1833 in Armstrong Co., PA. Moved to Vernon Co. in 1855 and married Emeline Moon in 1856. Moved to Black Earth for 3 years and then moved back. Served in Co. I., 12th Regt. WI Vol. Since that time Foreman lived in Lynn and Fayette Counties in Iowa. Moved to Seymour, MO in Spring of 1897 and died there on Dec. 24, 1899 from paralysis. Survived by wife, 7 children, a 91-year-old mother, 1 brother [James Foreman who resides near Kickapoo] and 1 sister [Mrs. Ransom Kellogg of Sugar Grove in Town of Kickapoo].
Forey	H. D.	DC, p2c2, 7/2/1887	Effie B. Clark married H. D. Forey on Wednesday in Victory. Alex Latshaw officiated. Their new home will be in Minneapolis per the 7/9/1887 issue of the newspaper.
Forey	H. D.	DC, p2c1, 11/27/1888	Died Nov. 17, 1888 of apoplexy in Duluth, MN. Born in Victory about 28 years ago. Married Effie Clark a year ago.
Forey	Hiland	DC, p3c4, 11/27/1888	Died Nov. 16, 1888 in Duluth, MN. His remains were taken to Victory. Married a year ago in June to Miss Effie Forey of Retreat.
Forseth	Ole	BD, p3c1, 9/23/1881	Died recently of spinal fever in Minnesota. Former resident of Boscobel.
Forseth	Ole B.	BD, p3c3, 5/24/1878	Ole B. Forseth married Martha Syverson on Tuesday. Groom from Boscobel. They departed for Minneapolis. The Rev. O. Nuess officiated.
Forseth	Ole B.	BD, p3c1, 10/24/1879	Former resident of Boscobel. Current resident of Minneapolis. Lost 3 fingers on his left hand.
Fortney	D. T.	DC, p3c2, 12/25/1886	Proprietor of Fortney Hotel in La Crosse. From Liberty Pole.
Fortney	Hans O.	RH, p4c3, 3/9/1899	One of the largest tobacco growers in the Town of Kickapoo. Sold his 1898 crop for over $900.
Fortney	Joseph	BD, p2c4, 11/26/1880	Grant County paid him a bounty for scalps turned into the county.
Fortney	Julia, Mrs.	RH, p4c2, 8/2/1900	Mrs. Fortney's funeral was held Tuesday. She was 97. Mr. and Mrs. J. T. Dregne of Readstown attended.
Fortney	Ole K.	DC, p2c2, 4/2/1887	Recently became the father of a boy. Resided at Liberty Pole.
Foshay	Geary	BD, p3c1, 11/27/1883	Resided in Patch Grove. An old resident of Grant Co. He was very ill at Sing Sing, NY where he had gone to visit.
Foster	Eliza M.	DC, p3c2, 11/19/1887	Eliza M. Foster married Willie Haverley on Nov. 25, 1887 at the residence of William Haverley of Red Mound. It was a double ceremony. Francis Haverley married George N. Angell, too.
Foster	George	DC, p2c3, 5/29/1888	Put up the third house in Cooley Valley, now occupied by W. F. Rose. Settled here 34 years ago. Now lives in Greene, IA. Visited former neighbors in the region.
Foster	George M.	DC, p3c2, 1/21/1888	Resided in De Soto for 34 years. Relocated to Greene, IA. Renewed subscription to the newspaper.
Foster	S. J.	BD, p3c2, 1/2/1880	The barns, sheds, farm equipment and crops of S. J. Foster were burned. Loss estimated at $2,000. Buildings were located next to S. W. Ranny's hotel in Wauzeka.
Fourt	boy	DC, p3c3, 5/8/1888	A son was born last week to C. S. Fourt.
Fourt	Charles	DC, p3c3, 3/3/1888	J. G. Kimberlin of Indiana visited his relative, Charles S. Fourt of the De Soto area.
Fourt	girl	DC, p3c4, 1/22/1887	A daughter was born on Wednesday to Charles S. Fourt of the De Soto vicinity.
Fourt	Lavinia	DC, p3c5, 9/4/1886	Lavinia Fourt recently married George Hammer at the home of John Valentine, the bride's uncle. Bride was formerly from Retreat. Groom from Battle Lake, MN.
Fowel	C. W.	RH, p5c3, 11/25/1897	Resided in Sylvan. Put new machinery in his sawmill.
Fowell	C. W.	RH, p4c2, 9/21/1899	Resident of Sylvan. Planned to move to Readstown.

Genealogical Events from Newspapers for Crawford, Vernon and Grant Counties, Wisconsin, 1870-1901

LAST NAME	FIRST NAME	NEWSPAPER, PAGE/COLUMN MONTH/DAY/YEAR	GENEALOGICAL DATA
Fowell	Charles W.	RH, p4c3, 2/7/1901	Fowell's steam saw mill and feed mill in Sylvan burned down. There was no insurance. The mill was worth about $1500. Wood and grain was also lost.
Fowell	W. T., Mrs.	RH, p4c1, 6/6/1901	Mrs. Fowell's funeral was held Tuesday in Sylvan.
Fowell	William	RH, p4c1, 4/25/1901	Moved from Sylvan to Readstown.
Fowell	William	RH, p4c3, 9/26/1901	Taylor and George Fowell of Sylvan visited their father, William Fowell of Readstown, who is "very low from the effect of a cancer in his eye." He had an operation performed about 6 months ago and thought that he would recover, but it has been growing worst for the past few months.
Fowell	William	RH, p4c1, 10/10/1901	Died of cancer on Oct. 19, 1901 from cancer. Born Sept. 1829 in Straffordshire, England. Moved to the America in 1852 and settled in Ohio. Married Rebecka Ables in Aug. 1856. She was the daughter of a Baptist minister. Moved to Vernon Co. in 1865 and to the town of Sylvan in Richland Co. in 1866, where he lived until May 1901. He was a member of the Church of England as a boy. In 1853 he united with the Christian Church in Ohio and later with the Methodist Episcopal Church. He was the father of 7 sons and 3 daughters. Eight children survive him. "When a boy he worked for 4 cents a day and managed to get a common school education and saved enough money at the age of 23 to bring him to America."
Fowler	boy	DC, p4c1, 3/12/1889	A son was recently born to Fred Fowler of De Soto.
Fox	George	RH, p5c3, 4/4/1901	Died Jan. 14, 1901. Extensive obituary published.
Fox	George O.	RH, p5c3, 11/18/1897	Former resident of Readstown. Enlisted in 14th Infantry of the U. S. Army. Lived in Vancouver, Washington.
Fox	Gertrude	RH, p5c3, 9/27/1900	Charles R. Moore married Gertrude Fox on Sept. 8, 1900 at the Christian Church in Crawfordsville, OR. Groom from Brownsville and attends Divinity School. Bride from Crawfordsville and has lived with Mr. and Mrs. J. F. Venner for the past 2 years.
Fox	girl	DC, p3c5, 2/3/1888	A "little daughter" of Mr. and Mrs. Lou Fox recently died in Victory.
Fox	Martha	BD, p3c2, 6/29/1883	Taught school in Boscobel.
Fralick	Frank	BD, p2c4, 11/26/1880	Grant County paid him a bounty for scalps turned into the county.
France	J. B.	BD, p3c1, 12/4/1883	Resided in Boscobel. Discovered lead on property in Crawford Co.
France	Johnnie	BD, p3c3, 12/16/1881	Hand was terribly lacerated by a circular saw at Ruka Brother's wagon factory last Saturday. Aged about 14 years.
Francisco	A.	BD, p3c4, 3/10/1882	Published a notice in the *Boscobel Dial* requesting all persons knowing themselves to be in debt to A. Francisco to call on T. Carrier, who has his books, and settle the debt.
Francisco	George M.	BD, p3c2, 12/9/1881	George M. Francisco married Fannie Cholerton at the home of the bride's father on Dec. 4, 1881. Groom from Boscobel. Bride from Richland Center.
Francisco	girl	BD, p3c3, 4/29/1881	A daughter was born to Andrew Francisco of Boscobel on April 13, 1881.
Francisco	Mary J., Mrs.	BD, p3c3, 9/9/1881	Died Sept. 6, 1881 in Boscobel from congestion. She was wife of N. J. Francisco.
Francois	Francis	BD, p2c3, 1/5/1883	Upon returning from doing his chores he was found to be acting like a "raving maniac." There were no signs of him returning to reason. He had a wife and one child. Lived in Town of Willow, Richland County. He was 45 years old.
Frank	Florence Celestia	BD, p3c1, 8/8/1879	Charles J. McKittrick married Florence Celestia Frank on August 5, 1879 in Pulaski, Iowa Co. Bride daughter of Major George R. Frank, former resident of Boscobel. Groom merchant in Muscoda. The Rev. William Stoddart officiated.
Franzeni	John, Mrs.	DC, p1c2, 5/24/1889	Mrs. John Franzeni and Daniel Buffa, both of Genoa, suffered with consumption.
Frater	Mrs.	DC, p3c4, 6/4/1887	Mrs. Frater, nee Haggerty, made a few remarks for the W.C.T.U. at a meeting in De Soto. Mrs. Frater taught school in De Soto between 1860 and 1865.
Frazier	Dora	DC, p2c2, 7/16/1887	Dora Frazier married Lincoln Reed on July 4, 1887. Bride and groom resided in Chaseburgh. The Rev. E. Trimin [Trumin?] officiated.
Frazier	J. H., Mrs.	RH, p5c4, 8/5/1897	New postmistress in Viola.
Frazier	John	RH, p4c2, 2/9/1899	Left Readstown for a position as a clerk at the State Capitol.

Genealogical Events from Newspapers for Crawford, Vernon and Grant Counties, Wisconsin, 1870-1901

LAST NAME	FIRST NAME	NEWSPAPER, PAGE/COLUMN MONTH/DAY/YEAR	GENEALOGICAL DATA
Frazier	John H.	RH, p5c3, 8/26/1897	Editor of the *Viola Intelligencer*.
Frazier	May	RH, p4c3, 11/14/1901	Howard Adams married May Frazier last week, per the Pleasant Valley news column.
Frazier	Pluma	DC, p2c2, 7/16/1887	Pluma Frazier married Henry Stodke on July 4, 1887. Bride and groom resided in Chaseburgh. The Rev. E. Trimin [Trumin?] officiated.
Frazier	William	BD, p3c2, 5/25/1883	Resided in Vernon County. Won a $1200 prize from the U. S. Dept. of Agriculture for producing the best samples of sugar from amber cane.
Free	Fred	DC, p2c1, 11/20/1886	Jennie Clawater married Fred Free on Nov. 14, 1886 at the residence of C. L. Ingersoll. Bride was the daughter of Hon. Wm. Clawater of Liberty Pole. Groom from Cobb, WI. The Rev. Thomas Crouch officiated.
Freehoff	James	DC, p3c3, 8/21/1886	Named principal of the De Soto Union School. Resided in Sigel, La Crosse Co.
Freehoff	Joseph	DC, p3c2, 10/9/1886	Elected President of the Lyceum in De Soto.
Freeman	Joseph	DR, p3c5, 1/12/1871	"Take notice: . . . my wife, Lucinda A. Freeman, has left my bed and board without cause or provocation, and that I will not pay any debts of her contracting after this date. Jan. 9, 1871 Joseph Freeman, De Soto."
Freeman	Joseph	DR, p3c3, 6/29/1871	Granted a divorce from Lucinda Freeman in Vernon County Courts. Mrs. Freeman got $280 worth of personal property. She was charged with adultery with Rev. Mr. Hill, a Methodist minister who was formerly stationed in De Soto. The charge was not sustained, as he had an alibi and exhonerated himself.
Freeman	Joseph	DR, p3c3, 7/13/1871	New information indicates that Mrs. Freeman was found guilty of adultery with Rev. Mr. Hill, who now lives in Pecatonica, IL. [More details are available on p3c4, July 24, 1871 issue.]
Freis	Judge	BD, p3c1, 2/20/1880	Died last Friday at an advanced age in Richland Center.
French	Bertha	RH, p4c2, 9/8/1898	Departed De Soto to teach school in Manning.
French	Corel B.	DR, p3c2, 9/21/1871	Died Sept. 18, 1871 of cholera infantum at the age of 16 months and 3 days. He was the son of N. E. and Sophia French of De Soto.
French	Frane?	BD, p3c1, 7/4/1879	Miss Frane[?] French of Fulton, NY visited her aunt and uncle, Mr. and Mrs. F. B. Burdick of Boscobel.
French	Minnie, Miss	DC, p3c1, 11/26/1887	Lived in De Soto. Visited grandfather, Mr. Gould of Genoa.
French	N. E.	DC, p3c1, 6/12/1886	Proprietor of a general store in De Soto.
French	N. E.	DC, p4c3, 4/5/1889	Sold on Saturday to Dr. Ewers the land west of the school building in De Soto, a strip 450 feet wide and extending from Main Street south to Dr. Ewers pasture, for $1000.
French	N. E.	DC, p4c2, 5/24/1889	Turned up solid silver spoons, forks and a knife while plowing in his field near De Soto.
French & McAuley		DC, p2c2, 2/19/1889	Large general merchandise store in De Soto. Buy and ship large quantities of potatoes and all kinds of farm products.
Friar	Thomas	BD, p3c2, 10/30/1883	Lizzie O'Brien married Thomas Friar on Oct. 22, 1883. Bride was the daughter of James O'Brien of Irish Ridge. Groom was from Woodman.
Frie	Ada, Mrs.	RH, p5c4, 1/13/1898	Resided in Kickapoo Center. Visited sister, Mrs. Ed Fry of West Lima.
Frier	John	BD, p3c1, 8/1/1879	Lost a hand after it was crushed while attempting to couple two railroad cars. Friere resided in Wauzeka.
Fritz	Casper	BD, p3c5, 7/27/1877	Published a notice that he was no longer responsible for his son, Henry Fritz. Resided in Fennimore.
Fritz	Fred	BD, p3c2, 1/13/1882	Last Saturday, James McHale, James McKown and Patrick Rogan played cards at the saloon owned by Fred Fritz in Boscobel. McHale broke a table leaf while playing. Fritz demanded payment for damages. McHale thought the amount Fritz demanded was too high and a fight commenced. A man by the name of Keller tried to stop the fight, to no avail. Harmon and Byron Peir and Albert Beam, boarders, were called by the women of the house to help stop the fight. The parties were prosecuted on Monday. Fritz, Rogan and Bean were each fined $3. McHale was fined $10.
Fritz	Fred	BD, p3c2, 12/20/1878	Charged with choking and beating his wife. Paid a $20 fine and costs. Resided in the Boscobel area.
Fritz	J. W., Mr. and Mrs.	BD, p3c1, 11/17/1882	Mr. and Mrs. Fritz of Flambeau, WI visited Mrs. Fritz' sister, Mrs. Richard Spiegelberg of Boscobel.

Genealogical Events from Newspapers for Crawford, Vernon and Grant Counties, Wisconsin, 1870-1901

LAST NAME	FIRST NAME	NEWSPAPER, PAGE/COLUMN MONTH/DAY/YEAR	GENEALOGICAL DATA
Fry	Jerome	RH, p5c2, 10/21/1897	Resided in Willow. Arrested for killing his neighbor, Dexter Johnson. Murder was ruled justifiable.
Frye	Ida, Mrs.	RH, p5c2, 5/11/1899	Resided in Kickapoo. Advertised carpetweaving services.
Fuka	Mr.	BD, p2c3, 12/4/1883	His house and barn in Vineyard Coulee [north of Prairie du Chien] was destroyed by a cyclone. W. Jelinek's home in the same coulee was also destroyed.
Funk		BD, p3c4, 2/22/1878	The Funk family of near Belle Center lost their home to fire last week Thursday.
Funk	Andrew A.	BD, p3c3, 12/24/1880	Andrew A. Funk married Mary Ruka at home of bride's father on Tuesday. Groom from Aurora, NB. Bride from Boscobel. The Rev. Frederick Mutschmann officiated at the German Lutheran Church. Kate and Charles Ruka were bride's siblings. Groom was previously employed in Boscobel as a salesman. The couple will live in Nebraska.
Funk	Fred	BD, p3c2, 2/23/1877	Recently died. He accidently drank bed bug poison, thinking it was whiskey. Resided in Wauzeka. Funeral to be held today or tomorrow.
Funk	Lewis	BD, p2c4, 4/4/1879	Resided in the Belle Center area. Had his neighbors, Mr. and Mrs. Dilley arrested. A year ago, while attending services house burned down. After examining the debris, concluded that feather bed and bedding was removed before the fire. He suspected the Dilleys, but had no proof. Dilleys recently prepared to move to Kansas and sold off furniture. Unsold items were placed in home of Mrs. Dilley's sister, Mrs. William Collins. Funk passed Dilleys on the road and saw his quilts. He got a warrant and the constable. More of his quilts were found. Mrs. Dilley confessed and was placed in jail. Husband did not confess. He was freed.
Funk	Lilly	DC, Supp, 10/23/1886	George J. Mann married Lilly Funk on Sept. 14, 1886 in a Catholic Church in Alma, WI. Rev. Father Hackner officiated.
Funk	Lizzie	BD, p2c3, 8/14/1883	The Grant County Circuit Court published a summons in the case, Lizzie Funk [plaintiff] vs. J. W. Funk [defendant].
Furderer	Henry	BD, p3c2, 6/18/1880	Died June 11, 1880. His funeral, sponsored by the Odd Fellows, was held on Sunday in Boscobel. Born July 16, 1838 in Neustadt, Baden, Germany. Emigrated to America in 1860. Englished in Company H, 7th WI Regiment Volunteers in 1861. He lost his right eye at South Mountain. The bullet remained in his head the remainder of his life. Member of the famous Iron Brigade. Survived by wife and 5 children.
Furman	Eddie	DC, p3c1, 12/10/1887	Returned home after a 15-month stay in Hubbard, MN.
Furman	G. W.	DC, p2c3, 8/28/1886	Advertised his availability to do light and heavy draying in De Soto.
Furman	George, Jr.	DR, p3c2, 11/2/1871	George Furman, Jr. and a daughter of Charles Smith were injured when returning to De Soto when they were thrown from their wagon.
Furman	Henry and Ed	DC, p4c2, 4/12/1889	Planned to work on the raft boat, *Ten Broeck*, this season. The *Ten Broeck* was called a steamboat on p4c3, 5/24/1889. Furmans were from De Soto.
Furman	May	DC, p3c3, 6/26/1886	Harlan T. Hare married May Furman on June 22, 1886 at the home of George W. Furman, the bride's father. Bride from De Soto. Groom from Mt. Pleasant, IA. Miss Cora Stogdill of La Crosse and Annie Caryle were the bridesmaids. The groomsmen were F. W. Hoadley and W. S. Milliken. the Rev. M. B. Balch officiated. A gift list was published.
GAR Camp Fire		DC, p3c4, 9/18/1886	The James Mason Post [De Soto] of the GAR held a Camp Fire. The following soldiers represented De Soto [company and regiment noted]: James H. Rogers, A, 25th WI; P. D. Bartholomew, A, 25th WI; W. F. Rose, B, 27th IA; G. W. Furman, I, 27th WI; C. S. Fonrt, K, 5th WI; D. Wilt, F, 43rd WI; O. Ewers, F, 41st WI; R. P. Pennell, B, 27th IA; Thomas De Lacy, A, 31st WI; Milo Whitney, K, 50th WI; W. G. Conklin, I, 6th IL [in Mexican War] Maj. end raised Co. I, 8th IL; James Voysey, I, 43rd WI; Edward Rogers, C, 18th WI; C. F. Bottom, D, 24th WI; Charles Pratt, D, 24th WI; William Miller, D, 18th WI; LeGrand Hickok, C, 18th WI; John W. White, I, 6th WI; Charles Tenney, K, 46th WI; William Green, H, 50th WI; A. E. Fosdick, I, 6th WI; C. F. Page, I, 6th WI and B, 8th WI; Z. T. Clark, B, 42nd WI; Fred Fowler, D, 48th WI; P. Peterson, D, 15th WI; S. D. Taylor, E, 3rd WI; Robert Boyce, B, 2nd Calvary WI; William G. Eddy, I, 6th MN; M. E. Lawrence, B, 42nd WI; Jason Phillips, E, 12th WI; James Whitney, B, 42nd WI and Smith Lane, 26th IA.
GAR Camp Fire		DC, p3c4, 9/18/1886	The James Mason Post [De Soto] of the GAR held a Camp Fire. The following soldiers represented Retreat [company and regiment noted]: G. W. Seymour, D, 156th NY; S. A. Mellen, B, 34th IL; E. J. Lees, 161 OH; J. S. Gibbs, B, 50th WI; F. B. White, unit unclear; M. Sallender, F, 8th WI; Fred Sallender, H, 10th WI; E. H. Ames, B, 50th WI; V. E. Aikens, B, 42nd WI and N. Cox, I, 4th KY [in Mexican War]. The following soldiers were from Mt. Sterling: Henry Moon, D, 31st WI; S. N. Brockway, A, 31st WI and J. S. Dudley, A, 31st WI. The following soldiers were from Red Mound: I. W. Rinehart, D, 31st WI; E. R. James, D, 31st WI and Charles Brown, C, 18th WI.

Genealogical Events from Newspapers for Crawford, Vernon and Grant Counties, Wisconsin, 1870-1901

LAST NAME	FIRST NAME	NEWSPAPER, PAGE/COLUMN MONTH/DAY/YEAR	GENEALOGICAL DATA
GAR Camp Fire		DC, p3c4, 9/18/1886	The James Mason Post [De Soto] of the GAR held a Camp Fire. The following soldiers [company and regiment noted] attended: B. F. Roberts, A, 25th WI and J. Billiard, I, 11th IN, from Victory; J. F. Van Emberg, G, 1st IA Calvary and S. D. Torrey, F, 149th NY and C. Maxwell, B, 27th IA from Lansing; William Witcraft, 10 IL, B. I. Witcraft, I, 42nd WI and George Backus, I, 42nd WI of Romance; Isaac Latimore, B, 75th OH and John Campbell, I, 6th WI and William Davis, C, 19th WI of Ferryville; C. P. Tower, I, 6th WI of Freeman; Gilbert Stewart of Seneca; C. J. Alden of Sparta; R. May, Lt. Col. 8th KY and Col. 7th KY and L L. Tongue, I. 6th WI of Viroqua; M. Minchan, L, 1st Cal. WI of Steamboat Rock; Capt. O. B. Thomas, D, 31st WI of Prairie du Chien and Peter N. Grenum, C, 17th WI of Bristow.
GAR Camp Fire		DC, p3c5, 9/18/1886	"James H. Rogers was the smallest, but livliest, William Davis the tallest and William Witcraft the largest soldier belonging to the James Mason Post."
GAR Installation		DC, p3c5, 1/15/1887	The James MasonPost No. 106 of the GAR in De Soto installed the following as officers: Charles F. Page, William Bates, Z. T. Clark, William M. Green, S. D. Taylor, James Whitney, Le Grand Hickok, J. H. Rogers and Charles S. Fourt.
GAR.		DC, p3c3, 12/31/1887	The Charles Green GAR. Post of Lynxville and Seneca swore in their officers. The officers were W. Pease, S. P. Prince, John Enright, George Newcomb, W. H. H. Black, E. Van Wormer, H. Porter and M. F. Nickerson.
Gadola	B.	DC, p3c4, 7/31/1886	Owned a saloon in Genoa.
Gadola	B.	DC, p3c3, 9/18/1886	B. Gadola sold his house and blacksmith shop in Genoa to Fred Morelli.
Gadola	B.	DC, p2c3, 5/1/1888	Planned to relocate next week with his family from Genoa to Washington Territory.
Gadola	Barney	DC, p3c4, 9/11/1888	Left Genoa last spring. Plans to start a business in Prescott, WI. Gadola is the brother-in-law of Fred Morrelli.
Gage	David	BD, p3c2, 1/17/1879	Died Jan. 2, 1879 in East Richford, VT at the age of 69. He was the father of Mrs. Hiram Favor.
Gaithwait	Ed	BD, p3c2, 6/22/1877	Resided in Woodman. Fined for selling liquor to minors.
Gardner	H.	DR, p3c1, 7/27/1871	He was the leader of the De Soto Coronet Band.
Gardner	H.	DC, p3c2, 4/17/1888	H. Gardner and Frank Riley "manned the ferry, *Potowonok*."
Gardner	H. L.	RH, p5c2, 7/8/1897	Graduated from the Stevens Point Normal this spring. He was a former principal of the Readstown schools.
Gardner	Henry	DR, p3c2, 2/16/1871	Waiting for legislative action to get a charter to operate a ferry in De Soto. Fred Miller of Prairie du Chien is also seeking a charter. Extensive article.
Gardner	Henry	DC, p2c1, 2/3/1888	In 1858-9 an influx of settlers from Maine and Massachusetts arrived in De Soto. Among this party were the Trotts, the Coards, Henry Gardner and Woodbridge Dyer.
Gardner	Henry	DC, p3c3, 5/29/1888	Died in St. Paul on Friday. Resident of De Soto. He and A. H. Wareham tried to board a cable car that failed to stop. Gardner slipped and was hit by the car. Died later that day at St. Joseph's Hospital. H. T. Hare and George Furman of De Soto went to St. Paul to retrieve the body. Mr. Gardner came to De Soto in 1857 and acted as engineer at the mill for years. He built the steamboats, *Comet, J. C. Thompson* and *Ruby*. Survived by wife [daughter of Mr. and Mrs. G. W. Furman] and 3 children [Ruby, Omer and Noel].
Gardner	Henry L.	RH, p5c2, 8/4/1898	Resided in Liberty Pole. He was the Republican candidate for Superintendent of Schools for Vernon Co. Graduated from Stephens Point Normal School. Taught school for 14 years.
Gardner	Omer	DC, p3c4, 7/3/1888	Died Sunday night in De Soto. He would have been 9 years old in October. He was the son of Mrs. Henry Gardner.
Gardner & Wareham		DR, p3c3, 1/26/1871	Henry Gardner and A. H. Wareham operated a ferry called the Comet between De Soto and Lansing. They made 2 trips each day.
Garlick	H. R.	RH, p4c3, 10/31/1901	Died Wednesday of Bright's disease at the home of his brother, Cy Garlick, who lived 2 miles south of Readstown. Garlick was an expert miller and recently leased the Readstown Flouring Mills.
Garner	Rev.	RH, p4c3, 11/8/1900	Resigned the pastorate in Kickapoo because of his poor health.
Garratt	G. H.	BD, p2c8, 1/5/1877	G. H. Garratt & Co.was a tannery, harness and leather store in Boscobel.
Garret	Clint	BD, p3c1, 9/10/1880	"Mr. Clint Garrett, of this city, has the traveling agency for Wisconsin to sell 'The Climax' upright hay knife. He will take orders for the hay knife from dealers, and will be pleased to show the workings of this valuable tool." Garrett resided in Boscobel.

Genealogical Events from Newspapers for Crawford, Vernon and Grant Counties, Wisconsin, 1870-1901

LAST NAME	FIRST NAME	NEWSPAPER, PAGE/COLUMN MONTH/DAY/YEAR	GENEALOGICAL DATA
Garret	George H.	BD, p3c3, 3/3/1882	Died Friday in Boscobel. Born Jan. 31, 1814 in Canton, CT. Started a harness and saddle trade in La Crosse, WI in 1858. Moved to Boscobel in 1872 and partnered with T. R. Seaton in the hardware business. Firm was sold to Ritter & Hubbell in 1874. With his son, he went back into harness business. Wife died "some years ago." She is buried in La Crosse.
Garrett	C. R.	BD, p3c1, 5/4/1883	Called back to Boscobel from Sparta to attend the funeral of his wife's mother, Mrs. E. Yocum.
Garrett	C. R., Mrs.	BD, p3c1, 2/25/1881	Traveled from her home in Boscobel area to visit mother in Sparta.
Garrett	G. H.	BD, p3c1, 12/10/1880	Returned to Boscobel after visiting his mother in Potosi. Mother celebrated her 90th birthday on Sunday.
Garrett	Mary A., Mrs.	BD, p3c2, 3/11/1881	Died in Boscobel on Mar. 3, 1881. Born in Madison Co., NY in 1831. Married T. W. Seaton in 1856 and moved to Potosi, Grant Co., WI. Lived there 13 years. Gave birth to 3 children. One buried in Potosi, others survive. Moved to Boscobel in 1870. Joined Congregational Church when she was 20 years old. She was the sister of ___ Garrett of Boscobel and Mrs. Blackwell of Potosi.
Garrett	Mary B., Mrs.	BD, p3c1, 1/7/1881	Died last Tuesday in Potosi at the residence of son-in-law, E. S. Rockwell. She was also the mother of G. H. Garrett and Mrs. T. R. Seaton, both of Boscobel.
Garrett & Son	G. D.	BD, p2c6, 10/22/1880	Made and sold saddles, harnesses, collars, whips, robes, etc. in Boscobel for the last 4 years. Previously, they ran a hardware business for 4 years.
Garvey	Ed	DC, p3c5, 8/7/1886	Garvey was building a dwelling across from the Catholic Church in Seneca.
Gates	David E.	BD, p3c2, 2/13/1880	George E. Gates married Josephine Storkson on Feb. 4, 1880. Bride and groom were from Fennimore. Otho Shrader, Esq. officiated.
Gates	Mr.	BD, p3c3, 5/25/1883	Resided in Crawford County. Loaded a railroad car with his belongings in Boscobel and departed for a new home in Dakota Territory.
Gates	O. J.	BD, p3c2, 8/23/1878	Resided in Fillmore Co., MN. Returned to Crawford Co. to visit friends and family.
Gay	Cora	DC, p2c2, 2/11/1888	Miss Cora Gays of Gays Mills went to Ft. Howard to visit her sister, Mrs. Loomis.
Gay	Frank E.	RH, p5c4, 11/4/1897	Frank E. Gay married Arilla M. Ely on Oct. 27, 1897 at Avalanch. Bride and groom from La Farge. Joseph Peacock officiated.
Gay	George, Dr.	BD, p3c1, 3/3/1882	Departed Muscoda for his new home in Phillips, a railroad station on the Wisconsin Central.
Geesa	Emma M.	DC, p2c2, 3/10/1888	Emma M. Geesa married George E. Woodhouse on Feb. 28, 1888 at the home of the bride's father, Frederic Geesa of Wheatland. Groom from Genoa.
Geese	Lizzie	DC, p2c2, 10/22/1887	Lizzie Geese married J. Sandlin on Thursday, per the Victory news column.
Genola	Frank, Mr. and Mrs.	DC, p3c3, 4/3/1888	Resided in Genoa. Their infant child recently died.
George	Indian	BD, p3c1, 9/1/1882	Indian George swore out a warrant against Blue Cloud. Blue Cloud accused of stealing $26. George received a note from Blue Cloud for $30. "The Winnebagos are now at peace."
German Lutheran Church		BD, p3c1, 4/4/1879	A confirmation ceremony is scheduled for Sunday in Boscobel at the German Lutheran Church. Rev. Helbig will confirm Caroline Fritz, Hulda Kreul, Lisetta Ruka, Mary Hinn, Hannah Kreul, Alice Christ, Mary Beinborn, Caroline Seeman, Amelia Helbig, Louie Mertz, Leonard Beiderman, Louie Schwab, George Ruka, Daniel Oswald, John Scheinpflug and George Kreul.
Gese	Mrs.	DC, p3c2, 11/20/1886	Resided in the Bad Axe Valley. Injured in a runaway accident.
Getter	Ben	DC, p3c3, 2/11/1888	Received $1108 pension back pay. Served in the 14th Regt. Wisconsin Infantry.
Getter	William	DC, p3c4, 8/28/1886	Getter's home in the Town of Sterling was destroyed by fire on Aug. 13, 1886.
Geurnsey	Jefferson M.	BD, p3c2, 9/13/1878	Jefferson M. Geurnesey married Martha J. Heberlin on Aug. 11, 1878. Bride and groom from Watertown. J. M. Davis of Blue River officiated.
Ghory	Mrs.	RH, p4c3, 5/9/1901	Mrs. Ghory's funeral was held Monday. She was from the La Crosse area but was a former resident of De Soto.
Gibbons	James	BD, p3c3, 8/30/1878	He was an "old blind man from Richland Co." In Boscobel selling subscriptions.
Gibbs	Harry	DC, p3c3, 10/15/1887	Harry Gibbs of Retreat took "French leave" of his parents. He left a letter saying he went to Dubuque.
Gibbs	Harry	DC, p4c2, 3/19/1889	Left Retreat for Verdon, Dakota.

Genealogical Events from Newspapers for Crawford, Vernon and Grant Counties, Wisconsin, 1870-1901

LAST NAME	FIRST NAME	NEWSPAPER, PAGE/COLUMN MONTH/DAY/YEAR	GENEALOGICAL DATA
Gibbs	John	DC, p2c3, 5/1/1888	Severly cut his foot with an ax, per Retreat news column.
Gibbs	Lucy, Mrs.	DC, p3c4, 4/17/1888	Recently died at Watertown, Dakota at the age of 81. Buried Sunday in the Retreat Cemetery. Survived by 4 children: John S. of Retreat, L. D. of North La Crosse, Mrs. Clara Melvin of La Crosse and Mrs. Mary Grosbeck of Watertown, Dakota. Mrs. Gibbs was born Dec. 7, 1806 in Cheshire Co., NH. Married Simeon Gibbs in 1827. Her father was a veteran of the War of 1812. Moved to Retreat in 1859.
Gibbs	Norman	BD, p3c1, 11/4/1881	Resided in Boscobel area. Sold 150 head of sheep for $2.50 each to a party in the Dakotas.
Gibbs	Norman	BD, p3c5, 10/13/1882	Norman Gibbs was the executor of the estate of Hiram Bliss [Buss?], late of Hickory Grove.
Gibbs	S., Mrs.	DC, p2c2, 8/13/1887	Departed Retreat for Watertown, Dakota to live with her daughter, Mrs. Mary Grosbeck.
Gibbs	Simeon	DC, p2c2, 7/30/1887	Died July 25, 1887 at the age of 82. Had a partial stroke 2 years ago. Survived by wife and 4 children -- [L?]indsley of La Crosse, John of Retreat, Mrs. Melvin and Mrs. Grosbeck of Watertown, Dakota. He was one of the earliest settlers in Retreat.
Gibbs	Thomas	BD, p2c4, 5/18/1883	Published a notice that he had given time to his son, William Gibbs of Marion, and that the father was no longer responsible for the son's debts.
Gienk	Charles	BD, p3c3, 7/19/1878	Lost his thumb in a planner at Wauzeka's Prairie du Chien Stave Factory.
Gilbert	William	BD, p3c6, 1/5/1883	Published a notice that he had taken up a cow in the Town of Scott, Crawford Co.
Gilbertson	Bell E.	BD, p3c2, 3/1/1878	O. J. How married Bell E. Gilbertson on Feb. 21, 1878 in Fennimore. Bride from Fennimore. Groom from Nobles Co., MN. The Rev. D. L. Hubbard officiated.
Gilbertson	John	DC, p3c3, 6/26/1886	He was a saloonkeeper in Lansing. Arrested for selling whiskey.
Gill	M. A., Mr. and Mrs.	RH, p4c1, 9/19/1901	Arrived in the area from their current home in Boulder, CO. Originally from Viola. Visited friends on the Kickapoo.
Gillas	Arthur	BD, p3c2, 9/15/1882	Robbed at Roth's Hotel in Woodman.
Gillett	Robert	BD, p2c5, 8/28/1883	A notice to creditors was published. The estate of Robert Gillette, late of Waterstown, was in probate.
Gillett	Thomas	DC, p3c4, 3/27/1888	Thomas Gillett and Charles Johnson of Genoa planned to leave for Washington Territory.
Gillette	Frank	DC, p1c2, 5/10/1889	Will entertain the Literary Society in Genoa with banjo solos.
Gilliam	William	BD, p2c4, 11/26/1880	Grant County paid him a bounty for scalps turned into the county.
Gilman	Byron	BD, p3c1, 1/14/1881	Resided in Fennimore. During a wolf hunt with George Smith, Smith's gun accidently discharged while crossing a creek. The bullet entered Gilman's knee. Gilman may lose the leg.
Gilman	Delia	BD, p3c3, 7/23/1880	Recently married Delia Gilman. Visited Mr. and Mrs. B. W. Coult in Boscobel. Planned to visit Bloomington and then depart for a new home in Steele City, NB.
Gilmore	J. T.	DR, p3c2, 12/14/1871	Proprietor of the American House at Bergen.
Glaiser	Charles J.	BD, p3c1, 7/23/1880	Started a newspaper in Bloomington called *The Record*.
Glass	Aaron	RH, p5c3, 4/14/1898	Glass and his son-in-law, Grant Williams of the Readstown area, went to Bad Ax to hunt wolves.
Glass	Aaron, Mrs.	RH, p5c3, 2/14/1901	Called from her home in Spring Valley to go to the bedside of daughter, Mrs. Grant Williams of Readstown, who is ill with heart trouble.
Glass	George	RH, p4c1, 2/21/1901	Glass' body arrived in Viroqua from Colorado. Killed by falling rock in a mine. He was the brother of Aaron and Thomas of Spring Valley. Funeral at Brookville.
Glass	John	RH, p4c2, 10/10/1901	Lived in Spring Valley. He planned to "start for Alabama soon."
Glass	Rosey	RH, p6c5, 9/2/1897	Benjamin Adams married Rosey Glass at Manning on Aug. 14, 1897. John Benson, J. P. officiated.
Glenn	Edward	BD, p3c2, 5/28/1880	Appointed to be a census enumerator in Wyalusing, Grant Co.
Glick	J. O.	RH, p5c2, 4/12/1900	The infant child of J. O. Glick died last Sunday in Sylvan while going home from church.

Genealogical Events from Newspapers for Crawford, Vernon and Grant Counties, Wisconsin, 1870-1901

LAST NAME	FIRST NAME	NEWSPAPER, PAGE/COLUMN MONTH/DAY/YEAR	GENEALOGICAL DATA
Glodery	A.	DR, p3c2, 12/29/1870	Sold dry goods, groceries, boots, shoes, hats, caps, etc. at his store in De Soto.
Glodery	Andrew	DR, p3c1, 9/14/1871	Sold his store and lot in De Soto to William Waldron. Planned to move to Iowa.
Glynn	P.	BD, p3c1, 4/27/1883	Chairman of the Woodman Town Board.
Gobin	Al	BD, p3c4, 8/4/1882	Lost a horse race to Will Harrington in Excelsior.
Gochenauer	Rufus	RH, p4c2, 9/20/1900	Resided in Sylvan. Passed through Readstown with a herd of registered Galloway cattle enroute to the Vernon Co. Fair.
Gochnour	H.	DC, p3c5, 6/19/1886	Dentist in Viroqua. Advertised monthly visits to De Soto to see patients.
Godfrey	M.	DR, p3c1, 3/30/1871	M. Godfrey, John Thompson, Willis Hickok and Thomas Peacock of Lansing returned home after spending the winter working in the pineries.
Godfrey	Mr.	DC, p1c2, 8/2/1889	Lived in Lansing. Visited sister, Mrs. C. P. White of Stoddard.
Godfrey	Vinnie	DC, p2c2, 10/2/1888	Vinnie Godfrey married Charles P. White Wednesday evening. Bride daughter of Mr. and Mrs. M. Godfrey of S. Lansing. Groom from Stoddard. Rev. Hutchenson officiated.
Godfrey	Will	DC, p3c3, 6/12/1886	Resided in Lansing, IA. His body was recently found. Drowned off the steamboat, *Ten Broeck* near Alma. He was a mate on the boat.
Godola	B.	DC, p2c2, 3/10/1888	Planned to leave Genoa for Washington Territory very soon.
Goehde	Herman	DC, p2c2, 10/1/1887	Killed by the cars [railroad] near Sparta on the 22nd. Survived by wife and 4 children in Liberty Pole.
Gokey	Ed	DC, p3c3, 1/1/1889	The Ed Gokey family moved to Trempealeau Co, WI where they rented a farm, per De Soto news.
Golden	George	DC, p3c2, 6/19/1886	Martha Arneson married George Golden on June 15, 1886. Bride from Sterling. Groom from Baraboo. Justice M. Loftus officiated.
Goman	Minnie, Miss	DC, p3c4, 7/31/1886	Returned to Genoa from Dakota.
Good Templar Lodge		DC, p3c4, 2/5/1889	The De Soto Good Templar Lodge elected the following as officers: W. H. Lewis, Ellen J. Lawrence, Cora Cooper, Mary Smith, C. W. Green, Mrs. W. K. Lowrie, W. M. Kalhar, Katie Haughton, Lyman Smith and H. H. Furman.
Goode	Richard	RH, p4c1, 9/20/1900	Richard Goode married Maude Dearman on Sept. 18, 1900. Groom from Manning. Bride from Readstown. Justice Benson officiated.
Goodridge	George	RH, p5c2, 7/15/1897	Recently gored to death by a bull in Platteville. Eighteen years ago, his brother-in-law, Elijah Bailey was killed in the same manner in the same place.
Goodvillage	George	BD, p3c2, 2/23/1883	George Goodvillage and troupe from "the Kickapoo" entertained at City Hall in Boscobel.
Gorden	C. B.	RH, p5c4, 3/16/1899	Recently died of heart failure in De Soto. Survived by wife, 3 sons and 1 daughter.
Gorder	C.	DC, p2c3, 2/26/1887	Planned to open a new drug store in De Soto in a portion of the J. M. Dunlevy building. Worked in a drug store in La Crosse.
Gorder	C.	DC, p3c3, 3/12/1887	Has decided to not open a drug store in De Soto.
Gorder	C. A.	DC, p3c3, 5/14/1887	Resided in Lansing. Visited De Soto before departing for Kansas.
Gorder	O. M.	DC, p3c4, 5/28/1887	Resigned as station agent in De Soto as it was "too much work for one man." E. B. Sperry of Genoa succeeded him.
Gorder	O. M.	DC, p3c3, 8/27/1887	Lived in the De Soto area. Presently working for the St. Paul & Duluth Railroad as a bill clerk in Cloquet, MN.
Gordon	C. E.	DC, p3c1, 11/26/1887	Resided in Waukon, IA. Purchased the J. E. McCrillis farms.
Gordon	Mrs.	DC, p2c1, 7/10/1888	At a Fourth of July celebration in Retreat, Mrs. Gordon exhibited a powder horn carried by John Rogers in the Revolutionary War and by his son in the War of 1812. Mrs. Gordon is a great-granddaughter of the original owner.
Gordon	Rev.	DC, p2c3, 10/9/1888	Resided at Rush Creek. Subscribed to the newspaper.
Gorman	Len	DC, p3c3, 1/8/1887	Len Gorman and Barney Gadola filled their icehouse in Genoa.
Gornan	Damace	BD, p2c4, 4/13/1877	Damace Gornan advertised house, sign and carriage painting services in Boscobel.

Genealogical Events from Newspapers for Crawford, Vernon and Grant Counties, Wisconsin, 1870-1901

LAST NAME	FIRST NAME	NEWSPAPER, PAGE/COLUMN MONTH/DAY/YEAR	GENEALOGICAL DATA
Gorsline	Alex	DR, p3c3, 12/21/1871	Badly hurt last week while working with a threshing machine on the farm of Ananias Smith outside Viroqua. He caught a knuckle and the skin was torn off his shoulder and the muscles wrenched very badly. Treated by Drs. Tinker and Chase. Will probably recover.
Gorsline	Asher	DC, p3c4, 5/21/1887	The Asher Gorsline family of Franklin took a train for Salem, OR.
Gorsline	Asher, Mrs.	DC, p3c5, 2/18/1888	Died Sunday night in Franklin. She was the daughter of Milton Southwick.
Gorsline	Will P.	DC, p2c2, 1/1/1887	Dora B. Pollard married Will P. Gorsline on Dec. 25, 1886 in Viroqua.
Gosling	H. C.	DC, p2c2, 8/7/1886	Will probably run for Sheriff in Vernon Co.
Gosling	Henry C.	DC, p2c1, 10/23/1886	Moved to Vernon Co. in 1852. Served in the 19th WI Vol. Lived in the Town of Franklin. Planned to run for office.
Gosling	John	RH, p5c5, 8/12/1897	Band teacher and tuba player. Lived in Viroqua.
Gosling	Sheriff	DC, p3c3, 3/27/1888	Sheriff Gosling, assisted by Thomas Mills and John Gosling, relocated 12 chronically insane people from Mendota to La Crosse where they will remain until the Vernon Co. asylum is completed. The following people were relocated: Anna O____son, Caroline Eerickson, John [Dasen?], Alice Bixton/Baxton, Hannah J. Davis, Henry Fitch, Mrs. Elizabeth Pol___d, T___ Tokkleson, Aurelia Gussetti, William Salie, George Partridge and Ole Selton.
Gott	Florence	DC, p3c2, 9/4/1888	Hired to teach at Crandon, Forrest Co., WI.
Gott	Florence M., Miss	DC, p3c3, 8/21/1886	Named teacher at the De Soto Union School. Resided in Viroqua.
Gott	L. R., Mrs.	DC, p2c2, 11/20/1886	Resided in Viroqua. Wrote weekly columns on the W.C.T.U. [Women's Christian Temperance Union] activities, plans and opinions.
Gott	Lydia R., Mrs.	DC, p3c4, 7/24/1886	She was the president of the Women's Christian Temperance Union in Viroqua. She organized a chapter with 29 members at the Methodist Church in Retreat. The officers were Mrs. S. J. Dustan, Mrs. M. J. Joran, Mrs. T. Scriffin, Miss Hattie Mellen and Mrs. D. P. Smith.
Gotting	Aug.	DC, p2c2, 3/19/1887	Died Feb. 26, 1887 of stomach cancer. He was a harness maker in Chaseburgh for the last 2 years.
Gould	Jay, Mrs.	DC, p3c3, 1/22/1889	Died Jan. 13, 1889 at her home, per De Soto news column.
Gould	Joseph	DC, p3c4, 2/18/1888	Early settler of De Soto. Current resident of Genoa.
Gould	Lizzie	DC, p2c2, 6/11/1887	May Devorce, Anna Schubert and Lizzie Gould graduated from Mound Ridge school this spring and passed the teacher examination.
Gould	Orange	BD, p3c1, 2/25/1881	Orange Gould married Tena Swiber on Tuesday in Boscobel. The Rev. T. M. Evans officiated.
Gould	Orange, Mrs.	BD, p3c1, 6/1/1883	Died May 27, 1883 during childbirth at 20 years of age. She was the eldest daughter of Mrs. Kate Schreiber of the Boscobel area.
Gould	S. J.	BD, p2c3, 5/26/1882	Served in the 6th WI Battery. Killed at New Madrid on April 26, 1862.
Gould	T. R.	BD, p3c1, 6/29/1883	Published a notice that a pocket book with valuable papers was lost between Boscobel and Wheatville.
Gould	T. Robert	BD, p3c1, 12/4/1883	T. Robert Gould married Lizzie Hughbanks on Thanksgiving Day in Boscobel. Bride from Boscobel. Groom from Whitewater. The Rev. T. W. Cole officiated.
Govier	John	BD, p2c4, 11/26/1880	Grant County paid him a bounty for scalps turned into the county.
Goyer	J., Dr.	RH, p2c1, 7/1/1897	Sold groceries, drugs and medicine at his store in Readstown.
Goyer	Joseph, Mrs.	RH, p4c2, 11/11/1897	Departed home in Readstown to visit brother, N. C. Bradley of Excelsior.
Goyer	Nettie	RH, p5c2, 1/27/1898	Published and copyrighted a piece of instrumental music titled "Thoughts of Springtime." Resided in Readstown.
Goyer	Nettie	RH, p3c2, 1/5/1899	Returned to Platteville from her home in Readstown to resume her studies in music.

Genealogical Events from Newspapers for Crawford, Vernon and Grant Counties, Wisconsin, 1870-1901

LAST NAME	FIRST NAME	NEWSPAPER, PAGE/COLUMN MONTH/DAY/YEAR	GENEALOGICAL DATA
Graduates		DC, p4c3, 3/12/1889	On March 8, 1889 graduates from Retreat and nearby school districts gathered at the Congregational Church. Lucinda Ames, Nellie Davis, Alice Cooley and Westley Bates graduated from Retreat No. 2 District school [Louise Bartholomew, teacher]. Olive Sterling, Kittie Bates and Lu Lombard graduated from Bishop Joint Dist. No. 5 school [Mary Rutter, teacher]. Josie E. De Lacy and Ella Eastman graduated from Cooley Valley Joint Dist. No. 5 school [Geo. F. Seymour, teacher]. Leo McClurg graduated from WestPrairie school [Wm. A. Morgan, teacher]. Emma E. Andrews graduated from Dist. No. 6 Sterling school [Ella Cooley, teacher].
Graduates		KC, Supp., 12/20/1900	Common school graduates of 1900: Town of Utica - Otto McCormick, Dora Hoffland, Mary Melvin, Florence Mitchell, Henry Tompson; Town of Seneca - Leona Lawrence, Sybil Noggle, Raleigh Leasle, Williette Mansfield, Dwight Randall, Dolly Randall, Henry Hand, Albert Hazen, Charles E. Scoville, Allie Peterson, Hannah Joy, Josie Mullany, Maggie Meagher, Mamie McNamara, Olive Thompson, Delia McNamara; Town of Clayton - Nina Rutter, Pearl Miller, Willie Bowe, Amelia Flynn, Maggy Mahony, Ethyl Mullikin.
Graduates		KC, Supp., 12/20/1900	Common school graduates of 1900: Town of Marietta - Pearl Rands, Roy Wood, Herbert Main, Gracie Christ, Nellie Chilson, Mattie Niland, Minnie Panders; Town of Freeman - Mary Thompson, Emma Felde, Stella Henderson, Mabel Campbell, Lulu Sterling, Dora Tonkfort, Eva Lyn Finley, Willie Finley; Town of Eastman - Michael Lenahan.
Graduates		KC, Supp., 12/20/1900	Common school graduates of 1900: Town of Haney - Frances Jenkins, Cora Vanhorn, Mabel McDaniel, Maud Sterns, Harvey Jenkins, Mammie Crowley, Fanny Dowling, Eva Peck, Jennie M. Lance; Town of Scott - Leta Byers, Jennie Brown, Donnie Greene; Town of Bridgeport - Ros Burrell, Albert Steinback.
Graduates		KC, Supp., 12/20/1900	Graded school graduates of 1900: Bell Center - Margie Rounds, Edith Whiteaker; Mount Sterling - Blanche Bennett, Bessie Clement, Bessie Briggs; Seneca - Willie A. Garvey, Archie W. Porter; Gays Mills - Leora Randall; Lynxville - Cora Copsey, Mary Davidson, Claudine Allen, Allie Bright; Eastman - Nellie J. Iverson; Ferryville - Olive Hutson, Grace Campbell.
Graduates		KC, Supp., 12/20/1900	High school graduates of 1900: Prairie du Chien - Lulu M. Chase, Caroline C. Griesbach, Nettie W. Martner, John F. McDonald, Harriet Wallin; Soldiers Grove - Ella Johnson, Mathias Monson, Frank Gander, Kneute Johnson, George Sampson
Graham	Carson	DR, p3c5, 5/18/1871	Worked as an attorney in Viroqua.
Graham	Charles	BD, p3c1, 10/15/1880	Charles Graham married Emma S. Mathews on Oct. 6, 1880 in Boscobel. Bride and groom from Mt. Ida.
Graham	Esther	BD, p3c1, 11/17/1882	Lew Alford married Esther Graham on Nov. 11, 1882 at the residence of Mr. A. McKinney in Boscobel. Groom from Madison. Bride from Boscobel. J. McLaughlin, Justice of the Peace, officiated.
Graham	Fred W.	DC, p2c3, 2/12/1887	Fred W. Graham married Belinda Johnson on Feb. 7, 1887. Groom from Houston Co., MN. Bride from Fillmore Co., MN. D. A. Steele, J.P., officiated at ceremony in De Soto.
Graham	T. J.	BD, p3c2, 6/29/1883	Departed Muscoda with a trainload of cattle. Headed for Montana.
Graham	T. J.	BD, p3c4, 9/11/1883	A Dissolution of Partnership notice was published for T. J. Graham and Jacob Bremmer of Muscoda.
Graiser	Tressa	BD, p3c1, 2/24/1882	A 50-pound tumor was removed from the breast of Tressa Graiser. Lived with her father near Fennimore. Died on Wednesday.
Grandstaff	Andrew	DC, p3c3, 6/5/1888	Arrested by a Pinkerton detective at the Jennings house in the Town of Liberty for the murder of the Reuben Drake family. He was lynched in Viroqua. Grandstaff was an illegitimate child. Father said to be a brother of the last murderer Vernon Co. sent to Waupon. He was 24 years old.
Grant	Nick	BD, p2c3, 7/28/1882	Nick Grant and family were residents of Mt. Sterling. Took rooms in Central House, Prairie du Chien to bid farewell to friends before departure for their new home in Dakota.
Grant	T. P.	DR, p4c2, 12/15/1870	Dealor in stoves, hardware, tinware, etc. in Lansing, IA.
Grass	H. C.	DC, p1c1, 7/26/1889	H. C. Grass married Alice Cooper on Wednesday, July 24, 1889 at the residence of the bride's mother in De Soto. Groom was a lawyer in Curry, MN. Bride taught school. The Rev. William Haughton officiated.
Graves	A.	BD, p3c1, 9/4/1883	Lost half of the barn roof in a storm on his farm located 6 miles north of Boscobel.
Graves	A. K.	BD, p2c3, 11/24/1882	A. K. Graves married Sallie Beach on Nov. 16, 1882. Bride and groom were from Prairie du Chien. Bride was the daughter of the Hon. H. Beach. Rev. A. McMaster officiated.
Graves	Ransom	BD, p3c2, 1/27/1882	About 80 years old. Near death at his home in Crawford Co. Former Superintendent of the Poor Farm in Grant Co. [25 years ago].

Genealogical Events from Newspapers for Crawford, Vernon and Grant Counties, Wisconsin, 1870-1901

LAST NAME	FIRST NAME	NEWSPAPER, PAGE/COLUMN MONTH/DAY/YEAR	GENEALOGICAL DATA
Gray	John	BD, p3c4, 12/28/1877	John Gray married Mattic Provin on Tuesday at the Methodist Episcopal parsonage. Groom from Boscobel. Bride from Belle Center. The Rev. G. W. Nuzum officiated.
Grazer	Susan	BD, p3c2, 2/21/1879	Susan Grazer married Mr. Brickler Thursday morning. Bride from Town of Fennimore. She was the daughter of Karel Grazer. Groom from Town of Marion.
Green	Clarence	RH, p5c4, 1/19/1899	Left De Soto for a new home in Plaine, MT where he had "secured a position."
Green	Cora A.	DR, p3c2, 1/4/1872	Charles E. Reiter married Cora A. Green on Jan. 1, 1872 at the residence of William Green in the Town of Freeman. Bride and groom were from the Town of Freeman. The Rev. D. L. Hubbard officiated.
Green	Daniel	BD, p3c2, 5/11/1883	Daniel Green married Jennie Seaton on May 8, 1883 at the residence of Mrs. Beebee in Boscobel. Bride from Boscobel. Groom from Potosi. The Rev. James Havens officiated.
Green	Emma E.	DC, p3c4, 8/28/1886	Richard Folie married Emma E. Green on Aug. 23, 1886 at the residence of the bride's parents in De Soto. Charles E. Woodbury, J.P., officiated. [See p3c3, 9/18/1886. Folie's real name was Dick Bennett. He was a married man from Genoa.]
Green	Lintner W.	BD, p3c1, 8/26/1881	Lintner W. Green married Rena Steele on Aug. 24, 1881 in Boscobel. Bride and groom from Scott, Crawford Co. The Rev. T. W. Evans officiated.
Green	Lorenzo	RH, p4c4, 4/27/1899	Died Tuesday in De Soto. Funeral held at the Methodist Episcopal Church.
Green	Lydia	RH, p4c3, 12/16/1897	Lydia Green married F. D. Woodcock at the residence of the bride's family. The marriage took place about 3 miles north of Readstown. C. W. Reeve officiated at the ceremony.
Green	Milton B.	BD, p3c1, 10/3/1879	Milton B. Green married Fanny C. Hubbard last Friday at the residence of Dr. William Stoddart in Boscobel. Bride from Fennimore.
Green	Nellie	DC, p3c3, 10/9/1886	Elected Secretary of the Lyceum in De Soto.
Green	Nellie	DC, p2c2, 5/7/1887	Native of the De Soto area. Taught school in the Howarth District.
Green	Nellie B.	DC, p3c2, 7/3/1886	Native of De Soto. Taught school in Sunnyside.
Green	Nellie B.	DC, p3c4, 8/27/1887	Hired to teach at Red Mound.
Green	Tompkins	DC, p1c6, 11/5/1887	Recently qualified for a pension [for his military service]. Resided in Boscobel.
Greene	L.	DC, p3c4, 3/20/1888	The L. Greene family tired of life in St. Paul and returned to their old home in De Soto.
Greenman	John W.	DC, p2c2, 11/27/1888	Former Treasurer in Vernon Co. Current resident of Salt Lake City. He was the brother of Mrs. Legrand Hickok of De Soto and Mrs. M. Monti of Genoa.
Gribble	Mary, Mrs.	RH, p5c3, 9/6/1900	Celebrated her 50th birthday last Tuesday. Lived in Kickapoo.
Griest	Lou, Miss	DC, p2c2, 10/8/1887	Returned to her home in Iowa. Spent most of the summer with sister, Mrs. Marston of Seneca.
Griest	Lucy, Miss	DC, p3c4, 1/15/1887	Resided in Clayton, IA. Visited her sister, Mrs. W. Marsten, per the Seneca news column.
Griffin	boy	DC, p3c3, 7/31/1888	A son was born Wednesday to Claud Griffon of Victory.
Griffin	Charley	RH, p5c4, 12/1/1898	Charley and May Griffin returned to Kickapoo after spending the summer working in Iowa.
Griffin	Claud	DC, p3c3, 3/19/1887	Bound over to appear in Circuit Court.
Griffin	Claud	DC, p2c1, 5/7/1887	Claud Griffin married Florence Ferguson on May 1, 1887. Bride and groom from Victory. Alex. Latshaw, J.P., of Victory officiated at the ceremony.
Griffin	George P.	DC, p2c2, 5/28/1887	Family departed for Clark Co. per Victory news column.
Griffin	Lydia, Mrs.	DR, p3c2, 3/9/1871	Died Feb. 26, 1871 in the Town of Genoa from consumption. She was 44 years old.
Griffin	May	RH, p5c4, 4/13/1899	May Griffin and Eva Downey, both of Kickapoo, went to Iowa for work. Planned to return.
Griffin	May	RH, p4c1, 12/28/1899	Guy Hopkins married May Griffin on Monday at the home of the bride's parents in Kickapoo. Groom from Viola.
Griffin	Samuel L.	DR, p3c5, 6/29/1871	Letters of administration were granted to Thomas D. Waller to handle the estate of Samuel L. Griffin, late of Vernon Co.
Griffis	John	BD, p3c3, 12/3/1880	The John Griffis family was severely injured when their team ran away while descending a hill. They were from Lower Grant.

Genealogical Events from Newspapers for Crawford, Vernon and Grant Counties, Wisconsin, 1870-1901

LAST NAME	FIRST NAME	NEWSPAPER, PAGE/COLUMN MONTH/DAY/YEAR	GENEALOGICAL DATA
Grimm	J. W.	RH, p5c2, 7/21/1898	Stock holder in the Sylvan Creamery.
Griswold	Walter H.	BD, p3c1, 1/7/1881	Walter H. Griswold married Mrs. Sarah A. Rogers on Dec. 30, 1880 in Boscobel at the Central House. Bride and groom from Chicago.
Grocery House		BD, p2c3, 10/22/1880	T. R. Seaton opened this business a few months ago.
Groom	George	BD, p3c2, 7/1/1881	Sentenced to 3 years at Waupon for manslaugher in the death of Vivian Groom of Grant Co.
Groom	Mary Jane	BD, p3c2, 9/27/1878	Mary Jane Groom married John Lyman Curtis on Sept. 25, 1878 at the home of the bride's parents in Marion. Groom from Fond du Lac Co. Rev. Dr. William Stoddart officiated.
Gross	Mary	DC, p3c3, 11/20/1888	Mary Gross recently married Arthur B. Baldwin. Bride and groom from Dubuque. Bride was a former resident of De Soto. Groom was freight conductor for the C. M. & St. Paul Railroad.
Grote	Anna	BD, p3c4, 5/18/1877	Died Sunday at the age of 14 in the Muscoda area. He suffered for years from a tapeworm.
Groves	Jno. S., Mrs.	DC, p2c4, 1/29/1887	Received a pension of $1859 for a son who died in the army. Resided in Viroqua.
Groves	John H.	DC, p3c3, 3/3/1888	Returned to home in Liberty. Spent nearly a year in Inkesty, Dakota.
Groves	Mrs.	RH, p7c2, 7/1/1897	Lived in Ross. Visited parents, Mr. and Mrs. Wilkinson of Readstown.
Groves	Will	RH, p4c1, 8/22/1901	Resided in Marietta. Visited parents, Mr. and Mrs. F. M. Groves of Readstown.
Gruber	Eva, Miss	DC, p3c5, 8/7/1886	Arrived in Cooley Valley from Minnneapolis for a short visit.
Gudhertz	Lizzie	BD, p2c4, 4/6/1883	The Grant County Circuit Court published a summons in the case, Lizzie Gudhertz [plaintiff] vs. John Gudhertz [defendant].
Guentzel	G.	BD, p2c7, 10/22/1880	Made saddles, harnesses and whips from boyhood, nearly 40 years. For the last 23 years he sold his goods in Boscobel.
Guist	girl	RH, p4c1, 4/12/1900	A daughter was born on April 9, 1900 to George Guist of Manning.
Guist	girl	RH, p4c3, 11/14/1901	A daughter was recently born to Sherman Guist of Pleasant Valley.
Guist	Mary	RH, p4c3, 3/9/1899	David B. Barrie married Mary Guist on Feb. 23, 1899 at the residence of John Tate, Esquire. Bride and groom from Kickapoo.
Guist	William	RH, p4c2, 9/6/1900	Returned to Readstown from Delevan, SD where he worked during the summer months.
Gullord	P. C.	DC, p2c2, 6/4/1887	The 3-year-old son of P. C. Gullord recently died of diphtheria in Chaseburgh. The 6-year-old daughter was sick, too, as was the father.
Gunderson	Emil	DC, p3c3, 3/10/1888	Squire McMichael recently sentence 4 young men [aged 16-18] from Genoa for carrying concealed weapons. Abram Morr was sentenced to 30 days of hard labor. Harry Spauling sentenced to 20 days of hard labor. Eli Barrett sentenced to the Industrial School at Waukesha. Emil Gunderson paid a fine.
Gunerus	Arne	RH, p4c2, 8/31/1899	Arrived from Fargo, ND to visit with old friends in Readstown. Former Readstown resident. Left when Dakota opened for settlement. Owns a 1/2 section beside the City of Fargo.
Guntzel	G.	BD, p2c8, 1/5/1877	Operated a harness services shop in Boscobel. Shop established in 1857.
Gupth	James	BD, p3c2, 9/7/1877	James Gupth married Isabella Cowan last Thursday in Boscobel. Bride was the daughter of George W. Cowan. The Rev. Dr. Stoddart officiated.
Guptill	Belle, Mrs.	DC, p2c2, 3/12/1887	Resided in Boscobel. Visited with Mrs. S. Haines of Seneca before departing for a new home in Fargo, Dakota.
Gurnsey	Jeff	BD, p3c1, 10/24/1879	Lost an index finger to a thresher at a farm near Sanders Creek.
Gussetti	Ben	DC, p3c4, 11/27/1886	Ben Gussetti recently married Ella Riley per the Genoa news column.
Gussetti	Ben	DC, p2c3, 11/26/1887	Ben Gussetti and family of Genoa went to Little Falls, MN to spend the winter.
Gussetti	Emma, Miss	DC, p1c2, 6/21/1889	Found dead in her bed on Monday in Genoa. She was the sister of Lewis Gussetti.
Gussetti	girl	DC, p2c2, 7/23/1887	A daughter was recently born to Ben Gussetti of Genoa.
Gustison	Gustie T.	DC, p3c2, 12/25/1888	Published a notice that he took up a stray steer in Ferryville.

Genealogical Events from Newspapers for Crawford, Vernon and Grant Counties, Wisconsin, 1870-1901

LAST NAME	FIRST NAME	NEWSPAPER, PAGE/COLUMN MONTH/DAY/YEAR	GENEALOGICAL DATA
Guthrie	John C.	BD, p2c4, 11/26/1880	Grant County paid him a bounty for scalps turned into the county.
Hackett		DR, p3c1, 10/19/1871	The 11-year-old daughter of widow Hackett died last Thursday on the highway crossing of Sugar Creek between the farms of Mr. Shea and Mr. Ralph Copper, Town of Freeman. Mrs. Hackett was returning home by wagon in the dark from Ferryville. The wagon ran off the bank and into the creek. The child was caught under a seat and drowned.
Hackney	Harry	BD, p3c1, 12/18/1883	Lived in Hunie, MO. Ten years ago he left Boscobel as a newly fledged lawyer. He later became a minister for the Methodist Episcopal Church.
Hackney	Mrs.	BD, p3c4, 8/29/1879	Mrs. Hackney [nee Hattie Muffley] arrived in Boscobel with her child to visit her father, J. R. Muffley. Mrs. Hackney lived in Merrillan.
Hadley	Orlando	RH, p4c3, 6/7/1900	Died Friday of suicide. Slit his throat with a jackknife. He was a 35-year-old farmer. Lived with George W. Burlin on a farm 5 miles northeast of Viola. Hadley's sister, Mrs. Geddes, found the body.
Haigh	George, Rev.	BD, p2c1, 10/11/1878	Named as new pastor of the Boscobel Methodist Episcopal Church. Replaced the Rev. George Nuzum.
Haigh	George, Rev.	BD, p3c3, 1/3/1879	Resigned as pastor of the Methodist Episcopal Church in Boscobel. Planned to become a Congregationalist. Haigh agreed to preach at Congregational churches in Avoca and Muscoda.
Haigh	George, Rev.	BD, p3c2, 1/10/1879	Departed with his family for a new home in Muscoda.
Haines	Walter H.	BD, p2c2, 12/9/1881	Walter H. Haines, formerly of Lancaster, was buried next to his mother. His mother died a few years ago. The body came from Delevan, where he worked with his father in a mercantile business. The remains were brought to the house of Mrs. J. O. Bartlett for prayer before burial.
Hainsworth	Daniel	DC, p2c2, 2/25/1888	Died Feb. 15, 1888 at Bergen.
Hainsworth	John	DC, p2c2, 6/18/1887	John Hainsworth and Joe Franzini found a grindstone quarry 1 mile above Genoa. John purchased a turning lathe and "has received orders for building stone."
Halderson	Albert	DC, p2c1, 4/30/1887	Albert Halderson married Rose Caswell last Sunday in Genoa.
Hale	Benjamin Daniel	RH, p4c2, 11/1/1900	He was the oldest settler in Readstown. Born in Ohio in 1814. Came to Wisconsin with his parents when he was a young man. Moved to Liberty Pole to farm. In 1852 moved to Readstown and built a flouring mill, the first in this section of the country. Farmers came from 50 miles around to use the mill. He was called "Uncle Dan" by everyone. He was a bachelor. His bride-to-be died when he was engaged at an early time. Survived by brother, N. D. Hale. Buried in Readstown Cemetery.
Hale	Charles	RH, p4c3, 9/21/1899	Charles Hale and family of Brownsville, IN planned to move to Readstown. He was the son of N. D. Hale.
Hale	Edwin	RH, p3c2, 2/15/1900	Married 19 years. Father of a new 10-pound boy. Passed out cigars all over Readstown.
Hale	Guy	RH, p4c2, 6/14/1900	Died June 14, 1900 after suffering 3 weeks with peretonitis. He was the youngest son of N. D. Hale.
Hale	Guy	RH, p4c3, 6/21/1900	Died June 14, 1900 of peretonitis. He was 9 years old, the youngest son of N. D. Hale. Since the death of his mother, he has been the constant companion of his Uncle Daniel Hale, now over 80 years of age. Buried in Readstown Cemetery.
Hale	John	BD, p2c2, 5/10/1878	Departed his home in Bloomington on April 29th to visit his former home in England and to attend the Paris Exposition.
Hale	John W.	BD, p3c2, 12/23/1881	John W. Hale married Elizabeth Wetmore at the Betts House in Boscobel on Dec. 21, 1881. Bride and groom from Little Grant. The Rev. E. L. Morse officiated.
Hale	Leona	RH, p4c3, 12/7/1899	Luther Salmon married Leona Hale on Dec. 4, 1899 at the home of the bride's parents in Readstown. Groom from Soldiers Grove. Planned to live in Soldiers Grove.
Hall	Ella	RH, p4c2, 5/9/1901	Ella Hall married Louis Larson on April 26, 1901 at the home of her father, John Hall of near Readstown. Bride and groom from Town of Kickapoo. Justice Davenport officiated.
Hall	Jennie, Mrs.	DC, p8c2, 7/26/1889	Mrs. Jennie Hall of California and Miss Eva Hall of Iowa visited their cousin, Mrs. Byron Lane of De Soto.
Hall	Jerome B.	DC, p3c4, 12/31/1887	Mary E. Joseph married Jerome B. Hall on Christmas Day 1887 at the residence of the bride's parents near De Soto. Groom from Alma Center, WI. The Rev. Thomas Crouch officiated.
Hall	John	RH, p5c3, 10/25/1900	Pathmaster in Spring Valley. Put in 2 new bridges last week.
Hall	John	RH, p5c4, 7/11/1901	Served as pathmaster in Spring Valley.
Hall	John, Mrs.	RH, p4c4, 10/28/1897	Left her Spring Green home to visit her daughter, Mrs. Will Drake of Barnum.

Genealogical Events from Newspapers for Crawford, Vernon and Grant Counties, Wisconsin, 1870-1901

LAST NAME	FIRST NAME	NEWSPAPER, PAGE/COLUMN MONTH/DAY/YEAR	GENEALOGICAL DATA
Halverson	Edward	RH, p5c4, 11/4/1897	Edward Halverson married Betsy Berg on Oct. 14, 1897 in Viroqua. Bride from Viroqua. Groom from Ferryville.
Halverson	Ole	RH, p4c3, 12/9/1897	Resident of Inkster, ND. He was shot on Nov. 27, 1897 by his "sweetheart" at the store where he worked as a clerk. Lived for 36 hours and then died. The girlfriend intended to kill herself. Halverson exonerated her of blame, nonetheless; she was arrested. Halverson was a cousin of H. J. Wamberg of the Park Hotel. Buried in Soldiers Grove.
Hamblin	George	BD, p2c3, 5/26/1882	Served in 11th IL Regt. during Civil War. He died early during the first day's battle at Pittsburg Landing on April 6, 1862. He was the son of Charles Hamblin of Richland Center.
Hamilton	Henry	BD, p3c1, 1/26/1883	Resided in Seneca. Called one of the largest stock raisers in Crawford Co. Recently purchased the stallion, Norman George, from L. Hammerly.
Hamilton	J. A.	BD, p3c1, 10/1/1880	Lived near Prairie du Bay. Recently found alone and sick and insensible. Removed to home of friends where he died Monday night.
Hamilton	John	BD, p3c2, 9/9/1881	John Hamilton and Charles McKinney were charged with burglary and assault with intent to kill in Crawford Co. Now case to be heard in the Grant Co. Circuit Court.
Hamilton	Mrs.	BD, p3c1, 2/9/1883	Recently died in Prairie du Chien. Former resident of Boscobel. Buried in Boscobel.
Hamilton	William	BD, p3c2, 12/31/1880	Worked as a freight train conductor. Died last Friday. He slipped while coupling cars and was run over. Wife was from Prairie du Chien. Funeral held at Milton.
Hamilton & Cole		BD, p2c5, 1/5/1877	Ran a dry goods store in Boscobel.
Hamilton & Cole		BD, p3c3, 2/2/1877	The Hamilton & Cole dry goods store in Boscobel announced the failure of the firm.
Hamilton & Cole		BD, p3c2, 4/13/1877	The "late firm" of Hamilton & Cole left on a train Tuesday for Michigan. They went out of business.
Hammer	George	DC, p3c5, 9/4/1886	Lavinia Fourt recently married George Hammer at the home of John Valentine, the bride's uncle. Bride was formerly from Retreat. Groom from Battle Lake, MN.
Hammond	Abner	BD, p3c3, 4/14/1882	He was a "horse thief, robber and jail breaker." Arrested again for horse stealing.
Hammond	Abner	BD, p3c3, 2/8/1878	Abner [or Avenor?] Hammond charged with burglary. Caught first by Charles Bennett of Lancaster. He escaped. Caught again by Messrs. Churchill and Brooks. Worked for Peter Hanson in Dubuque by peddling apples. Caught in Seelyberg by Bob Parker and Henry Wyant. Claimed Charles Bennett of Lancaster offered to split $200 of the stolen money with him for his silence. After Hammond escaped and was recaptured, Bennett helped him escape again. John Kintzinger, a brother-in-law of Peter Hanson, helped to negotiate terms with Bennett. Additional affadivits were published p2c2, 3/29/1878. Charles Bennett's testimony was published p2c3, 3/15/1878.
Hammond	G. S.	BD, p2c7, 10/22/1880	Advertised that he had taken up a colt on his land in the Town of Liberty Grove.
Hammond	Montraville, Mr.	BD, p3c2, 5/16/1879	Died May 9, 1879 in Watterstown. Born August 20, 1839 in Cataragus Co., NY. As a child he moved with his parents to Illinois. Joined Co. B, 33rd Regt. WI Volunteers during the war. Returned to Boscobel at close of war. Married Emma, daughter of Jacob Scott on March 4, 1866 in Boscobel. Survived by wife and 4 small children.
Hammond	Montreville, Mr.	BD, p3c5, 9/7/1879	Jacob Scott petitioned the Probate Court in Grant County to administer the estate of Montreville Hammond.
Hammond	Mrs.	RH, p5c5, 7/29/1897	Arrived from Dubuque to visit relatives in the Ross area. She was accompanied by her father, G. W. Wise and brother, Lute.
Hammond	William N.	BD, p3c1, 7/16/1880	William Hammond of Grant Co. recently married Minerva Ricks of Grant Co. at the residence of John Ricks in Boscobel. The Rev. W. W. Hurd officiated.
Hancock	G. A.	DC, p3c2, 6/19/1888	In charge of J. H. Rogers store in De Soto.
Hancock	G. H.	DC, p3c2, 5/29/1888	G. H. Hancock and family are leaving De Soto for a lucrative job in Dubuque. Had worked as a bookkeeper for W. F. Davidson.
Hankins		RH, p6c5, 9/2/1897	A son was recently born to Joe Hankins of Ross.
Hanks	William	RH, p4c2, 8/30/1900	Fire recently destroyed his house in La Farge. Neighbors saved the house of A. W. DeJean who lived 20 feet away.
Hanson	Austin	DR, p3c1, 1/12/1871	Austin Hanson married Elizabeth Johnson on Dec. 30, 1870 in Ferryville. The bride and groom were from Freeman. W. F. McMasters, J.P., officiated.
Hanson	boy	DC, p3c3, 1/28/1888	A son was recently born Mr. Hanson of Cooley Valley.
Hanson	Jane S.	BD, p3c2, 1/19/1877	Edward Oleson married Jane S. Hanson on Jan. 14, 1877 at the home of the bride's father. Bride and groom were from Hickory Grove. W. W. Reid, Esq. officiated.

Genealogical Events from Newspapers for Crawford, Vernon and Grant Counties, Wisconsin, 1870-1901

LAST NAME	FIRST NAME	NEWSPAPER, PAGE/COLUMN MONTH/DAY/YEAR	GENEALOGICAL DATA
Hanson	John	RH, p5c6, 7/15/1897	Moved to Bloomingdale from Cashton to try blacksmithing again.
Hanson	Lena	RH, p5c4, 11/3/1898	Adam Hocking recently married Lena Hanson, per Sugar Grove news column.
Hanson	Lewis	DR, p3c3, 1/26/1871	Thrown from a horse and died Tuesday. He lived with Mr. A. Goppers, about 7 miles from De Soto. He was a 20-year-old Norwegian.
Hanson	Louis	BD, p2c3, 4/28/1882	Aged 29 years. Son of a widow lady in Town of Franklin. Found dead in a field he was plowing for John Whitworth, east of Viroqua. A gun accident may have caused his clothing to catch on fire.
Hanson	Rev.	DC, p3c5, 10/30/1886	Caroline Runice married Rev. Hanson on Oct. 20, 1886 at the home of the bride's parents. Bride from WestPrairie. Groom from St. Paul.
Hanson	William	RH, p5c3, 1/13/1898	Fire destroyed the barn of William Hanson on his farm 3 miles east of Readstown. The farm was previously owned by Amos Pettit.
Hare	boy	DC, p3c3, 1/14/1888	Son born on Jan. 9, 1888 to H. T. Hare.
Hare	H. T.	DC, p3c2 9/3/1887	Lived in Burlington, IA. Subscribed to the *De Soto Chronicle*.
Hare	H. T.	DC, p3c2, 12/3/1887	Mr. and Mrs. H. T. Hare arrived from Burlington to spend the winter with Mrs. Hare's parent, Mr. and Mrs. G. W. Furman of De Soto.
Hare	H. T.	DC, p3c3, 1/8/1889	Opened a barbershop in De Soto.
Hare	H. T.	DC, p2c3, 2/19/1889	Ran a barbershop in De Soto.
Hare	H. T.	DC, p4c1, 4/12/1889	Resided in De Soto. Rumored to be the agent for the Diamond Jo line of steamers in De Soto.
Hare	Harlan T.	DC, p3c3, 6/26/1886	Harlan T. Hare married May Furman on June 22, 1886 at the home of George W. Furman, the bride's father. Bride from De Soto. Groom from Mt. Pleasant, IA. Miss Cora Stogdill of La Crosse and Annie Caryle were the bridesmaids. The groomsmen were F. W. Hoadley and W. S. Milliken. the Rev. M. B. Balch officiated. A gift list was published.
Hare	Mary A., Mrs.	DC, p3c2, 11/13/1886	Nee Furman. Arrived in De Soto [her hometown] from Mt. Pleasant, IA to visit friends.
Hare	Mary, Mrs.	DC, p3c4, 7/2/1887	Arrived from Mt. Pleasant, IA to visit sister, Mrs. Gardner of De Soto.
Harn	Rola T.	RH, p4c1, 9/20/1900	Recently died at Pagosa Springs, Colorado from a gunshot wound received on August 29th. He was the grandson of E. P. Bender of Viola.
Harn	Tom	RH, p5c3, 9/13/1900	Former resident of Readstown. Accidently shot by J. S. Brown on the Willett Brown ranch in Oregon. Harn and Albert Henderson were sleeping in a tent and heard noise among the chickens. Harn investigated, as did Brown. Brown accidently shot Harn. Harn doing fine.
Harper	Effie	DC, p2c4, 1/14/1888	Miss Effie Harper left Seneca to open a dressmaking shop in Prairie du Chien.
Harrington	E. D.	DC, p3c3, 4/2/1887	Victim of an "attempted" robbery outside De Soto.
Harrington	Eddie	DC, p3c6, 6/12/1886	Proprietor of the Eureka Barbershop in De Soto.
Harrington	G. H.	DC, p2c2, 5/28/1887	Worked as a blacksmith in Ferryville.
Harrington	Oc	DC, p3c3, 11/12/1887	Ran a shoemaker shop and basement restaurant in Newton.
Harris		RH, p5c4, 6/16/1898	A son was recently born to George Harris of Readstown.
Harris	Andrew	BD, p3c1, 11/6/1883	Andrew Harris married Mrs. Eldora Wright on Oct. 30, 1883 at Blue River Station. Bride and groom were from Blue River Station. The Rev. Q. R. Wright officiated.
Harris	Andrew	BD, p3c3, 7/27/1877	Former resident of Watterstown, WI. Resided in Lyons, Cass Co., KS. Sent specimens of wheat he raised on his new farm to the newspaper editor.
Harris	Anna	RH, p4c2, 11/9/1899	O. H. Larson married Anna Harris. Groom was a Kickapoo farmer. Bride was the daughter of Joseph Harris of Manning.
Harris	boy	RH, p7c2, 7/1/1897	A son was recently born to George Harris of the Readstown area.
Harris	C. C.	DC, p2c2, 1/1/1887	C. C. Harris married Anna Johnson at Bay State House in De Soto on Dec. 27, 1886. Groom from Minneapolis. Bride from Town of Freeman.
Harris	Charles	RH, p4c2, 6/8/1899	Arrived in Readstown to visit with relatives. He was from Manton, MI.

Genealogical Events from Newspapers for Crawford, Vernon and Grant Counties, Wisconsin, 1870-1901

LAST NAME	FIRST NAME	NEWSPAPER, PAGE/COLUMN MONTH/DAY/YEAR	GENEALOGICAL DATA
Harris	Ezra	BD, p2c4, 11/26/1880	Grant County paid him a bounty for scalps turned into the county.
Harris	John	BD, p3c1, 10/15/1880	John Harris married Linda Day on Oct. 7, 1880. Bride and groom from Wauzeka.
Harris	John	BD, p3c2, 9/27/1878	John Harris married Olive L. Taft on Sept. 22, 1878 at the Muffley House in Boscobel. Bride and groom from Crawford Co. Dr. William Stoddart officiated.
Harris	Late	BD, p3c2, 10/24/1879	Lived in Lone Rock. Died Friday night after falling under the cars as a freight train left Wauzeka. He was a brakeman. He was 22 years old. His wife was sick and not expected to live.
Harris	Mathew	RH, p4c2, 7/12/1900	Died Monday from dropsy "caused from complication of diseases resulting from a gun shot wound while in the country's service." Funeral held in Mauton, MI. Buried in Maple Hill Cemetery. Born in Pennsylvania and married twice. Survived by his wife, several children and 2 adopted sons, Frank and Charles Harris. Served with Co. I, 17th WI Vol. during the Civil War and marched to the sea with General Sherman. Resided in Cedar Creek for 21 years. He was nearly 72 years old. Former resident of Readstown.
Harrison	M., Mrs.	DC, p3c4, 12/25/1886	Mrs. M. Harrison and daughter, Ella, of La Crosse, visited her mother, Mrs. Regly, of Genoa.
Harrison	Richard	DR, p3c2, 3/2/1871	Richard Harrison married Elizabeth Parnell on Feb. 9, 1871 at the Methodist Episcopal Church at Oswego, KS. The bride and groom lived in Oswego. The Rev. Mr. Conley officiated.
Harrower	Robert	BD, p3c2, 9/10/1880	The 10 or 12-year-old son of Robert Harrower of near Millville lost two fingers in a circular saw accident.
Harrower	William	BD, p3c2, 9/13/1878	William Harrower married Ella A. Nye on Sept. 5, 1878 in Fennimore. The Rev. D. L. Hubbard officiated.
Hartwell	Sperry D.	BD, p3c3, 3/17/1882	Sperry D. Hartwell married Sadie J. Palmer on Mar. 12, 1882 at the residence of William F. Tuttle. Bride and groom from Fennimore.
Harvey	John B.	DR, p2c3, 5/11/1871	Proprietor of a harness and saddle shop in Lansing, IA.
Harvey	Mrs.	DR, p3c2, 1/4/1872	Died in Cass Co., MO at the age of 90 years. She was buried in Walnut Mount Cemetery, Retreat, WI.
Haskell	Charles	DC, p2c4, 1/14/1888	Mrs. Charles Haskell invited friends to her home in Red Mound to celebrate her husband's 35th birthday on Wednesday. The host received a patent rocking chair, a dressing case and a paper rack for his birthday.
Haskell	H. W.	DR, p2c3, 12/15/1870	Proprietor of the Sherman House in Viroqua.
Haskell	H. W.	DR, p3c2, 5/18/1871	Recently established a general store in Viola.
Haskell	H. W.	DC, p3c2, 12/25/1886	Arrived from Lone Rock to visit son, Charles of Red Mound.
Haskell	H. W.	BD, p3c1, 1/5/1877	Proprietor of the Towsley House in Lone Rock.
Haskell	Hiram	DC, p3c3, 9/10/1887	Hiram Haskell of Lone Rock visited his son, Charles of Red Mound.
Haskell	Hiram	DC, p3c2, 1/28/1888	Landlord of the Haskell House in Lone Rock.
Hasking	Wright	RH, p5c4, 11/4/1897	Wright Hasking married Francis Talcott on Oct. 24, 1897 at the home of the groom's parents in Soldiers Grove. H. Gardner officiated.
Haskins	J.	BD, p3c1, 12/29/1882	Brought 35 head of cattle from Crawford Co. to Boscobel for shipment to Chicago.
Haskins	J. F.	DC, p3c3, 2/11/1888	Owned 70 colts and horses on his Haney Valley farm.
Hastings	Clarence	RH, p6c2, 10/24/1901	Charged with assaulting a 13-year-old girl. Brought to Viroqua from Iowa where he was arrested.
Hatch	E. D., DDS	RH, p4c3, 2/7/1901	Advertised his dental services at his office in Viola.
Hatch	W. J.	BD, p3c2, 1/23/1880	Residence in Bloomington destroyed by fire. Partially insured.
Hauge	Lewis	RH, p4c3, 9/19/1901	Left home at Oak Ridge for North Dakota to look after his farming interests.
Haughton	J. W.	DC, p3c4, 5/1/1888	Admitted to the bar. He was the son of Rev. William Haughton.
Haughton	Joseph	DC, p3c2, 10/2/1888	Son of Rev. William Haughton of Retreat. Left for Watertown, Dakota to work for the winter.

Genealogical Events from Newspapers for Crawford, Vernon and Grant Counties, Wisconsin, 1870-1901

LAST NAME	FIRST NAME	NEWSPAPER, PAGE/COLUMN MONTH/DAY/YEAR	GENEALOGICAL DATA
Haughton	Katie	DC, p2c2, 9/18/1888	Left Retreat to attend school at the University in Madison.
Haughton	Katie, Mrs.	DC, p3c4, 4/2/1887	Planned to teach at Collins this summer.
Haughton	William, Rev.	DC, p3c3, 10/2/1888	Rev. William Haughton and E. T. Bishop attended the Congregational Convention at La Crosse.
Haughton	William	DC, p3c3, 8/7/1886	Served as pastor of the Congregational Church in De Soto and Cooley Valley.
Haughton	William, Rev.	DC, p3c4, 3/26/1887	Author of numerous poems published in various issues of the newspaper.
Haughton	William, Rev.	DC, p3c3, 3/10/1888	Organized a non-denominational church in the Cooley Valley on the 4th. It consisted of 20 members.
Haughton	William, Rev.	DC, p8c2, 8/9/1889	Reported that he had officiated at 131 marriages and 123 funerals since he settled in the vicinity.
Hauxshurst	Sidney	BD, p3c2, 9/13/1878	Sidney Hauxshurst recently married Julia N. Cottrell in Milwaukee. Groom lived in Boscobel during the war. Bride from Milwaukee.
Havens	Joe	BD, p3c3, 2/22/1878	Joe Havens married Henriett Ostrander on Feb. 8, 1878 at Fennimore. Bride and groom from Marion. R. F. Green, Esquire officiated.
Haverley	Francis	DC, p3c2, 11/19/1887	Eliza M. Foster married Willie Haverley on Nov. 25, 1887 at the residence of William Haverley of Red Mound. It was a double ceremony. Francis Haverley married George N. Angell, too.
Haverley	Willie	DC, p3c2, 11/19/1887	Eliza M. Foster married Willie Haverley on Nov. 25, 1887 at the residence of William Haverley of Red Mound. It was a double ceremony. Francis Haverley married George N. Angell, too.
Haverly	Anna	DC, p3c1, 6/11/1887	Anna Haverly married Clarence E. Bean on June 1, 1887. Bride was the daughter of William Haverly of Red Mount. The Rev. William Haughton officiated. Couple moved to De Soto.
Haverly	Will	DC, p3c2, 4/17/1888	Bought the L. F. Miller farm in Red Mound.
Hawes	Mrs.	DC, p3c3, 11/12/1887	Mrs. Hawes, Mrs Jones and Fred Jones arrived in Retreat to visit relatives. They were from Nebraska.
Hawkins	Pauline, Miss	RH, p4c4, 5/26/1898	Resided in Sylvan. Visited her sisters, Mrs. Charles Foreman and Mrs. John Chitwood of Kickapoo.
Hawley	George E.	BD, p3c2, 10/23/1883	Shipped 9 head of Galloway cattle from Boscobel to Scotland, Dakota.
Hayden	Ella	DC, p3c3, 3/20/1888	Died Mar. 11, 1888 in Sag City from lung fever. Survived by husband, Jessie Hayden, and 6 children. She was the daughter of T. C. Ankeny, a former De Soto resident.
Hayden	Emma	DC, p2c1, 5/7/1887	Charles Clark married Emma Hayden on May 1, 1887. Bride and groom from Town of Wheatland. Alex. Latshaw, J.P., of Victory officiated at the ceremony.
Hayden	Giles	DR, p3c3, 9/21/1871	From West Prairie. Bought the horse used by Capt. Worth in the brickyard when the yard was closed. The horse died enroute to West Prairie. The horse was too frail to ride.
Hayden	Giles	DC, p2c2, 10/1/1887	Mr. and Mrs. Giles Hayden returned to Victory after a visit with daughter, Mrs. Charlie Clark, in St. Paul.
Hayden	Giles	DC, p3c2, 1/14/1888	Resided in Wheatland. Settled in the area in 1855.
Hayden	J. B.	DC, p3c3, 9/4/1886	Brought to Viroqua for medical treatment. He was injured in the face at Miner's saw mill near Bloomingdale.
Hayden	John	RH, p5c3, 1/17/1901	Hayden's house in De Soto was recently destroyed by fire.
Hayden	Mr.	RH, p5c3, 1/24/1901	Died last Wednesday of heart trouble. Born in Retreat. Resided a few miles from De Soto.
Hayden	Samuel	DC, p3c2, 3/3/1888	Died at his home in Sterling last Saturday of lung fever. He was an early settler in the area. Aged 60 years. Left England 40 years ago and lived in WestPrairie for 32 years. Survived by wife and 12 children. Funeral held at Liberty Pole by his pastor, G. W. Nuzum.
Hayden	Sylvester, Mrs.	DC, p3c4, 8/28/1886	Resided in Dakota. Returned to visit in Retreat, her former home.
Haydon	S.	DC, p2c2, 10/8/1887	Owned extensive orchards in Kansas. Visited sisters, Mrs. Withee and Mrs. F. Haynes, in Seneca. Planned to visit other relatives in Grant Co.
Hayes	John	BD, p2c2, 5/12/1882	Resided in the Town of Eagle for the last 12 years. Served as coxswain on the U.S. War Sloop *Kearsarge* during the Civil War. Gave an account of the battle against the rebel war vessel *Alabama*. Give $700 as his portion of prize money for the destruction of the *Alabama*.
Haynes	F., Mrs.	DC, p2c2, 10/8/1887	Departed Seneca for Bloomington to visit her sister, Mrs. Brooks.
Hazeltine	Daniel	RH, p4c1, 9/7/1899	Sick with typhoid fever at his home in the Town of Kickapoo.

Genealogical Events from Newspapers for Crawford, Vernon and Grant Counties, Wisconsin, 1870-1901

LAST NAME	FIRST NAME	NEWSPAPER, PAGE/COLUMN MONTH/DAY/YEAR	GENEALOGICAL DATA
Hazeltine	Nettie	RH, p5c4, 4/28/1898	Grant Alexander married Nettie Hazeltine on April 17, 1898, per Sugar Grove news column.
Hazelton	George C.	BD, p3c1, 12/2/1881	The Hon. George C. and Mrs. Hazelton departed Boscobel for Washington, D. C. for the next session of Congress. Their sons, George and John, went with them.
Hazelton	George C.	BD, p3c1, 1/5/1877	Attorney in Boscobel.
Hazelton	George, Mrs.	BD, p3c2, 10/13/1882	Resided in Boscobel area. Summoned by telegraph to be at the bedside of her mother in Portland, ME.
Hazen	George	DC, p3c3, 7/23/1887	Rented the Merchants Hotel in Richland Center.
Hazen	George, Mrs. B.	BD, p3c2, 9/25/1883	Buried on Sept. 15, 1883 in Madison. She was the wife of George Hazen, a traveling salesman for Messrs. Ball and Goodrich of Milwaukee.
Hazen	Mr.	DC, p3c4, 8/28/1886	Sold his share of a Lynxville hardware store to Mr. DuChess of Prairie du Chien.
Hazen	R. E.	DC, p3c4, 8/21/1886	Operated a saloon in Lynxville.
Hazen	R. E.	DC, p2c1, 12/18/1886	Opened a billiard saloon in Stoddard.
Heal	Ellen, Mrs.	DC, p3c3, 5/8/1888	Resided in Viroqua. Recently buried her only son in the Retreat Cemetery.
Heal	J. H.	DC, p3c2, 7/3/1886	Taught school at Lycurgus, IA.
Heal	J. H.	DC, p2c3, 8/7/1886	Resided in Freeman. Expected to run for Superintendent of Schools in Crawford Co.
Heal	James H.	DC, p3c3, 9/3/1887	James H. Heal married Jane E. Lawrence on Monday at the N. Coe residence in De Soto. Groom taught school in Norwalk. The Rev. I. F. Nuzum of Mauston officiated.
Heal	William	RH, p5c4, 3/22/1900	Died Monday of heart failure at Elk Creek. The funeral was held at Sylvan Church by Rev. Bell.
Heald	William E.	DR, p2c3, 3/16/1871	Offered to sell his 180-acre farm near De Soto.
Hebard	Albert	RH, p4c1, 9/7/1899	Moved to Readstown from Otter Creek.
Hebard	E.	RH, p4c2, 11/14/1901	Resided in Ladysmith. Hebard's parents left their home in Vernon Co. and planned to live with their son.
Hebard	Ernest	RH, p4c1, 9/27/1900	Opened the Star Restaurant in the north end of Readstown.
Hebard	Lizzie	RH, p5c5, 10/7/1897	H. J. Mosher married Lizzie Hebard on Sunday, Oct. 3, 1897 at the home of the bride's parents in Kickapoo. Bride from Kickapoo, Vernon Co. Groom from Milton, Monroe Co. C. W. Reeve, J. P. officiated.
Hebard	W.	RH, p5c4, 11/18/1897	Resided in Readstown. Planned to move his blacksmith shop to Manning.
Hebbard	Albert	RH, p5c2, 11/3/1898	Worked as a stonemason. Built a wall for G. A. Ewers sawmill in Readstown.
Heberlin	Martha J.	BD, p3c2, 9/13/1878	Jefferson M. Geurnesey married Martha J. Heberlin on Aug. 11, 1878. Bride and groom from Watertown. J. M. Davis of Blue River officiated.
Heberling	Ella E.	BD, p3c1, 11/21/1879	Antoine L. Dunston married Ella E. Heberling on Nov. 18, 1879 in Boscobel. Peter Rae, Esquire officiated.
Heberling	Ida, Mrs.	BD, p3c4, 12/30/1881	Died Dec. 18, 1881 in Watterstown. She was the wife of Ed Herberling. Aged 24 years and 23 days. Mother of 3 small children.
Heffard	Ernest	RH, p5c3, 7/22/1897	Moved his family to Favor's stone quarry in the Viroqua area. Employed at the quarry.
Heil	Frank	RH, p5c4, 10/20/1898	Purchased a 160-acre farm "up north." Will leave his present home in Sugar Grove.
Heine	Antone	BD, p3c2, 12/25/1883	Antone Heine married Millie Stroh on Dec. 18, 1883 at the home of the bride's parents in Boscobel. Groom also from Boscobel. The Rev. T. W. Cole officiated.
Helgerson	Lewis	DR, p3c1, 12/29/1870	Merchant in Ferryville, Crawford Co.
Helgerson	Mrs.	DC, p3c3, 6/12/1886	Died last week on Thursday at her home north of Victory. She was the mother of 6 children. Thrown into a tree during a runaway accident. Funeral was held at the Norwegian Church at Bad Axe.
Helgerson	Thomas	DC, p2c2, 6/11/1887	Resided in the Town of Sterling. Lost 2 children to diphtheria.

Genealogical Events from Newspapers for Crawford, Vernon and Grant Counties, Wisconsin, 1870-1901

LAST NAME	FIRST NAME	NEWSPAPER, PAGE/COLUMN MONTH/DAY/YEAR	GENEALOGICAL DATA
Heller		BD, p3c2, 8/5/1881	A child of Mr. and Mrs. Heller of Boscobel died Wednesday night from the heat.
Heller	Anna	BD, p3c1, 12/18/1883	Charles Pulmann married Anna Heller on Dec. 13, 1883 at the residence of the bride's parents in Boscobel. Rev. Rami officiated.
Hellmand	A. C.	RH, p4c1, 9/28/1899	Opened a meat market in Readstown.
Hellmund	A. C.	RH, p2c1, 7/1/1897	Proprietor of the Readstown Meat Market.
Hellmund	A. C.	RH, p7c2, 7/1/1897	His new meat market in Readstown is finished and ready for business.
Helmond	A. C.	RH, p4c2, 2/14/1901	Erected a large icehouse this week in Readstown.
Helmund	Pearl	RH, p4c1, 9/27/1900	Cut his foot with an axe while helping his father at the slaughterhouse in Readstown.
Helpman	Irvin L.	DC, p2c3, 9/24/1887	Visited sister, Mrs. Rose of the Cooley Valley. Returned to his home in Shrevesport, LA.
Helpman	M.	DC, p3c3, 10/15/1887	Lived in Bourbon, IN. Visited daughter, Mrs. W. F. Rose of the Cooley Valley. This was his first visit in 19 years.
Hemenway	Bert	DC, p4c2, 5/17/1889	Resigned as a clerk at the store owned by W. F. Davidson. Planned to open a grocery store in De Soto.
Hemenway	George	DC, p4c3, 4/26/1889	The heirs of George Hemenway of De Soto received $1800 pension on account of his death in service.
Hemenway	Mrs.	DC, p3c3, 2/5/1887	Mrs. Hemenway's new residence in De Soto was destroyed by fire. The first floor household goods were saved. "The loss falls particularly heavy upon the family as they have denied much and worked hard to build this home."
Henderson	Allen W.	BD, p3c1, 7/23/1880	Allen W. Henderson married Mary Ann Murphy of Hickory Grove at the home of the bride's mother on July 15, 1880. The Rev. W. Stoddart officiated.
Henderson	boy	DC, p1c1, 6/7/1889	A son was born on Monday evening to H. Henderson of Ferryville.
Henderson	Clarissa B., Mrs.	BD, p3c3, 2/2/1877	Died Jan. 27, 1877 in Boscobel at 53 years, 3 months of age. Survived by husband, George W. Henderson, and 7 children. Funeral held at the Methodist Church.
Henderson	Henry	DC, p2c2, 5/28/1887	Recently erected a new store room in Ferryville.
Henderson	Henry	DC, p2c2, 12/25/1886	Planned to marry Mrs. Annie M. Lough in Ferryville. Wedding invitations were sent out.
Henderson	Henry	DC, p2c2, 1/1/1887	Henry Henderson married Miss Annie M. Lough on Dec. 27, 1886 at the residence of M. Lough of Freeman. Bride and groom from Ferryville. The Rev. Thomas Crouch officiated.
Henderson	Jake	DC, p3c3, 2/3/1888	Home in Victory destroyed by fire.
Henderson	Mr.	DC, p3c5, 8/14/1886	Operated a general store in Ferryville.
Henderson	William	RH, p5c4, 10/20/1898	Returned to his home in Kentucky after visiting with aunt, Mrs. N. E. French of De Soto.
Hendrick	D. D., Mrs.	DC, p3c3, 4/9/1887	Died on Mar. 25, 1887 at Markesan, WI. She was the mother of Mrs. A. Hersey.
Henika	Frank B.	RH, p5c3, 2/28/1901	Died Feb. 24, 1901 in Readstown. Born June 20, 1842 in NY. Served in Co. F, 2nd Wis. Calvary for 3 years and 9 months. Resident of Readstown for the last 3 years. Survived by 1 son, Dr. G. W. Henika. Brothers are unable to be here for the funeral. Remains taken to Madison. Will be buried by father and mother.
Henika	G. W., Dr.	RH, p5c2, 4/28/1898	Planned to move from Milwaukee to Readstown and occupy part of the Bliss Hotel.
Henika	G. W., Dr.	RH, p5c1, 8/31/1899	Advertised his services as a physician and surgeon in Readstown.
Henika	girl	RH, p4c1, 8/30/1900	A daughter was born on Thursday to G. W. Henika of Readstown.
Henrich	boy	BD, p3c1, 5/18/1883	A son was born on Friday to Paul L. Henrich of the Boscobel area.
Henry	O. S.	DC, p3c4, 2/5/1887	The O. S. [first initial may be wrong] Henry house at Monument Rock was burned. House was owned by Mrs. W. O. Johnson.
Henthorn	Ella, Miss	RH, p4c1, 10/11/1900	Resided in Sterling, NB. She was a guest of M. A. Andrews in Readstown.

Genealogical Events from Newspapers for Crawford, Vernon and Grant Counties, Wisconsin, 1870-1901

LAST NAME	FIRST NAME	NEWSPAPER, PAGE/COLUMN MONTH/DAY/YEAR	GENEALOGICAL DATA
Henthorn	Herman	RH, p5c3, 1/3/1901	Herman Henthorne married Gertie G. Randall on New Year's Day, per Sugar Grove news column.
Henthorn	Herman, Mr. and Mrs.	RH, p4c3, 2/7/1901	A kitchen party was held in their honor at their home in Sugar Grove. "The old folks took possession of the day time by helping the wife with quilts, etc. In the evening the young people were entertained with music after which they all partook of a well-set table. They received many useful presents."
Henthorn	Norman	RH, p4c2, 1/3/1901	Lived in Sylvan. Worked as a salesman for the Economy Gas Lamp Co. of Chicago.
Henthorn	Washington	RH, p5c4, 3/22/1900	Died last Sunday in Pardeeville, WI. He was an old resident of Sylvan. Many relatives remain in the area.
Herrick	Robert	DR, p3c5, 1/12/1871	He was an old resident of Rising Sun. Recently opened a blacksmith shop. To gain customers from a nearby competitor he reduced his rates. The competitor's friends entered Herrick's store, tore down a partition around the post office department, scattered mail, broke windows and set fire to the building. They fired a shot at Herrick and assaulted him. Two of the assailants were captured.
Hesler	Dora, Mrs.	RH, p4c2, 11/11/1897	Arrived from Balmoral, WI to visit sister, Mrs. Minnie Carter of Readstown, and uncle, Dr. C. W. Puff of Viola.
Hess	George	BD, p3c1, 8/4/1882	Resided in Montfort. Recently died of consumption. He was a wheelright by trade. Married Lucinda Schidee [sp.?] in 1850. He/she was child of Mrs. T. W. Dohme of Boscobel. Survived by widow, 3 daughters and 1 son. He was a prominent Mason.
Hess	Gottfried	BD, p2c3, 8/11/1882	Born in Prussia in 1824. Moved to U.S. in 1851. Stayed in the eastern U.S. for a short time and then moved to Grant Co., WI. Volunteered for Union Army service in Civil War. Died Aug. 2, 1882 in Montfort.
Heupel	Adam	BD, p3c2, 2/23/1877	An auction was held at the Adam Heupel residence last Wednesday.
Hewey	James	DR, p3c1, 10/26/1871	Wagon maker in Chaseburg.
Hewitt	Carlos M., Dr.	BD, p3c2, 2/17/1882	Died in Boscobel on Feb. 11, 1882 of heart and lung disease. Born July 1, 1808 in Sangersfield, Oneida Co., NY. When 15 he went to the Academy at Lewiston, NY and later to the State Medical University of NY at Fairfield. Graduated in 1838. Soon after graduation he married Elizabeth Nash of Walsingham [or Watsingham?], Upper Canada. All four of their children died in infancy. Moved to Potosi in 1840. Moved to Boscobel in 1859.
Hickey	Patrick, Mrs.	BD, p3c4, 2/17/1882	Resided in Boscobel. Fell and split the cap of her knee. Confined to bed. Has fallen several times in the past two years. May not recover use of her limb.
Hickok	David B.	DR, p3c3, 6/15/1871	Died June 14, 1871 at home in De Soto at the age of 22 years. Funeral held at the Congregational Church. He had heart disease for several years.
Hickok	David B.	DR, p3c2, 6/22/1871	Resided in De Soto. Recently died. Post mortem exam revealed he died from adhesion of lungs.
Hickok	David H.	DR, p3c4, 1/5/1871	The Vernon County Circuit Court was scheduled to hear summons for relief case, David H. Hickok, Legrand Hickok and David B. Hickok, plaintiffs vs. George Hewitt, defendant.
Hickok	Leland, Mrs.	RH, p3c4, 9/29/1898	Left home in De Soto for Pipin to visit daughter, Mrs. A. Canfield.
Hickok	Mrs.	DC, p3c2, 10/16/1886	A dance was given at Lyttle's hall for the benefit of Mrs. Hickok's house.
Hickok	S. G., Mrs.	DC, p2c2, 4/9/1887	Resided in De Soto. Visited sister, Mrs. M. Monti of Genoa.
Hickok	S. G., Mrs.	DC, p2c2, 4/9/1887	Arrived from De Soto to visit her sister, Mrs. M. Monti of Genoa.
Higinbotham	Daisy	RH, p5c3, 3/30/1899	Charles Turner recently married Daisy Higinbotham per Sugar Grove news.
Hill		DC, p3c2, 12/17/1887	Brother Hill was the first pastor of Methodist Church built on the Crawford Co. side of De Soto [possibly in the late 1850s]. Bro. Irish succeeded Bro. Hill.
Hill	Harvey	RH, p5c4, 3/29/1900	Arrived from Oregon to visit relatives in Kickapoo.
Hill	Isabel	DR, p3c3, 11/30/1871	Died recently at the residence of her son in Retreat. She was 69 years old. She was survived by her husband, John Hill.
Hill	J. M.	DC, p2c2, 11/5/1887	J. M. Hill, Frank Slater and Abram Bates returned to Retreat from Dakota.
Hill	J. M., Mrs.	DC, p1c2, 4/5/1889	The Retreat W.C.T.U. published a resolution of respect in the memory of Mrs. Hill.
Hill	John	DC, p3c4, 11/27/1886	John Hill and Clifton White returned to Retreat from Dakota.

Genealogical Events from Newspapers for Crawford, Vernon and Grant Counties, Wisconsin, 1870-1901

LAST NAME	FIRST NAME	NEWSPAPER, PAGE/COLUMN MONTH/DAY/YEAR	GENEALOGICAL DATA
Hill	John	DC, p3c3, 12/17/1887	Returned to Retreat from Dakota.
Hill	John	DC, p2c3, 4/3/1888	John Hill married Nettie M. Jacobus on Mar. 23, 1888. Bride and groom from Retreat. The Rev. Thomas Crouch officiated.
Hill	M. O.	DC, p3c3 8/27/1887	Lived in the De Soto area. Hired to teach school at Patch Grove, Grant Co.
Hill	M. O., Mr.	DC, p3c4, 12/4/1886	Taught school in the Brookville District per Liberty Pole news column.
Hill	M., Mrs.	DC, p2c3, 3/5/1889	Died Friday in Retreat.
Hill	Mr.	DC, p3c2, 3/26/1887	Poor Commissioner for Vernon Co. He transferred several children from the poor farm to the Dependent School in Sparta.
Hill	Mr.	DC, p3c5, 2/18/1888	Mr. Hill, age 94, is very ill. He is the father of Mrs. Welche of Ontario.
Hill	Nettie	BD, p3c1, 9/7/1879	Charles Hinn married Nettie Hill on Monday evening at the Lutheran Church in Boscobel. Bride from Marion.
Hill	O. P.	DC, p3c2, 11/20/1886	Selected to be Poor Commissioner for 1887.
Hill	O. P.	DC, p3c2, 9/17/1887	Lived in Viroqua. Received a pension for his military service.
Hinders	Hannah, Mrs.	BD, p3c2, 5/21/1880	R. J. Darnell married Mrs. Hannah Hinders on May 9, 1880 at the Forest House in the Town of Forest, Richland Co. This was Darnell's third marriage and Hinder's fourth marriage. They are both blind.
Hinds	J. H.	DC, p3c3, 8/14/1888	Celebrated his 84th birthday on August 6, 1888 in De Soto. Among those present were: Mrs. Blood [age 83], Mrs. Stanley [age 69], Judge Terhune [age 67], Mrs. Arnold [age 60] and Mrs. Hiram Hinds [and daughter, Alice of Purdy].
Hinds	J. H., Esq.	DC, p3c3, 1/7/1888	Pension application for military service was approved. He was 83 years old and very feeble.
Hinds	James H., Squire	DC, p4c2, 4/26/1889	Died April 22, 1889 in De Soto. Born in Malins [or Malms], Onondaga Co., NY on Aug. 6, 1804. Adopted by Mr. Gould Benedict Stewart of Hamilton College, Utica, NY. When he came of age he moved to Buffalo and worked in a law office. In 1832 he lost his wife, Julia Anna, and a 1-week-old baby. In 1837 he moved to Chicago. Moved to Racine in 1838, where he employed men to paint houses. Moved to Dubuque in 1817 [possibly 1847?] where children [Amy, Elizabeth and Wilna] died. Moved to De Soto in 1866. Lost his son, James, in 1863. James died from wounds in the Civil War. Second wife died in 1885. Lately stricken with paralysis. Cared for by his nieces, Sophia and Mary.
Hinds	Squire	DC, p3c2 8/13/1887	Celebrated 83 birthday on Aug. 6, 1887. The family of H. H. Hinds of Purdy came to visit him.
Hine	Anton	BD, p3c1, 11/6/1883	Employed as a harness maker by G. Guentzel of Boscobel. After returning from hunting he discovered his purse was missing along with $165.
Hiner	Henry	BD, p3c3, 4/5/1878	Henry Hiner married last week in Bloomington. Wife's name was not given.
Hinks	Linda	DC, p2c1, 7/2/1887	Miss Linda Hinks of La Grange, IL is the guest of her aunt, Mrs. Mary Lombard of Retreat.
Hinkst	May	DC, p3c4, 8/7/1886	Resided in Liberty Pole. Hired to teach school in Retreat.
Hinkst	May	DC, p3c4, 5/14/1887	Native of Liberty Pole. Taught school in the Bishop District.
Hinn	C. P.	BD, p3c2, 2/10/1882	C. P. Hinn of Boscobel and clerk at Parker, Hildebrand & Co. left for Fennimore to become a partner with Oswald and open a new store.
Hinn	Charles	BD, p3c1, 8/26/1881	Burned the carcasses of hogs that died from hog cholera. Resided in Marion.
Hinn	Charles	BD, p3c2, 3/21/1879	Managed the Boscobel Cornet Band.
Hinn	Charles	BD, p3c1, 9/7/1879	Charles Hinn married Nettie Hill on Monday evening at the Lutheran Church in Boscobel. Bride from Marion.
Hinn	Charles P.	BD, p3c2, 9/10/1880	Charles Hinn married Delphine Rothe on September 9, 1880 in Whitewater, WI. Groom from Boscobel. Bride from Whitewater.
Hire	Jacob J.	BD, p3c5, 7/27/1877	Jacob J. Hire married Lizzie McHarg yesterday at the home of the bride's father. Bride and groom from Wauzeka. The Rev. Dr. Stoddart officiated.
Hoadley	F. B., Mrs.	BD, p3c2, 4/13/1877	Mrs. Hoadley of Detroit, MI, formerly Mrs. James Armstrong, visited friends in Boscobel.

Genealogical Events from Newspapers for Crawford, Vernon and Grant Counties, Wisconsin, 1870-1901

LAST NAME	FIRST NAME	NEWSPAPER, PAGE/COLUMN MONTH/DAY/YEAR	GENEALOGICAL DATA
Hobis	Herman, Mrs.	BD, p3c2, 11/9/1877	Gave birth in Boscobel to a 12-pound daughter on election day.
Hockenbury	Dr.	DC, p3c2, 1/1/1887	Recently died in Bad Axe.
Hocking	Adam	RH, p5c4, 11/3/1898	Adam Hocking recently married Lena Hanson, per Sugar Grove news column.
Hocking	Addie	RH, p5c4, 10/20/1898	T. D. Risen married Addie Hocking on Oct. 16, 1898 at the residence of, and by, George Wise, Justice of the Peace. Bride and groom from Mound Park.
Hodge	W. A.	DC, p2c2, 6/4/1887	Advertised the sale of his homegrown nursery stock at Victory.
Hodge	W. A.	RH, p4c4, 2/2/1899	Suffered a stroke of paralysis last week at his home in Victory.
Hodge	W. A.	DC, p3c4, 11/27/1886	Erected a new store building in Victory. Sign on front of house says "Meals at all hours."
Hodges	Mr.	DR, p3c2, 10/5/1871	Operated a vineyard at Victory.
Hodgins	Eugene D.	BD, p3c1, 11/05/1880	Eugene D. Hodgins married Minnie M. Olmsted on Tuesday at Cherokee, IA at the Congregational Church. Bride was well known in Boscobel.
Hof	Philip J.	BD, p3c2, 8/25/1882	Died Aug. 15, 1882 in Boscobel from an abcess of the lungs. Born in 1811 in Bavaria. Orphaned when young. Raised by an uncle. Learned the tailor trade. Taught theology in Paris and studied in Geneva. Called to do missionary work among Germans in America. First served in Albany, NY, then in Detroit [9 years]. Preached to congregations in Ohio, Michigan and Wisconsin. "He left 8 childen, the two youngest of which will reside with their sister, wife of Rev. H. A. Penns, at Shumway, IL; the other children will remain in the city."
Hoff	Mrs.	BD, p3c2, 1/10/1879	Recently died of dropsy in Boscobel.
Hoffman	Ad.	RH, p5c4, 8/22/1901	Former resident of Viola. He "was one of the lucky ones in the recent drawing in Oklahoma, and has been offered $1500 for his claim. It is within a mile of the county seat."
Hoffman	C. A.	DC, Supp, 10/23/1886	Appointed postmaster in Belle Center.
Hoffman	Hallie	RH, p4c2, 10/17/1901	A surprise party was given in his honor. He will be moving to Ladysmith, WI next week. He was a member of the Comet Band. Fellow band members gave him the party. C. H. Davenport gave Hoffman a gold watch chain on behalf of the band.
Hoffman	Thomas	RH, p4c1, 6/1/1899	Recently moved from Bell Center to Readstown. Hoffman was a "shrewd businessman."
Hogle	Mr.	BD, p3c4, 12/13/1878	Per the Lamars Sentinel, Mr. Hogle and his wife, Hannah, have moved to Lamars, IA to spend the remainder of their days. They were 83 and 79 years old, respectively. They married in Genesee Co., NY and celebrated their golden wedding anniversary 11 years ago. They lived in Wisconsin for 35 years. They were the parents of Mrs. Lewis Crow, Mrs. M. F. Crouch and Mrs. Joseph Duncan of this county.
Holberg	J., Rev.	DR, p3c1, 2/23/1871	Former resident of Lansing, IA. Now lived in Salem, OR.
Holcomb	Cal	RH, p5c4, 1/20/1898	"The new pupils on the ice the last skating were Cal Holcomb and wife, and Miss Alta Benn, but, Cal they don't skate on their heads, stand up like a man." [From Kickapoo Center news column.]
Holcomb	Frank	RH, p5c4, 12/1/1898	Returned to Kickapoo from Iowa where he had been working the past summer.
Holcomb	Frank	RH, p5c3, 3/22/1900	Frank Holcomb married Lennie Wallace on March 19, 1900 at the home of the bride's parents, 2 miles east of Readstown.
Holcomb	Frank	RH, p4c2, 9/5/1901	Holcomb's house and household goods destroyed by fire. House located near Sugar Grove. There was no insurance.
Holcomb	Ursula	DC, p3c3, 4/17/1888	Mart Molly married Ursula Holcomb last week in Elroy. They planned to set up housekeeping on the Holcomb farm, about 2 miles from Ontario.
Hollinger	Minnie	DC, p2c2, 4/2/1887	Richard Vallant recently married Minnie Hollinger at the residence of J. Hollinger.
Holton	Theodore	BD, p3c1, 9/17/1880	Resided in Beeker Co., MN. Formerly from Castle Rock, Grant Co. Visited in Boscobel.
Homer	Ellen	BD, p3c5, 7/27/1877	David Baldrick married Ellen Homer on July 16, 1877 at Caseville. Bride and groom from Iowa. Henry Burgen officiated.

Genealogical Events from Newspapers for Crawford, Vernon and Grant Counties, Wisconsin, 1870-1901

LAST NAME	FIRST NAME	NEWSPAPER, PAGE/COLUMN MONTH/DAY/YEAR	GENEALOGICAL DATA
Honor Roll		DR, p3c3, 10/12/1871	The students on the De Soto School Honor Roll were Eddie Bean, William Benedict, Helen Lawrence, Elizabeth Kahler, Katie Saxe, Anna Miller, Clara Wait, Bertha Caldwell, Fanny Caldwell, Almeda Coffin, Emma Whitney and Mary Porter. The following students were removed from the Honor Roll [due to absence, tardiness, imperfect lessons, talking in class, etc.]: John Barr, Andrew Hemingway, George Wait, Frank Walker, Lovina Merrill, Martha Trott, Estella Furguson, Fanny Hemingway, Jennie Woodbury, Phebe Coffin, Bertha Everson, Florence Bevans, Anna Loftus, Alice Steele and Florence Glodery.
Honor Roll		DR, p3c3, 12/21/1871	The students on the De Soto School Honor Roll were Alfred McDowell, Frank Warren, Theodore Saxe, Estella Ferguson, Ida Lowrie, Ellen Lawrence, Elizabeth Kahlar, Anna Loftus, Alice Steele, Clara Wait, Frank Walker, Lorin Whitney, Frederick Stanley, Katie Saxe, Edwina Lowrie, Emma Whitney, Lena Lane, Mary Porter and Florence Glodery. The following students were removed from the Honor Roll [due to absence, tardiness, talking in class, etc.]: Charles McDowell, Jerome Caldwell, Andrew Hemingway, Charles Woodbury, Byron Lane, Thomas Bevan, Jennie Woodbury, Bertha Caldwell, Ada Daly, Lui Ankeny, George Furman, George Wait, Alvin Beck, Frank Pulver, Florence Bevans, Phebe Coffin, Della Furman and Martha Trott.
Hook	John	BD, p3c2, 3/15/1878	Escorted to Waupun [prison] from Lancaster. Sentenced to 1 year for breaking into a Washburn store.
Hoover	H. C.	DC, p3c2, 10/8/1887	Lived in Genoa. The government doubled his pension [for military service].
Hoover	John	DR, p2c3, 8/24/1871	Arrested by a vigilance committee in Vernon Co. for stealing cattle and horses. His companions, John Loper and Joe Miller, were also arrested.
Hooverson	Peter	BD, p3c1, 3/24/1882	The Hon. Atley Peterson returned to Soldiers Grove with his partner, Peter Hooverson, who went to Hot Springs, AR for his health. Hooverson's condition was hopeless. Peterson went to Arkansas to bring him back.
Hooverson	Peter	BD, p2c3, 4/21/1882	Died Mar. 20, 1882 in the home of his brother, Hoover, in the Town of Utica. Buried in the Lutheran Cemetery at Knute Hooverson's farm. Served as chairman of the last Crawford Co. Board and with the firm Peterson & Hooverson in Soldiers Grove. Born in Aardal, Norway on 1 July 1836. Came to America with his parents in 1837. Settled at Door Creek, Dane Co., WI. In 1852 the family moved to a farm 2 miles south of Soldiers Grove. Served in Civil War. Had a chronic liver complaint. Survived by wife and 2 small children.
Hopkins	Claudius Brainerd	BD, p3c1, 4/2/1880	Claudius Brainerd Hopkins married Elizabeth Ann Miller on Mar. 25, 1880 in Boscobel. Bride from Blue River. Groom from Hickory Grove.
Hopkins	girls	RH, p4c2, 8/9/1900	Twin girls were born last Saturday to Guy Hopkins of Kickapoo.
Hopkins	Guy	RH, p4c1, 12/28/1899	Guy Hopkins married May Griffin on Monday at the home of the bride's parents in Kickapoo. Groom from Viola.
Hopkins	Henry B.	RH, p4c2, 3/30/1899	Died March 27, 1899 in Viola. He was an invalid for many years. Lived in Sugar Grove until poor health forced him to move in with his son, Albert of Viola. Buried in the Sugar Grove Cemetery.
Hopkins	Thaddeus E.	DR, p3c4, 2/9/1871	Thaddeus Hopkins married Lizzie Fish in De Soto on Feb. 6, 1871. Bride and groom were from Lansing. The Rev. Mr. Hubbard of the Methodist Episcopal Church officiated.
Hoppin	Albert	BD, p2c3, 7/6/1877	Albert Hoppin married Bell Cliffton on June 25, 1877 in Muscoda. Bride from Washburn. Groom from La Crosse. Rev. Bishop Lench of Avoca officiated.
Hopwood	Stella	RH, p4c1, 11/23/1899	Resided in Steuben. Visited her uncle, A. C. Helmund of Readstown.
Horsfall	Joseph	BD, p3c2, 5/28/1880	Appointed to be a census enumerator in Millville, Grant Co.
Horsfall	Mrs.	BD, p2c2, 6/10/1881	Died Friday. She was a widow who lived in Millville, Grant Co. Mother of David Horsfall.
Horton	Lewis	RH, p6c2, 5/25/1899	Lewis Horton married Lula Kyser on May 18, 1899. Bride from Manning. Groom from La Farge.
Hosmer	General	DC, p2c2, 11/26/1887	In 1857 General Hosmer and his son built a "pretentious" dwelling in "Missouri," the southern part of De Soto located in Crawford Co. They also laid the foundation for a large flouring mill. Due to "hard times" the mill was never completed. After a year, they returned east and abandoned everything, not getting a penny for their outlay. When the war broke out the junior Hosmer entered the army. He received a wound that lamed him. After recovering he was attached to the Judge Advocate General's office in Washington where he applied his legal education. Hosmer conducted the prosecution of Writz of Andersonville notoriety and succeeded in getting him convicted and hung.
Host	Hattie	DC, p1c2, 5/17/1889	Taught summer school in Cooley School.

Genealogical Events from Newspapers for Crawford, Vernon and Grant Counties, Wisconsin, 1870-1901

LAST NAME	FIRST NAME	NEWSPAPER, PAGE/COLUMN MONTH/DAY/YEAR	GENEALOGICAL DATA
Host	Hattie	DC, p1c2, 8/9/1889	Lived in Retreat. Taught school in Ferryville.
Houghton	Charles	DC, p2c2, 10/29/1887	Lived in a comfortable home in De Soto in 1856. He was the father of Dr. Houghton, one of the village's proprietors.
Houghton	Dr.	DC, p2c1, 11/26/1887	In 1856 or 1857 De Soto's only physician was Dr. Houghton "whose chief, and in fact only remedy ws what he called 'Family Medicine.' A second doctor by the name of Hyde appeared in town about this time. He stayed about a year.
Houghton	Dr.	DC, p2c1, 2/3/1888	Dr. Houghton, one of De Soto's proprietors, moved away in 1859 and so did all "desire to make the New England element predominant."
Houghton	Dr.	DC, p2c2, 10/29/1887	Dr. Houghton operated De Soto's first hotel, the Winnesheik Hotel, at the foot of the street opposite Carlyle's store.
Houghton	E. B., Dr.	DR, p3c2, 12/29/1870	Laid out the village of De Soto in 1854. At that time the only building in De Soto was an old log cabin built by a French trader. Houghton was a former resident of Lansing, IA who purchased the land on which De Soto is located from John Mobley. Dr. Houghton opened the first store in De Soto.
Houghton	Edmund	DC, p2c2, 10/29/1887	Owned a wheelwright shop in De Soto in 1856 that he leased to Cyrus and Addison Worth.
Houghton	Katie	DC, p3c4, 12/4/1886	Taught school in the Van Wagner District per Liberty Pole news column.
How	O. J.	BD, p3c2, 3/1/1878	O. J. How married Bell E. Gilbertson on Feb. 21, 1878 in Fennimore. Bride from Fennimore. Groom from Nobles Co., MN. The Rev. D. L. Hubbard officiated.
Howarth	D.	DC, p3c2, 11/13/1886	D. Howarth of De Soto has hosted Miss S.J. Druver [Druier?] of 30 Toby St. Providence, RI for the last 4 months.
Howe	G. W., Mrs.	BD, p3c2, 8/17/1877	Nee Lizzie Lesler. Departed Boscobel for home in New Hampton, IA.
Howe	Henry	RH, p4c2, 5/9/1901	Died April 29, 1901 in Viroqua. Survived by wife and 2 children. Remains shipped to his late home in Deerfield. Mr. Howe of Readstown attended his brother's funeral.
Howe	Lizzie, Mrs.	BD, p3c1, 3/26/1880	Visited her parents before departing for a new home in Kansas City.
Howe	Will E., Mrs.	BD, p3c2, 4/6/1877	Nee Mary Carrier. Traveled from La Crosse to Boscobel to visit relatives and friends.
Howerth	Denis	RH, p5c4, 12/1/1898	Mrs. E. W. Brown of Dakota came to De Soto to visit her father, Denis Howerth.
Hoyt	Nina	DC, p3c2, 8/14/1888	Nina Hoyt married Bernhart Rannetsberger on Aug. 5, 1888. Bride was the daughter of Sen. J. W. Hoyt of Chaseburg.
Huard	William	DC, p1c1, 8/9/1889	Operated a lumberyard in Lynxville. "He is selling at the La Crosse retail prices."
Hubbard	D. L., Rev.	DR, p3c1, 6/8/1871	Pastor of the Methodist Church in De Soto.
Hubbard	Fanny C.	BD, p3c1, 10/3/1879	Milton B. Green married Fanny C. Hubbard last Friday at the residence of Dr. William Stoddart in Boscobel. Bride from Fennimore.
Hubbard	Rev.	DR, p2c4, 12/29/1870	Resided in De Soto. Planned to speak on temperance at the Congregational Church.
Hubbard	W. M.	DC, p3c4, 7/23/1887	Arrived from Ida Grove, IA. Visited his relatives in Retreat, the McClurg and Bishop families.
Hubbard	William	DC, p3c4, 7/31/1886	Visited relatives in Retreat. Made a living selling organs and sewing machines. Resided in Iowa.
Hubbell	A. H.	BD, p3c3, 10/18/1878	A. H. Hubbell of Columbus, OH visited his brother, H. W. Hubbell of Boscobel.
Hubbell	Frank A.	DC, p2c3, 3/19/1887	Lived in De Soto. Ddrowned last fall in Winona. $50 reward offered for the recovery of his body.
Hubbell	H. W., Mr.	BD, p3c2, 3/28/1879	Leader of the Forest City [Boscobel] Cornet Band. Purchased a new cornet.
Hubbell	T. N.	BD, P3c2, 4/23/1880	Sworn in as mayor of Boscobel.
Hudson	Eugene	DC, p3c4, 1/15/1887	Died Jan. 9, 1887 at the residence of L. G. Sterling per the Retreat news column. Funeral services held at the Christian Church by Rev. Houghton.
Huff	Willie	BD, p3c2, 9/11/1883	Departed from Appleton to attend Lawrence University.
Huffman	C. A.	DC, Supp, 10/29/1887	C. A. Huffman of Soldiers Grove, F. G. Barnum of North Star and M. E. Reynolds of Belle Center wrote letters endorsing the La Crosse Business College. The letterswere used in a newspaper advertisement.

Genealogical Events from Newspapers for Crawford, Vernon and Grant Counties, Wisconsin, 1870-1901

LAST NAME	FIRST NAME	NEWSPAPER, PAGE/COLUMN MONTH/DAY/YEAR	GENEALOGICAL DATA
Huffman	C. A.	RH, p4c1, 10/10/1901	Resided in Readstown. Bought the furniture store of Wallace & Ingle in Ladysmith, WI.
Huffman & Fowell		RH, p4c2, 11/9/1899	The partners were building a new stave factory in Readstown and in Sylvan.
Hufschmidt	Charles W.	DR, p3c1, 9/28/1871	Purchased the boat [steamboat?] *Johnny Schmoker* to run between Lansing and Prairie du Chien.
Hufschmidt	Emelie	DR, p3c2, 1/26/1871	Died Jan. 18, 1871 in Lansing from typhoid fever. She was the eldest daughter of C. W. and Rosalie Hufschmidt. Aged 17 years, 8 months and 24 days.
Hufschmidt	Hulda	DR, p3c2, 2/9/1871	Died yesterday of typhoid fever in Lansing. She was the daughter of C. W. Hufschmidt.
Hufschmidt	Robert	DR, p3c1, 1/12/1871	Taught a German language class in De Soto.
Hufschmidt	Robert	DR, p3c5, 2/23/1871	Offered to sell farm implements in De Soto.
Hughes	John	BD, p3c4, 6/3/1881	Friends of John Hughes expected to gather in Boscobel to seek vengeance on [John] Phillips for killing Hughes. Phillips was advised by his friends to leave town. Phillips left his business in the hands of Mr. Heller and departed with his family. Hughes supporters showed up but dispersed. A coroner's jury affirmed that Phillips shot in self-defense when Hughes charged at him with an axe.
Hulls	A. H.	DR, p2c4, 8/24/1871	Operated a hotel in Viola.
Hummel	Edith	BD, p3c1, 1/5/1883	Resided in the Boscobel area. Departed for school at Appleton College.
Hummel	H., Mrs.	BD, p3c2, 6/3/1881	Resided in Boscobel. Visited by her bother, Charles Zimmerman of Beaver Dam.
Hummel	Willie Johnnie	BD, p3c2, 11/11/1881	Died Nov. 5, 1881 in Boscobel at age 5 years, 6 months. He was the youngest son of Mr. and Mrs. Hummel. Funeral held at the Methodist Episcopal Church.
Hummell	Henry	BD, p2c4, 10/22/1880	Proprietor of a meat market in Boscobel. Established 14 years ago. Sells fresh and cured meats, fresh vegetables, lard, tallow, etc.
Humphrey	William	BD, p3c1, 3/23/1883	William Humprey and Walter Hickling of West Grant recovered a span of horses on which they held a chattle mortgage. The horses were sold to Lonahans in Boscobel.
Hunt		DC, p2c1, 2/5/1887	C. V. Porter wrote a series of articles on the Black Hawk War. In it he says "The army under Atkinson encamped on the night of August 1, at Mr. Hunt's place, Sec. 3, 3/4 mile north of the Indian camping ground. The spring where they obtained water is a quarter mile of a mile north of Hunt's house, in a ravine . . . It is said that a part of the army encamped on the ground where stands Mr. Hunt's house."
Hunt	Cyrus	DC, p3c3, 3/3/1888	Planned to send hoops from his home in Retreat to Chicago.
Hunt	George C., Mrs.	BD, p3c3, 9/20/1878	Nee Ella Benedict. Former Boscobel resident. Arrived from Walnut, IA to visit Mrs. Seeds in Boscobel.
Hunt	Kittie	RH, p5c2, 1/13/1898	Taught at Spring Valley. Spend the weekend at the Herman Davenport residence.
Hunt	Squire	DC, p2c3, 11/26/1887	Celebrated his 25th wedding anniversary last Thursday at his home in Retreat.
Huntington	Emma, Miss	DR, p3c1, 4/6/1871	Died April 5, 1871 from Billious fever. She was the daughter of S. F. Huntington of the Town of Freeman. Aged 23 years and 4 months.
Huntington	Fannie B.	DR, p3c2, 4/6/1871	Published the following notice: "I have seen a notice in The *De Soto Republican*, to the effect that I, the wife of H. R. Huntington, had 'left his bed and board.' It is false. Instead of that, he ordered me to pack my trunk, and took me and our child to my grandmother's gate and left me. But before leaving the wagon, he told me never to let him see my face in Iowa again." Signed, Fannie B. Huntington, The deserted Wife. The newspaper continued, "From the above, and what we have learned from other parties, we are led to believe that the said H. R. Huntington never did look a great deal after the comfort and convenience of his wife, and as a family man, was not a success. He is now supposed to be in Iowa and the deserted wife and child are stopping with relatives in the town of Freeman."
Huntington	Fanny B.	DR, p3c2, 8/17/1871	A Summons of Relief was published in Vernon Co. for the case of Fanny B. Huntington, plaintiff, vs. Hezekiah R. Huntington, defendant.
Huntington	H. R.	DR, p3c6, 3/30/1871	Resided in Rising Sun. Published a notice that his wife, Fannie B. Huntington, left his bed and board without just cause or provocation. He warned the public to not trust her on his account, as he would not be responsible for her debts.
Huntington	Hannah L., Mrs.	DC, p2c2, 2/25/1888	Died Feb. 6, 1888 at North Elba, NY at the home of her daughter-in-law, Mrs. Frank Huntington. She was 87. Lived in De Soto for nearly 30 years.

Genealogical Events from Newspapers for Crawford, Vernon and Grant Counties, Wisconsin, 1870-1901

LAST NAME	FIRST NAME	NEWSPAPER, PAGE/COLUMN MONTH/DAY/YEAR	GENEALOGICAL DATA
Huntington	Lee	DC, p3c3, 3/3/1888	Lee Huntington married Etta Hall on Feb. 22, 1888, per Genoa news column.
Huntington	Lizzie, Mrs.	DC, p3c2, 12/25/1886	Arrived in De Soto from Broken Bow, Custer Co., NB to attend her brother's funeral.
Huntington	Lizzie, Mrs.	DC, p3c4, 4/9/1887	Spent the winter in the De Soto area. Returned by train to Anselmo, NB.
Huntington	Luther	DC, p2c2, 7/30/1887	Died last Wednesday near Genoa.
Huntington	S. F., Mr. and Mrs.	DC, p3c4, 5/8/1888	Left the De Soto area for Lincoln, NB.
Huntington	S. S., Mr. and Mrs.	DC, p3c3, 1/21/1888	Arrived in De Soto from their residence in Lincoln, NB to visit Mrs. Huntington's parents, Mr. and Mrs. M. Kalhar.
Huntington	Samuel	DC, p2c2, 11/26/1887	Samuel and Hannah Huntington and their son, Frank, lived on a ridge near De Soto near the B. A. Stevens family in 1857.
Hurd	Cassie Lee	BD, p3c5, 9/7/1879	Died August 30, 1879 in Boscobel at the age of 2 months and 18 days. She was the daughter of G. A. and Lucretia R. Hurd.
Hurd	Frankie, Miss	BD, p3c2, 9/4/1883	F. E. Pearson married Miss Frankie Hurd on Sept. 1, 1883 at 7:00 A.M. The bride's brother, Rev. W. W. Hurd, officiated, at the wedding that was held at the home of another brother, Dr. R. W. Hurd, in Boscobel. Groom was also from Boscobel. The couple's new home will be in Madison where the groom works as a train dispatcher. Bride was daughter of Rev. Z. S. Hurd of Boscobel.
Hurd	Gardner A.	BD, p3c3, 5/24/1878	Gardner A. Hurd married Lucetta B. Bullock on May 20, 1878 at the residence of Philip Kelts of Lancaster. Groom from Boscobel. The Rev. W. L. Brown officiated.
Hurd	O. S.	BD, p3c2, 9/21/1877	Recently married in Farmington, IA. Visited his relative, Dr. Hurd of Boscobel.
Hurd	W. T.	BD, p3c1, 1/5/1877	Physician in Boscobel.
Hurd	Will T.	BD, p3c4, 8/9/1878	Will T. Hurd married Emily B. Casseboom on Aug. 6, 1878 at the Congregational Church in Boscobel. Rev. William Stoddart officiated.
Hurd	Willis	BD, p3c2, 2/2/1877	Rev. J. D. Searles selected him to preach at area Methodist churches.
Hurlbert	Mirtie	RH, p5c4, 7/15/1897	Installed as typo at the Herald office in Readstown.
Hurlburt	F. A.	DC, p3c3, 2/3/1888	Well-known traveling salesman in the area. Resided in Whitewater. Caught typhoid fever in California. Died. [per 2/11/1888 issue]
Hurlbut	A. L.	RH, p7c2, 7/1/1897	Resided in Crawford Co. Visited brother, Scott, in Readstown.
Hurlbut	Albert	BD, p3c1, 4/6/1883	Left Boscobel to open up a farm in Dakota.
Hurlbut	Albert	BD, p3c2, 11/6/1883	Planned to move his family from Boscobel to Aikin, MN.
Hurlbut	boy	BD, p3c1, 10/23/1883	A son was born last week to Henry Hurlbut.
Hurlbut	Henry	BD, p3c3, 9/20/1878	Planned to move from Boston to Boscobel to open a jewelry store.
Hurlbut	Hoffney	BD, p3c2, 7/24/1883	Recently died in Sextonville, Richland Co. Settled in Platteville before 1853, where he made threshing machines. Served as the Platteville postmaster. Moved to Boscobel in 1860. Father of two sons, Henry and Albert, who resided in Boscobel.
Hurlbut	L., Mrs.	BD, p3c2, 4/6/1877	Buried last Wednesday. She was 70 years old. Lived the last 10 years of her life living with her son, Albert Hurlbut of Boscobel.
Hurlbut	Mabel	RH, p4c2, 8/15/1901	Dan Phillips married Mabel Hurlbut on August 21, 1901 at the home of the bride's father, W. S. Hurlbut of Readstown. Groom from Mt. Sterling. Bride was the sister of Mrs. H. M. Pond. Couple planned to move to Dakota.
Hurlbut	W. S.	RH, p4c1, 12/14/1899	His father died on Saturday morning at Hurlbut's Corners.
Hurlbut & Infield		RH, p4c1, 5/11/1899	Recently "burned a fresh kiln of lime" in Readstown. Offered the product for sale.
Hurley		DC, p8c2, 6/28/1889	The infant son of M. Hurley died on Friday in De Soto. Buried in Rising Sun.
Hurley	Henry	BD, p2c2, 11/20/1883	Apointed night watchman for the Soldiers Grove.

Genealogical Events from Newspapers for Crawford, Vernon and Grant Counties, Wisconsin, 1870-1901

LAST NAME	FIRST NAME	NEWSPAPER, PAGE/COLUMN MONTH/DAY/YEAR	GENEALOGICAL DATA
Hurley	M.	DC, p2c2, 5/14/1887	The De Soto Village Board approved the application of M. Hurley for a retail liquor license. William F. Terhune was appointed Village attorney. D. B. Collins was appointed marsahll. James Thompson resigned as Trustee and then appointed Street Commissioner. David Collins was appointed night watchman at a salary of $24 per month, to be on duty from 10 p.m. to 4 a.m. each day.
Hurley	Mike	DC, p3c6, 6/12/1886	Dealer in wine and liquors in De Soto.
Hurley	Mike	DC, p3c2, 7/10/1886	Opened a brewery in De Soto.
Hurley	Mike	DC, p3c3, 3/3/1888	Relocated his saloon from Missouri [southern De Sota] into the Devlin Building on Main Street.
Huse	Charles W.	DC, p2c2, 8/6/1887	Resided in Stoddard. Arrested by Under Sheriff Tongue. Charged with ravishing the 12-year-old daughter of Mrs. Lydia Braley/Brally, a widow. Huse boarded at Mrs. Braley's boarding house. Huse was about 40 years old and had been married 2 times. He claimed to be a doctor and that he previously lived in La Crosse and Minneapolis. Bail set at $1000.
Hushka	L. V.	RH, p4c2, 3/17/1898	He was the son-in-law of F. L. Perham of Readstown and lived in the Sparta area. Departed for the Black River Falls area to join a party going to the Alaskan goldfields.
Huston	Daisy B.	RH, p4c3, 10/17/1901	Alva Strait married Daisy B. Huston on Oct. 9, 1901. Groom was a photographer in Readstown and the son of S. D. Strait of Otter Creek. Justice of the Peace W. J. Roberts officiated.
Huston	Mr.	RH, p4c1, 10/31/1901	Recently died in Otter Creek. He was the brother of Mrs. Alva Strait.
Hutchison	Ab. [Ob.?]	RH, p5c4, 7/22/1897	Planned to leave Readstown for Lowell, NB where he will spend the summer and autumn.
Hutchison	Alta, Mrs.	RH, p5c2, 6/23/1898	Operated the telephone exchange in Readstown.
Hutchison	boy	RH, p4c3, 9/19/1901	A son was recently born to Frank Hutchison of Spring Valley.
Hutchison	C. D.	RH, p4c2, 3/2/1899	Also known as Charles and Dick. Ran an engine on the Atchison, Topeka and Santa Fe Railroad between Paton and Las Vegas, NM and La Junta, CO.
Hutchison	Frank	RH, p4c2, 9/26/1901	Purchased the Gem Meat Market in Readstown from A. C. Helmund.
Hutchison	J. A.	RH, p5c2, 10/27/1898	Purchased a half interest in The [Readstown] Herald.
Hutchison	J. A.	RH, p5c4, 12/1/1898	Wrote a letter about the sites around Denver. It was published in the newspaper.
Hutchison	J. A.	RH, p4c3, 10/18/1900	Wrote a series of letters from the west. They were published in the newspaper.
Hutchison	Joe	RH, p5c4, 6/9/1898	Former resident of Readstown. Moved from Delta to Denver, CO where he works in a bicycle factory.
Hutchison	Joseph A.	RH, p4c2, 11/16/1899	Returned for a visit in his hometown, Readstown, from Colorado. On the way, he visited his brother, William, of Bristol, IA, whom he had not seen for several years. He also visited with Misses Grace and Belle Clancy at their Greene, IA millinery business.
Hutchison	Joseph H.	RH, p4c2, 10/4/1900	Enrolled in Denver [Colorado] Dental College. He was formerly of the Readstown Herald.
Hutchison	Mary A.	RH, p5c5, 7/15/1897	Born in Liberty Pole on Jan. 18, 1850 and died at the home of her brother, William Hutchison, in June of 1897 in Readstown. Moved with her parents to Readstown in 1855. Lived with Mrs. Fay P. Briggs of Soldiers Grove for about 3 years. Also lived with Mrs. Bliss and her sister, Mrs. Wallace Morley. After William Hutchison's wife moved to Viroqua, she kept house for the family who remained on the farm.
Hutchison	May	RH, p4c4, 8/25/1898	Died in Readstown on Aug. 17, 1898 from the effects of a snakebite she received 12 years ago. She was the daughter of William Hutchison. Born Feb. 23, 1870 in Readstown. Taught school in Readstown. When her father was elected Register of Deeds, she choose to stay on the farm with her brother, Will, and uncle, Albert, and keep house.
Hutchison	Pete	RH, p5c2, 4/21/1898	Received a bounty of $175 for wolf pelts.
Hutchison	R. A., Mrs.	RH, p4c3, 5/25/1899	Died May 17, 1899 at the home of her son, Frank Hutchison of Readstown. She was the wife of B. C. Hutchison, deceased. Born in Ohio 64 years ago. Came to Wisconsin with parents, Mr. and Mrs. Munyon, when she was a young girl. Married first to John Lowry, who died in the Civil War. They were the parents of 3 children. Several years later, she married B. C. Hutchison, who died a few years ago. They were the parents of Charles, Frank and Ella. Mrs. Hutchison was a member of the Methodist Episcopal Church.

Genealogical Events from Newspapers for Crawford, Vernon and Grant Counties, Wisconsin, 1870-1901

LAST NAME	FIRST NAME	NEWSPAPER, PAGE/COLUMN MONTH/DAY/YEAR	GENEALOGICAL DATA
Hutchison	Vernice	RH, p5c3, 1/13/1898	Died Sunday of typhoid fever. She was the 2-year-old daughter of Pete Hutchison. Buried in the Readstown Cemetery. Rev. Casper preached the funeral sermon.
Hutchison	Will	RH, p4c2, 3/22/1900	Left Readstown for Viroqua to learn the barber trade at the parlors of Potts & Curtis.
Hutchison	Will	RH, p4c2, 1/31/1901	Gone for 5 years. Will Hutchison and his daughter, Leola, of Bristow, Butler Co., IA were the guest of his mother, Mrs. C. C. Hutchison of Readstown.
Hutchison	William	RH, p5c4, 7/22/1897	Celebrated his 51st birthday in Readstown at a big party held in his honor. He was presented with an Oxford Bible. Served as Register of Deeds.
Hutchison	William	RH, p4c1, 8/1/1901	Given a surprise birthday party on July 20, 1901 to celebrate his 55th [?] birthday. Resided in Viroqua. Party received extensive coverage in the newspaper.
Hutchison	William, Jr.	RH, p4c2, 12/27/1900	William Hutchison, Jr. married Rose Crook on Dec. 23, 1900 at the home of the groom's parents, Mr. and Mrs. William Hutchison. Bride and groom from Readstown.
Hutchison	William, Jr.	RH, p4c2, 8/29/1901	Planned to move to Cleressa, MN and open a barbershop, per Readstown news column.
Hutchison	William, Mrs.	RH, p4c2, 5/10/1900	Cancer was removed from Mrs. Hutchison's breast by Drs. Trowbridge and Belt of Viroqua and Dr. Brown of Soldiers Grove.. Mrs. Hutchison lived in Readstown.
Hutson	B. D.	DC, p1c2, 8/9/1889	B. D. Hutson and his daughter, Carrie and Olive, all of Ferryville, went on a trip to Lansing.
Hyde	E. B.	DR, p3c1, 9/28/1871	Resided in Town of Sterling. Elected a lay delegate to Western Wisconsin Conference of the Methodist Episcople Church that meets in Mineral Point.
Infield	Lee	RH, p5c2, 8/11/1898	Went to South Dakota to work during the harvest.
Infield	Mr.	RH, p5c4, 12/16/1897	Mr. Infield of Scott, Crawford Co. visited his daughter, Mrs. W. S. Hurlbutt of Readstown. Mr. Infield's son, Lee, also went on the trip.
Ingebretson	Nels	RH, p5c2, 8/9/1900	A notice of application for final settlement of estate was published by the Vernon County Probate Court.
Ingebrigtin	Nils	RH, p5c4, 4/6/1899	Vernon County Probate Court published a notice regarding a case involving the proof of a will for Nils Ingebrigtin, late of the Town of Kickapoo. Peter Briggson submitted the will to the court.
Ingersol	C. L., Mr. and Mrs.	DC, p3c3, 4/2/1887	Returned to De Soto after visiting their daughter, Mrs. Ryan, who gave birth to their new grandson. The Ryan's lived in Hanover, WI.
Ingersol	C. L., Mrs.	DC, p3c2, 3/12/1887	Visited daughter, Mrs. Susie C. Ryan of Hanover, IL.
Ingersol	C. L., Mrs.	DC, p3c3, 11/6/1888	Mrs. C. L. Ingersol of De Soto and Miss Hattie Mellen of Retreat attended the W.C.T.U. convention in La Crosse.
Ingersol	Charles L.	DC, p2c3, 3/12/1887	The Vernon County Circuit Court published a summons for the case Charles L. Ingersol, plaintiff vs. Martin McCormick, defendant.
Ingersol Nine		DC, p3c4, 4/9/1887	The "Ingersol Nine" ball club in Victory was composed of Will Cooper, George Carlyle, Franie Dyer, Will Marker, Henry Furman, Elmer Marker, Ed Harrington and Corril Clark.
Ingersoll	C. L.	DR, p3c4, 12/15/1870	Published a notice asking all persons to settle their accounts with him. He was the proprietor of the De Soto Grain and Produce Market.
Ingersoll	C. L.	DR, p4c3, 12/15/1870	Advertised the sale of general merchandise in De Soto.
Ingersoll	C. L.	DR, p3c2, 12/29/1870	Store in De Soto sold dry goods, clothing, groceries, stoneware, tableware, cutlery, hardware, drugs, medicines and "everything you can think of."
Ingersoll	C. L.	DC, p2c1, 2/3/1888	Arrived in De Soto in 1859.
Ingersoll	C. L., Mr. and Mrs.	DC, p3c3, 1/28/1888	Miss Lizzie Stogdill of New York City and Miss Sarah Gibson of Greeley, CO were the guests of Mr. and Mrs. C. L. Ingersoll of De Soto.
Ingersoll	D. A.	DC, p3c4, 5/28/1887	Subscribed to the newspaper. Resided in Fort Dodge, IA.
Ingersoll	Mina M.	DC, p2c2, 11/27/1886	Died on Nov. 1, 1886 in Englewood, near Chicago, IL. She was the wife of William Stacey, Jr. and daughter of the late Robert S. Ingersoll of Evans, NY. She was about 50 years of age. She was noted for her prose, poetry and work with the W.C.T.U. She was related to the C.L. Ingersoll family of De Soto and William G. Conklin family of Diamond Mills.
Ingham	Sam	DC, p4c3, 3/19/1889	Home recently destroyed by fire in Seneca. He was unable to control the flames. Miss Lizzie was burned about the head and right arm while letting calves out of a barn.
Inman	David	DC, p2c2, 2/12/1889	He is logging on the headwaters of the Wisconsin River. Visited relatives in Victory.
Inman	Etta	DC, p3c4, 2/26/1887	Arrived from home in Tomah, WI to visit grandmother, Mrs. Conrad of Victory.

Genealogical Events from Newspapers for Crawford, Vernon and Grant Counties, Wisconsin, 1870-1901

LAST NAME	FIRST NAME	NEWSPAPER, PAGE/COLUMN MONTH/DAY/YEAR	GENEALOGICAL DATA
Ivey	Joseph	BD, p3c2, 9/15/1882	Joseph Ivey of Marion killed his son-in-law, Orlando Bacon, in self-defense. Bacon owed money to Ivey and promised to give him a partial payment when his grain was threshed. Ivey discovered that Bacon planned to dispose of the grain to other parties and had an attachment placed on the grain. This angered Bacon. Ivey turned himself in to authorities..
Ivey	Joseph	BD, p3c1, 9/18/1883	Joseph Ivey was found guilty of manslaughter in the third degree for murder of his son-in-law, Orlando Bacon.
Ivey	Joseph	BD, p3c1, 9/25/1883	Sentenced to two years in the State prison for the killing of Orlando Bacon.
Ivey	Joseph	BD, p3c4, 2/22/1878	Admitted to the bar. Resided in Lancaster.
Jackson	George Barren	BD, p3c4, 4/19/1878	Died April 10, 1878 in Boscobel at the age of 6. Son of George and Julia Jackson.
Jackson	George F.	DC, p3c2, 11/12/1887	Died Nov. 5, 1887 at the age of 81. He was an early settler of Harmony.
Jackson	Joseph	BD, p3c4, 1/16/1880	Commissioners Notice was published that the estate of Joseph Jackson, late of Hickory Grove, was in Probate.
Jackson	Joseph	BD, p3c3, 1/31/1879	Resided in the Boscobel area. Recently died. He was buried Tuesday. Lived over 70 years.
Jacobs	L. W.	BD, p3c2, 12/25/1883	Attended law school at the State University. Home for the holidays.
Jacobs	Lansil	BD, p3c3, 6/22/1883	Returned to Boscobel from Madison where he was studying at the State University.
Jacobs	Lansil W.	BD, p3c2, 6/17/1881	Resident of Boscobel. Sent a letter to the editor denying his participation in recent "rumored events."
Jacobs	Larry	BD, p2c4, 11/26/1880	Grant County paid him a bounty for scalps turned into the county.
Jacobson	girl	RH, p4c2, 6/28/1900	A daughter was recently born to Martin Jacobson of Readstown.
Jacobson	Martin	RH, p4c1, 9/6/1900	Sold his Readstown area property to Pete Sorenson. Jacobson was "compelled to leave Wisconsin's damp climate."
Jacobson	Martin	RH, p4c3, 10/3/1901	Died Sunday of consumption at the home of his parents near Readstown. Went to Colorado a year ago to regain his health. It was a temporary help. Returned home last spring. Funeral services were held at Folsom.
Jacobson Bros.		RH, p5c6, 9/9/1897	Advertised well drilling services in Readstown.
Jacobus	Charles	DC, p3c2, 7/3/1888	Jacobus was the 16-year-old son of P. Jacobus of Retreat. He went to La Crosse to get treatment for his eyes.
Jacobus	Delos	DR, p3c4, 3/9/1871	Hired to operate the telegraph office in De Soto.
Jacobus	Delos	DR, p3c1, 8/31/1871	Left De Soto for a new home in St. Paul.
Jacobus	Delos	DR, p3c2, 11/16/1871	Badly injured last week near Winona. His brother-in-law, Charley Stevens, went to see him. "Delos is an unfortunate youth of De Soto, always getting hurt . . ."
Jacobus	Elsworth	DC, p3c4, 11/27/1886	Recently married in Dakota. Former resident of Retreat.
Jacobus	Ida G.	DC, p2c3, 3/5/1887	Died Feb. 5, 1887 at the residence of her brother, Delos Jacobus, of Crookston, MN. She lived all but the last 2 of her 31 years in De Soto. She was an invalid for a number of years.
Jacobus	Katie	DC, p3c2, 5/7/1887	Native of the De Soto area. Taught school in the Powell District.
Jacobus	Mr.	DR, p3c2, 12/29/1870	Operated a wagon manufactory on Main Street in De Soto.
Jacobus	Peter	DC, p3c3, 11/20/1886	Peter Jacobus, his son, Charley, and Bert Bates returned to Retreat from a trip to Dakota.
James	Bill	BD, p2c3, 2/23/1883	Planned to move from [Richland Center area?] to Miner's Point, Dakota to open a hardware store.
James	Dora	DR, p3c3, 9/7/1871	Died of consumption on Sept. 5, 1871 in the Town of Freeman. She was the wife of Ethelbert E. James. Aged 24 years and 28 days.
James	N. L.	BD, p2c3, 3/17/1882	Established a wagon factory in Richland Center at Parfrey sawmill.
James	N. L.	RH, p4c3, 11/30/1899	Lived in Richland Center. He was General Manager for the Western Wisconsin Railroad, formerly called the Kickapoo Valley and Northern Railroad.

Genealogical Events from Newspapers for Crawford, Vernon and Grant Counties, Wisconsin, 1870-1901

LAST NAME	FIRST NAME	NEWSPAPER, PAGE/COLUMN MONTH/DAY/YEAR	GENEALOGICAL DATA
James	S. L., Mrs.	BD, p3c3, 10/4/1878	After visiting with daughter, Mrs. F. C. Jenkins of Boscobel, Mrs. S. L. James returned to her home in Janesville.
James	Thomas, Capt.	DC, p3c2, 3/12/1887	From New York. Visited his parents in Retreat after a trip to China and Japan.
James	Thomas, Captain	DC, p2c2, 9/18/1888	Visited parents in Retreat.
James	William	BD, p3c1, 8/4/1882	William James and John Crowley paid fines for disturbing the peace in Boscobel.
James Mason GAR. No. 65		DC, p3c2, 11/19/1887	The Women's Relief Corps of De Soto's James Mason GAR. Corps, No. 65 was formed by Mrs. Charity Rusk Craig and Mrs. E. Hazen. The officers were Mrs. Addie R. Page, Mrs. Amanda Clark, Almeda Whitney, Mrs. Maria L. Couch, Miss Ellen J. Lawrence, Mrs. Maty Witcraft, Mrs. Martha Blanchard and Mrs. Mary Lane.
Jameson	Miss	BD, p3c4, 6/27/1879	Prof. H. R. Smith married the daughter of William Jameson on June 15, 1879. Groom was principal at Muscoda. His parents lived in Baraboo.
Jefferson	James	RH, p3c4, 9/29/1898	Arrived home for a visit with his parents, Rev. and Mrs. James Jefferson of De Soto. He had been in Cuba.
Jeffries	W.	BD, p2c3, 8/24/1877	Sold fruit and candy in his store in Muscoda.
Jeide	John	BD, p3c1, 3/24/1882	Jeide and family lived in Lancaster. They were the guests of Henry Henkle of Boscobel.
Jencks		BD, p3c1, 7/8/1881	A daughter was born July 3, 1881 to Mrs. Mary E. Jencks of Milwaukee. The girl is the granddaughter of A. F. Snow of Boscobel.
Jencks	Clifford	BD, p3c2, 11/22/1878	Clifford Jencks married Mary at the residence of A. F. Snow last Thursday afternoon.
Jencks	S. R., Mrs.	BD, p3c2, 7/2/1880	Funeral held for Mrs. S. R. Jencks on Sunday at the Methodist Episcople Church in Boscobel. Body arrived by train from Milwaukee. She moved to Milwaukee one year ago. Died June 25, 1880 from an accident in Milwaukee. A frightened horse upset her buggy. She fell out and hit her head. Her stepson, Clifford Jencks, had parked the buggy. She was daughter of Rev. I. S. and Mrs. Hurd of Boscobel and sister of Dr. Watson Hurd of Madison and Dr. W. T. Hurd [dentist] of Boscobel.
Jenkins	Charles	BD, p3c3, 10/4/1878	Resided in Bosobel. Sent to Reform School.
Jenkins	F. C., Mr. and Mrs.	BD, p3c3, 7/1/1881	Left Boscobel to attend the funeral of Mr. Jenkin's mother in Janesville, WI.
Jenkins	Joe	BD, p3c5, 8/30/1878	Jenkins was rumored to have beaten his wife. He was said to have shot her, struck her with a brick and injured her hand and hit her with metal knuckles. Mrs. Jenkins said officers refused to issue a warrant for husband's arrest. The newspaper doubted the officers would refuse Mrs. Jenkin's request.
Jenkins	Joe	BD, p3c2, 5/23/1879	Joe Jenkins was arrested for injuring Eli Woodard in a knife fight in Boscobel. Woodard may lose his arm.
Jenkins	Joe	BD, p3c1, 6/6/1879	Joe Jenkins and Barney Hine were arrested for fighting in Boscobel by Marshal Kelty. Jenkins hit Hine with brass knuckles and fined $10.
Jenkins	Joseph	BD, p3c1, 10/6/1882	Jenkins and John Miles were arrested in Boscobel for assault with intent to steal.
Jenkins	Joseph	BD, p3c1, 11/24/1882	The case, Wisconsin vs. Joseph Jenkins and Uriah Jenkins, Jr. was continued.
Jenkins	Joseph	BD, p3c2, 2/16/1883	Joseph Jenkins and John Miles were found guilty of assaulting Bert Cheever [of Boscobel?] with intent to rob.
Jennings	Emily, Mrs.	DC, p3c4, 7/3/1888	Robbed of $800 while visiting a son on Trout Creek in Crawford Co. She was from the Town of Liberty. The burglars were captured.
Jetter	J.	BD, p3c1, 3/16/1883	J. Jetter married Mrs. J. Christ on Mar. 10, 1883 in Prairie du Chien. Bride from Marietta. Groom from Wauzeka. Major L. F. S. Viele officiated.
Jetter	J., Mrs.	BD, p2c2, 9/18/1883	Mrs. Jetter of Wauzeka offered to sell or rent the George Christ farm in Marietta, three miles north of Boscobel. 110 of the 220-acre farm were under cultivation.
Jewell	S. Virginia	DR, p3c3, 6/29/1871	C. D. Williams married S. Virginia Jewell on June 24, 1871 at the home of the bride's father. Groom from Liberty Pole. Bride from Town of Freeman.

Genealogical Events from Newspapers for Crawford, Vernon and Grant Counties, Wisconsin, 1870-1901

LAST NAME	FIRST NAME	NEWSPAPER. PAGE/COLUMN MONTH/DAY/YEAR	GENEALOGICAL DATA
John	Winnebago	BD, p3c2, 3/16/1883	Well known to residents in the area for over 40 years. He was an 86 year old Indian. His body was found a mile west of Woodman. John was hit by a train. He and his companion, Lewis Johnson [or Black Hawk], were drunk and sitting on the tracks when John was struck. An inquest into the death was initiated. He was the uncle of Mike Cloud. Authorities notified Indians living in the area. Burial rites were performed by Mike Cloud and his followers from Blue River and George Goodvillage and his attendants from the Kickapoo. He was buried in the cemetery in regular Indian fashion.
Johnson	Anna	DC, p2c2, 1/1/1887	C. C. Harris married Anna Johnson at Bay State House in De Soto on Dec. 27, 1886. Groom from Minneapolis. Bride from Town of Freeman.
Johnson	Anna	DC, p3c3, 3/27/1888	Declared insane. Taken to Mendota Asylum from her home in West Prairie by Sheriff Gosling.
Johnson	Austin	DC, p3c3, 11/13/1886	Sold a mortgaged team of horses in La Crosse for $212. Ole Torger, one of the mortgagors, found him and "compeled him to refund the money and return."
Johnson	Belinda	DC, p2c3, 2/12/1887	Fred W. Graham married Belinda Johnson on Feb. 7, 1887. Groom from Houston Co., MN. Bride from Fillmore Co., MN. D. A. Steele, J.P., officiated at ceremony in De Soto.
Johnson	Elizabeth	DR, p3c1, 1/12/1871	Austin Hanson married Elizabeth Johnson on Dec. 30, 1870 in Ferryville. The bride and groom were from Freeman. W. F. McMasters, J.P., officiated.
Johnson	Ella	DC, p3c3, 1/28/1888	Traveled from West Prairie to visit her sister, Mrs. T. Peterson of the De Soto area.
Johnson	Fred, M. D.	DC, p3c2, 6/19/1888	Returned from Cameron, WI for a visit in Retreat, his old home.
Johnson	George M.	DC, p2c4, 1/15/1887	George M. Johnson married Bertha O. Olson on Jan. 8, 1887 at De Soto. Groom from Waukon IA. Bride from Houston Co., MN. William F. Terhune officiated.
Johnson	Hans	BD, p3c2, 4/14/1882	Former resident of Port Andrew. Now from Hillsboro [Hillsbow?], Dakota. Visited Boscobel.
Johnson	Hiram	DC, p1c4, 5/3/1889	Resided in Ohio. Unmarried. Visited with brothers in Bad Axe City.
Johnson	J. C, Mrs.	DC, p2c2, 2/11/1888	Died Feb. 5, 1888. Born Christiana Otteson 24 years ago. Married less than a year. Wife of the Town of Sterling Treasurer. [also p3c3]
Johnson	J. C.	DC, p3c3, 8/14/1886	He was a candidate for Vernon Co. Treasurer. Resided in West Prairie.
Johnson	J. J.	DR, p3c2, 8/17/1871	He was a former resident of the De Soto area. Now lived in Madison, NB.
Johnson	J. O., Mrs.	BD, p3c2, 10/30/1883	Returned to Boscobel from Northfield, MN after receiving a telegram stating her mother was ill.
Johnson	John C.	DC, p3c4, 4/9/1887	John C. Johnson married Christina Otteson last Thursday in West Prairie.
Johnson	John C.	DC, p2c1, 5/21/1887	The John C. Johnson wedding took place on Mar. 31, 1887 at the home of the bride's parents in Mt. Sterling. A large list of gifts and the names of those who gave them was published. [Married Christina Otteson.]
Johnson	John O.	RH, p4c1, 7/5/1900	John O. Johnson married Christe Verson on July 1, 1900 at De Soto. Bride from West Prairire. Groom well-known in Readstown.
Johnson	John, Mr. and Mrs.	BD, p3c2, 2/8/1878	Mr. and Mrs. John Johnson and brother, Matt Johnson, of Jamestown, were called insane. Insanity caused by their intense religious feelings. In their zeal, they wre found to be neglecting their children. They were Catholic.
Johnson	John, Mrs.	BD, p3c2, 5/4/1877	Arrived from Northfield, MN to visit in Boscobel, her former residence.
Johnson	Julia	BD, p2c3, 7/29/1881	Died July 5, 1881in her home in Port Andrews. Born about 26 years ago in Norway. Sister of Hans.
Johnson	Lewis	DR, p3c2, 12/14/1871	Moved away from Ferryville. The editor hoped he got the smallpox because he left without paying for his newspaper subscription.
Johnson	Maggie	BD, p2c5, 1/13/1882	Court summonds published for the case, Maggie Johnson, plaintiff, vs. John Johnson, defendant. They were residents of the Boscobel area.
Johnson	Maggie	DC, p3c3, 9/18/1886	Recently married T. Peterson of Soldiers Grove. She was the daughter of John C. Johnson of West Prairie.
Johnson	Martin A.	DC, p2c2, 9/17/1887	Lived in Kelso, Dakota. Subscribed to the *De Soto Chronicle*.
Johnson	O. M., Rev.	DC, p3c5, 9/25/1886	Preached his farewell sermon at [?].
Johnson	Ole	BD, p2c1, 7/18/1879	Denied a pension for his military service. Discharged in 1864 at Harpers Ferry. Soon after he lost an arm due to earlier injuries. Departed his home in Lancaster for Washington, D.C. to plead his case.

Genealogical Events from Newspapers for Crawford, Vernon and Grant Counties, Wisconsin, 1870-1901

LAST NAME	FIRST NAME	NEWSPAPER, PAGE/COLUMN MONTH/DAY/YEAR	GENEALOGICAL DATA
Johnson	Ole J.	DC, p3c3, 1/28/1888	Died at the Mendota asylum. Buried Wednesday in West Prairie.
Johnson	S.	BD, p3c3, 11/16/1877	Robbed of $2000 after returning from Chicago where he sold cattle. Resided in Black Earth. Made a living as a cattle dealer.
Johnson	William	BD, p3c1, 3/11/1881	Died at age 84 on Feb. 20, 1881 in Bloomington. He asked that no ladies attend his funeral.
Johnson	William O.	DC, p3c2, 7/24/1886	Died at his home near Monument Rock on July 15, 1886 in his 41st year of life.
Johnsroot	Mons O.	BD, p3c1, 6/22/1883	Resided in Castle Rock. Sold his tobacco crop in Boscobel to William Nelson of Boscobel.
Johnstone	Sam, Mrs.	BD, p2c2, 7/6/1883	Editor of the newspaper published a letter authored by Mrs. Johnstone describing her train trip between Boscobel and Butte, Montana. Mrs. Johnstone apparently grew up in Boscobel and now lives in Butte.
Johnstone	William	RH, p4c2, 11/11/1897	Departed Readstown for the northern woods to find work in the pineries or dispose of his team.
Jones	Bertha, Mrs.	RH, p5c4, 2/15/1900	Mrs. Jones' funeral held at the Christian Church in Sugar Grove on Tuesday. Buried in Sugar Grove Cemetery.
Jones	boy	RH, p4c1, 3/2/1899	A son was recently born to William Jones of Readstown.
Jones	Clarissa	BD, p2c4, 4/19/1878	A hearing was scheduled by the Grant Co. Probate Court for the estate of Clarissa Jones.
Jones	Clarissa	BD, p2c4, 10/11/1878	Grant County published a probate notice for Clarissa Jones, deceased. George Cannon to be executor.
Jones	Clarissa	BD, p3c2, 4/13/1877	Died Sunday afternoon. Funeral was held at the Baptist Church. She was the sister of Miss M. M. Jones in Boscobel.
Jones	Clarissa	BD, p2c4, 5/3/1878	Born March 28, 1828 in Gerry, Chautauqua Co., NY. She was the ninth child of Stephen and Clarissa Jones. Joined the Baptist Church in Fredonia in 1852. Removed to Wisconsin in 1857. Died April 8, 1877 from "melanosis of lungs and heart disease." Martha M. Jones provided an account of her deathbed activities.
Jones	Ira C.	BD, p3c2, 1/5/1877	Planned to sell farm stock, implements and household goods at his home in Hickory Grove.
Jones	James	BD, p3c4, 10/29/1880	James Jones of Grant Co. was discharged by writ of habeous corpus. Had been held in custody of Grant Co. sheriff by order of Superintendent of the Lunatic Asylum in Madison.
Jones	James	BD, p3c1, 7/22/1881	Taken from Boscobel to the asylum in Madison.
Jones	James	BD, p2c7, 10/22/1880	State of Wisconsin vs. James Jones. "The above named James Jones was this day discharged by me on a hearing upon a writ of habeas corpus issued by me, in the above matter, he being held in custody by the sheriff of Grant county on an order from the Superintendent of the Lunatic Asylum at Madison and from which he was discharged." A. P. Thompson, Circuit Court Commissioner, Grant Co. Oct. 14, 1880
Jones	James	BD, p3c1, 1/5/1877	Proprietor of the Carrier House in Boscobel.
Jones	Rev.	RH, p7c1, 7/1/1897	Pastor of the Church of Christ in Readstown.
Jones	Robert C.	BD, p3c2, 1/24/1879	Robert C. Jones married Eliza E. Colburn at the residence of the bride's father on Jan. 15, 1879. Bride from Crawford Co. Groom from Mt. Ida. The Rev. W. Stoddart officiated.
Jones	S. N., Mrs.	BD, p3c1, 6/16/1882	Died a week ago Monday in Fennimore of heart disease while "engaged out in a washing."
Jones	T. J.	BD, p3c2, 5/28/1880	Appointed to be a census enumerator in Hickory Grove, Grant Co.
Jones	T. T.	DC, p3c2, 7/17/1886	Resided in De Soto. His parents, Mr. and Mrs. T. C. Jones of Minnesota, came to visit him. T. C. graduated from a musical college in Fayette.
Jones	Thomas	RH, p5c3, 11/4/1897	Lost his barn, hay, grain, team and harness to a fire in Sugar Grove.
Jones	Tim	DC, p3c2, 10/23/1886	Completed work on the spire of the Catholic Church in Rising Sun.
Jones	William	RH, p5c3, 1/20/1898	Resided in Readstown. Purchased a newspaper subscription for his brother in Dakota.
Jope	Robert	BD, p2c3, 6/3/1881	Aged 88. Destitute. Passed through Lone Rock on foot on his way to Pittsburgh, PA. Started from Wauzeka where his son-in-law, Fin Seely, lived.
Jordan	James	DC, p2c3, 8/20/1887	James Jordan recently married Marcia Wightman of Oregon.

Genealogical Events from Newspapers for Crawford, Vernon and Grant Counties, Wisconsin, 1870-1901

LAST NAME	FIRST NAME	NEWSPAPER, PAGE/COLUMN MONTH/DAY/YEAR	GENEALOGICAL DATA
Jordan	James, Mrs.	DC, p3c2, 12/24/1887	Traveled from Retreat to Neilsville to visit her brother.
Jordan	L. S.	RH, p4c1, 1/18/1900	Employed by the Readstown Broom Factory. Resided in La Farge.
Jordan	R. W.	DR, p3c2, 1/4/1872	Sold his farm in the Town of Sterling to Mr. Miner of Connecticut.
Jordon	girl	DC, p3c3, 6/19/1888	A daughter was recently born to James Jordon of Retreat.
Jordon	James	DC, p3c4, 2/5/1887	James Jordon of Greene, Iowa visited his sister, Mrs. C. C. Bishop of Retreat.
Joseph	Alice	RH, p5c4, 10/6/1898	Delbert Neeley married Alice Joseph at the home of the bride's parents in De Soto on September 28, 1898. Groom from La Crosse. The Rev. James Jefferson officiated.
Joseph	Charles	RH, p4c2, 9/8/1898	Nettie Wilford married Charles Joseph at the home of the bride's parents on August 2, 1898, per De Soto news column.
Joseph	Maggie	DC, p3c2, 12/11/1888	Maggie Joseph married Ed Angell on Nov. 29, 1888 at home of the bride's brother, William Joseph of Cooley Valley. Groom son of Robert Angell. Planned to live in Michigan. [and p3c4, 12/18/1888] Rev. William Haughton officiated.
Joseph	Mary E.	DC, p3c4, 12/31/1887	Mary E. Joseph married Jerome B. Hall on Christmas Day 1887 at the residence of the bride's parents near De Soto. Groom from Alma Center, WI. The Rev. Thomas Crouch officiated.
Joseph	W. M.	DR, p3c4, 8/31/1871	Published a notice that he took up two stray colts in the Town of Wheatland.
Joseph	William, Sr.	DC, p2c3, 5/29/1888	Seriously ill with inflamatory rheumatism in Cooley Valley.
Jrmbois	Media	DC, p2c3, 9/17/1887	Media Jrmbois [newspaper typo?] and family left Genoa for St. Croix Falls to open a boarding house.
Judge	Patrick	BD, p3c1, 9/18/1883	Patrick Judge, Patrick Battle, John Judge and John Judge, Jr. were found guilty of manslaughter in the fourth degree for the death of the negro Gatlin in Lancaster.
Judkins	J. C.	BD, p2c6, 10/22/1880	Proprietor of the art car in Boscobel. "Mr. Judkins makes a specialty of the silver-type production of the human face and form known to art . . ."
Juelson	Peter	BD, p2c4, 11/26/1880	Grant County paid him a bounty for scalps turned into the county.
Kaitenbach	Mary	BD, p3c2, 2/18/1881	George Kendall married Mary Kaitenbach on Feb. 17, 1881 at the residence of Mrs. Cornelia Dyer. The Rev. Charles Schraudenbach officiated. Groom from Boscobel. [Kaltenbach?]
Kalenbach	Thressa	BD, p3c3, 7/22/1881	Arrived in Boscobel from Potosi to visit her sister, Mrs. William Dyer.
Kalhar	D. J.	DC, p3c3, 7/3/1888	Served as assistant to the editor of the *De Soto Chronicle*.
Kalhar	D. J.	DC, p4c3, 3/19/1889	Departed De Soto for Omaha. Planned to go to Oklahoma when the land is opened and set up a farm.
Kalhar	D. J.	DC, p2c1, 5/10/1889	Wrote 2 letters from Oklahoma that described the Oklahoma land rush. They were published in the newspaper.
Kalhar	D. M.	DC, p3c2, 10/16/1886	Arrived in De Soto from Nogales, AZ to visit friends.
Kalhar	Dan	DC, p8c2, 6/21/1889	Returned to De Soto from Oklahoma. Planned to be gone for 2 years, but saw all he wanted to see in 2 months.
Kalhar	Dan J.	DC, p2c1, 10/2/1888	Purchased the *De Soto Chronicle* from Fred Z. Alexander.
Kalhar	Dan J.	DC, p2c1, 3/5/1889	Sold the *De Soto Chronicle* to Frank A. Carr.
Kalhar	Dennis	DC, p3c3, 12/18/1886	Died Dec. 12, 1886 from a gun shot in Nogales, AZ.
Kalhar	Dennis M.	DC, p2c2, 12/25/1886	Died Dec. 11, 1886 in Nogales, AZ. Worked as a railroad agent. Shot by Inspector Hambleton after a quarrel in the U.S. Custom House. Born in Port Washington, WI on Sept. 10, 1855. Moved with his parents to De Soto in 1857. Brother, Robert, brought the body back to Wisconsin for burial. [Lengthy article.]
Kalhar	Inez, Mrs.	DC, p3c3, 5/21/1887	Resided in De Soto. Visited her parents, Mr. and Mrs. J. B. McClurg of WestPrairie.
Kalhar	Robert	DC, p3c4, 12/11/1886	Resided in De Soto. Received a telegram that his brother, Dennis Kalhar, was shot at Nogales, AZ. The wound was probably fatal. Robert left on a train for Nogales.
Kalhar	Robert	DC, p3c4, 12/25/1886	Returned to Nogales to settle his brother's affairs, including a $5000 accident insurance policy.

Genealogical Events from Newspapers for Crawford, Vernon and Grant Counties, Wisconsin, 1870-1901

LAST NAME	FIRST NAME	NEWSPAPER, PAGE/COLUMN MONTH/DAY/YEAR	GENEALOGICAL DATA
Kalhar	Robert, Mr. and Mrs.	DC, p3c4 8/13/1887	Departed De Soto for a new home in eastern Wisconsin.
Kalish	H.	DC, p2c1, 12/18/1886	Sold milk and honey in Stoddard.
Kaltenback	Frank	BD, p3c1, 5/20/1881	Arrived from Harvard, NB to visit friends in Boscobel. [Kaitenback?]
Kalvestran	O. A., Mrs.	RH, p4c2, 10/10/1901	Resided in Readstown. Entered several pieces of "fancywork" and paintings at the Gays Mills Fair.
Kanable	Myrtle M.	RH, p5c4, 3/16/1899	George A. Benn married Myrtle M. Kanable last Sunday per the Sugar Grove news column.
Kanable	Oscar	RH, p4c2, 3/2/1899	Came from Berlin, MO to visit E. P. Kellogg of Readstown.
Kanable	Owen	RH, p4c4, 7/21/1898	Ed Smith and Owen Kanable of Kickapoo bought out the shares of L. R. Gribble and John Downey in a threshing machine. They will operate it this fall.
Kane	Con, Jr.	DC, p3c4, 2/19/1887	Dangerously ill at his home in Seneca.
Karrigan	Mary	BD, p3c3, 8/13/1881	Died Friday after hanging laundry in the high heat at the Railway House in Prairie du Chien. Recently arrived from the "old country."
Kast	J. N.	BD, p3c1, 6/11/1880	J. N. Kast married Emily Brickner last Monday in Boscobel. Justice DeWitt officiated.
Kast	Martha	RH, p4c2, 5/9/1901	Harvey Schovill[e] married Martha Kast on May 5, 1901 at the home of the bride's parents, Mr. and Mrs. George Kast of Readstown. Groom from Crawford Co.
Kau [Kan?]	Kate, Miss	BD, p3c3, 7/25/1879	Arrived from Milwaukee to visit sister, Mrs. E. O. Speigelberg of Boscobel. Mrs. J. Schaurnacher of Portage City arrived to visit daughter, Mrs. E. O. Speigelberg.
Kavanaugh	Grant	BD, p3c3, 9/10/1880	Died Aug. 26, 1880. He was the son of William Kavanaugh of Blue River Station.
Kayo	L.	DC, p3c3, 9/18/1886	Just completed a foundation under his store building in Lynxville and will erect an adjoining wing.
Kazda	John	BD, p3c1, 8/25/1882	John Kazda married Delia Richmann on Aug. 17, 1882 in Boscobel at the Wisconsin Hotel. Bride and groom from Wauzeka. J. McLaughlin, J.P. officiated.
Keene	Rossie	BD, p3c7, 3/2/1877	A sheriff's sale was ordered to settle a foreclosure in the case John P. Lewis vs. unknown heirs of Rossie Keene of Lancaster, deceased.
Keily	James	BD, p3c4, 2/22/1878	Died last Monday while returning to Little Grant from Bridgeport where he went to sell pork. Rode home with Benj. Garthwaite who was unable to revive him. Wife died one or two years ago. Survived by a large family of children.
Keiren	Thomas	BD, p3c1, 10/24/1879	While working at the hoop and strap factory of Thomas Seaton he got the end of his thumb too close to the machinery.
Keirin	Vina	DC, p3c4, 12/4/1886	Taught school in the Gorrell District per Liberty Pole news column.
Kellar	J. A.	DC, p3c3, 10/23/1886	Rented Tuttle's Restaurant in De Soto.
Kelley	child	BD, p3c2, 1/10/1879	A child of Mr. and Mrs. Kelley recently died of scarlet fever in Boscobel.
Kellicut		RH, p5c4, 9/16/1897	A daughter was recently born to Ed Kellicut of the Ross area.
Kellicut	Lan	RH, p4c4, 10/28/1897	Hired to do carpentry work on a new barn for Will Groves of Ross.
Kellogg	C. L., Mr. and Mrs.	BD, p3c1, 7/11/1879	Mr. and Mrs. C. L. Kellogg [nee Mame Rice] visited Boscobel, the wife's former home.
Kellogg	Charles	BD, p3c2, 4/29/1881	Home in Dry Hollow, near Boscobel, was destroyed by fire. Insurance will cover the loss.
Kellogg	Charles L.	BD, p3c3, 12/14/1877	Charles L. Kellogg married Mame Rice on Dec. 12, 1877 at the home of the bride's uncle, J. H. Sarles, in Boscobel. Planned to live in Oconomowoc. The Rev. W. M. Stoddart officiated.
Kellogg	H. R.	RH, p4c2, 1/31/1901	Opened a shoe repair business in Readstown.
Kellogg	Hiram	RH, p4c1, 11/4/1897	Advertised building moving servie in Readstown.
Kellogg	Hiram	RH, p5c2, 4/14/1898	Thrown off his horse while racing. He broke his collarbone.
Kellogg	L. S., Mr. and Mrs.	RH, p4c1, 7/11/1901	Mr. and Mrs. L. S. Kellogg, J. W. Sutherland and Mr. N. Davenport attended the reunion of the 12th WI Vol. Regt. at Boscobel from July 3 - 5, 1901.

Genealogical Events from Newspapers for Crawford, Vernon and Grant Counties, Wisconsin, 1870-1901

LAST NAME	FIRST NAME	NEWSPAPER, PAGE/COLUMN MONTH/DAY/YEAR	GENEALOGICAL DATA
Kellogg	Louis	RH, p2c1, 7/1/1897	Advertised services as a carriage and wagon maker in Readstown.
Kellogg	Nellie	RH, p4c2, 7/8/1897	Advertised services as a fashionable dressmaker in Readstown.
Kellogg	Nellie	RH, p5c4, 12/9/1897	Lived in Readstown. Advertised her willingness to "sew by the day."
Kellogg	Nellie	RH, p4c3, 1/4/1900	Nellie Kellogg recently married James O'Leary at St. James Church. Rev. Duffey officiated. The couple is well known in Readstown.
Kellogg	Neut, Mrs.	RH, p5c4, 6/16/1898	Arrived from Worley, WI to visit relatives in Readstown.
Kelsey	Emma L.	BD, p3c1, 9/4/1883	Joseph Clark married Emma L. Kelsey on Aug. 31, 1883. Bride from Rock Co., WI. Groom from Crawford Co. J. McLaughlin, J.P., officiated at the wedding in Boscobel.
Kelts	Philip	BD, p3c4, 7/21/1882	Died July 14, 1882 in Boscobel. Born May 7, 1815 in Madison Co., NY. Orphaned when 4 years old. Moved west in 1839, first to Illinois, later that year to Lancaster, WI. Married Oct. 12, 1840 to a sister of the late William Dyer of Lancaster. Had no children, but raised 4 boys, one of whom, James Kelts, was adopted. Alternated his residence between Boscobel and Lancaster.
Kelty	Emma Fancher	BD, p3c2, 8/19/1881	Died in Boscobel on Aug. 11, 1881. Born in Dayton, OH on Feb. 9, 1827. Married John Kelty in Mar. 1852 in Mineral Point, WI. Moved to Boscobel in 1855. Moved to house on the corner of Freemont and Chestnut in 1865. Died from congestion.
Kelty	John	BD, P3c2, 4/23/1880	Sworn in as marshall of Boscobel.
Kelty	John	BD, p3c2, 10/16/1883	Father of Sylvia Kelty and Mrs. Fletcher DeLap. Accidently killed by a gun while hunting in Jamestown, Dakota on Monday morning. He was born at Peach Bottom, York Co., PA in March 1834. Moved to Boscobel over 20 years ago to a farm southeast of town. Held various officies of respect. Served as a soldier in Co. B., 33rd WI Inf. His wife died in the spring of 1882. Soon after his wife's death, he and daughter, Sylvia, moved to a farm in Stuttsman Co., Dakota. He had a life insurance policy.
Kelty	John	BD, p3c1, 4/18/1879	Lead was discovered in Crawford Co. on land owned by John Kelty and James Wayne. David May will "work the project."
Kelty	John, Mrs.	BD, p3c1, 7/22/1881	Sold birds in Boscobel.
Kemper	Henry	BD, p2c4, 9/8/1882	Petitioned the Grant County Court to admit the the last will and testament of Philip J. Hof to probate.
Kendall	boy	BD, p3c1, 1/13/1882	A son was born on Tuesday to George Kendall in Boscobel.
Kendall	George	BD, p3c2, 2/18/1881	George Kendall married Mary Kaitenbach on Feb. 17, 1881 at the residence of Mrs. Cornelia Dyer. The Rev. Charles Schraudenbach officiated. Groom from Boscobel. [Kaltenbach?]
Kendall	George	RH, p5c3, 12/8/1898	Hosted prayer meetings at his home in the Mound Park area.
Kendall	George, Mrs.	BD, p3c1, 8/8/1879	Buried last Sunday. She was an old resident of Boscobel.
Kendall	H. P.	DR, p3c3, 5/11/1871	Taught the higher department in the De Soto school.
Kendall	Mr.	DR, p3c4, 1/12/1871	Served as principal in the De Soto school.
Kendall	Mrs.	DC, p2c2, 5/21/1887	Died Sunday at the residence of her daughter, Mrs. Morgan, per the Retreat news column. Funeral held at the Congregatioal Church by Rev. Haughton. She was the mother of Henry Kendall of Green, IA.
Kendall	Nathaniel	BD, p2c4, 8/3/1877	The Grant County Circuit Court published a summons to appear in the case, Nathaniel W. Kendall, plaintiff, vs. Winfield S. Aldrich, Levi Gulliford, Daniel W. Gale and Frances P. Van Wyck, defendants.
Kenefic	Annie	DC, p2c4, 2/19/1887	Annie Kenefic married William Downey last Thursday. Father Wurtz of Genoa officiated.
Kenefic	D. W.	DC, p3c4, 1/22/1887	Nettie Lane married D. W. Kenefic on Jan. 16, 1887. Bride from De Soto. Groom from Lansing. Gift list and the names of the givers was published. The Rev. William Houghton officiated.
Kent	B. F.	DR, p3c2, 1/4/1872	B. F. Kent, Esquire married Mary J. Kendall on Jan. 1, 1872 at the residence of the bride's father. Bride from Wheatland, WI. Groom from Pleasant Grove, IA. The Rev. James M. Mitchell officiated.
Kenyon	G. P., Mrs.	BD, p3c1, 2/6/1880	Resided in Wonewoc. She and son, Paul, and daughter, Maud, visited her brother, Hon. J. H. Sarles, in Boscobel. Planned to visit parents in Fennimore.

Genealogical Events from Newspapers for Crawford, Vernon and Grant Counties, Wisconsin, 1870-1901

LAST NAME	FIRST NAME	NEWSPAPER, PAGE/COLUMN MONTH/DAY/YEAR	GENEALOGICAL DATA
Keop	Mr.	DC, p2c2, 12/11/1886	Opened a general store in Stoddard. Former resident of Eastman.
Kermott	Rev.	BD, p3c1, 3/28/1879	Rev. Kermott baptised by immersion last Sunday in Boscobel the following: Mr. and Mrs. Popejoy, Miss Cora Butler, Miss Ida Bailey, Miss Patten and Mr. French.
Kerndt	Julius	DR, p3c3, 3/9/1871	Died Mar. 5, 1871. He was an early settler of Lansing, IA. The funeral was conducted by the Odd Fellows. Survived by a wife and 5 children.
Kerndt	Julius	DR, p3c2, 3/16/1871	Over a 1000 people attended the Kerndt funeral. He was 37 years old.
Kerr	James	BD, p3c1, 9/15/1882	James Kerr married Margaret Collins on Sept. 10, 1882 in Muscoda. Bride and groom from Boscobel. The Rev. I.[J.?] J. Wright officiated.
Ketch	M. M.	BD, p3c1, 2/20/1880	Died Feb. 16, 1880 in Montfort. Aged 27 years. At one time he worked at the Boscobel Bank under F. McSpaden.
Ketchum	May	DC, p3c3, 7/3/1886	Byron D. Lane planned to marry May Ketchum on July 14, 1886. Bride from near Princeton. Groom from De Soto.
Keyes	Catherine	BD, p2c2, 7/2/1880	Court Summons published. Catherine Keyes, plaintiff vs. Sylvestor Keyes, defendant.
Keyes	Charles H.	BD, p3c1, 4/15/1881	Charles H. Keyes married Nellie E. Brown at the home of the bride's father in the Town of Scott on April 12, 1881. Rev. W. Stoddart officiated. Groom from Excelsior.
Keys	Catherine	BD, p3c2, 2/27/1880	"Sylvester Keys of this town [Woodman] publishes in The *Boscobel Dial*, under date of February 18, 1880, a notice accusing me of leaving his bed and board, etc., and forbidding all persons from giving me credit, etc. and in answer thereto, I reply: That the bed I occupied while under his roof was my own; and the maintenance, poor as it was, I received, while in his poorer society mostly came from my own providing. He will have to work for his living now, and he need not trouble himself about my making a better living without him. I shall have one less mouth to feed and one less idle person to look after; and I hereby notify all persons not to trust him on my account, as I will support him no longer."
Keys	Sarah	BD, p3c1, 12/3/1880	Charles Wepking married Sarah Keys on Nov. 28, 1880. Bride and groom from Fennimore.
Keyser	Peter	RH, p5c2, 10/7/1897	The Peter Keyser family home in Readstown was quaranteed. They had diphtheria.
Kickapoo Athletic Club		RH, p4c2, 1/31/1901	The officers of the newly formed Kickapoo Athletic Club were John Goode, Albert Hebard, Stanley Morris, Earl Bishop, Will Hutchison and N. Farmer. It was a boxing club, based in Readstown at Davenport Bros. tin shop.
Kid	V., Mr.	DC, p8c2, 8/9/1889	Hired to teach school in De Soto next year.
Kieren	Anton	BD, p2c8, 1/5/1877	Anton Kieren was a tailor in Boscobel.
Kimball	Miss	DC, p2c2, 5/28/1887	George Allen married Miss Kimball on May 8, 1887, per Lynxville news column.
Kimberlin	I. G.	DC, p3c3, 4/3/1888	Planned to move from Indiana to a new home in De Soto.
Kimgry	Angaline	BD, p3c1, 3/3/1880	Robert B. Newberry recently married Angaline M. Kimgry. Bride from Patch Grove. Groom from Breckenridge, MN.
Kincannon		BD, p3c1, 9/4/1883	Kincannon's string band was scheduled to furnish the music at a social dance to be held at Ruka's Hall in Boscobel.
Kincannon		BD, p2c2, 12/9/1881	A skeleton was found in the desert near the surveyed line of the Salt Lake and Western railroad, 15 miles from Fish Springs in Utah. The bones and clothes were bleached white from time and sun. In the coat were found numerous papers and letters, a toothbrush, looking glass, pencil, razor, etc. The letters appeared to be written to his wife or soon-to-be wife. Her name was given as Jane Badger, Fairplay, P.O., Grant Co., WI. The man died of hunger and thirst about 1863 according to a date on a receipt. Mr. George Whitcomb of St. Louis forwarded this item to the *Boscobel Dial* and mentioned that one of the Kincannon boys left home about the time of the war and was either married to, or going with, a girl of about the same name as the one mentioned above.
Kinder	boy	RH, p4c2, 3/2/1899	The 2-year-old son of Peter Kinder was buried last Friday in Viola.
King	Harry	BD, p2c3, 2/16/1883	He was well known for his energy. After each snowfall, without solicitation, he used his horse and snowplow to break paths throughout the upper and lower town in Prairie du Chien.
Kingsland	N. W., Mrs.	DC, p2c1, 9/17/1887	Traveled from Lynxville to join her husband in Webber, Dakota.
Kingston	Mrs.	DC, p3c2, 3/26/1887	Died last week at the age of about 72 at her home in Bergen. Survived by her 96-year-old mother. Her son, William, came from Madison for the funeral.

Genealogical Events from Newspapers for Crawford, Vernon and Grant Counties, Wisconsin, 1870-1901

LAST NAME	FIRST NAME	NEWSPAPER, PAGE/COLUMN MONTH/DAY/YEAR	GENEALOGICAL DATA
Kingston	Robert	DC, p2c2, 7/2/1887	Lost his home to fire in Chaseburgh.
Kinney	George	BD, p3c1, 8/25/1882	From Potosi. Candidate for County Treasurer in Grant Co.
Kinney	Thomas F.	BD, p3c2, 5/28/1880	Appointed to be a census enumerator in Potosi, Grant Co.
Kinzie	Mr.	BD, p2c3, 1/13/1882	Mr. Kinzie's store in Avoca was destroyed by fire last Monday. The second floor was occupied by Prof. R. J. Porter and family. Porter most regretted the loss of his library and private papers.
Kipp	William	DC, p7c4, 6/21/1889	Convicted in Crawford County Circuit Court of assault with intent to kill Cyrus Lathrop. Asked for a new trial. Claimed one of the jurors was incompetent.
Kirby	Kate	BD, p3c1, 6/27/1879	Alex Provis married Kate Kirby last Thursday in Spring Green. Bride from Spring Green. Groom was a lawyer in Boscobel.
Kirkpatrick	Frank C.	BD, p3c3, 6/15/1877	Died June 2, 1877 at the age of 82 in the Town of Clifton, Grant Co. He was born in Georgia and moved to Illinois early in his life. Moved to Wisconsin in 1827. Served in the Black Hawk War.
Kish	boy	DC, p3c4, 8/7/1886	A son was recently born to William Kish of Victory.
Kish	William	DC, p3c2, 7/31/1886	The skiffs owned by William Tipplets and William Kish of Victory were recently stolen.
Kish	William	DC, p2c2, 11/19/1887	William Kish and family moved on an island near De Soto.
Kissack	Thomas	BD, p2c3, 3/10/1882	Kissack's house destroyed by fire. Located 2 miles east of Soldiers Grove. Fire started in a stovepipe when 2 daughters were home alone. Only a bureau and bedstead were saved. There was no insurance.
Kistler	D., Mrs.	BD, p3c2, 11/7/1879	Accidently shot her ankle while taking down a loaded gun. Lived in Boscobel.
Kistler	D., Mrs.	BD, p3c2, 11/21/1879	Died Sunday from lockjaw produced by a gunshot wound. Survived by husband and 3 children in Boscobel.
Kitch	M. M.	BD, p3c4, 1/19/1877	Former resident of Boscobel. He abandoned his wife and child. Found in Rockford, IL with Nettie Newcome, the daughter of a Grant Co. farmer. [The relationship with Newcome was denied in the newspaper the following week, p3c2, 1/26/1877.]
Kitch	Milton	BD, p2c2, 6/29/1877	Milton Kitch married Fanny Wells two weeks ago in Fennimore. The bride was from the Town of Wingville.
Klanskey	John	DC, p1c2, 8/2/1889	Lived in Green Bay. Visited sister, Mrs. Henry Kloak of Cooley Valley.
Klansky	Hattie, Miss	DC, p2c2, 7/2/1887	Returned to here home near Green Bay after a 2-year visit with her sister, Mrs. H. Kloak of Cooley Valley.
Klegg	S., Corp.	DC, p2c3, 7/31/1886	Reported on the success of soldiers ____ in Readstown.
Kline	Eliza	DR, p3c3, 5/11/1871	Taught the lower department in the De Soto school.
Kline	Eliza, Miss	DC, p2c2, 7/23/1887	Taught school in De Soto 10 or 12 years ago. Recently visited her old boarding place with Mrs. E. Houghton. Current resident of Denver, CO. Visited her sister, Mrs. A. Baldwin of Viroqua.
Kloak	John	DC, p3c5, 9/18/1886	Built a smokehouse at his place in Cooley Valley. He has also dug a cellar for a new house.
Klok	Fred	RH, p4c2, 9/8/1898	Planned to start a blacksmith shop on River Street in De Soto.
Klook	Henry, Mrs.	DC, p1c1, 6/28/1889	Resided in Cooley Valley. Received a telegram from St. Paul saying her sister, Miss Hattie Klausky had died. Mrs. Klook departed by train for St. Paul.
Knapp	Lois, Mrs.	RH, p5c6, 7/15/1897	Resided in Bloomingdale. Died Tuesday. Funeral help at Sugar Grove.
Knapp	William, Rev.	DC, p3c2, 12/4/1886	Died Nov. 23, 1886 at Richland City at the age of 87. "He was probably the oldest army chaplain in the West, having been chaplain of the 19th WI Infantry.
Knaub	Louis	BD, p3c1, 2/18/1881	From the Boscobel area. Buried Friday.
Knight	George	BD, p2c3, 6/9/1882	Died last Saturday night [originally published in the *Richland Rustic* on 6/3/1882] in Richland Center area. He was the main support of his widowed mother. Aged 20 years. Managed family farm and attended public high school. Funeral held at the Baptist Church.
Knower	Ella Osgood	DC, p3c3, 8/7/1886	Died of consumption on July 6, 1886 at the home of her parents in Genoa. She was the wife of George Knower of Cooley Valley. Died at the age of 28.
Knower	George	DC, p3c4, 2/18/1888	Recently married Cora Tenney in Taylor Co. Bride from De Soto. Groom from Genoa.

Genealogical Events from Newspapers for Crawford, Vernon and Grant Counties, Wisconsin, 1870-1901

LAST NAME	FIRST NAME	NEWSPAPER, PAGE/COLUMN MONTH/DAY/YEAR	GENEALOGICAL DATA
Knower	Martha Buchanan, Mrs.	DC, p2c1, 5/14/1887	Mrs. Martha Knower died May 5, 1887 at Chelsea, Taylor Co., WI. She was the daughter of Frank Buchanan of Victory and a former teacher. She was 24 years old. Remains were brought to Victory for burial.
Knower	Mr.	RH, p4c3, 2/14/1901	Fined $30 for ill treatment of his 12-year-old boy. The boy was sent to reform school. Knower lived in the De Soto area.
Knower	Mr. and Mrs.	DC, p1c3, 5/3/1889	Collected 3 children who have lived with their grandfather, Mr. Joseph Gould of Genona, for the last 3 years. Knower lived in Taylor Co., WI.
Knower	W. H.	DC, p3c3, 7/17/1886	He was the Vernon Co. Surveyor.
Knowlton	Oliver Perry	BD, p3c3, 1/30/1880	Died last Sunday in Boscobel. Born Aug. 23, 1822 in Woodstock, VT. When 2, moved with parents to Ohio. Later moved to Missouri. Moved to Wisconsin in 1845 and settled near Wingville. In the gold rush of 1849, he and D. R. Sylvester and Mr. Stephens went by ox team to California. Returned 2 years later by way of Panama. Moved to Castle Rock in 1852 and built a flouring mill. Partnered with D. R. Sylvester and Stephen Knowlton, Oliver's brother. Opened hardware store in Boscobel 5 years later. Served as postmaster. Sold store to F. McSpaden before war broke out. Went into dry goods business with J. McLaughlin [Knowlton & McLaughlin]. Closed the store. Married twice. Survived by his widow and three children. One son, Edward, is grown and lives out in the mountains. Five children dead. Member of Boscobel City Council and the Congregational Church.
Knutson	Henry	BD, p3c2, 9/13/1878	Henry Knutson married Linda Walker on Sept. 3, 1878 in Boscobel. Bride and groom from Hickory Grove. The Rev. Z. S. Hurd officiated.
Knutson	Jane	BD, p3c1, 2/3/1882	F. F. Nilson [Nelson?] married Jane Knutson on Jan. 28, 1882 at Muscoda. Groom from Lincoln, IA. Bride from Hickory Grove. The Rev. T. M. Evans officiated.
Knutson	Ole	BD, p3c2, 3/14/1879	The Ole Knutson store in Pine Grove [Soldiers Grove] was destroyed by fire. Most of the goods were saved.
Koepet	Albert	BD, p2c3, 11/4/1881	Jailed in Prairie du Chien. Threw a stone into a saloon window in Wauzeka.
Kohn		DR, p2c6, 8/24/1871	Died at Lansing last Tuesday when an embankment caved in. He was a railroad laborer.
Kolb	Gussie	DC, p3c4, 4/9/1887	Left Hillsborough to spend the summer out West
Korber	Henry	BD, p2c4, 11/26/1880	Grant County paid him a bounty for scalps turned into the county.
Kot	Francis	BD, p3c2, 2/2/1883	Francis Kot married Sophia Tohsh [or Tolish] on Jan. 13, 1883. Bride and groom were from Hickory Grove. The Rev. Charles Schroudenback officiated.
Kraemer	Peter	BD, p2c3, 2/16/1883	Died Saturday [per the Muscoda News of 2/8/1883] at the residence of his son, John Kraemer of Muscoda. Born in Luxemburg, Germany. Immigrated to U.S. about 1850 and moved to Muscoda. He was 61 years old.
Kratchwell	V. J.	BD, p2c3, 4/20/1877	The bankruptcy case of V. J. Kratchwell of Boscobel was scheduled for May 15, 1877 in Madison.
Kratochwill	V. J.	BD, p2c4, 10/22/1880	Has 23 years experience in the boot and shoe business. Worked in the business in Boscobel for the last 20 years, 8 of which he has been doing business for himself.
Kretsch	Charles	BD, p2c4, 4/19/1878	Died April 8, 1876 in Boscobel. Magdalena Kretsch of Boscobel, the widow, petitioned to administer the estate.
Kreul	Hannah	BD, p3c2, 2/24/1882	Christ Beckler married Hannah Kreul on Feb. 16, 1882 at the home of the bride's parents in Fennimore. Rev. Mutchman officiated.
Kronschage	girl	BD, p3c3, 4/29/1881	A daughter was born to Theo Kronschage of Boscobel on April 17, 1881.
Kronshage	Ben	BD, p3c2, 7/9/1880	Arrived in Boscobel after a year's absence.
Kronshage	Th.	BD, p2c5, 10/22/1880	Dealer of guns, pistols, cutlery, ammunition, etc. in Boscobel. Opened for business 8 years ago. Also sold shelf hardware and sewing machines. Dealt in hides, pelts and furs.
Kronshage	Theo.	BD, p2c7, 1/5/1877	Sold hardware in Boscobel.
Kronshage	Thomas	BD, P3c2, 4/23/1880	Sworn in as treasurer of Boscobel.
Krouse		DC, p2c2, 7/16/1887	A child of Albert Krouse of La Crosse died July 11, 1887. It was buried in Chaseburgh.
Kurtz	John C.	DC, p2c1, 11/26/1887	John C. Kurtz and George H. Hale put up a hotel in De Soto in 1856 and called it the De Soto House.

Genealogical Events from Newspapers for Crawford, Vernon and Grant Counties, Wisconsin, 1870-1901

LAST NAME	FIRST NAME	NEWSPAPER, PAGE/COLUMN MONTH/DAY/YEAR	GENEALOGICAL DATA
Kurtz	John C.	DC, p2c1, 5/1/1888	In the late 1850s, John C. Kurtz suggested that a mock Senate be created in De Soto as a form of amusement. The idea was well received. Members selected various states to represent and submitted bills for debate. The members were Robert Mulhern, William Mulhern, Daniel Mulhern, Charles Whiting, George G. Van Wagoner, John C. Kurtz, Adam Carlyle, John C. Davis, Anthony Vallee, Frederick Carr, D. A. Steele, Cyrus Worth, Addison Worth, C. B. Stevens, George H. Hale, Williard Blake, Dr. Sperry, Johnny Radcliff, George D. McDill and Nathan Tilden. Radcliff was from Alabama and apparently represented that state. Anthony Valley was a great admirer of General Andrew Jackson. Valley sported a watch-chain made of United States ten-cent pieces.
Kussel	I.	BD, p3c1, 5/7/1880	Moved his clothing stock from his store in Boscobel to a new store in Green, IA.
Kyes	Mrs.	DC, p2c1, 4/16/1887	Died Saturday at the home of her daughter, Mrs. Dr. Miller of Ontario.
Kyser	Lula	RH, p6c2, 5/25/1899	Lewis Horton married Lula Kyser on May 18, 1899. Bride from Manning. Groom from La Farge.
Kyser	Lyman	RH, p4c1, 10/24/1901	Shipped his household goods from Readstown to his new home in Ladysmith, WI.
La Flash	Levi	DC, p3c3, 8/21/1886	Thrown in the cylinder of a thrashing machine in Harmony on Aug. 11, 1886. A portion of his head was taken off.
Lacy	Jesse M.	BD, p3c1, 1/26/1883	Recently died. He was 3 years, 2 months and 23 days old. His father was T. W. Lacy, editor of the Prairie du Chien Union.
Ladies Mite Society		DC, p3c3, 1/28/1888	The officers of the Retreat Ladies Mite Society were Mrs. A. D. Bean, Mrs. C. C. Bishop, Mrs. S. J. Duston and Mrs. S. A. Seymour.
Laheurty	John	BD, p3c3, 1/19/1877	Resided in Clyde, Iowa Co. Died last week in an accident.
Laird	Thomas	BD, p3c3, 5/18/1877	Died last week in Wingville.
Laird	Thomas	BD, p2c1, 6/8/1877	Recently died in Wingville. Born in Ireland in 1815. Of Scotch descent. Moved to Galena in 1844. Moved to Jamestown, Grant Co. in 1845. Later moved to Potosi and Wingville. Survived by 8 of his 14 children. Former Chairman of the Town Board in Wingville.
Lake	Will	DC, p2c4, 1/29/1887	Resided in Viroqua. Sold tombstones in De Soto.
Lamb	Joseph, Mrs.	DC, p3c3, 11/20/1886	Mrs. Joseph Lamb and daugher, Angie, formerly of Victory, but now of Dakota, were expected to return to Victory for a visit with friends and relatives.
Lamb	Mrs.	DC, p1c3, 4/12/1889	Mrs. Lamb of Yankton, Dakota visited her sister, Mrs. C. C. Coleman of Genoa.
Lambert	George	BD, p3c1, 8/25/1882	Landlord of the Mt. Hope House [a hotel].
Lambert	Lena	BD, p3c1, 5/13/1881	Daniel Oscar Taft married Lena Lambert on May 4, 1881 in Boscobel. J. McLaughlin, J.P. officiated.
Lambert	Matt	BD, p3c6, 3/24/1882	Worked as an assistant to the owners of Oswald & Hinn, a general store in Fennimore.
Lamphire	F. A., Mrs.	BD, p3c2, 8/24/1877	Mrs. Lamphire and her 2 sons arrived in Boscobel from Galesburg, IL to visit her brother, Dr. Carley. She taught school for the last 30 years.
Lamprict	Henry	DC, p2c2, 5/7/1887	Henry Lamprict married Amelia Schurbert on May 3, 1887. Groom partner in the firm Barnetsburger and Lamprict. Bride was the daughter of Edward Schurbert of the Town of Genoa. Bride was a former teacher.
Lanam	Fred	RH, p4c2, 4/5/1900	Planned to hold an auction sale oif his household goods in Readstown. He will move to Zanesville, OH, his birthplace, to spend his remaining days.
Lance		BD, p3c2, 10/30/1883	Messrs. Lance and Neely operated a limeworks in Werley.
Lance	Joseph	BD, p3c1, 2/4/1881	Joseph Lance married Louisa Neely on Feb. 2, 1881 in Boscobel at Betts House. Bride and groom from Mt. Ida. The Rev. William Stoddart officiated.
Lane	boy	DC, p3c2, 12/17/1887	A son was born on Dec. 11, 1887 to Byron D. Lane of De Soto.
Lane	Byron	DC, p2c3, 2/19/1889	Delivered freight and baggage in De Soto. He was also the Village marshall.
Lane	Byron D.	DC, p3c3, 7/3/1886	Byron D. Lane planned to marry May Ketchum on July 14, 1886. Bride from near Princeton. Groom from De Soto.
Lane	Byron D.	DC, p3c4, 7/24/1886	Resided in De Soto. Recently married.

Genealogical Events from Newspapers for Crawford, Vernon and Grant Counties, Wisconsin, 1870-1901

LAST NAME	FIRST NAME	NEWSPAPER, PAGE/COLUMN MONTH/DAY/YEAR	GENEALOGICAL DATA
Lane	Nettie	DC, p3c5, 7/24/1886	Nettie Lane and Mrs. Jane Cooper announced an upcoming meeting of the Winneshiek Lodge No. 386, I.O.G.T. [International Order of Grand Templars]
Lane	Nettie	DC, p3c4, 1/22/1887	Nettie Lane married D. W. Kenefic on Jan. 16, 1887. Bride from De Soto. Groom from Lansing. Gift list and the names of the givers was published. The Rev. William Houghton officiated.
Lane	Smith	DC, p3c3, 5/21/1887	Granted an increase in his pension. Resided in De Soto.
Lane	Smith	DC, p3c4, 4/3/1888	Died March 30, 1888 in De Soto of a complaint contracted during the Civil War. He served in Co. G, 26th Regt. Iowa Vol. Father of Mrs. Lena Hall of Williamston, IA and Mrs. Nettie Kenefick of Lansing. He was 58 years, 6 months and 1 day old. Survived by wife and children.
Lane	Smith	DC, p3c2, 3/27/1888	Smith Lane is very ill and may not recover. His daughters arrived from Iowa.
Lang	Paul	RH, p5c4, 1/13/1898	Worked for Jim Mathews in Kickapoo Center.
Langdon	May	DC, p3c4, 3/5/1887	May Langdon and Hattie Tompson, both of Seneca, intend to start for Nebraska in a few days.
Lange		RH, p5c3, 9/20/1900	A 12-pound son was recently born to Paul Lange of Kickapoo.
Lange	C. W.	RH, p4c2, 9/1/1898	Mrs. Frank Ibach of Preston, MN visited her parents, Mr. and Mrs. C. W. Lange of Kickapoo.
Lange	Paul	RH, p5c4, 2/23/1899	Left Kickapoo for Minnesota where he expects to work for the summer.
Lange	Paul	RH, p5c3, 3/22/1900	Paul Lange married Sabra Andrews on March 18, 1900. Bride and groom were from Kickapoo.
Lange	Paul	RH, p5c4, 3/22/1900	Paul Lange married Sabra Andrews on March 11, 1900. C. H. Davenport officiated at the ceremony.
Langford	E. D.	BD, p3c1, 1/16/1880	Married Isabel Wilson on Dec. 25, 1879 at residence of bride's parents. Groom from Kentucky. Bride from Town of Marion. J. McLaughlin, Esq. officiated.
Langlais	Thomas	BD, p1c8, 4/12/1878	Resident of the Town of Scott. Found 2 miles from his home in "dying condition" the other day. He had three wounds to his head and a pounding all over his body. After the death, neighbors began a search to "trace the affair." A hat and stick with blood on it was found in the cellar of a partially burned house adjoining the home of Henry Lengele, a saloonkeeper. Lengele's wagon showed evidence it had transported Langlais. Lengele and his 3 sons were arrested.
Lankford	Cornelius	DC, p3c2, 9/3/1887	Died of diphtheria on Aug. 22, 1887 at Ferryville at the age of 9 years. He was the son of B. D. and Olena Lankford.
LaRoque	Joe	BD, p2c2, 11/13/1883	Lived in Prairie du Chien. Experienced a hunting accident when his gun discharged in to both hands. Two fingers have been amputated from one hand. The other hand may have to be amputated, too.
Larson	Bert B.	BD, p3c1, 1/26/1883	Bert B. Larson married Helen Thompson on Jan. 18, 1883 in Boscobel. Groom from Dakota. Bride from Marion, WI.
Larson	Hans	RH, p4c2, 5/2/1901	Recently sold his Readstown area farm to his son, Louis. Louis recently married Ella Hall. Hans reserved 6 acres for himself and is now building another home.
Larson	John L.	RH, p5c3, 3/17/1898	Former District Attorney for Vernon Co. Died March 13, 1898 in San Bernado [Bernadino?], CA of consumption. Went to California last fall to improve his health. Resided in Viroqua.
Larson	Louis	RH, p4c2, 5/9/1901	Ella Hall married Louis Larson on April 26, 1901 at the home of her father, John Hall of near Readstown. Bride and groom from Town of Kickapoo. Justice Davenport officiated.
Larson	Matt	DC, p2c2, 5/7/1887	Blacksmith in Chaseburgh. Father of a 12-pound newborn boy.
Larson	O. H.	RH, p4c2, 11/9/1899	O. H. Larson married Anna Harris. Groom was a Kickapoo farmer. Bride was the daughter of Joseph Harris of Manning.
Latamore [Lattimore]	Issac	DC, p3c3, 10/30/1886	Caught by the rebels seven times during the Civil War. He always escaped. Wounded during the War, yet he was recently denied a pension. Served 4 years, 7 months and 16 days. Resided in Ferryville.
Lathrop	Flora	BD, p3c2, 6/7/1878	James Crouch married Flora Lathrop last Tuesday. Bride was from Boscobel. The Rev. G. W. Nuzum officiated.
Lathrop	Flora A.	BD, p3c2, 5/11/1877	From Boscobel. Baptised by the Rev. Jesse D. Searles of the Methodist Episcopal Church in Sanders Creek.
Lathrop	George	RH, p4c2, 11/22/1900	Sold his farm in Gays Mills and moved to Readstown where he worked as a carpenter at the tobacco warehouse.
Latimer		DC, p1c2, 6/29/1889	"A raft of ties belonging to Hoyt and Latimer start down the river today under the management of Ed. Cox, Sr.", according to the Genoa news column.

Genealogical Events from Newspapers for Crawford, Vernon and Grant Counties, Wisconsin, 1870-1901

LAST NAME	FIRST NAME	NEWSPAPER, PAGE/COLUMN MONTH/DAY/YEAR	GENEALOGICAL DATA
Latimer	Mr.	DC, p1c3, 4/26/1889	Lived in Genoa. Purchased railroad ties in Ferryville.
Latimer	Thomas	DC, p3c4, 9/11/1888	Went down river with Ed Cox on his raft of ties, per the Genoa news column.
Latimore		DC, p3c3, 9/10/1887	A child of Isaac Latimore died last week in Ferryville of diphtheria.
Latimore	Enoch	DC, p3c4, 10/16/1888	Latimore's house in Retreat destroyed by fire. Most furniture saved. He was in process of moving out when fire took place. There was no insurance.
Latimore	Isaac	DC, p1c1, 6/21/1889	"A few weeks since the wife of Mr. Isaac Latimore left him in a mysterious and unaccountable manner giving no reason for her strange conduct and made arrangements for him to meet her at the depot when she expected to return. At the same time she knew and did not expect to come back. Mr. L. is a highly esteemed farmer of this vicinity and the unreasonable actions of his wife has deeply grieved him and the general feeling is against Mrs. L. as the public does not approve of any such actions as she left him just when she should have been with him to assist him with the work for Mr. L. is not very healthy and to leave him alone in the busy time of the year shows a very poor principle in her. She could have told him at least that she would not return. But it is not very surprising in her as she has done this same thing before. But Mr. L. has always acted the past of a good and kind husband to the certain knowledge of those who knew him least. Mr. Latimore has the sympathy of the entire neighborhood." [Lived in Town of Freeman.]
Latimore	J., Mrs.	DC, p1c1, 5/31/1889	Lived in Ferryville. She has not been heard from for quite awhile. Unknown to her husband, she sent most of her things away. "Mr. L. can have clear sailing now and no opposition." [Per 5/24/1889, Mrs. Latimore went to La Crosse and Mr. L. was worried she wouldn't return.]
Latshaw	Albert	DC, p2c2, 4/2/1887	Resided in Rising Sun. Departed for a one-year visit in Kansas City.
Latshaw	Albert	DC, p2c2, 6/4/1887	Returned to Victory after visiting Kansas.
Latshaw	Alex, Mr. and Mrs.	DC, p3c2, 11/5/1887	Left De Soto for a visit with relatives in Oaktown, IN, Terre Haute, IN and Marshall, IL.
Latshaw	Budd	DC, p1c1, 8/16/1889	Budd Latshaw and Will Quinn of Victory worked for the last 6 weeks on the *Gile* [a steamboat?].
Latshaw	C. B.	DC, p2c2, 11/19/1887	Returned to Victory from Nebraska.
Latshaw	Claire B.	DC, p2c2, 9/17/1887	Left Victory for Farlington, KS to spend the winter with sister, Dr. Kate Parker, and to attend school.
Latshaw	James	DC, p2c2, 3/26/1887	Returned to Victory from a trip to Indiana where he visited relatives.
Lattie	Dave	RH, p5c3, 11/29/1900	"If anyone is in need of an embalmer, call on Dave Lattie, he is an expert at the business." From Spring Valley news column.
Lattie	David	RH, p4c3, 9/27/1900	Worked for Andrew Vold. Cut corn in Spring Valley.
Lavis	W. H.	DC, p3c3, 10/9/1888	A surprise 26th birthday party was held for him at the Bay State House in De Soto.
Law	Abbie H.	DR, p2c3, 6/1/1871	Abbie H. Law of Chicago petitioned the Vernon County Probate Court to administer the estate of her husband, the late Emerson Law.
Lawrence	Alice	DC, p3c4, 5/8/1888	Taught school in Red Mound.
Lawrence	Alice Z.	DC, p3c4 8/27/1887	Hired to teach at Ferryville.
Lawrence	Charley	DC, p3c2, 8/7/1888	Owned a relic of the Harrison campaign -- a watch. It was worn by his father-in-law, Col. Stanley in the Tippecanoe campaign. Lawrence resided in De Soto.
Lawrence	D. R.	BD, p3c2, 7/23/1880	Resident of Crawford Co. Recently found two mastodon teeth. One weighed over 12 ½ pounds. Planned to send them to the Historical Society.
Lawrence	D. R.	BD, p3c1, 12/1/1882	Exchanged his Crawford Co. farm on the Kickapoo River for the water cure established in Boscobel.
Lawrence	Ellen J.	DC, p3c3, 11/20/1886	Resided in De Soto. Her article, "How to Maintain Interest in Primary and Middle Forms" was published in the newspaper.
Lawrence	Ellen, Miss	DC, p3c3, 8/21/1886	Named intermediate teacher at the De Soto Union School.

Genealogical Events from Newspapers for Crawford, Vernon and Grant Counties, Wisconsin, 1870-1901

LAST NAME	FIRST NAME	NEWSPAPER, PAGE/COLUMN MONTH/DAY/YEAR	GENEALOGICAL DATA
Lawrence	Henry	DC, p2c1, 6/12/1888	Thought he found oil in a swampy area near the Mississippi River, about 6 miles south of De Soto. Adam Carlyle, John C. Kurtz, William West, Charles E. Woodbury and Charles Whiting were told of the "discovery" and planned to partner with Lawrence and develop the site. A visit to the site indicated the area contained muck and decayed vegetation, not oil. Martin Loftus was hired to "dig a hole and stone it around" to help confirm the assessment. Nothing was found. [Long, interesting story.]
Lawrence	James	DC, p3c3, 12/3/1887	An auction sale was advertised to settle the estate of James Lawrence. This was in accordance with his will, per James W. Lawrence, Executor. The land was 1 mile southeast of De Soto in Crawford Co.
Lawrence	James, Sr.	RH, p4c4, 2/16/1899	Dislocated his hip when a wagon he was driving hit the side of a bridge on Rush Creek and over turned. He hit the ice. Treated by Dr. Andrew. Resided in De Soto.
Lawrence	Jane E.	DC, p3c3 8/27/1887	James H. Heal married Jane E. Lawrence on Monday at the N. Coe residence in De Soto. Groom taught school in Norwalk. The Rev. I. F. Nuzum of Mauston officiated.
Lawrence	M. H.	DC, p3c3, 3/5/1887	Moved to La Crosse from De Soto to work in sales at Quinn & Batchelor's boot and shoe house.
Lawrence	Mary Williams, Mrs.	DC, p3c4, 3/12/1887	Died Mar. 7, 1887. Born Feb. 5, 1805 in Caldicut, Monmouthshire, England. Married James Lawrence in 1832. Moved to America in 1851 and settled in Liberty Pole. They moved to their ridge farm near De Soto 3 years later. She was widowed in Aug. 1883. She contracted pneumonia while visiting her daughter, Mrs. N. Coe of Viroqua. All her children were present at her deathbed: Thomas, James, Mathew, Jane, Mrs. N. Coe and Mrs. N. J. Miller. Buried in Mt. Vernon Cemetery.
Lawrence	Mattie	DC, p3c2, 9/11/1886	Went to Chicago to attend high school.
Lawrence	Mr.	DC, p2c2, 7/2/1887	Sold his livery stable in Lynxville to Davidson and Noggle and returned to Boscobel.
Lawrence	Nellie	DC, p2c3, 1/22/1887	Wrote a poem called "In Memory of W. T. Lawrence." It was published. The first lines were: "One year ago, the sixth, Willie, Called from your home away, To your Father's house in Glory,".
Lawrence	Polly M., Mrs.	BD, p3c1, 12/3/1880	Died Nov. 28, 1880 in Bell Center. Aged about 70 years. She was the mother of Daniel Lawrence, formerly of Boscobel.
Lawrence	Thomas	DC, p3c4, 7/3/1886	Almost drowned when his horses were startled at the levee in De Soto by engine #4 of the new railroad. Lawrence couldn't swim. The horses, valued at $250, were drowned.
Lawrence	Thomas, Mr. and Mrs.	DC, p3c3, 5/1/1888	Recently celebrated their 30th wedding anniversary at their home a mile outside of De Soto.
Lawrence	William	DC, p3c3, 8/7/1888	Died July 31, 1888 at his home in Victory. Resident of Vernon Co. for about 28 years. His first residence in the area was in De Soto. After 5 year there, he moved to Victory. Survived by wife and 4 children. He had been sick for the last 3 years and confined to his bed for the last year.
Lawrence	William	DC, p2c4, 1/15/1887	Maria Cooley [Conley?] recently married William La____ [Lawrence?]. Bride from De Soto. Groom from Boscobel. Married in Boscobel.
Lawson	S.	BD, p2c3, 1/13/1882	S. Lawson and J. O. Davidson announced plans to build a 3 story building for stores, offices and halls in Soldiers Grove. Will measure 46' by 60'.
Lawton Bros.		DR, p2c4, 8/24/1871	Operated a steam saw mill in Viola.
Lawver		BD, p3c3, 6/8/1877	Pat Ryan, Homer Nelson Taft [found guilty of a murder attempt on James Harris on Wauzeka], Mr. Nichols and 2 Lawvers escaped from jail in Prairie du Chien.
Laydan	James	DC, p3c3, 3/3/1888	The James Laydan children of Genoa have diphtheria.
Layer	Herman	RH, p4c2, 5/23/1901	Herman Layer recently married Queen Cass. Bride and groom from Viroqua. Ceremony was held at the home of the bride's parents, Mr. and Mrs. James Cass of SumnerIA. Groom was a partner with Mr. Mellum in a clothing business.
Laylan		DC, p3c3, 1/28/1888	A child was born Saturday to James Laylan of Caledonia Junction. Child died of measles.
Laylan	Cyntha, Mrs.	DC, p2c3, 5/1/1888	Died last Tuesday in Genoa after a long illness. She was buried in the "old burying ground." Rev. Brown of Bergen preached the funeral sermon.
Laylan	James	DC, p2c2, 3/10/1888	Four more of the James Laylans are down with diphtheria in Genoa.
Laylans	girl	DC, p3c4, 10/30/1888	A daughter was recently born to Ike Laylans of Genoa.
Layne	P. J.	DR, p2c6, 12/15/1870	Advertised his services as the clerk of court and licensed conveyancer in Viroqua.

Genealogical Events from Newspapers for Crawford, Vernon and Grant Counties, Wisconsin, 1870-1901

LAST NAME	FIRST NAME	NEWSPAPER, PAGE/COLUMN MONTH/DAY/YEAR	GENEALOGICAL DATA
Layton	L. D.	DR, p1c5, 2/23/1871	Operated a boarding school for young men attending the Mt. Sterling Academy.
Lazenby	William	DR, p2c2, 9/14/1871	He committed suicide last Thursday on his farm on Warner Creek, about 9 miles from Ontario. He was a single man. Information reprinted from the *Ontario Sunrise*.
Leamere	T.	BD, p2c2, 3/24/1882	Lived in Town of Eastman. His team of mares, harness and buggy were stolen.
Leasman	Augusta	BD, p3c1, 9/4/1883	Augusta Leasman received new goods for her millinery store in Boscobel.
Leatherberry	Pete	BD, p2c3, 5/20/1881	Purchased a mail route from Mr. Pier in Richland Co. nine years ago. Also purchased a team of horses from Pier that he still uses.
Lee	Clayton E.	BD, p3c1, 2/3/1882	Clayton E. Lee married Nellie N. Jennings at Blue River on Dec. 31, 1881. Groom from Oshkosh. Bride from Blue River. The Rev. T. M. Evans officiated.
Lee	Emogine	BD, p3c2, 2/1/1878	John Scott married Emogine Lee on Jan. 29, 1878 at the home of the bride's father in Blue River Station. The Rev. Z. S. Hurd officiated.
Lee	Lucinda	BD, p3c1, 4/8/1881	Edward G. Williams married Lucinda Lee on Mar. 3, 1881 at the residence of Joseph Lee in Watterstown. Bride and groom from Watterstown.
Leech	Jack	BD, p3c2, 4/13/1877	Accused of murder in a Dodgeville saloon last spring. He was taken to Richland Co. for trial.
Lees	E. G.	DC, p3c3, 4/16/1887	Planned to hold an aution of household goods and livestock at his place on Rush Creek.
Leiving	George W.	DC, p3c4, 8/21/1886	Died Aug. 18, 1886 of sunstroke while watching a raft of logs on the river. Survived by a brother in Louisville, KY. Buried in De Soto.
Lemen		DC, p2c1, 1/29/1887	Gen. Atkinson's troops fought Black Hawk's braves during the Black Hawk War on what is today the Lemen farm [between Battle Hollow and the Bad Axe?].
Lemen	Robert E.	DC, p2c1, 2/5/1887	In a series on the Black Hawk War, C. V. Porter writes, "When about three miles from the present village of Victory the Indian outpost was attacked very near the spot where later Robert E. Lemen on Section 35, Town 12, Range 7, built a house of logs set upright and which partly sided up, still stands. Here in 1846, Mr. Le Grand Sterling saw twelve skeletons of Indians. And in 1852 H. H. McAuley saw the bones of an Indian with a bullet hole in the topof the skull. C. M. Sterling informs me that the trail from the Lemen house as seen by his father, Lewis Sterling, passed west across Section 35, 34 and 33 and struck the river bank at the low place in the bluff below Conway's house whichis about ¼ mile north of Battle Hollow.
Lemon	Richard, Mrs.	DC, p2c2, 6/5/1888	Resided in Viroqua. Visited parents, Mr. and Mrs. Arnold of Cooley Valley.
Lemon	Robert E.	DC, p3c2, 12/17/1887	"Robert E. Lemon, who sailed a wood-boat between De Soto and Victory, was a good deal of a joker, and he would repeat at the latter town what we said about it, and on the return trip would bring us what the Victorians [residents of Victory] said about us [residents of De Soto]." These events apparently took place in the 1850s.
Lemon	Tillie, Mrs.	DC, p3c2, 10/9/1888	From Viroqua. Visited parents, Mr. and Mrs. Sam Arnold of near De Soto.
Lemy	M. P.	DC, p3c2, 10/16/1886	Native of Waterford, Ireland. Visited with his relative, Mrs. Peter Loftus.
Lenahan	Dennis	BD, p3c3, 8/19/1881	Death announced at the Boscobel City Council meeting where he served as an alderman.
Lenehan	D.	BD, P3c2, 4/23/1880	Sworn in as an alderman of Boscobel.
Lenehan	D.	BD, p2c3, 5/30/1879	Received a license to operate a tavern in Boscobel.
Leoby	Henry	BD, p3c2, 2/2/1883	Henry Leoby married Mary Elizabeth Anderson on Dec. 16, 1882. Groom from Prairie du Chien. Bride from Boscobel. The Rev. Charles Schroudenback officiated.
Lesler	J.	BD, p3c1, 4/6/1883	Lesler and his family departed Boscobel for a new home in Stanton, NB.
Lesler	J.	BD, p3c2, 11/20/1883	Died Nov. 11, 1883 in Stanton, NB of a self-inflicted pistol shot. He was in failing health and approaching blindness. Assumed he had melancholoy. Settled in Potosi, WI about 40 years ago, later moving to Boscobel. Last spring he and his wife moved to Nebraska to be with his married daughters. Father of Lou P. Lesler.
Lesler	Jacob	BD, p3c2, 11/27/1883	Died of suicide last Saturday [per an article reprinted from the Stanton, Nebraska *Weekly Register*]. He was born in France 76 years ago and came to America when he was young. Weakened by consumption. Partially deaf and blind. Had chronically sore eyes. Resided with A. Wagner. Mrs. W. H. Smith was a daughter.
Lesler	Josephine	BD, p3c3, 9/20/1878	Departed Boscobel for Mt. Sterling, IL to spend the winter with her sister, Mrs. Smith [nee Fannie Lesler].

Genealogical Events from Newspapers for Crawford, Vernon and Grant Counties, Wisconsin, 1870-1901

LAST NAME	FIRST NAME	NEWSPAPER, PAGE/COLUMN MONTH/DAY/YEAR	GENEALOGICAL DATA
Lesler	Josie	BD, p3c3, 10/26/1877	Hired to teach school in the German District, 8 miles southwest of Wauzeka.
Lesler	Lou P.	BD, p3c2, 6/1/1883	Died May 27, 1883 in Boscobel. He was the owner of the *Boscobel Dial*. Born Nov. 8, 1844. Raised in Grant Co. He clerked at a Lancaster store for John P. Lewis when he was 17. Enlisted as a private in Co. A, 41st Regt. WI Vol. Moved to Boscobel to work for D. T. Parker. Leg was crippled in an accident. Worked as a bookkeeper for Meyer Bros. in 1871. Married Eda [Edith] A. Meyer on April 17, 1875. Fathered a son and a daughter. Served as County Treasurer. Funeral was attended by Lizzie Howe of Stanton, NB [sister] and the following citizens of Lancaster -- R. B. Lesler of Neilsville, J. P. Lewis, James McMahan, John F. Lane, Capt. H. D. Farquharson, J. L. Rewey.
Lesler	Lou P., Mrs.	BD, p2c1, 6/1/1883	She announced that she would continue publication of the *Boscobel Dial* following the recent death of her husband, the former owner. It was her only source of income.
Levergreen	Hettie Olivia	RH, p4c3, 11/8/1900	Hettie Olivia Levergreen married the Rev. Elmer Octavius Chapel at the home of the bride's parents on Wednesday evening. Bride was the daughter of Isaac Levergreen and was employed as a milliner. Groom was the Congregational minister in Readstown. C. Melbourne Chapel of Chicago was the groom's brother. Couple planned to live in Readstown. The Rev. C. A. Randolph of Schickley, NB officiated. Reprinted from an article in the *Aurora Beacon*.
Levings	Mrs.	BD, p3c1, 9/11/1883	Advertised her desire to open a kindergarten in Boscobel for 3 to 7-year-old children. She had previous kindergarten experience in Potosi.
Lewis	Andrew	DC, p3c2, 2/11/1888	Resided in Bloomington. Visited brother, Walter of De Soto.
Lewis	Bill	BD, p3c3, 8/14/1883	Lived near Muscoda in Richland Co. Claimed to be Frank Bennett to get a job as a raftsman to take logs down the Wisconsin River to St. Louis. He lied to Ike Woodard, marshall, who was trying to arrest Bennett.
Lewis	Catherine, Mrs.	RH, p4c2, 1/31/1901	Died Jan. 30, 1901 in Readstown. She was the mother of Mrs. Sarah McClaran of Minneapolis.
Lewis	Catherine, Mrs.	RH, p5c3, 2/7/1901	Died Jan. 30, 1901 at her home 1 mile east of Readstown. Born Feb. 4, 1816, nee Brady, in the County of Monahan, Town of Carley, Ireland. Came to American when she was 21. Married Ferdinand L. Lewis on Sept. 20, 1854 in Simcoe, Canada. The Rev. Salmon Reeter of the English Episcopal Church officiated. Moved to Readstown in 1862. Mr. Lewis enlisted as Veterinary Surgeon in the Civil War, leaving behind a wife and 4 children. [Apparently he died during the war.] After much difficulty, Mrs. Lewis received a widow's pension and a few hundred dollars of backpay, from which she purchased a 30 acre farm, built a house, gave her children a good common school education and lived to see all married and comfortable. She lost her sight a few years ago and moved in with her daughter, Mrs. William Jones. Funeral held at Methodist Episcopal Church in Readstown. Buried in Readstown Cemetery, next to eldest son, George, who died 25 years ago. She was the mother of George, F. J. Lewis, Mrs. W. D. Jones and Mrs. W. A. McClaran.
Lewis	F.	BD, p3c1, 1/5/1877	Jeweler in Boscobel.
Lewis	F., Mr.	BD, p3c2, 9/18/1883	Resided in Boscobel. Had a bad accident. A horse caught Lewis by the cheek, tearing lose the flesh from the bones on his face.
Lewis	H. Burt	BD, p3c3, 11/30/1877	H. Burt Lewis married Olive L. Earl on Thursday last week at the house of the bride's father, Rev. H. H. Earl. Bride and groom from Fennimore. The Rev. D. L. Hubbard officiated.
Lewis	H. H., Mrs.	RH, p4c2, 6/21/1900	Mr. Lewis and her daughter, Helen, visited parents, Mr. and Mrs. Bell of Mt. Sterling.
Lewis	Marvin	BD, p3c4, 1/30/1880	Died Jan. 28, 1880 in Harvard, IL. He was the son of Frank Lewis of the Boscobel area. Aged 28 years, 9 months and 20 days. Had inflamation in both lungs. Born in Bristol, CT. Moved to Platteville in 1855 and to Boscobel in 1856. Married two years ago to Ella Donahue of Harvard, IL. Buried in Boscobel.
Lewis	Rev.	RH, p4c2, 11/11/1897	Rev. Lewis of the Church of Christ in Viroqua conducted revival meetings in Readstown.
Lewis	Simon	BD, p3c7, 3/2/1877	A sherriff's sale was held for John S. Lewis and Mary C. Lewis, executors of Simon K. Lewis, deceased vs. Samuel Long, Margaretta Long [his wife] and John P. Lewis.
Lewis	W. H.	DC, p2c2 7/23/1887	Hired by the De Soto school board to serve as principal. He was from Patch Grove, WI. Ellen J. Lawrence and Miss Gott were hired as teachers.
Lewis	W. H.	DC, p5c1, 7/19/1889	Worked as an agent for the New York Life Insurance Co. in De Soto.
Lewis	Walter	BD, p3c3, 5/25/1883	Resided in Kansas. Visited
Lewison		DC, p3c2, 2/12/1887	Two children of Ole Lewison died last week from diptheria in Rush Creek.

Genealogical Events from Newspapers for Crawford, Vernon and Grant Counties, Wisconsin, 1870-1901

LAST NAME	FIRST NAME	NEWSPAPER, PAGE/COLUMN MONTH/DAY/YEAR	GENEALOGICAL DATA
Lewison		DC, p2c2, 9/17/1887	Ole Lewison's 3-month-old child died Tuesday in De Soto.
Lewison	Lena	RH, p5c4, 11/17/1898	Lena Lewison and Sarah Paulson departed De Soto for jobs in Grant Co., MN.
Lien	Melia, Mrs.	BD, p3c1, 8/28/1883	Died Aug. 20, 1883 in Stoughton, WI. She was the daughter of Mrs. A. Folson of Boscobel and niece of William Nelson of Boscobel.
Limbocker	G. W.	BD, p3c4, 6/14/1878	Bought a 160-acre farm in Harvard, Clay Co., NB. Family in Boscobel will join him. He was a Captain in the Civil War.
Limbocker	G. W.	BD, p3c5, 6/14/1878	Capt. G. W. Limbocker wrote a letter to the editor of the *Boscobel Dial* from Harvard, Clay Co., NB. Limbocker mentions several people he knew from Wisconsin who had relocated to Nebraska. He ran into Tommy Dowd, who he knew during the Civil War. Dowd served in Co. F. Algie Hill was in Hastings, as was Capt. Harlocker. Marion Sylvester and Bob Coates were in Harlan Co. While visiting an area 12 miles north of Harvard, found a colony from Grant Co., Wis: 1) E. Sonard, John Sonard, a son-in-law of E. Sonard -- all of Millville; 2) George Cutts, W. M. Sylvester, Frank Winayack and others from Castle Rock; 3) James Williams and others from Wisconsin whom he didn't get to visit and 4) a Norwegian family named Allingson that recently arrived in the area. The Allingsons were from Boscobel.
Limbocker	George, Capt.	BD, p2c3, 8/2/1878	Letter he wrote published in newspaper. Described his trip west to Iowa and Nebraska. Spent two weeks visiting friends and relatives in southern Iowa, at his old house, which he had not seen in 10 years.
Limbocker	Lill	BD, p3c2, 3/24/1882	Lill Limbocker, formerly Mrs. Lillian Turner of Boscobel, moved with her parents [Capt. and Mrs. Limbocker] to Harvard, NB three years ago after deserting her husband. They had been married 4 years. Lill reported to have eloped with A. Gohring. They went to Superior, Nickolls Co. Gohring said to have deserted his wife a year ago. [Lillian denied this report in a letter published on 3/31/1882.]
Lincoln	Mrs.	BD, p3c2, 1/10/1879	Recently died of consumption in Boscobel.
Lind	Charles	DC, p3c2, 6/19/1886	Returned to De Soto for a position at C. Lytlle's store. Spent the last year in La Crosse doing a clerkship.
Lind	Charles	DC, p3c4, 5/7/1887	Clerk. Slept in the P. S. Davidson store in De Soto. Scared away a burgler.
Linderman	Regna	RH, p5c4, 11/4/1897	Dr. M. M. Trowbeidge planned to marry Regna Linderman on Nov. 7, 1897 at the home of the bride's parents in Viroqua.
Linn	A. B.	BD, p2c2, 2/15/1878	Fire destroyed Linn's goods that were housed at the railroad depot in Woodman. Arson suspected. Linn resided in Mt. Hope.
Linn	boy	RH, p5c3, 1/24/1901	A son was recently born to Mr. and Mrs. Linn of De Soto. He weighed 11 pounds.
Liscum	Elliott H., Capt.	BD, p3c1, 10/29/1880	Died in Richland Center. Formerly of Lancaster. Aged 48 years. Enlisted in 33 Wisc. Regiment as a Lieutenant. Later enlisted in the 49th Regiment as a Captain. Survived by wife, 3 daughters and 1 son.
Liseum	Will	BD, p3c2, 11/3/1882	Will Liseum, Al Hamilton, George McPheters and Frank Walworth were arrested for arson and pillaging of the railroad depot in Richland Center.
Literary Society		DC, p3c4, 8/7/1886	The new officers of the Literary Society in De Soto were J. T. Morgans, F. Z. Alexander, Nellie Green, Mrs. M. B. Balch and Emma Bevan. The library was housed in Mrs. Balch's residence. The following participated in the Literary Society program: Mrs. Balch, James Lawrence, Mary Woodbury, Ara Bartholomew, Anna Carlyle, Emma Bevan, Mr. and Mrs. Jones, Alice Cooper, Nettie Lane, D. Kenefick, Mattie Lawrence and Mr. and Mrs. Gardner.
Lockwood		BD, p3c2, 4/29/1881	Lockwood & Hayes recently leased the Avery mills near Excelsior.
Loftus	Anna	DC, p8c2, 8/2/1889	Anna Loftus, daughter of Mr. and Mrs. Peter Loftus of De Soto, visited her parents, brother and sister. She is now a nun of the Franciscan order with the name Sister Cleofa. Went to Mt. Carroll, IL to teach in a large school.
Loftus	Edward	DC, p2c4, 2/26/1887	Died Feb. 22, 1887 in Minneapolis at the age of 4. He was buried in De Soto. His parents were James and Ann Loftus.
Loftus	James	DR, p1c1, 12/15/1870	Proprietor of the De Soto Restaurant in De Soto, WI.
Loftus	James	DR, p3c1, 12/15/1870	While digging holes for trees on his premises, he found a skeleton. It is probably from the Black Hawk War.
Loftus	James	DR, p3c1, 4/27/1871	Sold his saloon and fixtures in De Soto to Peter Barthelomew.
Loftus	James	DC, p2c3, 9/3/1887	Died in Minneapolis on Aug. 24, 1887 when he was 37 years old. Served in Co. I, 50th WI Inf. when he was 14 years old. Survived by father, sisters, wife and 3 children.

Genealogical Events from Newspapers for Crawford, Vernon and Grant Counties, Wisconsin, 1870-1901

LAST NAME	FIRST NAME	NEWSPAPER, PAGE/COLUMN MONTH/DAY/YEAR	GENEALOGICAL DATA
Loftus	James H.	DC, p2c1, 3/27/1888	Resided in De Soto. Enlisted in Civil War at the age of 14 years, 7 months and 13 days on March 8, 1865. Born July 25, 1850. Served in Co H. 50th Regt. WI Vol. Died last fall. He was the brother of Martin Loftus.
Loftus	Kate	DC, p3c4, 7/2/1887	Daughter of Martin Loftus of De Soto. Recently left $50,000 in her own name by the death of her father-in-law, Mr. Orth of Minneapolis.
Loftus	Martin	DC, p3c3, 6/26/1886	Opened a boarding house near the new depot in De Soto.
Loftus	Martin	DC, p3c4, 7/3/1886	Installed inside running water from a hillside spring at his home in De Soto.
Loftus	Martin	DC, p3c2, 7/17/1886	Loftus' children [Clara, Mary, George and James] arrived in De Soto from Minneapolis..
Loftus	Martin	DC, p8c2, 6/14/1889	Built a reservoir to hold spring water on the hillside behind his house in De Soto.
Loftus	Mary	DC, p3c2, 7/3/1886	Returned to De Soto after teaching in Stoddard.
Loftus	Mary	DC, p3c2, 11/27/1886	From De Soto. Taught school at Bergen.
Loftus	Mary, Miss	DC, p3c3, 9/11/1888	Attended Catholic school in Prairie du Chien.
Loftus	Peter	DC, p8c2, 8/9/1889	Church services were held in the Peter Loftus home in De Soto by Rev. Father Wirtz of Genoa.
Loftus	R. P.	DC, p2c2, 2/26/1889	In charge of the water works in De Soto and Stoddard for the C. B. & N. Railroad.
Logan	James, Jr.	DR, p3c2, 12/22/1870	Died of consumption on Dec. 8, 1870 in Lansing, IA. He was 32 years old.
Logan & Coumbe		BD, p3c3, 1/19/1883	"The firms of Logan & Coumbe and B. F. Washburn [of Excelsior] are buying large stocks of [railroad] ties which they will raft to the tie yards at Green River, Lyons, Iowa and other places"
Lombard	Frank	DC, p3c4, 8/7/1886	Frank Lombard and Bert Bates of Retreat recently "started for Dakota."
Lombard	Frank	DC, p2c2, 11/19/1887	Frank Lombard and John L. Davis, both of Retreat, went to Janesville, WI to attend the school of telegraphy.
Lombart	Frank	DC, p3c2, 2/12/1887	Returned to Retreat from Dakota.
Loney	C. W.	BD, p3c4, 3/24/1882	Pioneer of Fennimore and first businessman of the town. Served as town clerk for many years.
Long	Minnie C.	BD, p3c1, 6/2/1882	Robert W. Brown married Minnie C. Long on May 28, 1882 at Boscobel. J. McLaughlin, J.P. officiated.
Long	William	BD, p2c3, 5/5/1882	Capt. Hurley captured Long while burglarizing in Prairie du Chien.
Longbottom	John	BD, p3c2, 5/28/1880	Appointed to be a census enumerator in Paris, Grant Co.
Longmire	William	RH, p4c2, 9/12/1901	Lived in Knapp's Creek. After delivering cattle to Readstown, he spent the night in the Park Hotel, where he was robbed of $35.
Loomis	Emma E.	BD, p3c2, 11/20/1883	Oscar G. Meyer married Emma E. Loomis on Nov. 14, 1883 at Werley, WI. Groom was the second son of Gustav Meyer of Boscobel. He worked as a bookkeeper for J. H. Sarles. Bride was from Werley. The Rev. T. W. Cole officiated.
Loomis	Mr.	BD, p3c2, 12/20/1878	Shot a bald-headed eagle. Resided in Mt. Hope. Bird was purchased by M. D. Tillotson and shipped to Chicago for preservation.
Loper	A.	DR, p2c4, 6/29/1871	Published a notice. He took up a lost bay horse at Warner's Landing in Vernon Co.
Lord	Rufus	BD, p3c2, 6/8/1877	Rufus Lord married Mary Peer on June 2, 1877 in Boscobel. Groom from Sextonville. Bride from Watterstown. Rev. Z. S. Hurd officiated.
Lorimer	William	BD, p3c1, 8/13/1881	Seventeen-year-old son of John Lorimer of Hickory Grove. Broke his collarbone after being thrown from a wagon.
Lough	Annie M., Miss	DC, p2c2, 1/1/1887	Henry Henderson married Miss Annie M. Lough on Dec. 27, 1886 at the residence of M. Lough of Freeman. Bride and groom from Ferryville. The Rev. Thomas Crouch officiated.
Lough	Annie M., Mrs.	DC, p2c2, 12/25/1886	Planned to marry Mrs. Annie M. Lough in Ferryville. Wedding invitations were sent out.
Love	Jonah	DC, p3c4, 2/26/1887	Stabed and killed Ole N. Nelson at Bristow, 10 miles east of De Soto, at the store of Mr. Fortune following a quarrel while playing cards. G. Esperseth's wrist was badly damaged; he may lose use of the hand. Jonah Love married a sister of Will and Capt. Owen. Ole was single and 26 years old.

Genealogical Events from Newspapers for Crawford, Vernon and Grant Counties, Wisconsin, 1870-1901

LAST NAME	FIRST NAME	NEWSPAPER, PAGE/COLUMN MONTH/DAY/YEAR	GENEALOGICAL DATA
Love	Jonah	DC, p2c1, 5/7/1887	Found guilty of murder in the second degree for the murder of Ole N. Nelson at Bristow last February.
Love	Jonah	DC, p3c2, 5/14/1887	Sentenced to 15 years of hard labor.
Lowers	Mrs.	DC, p3c3, 10/29/1887	Buried Saturday. She was 89 years old. [Per Ontario news column]
Lowrie	Grace	RH, p5c3, 12/13/1900	Grace Lowrie recently married Guy Sharp. Bride from De Soto. Groom from Dakota.
Lowrie	Pitt, Mrs.	DC, p3c3, 10/2/1886	Resided 5 miles west of Viroqua. Became violently insane on Monday. Now nearly sane.
Lowrie	W. K.	DC, p3c2, 4/10/1888	Went to La Crosse to have a physician cut away cancer from his lower lip.
Lowrie	W. K., Mrs	DC, p3c3, 9/10/1887	Called from De Soto to Rock Falls, IL. Her daughter, Mrs. Alfredda Nims, was very ill.
Lubke	William, Mrs.	DC, p3c3, 11/13/1886	Died in Retreat on Nov. 9, 1886 of apoplexy.
Lucas	Isaac	BD, p3c1, 9/4/1883	The Isaac Lucas funeral was held Wednesday at the Methodist Episcopal Church in Boscobel. Lucas was a Grant Co. resident for many years. Moved to Platteville in 1844.
Lucas	James, Mrs.	BD, p3c2, 11/24/1882	Recently died in Boscobel. Born in Warwickshire, England. Moved to Ohio. Settled in Boscobel 26 years ago. Husband died in 1865. Lived with youngest son in the old homestead. The youngest son will move in with his sister, Mrs. Woolstenholme of Liberty. Survived by [an additional?] 2 sons and 2 daughters who live in Iowa.
Lucas	Mrs.	BD, p3c2, 11/17/1882	Found dead Friday morning at her home in Boscobel. Died of asthma. She was an old lady. Funeral took place at the Congregational Church.
Lucis	Olive Elender	BD, p3c2, 12/9/1881	Charles Wesley Beaumont married Olive Elender Lucis on Dec. 8, 1881. Groom from Boaz, Richland Co. Bride from Boscobel. The Rev. T. M. Evans officiated.
Luckey	Miss	BD, p3c2, 11/14/1879	Crad Barnett recently married Miss Luckey. Bride from Independence, IA. Groom was a former resident of Boscobel but now lived in Independence, IA. Planned to live in Williamsport, PA, the groom's native state.
Lull	Martha	BD, p3c1, 5/7/1880	William Snow of Boscobel married Martha Lull of Boscobel on Monday afternoon at The Carrier House. Prof. John Allison officiated.
Lund	Miss	DC, p3c2, 12/3/1887	Miss Lund married Mr. Arneson on Thanksgiving Day at Purdy. "Miss Lund's mother was present from Chicago where she lives in affluence."
Lunde	Eric	DC, p3c3, 12/31/1887	Taught Norwegian school in Freeman.
Luth	John	DR, p2c5, 12/22/1870	Proprietor of a saddle and harness business in De Soto.
Luth	John	DR, p3c2, 12/29/1870	Recently opened a new harness and saddle manufactory in De Soto. He is very busy with work.
Luth	John	DR, p3c2, 11/2/1871	John Luth married Carthegnia McAuley on Oct. 17, 1871. Luth was a harness maker. Bride was from the De Soto area.
Luxom	Jim	RH, p5c3, 10/14/1897	Found metal ore in his Bear Creek mine. He believes it is gold.
Lyman	Alonzo, Mr. and Mrs.	BD, p3c3, 10/1/1880	Arrived from Rushford, NY to visit Mr. and Mrs. N. R. Miller of Boscobel. Mrs. Lyman and Mr. Miller were siblings.
Lyman	Charles, Dr.	BD, p3c3, 7/23/1880	Recently married Delia Gilman. Visited Mr. and Mrs. B. W. Coult in Boscobel. Planned to visit Bloomington and then depart for a new home in Steele City, NB.
Lynxville		DC, p1c1, 7/26/1889	Lynxville was preparing to incorporate as a village. The following list of candidates were expected to win office: County Supervisor, S. Armstrong; President, A. N. Searle; Trustees, Wm. Huard, T. C. Bright, S. H. Vanderbilt, D. L. Heligas, Geo. Pease, and Geo. Sutton; Assessor, Frank Haskell; Clerk, A. E. Wolcott; Treasurer, John Vanderbilt, Sr.; Police Justice, Frank Haskell; Justice of the Peace, L. B. Allen; and Constable, Edward Noggle.
Lyons	Will	RH, p4c2, 8/23/1900	Died August 21, 1900 of typhoid fever at his home in Brookville. He worked there for the last 2 months as a carpenter. He was the brother of Mary Welch, per RH, p4c3, 11/8/1900.
Lyster	Frank	BD, p3c2, 5/28/1880	Appointed to be a census enumerator in Jamestown, Grant Co.
Lytle	J. O.	RH, p6c3, 1/5/1899	Returned to Medford after visiting family in De Soto.
Lytle	Maud	RH, p4c3, 9/26/1901	Charley Collins married Maud Lytle last week in La Crosse. Bride and groom from De Soto.
Lyttle		DC, p3c4, 8/21/1886	C. Lyttle & Co. sold a Lynxville lumberyard to the Lansing Lumber Co.

Genealogical Events from Newspapers for Crawford, Vernon and Grant Counties, Wisconsin, 1870-1901

LAST NAME	FIRST NAME	NEWSPAPER, PAGE/COLUMN MONTH/DAY/YEAR	GENEALOGICAL DATA
Lyttle	Alice, Mrs.	DC, p3c4, 12/11/1886	Taught embroidery lessons.
Lyttle	baby	DC, p3c3, 2/19/1889	The 6-month-old baby of John Lyttle of De Soto died Thursday. Buried in Lansing.
Lyttle	boy	DC, p2c1, 8/21/1888	A son was born to John Lyttle of De Soto on August 12, 1888.
Lyttle	C.	DC, p3c3, 7/3/1886	Received the first load of freight [lumber from Onalaska] on the new railroad in De Soto.
Lyttle	Charles	DC, p2c3, 4/2/1887	Retired from a partnership between himself and Payton S. Davidson of La Crosse.
Lyttle	Charles and John	DC, p2c3, 10/29/1887	Returned to De Soto from their railroad work in northern Michigan.
Mackie	C. E., Miss	RH, p4c2, 1/4/1900	M. A. Andrews married Miss C. E. Mackie on Dec. 25, 1899 at the home of the bride's mother. Groom was the Town Treasurer in Readstown for many years. He was also the depot agent, Secretary and Treasurer for Readstown Broom Company and President of Readstown Telephone Company. Bride lived at 37 Elm Street, Toronto, Canada.
Maeby	Jennie	DC, p3c3, 8/7/1888	Died July 30, 1888. Survived by husband and an infant. Buried in Viroqua. Mr. and Mrs. W. D. Maeby lived in Newton [per p3c3, 7/31/1888]
Maeliotka	Casper	BD, p3c1, 12/10/1880	Casper Maeliotka married Josephine Brindler on Dec. 8, 1880 in Boscobel. Bride from Hickory Grove. Groom from Muscoda.
Mahoney		DC, p2c2, 3/19/1887	A few weeks ago a 12-year old son of Patrick and Mary Mahoney of the Town of Blooming Grove died of diphtheria. Sunday evening a sister, Nellie, died at her boarding house in Madison. "She attended her brother's funeral, and contracted the disease, no doubt." They are survived by brothers, D. O. Mahoney of Viroqua and P. W. Mahoney of La Crosse.
Mahoney	D. O.	DC, p3c2, 6/19/1886	Served as County Superintendent of Schools.
Mahoney	D. O.	DC, p2c2, 8/7/1886	Will probably run for Co. Superintendent in Vernon Co.
Mahoney	Paul W.	DC, p2c2, 8/20/1887	Paul W. Mahoney married Alice De Hart on Aug. 17, 1887. Bride from West Lima. Groom was a lawyer in North La Crosse.
Maiben	Arabilla	RH, p4c4, 4/7/1898	The Vernon County Probate Court published a notice that George L. Maiben had petitioned to administer the estate of Arabilla Maiben.
Maiben	George	RH, p4c2, 6/21/1900	Left Readstown for Grand Junction, CO "in search of health."
Maiben	George	RH, p4c3, 9/13/1900	Health has improved since his move to Colorado. Planned to make Grand Junction home. Mrs. Maiben will join her husband about Oct. 30th. She is selling the residence and household effects.
Maiben	George, Mrs.	RH, p5c3, 1/20/1898	Resided in Lancaster. Visited relatives in Readstown.
Maiben	girl	RH, p5c3, 7/8/1897	A daughter was recently born to George Maiben of Readstown.
Maiben	H.	RH, p5c2, 3/17/1898	H. Maiben, James Maiben and Ed Kellogg of Readstown are making sugar.
Main	Cortland	BD, p3c1, 4/7/1882	Cortland Main married Emma M. Zillinger on April 2, 1882 in Boscobel. The bride and groom were from Crawford County. J. McLaughlin, J.P. officiated.
Main	William	BD, p3c1, 6/30/1882	Resided in Boscobel. Received a patent for a trace carrier.
Main	William H.	BD, p3c3, 12/8/1882	Inventor. A stock company was formed by Boscobel residents to manufacture his safety trace carrier.
Main	William H.	BD, p3c2, 7/28/1882	Boscobel inventor. Discovered a way to obviate washing of canal banks by boats.
Maine	W. N.	BD, p3c3, 5/21/1880	Resided in Boscobel. Received a patent for a wheel harrow.
Malin	Joseph	DC, p2c2, 3/10/1888	Sick with lung fever in Genoa.
Malin	Paul	DC, p2c1, 4/16/1887	Sold his farm in Genoa to Carlo Maltrasia and moved to La Crosse to work as a stone mason.
Mallalley	Michael, Sr.	BD, p2c3, 1/5/1883	Resided near Bloomington. Broke his ribs and received internal injuries when his sleigh overturned. He was over 80 years old.
Manger	William	DR, p4c5, 12/15/1870	Sold furniture in Lansing, IA.

Genealogical Events from Newspapers for Crawford, Vernon and Grant Counties, Wisconsin, 1870-1901

LAST NAME	FIRST NAME	NEWSPAPER, PAGE/COLUMN MONTH/DAY/YEAR	GENEALOGICAL DATA
Manley	Cyrus	BD, p3c1, 7/13/1883	Came to Boscobel with his sick child seeking medical attention. Dr. Armstrong's diagnosis was measles.
Manlon	O. P.	BD, p3c2, 5/28/1880	Appointed to be a census enumerator in Muscoda, Grant Co.
Mann	Emma	BD, p3c1, 12/4/1883	Thomas Bailey married Emma Mann on Dec. 2, 1883 in Prairie du Chien. Groom from Boscobel. Bride from Prairie du Chien.
Mann	George J.	DC, Supp, 10/23/1886	George J. Mann married Lilly Funk on Sept. 14, 1886 in a Catholic Church in Alma, WI. Rev. Father Hackner officiated.
Mann	Minnie	BD, p3c2, 6/21/1878	Minnie Mann married Frank McLimans on June 18, 1878. Bride and groom were from Liberty, Grant Co. The Rev. D. L. Hubbard officiated.
Manning	W. S.	RH, p4c2, 5/30/1901	Appointed County Judge for the new county of Gates. He was a former resident of Soldiers Grove.
Mansfield	Samuel	DC, p2c2, 3/19/1887	Native of Lynxville. He was an old resident. Died last week.
Mansfield	Wesley	DC, p2c1, 9/17/1887	Lived in Lynxville. Buried September 1, 1887.
Mara		BD, p2c3, 12/4/1883	A log house on the Hromatka farm, north of Wauzeka Road, was blown down in a storm. Mr. and Mrs. Mara occupied it. Mrs. Mara was killed.
Marin	R. W.	DC, p3c4, 1/15/1887	R. W. Marin recently married Emma Bennett per the Seneca news column.
Marker	Elmer	DC, p3c3, 5/7/1887	Learning the butcher trade.
Marker	Elmer	DC, p2c1, 7/23/1887	Lost several fingers when he was young. A dynamite cartridge exploded in his hand. Last winter, he accidently shot a piece off of one of the crippled fingers. On Friday a horse kicked him in the face and knocked out several teeth.
Marker	James	DC, p3c3, 11/13/1886	Died Oct. 26, 1886 in Lambert, NB. Mrs. Marker died about a year ago. They were old "Jefferson neighbors" of W. T. McConnell of Viroqua. James Marker was the brother of S. Marker of De Soto.
Marker	James	DC, p3c3 8/13/1887	James Marker and Charles Brunk purchased ½ interest in the Graham Sawmill in the Town of Liberty.
Marker	James	DC, p3c2, 11/5/1887	Moved his family to Liberty where he and Charles B_____ operated a sawmill.
Marker	Sarah E., Mrs.	RH, p4c3, 5/26/1898	Died at her Viola home on May 17, 1898. Buried next to her mother in the Salem County [Cemetery?]. She was the sister of W. C. T. Adams of Readstown and Oscar G. Adams of Avalanche. Father lived in Chippewa Co. Survived by husband and infant baby. Member of Christian Church in Viroqua. Born in the Town of Webster, Vernon Co. on May 13, 1874. Married Elmer Marker 2 years ago.
Markham	E. F.	BD, p3c2, 9/19/1879	E. F. Markam married Miss E. A. Brown last Sunday at Muscoda. Bride from Watterstown. Groom from Boscobel. The Rev. George Haigh officiated.
Markham	Mark	BD, p3c2, 8/11/1882	Mark Markham of Clairmount, IA visited his brother, Frank of Boscobel. This was their first visit in 12 years. Frank did not recognize Mark.
Markle	J. C.	DC, p2c2, 3/19/1887	Held an auction at his home in Chaseburgh. Left for Colorado. His family is to follow.
Marks	N.	DC, p3c4, 8/14/1886	Home in Retreat destroyed by fire.
Marks	N.	DC, p3c4, 11/13/1886	Published a notice that he had taken up a cow at his farm in Retreat, Town of Sterling.
Marks	William	BD, p3c1, 12/25/1883	Fell through ice on the Wisconsin River and almost lost a valuable span of horses. Prompt assistance from others saved them.
Markt	Frank	BD, p2c3, 8/24/1877	Lost his Muscoda area farmhouse to fire.
Marsh	Rebecca	BD, p2c6, 3/19/1880	Grant Co. Circuit Court published a summons for Rebecca Marsh, plaintiff vs. White Marsh, defendant.
Marshell	Amy	RH, p5c2, 7/13/1899	William Miller married Amy Marshell last week. Bride from Rockton. Groom from Sugar Grove.
Marston	Eugene	DC, p2c2, 5/7/1887	Eugene Marston, Frank Stephenson and C. W. Nichols "have caught the Spokane Fever and will probably go to Washington Territory in May."
Marston	Mrs.	DC, p2c2, 5/7/1887	Mrs. Marston, of Seneca, received a visit from her cousin, Roland Spencer of Pennsylvania.
Marston	W., Mrs.	DC, p2c2, 5/7/1887	Mrs. W. Marston and Miss Griest left Seneca for Clayton, IA to visit their parents.

Genealogical Events from Newspapers for Crawford, Vernon and Grant Counties, Wisconsin, 1870-1901

LAST NAME	FIRST NAME	NEWSPAPER, PAGE/COLUMN MONTH/DAY/YEAR	GENEALOGICAL DATA
Marston	Wilford, Mrs.	DC, p2c2, 9/24/1887	Departed Seneca to visit parents in Clayton, IA.
Marten	Oscar	RH, p4c2, 1/4/1900	Oscar Marten married Rosa Umback last Monday at the home of George Sutherland. C. H. Davenport officiated.
Martin	Emma Bennett, Mrs.	DC, p2c3, 2/11/1888	Died Feb. 2, 1888 at the Biglow House, Seneca, WI. Survived by a week-old baby. She was a farmer, teacher and sister of E. M. Bennett who died last October.
Martin	girl	RH, p4c4, 2/2/1899	A girl was recently born to Daniel and Jennie Martin of Sugar Grove.
Martin	J. W., Mrs. Rev.	DC, p8c2, 6/7/1889	Left De Soto for Nebraska. Received a telegram stating her mother was very ill.
Martin	John	BD, p3c2, 7/7/1882	Died July 4, 1882 at home of his son, Jacob. Resided in Boscobel. Born Nov. 23, 1802 in Germany. Emigrated to America in 1856. Moved to Grant Co. He was the father of 10 children. Survived by 7 children: John Martin, Jr.; Jacob Martin; Mrs. Elizabeth Sanger; Mrs. Margaret Ruka; Mrs. Eliza Scheinpflug; Mrs. Kate Seeman and Mrs. Caroline Boldt. Funeral held at the German Lutheran Church.
Martin	Mr. and Mrs.	DC, p2c2, 4/2/1887	Departed Seneca for a trip to the West. Planned to visit friends in La Mars, IA and then travel to Omaha, NB.
Martin	Mrs.	BD, p2c3, 1/12/1883	Her millinery shop in Richland Center was saved from fire by a bucket brigade.
Mason	F. M.	BD, p2c4, 11/26/1880	Grant County paid him a bounty for scalps turned into the county.
Mason	James	DC, p3c5, 7/24/1886	The James Mason Post No. 106, Grand Army of the Republic [GAR] met at the Odd Fellows Hall in De Soto and elected C. S. Fourt and O. Ewers as officers.
Mason	Sargeant	BD, p3c2, 3/31/1882	Petition circulated asking for a reduction in the sentence of Sargeant Mason.
Masonic Lodge		BD, p3c4, 1/5/1877	Officers of the Masonic Lodge in Boscobel: T. N. Hubbell, G. W. Parker, M. N. Sawyer, B. W. Coult, W. B. Phillips, D. C. Perrigo, M. B. Pittman, James S. Clark and A. [H.?] Alden.
Massiker		DR, p3c1, 7/20/1871	Two Massiker children, aged 12 and 13, drowned in the Mississippi River off Lansing, IA.
Masten	Mat	RH, p4c2, 8/30/1900	While doing repairs, he found the skeletons of a man and 2 boys under the floor of an old residence at Bell Center. It was the oldest house in the area. Built by early settlers and occupied by many families over the years. Murder was certainly involved.
Mathews	Dick	BD, p3c2, 7/26/1878	Mathews' livery and stable in Prairie du Chien was struck by lightening.
Mathews	Ed	RH, p6c4, 9/22/1898	From Kickapoo. Bought land "up north" for a new home.
Mathews	Ed	RH, p5c4, 9/29/1898	Started for the "north" with 3 prairie schooners. Left his home in Kickapoo.
Mathews	John	BD, p2c4, 11/26/1880	Grant County paid him a bounty for scalps turned into the county.
Mathews	Thomas, Mrs.	BD, p2c3, 9/9/1881	Died Aug. 23, 1881 in Orion, Richland Co. Born in 1825 in Illinois. Moved to Wisconsin in 1839. Married Thomas Mathews in 1840. Moved to Orion in 1842. Thomas is now the "oldest settler" in Richland Co., with the exception of John Combe of Port Andrew who came to the county a year before Mathews.
Maxum	Orville	BD, p3c2, 6/13/1879	Died May 29, 1879 in the Town of Hickory Grove. Fell in a cistern and drowned. He was 5 ½ years old. Son of Henry and Josephine Maxum.
Maxwell	C.	DC, p3c3, 10/2/1886	Resided in Lansing. He was a veteran of the Mexican and Civil Wars.
Maxwell	C.	DC, p3c4, 7/16/1887	Resided in Lansing. Served in the Mexican War and was recently allowed a pension.
May	Col.	DC, p3c2, 1/22/1887	Col. May of the Town of Jefferson recently received arrearages for his pension of $6400 or $125 per month for 21 years and 4 months.
May	D. R.	DC, p1c6, 10/8/1887	Resided in Boscobel. Qualified for a pension for military service.
May	David	BD, p3c1, 8/6/1880	Came from Crawford Co. to sell the season's first load of wheat in Boscobel. Sold for 60 cents a bushel.
May	Frankie	DC, p2c2, 2/11/1888	Resided in English Bench, IA. Visited uncle, W. R. Rose of Cooley Valley.
May	R., Col.	DC, p3c2, 3/26/1887	Resided in Jefferson. Returned from a trip to Missouri, Kansas, Nebraska and Iowa. He visited a sister he had not seen for 32 years. He visited a brother and sister he had not seen for 27 years.

Genealogical Events from Newspapers for Crawford, Vernon and Grant Counties, Wisconsin, 1870-1901

LAST NAME	FIRST NAME	NEWSPAPER, PAGE/COLUMN MONTH/DAY/YEAR	GENEALOGICAL DATA
Mayhan	Mary, Mrs.	RH, p5c5, 10/7/1897	J. P. Dearman married Mrs. Mary Mayhan on Oct. 3, 1897. Bride and groom from Arbor, Vernon Co. Charles W. Reeve, J. P. officiated.
McAfee	Mrs.	RH, p4c1, 11/29/1900	Arrived from Osage, IA to visit relatives in Readstown.
McAllister	Nelson	BD, p3c1, 11/7/1879	Home destroyed by fire. No insurance. Lived 4 miles east of Muscoda.
McAuley	Carthegnia	DR, p3c2, 11/2/1871	John Luth married Carthegnia McAuley on Oct. 17, 1871. Luth was a harness maker. Bride was from the De Soto area.
McAuley	H. W.	DR, p2c1, 8/24/1871	A tombstone was stolen from him. [Not clear if tombstone was taken from a living person or from a grave.]
McAuley	H. W., Esq.	DR, p3c1, 10/26/1871	Moved from De Soto to Viroqua to practice law.
McAuley	Henry	DC, p2c2, 2/5/1887	Cut wood in 1852 on Battle Island, site of the Battle of Bad Axe during the Black Hawk War. He said the trees were literally full of bullets. McAuley told the story about a soldier killed in the fight. He was buried on the island by two brothers. At the head of the grave they buried an iron kettle containing quite a sum of silver money. "Over the kettle they stuck down a cottonwood slip which grew to be a large tree. Years after the battle the two men came and dug up the money."
McAuley	John	DC, p3c4, 2/19/1887	Former resident of Seneca, but now of Mitchell, Dakota. Visited friends in Seneca.
McAuley	John	RH, p4c2, 9/8/1898	Departed De Soto for La Crosse to finish coursework at the Wisconsin Business University.
McAuley	R. M.	DC, p4c2, 4/19/1889	R. M. McAuley and Charles McDowell of De Soto trapping and fishing stories published.
McAuley	R. M.	RH, p4c2, 9/8/1898	Planned to leave De Soto in the spring. He will go to Gays Mills where he recently purchased property.
McAuley	R., Mrs.	DC, p1c1, 6/7/1889	Lived in De Soto. Visited her sister, Mrs. Arthur James of Retreat.
McBergh	Marcus C.	DC, p2c1, 10/2/1888	Former resident of De Soto. He was a Republican candidate for Vernon Co. sheriff.
McCarthy	Belle	BD, p3c2, 5/21/1880	William Bliss married Belle McCarthy on Saturday in Boscobel at the Muffley House. Bride from Bell Center, Crawford Co. Prof. J. Allison officiated.
McCarthy	T. M.	BD, p3c2, 6/1/1877	T. M. McCarthy and J. H. Wigley planned to set up a general merchandise store in Boscobel.
McCarty	J. H.	DC, p2c2, 8/7/1886	Will probably run for Register of Deeds in Vernon Co. Resided in the Town of Kickapoo.
McCarty	James	RH, p5c2, 7/13/1899	James McCarty recently married Mary E. Hale. Groom from Sugar Grove.
McCarty	James	RH, p4c2, 8/17/1899	Fire completely destroyed his house in Readstown.
McCarty	John J.	DC, p2c1, 10/2/1888	Republican candidate for Vernon Co. Registrar. He was a "gentleman who is a well known teacher and businessman of Readstown. He is lame and not capable of doing manual labor."
McCarty	John J.	DC, p3c4, 10/30/1888	Candidate for Registrar of Deeds. Engaged in a mercantile business in Readstown. Badly crippled by rheumatism.
McCarty	John J.	DC, p3c3, 2/12/1889	Died last Wednesday in Viroqua.
McCarty	Len	RH, p4c1, 12/28/1899	Len McCarty married Belle Randall on Dec. 19, 1899. Groom from Soldiers Grove. Bride from Sugar Grove.
McCarty	Leota	RH, p4c2, 5/3/1900	Resided in Readstown. Hired to teach in Cashton.
McCarty	Mattie	RH, p4c3, 3/23/1899	Jesse Ewers married Mattie McCarty on March 17, 1899. Bride and groom from Readstown. The Rev. George Nuzum of Viroqua officiated.
McCaskey	Josiah	BD, p3c2, 3/30/1883	Appointed to be postmaster by President Pierce in 1855 in Fancy Creek, Richland County. John Hart succeeded him.
McClaran	H. O.	RH, p4c2, 11/11/1897	Resided in Manning. Paid for a *Herald* subscription for his brother, A. W. McClaran, of Minneapolis.
McClaran	H. O.	RH, p3c2, 1/5/1899	Returned to the D. L. Moody Institute in Chicago from his home in Manning to resume his theological studies.
McClaran	W. A.	RH, p4c2, 7/20/1899	Visited relatives in Readstown. Moved to Dakota 15 years ago when the territory was first opened for settlement. Ran a mercantile business in Aberdeen, SD and a cattle ranch outside the city.

Genealogical Events from Newspapers for Crawford, Vernon and Grant Counties, Wisconsin, 1870-1901

LAST NAME	FIRST NAME	NEWSPAPER, PAGE/COLUMN MONTH/DAY/YEAR	GENEALOGICAL DATA
McClaran	W. A., Mrs.	RH, p4c1, 7/20/1899	Arrived in Readstown from Mound City, SD to visit with mother, Mrs. C. Lewis.
McClary		BD, p3c3, 4/13/1877	Defendant in an arson case in Richland Co. Accused of burning Mr. Rodolf's mill.
McClurg	Mabel, Miss	DC, p3c3, 9/18/1888	Arrived in De Soto from West Prairie to visit sister, Mrs R. J. Kalhar.
McClury	Leora	DC, p3c3, 3/19/1887	Hired to teach school in the TeWalt District this summer.
McCollum	L. C.	BD, p2c3, 2/9/1883	Nellie Akey married L. C. McCollum last Sunday at the home of the bride's parents, Mr. and Mrs. Lemuel Akey of Buena Vista, Richland Co. Groom from Fifield, Price Co., WI. This was a double wedding with Mattie Akey and N. H. Burgor. Groom from Viola. The Rev. Pearce of Richland Center officiated.
McCord	James	BD, p3c2, 5/11/1877	From Boscobel. Baptised by the Rev. Jesse D. Searles of the Methodist Episcopal Church in Sanders Creek.
McCord	Mrs.	BD, p3c1, 9/2/1881	Struck by lightening in her Boscobel home.
McCord	Walker	BD, p3c2, 12/2/1881	Died Nov. 23, 1881. Born Dec. 3, 1798 in Mercer Co., PA. Married Jeannett Moore in spring of 1825 in Mercer Co. PA. Moved to Platteville in 1843 and to Boscobel in 1848. He was the third family to live in the Town of Boscobel. Preceeded by the Wayne and Powell families. Survived by his wife and 7 of his 8 childen. Member of Baptist Church.
McCord	William	BD, p3c2, 6/8/1883	McCord and Benjamin Bull were arrested for disturbing the peace in Boscobel.
McCormick	John	DC, p3c2, 5/22/1888	John McCormick and George Alcorn opened a restaurant in De Soto in Devlin's former butcher shop.
McCormick	John	DC, xxxx, 7/19/1889	John McCormick married Josie McDonald on July 15, 1889 at St. Phillips Church. Bride from Soldiers Grove. Rev. Father Conley officiated.
McCormick	Michael	BD, p3c1, 2/27/1880	Last Saturday the three sons of Michael McCormick of Rolling Ground were injured while hauling corn stalks. The team ranaway. John died the next day after the accident.
McCouey	Tom	RH, p4c2, 12/27/1900	Shot and seriously wounded his father-in-law, William Dearman, on Christmas night in Readstown at the postoffice. McCouey and Dearman were both intoxicated. [A follow up article from 1/3/1901 said only McCouey was drunk.] McCouey was arrested. Dearman was critically ill.
McCrillis	Della	DC, p2c5, 1/14/1888	Edwin Stolp married Della McCrillis on Dec. 26, 1887 in Mt. Sterling at the home of the bride. Rev. Wm. Haughton officiated.
McCrillis	J. E.	DC, p3c2, 10/1/1887	Planned to sell his farm at auction on Oct. 19th. Farm located 5 miles southeast of De Soto. Had a similar auction in Vermont 33 years ago. Will go to Dakota.
McCrillis	J. E.	DC, p2c2, 12/3/1887	Injured when his wagon tipped over. The wagon was loaded with household goods being sent to Buffalo Gap, Dakota.
McCrillis	Joseph E., Mr. and Mrs.	DC, p3c4, 7/16/1887	Celebrated their golden wedding anniversary on Friday. Resided in Freeman. Married July 9, 1887 in Providence, RI. Came to Wisconsin in the 1850s and settled at Mt. Sterling. Moved to their present home, about 5 miles southeast of De Soto in 1874. Received $5 pieces from W. G. Conklin and a brother at Malborrough [Marlborough?], MA.
McDaniel	Gertrude Drake, Mrs.	RH, p5c2, 5/31/1900	Died at her father's home on May 28, 1900 in Sugar Grove. She was 18. Funeral conducted by Elder Wells.
McDaniel	James	RH, p4c4, 11/11/1897	Ill with typhoid fever in Clinton Center. Further down the news column it stated, Mr. and Mrs. McDaniel died of typhoid a few weeks ago.
McDaniel	Monroe	RH, p5c4, 1/20/1898	Monroe McDaniel, Lester Smith and Alex McEathron of Sugar Grove spent last summer in the west and have now returned.
McDaniel	Monroe	RH, p5c4, 11/23/1899	Returned to Sugar Grove from the west where he had worked for the past summer. His hand was caught in a corn sheller.
McDaniel	Monroe	RH, p5c3, 10/11/1900	Monroe and O. H. McDaniel, Roy Morrow and Jesse Drake left Sugar Grove by train for Illinois to work in a stave factory for the winter.
McDaniel	Monroe	RH, p5c3, 2/21/1901	Monroe McDaniel married Alice Pettit on Monday. Bride and groom from Sugar Grove. Bride granddaughter of Reuben Alexander. Groom son of William McDaniel. Squire Ward officiated at the ceremony.
McDermott	John	BD, p3c1, 8/14/1883	John McDermott was named President of the newly formed GAR Post in Boscobel.
McDermott	John	BD, p3c1, 9/25/1883	The John McDermott Post 101, GAR was chartered on August 15, 1883 with 44 members. It now has 71 members.

Genealogical Events from Newspapers for Crawford, Vernon and Grant Counties, Wisconsin, 1870-1901

LAST NAME	FIRST NAME	NEWSPAPER, PAGE/COLUMN MONTH/DAY/YEAR	GENEALOGICAL DATA
McDermott	John, Capt.	BD, p3c3, 8/21/1883	The John McDermott Grand Army of the Republic [GAR] Post 101 was organized in Boscobel on Aug. 15, 1883. The charter members were John Stahel, William Cook, James B. Ricks, L. G. Armstrong, Charles E. Cook, John V. B. France, N. J. Francisco, J. McLaughlin, E. B. Smith, G. B. Murphy, G. C. Wurstur, J. W. Nice, John Barbeaux, M. Ableiter, F. Kumrein, R. B. Rice, James Grant, W. L. Huff, Isaac Woodard, James L. Taylor, D. B. Richardson, Wallis W. Young, N. E. Bircherd, D. R. Lawrence, Isaac Peterson, D. W. Carley, Louis Reichel, Geo. W. Cowan, Charles B. Miller, A. F. Henderson, M. A. Sawyer, Thomas Tuffley, G. H. Winn, F. W. Dohme, George Tuffley, A. McKinney, W. C. Scott, A. J. Renshaw, Joseph J. Clark, William Gribble, Joseph Gribble, Amos Devoe, E. F. Devoe and Harvey Clark. The Post was named after one of the "best soldiers that ever left Grant county, and one who bravely laid down his life for his country -- Captain John McDermott, of Company C, 20th Wisconsin Infantry". [Each soldier's company and regiment were provided in the original article.]
McDill	George	DR, p3c3, 5/11/1871	Appointed town clerk in De Soto. Replaced William Coffin, who is moving to Charles City, IA to work in a grocery house. [p3c4]
McDill	George	DR, p3c3, 6/15/1871	Admitted to the bar in Crawford County. Studied law with T. C. Ankeny of De Soto.
McDill	George D.	DR, p3c2, 12/7/1871	George D. McDill married Emma Ankeny on Nov. 25, 1871 at the parsonage by Rev. J. M. Mitchell. Bride and groom were from De Soto.
McDill	Hugh	DC, p2c2, 11/26/1887	The Hugh McDill family arrived in De Soto in 1857.
McDonald	Art	BD, p3c4, 8/10/1877	Arrived from the Black Hills for a visit at former home in Prairie du Chien. A. E. Frank [of Prairie du Chien] and H. H. Whaley [of ?] were also in the Black Hills.
McDonald	C.	BD, P3c5, 1/5/1877	Advertised a billards room in Boscobel.
McDonald	Charles	BD, p3c2, 5/4/1877	Retired from the saloon business in Boscobel. Planned to work as a traveling salesman.
McDonald	Charles	BD, p3c1, 5/30/1879	Departed the area for a new job in La Crosse running a billiards room.
McDonald	Charlies	BD, p3c2, 8/2/1878	Ran billard rooms at the Central House in Boscobel.
McDonald	E.	BD, p3c3, 11/30/1877	Mr. E. McDonald, his wife, his son [Burr] and daughter [Jody] returned to Lone Rock after living in Beloit for 3 years. Mr. McDonald is now blind. Ran Lone Rock's principal hotel.
McDonald	Gertie E.	BD, p3c2, 6/23/1882	Died last evening, per a 6/15/1882 issue of the *Eau Claire Leader*. She was the 8-year-old daughter of Charles and Josephine McDonald and a former resident of Boscobel and La Crosse.
McDonald	Ida	BD, p3c3, 1/13/1882	Prof. C. R. Showalter married Ida McDonald at the home of the bride's mother on Jan. 10, 1882. Groom taught at the Fennimore High School. Bride from Fennimore.
McDonald	Isaac	BD, p2c4, 4/13/1877	In the case, H. A. W. McNair, plaintiff, vs. Isaac McDonald, defendant, the Grant Co. courts ordered that land in Grant Co. be sold at public auction to satisfy a debt.
McDonald	Janey	DC, p3c4, 11/27/1888	Hired to teach school in the Patridge District.
McDonald	Josie	DC, xxxx, 7/19/1889	John McCormick married Josie McDonald on July 15, 1889 at St. Phillips Church. Bride from Soldiers Grove. Rev. Father Conley officiated.
McDonald	R. A.	DR, p3c4, 12/14/1871	Died Dec. 11, 1871 at Victory, WI at the age of 8 years, 3 months and 24 days. Child of Ensign and Emily McDonald.
McDonald	William	DC, p2c2, 5/21/1887	Returned to Lynxville to visit old friends. Current resident of Running Water, Dakota.
McDowell	A., Mrs.	DC, p3c2, 10/15/1887	Lived in the De Soto area. Went to Jersey City, NJ to visit her sister.
McDowell	Al, Mrs.	DC, p3c4, 2/3/1888	Returned to the De Soto area after a 4-month visit at Newburg, NY and Jersey City, NJ.
McDowell	Albert	BD, p3c3, 7/12/1878	Found the body of a newborn child in the road while traveling to Boscobel on the ridge from Belle Center, near the Cass place.
McDowell	Alexander	DC, p3c2, 8/28/1888	In 1840 he lived in Orange Co., NY and voted for Harrison to be President.
McDowell	Battey	DR, p3c1, 5/11/1871	He was a long time resident of De Soto. Departed for a new home in the west.
McDowell	Ben	BD, p3c2, 8/5/1881	Edward McDowell of Town of Scott, Crawford Co. received a telegram Saturday that his son, Ben McDowell, drowned in Lake Pepin and was buried. McDowell and friends were on their way to the northern wheatfields to help harvest. They took deck passage on a boat. It is believed that McDowell fell off the boat when he was partially awake and walking around.

Genealogical Events from Newspapers for Crawford, Vernon and Grant Counties, Wisconsin, 1870-1901

LAST NAME	FIRST NAME	NEWSPAPER, PAGE/COLUMN MONTH/DAY/YEAR	GENEALOGICAL DATA
McDowell	Charles	DC, p3c6, 6/12/1886	Proprietor of a blacksmith shop in De Soto.
McDowell	Charles	DC, p2c2, 2/26/1889	Operated a blacksmith and wagon making shop in De Soto.
McDowell	Elmer	RH, p5c4, 7/8/1897	Elmer McDowell won first place and William Aikins won second place at the horse race in Readstown during the 4th of July celebration.
McDowell	Elmer	RH, p4c2, 11/15/1900	Recovering from typhoid fever in Readstown.
McDowell	Gertrude	RH, p4c2, 5/25/1899	Gertrude McDowell married Levi Adkins on May 22, 1899 at the home of the bride's parents, Mr. and Mrs. M. McDowell of Readstown. Groom from Werley, Grant Co. C. H. Davenport, Justice of the Peace, officiated.
McDowell	Myrtle	RH, p5c4, 2/16/1899	Died of measles on Feb. 11, 1899 in Readstown at the age of 17 years and 8 months. She was the youngest daughter of Madison and Mary E. McDowell. Funeral held at the U.B. Church in Sylvan by Rev. Perry. Buried in the Sylvan Cemetery.
McEathron	Alex	RH, p5c4, 11/30/1899	Alex McEathron planned to marry Kittie Alexander tomorrow [Thursday] per the Sugar Grove news column.
McEathron	Fred	RH, p5c2, 1/13/1898	Mertie Nixon married Fred McEathron on Jan. 8, 1878 at the home the bride's parents in Star, MN. The Rev. T. M. McClung officiated.
McEathrun	Lucinda, Mrs.	RH, p4c4, 2/16/1899	Mrs. McEathrun and son, John, left Sugar Grove for a new home [possibly a temporary home] in Omaha.
McEvoy	Mrs.	DC, p3c2, 1/1/1887	Resided in De Soto. Dangerously ill with lung fever. Mother of Mrs. Banks and Mrs. Downey.
McEvoy	Nellie	DC, p3c2, 10/9/1888	Received the latest fall and winter styles, patterns, hats and bonnets. Has a large selection of ostrich tips and plumes, fancy feathers, silks, plushes, etc.
McEvoy	Nellie, Miss	DC, p3c3, 7/31/1886	Came from Harper's Ferry, IA to visit her sister, Mrs. Banks of De Soto.
McFadden	G., Dr.	BD, p3c4, 2/22/1878	Former resident of Lancaster. Husband of Julia Hyde. Elected county clerk of Wilson Co., KS.
McFarland	M. E., Mrs.	BD, p3c2, 3/14/1879	Died Feb. 24, 1879 in Napa, CA. Lived in Boscobel for 3 years. Nee Lizzie Lowell. Wife of A. McFarland, Esq.
McFarland	Mrs.	BD, p3c1, 3/14/1879	Died Feb. 23, 1879 in Nappa [Napa?] City, CA. Nee Lizzie Lowell.
McGinnis		DC, p3c4, 1/21/1888	The McGinnis and Cooper families were quarantined in De Soto. Seymour Marker submitted a bill to the village Board for attending them.
McGinnis	John	DC, p8c2, 7/19/1889	Opened a meat market in De Soto. He was a former resident of De Soto. Current resident of Victory.
McGinnis	Maggie	DC, p3c2, 12/24/1887	Died Dec. 17, 1887 in De Soto at the age of 6 years.
McGinnis	Nellie	DC, p3c2, 11/20/1886	Nellie McGinnis and Mrs. Banks gave rag baby parties in De Soto.
McGonigal	William	BD, p3c4, 9/13/1878	Announced a meeting in Lancaster of the Old Settlers Association of Grant County, Wisconsin.
McGowan		BD, p3c2, 1/19/1877	Hanged himself last Saturday in his father's stable in Port Andrew. Aged about 20 years.
McGranahan	James	BD, p3c2, 11/1/1878	Injured in a powder mill explosion 5 weeks ago. Recovering and out on the streets of Boscobel again.
McGraw	George	BD, p3c2, 3/22/1878	George McGraw married Fannie Shaw on Mar. 7, 1878. Bride from Mt. Ida. Groom from Boscobel. The Rev. G. W. Nuzum officiated.
McGraw	John	BD, p3c1, 1/23/1880	Hand badly smashed two weeks ago while coupling railroad cars in Woodman. Under the care of Dr. L. G. Armstrong of Boscobel.
McGraw	Ransom, Mr. and Mrs.	BD, p3c3, 3/21/1879	A charivari was held for Mr. And Mrs. Ransom McGraw [of near Boscobel] who recently resumed living together after spending 1 ½ years apart.
McGrew	Senator	BD, p2c3, 4/6/1883	The *Republican and Observer* noted that ex-senator McGrew was not in an Ohio insane asylum as rumored. He was visiting with sisters in Steubenville, OH for health reasons.
McGuigan	Bernard	BD, p3c2, 1/10/1879	Bernard McGuigan married Ellen Cull on Jan. 1, 1879. Bride and groom from Woodman. The Rev. Charles Schraudenbach, a Catholic priest in Boscobel, officiated.
McGuinness	John	DC, p3c2, 4/9/1887	Resided near De Soto. His 9-month-old son died Saturday.
McGuinnis	Nellie	DC, p3c3, 10/2/1888	Nellie McGuinnis married Matt J. Myers on Tuesday. Groom, an agent for C. B. & N. Railroad, was from Victory. Rev. Haughton officiated.
McHarg	Lizzie	BD, p3c5, 7/27/1877	Jacob J. Hire married Lizzie McHarg yesterday at the home of the bride's father. Bride and groom from Wauzeka. The Rev. Dr. Stoddart officiated.

Genealogical Events from Newspapers for Crawford, Vernon and Grant Counties, Wisconsin, 1870-1901

LAST NAME	FIRST NAME	NEWSPAPER, PAGE/COLUMN MONTH/DAY/YEAR	GENEALOGICAL DATA
McHugh	Frank	BD, p3c2, 9/25/1883	Resided in Watertown. Visited his uncle, M. T. Carrier of Boscobel.
McIntyre	B. M.	BD, p2c1, 10/11/1878	McIntyre home in Blue River destroyed by fire. It was occupied by Carl Fursch. Building was insured by P. A. Daggett's agency at Muscoda.
McKay	John, Rev.	DC, p1c2, 6/14/1889	Arrived from Madison to visit brother, R. McKay of Retreat.
McKay	Laura Davis, Mrs.	DC, p3c3, 10/2/1888	Died Aug. 15, 1888. The Retreat W.C.T.U. published a resolution of sympathy.
McKay	Laura, Mrs.	DC, p2c3, 8/28/1888	Died August 15, 1888 of apoplexy at the residence of Dr. Davis of Dubuque, IA. Wife of a merchant in De Soto. Remains brought to De Soto for a funeral at the Methodist Episcopal Church.
McKay	Mary, Miss	DC, p3c3, 9/4/1888	Nominated for County Superintendent of Schools in Richland Co. She was a resident of Richland Center.
McKay	R. N.	DC, p3c2, 4/2/1887	Returned to Retreat after his property in Hurley [WI?] burned.
McKay	R. N., Mrs.	DC, p3c3, 11/13/1886	Formerly of Richland Center. She is spending a few weeks with her parents, Mr. and Mrs. J. L. Davis, before moving to Hurley, WI [per Retreat news column].
McKay	Vernie	DC, p8c2, 8/9/1889	Left De Soto for his home in Dakota by way of La Crosse where he took in the circus.
McKee	John	RH, p4c4, 11/11/1897	Departed home in Ross to go to Ohio to see his critically ill mother.
McKee	Robert	BD, p3c4, 8/3/1877	Opened a store in Boscobel to sell a stock of goods from a bankruptcy.
McKee	Robert	BD, p3c2, 9/6/1878	Moved to Boscobel to open a store.
McKinney	Ella, Miss	BD, p3c3, 11/9/1877	Dies Tuesday in Boscobel. She was "on the sunny side of 20" and a member of the Methodist Church.
McKinney	Estella C.	BD, p3c2, 3/31/1882	Died Dec. 17, 1881 when 6 years, 9 months and 6 days old. She was daughter of J. P. and Rebecca McKinney of Towerville, Crawford Co.
McKinney	J.	BD, p3c3, 11/15/1878	The J. McKinney family departed Boscobel for Fayette, IA where McKinney was engaged in the hoop business.
McKinney	James	BD, p3c2, 8/5/1881	The 14-year-old son of Mr. J. S. McKinney of Excelsior accidently shot a ball into his thigh last Sunday. The doctor has not yet extracted the ball.
McKitrick	Samuel	RH, p6c2, 9/22/1898	He was very ill and not expected to live. Resided in Topeka, KS. Worked in the lumber business in Readstown 16 years ago.
McKitrick	Samuel	RH, p5c3, 9/29/1898	Died Tuesday at his home, 1131 Van Buren St., Topeka, KS. Buried in the Topeka Cemetery.
McKitrick	Samuel, Mrs.	RH, p5c3, 11/10/1898	From Topeka, KS. Visited with friends and relatives in Readstown. Left Readstown 16 years ago.
McKitrick	Samuel, Mrs.	RH, p4c1, 11/15/1900	Resided in Topeka, KS. Visited friends in Readstown and then left for La Crosse to visit parents, per RH, p4c2, 11/22/1900.
McKittrick	Charles J.	BD, p3c1, 8/8/1879	Charles J. McKittrick married Florence Celestia Frank on August 5, 1879 in Pulaski, Iowa Co. Bride daughter of Major George R. Frank, former resident of Boscobel. Groom merchant in Muscoda. The Rev. William Stoddart officiated.
McLaine	Garrett	BD, p3c3, 2/13/1880	Died Feb. 4, 1880 in Geary, Dakota. Former resident of Boscobel. Remains taken to home of Mrs. Farris, his sister-in-law. Wife and child died of small pox 6 years ago in Boscobel. Buried in Boscobel by the Odd Fellows. No blood relations remain in this area.
McLamans	James	BD, p3c2, 11/2/1877	Died Oct. 25, 1877 at Fennimore at 83 years of age. Survived by wife and 8 children.
McLean	Ida	BD, p3c1, 8/1/1879	Dr. D. O. Pickard married Ida McLean on Tuesday evening. Groom from Fennimore. Bride was the adopted daughter of Mr. A. Palmer of Boscobel. The Rev. William Stoddart officiated.
McLiman	Alameda	BD, p3c1, 11/26/1880	Robert Brandon married Alameda McLiman on Nov. 18, 1880 in Boscobel. Bride and groom were from Grant Co. Peter Rae, Esquire officiated.
McLimans	Frank	BD, p3c2, 6/21/1878	Minnie Mann married Frank McLimans on June 18, 1878. Bride and groom were from Liberty, Grant Co. The Rev. D. L. Hubbard officiated.
McMahon	James	BD, p3c2, 6/3/1881	Supervisors James McMahon, James McCormick, Archie Brown, Thomas Watson and C. Shuttleworth were in Boscobel to attend to their duties as county road commissioners.
McMahon	Thomas	BD, p3c1, 8/25/1882	Candidate for County Treasurer in Grant Co. Imprisoned in Andersonville during Civil War.
McMahon	Thomas	BD, p3c2, 5/28/1880	Appointed to be a census enumerator in Harrison, Grant Co.

Genealogical Events from Newspapers for Crawford, Vernon and Grant Counties, Wisconsin, 1870-1901

LAST NAME	FIRST NAME	NEWSPAPER, PAGE/COLUMN MONTH/DAY/YEAR	GENEALOGICAL DATA
McManamy	Catherine	DC, p3c4, 12/4/1886	Taught school in the Ole Targer District per Liberty Pole news column.
McMillan	F. E.	RH, p4c2, 4/5/1900	F. E. McMillan and J. R. Chitwood formed a partnership in Readstown to do carpentry work.
McMillen	Nellie, Mrs.	DC, p2c2, 4/2/1887	Visited her parents, Mr. and Mrs. F. Clark of Victory.
McMillin	Rev., Mrs.	RH, p4c1, 7/4/1901	Died about 2 weeks ago and buried at Fancy Creek, Richland Co., per her son, William McMillin of Shortville, Clark Co. Rev. McMillin was pastor of the Readstown Methodist Church about 20 years ago.
McMullen	Charles	BD, p3c2, 8/11/1882	Charles McMullen and Martin Carlin were arrested for disorderly conduct in Boscobel.
McMurray	John	BD, p3c1, 11/25/1881	In the Grant Co. courts the case, State of Wisconsin vs. John McMurray was heard. This was a case involving bastardy. Mrs. Nancy Yeager was called to testify.
McNair	H. A. W.	BD, p3c2, 9/18/1883	In the case H. A. W. McNair vs. J. L. Rewey, there was a verdict of $2800 in favor of the plaintiff in Grant County Circuit Court.
McNair	H. A. W.	BD, p3c4, 3/24/1882	Visited Fennimore in 1842 and moved on to the farm in which he now resides in June 1848. Held several offices: town chairman in 1853 and 1858, County Commissioner in 1866 and 1867 and county surveyor from 1861-1864. He also served in the Wisconsin State Legislature in 1852, 1867 and 1870.
McNamee	Mathew	BD, p3c2, 2/9/1877	Lived near Mt. Hope. Planned to sell farm items at public auction.
McNelly	H. F.	BD, p3c4, 7/31/1883	He was arrested in Dakota Territory for the rape of a 10-year-old girl that took place 11 months ago in Muscoda.
McNelly	H. T.	BD, p2c2, 3/24/1882	Lawyer in Muscoda. Charged with raping the 10 year old daughter of Mr. Dickinson, a farmer who lived a mile outside of Muscoda. McNelly skipped the country.
McPherson	Jessie, Mrs.	DC, p2c4, 1/14/1888	Mrs. Jessie McPherson, nee Kellogg, who has been living in Dakota during the past few years is in Seneca visiting old acquaintances. She intends to return the first of March.
McQueen	John and Doda	DC, p2c2, 3/12/1887	Departed Seneca for Iowa.
McRenolds	Henry	BD, p3c2, 3/31/1882	Planned to open a restaurant in the Nelson Store Building in Boscobel. Mrs. McRenolds and Miss Alice will assist him.
McReynolds	Franklin L., Rev.	BD, p3c4, 1/4/1878	Rev. Franklin L. McReynolds died Nov. 21, 1877 in Grant Co. at theage of 33 years and 5 months. Died of cancer.
McReynolds	Henry	BD, p3c4, 4/28/1882	Placed an advertisement in the newspaper for his Boscobel restaurant that also sold ice cream, confectionery, canned goods, cigars, tobacco and baked goods.
McReynolds	Thomas Wesley	BD, p3c4, 1/30/1880	Died Jan. 19, 1880. Celebrated 23rd birthday last November. Married about a year ago to Olive Quincey, daughter of S. A. Quincey [who moved from Mt. Hope to Ashland, NB last spring]. Thomas was the brother of Henry McReynolds of Boscobel and son of Thomas McReynolds. Reared near Boscobel. Died of consumption.
McReynolds	Thomas Wesley	BD, p3c2, 1/3/1879	Thomas Wesley McReynolds married Olive E. Quincy Dec. 26, 1878 at the home of the bride's parents. Rev. Z. S. Hurd of Boscobel officiated.
McReynolds	Thomas, Mrs.	BD, p3c3, 10/26/1877	Died Saturday night in Boscobel.
McShore	David	BD, p2c2, 12/11/1883	Died Nov. 25, 1883 at his home in Richwood, Richland Co. He was 67. Settled on his farm in 1846. Survived by wife, 4 sons and 3 daughters. Three sons and 2 daughters were married. He was buried by the roadside on his farm.
McSpaden	F., Mrs.	BD, p3c2, 12/5/1879	Wrote a letter to the editor challenging the newspaper's statements in a story about her son's conviction of a crime. She claimed that because the trial was not fair, her son is going to reform school.
McSpaden	Henry	BD, p3c2, 5/12/1882	McSpaden was "loaded into a wheelbarrow and under the guidance of Marshall Woodard was safely laid away in the calaboose" for being drunk and disorderly on the Boscobel streets. Sentenced to 30 days.
McSpaden	Jim	BD, p3c3, 7/20/1883	Former resident of Boscobel. Current resident of Omaha. Arrived in town for a visit.
McSweeney	Daniel	BD, p2c4, 1/5/1877	By judgement of the Grant Co. Circuit Court, a Sheriff's sale of land in Boscobel was scheduled to be held on Feb. 3, 1877. This involved the case George F. Hildebrand and George W. Parker, plaintiffs vs. Daniel McSweeney, defendant; foreclosure.
McSweeney	Daniel, Mrs.	BD, p3c1, 10/24/1879	Died Friday from complications of childbirth in the Boscobel area.
McSweeney	Ed	BD, p3c1, 8/4/1882	Fined $5 for cruelty to animals in Boscobel. His father paid the fine.

Genealogical Events from Newspapers for Crawford, Vernon and Grant Counties, Wisconsin, 1870-1901

LAST NAME	FIRST NAME	NEWSPAPER, PAGE/COLUMN MONTH/DAY/YEAR	GENEALOGICAL DATA
McSweeney	Edward	BD, p3c1, 7/6/1883	Ed McSweeney and Matt Carrigan were fined for disturbing the peace in Boscobel.
McSweeney	John	BD, p3c1, 7/21/1882	Sweeney and Samuel Yeager, Jr. had a fist fight in Excelsior.
McVay	Adelia	RH, p4c4, 11/11/1897	Finished teaching a school term on Nov. 5, 1897 in the Quinn District.
McVey	Sherman	RH, p4c2, 10/31/1901	Nellie Flanagan married Sherman McVey on Oct. 19, 1901. Bride lived in Estherville, IA; however, she was a former resident of Readstown. Groom from Rockton, WI. Planned to live in La Crosse.
McWilliams		BD, p3c2, 7/22/1881	The McWilliams stave factory was shut down for the season for want of wood. Unable to meet demand.
McWilliams	boy	BD, p3c2, 8/18/1882	Son born Tuesday to Billy McWilliams of Boscobel area.
McWilliams	girl	BD, p3c1, 3/31/1882	Daughter born Saturday night to Charles McWilliams of the Boscobel area.
McWilliams	Mary	BD, p3c3, 7/1/1881	A. C. Vanderpool recently married Mary McWilliams. Bride daughter of Thomas McWilliams of Boscobel. Groom from Eagle, WI. Guest list printed.
McWilliams	Ned	BD, p3c1, 7/31/1883	Died Tuesday from convulsions, "superinduced" by teething. He was the youngest son of William and Sarah McWilliams of the Boscobel area.
McWilliams	Thomas, Mrs.	BD, p3c3, 7/29/1881	Departed Boscobel for Eagle to visit her daughter, Mary.
McWilliams	W.	BD, p3c6, 11/2/1877	W. McWilliams & Co. advertised the opening of a new stave factory in Boscobel. F. McSpaden was hired to be his agent.
McWilliams	William	BD, p3c2, 10/13/1882	Left Boscobel to attend the funeral of his mother-in-law, Mrs. M. B. Pittman, in Eagle. His father-in-law died two weeks ago.
McWilliams	William	BD, p2c5, 10/22/1880	Operated a stave factory on the north bank of the Wisconsin River across from Boscobel. [Staves are used by coopers to make barrels.]
McWilliams	William	BD, p3c2, 1/24/1879	The McWilliams stave factory in Boscobel was destroyed by fire. Mr. V. Petty discovered the flames.
Meacham	Flora	DC, p2c1, 6/18/1887	Taught school in Chaseburgh.
Medary	T. C.	DR, p1c1, 12/15/1870	Editor and publisher of the *De Soto Republican* in De Soto, WI.
Medary	Thomas C.	DR, p2c1, 1/18/1872	Announced he would stop publication of the newspaper. The subscribers were not paying their bills. Planned to return to his home in Lansing and publish a new paper called *The Iowa North-East*.
Meechan	Billy	DC, p2c2, 2/3/1888	Sold his load of wheat in De Soto in 1859.
Meeker	J. D.	BD, p3c3, 5/18/1877	Former Town Treasurer in Boscobel. Died May 2, 1877 in Loyalton, CA at the home of his son, Thomas.
Mellen	S. S.	DC, p2c1, 12/18/1886	Resided in Groton, Dakota. Ill with pneumonia. Brother of Dr. Mellen of Retreat.
Melton	W. H.	DC, p1c2, 4/19/1889	Ran a delivery wagon in Ferryville.
Melton	William	DC, p2c2, 12/11/1886	Opened a lumberyard in Ferryville.
Melton	William	DC, p3c4, 1/15/1887	William Melton and William Davis opened a new store this week at the lumberyard and intend keeping a full stock of groceries, per Ferryville news column.
Melvin	Clara, Mrs.	DC, p3c4, 10/30/1886	Lived in Watertown, Dakota. New subscriber to the *De Soto Chronicle*.
Melvin	Nellie	RH, p5c5, 7/15/1897	John Standiford recently married Nellie Melvin in the Otter Vale area.
Menkhausen	Anna	BD, p3c3, 12/1/1882	Lou Eberly married Anna Menkhauser at the Catholic Church on Tuesday. Bride was the daughter of Mr. and Mrs. Charles Minkhausen of Boscobel. Groom was from Montfort. [more details in BD, p3c2, 12/8/1882]
Menkhausen	C. W. [?]	BD, p2c4, 11/26/1880	Grant County paid him a bounty for scalps turned into the county.
Merchant	Warren	BD, p3c1, 4/16/1880	Sentenced to 4 years at Joliet for burning the Sherwood barn and robbing the Mt. Sterling post office. Claimed he had 3 confederates.
Merrick	boy	DC, p2c3, 8/6/1887	Son born Wednesday to Calvin Merrick of Victory.

Genealogical Events from Newspapers for Crawford, Vernon and Grant Counties, Wisconsin, 1870-1901

LAST NAME	FIRST NAME	NEWSPAPER, PAGE/COLUMN MONTH/DAY/YEAR	GENEALOGICAL DATA
Messersmith	J., Mrs.	DC, p2c3, 11/26/1887	Has broken up house-keeping since the death of her mother, Mrs. Matilda Clark. She is now visiting at the home of her uncle, L. G. Sterling of Retreat.
Metcalf	Clinton	DC, p3c3, 10/2/1888	Left his home in Lansing, IA for Ann Arbor, MI to attend dental school.
Methodist Ministers		DC, p3c4, 10/8/1887	The Methodist ministry assignments for the coming year are: E. E. Cough, Platteville; Thomas Crouch, De Soto; L. N. Wooley, Melrose; A. B. Scoville, Mt. Sterling; G. W. Nuzum, Springville; J. T. Morgans, Onalaska; J. H. Avery, Viroqua; W. McMillan, Bloomingdale; D. Clingman, Fairchild; W. W. Hurd, Prescott; W. J. McKay, Madison; T. J. Snodgrass, Merrimac; W. F. Delap, Elroy; I. F. Nuzum, Mauston; E. Trimm, Necedah; H. D. Jencks, New Lisbon; and I. B. Bichford, Reedsburg. Rev. George W. Chase is Presiding Elder for the district and Rev. M. B. Balch of De Soto will move to Madison.
Metic	Clark	DC, p2c2, 11/19/1887	Clark Metic and sister, Mrs. Edward Baily, returned to their homes in Victory after visiting parents in Mt. Sterling.
Metric	boy	DC, p2c2, 3/26/1887	Son recently born to Calvin Metric of Victory.
Mettic		DC, p2c1, 4/16/1887	A son was recently born to Calvin Mettic of Victory.
Metz		BD, p3c2, 12/3/1880	The son of Fred Metz of Boscobel shot a large brown eagle. It measured 10 feet from tip to tip.
Meyer	Adolph, II	BD, p3c2, 5/31/1878	Adolph Meyer, II and Thomas Bailey, both of Boscobel, departed this morning for Bismark to "accumulate wealth." Arthur Moulton will soon depart for the East.
Meyer	Clara	BD, p3c2, 5/27/1881	Henry Walter recently married Clara Meyer. Bride youngest daughter of Gustav Meyer of Boscobel and sister of Mrs. Lou P. Lesler [p3c2]. Groom was a teller at the bank of A. J. Pipkin of Boscobel [p3c3].
Meyer	Ed, Mrs.	BD, p3c2, 4/13/1877	Mrs. Ed Meyer left Boscobel with her children to visit relatives in Decatur, IL.
Meyer	Edward	BD, p3c2, 5/10/1878	Ed Meyer, M. B. Pittman, J. D. Wilson, George Gunderson, Hiram Favor and Louis Ruka, II, departed Boscobel for Algona, IA to meet Seth Curry and Fred Mortimer. They planned to explore wild lands on which to relocate.
Meyer	Hattie L.	BD, p3c4, 12/21/1877	John D. Wilson married Hattie L. Meyer last Tuesday at the home of the bride's father in Boscobel. Bride was daughter of Gustave Meyer. Groom was an attorney in Boscobel.
Meyer	Oscar G.	BD, p3c2, 11/20/1883	Oscar G. Meyer married Emma E. Loomis on Nov. 14, 1883 at Werley, WI. Groom was the second son of Gustav Meyer of Boscobel. He worked as a bookkeeper for J. H. Sarles. Bride was from Werley. The Rev. T. W. Cole officiated.
Meyer	Otto	BD, p3c2, 8/28/1883	Arrived from his home in Milwaukee to visit his uncles, G. and Ed Meyer, in Boscobel.
Meyer Bros.		BD, p2c6, 10/22/1880	Operated a store in Boscobel that sold dry goods, clothing, boots and shoes, caps and groceries. They were also dealers in produce, stock of all kinds, wool, grain, hoop poles and railroad ties. Opened as Fette & Meyer in 1857. The name was changed to Meyer, Hildebrand & Co. 14 years ago. The name was changed again in 1870, this time to Meyer Bros.
Meyer Brothers		BD, P3c5, 1/5/1877	Advertised a dry goods store in Boscobel.
Meyer Brothers		BD, p3c4, 4/13/1877	In the case Meyer Brothers et al vs. R. Anderson, judgement was found for the plaintiff at the Iowa term of the Circuit Court held in Dodgeville. This was a case from Grant Co.
Michaels	August	BD, p3c2, 5/28/1880	Appointed to be a census enumerator in Lancaster, Grant Co.
Middleton	boy	RH, p4c1, 3/2/1899	A son was recently born to G. K. Middleton of Readstown.
Middleton	C. K.	RH, p7c1, 7/1/1897	Advertised services as a blacksmith in Readstown.
Middleton	Frank	RH, p4c2, 2/9/1899	Left Readstown for a new position at a machine shop in Milwaukee.
Middleton	G. K.	RH, p5c3, 7/8/1897	Planned to erect a new blacksmith shop in Readstown.
Middleton	Mrs.	RH, p5c2, 10/27/1898	Left her home in Readstown to visit her mother in Chicago.
Midthum	Grace	RH, p4c1, 11/29/1900	John Drake married Grace Midthum on Nov. 28, 1900. Bride and groom were from Spring Valley. The Rev. G. W. Nuzum officiated.
Midthum	Jno., Mrs.	RH, p5c3, 11/29/1900	Died Thursday from a long and lingering illness at her home in Spring Valley. Funeral was held at the cemetery of the United Lutheran Church at Folsom.
Midthum	John, Sr.	RH, p4c3, 5/30/1901	John Midthum married Mrs. Natwick last Friday. Bride from Liberty Pole. Groom from Black Bottom. They were serenaded by a charivari.

Genealogical Events from Newspapers for Crawford, Vernon and Grant Counties, Wisconsin, 1870-1901

LAST NAME	FIRST NAME	NEWSPAPER, PAGE/COLUMN MONTH/DAY/YEAR	GENEALOGICAL DATA
Miles	John, Mrs.	BD, p3c2, 2/24/1882	Departed home in Lancaster to visit sister, Mrs. J. P. Miller. Mrs. Miller lived 3 miles from the Werly Station. It got dark before Mrs. Miles arrived. She and her 1-year-old and 3-year-old children got lost in a storm. They walked until dawn at which time they found themselves 2 miles from Mrs. Miller's home.
Miles	Margaret J.	DC, p1c5, 11/26/1887	Granted a pension for the military service of her deceased husband, Ezra Edgecomb [Edgcomb?]. Resided in Boscobel.
Milham	Albert N.	BD, p2c2, 9/10/1880	Foreclosure sale notice was published, Albert N. Milham, plaintiff, vs. Samuel P. Briggs, defendant. Ordered by Grant County courts.
Millard	O. H.	DC, p3c2, 10/16/1886	Founder of the village of Ontario. Sold his home and store to D. Timmerman. Planned to move to Califomnia.
Millard	O. H.	DC, p2c2, 11/27/1888	Former Vernon Co. resident. Current resident of San Diego, CA.
Miller	A. N., Mrs.	DC, p3c6, 6/12/1886	Proprietor of the De Soto House in De Soto.
Miller	A. N., Mrs.	DC, p3c2, 10/8/1887	Hosted an unexpected family reunion with her daughters, Miss Mary and Mrs Annie Farrell, from Chamberlain, Dakota, and cousins, Mrs. Sargent and Mr. and Mrs. Clark, who were enroute from Vermont to their home in Caledonia, Dakota.
Miller	A. N., Mrs.	DC, p3c2, 10/2/1888	She was the new landlady of the Bay State House.
Miller	Adam B.	DC, p3c4, 5/7/1887	Former De Soto teacher. Married an Ohio girl a few weeks ago.
Miller	Anna Barbara	DC, p2c2, 7/16/1887	Died July 2, 1887 at her home in Harmony at the age of 62. She was the wife of Henry Miller.
Miller	Ben	BD, p3c2, 4/8/1881	Resided in Patch Grove. Died of consumption on Wednesday in Boscobel.
Miller	Bertha	DC, p4c2, 5/3/1889	Departed De Soto for St. Paul to work in a law office.
Miller	boy	BD, p3c1, 8/26/1881	Son recently born to John Peter Miller of the Boscobel area.
Miller	C. A., Mrs.	RH, p4c2, 7/26/1900	Lived in Bell Center. She was in great agony. Bit by a yellow rattlesnake a week ago.
Miller	C. W.	RH, p4c2, 9/26/1901	Former editor of *Soldiers Grove Advance*. Now employed by *Burnett County Journal* in Grantsburg. The *Advance* is now edited by G. L. Miller, the father of C. W. Miller.
Miller	Charles	RH, p5c2, 1/27/1898	Resided in Richland County. He was born in 1799 and was still in good health, per *Highland Press*.
Miller	Chris	BD, p3c3, 9/19/1879	Died last Tuesday. He was one of Muscoda's oldest citizens. Miller was also known as Muller. Funeral services were conducted by the Odd Fellows.
Miller	Don	RH, p5c4, 4/7/1898	Returned to Readstown from Seattle. There were 50 men for each job in Seattle.
Miller	E. K.	DR, p4c4, 12/15/1870	He was a manufacturer and dealer in bed steads, chairs, tables, etc. in De Soto.
Miller	E. K., Mrs.	DR, p3c4, 1/26/1871	She was the proprietor of the De Soto Bazaar. Sold pictures, books, jewelry, toys, candy and "Yankee Notions."
Miller	E. K., Rev.	DR, p3c3, 6/15/1871	Arrived in De Soto to visit his father, Joseph Miller. Resided in Oak Creek, near Milwaukee. Delivered a sermon in the Congregational Church.
Miller	Elizabeth	BD, p3c3, 2/22/1878	William E. Sleightam [Slightam?] married Elizabeth Miller on Feb. 13, 1878. Bride from Prairie du Chien. Groom from Madison. Rev. Mr. Samuels of the Episcopal Church officiated in a ceremony held at the home of the bride's mother in Prairie du Chien. Katie and Agnes Overton provided music with the assistance of Miss Taylor and Belle Beck of Madison and Charles and John Sleightam [brothers of the groom]. Groom was an engineer on Engine #104.
Miller	Elizabeth Ann	BD, p3c1, 4/2/1880	Claudius Brainerd Hopkins married Elizabeth Ann Miller on Mar. 25, 1880 in Boscobel. Bride from Blue River. Groom from Hickory Grove.
Miller	Fred	DR, p3c1, 6/8/1871	"The *Ella* takes away considerable wheat from De Soto. She is in good repair this season, and her jolly Captain, Fred Miller, know how to manage her."
Miller	Fred J.	DR, p2c2, 3/9/1871	Resided in Prairie du Chien. A letter explaining his business reasons for wanting a state ferry charter was published.
Miller	Fred J.	BD, p2c2, 2/9/1883	Died Jan. 27, 1883 in Topeka, KS. Fell while painting in his new house. Born Oct. 27, 1832 in Pennyan, Yates Co., NY. Moved to Illinois in 1841 and Prairie du Chien in 1843. Moved to Topeka last fall. He clerked at the Green Bay Fur Company under Co. B. W. Brisbois when he was young. He was part owner of the steamboat *Ella* on the Mississippi River at one time. Buried in Prairie du Chien.

Genealogical Events from Newspapers for Crawford, Vernon and Grant Counties, Wisconsin, 1870-1901

LAST NAME	FIRST NAME	NEWSPAPER, PAGE/COLUMN MONTH/DAY/YEAR	GENEALOGICAL DATA
Miller	girl	RH, p4c1, 4/12/1900	A daughter was born on April 7, 1900 to Gene Miller of Readstown.
Miller	H. P., Dr.	DC, p2c2, 3/12/1887	Physician from Ontario, WI.
Miller	Henry	DR, p3c5, 12/15/1870	He was 87 years old. He was the first subscriber to the new newspaper, *De Soto Republican*.
Miller	Henry K.	DR, p3c2, 12/29/1870	Sold groceries, dry goods, boots, shoes, hats queensware, etc. Started his trade in De Soto a few months ago.
Miller	Howard C.	DC, p2c2, 3/12/1887	Clerked in E. E. Dailey's bookstore in La Crosse. He was the son of Dr. H. P. Miller of Ontario.
Miller	Joseph	DR, p3c3, 12/29/1870	"Mr. Joseph Miller is the only cabinet maker in the village [of De Soto], consequently he has all the work he can attend to."
Miller	Maggie	BD, p3c3, 11/2/1877	Aged 2. Daughter of Peter Miller. Recently died in the Boscobel area.
Miller	N. B.	BD, p3c3, 5/28/1880	"Saloon and Restaurant at the old and well-known Stand, North of the Railroad Track. At which place may always be found Very Best Wines, Liquors, and Cigars to be had in the City. Meals! N. B. Miller, Proprietor. Boscobel, Aug. 7, 1874."
Miller	N. B.	BD, P3c6, 1/5/1877	Advertised his saloon and restaurant in Boscobel.
Miller	N. B.	BD, p3c2, 7/12/1878	Left Boscobel for Cuba, NY to see his 78-year-old father who was recently injured in a wagon accident.
Miller	N. B.	BD, p3c2, 7/19/1878	Father died July 8, 1878 in Cuba, NY. Miller arrived from Boscobel to see his father before his death.
Miller	N. B., Mrs	BD, p3c4, 8/29/1879	Departed Boscobel for Stevens Point to visit sister, Mrs. Scott.
Miller	Owen	BD, p3c1, 10/17/1879	Departed Boscobel for a new job in Prairie du Chien.
Miller	Peter J.	BD, p3c2, 10/26/1877	The 3-year-old son of Peter J. Miller died last Saturday.
Miller	Phillip	BD, p3c2, 5/11/1877	Phillip Miller and Ben Rozencranz [Rosencrans?] left Wauzeka on Wednesday for the Black Hills.
Miller	W. W.	DC, p3c4, 11/13/1886	Resided in De Soto. Advertised the loss of a cow that had strayed from his farm.
Miller	William	RH, p5c2, 7/13/1899	William Miller married Amy Marshell last week. Bride from Rockton. Groom from Sugar Grove.
Millett	V., Mr.	BD, p3c2, 11/17/1882	Suffered a severe stroke while drawing water. His wife helped him to the house. He was over 70 years old. Lived in Crawford Co.
Milliken	W. S.	DC, p3c2, 12/18/1886	Left De Soto for his home in Fairfield, IA.
Mills	Eli	DC, p2c2, 6/18/1887	Cora Rose married Eli Mills on June 19, 1887. Bride of Cooley Valley, formerly of Village Creek, IA. Groom from Viroqua. The Rev. William Haughton officiated.
Mills	Eli O., Mr. and Mrs.	DC, p3c3, 6/19/1888	Resided in Viroqua. Visited parents, Mr. and Mrs. Rose of Cooley Valley.
Mills	Thomas	DC, p3c3, 11/27/1886	Served as Secretary of the Crawford County Agricultural Society.
Miner	Susan	BD, p2c3, 5/9/1879	William Dyer requested the Grant County Probate Court to admit the will of Susan Miner, late of Boscobel.
Ministerial Appointments		DR, p2c2, 11/2/1871	The following are appointments for the Prairie du Chien District of the West Wisconsin Conference of the Methodist Episcopal church made at Mineral Point: Rev. Alfred Brunson, D.D., Presiding Elder; Prairie du Chien -- I. S. Leavitt; Patch Grove -- J. D. Brothers; Beetown -- N. S. Austin; Boscobel -- C. P. Hackney; Avoca -- W. W. Wheaton; Spring Green -- H. J. Walker; Sextonville -- W. R. Irish; Arion -- J. J. Clifton; West Branch -- N. C. Bradley; Viroqua -- W. F. Delap; Newton -- to be supplied; Springville -- J. Medd; De Soto -- Delos Hubbard; Wauzeka -- E. H. Sackett; Mount Hope -- B. L. Jackson; Bell Center -- O. Burnett and Mount Sterling -- W. J. McKay.
Minor	Thomas	DC, p1c2, 4/26/1889	Suffered a slight stroke of palsy. He is now speechless. Lived in Retreat.
Minor	W., Mr.	DC, p1c2, 5/10/1889	Mr. W. Minor of Great Ranington, MA visited his father, Mr. T. Minor of Retreat. "The old gentleman [Mr. T. Minor] is some better but still speechless."
Minor	Watson	DC, p3c3, 11/20/1886	Recently married. "Watson Minor, and his bride, of Viroqua, were visiting relatives and receiving the congratulations of their hosts of friends, at Retreat, Saturday and Sunday."

Genealogical Events from Newspapers for Crawford, Vernon and Grant Counties, Wisconsin, 1870-1901

LAST NAME	FIRST NAME	NEWSPAPER, PAGE/COLUMN MONTH/DAY/YEAR	GENEALOGICAL DATA
Minor	Will	RH, p7c2, 7/1/1897	Lived in Westby. Came to Readstown to look after his lumber business.
Mitchel	August	DC, p2c2, 3/10/1888	A criminal case was held in the Justice Parkin's court, State of Wisconsin vs. August Mitchel, for abusing his wife. He was fined $1.00 and costs, per Chaseburgh news column.
Mitchell	Emma L.	BD, p3c2, 10/23/1883	George Proudfit married Emma L. Mitchell on Oct. 17, 1883 at the residence of the bride's parents in Seward Co., [Nebraska?]. The Rev. S. G. Lamb officiated. Bride was the daughter of J. B. Mitchell, a druggist.
Mitchell	Frank	DC, p3c3, 8/21/1886	Barn damaged [destroyed?] by fire in Harmony.
Mitchell	Mr., Rev.	DR, p3c1, 6/8/1871	Pastor of the Congregational Church in De Soto.
Mithum	John	RH, p5c3, 10/24/1901	A large crowd serenaded him and his wife on Saturday night at their home at Oak Ridge. John was prepared for them, for they were treated to refreshments.
Mithum	John, Jr.	RH, p5c3, 10/17/1901	Lived at Oak Ridge. "... Drove to the Mississippi River last Saturday and on returning took unto himself a wife."
Mitscher	A., Mrs.	DC, p2c3, 3/5/1887	Died Feb. 24, 1887 at the age of 54 in Hillsborough.
Moe	Ole T.	RH, p4c1, 7/21/1898	Advertised services as a shoemaker in Readstown.
Moffit	Olga	DC, p2c3, 3/5/1887	Died Feb. 20, 1887 of scarlet fever at the home of A. Mitscher [of Hillsborough?]. She was the daughter of Mr. and Mrs. F. A. Moffit of Waterloo, WI.
Molie	Nellie, Miss	BD, p2c5, 10/22/1880	Dealer in millinery and fancy goods in Boscobel. Went into business last May.
Mollie	Will	BD, p3c2, 12/17/1880	Will Mollie, second son of Mrs. C. J. Mollie of Boscobel, was injured in Rushford during a train accident on Sunday evening. Died on Monday. Mollie was a brakeman on the train. Will Woodard of Boscobel was with him when the accident took place.
Molly	Mart	DC, p3c3, 4/17/1888	Mart Molly married Ursula Holcomb last week in Elroy. They planned to set up housekeeping on the Holcomb farm, about 2 miles from Ontario.
Monroe	Mrs.	RH, p5c4, 4/6/1899	Died Wednesday night in De Soto from lung fever.
Montague	Cyriel L.	DC, p3c2, 1/29/1887	Did watch repair work at the De Soto House.
Monti	boy	DC, p2c3, 5/1/1888	A son was recently born to Joe Monti of Genoa.
Monti	boy	DC, p3c3, 12/25/1888	A son was recently born to Lewis Monti of Genoa.
Monti	Joseph	RH, p5c4, 4/14/1898	Anna Brannon and Joseph Monti sent out invitations to their wedding, per De Soto news column.
Monti	Joseph, Mrs.	DC, p1c2, 4/26/1889	Mrs. Joseph Monti of Genoa and her brother, J. Page visited friends in Newton
Monti	M.	DC, p3c4, 7/31/1886	Kept boarders in Genoa.
Monti	Mathew	DC, p2c3, 3/19/1887	Resided in Genoa. Worked as a land agent for Frederickson & Co. properties of Swift Co., MN.
Montieth	Andrew	BD, p3c2, 5/31/1878	Died May 18, 1878 in Fennimore near Ebenezer Church at the residence of his son. He was 84. Survived by his 84-year-old wife and 8 children.
Montson	Henry	DC, p1c1, 6/28/1889	Spent the last 6 years "in the woods." Returned to Ferryville.
Moody	Nathan	DR, p3c6, 9/28/1871	Nathan Moody married Martha ____ on Sept. 28, 1871 in Viroqua. Bride and groom from Viroqua. Rev. G. W. Nuzum officiated.
Mookrie	Mr.	RH, p5c2, 1/27/1898	Planned to open another store in Readstown in the Bliss Building. He also operated a store in Folsom.
Moon	Jay	RH, p5c2, 12/1/1898	Resided in Soldiers Grove. Planned to open a barbershop in Readstown.
Moon	William	RH, p5c3, 8/5/1897	Planned to move from Readstown for LaValle, WI where he has rented a hotel. Operated the west side hotel in Readstown.
Moore	A. J.	DR, p3c1, 12/22/1870	Former resident of De Soto. Now keeping hotel in Baraboo, WI.
Moore	Alfred	DC, p2c3, 2/3/1888	Resided in West Prairie in the early 1860s. Came to De Soto to sell beef and vegetables periodically. He played fife and drums and stuttered.
Moore	Alice, Miss	RH, p5c3, 8/18/1898	Resided in Soloan, northwest Iowa. Visited in Readstown, her hometown.

Genealogical Events from Newspapers for Crawford, Vernon and Grant Counties, Wisconsin, 1870-1901

LAST NAME	FIRST NAME	NEWSPAPER, PAGE/COLUMN MONTH/DAY/YEAR	GENEALOGICAL DATA
Moore	Charles R.	RH, p5c3, 9/27/1900	Charles R. Moore married Gertrude Fox on Sept. 8, 1900 at the Christian Church in Crawfordsville, OR. Groom from Brownsville and attends Divinity School. Bride from Crawfordsville and has lived with Mr. and Mrs. J. F. Venner for the past 2 years.
Moore	D. E., Mr. and Mrs.	RH, p4c3, 10/3/1901	Played violin, mandolin, guitar and washboard at a concert given by the Readstown Band last Saturday.
Moore	Emma B.	DC, p3c3, 11/12/1887	Emma B. Moore married Charles O. Carpenter on Nov. 5, 1887 in De Soto. Bride and groom from Lansing, IA. The Rev. Thomas Crouch officiated.
Moore	James	BD, p3c4, 5/18/1877	James Moore and W. Fayant left Muscoda for Deadwood, Black Hills.
Moore	Rena, Mrs.	BD, p3c3, 5/21/1880	Committed suicide last Saturday at the home of Mr. Lambert of Mt. Hope. She was the wife of John Moore of Mt. Ida. Suicide caused by domestic trouble. A child that was also given poison may recover.
Moore	Sam W.	DC, p3c2, 5/28/1887	Settled in 1858 on his 500-acre farm in Harmony, Vernon Co.
Moran	Catharine	BD, p3c3, 4/27/1877	The wedding party of O. W. Flynn and Catharine Moran was held at the Central House in Boscobel on Tuesday. Bride from Wauzeka. Groom was the brother of P. Flynn of "narrow gauge railroad fame."
Moreland	Ben	RH, p5c4, 1/20/1898	Lost a horse after it was kicked by another horse, per Kickapoo Center news column.
Morelli	Dode	DC, p1c2, 5/24/1889	Dode Morelli and Frankie Riley worked on the steamboat, *Nellie*. Lived in Genoa.
Morgan	Achsah, Miss	DC, p3c2, 11/12/1887	Sold her Red Mound farm for $1200 to L. F. Miller. Planned to move to California where a brother, H. H. Morgan, lived.
Morgan	J.	DR, p3c6, 4/13/1871	Advertised the sale of Norway oats. Resided in Sterling, WI.
Morgan	J. T., Mrs.	DC, p3c3, 3/27/1888	Visited the Crouch farm last week in De Soto. She was the sister of Mr. Crouch.
Morgan	Joseph, Mrs.	DC, p3c3, 6/4/1887	Resided in Retreat. Received visit from sister, Mrs. George C. Pierce of Santiago, CA.
Morgan	Mary W.	DC, p3c5, 10/30/1886	Mary W. Morgan recently married W. W. Minor at Ontario, CA. Bride former resident of Red Mound, WI. Groom from Viroqua.
Morgan	W. P.	DC, p3c1, 11/26/1887	From Red Mound. Spent the summer in Ashton, Dakota. Now visiting his uncle, H. H. Morgan of Ontario, CA.
Morgan	Will	DC, p3c4, 3/27/1888	Returned to Retreat. Had been absent for a year in Dakota.
Morgan	Will and Wendall	DC, p3c2, 4/2/1887	Will Morgan, Wendall Morgan and Homer Lombard departed from the De Soto train station for teaching jobs in Groton, Dakota.
Morgan	William H.	DC, p3c4, 5/28/1887	Subscribted to the newspaper. Resided in Northville, Dakota.
Morgans	J. T.	DC, p3c3, 8/7/1886	Served as pastor of the Methodist Episcople Churches in De Soto and Retreat.
Morgans	J. T., Rev.	DC, p3c2, 9/18/1886	Scheduled to preach his farewell sermon this Sunday.
Mork	girl	RH, p5c4, 11/25/1897	A daughter was recently born to Thomas Mork, former principal of schools in Readstown.
Mork	T. O.	RH, p4c3, 10/18/1900	Campaigned as a Republican candidate for Register of Deeds in Vernon Co. Picture published.
Morley	Elmer	RH, p4c1, 10/4/1900	Returned home to Readstown after spending the summer working at a farm in Orchard, IA.
Morley	Elmer	RH, p4c2, 10/18/1900	Elmer Morley married Nina Pond last Sunday at the home of Justice Winn in Soldiers Grove. Bride and groom from Readstown.
Morley	Elmer	RH, p4c1, 8/22/1901	Recently found a pearl worth $50 in a Kickapoo River clam.
Morley	James	RH, p4c2, 9/20/1900	Former resident of Readstown. A son was recently born to Morley, who now lives in Ashville, NC. The boy weighed 11 1/2 pounds.
Morley	Jim	RH, p5c2, 10/20/1898	Left his home in Readstown for a new position in North Carolina where he will be a telephone company lineman.
Morr	Abram	DC, p3c3, 3/10/1888	Squire McMichael recently sentence 4 young men [aged 16-18] from Genoa for carrying concealed weapons. Abram Morr was sentenced to 30 days of hard labor. Harry Spauling sentenced to 20 days of hard labor. Eli Barrett sentenced to the Industrial School at Waukesha. Emil Gunderson paid a fine.

Genealogical Events from Newspapers for Crawford, Vernon and Grant Counties, Wisconsin, 1870-1901

LAST NAME	FIRST NAME	NEWSPAPER, PAGE/COLUMN MONTH/DAY/YEAR	GENEALOGICAL DATA
Morris	Ed	BD, p2c3, 8/11/1882	Resided in Richland Center area. Lost sight in an eye. Three weeks ago felt pain in eye while harvesting. Dr. Bickford later found the eye had burst. Confined to bed with malaria.
Morrison	I. C., Miss	BD, p3c4, 7/7/1882	Misses I. C. Morrison, F. I. McDonald, V. B. Strother and F. Barton graduated from St. Mary's Institute in Prairie du Chien.
Morrow	Dr.	BD, p2c5, 2/3/1882	From Gillingham. Reported an outbreak of rubeola on Fancy Creek in Richland Co.
Morrow	Henry	RH, p5c4, 8/5/1897	Planned to open a bakery in Viola.
Morrow	James	RH, p4c3, 8/29/1901	Died Aug. 18, 1901 at his home in Mound Park. Born Apr. 6, 1847 in Carl [Carroll?] Co., OH. Married Sarah E. Williams on Oct. 29, 1869. Survived by 5 of his 11 children: Maggie, Samuel, Will, Nettie and Grace. Also survived by wife, 6 brothers and 4 sisters. After marriage, Morrow moved to Kansas. Moved to Richland Co, WI on March 10, 1874, where he resided until his move to Mound Park. Served in 12th OH Vol. Calvary for nearly 3 years. Member of the Methodist Church in Viola for last 12 years. Buried in the village cemetery.
Morse	A. C.	BD, p3c2, 5/28/1880	Appointed to be a census enumerator in Fennimore, Grant Co.
Morse	Alice, Mrs.	DC, p3c2, 4/2/1887	Mrs. Alice Morse and daughter, Miss Carrie I. Rose, departed De Soto by train for a new home in Huron, Dakota. Natives of Cooley Valley [p2c2, 49/1887].
Morse	Allie, Mrs.	DC, p3c4, 11/27/1886	Mrs. Allie Morse and daughter of Huron, Dakota visited grandparents, Mr. and Mrs. W. B. Conklin of Cooley Valley.
Morse	Allie, Mrs.	DC, p1c2, 8/2/1889	Mrs. Allie Morse and daughter, Marian, returned to Elgin, IL after visiting her grandparents, Mr. and Mrs. W. G. Conklin of Cooley Valley.
Morse	C.	DC, p2c4, 1/14/1888	Mr. C. Morse surprised the people of Cooley Valley when he arrived from Dakota.
Morse	E. L., Rev.	BD, p3c1, 1/5/1883	Resigned his position as minister for the Boscobel Congregational Church.
Mortimer	F. M., Mrs.	BD, p3c2, 6/29/1883	Mrs. F. M. Mortimer and her son, John, and her servant left Boscobel for a new home in Palo Alto Co., IA.
Mortimer	Fred	BD, p3c2, 5/13/1881	Fred Mortimer married Alice Carrier at the home of the bride's father on May 9, 1881. Bride from Boscobel. Took train to Milwaukee after the ceremony. Rev. William Stoddart officiated.
Mortimer	Fred	BD, p3c1, 3/23/1883	Departed Boscobel for a new home in Emmetsburg, IA.
Mortimer	Mary, Miss	BD, p3c2, 7/20/1877	Recently died. She was the founder of the Milwaukee Female Academy. She was the aunt to Mr. Fred [Mortimer?] of Boscobel.
Morton		DC, p3c4, 10/2/1886	A 3-year-old child of William Morton of Retreat lost the forefinger on the left hand from a bucksaw accident.
Morton	G. I.	BD, p2c3, 1/27/1882	Lived in Richland Co. Horses stolen from him. William and Adam Zeirfuss [or Guilfuss per April 28, 1882 issue] of Myers Grove, Stearn Co., MN were captured with the horses in Minnetaska, MN. They were Prussian and spoke little English. They claimed to have purchased the horses from a man near Morton's farm the night they were stolen. Trial was ordered. [They were acquitted, per April 28, 1882 issue of the newspaper.]
Moses	Alice	RH, p6c3, 5/23/1901	Randolf Randall married Alice Moses on Saturday. Groom from Trout Creek. Bride from Sugar Grove. Cannons and cowbells were used during their charivari.
Moses	Mary	RH, p5c4, 4/28/1898	Hired to teach at Sugar Grove.
Mosher	H. J.	RH, p5c5, 10/7/1897	H. J. Mosher married Lizzie Hebard on Sunday, Oct. 3, 1897 at the home of the bride's parents in Kickapoo. Bride from Kickapoo, Vernon Co. Groom from Milton, Monroe Co. C. W. Reeve, J. P. officiated.
Moshier	W. G.	BD, p2c3, 8/11/1882	Well known miller in Excelsior. Sold his mill. Seeking a new home in Prairie du Chien. Moshier built the Douseman Mill in Mill Coulee, Prairie du Chien.
Moshier	W. G.	BD, p3c3, 8/30/1878	Owned the racehorse, Granville. Lived in Excelsior. He was in Boscobel to work with his horse.
Moshier	W. G., Mrs.	BD, p3c1, 6/22/1883	Buried Tuesday in Prairie du Chien.
Moshier	William	BD, p3c1, 3/25/1881	Received 50,000 trout from the State Fish Hatchery to be stocked in Richland County streams.
Moshier	William G.	BD, p2c3, 3/2/1877	Lived in Excelsior. Prepared to stock English Creek in Town of Clayton, Crawford Co. with 15,000 speckled trout.
Mosholder	George	DC, p3c3, 7/9/1887	Erected a 16 x 24 foot dwelling in De Soto.
Mosier	Paul	RH, p5c3, 12/8/1898	Lived in Mound Park. Employed at a flouring mill at Boscobel.

Genealogical Events from Newspapers for Crawford, Vernon and Grant Counties, Wisconsin, 1870-1901

LAST NAME	FIRST NAME	NEWSPAPER, PAGE/COLUMN MONTH/DAY/YEAR	GENEALOGICAL DATA
Moss	H.	DC, p2c2, 3/10/1888	Mr. H. Moss and family of the Cooley Valley area left Tuesday for a new home in Mosinee, Wisconsin.
Mossholder	George	DC, p8c3, 8/2/1889	Built a porch on the home of J. H. Rogers in De Soto.
Moulton	A. C.	BD, p3c3, 10/4/1878	Former resident of Boscobel. Now engaged in the hotel business in Longwood, CO.
Moulton	Arthur	BD, p3c2, 8/23/1878	Once lived in Boscobel. Now lives in Berthound, Larimer Co., CO.
Mt. Sterling Academy		DR, p1c4, 12/22/1870	Academy building and church finished in Fall of 1867. School opened in Mt. Sterling in January 1868. The school is not sectarian, nor are any efforts made to change the religious beliefs of the students.
Mt. Zion M.E. Church		BD, p2c2, 9/16/1881	The Mt. Zion Methodist Episcopal Church was dedicated on Sept. 4, 1881. Church was built near the town house for the Town of Scott. The Rev. J. E. Irish, D.D., Presiding Elder and Rev. Isaac N. Adrian, preacher in charge and visiting preachers participated. Sister W. B. Walton presided at the organ. A collection was received from the congregation that released the debt. Jacob Graham, John P. Coleman and W. B. Walton were trustees. On behalf of the congregation, George Meyers and Joseph Barto gave Adrian a subscription of $30.
Mueller	A.	DR, p3c2, 2/2/1871	Ran a general store in Victory, WI.
Mueller	A.	DR, p3c4, 12/14/1871	Published a notice asking his creditors to settle up. "I must have my dues in order to save my credit." Lived in Victory.
Mueller	C. L.	DC, p3c5, 9/11/1886	Advertised he would pay the best prices for hoop poles and shaved flour barrel hoops. Resided in De Soto.
Mueller	C. L.	DC, p2c2, 2/26/1889	Lived in La Crosse. Ran the hooppole shaving business in De Soto.
Mueller	C. L.	DC, p4c3, 3/12/1889	Published a notice. "I have given my son, Otto Mueller, his time and will not be responsible for any bill that he may contract . . . La Crosse, March 9, 1889."
Mueller	Charles	DR, p3c2, 7/20/1871	Worked as a cooper in Lansing, IA.
Mueller	Jennie, Miss	DC, p3c4, 9/4/1886	Miss Mueller and her brother left Victory to visit their father in Rochester, MN.
Mueller	Johanna	DC, p3c4, 11/27/1886	Taught school in the Asbury Ridge per Victory news column.
Mueller	Johanna and Hulda	DC, p3c3, 4/16/1887	Planned to leave Victory for new homes in Rochester, MN. They left with their mother, Mrs. A. Mueller, an area resident for the last 18 years.
Muffley	Frank	BD, p3c1, 11/17/1882	Resided in Boscobel. For the second time, he was taken to the asylum in Madison for treatment.
Muffley	J. R.	BD, p2c7, 10/22/1880	Opened a furniture and undertaking business in Boscobel 23 years ago. He was a "practical" cabinetmaker.
Muffley	J. R. and L.	BD, p3c1, 4/16/1880	Planned to run the Boscobel carding mills the ensuing season.
Muffley	John R.	BD, p3c1, 4/28/1882	Left Boscobel for his farm in Dakota.
Muffley	L.	BD, p3c4, 4/12/1878	George Cannon, J. H. Clark, L. Muffley, D. Lenehan, M. O. Brekke, B. M. Coats and L. J. Woolley received payments for services they provided to paupers in Grant Co.
Muhr	Barnhart	DR, p3c2, 12/7/1871	Took up a red cow in the Town of Bergen, Vernon Co.
Mulhair		BD, p3c3, 3/26/1880	Old man Mulhair [Malhair?] who lived across from Boscobel was arrested for horse stealing in LaFayette County.
Mulhair	Mary Anna	BD, p3c2, 1/10/1879	James O'Kane, Esquire, married Mary Anna Mulhair on Jan. 1, 1879. Bride from Boscobel. Groom from Marietta. Rev. Charles Scraudenbach, a Catholic priest, officiated.
Mulhair	William	BD, p3c6, 1/5/1883	Published a notice that he had taken up a heifer in the Town of Marietta, Crawford Co.
Mulhern	Denis	DC, p3c2, 12/17/1887	Elder Denis Mulhern was a Baptist preacher in De Soto in the 1850s. Services were held at the schoolhouse. No other denominations were active at the time. People of other beliefs attended the services. The De Soto town proprietors [Powers, Houghton and Osgood] were closed communion Baptists. After a church scandal and the expulsion of a prominent member the society started to fade away.
Mulhern	Dennis, Rev.	DC, p2c1, 3/20/1888	Town of Wheatland Superintendent of Schools in 1857/8. Moved away from the De Soto area in 1859.
Mulhern	Elder	DR, p3c3, 9/21/1871	Preached in a De Soto schoolhouse in 1856, as there were no church buildings.

Genealogical Events from Newspapers for Crawford, Vernon and Grant Counties, Wisconsin, 1870-1901

LAST NAME	FIRST NAME	NEWSPAPER, PAGE/COLUMN MONTH/DAY/YEAR	GENEALOGICAL DATA
Mumford	Mr.	DR, p3c3, 8/31/1871	He was the Crawford County Superintendent of Schools.
Munson	M.	DC, p3c5, 8/14/1886	Operated a saloon in Ferryville.
Munyon	Henry	DC, p2c3, 8/27/1887	Henry Munyon and J. Love, "two old citizens of West Vernon," bought tickets for Chamo, NM.
Murley	T.	BD, p3c1, 3/3/1882	Left Boscobel with his brother-in-law, Seth D. Curry to visit Curry's family in Dakota.
Murphy	Catherine	BD, p3c4, 3/28/1879	Published a notice that her son, Grant, had left home and that she would not be responsible for his debts. Resided in Hickory Grove.
Murphy	J. O.	DC, p3c4, 12/4/1886	Taught school in the Larson District per Liberty Pole news column.
Murphy	J. R.	BD, p2c2, 2/15/1878	Fire destroyed Murphy's residence in Woodman. Arson suspected.
Murphy	James	BD, p3c4, 11/22/1878	Died Oct. 15, 1878 from a horse fall in Hickory Grove. Settled in Hickory Grove during the fall of 1855. Born in Clinton Co., NY where he married. He was 54 years old. Survived by wife and 8 children. Served as chairman of town board.
Murphy	John	BD, p2c2, 2/15/1878	Citizens demolished Murphy's saloon in Woodman to stop the spread of flames that consumed several adjacent buildings. Arson suspected.
Murphy	Mary	BD, p3c3, 12/10/1880	George Weggins married Mary Murphy on Dec. 3, 1880 in Boscobel. Bride and groom were from Postville, IA.
Murphy	Mary Ann	BD, p3c1, 7/23/1880	Allen W. Henderson married Mary Ann Murphy of Hickory Grove at the home of the bride's mother on July 15, 1880. The Rev. W. Stoddart officiated.
Murphy	Pelagie M.	BD, p3c5, 9/7/1879	Died Aug. 21, 1879 at the age of 7 months. She was the daughter of John R. and Mary M. Murphy of Woodman.
Murray	John	BD, p2c1, 10/5/1877	Taken to Waupon for an 18-month sentence by Sheriff Birchard. His crime was burglary.
Murry	Thomas	BD, p2c3, 11/24/1882	Residence in Bear Valley, Richland Co. was blown down in a storm.
Musgrove	Frank	RH, p5c4, 11/4/1897	Frank Musgrove married Jessie Walters on Oct. 24, 1897 at Wauzeka. Bride and groom from La Farge.
Myer	Gustave and Edward	BD, p2c4, 1/5/1877	By judgement of the Grant Co. Circuit Court, a Sheriff's sale of land in Boscobel was scheduled to be held on Feb. 3, 1877 in Darlington, Lafayette Co. This involved the case Gustave and Edward Myer, plaintiffs vs. W. B. Phillips, Smith Roundy & Co., Steel & Price, H. Hibberd & Co., I. Z. Farewell, defendants.
Myers	girl	DC, p1c2, 5/31/1889	A daughter was born last Sunday to Matt J. Myers, the C. B. & N. agent at Victory.
Myers	Matt J.	DC, p3c3, 10/2/1888	Nellie McGuinnis married Matt J. Myers on Tuesday. Groom, an agent for C. B. & N. Railroad, was from Victory. Rev. Haughton officiated.
Naler	Andy	BD, p2c1, 10/5/1877	Taken to Waupon for an 18-month sentence by Sheriff Birchard. His crime was burglary.
Names	Carter	DC, p4c1, 5/3/1889	Pension approved for military service. Resided in Retreat.
Nash	Ole T.	BD, p2c3, 11/24/1882	Chairman of the Freeman Town Board in Crawford Co. He was taken violently insane while attending a county board meeting.
Natwick	Mrs.	RH, p4c3, 5/30/1901	John Midthum married Mrs. Natwick last Friday. Bride from Liberty Pole. Groom from Black Bottom. They were serenaded by a charivari.
Nauert	Anna	BD, p3c1, 7/5/1878	Calvin Schmahlenberger married Anna Nauert on June 27, 1878 at the Henry Furderer residence in Boscobel. Bride from Fennimore. Groom from Hickory Grove. J. McLaughlin, Esquire officiated.
Nauert	W. J. F.	BD, p3c3, 5/10/1878	The Boscobel City Council approved bonds for the saloons of W. J. F. Nauert, O. C. Christopherson, A. Bobel, Jacob and Richard Lesler and J. N. Comstock.
Nauert	William	BD, p3c3, 9/13/1878	Nauert's Boscobel saloon was robbed of a new gun, $8, cigars and liquor.
Nauert Bros.		BD, p3c2, 7/24/1883	Purchased property from Henry Leasman. Planned to build a two-story building. The first floor would be used as a saloon. The second floor would be a public hall.
Neeley	Delbert	RH, p5c4, 10/6/1898	Delbert Neeley married Alice Joseph at the home of the bride's parents in De Soto on September 28, 1898. Groom from La Crosse. The Rev. James Jefferson officiated.
Neely	Louisa	BD, p3c1, 2/4/1881	Joseph Lance married Louisa Neely on Feb. 2, 1881 in Boscobel at Betts House. Bride and groom from Mt. Ida. The Rev. William Stoddart officiated.
Neil	Louis	BD, p3c3, 7/22/1881	Arrived in Boscobel from Fargo, Dakota to visit friends.

Genealogical Events from Newspapers for Crawford, Vernon and Grant Counties, Wisconsin, 1870-1901

LAST NAME	FIRST NAME	NEWSPAPER, PAGE/COLUMN MONTH/DAY/YEAR	GENEALOGICAL DATA
Nell	Louis, Mrs.	BD, p3c3, 7/20/1883	Nee Emma Cowan. Arrived from Fargo, Dakota to visit her old home in Boscobel.
Nelson	Caroline	DC, p2c2, 5/21/1887	Died May 4, 1887 at the age of 2 years and 8 months. She was the only daughter of Stephen and Lizzie Nelson.
Nelson	Carrie	BD, p3c2, 6/25/1880	Andrew F. Oleson of Boscobel married Carrie Nelson on June 20, 1880 at the East Koshkonong Church in Dane Co., WI.
Nelson	Charles	BD, p3c1, 11/26/1880	Died Monday of consumption in Boscobel.
Nelson	Charles	BD, p3c2, 5/31/1878	Charles Nelson married Mina Peterson on Tuesday. Groom from Boscobel and worked for the firm, Nelson & Son.
Nelson	George	RH, p4c2, 10/24/1901	Departed Readstown with his family for new home in Ladysmith. They planned to drive through and expected the trip to take about 3 weeks, if the weather is cooperative.
Nelson	girl	DC, p2c2, 7/16/1887	Daughter recently born to Steve Nelson in Chaseburgh.
Nelson	H.	BD, p2c8, 1/5/1877	H. Nelson & Co. was a lumberyard in Boscobel.
Nelson	Hans	RH, p5c3, 2/14/1901	Hans Nelson and Albert Jacobson of Spring Valley plan to go to Tennessee for their health.
Nelson	John	RH, p4c2, 10/31/1901	John Nelson and Samuel Neeley were involved in a lawsuit over a horse trade before Judge Davenport. Each paid attorney fees and court costs and agreed to disagree and went home good friends after a days' entertainment.
Nelson	L. M.	DR, p1c1, 12/15/1870	Advertised cutlery and sissor sharpening services at his barbering and bathrooms in Lansing, IA.
Nelson	Minnie	BD, p3c4, 1/13/1882	Applied to administer the estate of Charles Nelson, late of Boscobel.
Nelson	Mrs.	BD, p3c1, 2/25/1881	Resided in Boscobel area. Her funeral was held on Wednesday.
Nelson	N. E., Mrs.	RH, p4c4, 9/22/1898	Resided in Liberty Pole. Opened a millinery shop in the McDowell Building, north of the postoffice in De Soto.
Nelson	Uriah	DC, p2c2, 6/18/1887	Georgetta Swan married Uriah Nelson on June 19, 1887 at the Bay State parlors in De Soto. Bride and groom from Village Creek, IA. D. A. Steele, Esquire officiated.
Nelson	William	BD, p3c2, 1/16/1880	Home in Boscobel robbed of $20.
Nelvin	Thomas	DC, p2c2, 6/4/1887	Thomas Nelvin [Melvin?] married Tillie A. Nelson on May 25, 1887 at the Lutheran Church in Chaseburgh. Bride from Chaseburgh. Groom from Hatton, Dakota.
Nemmick	Joe	BD, p2c1, 10/5/1877	Taken to Waupon for a 6-month sentence by Sheriff Birchard. His crime was housebreaking.
Nevill	John A.	BD, p3c2, 5/28/1880	Appointed to be a census enumerator in Potosi, Grant Co.
Newberry	Robert B.	BD, p3c1, 3/3/1880	Robert B. Newberry recently married Angaline M. Kimgry. Bride from Patch Grove. Groom from Breckenridge, MN.
Newbury	Fred E.	BD, p3c3, 10/24/1879	Fred E. Newbury married Emma J. Comstock on Wednesday evening at the Congregational Church. Bride from Boscobel. Groom from Southbridge, MA. Extensive coverage of wedding and guests.
Newell	Emma	DR, p3c4, 6/8/1871	T. G. Orr married Emma Newell on June 1, 1871. Bride from Waukon, IA and groom from De Soto. The Rev. L. L. Frisk officiated.
Newell	James E.	DC, p3c3, 5/21/1887	Recently died in Osage, KS. Pioneer and ex-county judge in Vernon Co.
Newick	Samuel	BD, p3c1, 4/25/1879	Died April 14, 1879 in Beetown. Served as Town Clerk for many years.
Newlin	Annie B.	BD, p3c1, 7/11/1879	John DeLos Emery married Annie B. Newlin on July 4, 1879. Bride and groom from Wauzeka. Justice J. McLaughlin officiated.
Newman	John	RH, p4c2, 2/1/1900	Home and household goods lost to fire last Tuesday. The residence was located 2 miles east of Readstown.
Newman	John A.	RH, p5c3, 12/1/1898	Called on the New Store in Readstown. He was one of the oldest residents in the Town of Kickapoo.
Newman	John A.	RH, p4c3, 12/28/1899	One of the oldest residents in the Town of Kickapoo. He has "paid taxes there for 46 years." Paid for a newspaper subscription for his sister, Mrs. J. M. Price of Diller, NB.

Genealogical Events from Newspapers for Crawford, Vernon and Grant Counties, Wisconsin, 1870-1901

LAST NAME	FIRST NAME	NEWSPAPER, PAGE/COLUMN MONTH/DAY/YEAR	GENEALOGICAL DATA
Newspaper Subscribers		DC, p3c4, 5/7/1887	The following people paid for subscriptions to the *De Soto Chronicle*: Thomas Latimer, Genoa; Edw. Schubert, Genoa; H. C. Haskell, Ontario; C. E. Whitney, Viroqua; E. B. Homsted, Newry; Carlos Farr, Newton; O. S. Harrington, Newton; Sam. W. Moore, Chaseburgh; Willis Owen, De Soto; Thomas Tenney, De Soto; Carrie I. Rose, Wolsey, Dakota; Irvin L. Helpman, Shrevesport, LA; P. Connor, Retreat; Frank Gross, Retreat; P. Finney, West Prairie; William Coffin, Lincoln, NB.
Newton		DC, p2c2, 4/2/1887	The little daughter of James Newton died last Wednesday of diphtheria in Retreat.
Newton	C. A.	DC, p3c3, 2/3/1888	Resided in Retreat. Lost 2 fingers from a buzz saw accident.
Newton	girl	DC, p2c4, 1/14/1888	A daughter was born to A. Newton of the Retreat area on Jan. 2, 1888.
Newton	J. A.	BD, p2c1, 7/1/1881	Died Friday in Prairie du Chien. Funeral was held at the Congregational Church.
Newton	Jasper	DC, p2c2, 5/28/1887	Jasper Newton is dangerously ill with diphtheria, per Freeman news column.
Nichols		BD, p3c3, 6/8/1877	Pat Ryan, Homer Nelson Taft [found guilty of a murder attempt on James Harris on Wauzeka], Mr. Nichols and 2 Lawyers escaped from jail in Prairie du Chien.
Nichols	C. H.	BD, p3c3, 11/1/1878	Published an ad asking for the return of his artificial teeth that he lost in Boscobel.
Nichols	C. W.	DC, p3c5, 8/7/1886	C. W. Nichols of Mt. Sterling goes to De Soto this week to work on C. Lyttle's warehouse and dwelling.
Nichols	C. W.	DC, p3c5, 8/21/1886	C. W. Nichols married Genevra Sears on Aug. 15, 1886 at the Bay State House in De Soto. Bride and groom from Mt. Sterling. The Rev. J. T. Morgans officiated.
Nicholson		RH, p5c2, 12/15/1898	The lawsuit, Nicholson [represented by Kast of Bell Center] vs. Oatfield [represented by Jarvis of Soldiers Grove], was heard in Readstown.
Nicholson	George W.	RH, p5c4, 3/16/1899	The court case, George W. Nicholson of Crawford Co., plaintiff vs. Charles Oakfield, tenant on the Louis Wagner farm, defendant, concerned a buggy.
Nicholson	Thomas	BD, p3c3, 1/11/1878	Dislocated his hip while riding in a wagon with Mr. Mitchell. Mitchell was drunk and drove the team too fast. Drs. Armstrong and Pickard attended him. Mitchell and Nicholson were from Rolling Ground.
Nickerson	L. S., Mrs.	BD, p3c3, 8/14/1883	Recently killed herself by hanging in the Town of Seneca. She didn't want to be a burden to her relatives. Before the hanging, Mrs. Nickerson arranged to have her daughter, Mrs. James A. Porter, leave the home with the grandchildren for a visit with Mrs. Porter's sister-in-law, Mrs. Hugh Porter. The oldest daughter was left to keep Mrs. Nickerson company. Mrs. Nickerson was 68 years old and came to Prairie du Chien in 1840, where she continued to reside.
Nickerson	M., Mrs.	DC, p3c4, 2/19/1887	Departed Seneca to visit her son in Philadelphia.
Nickerson	Mr.	DC, p3c4, 2/19/1887	Mr. Nickerson of Seneca received a pension [for military service].
Nikil [or Nihil]	J. J.	DC, p3c2, 10/22/1887	Subscribed to the *De Soto Chronicle*. Resided in Calmer, IA.
Nilson	Anna	DR, p3c4, 2/9/1871	Charles Bock married Anna Nilson on Feb. 8, 1871. Bride and groom were from Lansing. J. H. Hinds, J.P., officiated.
Nilson	F. F.	BD, p3c1, 2/3/1882	F. F. Nilson [Nelson?] married Jane Knutson on Jan. 28, 1882 at Muscoda. Groom from Lincoln, IA. Bride from Hickory Grove. The Rev. T. M. Evans officiated.
Nixon	Mertie	RH, p5c2, 1/13/1898	Mertie Nixon married Fred McEathron on Jan. 8, 1878 at the home the bride's parents in Star, MN. The Rev. T. M. McClung officiated.
Nobel	Rebecca	BD, p3c1, 11/3/1882	Samuel Buchanan married Rebecca Nobel on Oct. 28, 1882 at the Central House in Boscobel. Bride and groom from Excelsior. The Rev. E. L. Morse officiated.
Nobis	Max	BD, p3c2, 9/23/1881	Max Nobis, W. J. Sherrard, D. Sherrard, L. P. Wonsor and Mrs. W. Wonzor published a notice that the barbers in Boscobel will henceforth be closed on Sundays.
Noble	L.	DC, p2c2, 5/7/1887	L. Noble of Newton planned to start for the West.
Noble	Maria	BD, p3c1, 10/30/1883	Oscar David married Maria Noble on Oct. 24, 1883 at the Central House in Boscobel. The bride and groom were from Excelsior. The Rev. W. Fletcher DeLap officiated.
Noggle	David, Judge	BD, p3c2, 7/26/1878	Died July 18, 1878 in Janesville. He was the father of Mrs. Charles G. Williams.
Noon	Martin	BD, p3c1, 3/10/1882	Martin Noon and John Bray were arrested for assaulting Mr. Crowley. [Charges were dropped against Bray [and Martin Noon?] per BD, p3c1, 3/17/1882.]
Noon	P. C.	BD, p3c1, 9/22/1882	In the case, Wisconsin vs. P. C. Noon, Martin Noon, John Adams and John Shields, a grand jury ruled insufficient evidence existed to proceed.

Genealogical Events from Newspapers for Crawford, Vernon and Grant Counties, Wisconsin, 1870-1901

LAST NAME	FIRST NAME	NEWSPAPER, PAGE/COLUMN MONTH/DAY/YEAR	GENEALOGICAL DATA
Noon	Patrick	BD, p3c2, 3/10/1882	Patrick Noon, John Adams and John Shields, all of Marietta, Crawford Co., were charged with assault [Adams and Shields -- aiding in assault] on John Crowley in Boscobel. They threw stones at him while drinking at Crowley's Hotel.
Norris	M. E.	BD, p3c1, 2/2/1883	Previously served as Crawford County Superintendent of Schools. He is now a businessman in Prairie du Chien.
Norton	John	BD, p3c3, 7/29/1881	John Norton and son, formerly of Fennimore, now live on a 640-acre farm 12 miles west of Shenandoah, IA.
Nottingham	Tom	DR, p3c3, 1/12/1871	Tom Nottingham and son provided music for the Christmas dance in Ferryville.
Nottingham	W. T.	DC, p3c3, 11/20/1886	The W. T. Nottingham String Band performed for a dance at Lyttle's Hall in De Soto.
Nowotny	Jacob	BD, p3c5, 3/10/1882	George F. Hildebrant petitioned the Probate Court in Grant Co. to administer the estate of Jacob Nowotny, late of Hickory Grove.
Nutt	Orlando	BD, p2c4, 11/26/1880	Grant County paid him a bounty for scalps turned into the county.
Nye	Ella A.	BD, p3c2, 9/13/1878	William Harrower married Ella A. Nye on Sept. 5, 1878 in Fennimore. The Rev. D. L. Hubbard officiated.
Obereder	F., Dr.	DR, p1c1, 12/15/1870	Physician in Lansing, IA. Advertised services in the *De Soto Republican*. Practiced many years in Germany and America. Saw patients in Crawford and Vernon Counties.
Obreight	James	BD, p3c1, 2/3/1882	Resident of Town of Haney, Crawford Co. Fatally shot Tuesday. He was 21 years old. Brother died recently, after the Boscobel fair.
O'Brien	Lizzie	BD, p3c2, 10/30/1883	Lizzie O'Brien married Thomas Friar on Oct. 22, 1883. Bride was the daughter of James O'Brien of Irish Ridge. Groom was from Woodman.
Ochsenberger	Mrs.	BD, p2c2, 5/27/1881	Resided in Town of Clayton, just across Sylvan town line. Died very suddenly last February. Shortly after her death, husband took childen to the home of her wife's parents in Indiana and left them. Departed for "parts unknown." The dead woman's father was suspicious of foul play and came to Wisconsin and had the body exhumed and examined by Dr. Dinsdale of Soldiers Grove and Dr. Haskell of Sylvan. They found strychnine in her stomach. Further developments to be reported when they become available.
Odd Fellow Lodge		BD, p3c3, 3/8/1878	An Odd Fellow Lodge was instituted in Excelsior. Named Richwood Lodge No. 276. Mr. Washburn organized an oyster supper. There were 11 candidates. The officers were J. J. Lewis, Levi Persinger and A. H. Avery.
Officer	W. H.	DC, p3c4, 2/5/1887	Former resident of Vernon Co. Recently died at Austin, MN. Engaged in a milling business. Served in the Wisconsin and Minnesota legislatures.
Ogden	Marion	RH, p4c2, 6/6/1901	Died of heart failure on Tuesday night at his home in Viroqua. Former resident of Sylvan. Moved to town about 5 years ago to provide an education for his children.
Oine	Peter	DR, p3c4, 11/30/1871	Published a notice that he took up a lost cow at his farm in the Town of Wheatland.
O'Kane	James	BD, p3c2, 1/10/1879	James O'Kane, Esquire, married Mary Anna Mulhair on Jan. 1, 1879. Bride from Boscobel. Groom from Marietta. Rev. Charles Scraudenbach, a Catholic priest, officiated.
Old Settlers Association		BD, p3c1, 6/3/1881	William McGonigal, Sec., published a notice for the annual meeting of the old settlers of Grant County to take place at the Courthouse in Lancaster.
Olds	Frank H.	BD, p3c2, 12/7/1877	Died last Sunday of small pox in Milwaukee. Former resident of Boscobel.
O'Leary		RH, p4c2, 10/7/1897	The O'Leary sisters advertised their millinery store in Readstown.
O'Leary		RH, p5c5, 10/28/1897	The O'Leary brothers operated the Riverside Hotel in Readstown.
O'Leary	James	RH, p4c3, 1/4/1900	Nellie Kellogg recently married James O'Leary at St. James Church. Rev. Duffey officiated. The couple is well known in Readstown.
O'Leary	James	RH, p5c3, 3/22/1900	The business partnership between James O'Leary and William O'Leary was dissolved. James O'Leary continued in the well drilling service by himself.
O'Leary	Julia	RH, p4c2, 1/17/1901	Henry Sutherland married Julia O'Leary on Sunday at the residence of Vol Wilkinson in Readstown. Justice Davenport officiated.
O'Leary	Norah	RH, p5c4, 3/24/1898	Vol Wilkinson married Norah O'Leary last week. C. W. Reeve officiated at the ceremony.
O'Leary	Rose	RH, p4c3, 4/13/1899	Jefferson Sutherland married Rose O'Leary on April 8, 1899 at the residence of C. H. Davenport, Justice of the Peace. Bride and groom from Readstown.
O'Leary	William	RH, p5c3, 3/22/1900	William O'Leary published a notice that his wife, Cora O'Leary, had left his bed and board without just provocation. He warned the public from giving her credit, as he would not pay any bills contracted by her.

Genealogical Events from Newspapers for Crawford, Vernon and Grant Counties, Wisconsin, 1870-1901

LAST NAME	FIRST NAME	NEWSPAPER, PAGE/COLUMN MONTH/DAY/YEAR	GENEALOGICAL DATA
O'Leary	William, Mrs.	RH, p4c2, 5/31/1900	Arrived from Iowa to visit parents, Mr. and Mrs. L. W. Pettygrove of Readstown.
Oleson		BD, p3c1, 3/19/1880	A carload of tobacco raised in this vicinity by Messrs. Oleson, Christopherson and Nelson was shipped from Boscobel.
Oleson	Andrew F.	BD, p3c2, 6/25/1880	Andrew F. Oleson of Boscobel married Carrie Nelson on June 20, 1880 at the East Koshkonong Church in Dane Co., WI.
Oleson	Christian	BD, p2c3, 5/5/1882	Resident of Soldiers Grove. Leg crushed by a wagon wheel accident. He may lose it.
Oleson	Edward	BD, p3c2, 1/19/1877	Edward Oleson married Jane S. Hanson on Jan. 14, 1877 at the home of the bride's father. Bride and groom were from Hickory Grove. W. W. Reid, Esq. officiated.
Oleson	Isabel P., Mrs.	BD, p3c2, 11/22/1878	Died Monday of consumption in the Boscobel area. Wife of Andrew F. Oleson. Aged 30 years, 1 month and 2 days.
Oliason	Ole	RH, p5c3, 11/11/1897	Accidently shot himself in the leg with a musket on Oct. 29, 1897. The leg was amputated. Resided in the Town of Jefferson.
Oliver		DC, p3c4, 8/7/1886	A child of Mr. Oliver of Asbury Ridge was recently buried in the Retreat Cemetery. Died of diptheria.
Olliver	Pearl, Mrs.	DC, p2c3, 7/3/1886	Resided in Genoa. She was "lying at the point of death." She was the mother of Mrs. Frohawk of MN. Attended by Dr. Rily of Brownsville.
Olmsted	Minnie M.	BD, p3c1, 11/05/1880	Eugene D. Hodgins married Minnie M. Olmsted on Tuesday at Cherokee, IA at the Congregational Church. Bride well known in Boscobel.
Olsen	Andrew, Mrs.	BD, p3c2, 10/13/1882	Left her home in Boscobel for a visit with parents in Clinton, Jefferson Co., WI.
Olson	Andrew	BD, p3c1, 6/10/1881	A son was recently born to Andrew Olson of Boscobel.
Olson	Andrew, Mrs.	BD, p3c3, 8/19/1881	Left Boscobel to visit relatives in Jefferson, Dane Co.
Olson	Engbert	BD, p2c5, 1/2/1880	Published an announcement that he has several stray sheep on his property in Town of Marion.
Olson	John A. [or H.]	RH, p4c2, 9/13/1900	Nearly killed when kicked by a horse. Resided in Readstown.
Olson	Jos. O.	DC, p2c2, 5/28/1887	Sold a small stock of goods and stationary in his Ferryville store.
Olson	Jos. S.	DC, p2c2, 5/28/1887	Resided in Rising Sun. Bought a lot in Ferryville on which to build a machinery depot and warehouse.
Olson	Lena, Miss	DC, p1c2, 4/19/1889	Arrived in Ferryville from Jamestown, Dakota for a visit.
Olson	Mrs.	BD, p3c4, 4/12/1878	Received help from the Boscobel pauper fund.
Olson	Ole	RH, p5c3, 2/14/1901	Resided in Spring Valley. Killed in the pineries. Funeral scheduled to be held at the home of Mr. Ophtodahl.
Olson	Ole	RH, p5c3, 2/21/1901	Recently died in the northern part of the State. Killed by a rolling log. He was about 30 years old. Came here from Norway about 2 years ago and lived with relatives in Spring Valley. Remains taken to Viroqua. Funeral held in Folsom.
Olson	Ole E.	DC, p3c3, 11/6/1886	Resided 2 miles north of Ferryville. Held an auction of animals, farm equipment and household goods.
O'Neil	Daniel, Mr. and Mrs.	BD, p2c3, 8/5/1881	Resided near Mt. Sterling. "Nearly robbed" on July 23rd. After covering Mrs. O'Neils face, the hired man, Will Hardin, who lived nearby, removed $500 from the woman's bedclothes while she was in bed. Mrs. O'Neil got a look at him before he left.
O'Neil	Michael	BD, p2c3, 7/8/1881	Buried Tuesday in the Catholic Cemetery in Prairie du Chien. He was one of the area's earliest settlers.
O'Neill	Tom	DC, p3c4, 10/23/1886	Bought a saloon built by the Crago Bros. at Mt. Sterling.
Oppreicht	B.	DC, p3c4, 7/24/1886	Resided in Haney. Owned a herd of 150 Holstein cattle.
Oram	Hannah F.	BD, p3c2, 11/14/1879	John Parker married Hannah F. Oram on Nov. 5, 1879 in Prairie du Chien. Bride from Prairie du Chien. Groom from Wauzeka. He was the brother of George Parker of Boscobel.
O'Riley	Daniel	DC, p3c4, 12/31/1887	Annie Dermody married Daniel O'Riley on Dec. 27, 1887 at Genoa. Bride from De Soto. Groom from National, IA. Father Wirtz officiated. A present list was published.
Orr	T. G.	DR, p3c4, 6/8/1871	T. G. Orr married Emma Newell on June 1, 1871. Bride from Waukon, IA and groom from De Soto. The Rev. L. L. Frisk officiated.
Orrison	I. D.	RH, p4c2, 12/7/1899	Quite the stage business to sell for Alonzo Bliss Medicine Company, per Readstown news items.

Genealogical Events from Newspapers for Crawford, Vernon and Grant Counties, Wisconsin, 1870-1901

LAST NAME	FIRST NAME	NEWSPAPER, PAGE/COLUMN MONTH/DAY/YEAR	GENEALOGICAL DATA
Orrison	J. D.	RH, p4c2, 12/7/1899	Sold native herbs, per Readstown news items.
Orth	Ed, Mr. and Mrs.	DC, p4c3, 5/10/1889	Mr. and Mrs. Ed Orth and their daughter, Maud, arrived in De Soto. They spent the winter in Monteray, Mexico. Mr. Orth returned to Minneapolis. Mrs. Orth visited relatives in De Soto.
Orth	Kate, Mrs.	DC, p3c2, 9/3/1887	Lived in Minneapolis. Subscribed to the *De Soto Chronicle*
Ortscheid	Andrew	BD, p3c1, 4/30/1880	His house in North Andover, Grant Co. was destroyed by fire on April 14th. It was insured.
Orvis	J. S.	DR, p3c4, 12/29/1870	Resided in Warren, IL. Purchased George Morgan's photographic stock in Lansing, IA.
Orvis	R. A.	DR, p3c3, 12/22/1870	From Baraboo. Committed suicide at South Bend, IN by drowning. He was assumed to be temporarily insane. Survived by a wife and 2 children.
Osborn		RH, p4c3, 6/16/1898	A daughter was recently born to Joe Osborn of De Soto.
Osborn	Addie, Mrs.	DC, p2c2, 5/28/1887	Departed Victory for Grant Co. to see an ill sister who was not expected to live.
Osborn	E.	DC, p3c3, 12/18/1886	Arrived from home in Excelsior to visit his son, Eli Osborn of Victory.
Osborn	Eli	DC, p3c3, 2/19/1889	Started for California, per Victory news column.
Osborn	Elmer	RH, p4c3, 9/5/1901	Arrived in De Soto from Cadott, WI to visit with his brother.
Osborn	Joseph	RH, p5c4, 10/6/1898	Resided in De Soto. Pulled 200,000 feet of lumber from the channel for Frank Woodbury's lumberyard.
Osborn	Richard Henry	RH, p5c3, 9/15/1898	Nora Tower married Richard Henry Osborn on August 21, 1898 at the home of the bride's parents near Readstown. C. H. Davenport, Justice of the Peace, officiated.
Osborn	son	BD, p3c3, 4/29/1881	A son was born to Henry Osborn of Boscobel on April 22, 1881.
Osborn	William, Mrs.	BD, p3c2, 8/28/1883	Left Boscobel to visit relatives in Mineral Point.
Osborne	Eli	RH, p4c4, 1/26/1899	Planned to move from De Soto to Cadott, Chippewa Co.
Osborne	Robert	DC, p3c4, 2/18/1888	Shot Andrew Grandstaff and cut the legs of James Wilder during a quarrel at Osborne's store in Kickapoo Center.
Osborne	Sherman	DC, p2c2, 4/9/1887	Departed Victory for Dakota.
Osborne	Sherman	DC, p2c2, 4/9/1887	Sherman Osborne "has gone to Dakota," per Victory news column.
Osborne	William, Mrs.	RH, p4c4, 1/26/1899	Resident of Victory. In the last stages of consumption. Mrs. Osborne's mother, Mrs. George Wilder of Kickapoo, was caring for her.
Osgood	Dr.	DC, p2c1, 10/29/1887	The De Soto town proprietors were Dr. Powers, Dr. Houghton and Dr. Osgood. Dr. Powers was the businessman of the three. Dr. Houghton owned much of the land. Dr. Osgood was in ill health [1856] and had but little to say or do in the way of building up the town. He corresponded with a leading agricultural paper in Massachusetts, by which a number of settlers came to De Soto. De Soto was intended to be a "New England" village.
Osgood	Dr.	DC, p2c2, 2/3/1888	In 1859 Dr. Osgood died and "later on" his wife and Dr. Powers moved away.
Osgood	J.	DR, p3c2, 12/29/1870	Dr. E. B. Houghton, J. Osgood, S. D. Powers and C. B. Worth, were among the "First Families" who settled in De Soto in 1854. In 1870, C. B. Worth was the only pioneer from this group still in De Soto.
Ostrander	Henriett	BD, p3c3, 2/22/1878	Joe Havens married Henriett Ostrander on Feb. 8, 1878 at Fennimore. Bride and groom from Marion. R. F. Green, Esquire officiated.
Ostrander	Mary S.	BD, p3c1, 1/9/1880	Married Isaac S. Pettit on Jan. 1, 1880 in Fennimore. Bride and groom from Hickory Grove. Otho Shrader, Esq. officiated.
Oswald		BD, p2c6, 1/13/1882	Notice published for a dissolution of partnership between Martin Oswald and C. Shuttleworth of Fennimore.
Oswald	W. L., Mrs.	BD, p3c4, 9/14/1877	Widow. Operated her deceased husband's store in Wauzeka.
Oswald & Shuttleworth		BD, P3c7, 1/5/1877	Advertised their dry goods store in Fennimore Center.
Ott		DC, p2c1, 4/16/1887	A young child of Henry Ott was buried on Saturday in Genoa.

Genealogical Events from Newspapers for Crawford, Vernon and Grant Counties, Wisconsin, 1870-1901

LAST NAME	FIRST NAME	NEWSPAPER, PAGE/COLUMN MONTH/DAY/YEAR	GENEALOGICAL DATA
Ott	Charles	DC, p3c4, 10/9/1886	He was in the process of building a warehouse in Genoa.
Ott	Charles	DC, p2c3, 7/3/1888	A train ran into a drove of hogs belonging to Charles Ott of Genoa, killing one and hurting several others that had to be killed later.
Ott	Henry	DC, p3c5, 2/18/1888	Died Feb. 12, 1888 in Genoa. Thirty teams were in line at the funeral.
Otteson	Christina	DC, p3c4, 4/9/1887	John C. Johnson married Christina Otteson last Thursday in West Prairie.
Otteson	Jacob	DC, p3c3, 2/11/1888	The funeral for Mrs. Johnson and her brother, Jacob Otteson, were held together at the Norwegian Church in West Prairie. He died one day before his sister.
Owen	Ed	DC, p3c2, 4/10/1888	The Town of Wheatland road overseers were Ed. Owen, Arvin Chase, Fred Elton, J. W. Caldwell, S. D. Taylor, William H. Shisler and W. J. Van Zant.
Owen	H. A.	DR, p2c1, 8/3/1871	He was a hotelkeeper, merchant and farmer in Liberty Pole.
Owens	Francis B.	BD, p3c1, 3/9/1883	Francis B. Owens married Luella Angeline Stanton on Mar. 4, 1883 at the residence of Calvin C. K_____ in the Town of Scott. Bride and groom were from Richland Co. E. A. Brown, J.P., officiated.
Owsley	Manley	BD, p3c2, 9/1/1882	Arrived from Decorah to visit in his former hometown, Boscobel.
Page	Charles, Mrs.	DC, p4c1, 3/12/1889	Sick with rheumatism. Lived in De Soto.
Pake	Edmond M.	BD, p3c4, 12/3/1880	Lived in the Town of Haney, Crawford Co. Published notice he had taken up a stray steer.
Palmer	Fanny, Mrs.	RH, p4c2, 6/27/1901	Nee Laughlin. Died of heart failure on June 20, 1901 in Walker, IA. She was a former resident of Viola.
Palmer	Lizzie A.	BD, p3c2, 2/21/1879	William E. Tuttle married Lizzie A. Palmer on Feb. 19, 1879. Bride from Fennimore. Elder Shears performed the ceremony at the Shears residence.
Palmer	Robert	DC, p3c4, 2/26/1889	Recently killed in Dubuque. Worked as a brakeman on the St. P. and K. C. Railroad. Two wives attended his funeral. He married Amanda J. Morris in 1880 in Waterloo, IA. Married Nellie Snyder in 1886 in De Soto. His second wife filed a petition to adminster his estate. The first wife contested the will. "Palmer supposed the latter to be dead when he married the former."
Palmer	Sadie J.	BD, p3c3, 3/17/1882	Sperry D. Hartwell married Sadie J. Palmer on Mar. 12, 1882 at the residence of William F. Tuttle. Bride and groom from Fennimore.
Parce	C.	BD, P3c2, 4/23/1880	Sworn in as an alderman of Boscobel.
Parce	C., Mrs.	BD, p3c1, 2/6/1880	Buried Tuesday in Boscobel. She and Mr. Parce had been married for 51 years.
Parce	Freeman	BD, p3c1, 8/6/1880	Crawford Co. resident. Accidentally shot himself in the leg while fooling around with an old-fashioned pepperbox revolver. He was the grandson of Alderman Parce of Boscobel.
Parce	John	BD, p3c1, 6/17/1881	Resided in Boscobel. Sent to the State Hospital for the Insane.
Parfrey	A. C.	BD, p2c2, 11/20/1883	The safe at his mill in Richland Center was blown open. Lost $332.
Parfrey	Elizabeth, Mrs.	BD, p2c3, 2/2/1883	Died last Sunday in Richland Center at the home of her daughter, Mrs. Henry Toms. She was the mother of Mr. A. C. Parfrey and Mrs. H. Toms, both of Richland Center, and F. W. Parfrey of Nebraska. She was one of the earliest settlers in the area.
Parish	George	BD, p3c1, 8/6/1880	Two sons of George Parish [resident of Wingville], aged 9 and 11, died when a wagon full of zinc ore overturned at a railroad crossing and buried them. They were on driving the wagon to Mineral Point. [The Aug. 31, 1880 edition, page 3c1, said that George Parish was the son of Richard Parish. George fell asleep and the team wandered from the road.]
Parker	Ada, Mrs.	DC, p3c3, 6/4/1887	Visited father, Wm. P. Daly of De Soto. Present residence is in Fargo, Dakota. She was a former typo on the paper published here by B. J. Castle.
Parker	D. T.	BD, p3c5, 3/24/1882	"D. T. Parker, deceased, in 1867, opened up the first general merchandising store [in the village of Fennimore] in the building now occupied by Messrs. Oswald & Hinn."
Parker	Dwight T., Jr.	BD, p3c1, 10/22/1880	Dwight T. Parker, Jr. married Cora Anderson on Oct. 13, 1880 at the home of the bride's father in Ripon. Groom and bride were "well known" in Boscobel.
Parker	Dwight, Jr.	BD, p3c4, 2/3/1882	A Grant Co. court summons was published for the case, Dwight Parker, Jr. [plaintiff] vs. John S. Townsend and Millie Townsend, his wife [defendants].
Parker	Frank	BD, p3c3, 3/15/1878	Departed Boscobel for Nebraska. He may stay there.

Genealogical Events from Newspapers for Crawford, Vernon and Grant Counties, Wisconsin, 1870-1901

LAST NAME	FIRST NAME	NEWSPAPER, PAGE/COLUMN MONTH/DAY/YEAR	GENEALOGICAL DATA
Parker	Frank	BD, p3c1, 7/4/1879	Returned to Boscobel. Attended the Commercial College at Poughkeepsie, NY.
Parker	J. L.	BD, p2c2, 2/15/1878	Fire destroyed Parker's store in Woodman. Arson suspected. Parker was Woodman's Postmaster and Town Treasurer.
Parker	John	BD, p3c2, 9/2/1881	Former merchant in Woodman. Now resident of Sheldon, IA. Lost his entire crop during a hailstorm. Bad weather has ruined his crops for the last 4 years.
Parker	John	BD, p3c2, 11/14/1879	John Parker married Hannah F. Oram on Nov. 5, 1879 in Prairie du Chien. Bride from Prairie du Chien. Groom from Wauzeka. He was the brother of George Parker of Boscobel.
Parker	M. Leavitt	BD, p3c2, 11/7/1879	M. Leavitt Parker married Cora J. Clark on Wednesday at the home of the bride's parents. Bride from Boscobel. Took a train to their future home in Sheldon, IA.
Parker	O.	BD, p3c5, 7/27/1877	O. Parker married Laura M. Davis on July 4, 1877 at Patch Grove. Bride and groom from Patch Grove. J. A. Davis, Esq. officiated.
Parker	Thomas E.	DC, p3c3, 7/24/1886	Named station agent in De Soto.
Parker & Wayne		BD, p3c4, 9/14/1877	Operated a barrel factory in Wauzeka.
Parker, Hildebrand & Co.		BD, p2c2, 10/22/1880	Mercantile established in 1857 in Boscobel. Occupies a large stone store, 90' by 35', two stories high, with basement. Stocked dry goods, clothing, boots, shoes, hats, caps, groceries and notions. Firm deals in wool, grain, stock, hoop-poles, staves and ties.
Parker, Hildebrand & Co.		BD, p2c5, 1/5/1877	Ran a dry goods store in Boscobel.
Parnell	Elizabeth	DR, p3c2, 3/2/1871	Richard Harrison married Elizabeth Parnell on Feb. 9, 1871 at the Methodist Episcopal Church at Oswego, KS. The bride and groom lived in Oswego. The Rev. Mr. Conley officiated.
Parnell	William	BD, p3c1, 4/8/1881	Opened a blacksmith shop on La Belle Street in Boscobel.
Parnell	William	BD, p3c2, 8/11/1882	Blacksmith in Boscobel. His watch was stolen by Steve Woods, also of Boscobel. Woods sold it to Edward Schuchart of Woodman for $4. George Woods, brother, paid $10 for the watch.
Parr	Thomas	BD, p3c3, 7/1/1881	Moved to Boscobel. Graduate of the State University.
Parr	Thomas W.	BD, p3c1, 10/22/1880	Thomas W. Parr married Lill L. Coates on Oct. 15, 1880 at the home of the bride's mother. Bride from Boscobel. Groom from Madison. The Rev. W. Stoddart officiated.
Partridge	A. D.	RH, p4c2, 9/13/1900	Arrived in Readstown from La Crosse to visit at the Davenport home.
Partridge	Mrs.	DR, p3c3, 9/7/1871	Lost a valuable shawl in De Soto. She offered a reward for its return.
Partridge	William	BD, p3c2, 3/9/1877	William Partridge married Mrs. Mary E. Brown on Mar. 7, 1877. Bride and groom from Boscobel. The Rev. George Nuzum officiated.
Patrick	Ella G.	DC, p3c3, 5/8/1888	Spencer L. Alexander planned to marry Ella G. Patrick [niece of W. S. Salyer] on May 16, 1888 in Spokane Falls, Washington Territory.
Patridge	Mrs.	RH, p5c4, 4/14/1898	Recently died in De Soto. Survived by a 2-week-old baby. Funeral held at the Methodist Episcopal Church.
Patten	J. E.	BD, p2c1, 11/20/1883	Resided in Soldiers Grove. Offered a reward for the return of a 3-year-old stray mare.
Patterson	E. E., Mrs.	RH, p4c1, 7/8/1897	Proprietor of the Patterson House in Readstown.
Patterson	John	DC, p3c4, 11/27/1886	Resided in Genoa. His father died Nov. 22, 1886 and was buried at Chaseburg.
Paulson	Peter	BD, p3c1, 11/27/1883	Died Monday after he was thrown from a wagon he was driving home to Hickory Grove from Boscobel. He was the 13-year-old son of Giftram Paulson.
Payne	Frank	BD, p2c2, 4/4/1879	Frank Payne married Alice Coleman at Rolling Ground on March 31, 1879.
Payne	Henry	BD, p2c3, 2/17/1882	Aged 26 years. Died Thursday [according to the Feb. 9, 1882 issue of the *Republican and Observer*]. Resided in Dayton. Accidently shot himself while hunting. Mr. Dobson, his brother-in-law, brought his remains to Indiana for burial.
Peacock	Thomas	DR, p3c1, 5/11/1871	Thomas Peacock married Emma Elder last Sunday. Bride and groom were from Lansing. D. A. Steele, J.P., officiated.
Pearson	F. E.	BD, p3c2, 9/4/1883	F. E. Pearson married Miss Frankie Hurd on Sept. 1, 1883 at 7:00 A.M. The bride's brother, Rev. W. W. Hurd, officiated, at the wedding that was held at the home of another brother, Dr. R. W. Hurd, in Boscobel. Groom was also from Boscobel. The couple's new home will be in Madison where the groom works as a train dispatcher. Bride was daughter of Rev. Z. S. Hurd of Boscobel.

Genealogical Events from Newspapers for Crawford, Vernon and Grant Counties, Wisconsin, 1870-1901

LAST NAME	FIRST NAME	NEWSPAPER, PAGE/COLUMN MONTH/DAY/YEAR	GENEALOGICAL DATA
Pease	D. G., Mr. and Mrs.	BD, p2c3, 2/9/1883	Celebrated their 25th wedding anniversary on Jan. 22, 1883 in Richland Center.
Peckham	Charles	RH, p5c3, 3/17/1898	Young man from the Town of Bloom. Sent to the State Asylum a few weeks ago. He was rapidly recovering.
Peer	Mary	BD, p3c2, 6/8/1877	Rufus Lord married Mary Peer on June 2, 1877 in Boscobel. Groom from Sextonville. Bride from Watterstown. Rev. Z. S. Hurd officiated.
Peer	Miller	BD, p3c2, 1/24/1879	The Peer residence in the Town of Clayton, Crawford Co. was destroyed by fire.
Peer	Morris	BD, p3c1, 2/4/1881	Morris Peer married Helen Updike on Jan. 27, 1881 at Hickory Grove. Groom from Watterstown. James Henderson, Esquire officiated.
Pennell	John	DC, p3c1, 2/3/1888	Returned to De Soto from Montana.
Pennell	John	DC, p3c2, 12/11/1888	Ida Bates married John Pennell on Nov. 30, 1888 at home of bride's parents in De Soto. Martin Loftus officiated.
Pepper	John	BD, p3c2, 2/27/1880	Former alderman. Left Boscobel to visit Missouri, Kansas, Nebraska, Iowa and Dakota. Looking for a new place to live.
Pepper	John	BD, p3c1, 5/5/1882	Departed Boscobel for Billings, MT to start up a cattle business.
Pepper	John	BD, p3c2, 9/13/1878	Ran a cattleyard in Boscobel.
Pepper	John, Mr. and Mrs.	BD, p3c2, 1/3/1879	Departed Boscobel to attended the wedding of their niece, Emma Shrader of Lancaster.
Pepper	Laura B.	BD, p3c2, 7/13/1883	Laura B. Pepper married Judson P. Walker on Wednesday in Boscobel. Bride was daughter of Mr. and Mrs. John Pepper of Boscobel. Groom was a bookkeeper at Parker, Hildebrand & Co. in Boscobel. Bride was a Boscobel teacher for the last 5 years.
Pepper	Laura, Miss	BD, p3c3, 10/19/1877	Engaged to teach school 3 miles south of Fennimore. Graduated from Boscobel High School last spring.
Perham	Charles & Ed	RH, p5c4, 5/19/1898	Resided in Readstown. Assigned to Co. L, 3rd Wisconsin Vol. At Chickamagua. Charles was promoted from Corporal to Sargent.
Perham	Charley	RH, p4c4, 10/6/1898	Wrote letter to his mother from "Porto Rico." It was published in the newspaper.
Perham	Ed	RH, p5c2, 10/14/1897	Returned to Readstown after selling his interest in a restaurant in Sparta.
Perham	Ed	RH, p5c3, 4/28/1898	Resided in Viroqua. Sold his restaurant to La Force Terhun and joined the army.
Perham	Ed	RH, p5c2, 10/6/1898	Sick with typhoid fever.
Perham	Ed	RH, p4c2, 1/19/1899	Ed Perham and sister, Mrs. E. V. Wolfe of Viroqua, visited their mother, Mrs. F. L. Perham of Readstown.
Perham	Ed	RH, p4c2, 3/2/1899	Worked as an apprentice to Joseph Boebrer of Viroqua. Boebrer ran a jewelry store.
Perham	F. L., Mrs.	RH, p4c2, 2/7/1901	Returned to Readstown after caring for her daughter, Mrs. Louis Huschka of Sparta, who has been ill.
Perham	Helen	RH, p6c3, 9/2/1897	Resident of Readstown. Hired to teach in the Thompson School.
Perham	Helen	RH, p4c2, 9/13/1900	Helen Perham married Ole Anderson on Sept. 9, 1900. Bride and groom from Readstown. Rev. G. W. Nuzum of Viroqua officiated.
Perham	Kittie	RH, p4c3, 3/9/1899	Kittie Perham married Grant Pierce at the home of the bride's sister, Mrs. Carrie Chase of Viroqua. Bride daughter of Mrs. F. L. Perham of Readstown. Groom from Viroqua. Planned to live in Viroqua.
Perkins	John G.	BD, p3c3, 5/28/1880	Resided in Fennimore. Published a notice in the newspaper that he would not be responsible for the debts of his son, Elsworth Perkins.
Perkins	John G.	BD, p3c5, 3/24/1882	After statehood, several of Fennimore's forefathers moved to the area. They were John G. Perkins, Thomas Tormey, Henry Dankleff, G. Wehrley, John Varrell and Wm. Marsen. Perkins moved a building onto the present site of the village of Fennimore in 1862 and opened the first hotel. That building is now called the Byerley House and is occupied by John Phillips. In 1866 W. W. Field, M. Bower, H. W. Wiefel and John G. Perkins plated 16 blocks and laid out the streets of Fennimore.
Perkins	L. B.	DC, p1c3, 4/12/1889	Mr. L. B. Perkins of Cashton visited his daughter, Mrs. Thomas Latimer of Genoa.
Perkinson	John	DR, p3c4, 2/16/1871	Lived in the Town of Sterling. Planned to hold an auction of land, grain, stock and household furniture.

Genealogical Events from Newspapers for Crawford, Vernon and Grant Counties, Wisconsin, 1870-1901

LAST NAME	FIRST NAME	NEWSPAPER, PAGE/COLUMN MONTH/DAY/YEAR	GENEALOGICAL DATA
Pester	Leonard	DC, p3c4, 6/11/1887	Native of St. Louis. Fell off a barge and drowned.
Peterson	Atley	DC, p2c2, 8/7/1886	Expected to run for Crawford Co. Railroad Commissioner. Resided in Soldiers Grove.
Peterson	Atley	DC, Supp, 10/16/1886	Native of Norway. Moved to Wisconsin in 1852. He briefly lived in Vernon Co. Moved to Soldiers Grove. Served as a member of the Wisconsin Assembly in 1879, 1880, 1881 and 1882. He was a lumber manufacturer and farmer. Running for Railroad Commissioner in Crawford Co.
Peterson	girl	RH, p4c3, 5/9/1901	A daughter was recently born to Knudt Peterson of the Readstown area.
Peterson	Mina	BD, p3c2, 5/31/1878	Charles Nelson married Mina Peterson on Tuesday. Groom from Boscobel and worked for the firm, Nelson & Son.
Peterson	Nels	BD, p3c2, 12/2/1881	Died of scarlet fever on Wednesday. He was the son of Peter Peterson, formerly of Boscobel, but now of Lone Rock. Nels had been working in Osage, IA. Came home when he got sick.
Peterson	Ole, Mrs.	BD, p2c2, 5/3/1878	Lived on a farm about ¼ mile from Bloomingdale with her husband and several children. Killed herself. Body found in a cistern on the farm. She was about 35 years old.
Peterson	Peter	BD, p3c1, 4/13/1883	Former partner in Dyer & Peterson of Boscobel. Left town for a new home in Ellendale, Dakota.
Peterson	Peter	RH, p4c1, 8/1/1901	Peter Peterson married Nettie Sime on July 30, 1901 at the home of the bride's parents, Mr. and Mrs. H. H. Sime. The Simes lived 4 miles southeast of Viroqua. Groom from Readstown. About 300 guests attended the wedding.
Peterson	Sem	RH, p4c2, 3/21/1901	Returned to Folsom to work on his father's farm. Previously worked in Madison where he made plows.
Peterson	T.	DC, p3c3, 9/18/1886	Returned to Soldiers Grove from Dakota where he proved a claim. Recently married Maggie Johnson, the daughter of John C. Johnson of WestPrairie.
Peterson & Son		RH, p7c1, 7/1/1897	Advertised hardware store in Readstown.
Petitt	Richard	BD, p3c2, 2/23/1877	An auction was scheduled for Mar. 1, 1877 at the Richard Petitt home in Hickory Grove.
Pettey	Mable	BD, p3c4, 1/19/1883	Died in Boscobel on Jan. 16, 1883. She was one of the twin children of Mr. and Mrs. V. Pettey. Died of scarletina when she was 4 years and 9 months old.
Pettit	Alice	RH, p5c3, 2/21/1901	Monroe McDaniel married Alice Pettit on Monday. Bride and groom from Sugar Grove. Bride granddaughter of Reuben Alexander. Groom son of William McDaniel. Squire Ward officiated at the ceremony.
Pettit	Amos	RH, p5c4, 1/27/1898	Passed through Kickapoo Center on his way to a new home in the north.
Pettit	Isaac S.	BD, p3c1, 1/9/1880	Married Mary S. Ostrander on Jan. 1, 1880 in Fennimore. Bride and groom from Hickory Grove. Otho Shrader, Esq. officiated.
Pettit	Vern	RH, p4c1, 2/7/1901	Son of Amos Pettit of Valley Junction. Visited his grandparents, Mr. and Mrs. Ruben Alexander of Sugar Grove.
Petty	H., Mrs.	BD, p3c1, 7/2/1880	Mrs. H. Petty and family departed Boscobel for a new home in Stevens Point, WI.
Petty	Henry	BD, p2c3, 10/11/1878	Henry Petty married Mrs. Hattie Bennett on Sept. 30, 1878 at the home of the bride's father. Bride and groom from Boscobel.
Petty	William	BD, p3c4, 1/25/1878	Died Jan. 19, 1878 in Boscobel when he was 72 years, 5 months and 26 days old. His wife of 47 years and 5 of his 10 children survive him.
Pettygrove	John	RH, p4c2, 7/12/1900	A hearing was held at the county seat for John Pettygrove and Charles Carter of Readstown. Pettygrove was bound over until the fall term.
Pettygrove	William H.	RH, p4c3, 10/19/1899	Died Oct. 14, 1899 from inflamation of the bowels. He was the son of L. W. Pettygrove of Readstown. Born Oct. 15, 1874 in the Town of Sterling, Vernon Co. Moved with his parents to Readstown in 1897. He was supposed to marry Sarenta Sutherland on Oct. 15, 1899. Buried in Liberty Pole. Funeral held by Rev. Bell at the Methodist Episcopal Church.
Peugh	Mary A.	BD, p2c5, 4/29/1881	Summons notice for Grant Co. Courts published. Mary A. Peugh, plaintiff, vs. Joseph Peugh, defendant.
Phelps	Dele	BD, p3c2, 5/27/1881	John Street recently married Dele Phelps. Street moved to Lancaster about a year ago and is connectd with the woolen mill. Bride is daughter of Fred Phelps. Bride is niece of John Pepper of Boscobel.
Phelps	J. O.	BD, p3c4, 11/22/1878	Died Wednesday in Spring Green.
Phelps	Mrs.	BD, p3c1, 10/29/1880	Daughter of Jessie D. Sarles. Returned to her home in Racine after father's funeral.

Genealogical Events from Newspapers for Crawford, Vernon and Grant Counties, Wisconsin, 1870-1901

LAST NAME	FIRST NAME	NEWSPAPER, PAGE/COLUMN MONTH/DAY/YEAR	GENEALOGICAL DATA
Phelps	Mrs.	BD, p3c2, 8/30/1878	Died at the residence of her daughter on Aug. 18, 1878. She was over 90 years old. Resided in Lancaster. Mother of Fred Phelps.
Philips	George W.	BD, p3c1, 10/15/1880	George W. Philips married Annie Coleman on Oct. 7, 1880 in Boscobel. Bride and groom from Town of Scott, Crawford Co.
Phillamalee	James	BD, p3c1, 4/4/1879	James Phillamalee recently married Mary McClimans. Bride from Lancaster. Groom from Seneca, Crawford Co. James M. David, Esquire of Blue River officiated.
Phillips	Achilles	BD, p3c2, 4/27/1883	Left Boscobel for Dakota a year ago. Taught school in Aberdeen. Has now taken out a claim near Westport and planned to farm.
Phillips	Dan	RH, p4c2, 8/15/1901	Dan Phillips married Mabel Hurlbut on August 21, 1901 at the home of the bride's father, W. S. Hurlbut of Readstown. Groom from Mt. Sterling. Bride was the sister of Mrs. H. M. Pond. Couple planned to move to Dakota.
Phillips	Elder	DC, p2c1, 4/16/1887	Recenly lost his cow. His neighbors in Ontario bought him another cow.
Phillips	John	BD, p3c3, 5/27/1881	Reported to have shot and killed John Hughes of Citron Valley, Crawford Co. on Wednesday morning near the Shamrock House in Boscobel. Hughes was known to be quarrelsome when drunk. Hughes was about 60 years old. Hughes was a former resident of Waukesha. Phillips moved to area about 2 years ago from Iowa Co. Phillips found to have acted in self-defense. Witnesses were Mr. Leb Muffley, Mrs. Enright and Mrs. Honn.
Phillips	John	BD, p3c1, 9/23/1881	Resided in Boscobel. Acquitted in shooting of John Hughes.
Phillips	W. B.	BD, p3c2, 8/19/1881	Hired to teach by the Mt. Hope School Board.
Phillips	W. B.	BD, p3c2, 11/23/1877	Resided in Boscobel. Secured a new position as the principal of Mount Hope High School.
Phillips	Walter B.	BD, p3c2, 5/28/1880	Appointed to be a census enumerator in Wingville, Grant Co.
Pickard	D. O.	BD, p3c1, 1/5/1877	Physician in Boscobel.
Pickard	D. O., Dr.	BD, p3c1, 8/1/1879	Dr. D. O. Pickard married Ida McLean on Tuesday evening. Groom from Fennimore. Bride was the adopted daughter of Mr. A. Palmer of Boscobel. The Rev. William Stoddart officiated.
Pickard	J.	RH, p7c3, 7/1/1897	Lived in Richland Center. Planned to open an excelsior factory in Readstown. He used to own an excelsior factory in Soldiers Grove.
Pidcock	Monroe	BD, p3c1, 4/27/1883	Elected street commissioner in Boscobel.
Pierce	Grant	RH, p4c3, 3/9/1899	Kittie Perham married Grant Pierce at the home of the bride's sister, Mrs. Carrie Chase of Viroqua. Bride daughter of Mrs. F. L. Perham of Readstown. Groom from Viroqua. Planned to live in Viroqua.
Pigg	Thad	BD, p3c2, 1/13/1882	Resided in Fennimore. Accidently shot himself in the upper arm. Amputated by Dr. Pickard, Dr. Wolff and Dr. McDermott. He was not expected to survive. He was the brother-in-law of Mr. Worden Stephens.
Pike	Ed	BD, p3c1, 9/16/1881	Ed Pike of Boscobel shipped 20 barrels of honey.
Pike	Ed	BD, p3c2, 7/27/1877	Delivered to the newspaper editor a sample of honey produced by his bees.
Pike	Edward	BD, p3c1, 4/14/1882	Alderman Edward Pike, Messrs. J. W. Nice, M. V. Petty and A. C. Phillips started on a prospecting trip west. They planned to look over the Rosebud country in Montana. They were residents of the Boscobel area.
Pike	Edwin	BD, p3c1, 9/25/1883	Shipped 12,000 pounds of extracted honey to New York City.
Pike	Lora Adella	BD, p3c3, 3/29/1878	Died Mar. 23, 1878 of scarlet fever in Boscobel. Aged 9 years, 1 month and 15 days. Daughter of Edwin and Ellen E. Pike.
Pike	Samuel	DR, p3c1, 9/7/1871	He was a long time resident of the Town of Wheatland. Moved to Chickasaw Station, IA.
Pike	Theo	DC, p3c2, 6/19/1888	Lived in Prairie du Chien. Bitten by a rattlesnake he kept as a pet. Former resident of Liberty Pole.
Pilz	Ed	BD, P3c2, 4/23/1880	Sworn in as an alderman of Boscobel.
Pion	John B.	BD, p2c3, 12/15/1882	Died Dec. 1, 1882 in Prairie du Chien. Born 1821 in Prairie du Chien. Ten of his 11 children survive him. He was of French heritage.
Pipkin	A. J.	BD, p3c4, 1/16/1880	Banker. Announced he was the successor to the failed First National Bank in Boscobel.

Genealogical Events from Newspapers for Crawford, Vernon and Grant Counties, Wisconsin, 1870-1901

LAST NAME	FIRST NAME	NEWSPAPER, PAGE/COLUMN MONTH/DAY/YEAR	GENEALOGICAL DATA
Pipkin	A. J.	BD, P3c2, 4/23/1880	Sworn in as an alderman of Boscobel.
Pipkin	A. J.	BD, p2c5, 10/22/1880	The First National Bank of Boscobel was organized in 1871. In 1879 the officers and stockholders approved Mr. Pipkin's request to reopen the bank. Mr. Pipkin spent many years in the wholesale grocery trade of Milwaukee.
Pitcher	Lyman, Mr. and Mrs.	DC, p3c2, 11/6/1886	Arrived in De Soto from Lowville, NY to visit Mrs. Pitcher's sister, Mrs. A. N. Miller.
Pittenger	John	BD, p3c1, 2/28/1879	Resident of Boscobel. Worked for Ed Ayer of Harvard, IL as the tie-man "for this section."
Pittinger	John	BD, p3c2, 11/20/1883	Prepared to move his family from Boscobel to Aikin, MN.
Pittinger	Matilda, Mrs.	BD, p3c1, 12/22/1882	Died Monday in Marion at the home of her daughter, Mrs. J. P. Miller. She was 75 years old. Funeral was held at home of her son, John of Boscobel.
Pittman	Emma	BD, p3c1, 2/7/1879	A daughter was born on Sunday to M. B. Pittman of Boscobel. She was named Emma.
Pittman	M. B.	BD, p2c3, 10/1/1880	Resided in Boscobel. Published notice that two of his cows were stolen or strayed.
Pittman	M. B., Mr.	BD, p2c2, 4/26/1878	A party was held at the home of Pittman's parents, Mr. And Mrs. T. W. Pittman on April 16, 1878 in Eagle. M. B. Pittman lived in Boscobel. The party was held in honor of one of his relatives. Many elderly relatives, especially Bovee relatives, were mentioned in the article.
Pittman	M. B., Mrs.	BD, p3c2, 8/17/1877	Visited friends in Eagle and Oconomowoc.
Pittman	Thomas	BD, p3c1, 9/22/1882	Thomas Pittman recently died in Eagle. He was 85 years old and a respected citizen of Waukesha Co. He was the father of Matt B. Pittman of Boscobel area.
Pittman & McWilliams		BD, p2c5, 1/5/1877	Ran a drug store in Boscobel.
Pittman and McWilliams		BD, p2c5, 10/22/1880	Opened a drug and grocery house 15 years ago in Boscobel. Operated out of two-story, 26" by 100" building with a basement -- the largest in town. Stock included drugs, medicines, toilet articles, paints, oils, books, stationary, staple and fancy groceries, wallpaper, crockery and glassware.
Plato	B. P.	BD, p2c3, 8/11/1882	Fell on stairs and was found unconscious. Died Tuesday [per *Republican & Observer*, 8/3/1882]. Resided in Richland Co. for 12 to 14 years. Would have been 70 years old on Nov. 5th. Buried in Janesville. Father of Mrs. Dr. Wall of Lone Rock.
Plum	Mr. and Mrs.	DC, p1c1, 6/28/1889	Visited the Angell family and Mr. Conklin in Cooley Valley and then departed for California.
Plummer	Washington, Capt.	DC, p2c2, 11/12/1887	In 1856 he owned the De Soto Lime and Barrel Company a mile up the valley from De Soto. Capt. Plummer was a retired, "wealthy New England sea captain." The company collasped a year later. Plummer went east, ostensibly to get money, but never returned and many debts went unpaid.
Podewetz	Jacob	DC, p3c5, 2/18/1888	Charged with bastardy. Complaint was made by Bertha Veighland, a deaf and dumb girl, per *Viroqua Censor*.
Poehler	Charles	DC, p2c3, 7/9/1887	Jennie Baty married Charles Poehler on July 4, 1887. Bride and groom from Lansing, IA. Police Justice Ingersoll officiated.
Poff	boy	BD, p3c5, 7/26/1878	The infant son of M. J. and Silas Poff died July 5, 1878 in Belle Center.
Poff	C. M., Dr.	RH, p5c3, 5/26/1898	Former resident of Readstown. Recently relocated to Carlisle, Clark Co., where he is Deputy Postmaster.
Pollard	Dora B.	DC, p2c2, 1/1/1887	Dora B. Pollard married Will P. Gorsline on Dec. 25, 1886 in Viroqua.
Pollard	Poor Commissioner	DC, p3c2, 7/17/1886	Pollard was in town [De Soto] "looking after his charges."
Pollard	S. R.	DC, p2c2, 8/7/1886	Will probably run for Sheriff in Vernon Co.
Pollock	John	BD, p3c6, 11/2/1877	Worked as a wagon maker and blacksmith in Lancaster.
Pomery	H. N.	RH, p5c4, 11/4/1897	Arrested for embezzlement. Former resident of Readstown. He worked as a collector for E. H. Gochenaur, cigar maker of Viola. He was accused of taking $267.60.
Pommey	Matilda	BD, p3c1, 8/25/1882	John Henry Winn [Wynne] married Matilda Pommey on Tuesday at the Betts House in Boscobel. Bride was from Montello, WI. The Rev. E. L. Morse officiated.
Pond		RH, p4c2, 1/26/1899	An infant child of H. M. Pond died on Tuesday. It was buried in the Readstown Cemetery.

Genealogical Events from Newspapers for Crawford, Vernon and Grant Counties, Wisconsin, 1870-1901

LAST NAME	FIRST NAME	NEWSPAPER, PAGE/COLUMN MONTH/DAY/YEAR	GENEALOGICAL DATA
Pond	Andrew	RH, p4c2, 1/24/1901	Bought 320 acres of land in Elk Mount, Dunn Co. Planned to move his family there in about 2 months.
Pond	Andrew	RH, p5c2, 10/31/1901	Pond and family left Readstown for Ladysmith, WI.
Pond	Andy	RH, p5c2, 12/15/1898	Returned from La Crosse with his bride to live in Readstown. He recently married.
Pond	Ella, Mrs.	RH, p4c3, 8/31/1899	Mrs. Ella Pond and her daughter, Nina, returned to Readstown after visiting Mrs. Pond's father, Mathew Harris of Manton, MI.
Pond	Ellis	RH, p4c2, 10/26/1899	Visited relatives in Readstown with son-in-law, Bert Sommers of Viola. Pond was a former resident of Readstown. Lived there over 20 years. Moved to Patch Grove, Grant Co. in 1894. Later moved to Muscoda, his present home.
Pond	girl	RH, p5c3, 12/1/1898	A daughter was recently born to M. Pond of Readstown.
Pond	H. M.	RH, p4c1, 5/11/1899	Started a stave mill in Readstown.
Pond	H. M.	RH, p4c3, 8/10/1899	Purchased a general store in Steuben. Moved away from Readstown.
Pond	Holley	RH, p5c3, 10/13/1898	Bought the Charles Aikins property, formerly owned by Pond's grandfather.
Pond	J.	RH, p5c3, 11/18/1897	Slowly recovering from typhoid fever at his home in Readstown.
Pond	J. L.	RH, p2c1, 7/1/1897	Advertised services as a contractor, builder and cooper in Readstown.
Pond	J. L., Mrs.	RH, p5c2, 7/15/1897	Left her home in Readstown to visit her son, Hiloy of Mt. Sterling.
Pond	John L.	RH, p7c3, 7/1/1897	Started a bee business in Readstown.
Pond	Mary, Mrs.	RH, p4c2, 2/7/1901	Died Monday at her home in Muscoda. She was the wife of Ellis Pond and a former resident of Readstown. She was the sister of Mrs. Perham and Mrs. Angell of Readstown.
Pond	Nina	RH, p4c2, 10/18/1900	Elmer Morley married Nina Pond last Sunday at the home of Justice Winn in Soldiers Grove. Bride and groom from Readstown.
Pool	Ed	DR, p3c5, 6/1/1871	Resided in Lansing area. Offered a reward of $40 for the return of a stolen raft of hardwood logs.
Pool	George W., Sr.	RH, p4c3, 8/23/1900	Killed himself with a rifle on Aug. 11, 1900. Left a note. He was disappointed in a love affair. Resided in the Town of Eagle.
Pool	Joel	BD, p2c2, 3/23/1883	According to the March, 17, 1883 issue of the *Richland Rustic*, Pool died yesterday. Pool was hit by a log that rolled down a hill, hit a rock and was thrown into the air. Pool was driving a wagon. Mrs. Pool also died. They are survived by a 10-year-old son. Accident took place on a bluff area near Buck Creek Mills that was being worked by N. I. James' logging hands.
Poole	Byron	BD, p2c4, 1/27/1882	Byron Poole recently married Effie Case. Bride was from Richland Co. "Uncle Freeman" gave the bride an Estey organ.
Porter	C. V., Dr.	DC, p2c1, 1/28/1888	Dr. C. V. Porter recently married Mrs. E. H. Robertson. The bride was a "lady farmer" from Viroqua.
Porter	Charles	BD, p3c1, 1/20/1882	Resided in Boydtown. Shipped the largest hog of the season from Boscobel.
Porter	H.	DC, p2c1, 12/11/1886	The 1887 officers of the Crawford County Agricultural Society were H. Porter, Fergus Mills, A. Mills, D. G. Twining and James Low.
Porter	H., Mrs.	DC, p3c3 8/27/1887	Mrs. H. Porter of De Soto left for near Manchester, NH, the place of her girlhood days, to visit an ill sister.
Porter	Hugh	DC, p2c2, 10/30/1886	Republican candidate for Wisconsin Assembly. The *Prairie du Chien Courier* stated was a chief of the Good Templars in Seneca and a prohibitionist. This was reported to be false. "Mr. P. is not a drunkard or a free whiskey man by any means but believes with the majority of people that the liquor traffic should be restrained by good and effective laws."
Porter	Hugh	DC, p2c3, 10/9/1888	Re-nominated to the Assembly to represent Crawford Co.
Porter	J. Flint	DC, p2c1, 10/29/1887	When C. B. Whiting [a native of New York] and J. C. Valentine [a native of New Jersey] first arrived in De Soto in 1856 they stayed at a barn that served as a hotel. The barn was owned by Seth Crowell. Others occupying the barn were J. Flint Porter, a son-in-law of Mr. Crowell, Henry Porter, his brother, a young man named Herman L. Morse and possibly James B. Ashley. A man named Alexander also stayed there. He made and mended shoes. Morse was sick and unemployed. Ashley was a carpenter.

Genealogical Events from Newspapers for Crawford, Vernon and Grant Counties, Wisconsin, 1870-1901

LAST NAME	FIRST NAME	NEWSPAPER, PAGE/COLUMN MONTH/DAY/YEAR	GENEALOGICAL DATA
Porter	Lillian, Miss	DC, p3c2, 12/17/1887	Departed De Soto to join her mother in Manchester, NH. The mother was caring for a sick sister.
Porter	Lillian, Miss	DC, p3c3, 3/10/1888	Miss Lillian Porter of De Soto area recently married a gentleman in the East.
Porter	Pricilla, Mrs.	DC, p3c3, 12/3/1887	Plans to move from Seneca to the home of her daughter, Mrs. Bennett of Mt. Sterling. Mr. Bennett recently died after a fall from the cars [railroad cars].
Posey	Joe	RH, p5c2, 7/22/1897	Worked on the Gays Mills section of the KV & N Railroad. His foot was mashed by a rail. It was partly amputated.
Post	Alvin	RH, p5c5, 7/15/1897	Departed Otter Vale for La Crosse to work as a photographer.
Postle	Mr.	BD, p3c3, 4/5/1878	Bought Mr. Hale's building in Muscoda. Hale planned to leave for Dakota. P. A. Dagget will occupy the building.
Potter	E. M.	RH, p4c2, 9/26/1901	Departed Readstown for Lancaster to appear as a witness at a lawsuit.
Potter	E. M.	RH, p4c1, 10/17/1901	Walter Potter of Dell and Frank Heart of Marshfield visited with E. M. Potter in Readstown.
Potter	Lena	BD, p3c2, 6/7/1878	Henry W. Young married Lena Potter on June 3, 1878 at the home of the bride's mother. Bride from Boscobel. Groom from Cresco, IA. They departed for a home in Iowa. The Rev. G. W. Nuzum officiated.
Potts	S. A., Rev.	BD, p3c2, 1/23/1880	Died Thursday in Woodman. Aged 60 years. Buried in Boscobel. Lived in Woodman for last 13 or 14 years. Survived by 5 daughters and 1 son. One daughter, who taught school, was unable to get to Boscobel in time for burial.
Powell	John	BD, p3c4, 5/18/1877	Died last Monday at his home near Mazomanie. He was a laborer on the wood train. Survived by wife and 3 children.
Powers	S. D.	DR, p3c2, 12/29/1870	Dr. E. B. Houghton, J. Osgood, S. D. Powers and C. B. Worth, were among the "First Families" who settled in De Soto in 1854. In 1870, C. B. Worth was the only pioneer from this group still in De Soto.
Powers	Theodore	DC, p2c1, 2/3/1888	Established a tin-ware store in De Soto in 1857.
Prater		BD, p3c1, 8/18/1882	A child of Mr. and Mrs. Prater of Boscobel was drowned Tuesday in a tub of water while mother had stepped away.
Pratt	Charles	DC, p3c4, 5/28/1887	Died in the La Crosse jail last week while suffering from "delirum tremens." He had charge of a water tank engine in De Soto until a short time ago. Served in Co. D. 24th Regt. WI Vol.
Pratt	H. A.	BD, p2c1, 10/30/1883	The Boscobel Common Council authorized the payment of $1 to H. A. Pratt, pauper.
Preiner	Silas	DC, p3c2, 7/2/1887	Quite his job on the Viroqua stage route. His father runs the La Crosse stage route in Coon Valley. Elias Lund has the Purdy route.
Prentice	George	DC, p3c3, 3/19/1887	Sold groceries in Ontario, WI.
Prentis	L. D.	DC, p4c1, 5/3/1889	Pension approved for military service. Resided in Ontario.
Prescott	J. R.	DR, p3c1, 9/7/1871	Lived in Retreat. Advertised the sale of grapes at six cents a pound.
Prescott	J. R.	DR, p3c2, 9/21/1871	Planned to open a cabinet shop and furniture store in Retreat.
Prestgard	Christena	RH, p4c1, 10/3/1901	Employed by Ole Fortney at Oak Ridge. Doing housework.
Preston	B. W., Dr.	BD, p3c5, 8/3/1877	Left Muscoda for his father's funeral in Pennsylvania.
Price	A. L.	DC, p3c3, 3/19/1887	Planned to relocate from the De Soto area to California in a few days.
Price	A. L.	DC, p3c2, 7/24/1886	Hired by John Devlin to help in the meat market in De Soto.
Price & Brewer	Drs.	BD, p2c6, 1/5/1877	Advertised in the newspaper their desire to see patients in Boscobel, Richland Center and Mazomanie.
Prince	S. C.	DC, p3c4, 8/21/1886	Ill health forced the closure of his store in Lynxville.
Prince	S. P.	DC, p3c3, 9/18/1886	Has a contract to dam Harper Channel near Lynxville.
Prindle	Charles	DC, p2c3, 5/1/1888	The Charles Prindle family are new residents of Genoa. They moved into the house vacated by Frank Riley.

Genealogical Events from Newspapers for Crawford, Vernon and Grant Counties, Wisconsin, 1870-1901

LAST NAME	FIRST NAME	NEWSPAPER, PAGE/COLUMN MONTH/DAY/YEAR	GENEALOGICAL DATA
Pritchard	Stella	BD, p2c5, 2/3/1882	Died last week at the residence of T. Savage. She was a resident of Bellmont, IA and a summer student at St. Mary's Institute in Prairie du Chien.
Privott	Sam	BD, p3c3, 8/14/1883	Lived in Orion. Called the "best river pilot that ever dipped an oar in the creek".
Proctor	Alfred	DR, p3c3, 12/14/1871	Resided in De Soto. Offered to sell dry white oak posts.
Proctor	James	DC, p3c3, 10/16/1888	Returned to De Soto after a 2-year stay in western Montana.
Proctor	Olive D.	DC, p2c3, 2/12/1887	Olive D. Proctor married James N. Boise on Feb. 6, 1887. Bride from Wheatland. Groom from La Crosse. The Rev. T. Crouch performed the ceremony in Wheatland.
Proudfit	Anna	BD, p3c1, 10/22/1880	Departed Boscobel for Friend, NB. Had interim stop at Blanchard, IA. Her sister, Libbie, went directly to Friend.
Proudfit	George	BD, p3c2, 10/23/1883	George Proudfit married Emma L. Mitchell on Oct. 17, 1883 at the residence of the bride's parents in Seward Co, NB. The Rev. S. G. Lamb officiated. Bride was the daughter of J. B. Mitchell, a druggist.
Proudfit	George	BD, p3c2, 8/2/1878	Visited his mother and sisters in Boscobel and then returned to his home in Nebraska.
Proudfit	Will	BD, p3c1, 2/6/1880	Resident of Friend, NB. Arrived in Boscobel to visit family and friends.
Provin	Mattic	BD, p3c4, 12/28/1877	John Gray married Mattic Provin on Tuesday at the Methodist Episcopal parsonage. Groom from Boscobel. Bride from Belle Center. The Rev. G. W. Nuzum officiated.
Provis	Alex	BD, p3c1, 6/27/1879	Alex Provis married Kate Kirby last Thursday in Spring Green. Bride from Spring Green. Groom was a lawyer in Boscobel.
Puckett	J. B.	BD, p3c1, 12/11/1883	Resided in Excelsior. Received three thoroughbred draft horses [a Clydsdale and 2 Normans] from the railroad cars at Boscobel. The horses cost him $4500.
Puckett	L. B.	BD, p3c3, 12/9/1881	Puckett, of Des Moines, IA, arrived in Boscobel with a beautiful Norman horse worth $800. Taken to his brother's home in Excelsior.
Pugh	A. J.	RH, p4c4, 4/27/1899	Resided in De Soto. As soon as the water went down, he planned to move on the island where his family has taken a homestead. They will remain there for the summer.
Pugh	J. C.	RH, p5c4, 11/3/1898	Worked as a stockman in Sugar Grove.
Pugh	J. C.	RH, p5c3, 12/1/1898	Resided in Sugar Grove. Pugh "has been engaged in the buying and selling of stock for the past 6 years and is a hustler . . ."
Pugh	Sarah	RH, p4c3, 1/13/1898	Left De Soto for a teaching position at Genoa.
Pugh	Sarah	RH, p4c3, 6/16/1898	Left De Soto for Readstown to work with Miss Nellie Kellogg in the millinery trade.
Pulham	boy	DR, p3c3, 1/12/1871	The 4-year-old son of William and Martha A. Pulham died on Jan. 2, 1871 of croup in the Asbury neighborhood [De Soto?].
Pulley	Rev.	DC, p3c4, 2/18/1888	Scheduled to preach at the Christian Church in Retreat. He was a "colored gentleman."
Pullman	Mrs.	DC, p2c2, 11/27/1886	Died Nov. 18, 1886 at De Soto at the age of about 70. She was the mother of Mrs. N. E. French.
Pulmann	Charles	BD, p3c1, 12/18/1883	Charles Pulmann married Anna Heller on Dec. 13, 1883 at the residence of the bride's parents in Boscobel. Rev. Rami officiated.
Puls	C.	DC, p3c2, 3/19/1887	Planned to relocate from West Prairie to Palouse Junction, Washington.
Puls	Chris	DC, p3c2, 6/11/1887	Former resident of the De Soto area. Recently purchased a ranch in Sprague, Washington Territory.
Pulver	Ben and wife	DC, p3c3, 12/31/1887	Resided in Haldane, IL. Visited Mr. Pulver's sister, Mrs. John M. White of De Soto. Ben used to live in Bad Axe City.
Pulver	Claud	DC, p2c1, 4/30/1887	Departed Genoa for La Crosse. Planned to run down a raft of logs for the coal yard.
Pulver	Claude	DC, p2c2, 10/2/1888	Died Sept 7, 1888. He was hit by lightning. Lived in Genoa. He was son-in-law of Mr. and Mrs. Monti of Genoa. Survived by wife, daughter, parents, 2 brothers and 1 sister.
Pulver	Claude, Mr. and Mrs.	DC, p3c2, 9/11/1888	Caught in a storm while fishing on an island across from De Soto. Mr. Pulver struck by lightning and killed at noon on Friday. Resided in Genoa.
Pulver	Frank	DC, p3c2, 12/11/1886	Taught school at Sunnyside.
Pulver	Frank H.	DC, p3c2, 9/18/1888	Frank H. Pulver married Josie B. White on Sept. 4, 1888 at the home of Rev. J. K. Eckman in Osborne, KS. Bride from Bloomington.

Genealogical Events from Newspapers for Crawford, Vernon and Grant Counties, Wisconsin, 1870-1901

LAST NAME	FIRST NAME	NEWSPAPER, PAGE/COLUMN MONTH/DAY/YEAR	GENEALOGICAL DATA
Pulver	John	DR, p3c4, 5/11/1871	Resided in De Soto. While working at Hemenway Wood & Co.'s mill in Lansing, he backed into a circular saw. Received a 4" x 6" deep cut in his rear end.
Pulver	Joseph	DC, p3c2, 11/12/1887	Joseph Pulver married Mrs. Paulina Chase on Nov. 2, 1887 in Viroqua.
Pulver	Nono, Mrs.	DC, p3c3, 12/18/1886	Shipped her household goods from Genoa to Drywood, WI.
Punnell	Mr.	DR, p3c3, 4/20/1871	Worked as a painter in Lansing. Beaten by the Trayer brothers, his wife's brothers, as retribution for on-going wife beating.
Putman	J.	DC, p1c6, 10/8/1887	Resided in Boscobel. Qualified for a pension for military service.
Quackenbush	G., Mr.	DC, p3c3, 12/17/1887	Visited his sister, Mrs. Hart [per Ontario news column].
Quamme	Tosten O.	DR, p2c3, 9/21/1871	Resided in Towerville. Published a notice that two of his cows had wondered off.
Quincy	Olive E.	BD, p3c2, 1/3/1879	Thomas Wesley McReynolds married Olive E. Quincy Dec. 26, 1878 at the home of the bride's parents. Rev. Z. S. Hurd of Boscobel officiated.
Quincy	S. A.	BD, p3c2, 5/2/1879	Pioneer in Grant Co. Came here 33 years ago from Vermont. The family has lived near Werley Station for the last 23 years. Departed Wednesday for Ashland, NB.
Quinn	girl	BD, p3c3, 10/25/1878	A daughter was born to Larry Quinn [depot watchman] of Prairie du Chien on Sunday morning.
Quinn	Josephine, Mrs.	DC, p3c4, 7/2/1887	E. V. Wernick married Mrs. Josephine Quinn on June 16, 1887. Groom was the principal of Hillsboro High School.
Quinnett	Dan	BD, p3c2, 7/20/1883	Dan Quinnett and John Hanks were arrested for stealing a horse from George Christ in Marietta.
Rabbitt	E. W.	RH, p4c4, 2/9/1899	Died Wednesday last week at the age of 78. His sons, George of Oaio [Ohio?] and Benjamin of Wonewoc arrived in time to see him before he died. Jim Rabbitt, a brother, lived in Kickapoo.
Rabbitt	Jim	RH, p5c4, 1/19/1899	Jim Rabbitt, Cora Rabbitt, Eva Downey and Gusta Benn were Sunday School teachers in Kickapoo.
Rabbitt	Lemuel	RH, p5c5, 7/15/1897	Lemuel Rabbitt married Carrie Melva Sommars at the home of the bride's sister, Mrs. Fred Lepley, per Viola news column. Rev. Hitchcock of West Salem officiated.
Rabbitt	Sarah, Mrs.	RH, p5c4, 10/27/1898	Died in Kickapoo on Oct. 18, 1898. She was born Sarah Hibbard on Aug. 17, 1836 in Ohio. Married Horace Devol on Jan. 16, 1855. He died July 1, 1878. Married Edwin Rabbitt on August 20, 1882. Joined the Baptist Church in Richland Center in 1875. Survived by husband, 2 brothers, 2 sisters and 4 grandchildren. Buried in Kickapoo Cemetery.
Rabbitt	Will	RH, p5c3, 5/5/1898	Resided in Bloomingdale. Visited his mother, Mrs. Dave Orrison of Readstown.
Rae	Carrie	BD, p3c2, 8/29/1879	Will Stillwell married Carrie Rae on Tuesday evening at the residence of the bride's father. They took a train for Rushford, MN after the wedding. The Rev. John Allison officiated.
Rae	Flora, Miss	BD, p3c2, 7/30/1880	Resided in Boscobel. Visited her sister, Mrs. Lizzie Mankey of Village Creek, IA.
Rae	Peter	BD, p3c2, 5/18/1883	Left Boscobel area for a new home in Aitkin, MN.
Rae	William	BD, p3c3, 4/27/1877	Committed suicide on April 21, 1877. He was about 59 years old. His wife died 2 years ago. He was very despondant. At one time he owned a farm near Palmyra, WI. For the last 18 months he stayed with George Kendall in Boscobel. Mrs. Kendall was Rae's sister.
Randall	Belle	RH, p4c1, 12/28/1899	Len McCarty married Belle Randall on Dec. 19, 1899. Groom from Soldiers Grove. Bride from Sugar Grove.
Randall	Bessie	RH, p5c3, 7/8/1897	Milton Buroker married Bessie Randall last Thursday at the home of Dr. Randall, the bride's parents. Bride and groom from Sugar Grove.
Randall	Frank	RH, p5c2, 11/11/1897	Entered nursing school in Battle Creek, MI.
Randall	Gertie G.	RH, p5c3, 1/3/1901	Herman Henthorne married Gertie G. Randall on New Year's Day, per Sugar Grove news column.
Randall	J.	RH, p5c2, 7/15/1897	Repaired watches in Readstown.
Randall	J., Mrs.	RH, p4c1, 11/22/1900	Suffered with typhoid fever at her home in Readstown.
Randall	Joseph	RH, p4c4, 3/29/1900	Advertised his services as a contractor and builder in Readstown.
Randall	Joseph	RH, p4c3, 4/25/1901	Died Wednesday evening in Readstown. He kept a small jewelry store in southtown. Buried in Readstown Cemetery by his wife who died a few months ago.

Genealogical Events from Newspapers for Crawford, Vernon and Grant Counties, Wisconsin, 1870-1901

LAST NAME	FIRST NAME	NEWSPAPER, PAGE/COLUMN MONTH/DAY/YEAR	GENEALOGICAL DATA
Randall	Joseph	RH, p5c4, 7/25/1901	Probate notice was published regarding the estate of Joseph Randall, late of Readstown. Herman Erickson applied to administer the estate.
Randall	Joseph, Mrs.	RH, p4c2, 1/10/1901	Died on Jan. 5, 1901 in Readstown. Funeral was held at the Methodist Episcopal Church. Buried in Readstown Cemetery.
Randall	Randolf	RH, p6c3, 5/23/1901	Randolf Randall married Alice Moses on Saturday. Groom from Trout Creek. Bride from Sugar Grove. Cannons and cowbells were used during their charivari.
Randall	Walter	DC, p3c4, 8/14/1888	Former citizen of Genoa. His body was brought back from Milwaukee on August 9th for burial in Bergen.
Rannetsberger	Bernhart	DC, p3c2, 8/14/1888	Nina Hoyt married Bernhart Rannetsberger on Aug. 5, 1888. Bride was the daughter of Sen. J. W. Hoyt of Chaseburg.
Ranney	Flora	BD, p3c1, 3/28/1879	Joseph Richards married Flora Ranney on Mar. 18, 1879 at the residence of the bride's father. Bride from Wauzeka. Groom from Cresco, IA. The Rev. William Stoddart officiated.
Ranney & Wilharbor		BD, p3c4, 9/14/1877	Operated hotels in Wauzeka.
Ransom	Leonard	BD, p3c3, 9/13/1878	Ranson's 10-year-old daughter was raped by a tramp. The tramp was arrested, according to J. A. Walsh, J.P. of Mt. Hope. Ransom lived in Mt. Hope.
Rastall	Benjamin	RH, p5c2, 11/3/1898	Operated a plant nursery 2 miles south of Viola.
Ray	Rosa V.	BD, p3c2, 7/7/1882	Died June 23, 1882 in Marrietta. Aged 19 years, 10 months, 22 days. She was the wife or S. E. Ray. Her mother died Sept. 4, 1881 and sister died Dec. 17, 1882. Her child died April 26, 1882.
Readstown		RH, p5c2, 1/20/1898	On Jan. 10,.1898 a court for the Independent Foresters was created in Readstown. The officers were C. W. Reeve, J. Fish, C. Carter, G. A. Ewers, W. Jones, L. N. Wood, C. H. Davenport, W. C. T. Adams, F. H. Rogers, W. C. Rosson, A. Glass, H. B. Andrews and M. Andrews. H. J. Wamburg and Chas. Moore were the trustees.
Readstown		RH, p5c3, 1/20/1898	Officers and teachers of the Sunday School [at a Readstown church] for this year are R. McCracken, Mrs. Emma Dyer, Leota Rogers, Mrs. F. L. Perham, Bessie Cowden [organist], W. C. T. Adams, Lilly Patterson, and Minnie Aikans.
Readstown		RH, p4c1, 7/13/1899	Three years ago, when the railroad came through, Readstown was occupied by 150 people. Now there are 400 people in the town.
Readstown		RH, p4c1, 8/31/1899	The Readstown Village officers were: President, J. M. Craigo; Trustees, William Crook, L. D. Kellogg, A. C. Helmund, Jerome Fish, W. H. Maiben, J. T. Dregne; Village Clerk, S. S. Thompson; Treasurer, G. W. Henika; Assessor, W. C. Craigo; Supervisior, Frank Henika; Street Commissioner, M. McDowell; and Marshall, William Johnstone.
Readstown		RH, p4c3, 11/11/1897	Readstown experienced a building boom in the last 13 months: homes were built for Louis Kellogg, M. McDowell, J. Randall, W. S. Hurlbut, David Orrison, David Orrison, Holly Pond, Finley Dyer, Ed. Van Winter, Jake Chitwood, Tom Davenport, I. Vernon, Lee Tate, Ed Kellogg; O. C. Hellmund a model meat market; J. Peterson & Son a hardware store; Wm. Crooks a general store; J. T. & J. S. Dregne a general store; Dr. Goyer a variety store; The Improvement Co. a large double store; Herman Davenport a dwelling and tinshop; Wm. Dearman a temperance saloon; Gladney Ewers a store, restaurant, and will erect a dwelling this fall; G. Middleton a stone blacksmith shop; H. J. Wamberg a hotel; Henry Maiben a store and Wm Crooks a warehouse. J. M. Craigo & Son erected a gristmill. The KV & N Railroad built a new depot. Shortly before this time residences were built for Jerome Fish, A. C. Hellmund and Wm. Johnstone.
Readstown Ball Team		RH, p4c2, 9/5/1901	The Readstown ball team was reorganized under the management of Martin Howe. The players were Elbert Wilkinson, W. B. Van Winter, Guy Fisher, Julius Sime, Elmer McDowell, Elmo Hale, Dick Henthorn, Ole Anderson, Ernest Hebard and Joe Dull.
Readstown Band		RH, p5c5, 8/12/1897	Readstown organized a band comprised of: Henry Maiben, B flat cornet; Willie Ward, B flat cornet; Earl Hutchison, B flat cornet; W. C. T. Adams, E flat alto; Walter Hutchison, E flat alto; Frank Randall, E flat alto; Frank Salmon, tenor; Finley Dyer, tenor; Jake Chitwood, baritone; Herman Davenport, tuba; Fred Goyer, snare drum; and Walter Van Winter, base drum.
Readstown School Board		RH, p5c2, 7/8/1897	The following served on the Readstown School Board: J. M. Craigo, Director [replaced N. D. Hale]; Ben Salmon, Treasurer [replaced Wm. Hutchison who moved to Viroqua]; and C. H. Carter, clerk [replaced J. E. Silbaugh who moved to Viroqua].
Readstown Teachers		RH, p5c2, 2/15/1900	The teaching staff in Readstown were: Minnie Tulley, Bessie Cowden, Elma Wilson, Millie Hetland, Amy Buxton, Celia Tollefson, Effie Rogers, Ina Eastman, Edna Henry, Ida Wettie, Jessie Brott and Helen Gott.
Readstown Town Board		RH, p7c1, 7/1/1897	The Readstown Town Board consisted of: Louis Thompson, Chairman; Ben Adams, Supervisor; Briggs Sutherland, Supervisor; Clarence Carter, Clerk; Morley Andrews, Treasurer; Aaron Glass, Assessor; C. W. Reeves, Justice.

Genealogical Events from Newspapers for Crawford, Vernon and Grant Counties, Wisconsin, 1870-1901

LAST NAME	FIRST NAME	NEWSPAPER, PAGE/COLUMN MONTH/DAY/YEAR	GENEALOGICAL DATA
Readtown I.O.G.T. Officers		RH, p5c4, 11/25/1897	The officers of the Readtown I.O.G.T.[Good Templars] are J. O'Leary, Helen Carter, Nona Hale, W. Babcock, Helen Perham, Minnie Crook, James O'Leary, W. Van Winters, Mabel Hurlbut and Leota Rogers.
Redmain	Mathew	BD, p3c1, 4/29/1881	Died Tuesday evening at Lenahan's hotel. Aged 62 years. Not relatives in this country.
Redmayne	Mathew	BD, p3c3, 4/29/1881	Resided in Town of Scott, Crawford Co. Died April 26, 1881 in Boscobel from paralysis. A friend, C. Shuttleworth, brought him to Boscobel for better care as he was a bachelor. Born in Yorkshire, England. Moved to Wisconsin in 1857. Resided in Crawford Co. about 20 years. Left his 120-acre farm to a brother in England. Shuttleworth was given power of attorney.
Reed	David	BD, p3c2, 9/27/1878	Age 13. Taken to the Reform School in Waukesha.
Reed	Elizabeth, Mrs.	RH, p5c2, 11/18/1897	Departed Readstown for a new home in California. Joined in Sparta by her daughters, Mattie and Edna.
Reed	George and Sarah, Mr. and Mrs.	BD, p3c3, 8/29/1879	Arrested for operating a whorehouse in Boscobel. Mary Evans was arrested on the same charge. They were sent to jail in Lancaster.
Reed	James	BD, p3c1, 2/10/1882	James Reed and Ed. Honstain were given a contract to build the Blue River Bridge.
Reed	Lincoln	DC, p2c2, 7/16/1887	Dora Frazier married Lincoln Reed on July 4, 1887. Bride and groom resided in Chaseburgh. The Rev. E. Trimin [Trumin?] officiated.
Reed	Rollin	BD, p3c3, 8/9/1878	Age 22. Dove into shallow water near the old Soldiers Grove mill on the west Kickapoo on July 14, 1878. It may cost him his life.
Reed	Wallace W.	BD, p2c2, 8/28/1883	Charles A Blanchard, Guardian, published an announcement that he had applied to settle the estate of Wallace W. Reed, an insane person.
Reep	Sever	DC, p2c2, 5/7/1887	Sever Reep and family departed Genoa for Dakota.
Reese	P.	DC, p2c2, 4/9/1887	P. Reese recently married Carrie Tippitts. Groom from Lansing, IA. Bride from Victory.
Reeve	C. M.	RH, p5c3, 9/30/1897	Replaced Thomas Flanagan as postmaster in Readstown.
Reeve	C. W.	RH, p2c1, 7/1/1897	Advertised services as a Notary Public Justice and collection agent in Readstown.
Reeve	C. W.	RH, p4c3, 3/2/1899	C. W. Reeve, C. H. Davenport, Helen Perham, Elva Adams, Grace Wilson, C. H. Carter, and Minnie Aikins were selected as officers of the Epsworth League in Readstown. The League was instituted by Rev. Frank Bell of the Methodist Episcopal Church.
Reeve	C. W.	RH, p4c2, 3/14/1901	Postmaster in Readstown. Entertained his brother, Eugene of Ironton, WI and his sister, Mrs. Martha Allen of Watertown, SD, whom he has not seen for 10 years. Reeve's was selling telephone service for the Readstown Telephone Company and "making more money than ever before."
Reeve	C. W., Mrs.	RH, p5c2, 9/15/1898	Left Readstown to visit her sister, Mrs. Ed. Bender of Bender Ridge.
Register of Deeds		BD, p3c3, 1/13/1882	The Grant County Register of Deeds reported that only half of all marriages in the county were officially recorded.
Register of Deeds		BD, p3c2, 3/9/1883	Informed a newspaper reporter that there was a bushel of old papers in the Richland County Register of Deeds office consisting of original deeds, mortgages, patents and other valuable documents that have been accumulating since 1852. These documents had been sent in by mail to be recorded; however, the proper fees did not accompany the documents. Consequently, they have not been recorded.
Reichel	Daniel	BD, p3c4, 12/23/1881	Died Dec. 16, 1881. Aged 15 years and 9 months. Funeral held at the Boscobel Methodist Episcopal Church.
Reichman	Henry	BD, p3c1, 4/14/1882	Henry Reichman married Julia Bower in Boscobel on April 6, 1882. Groom from Wauzeka. Bride was the daughter of George Bower of Marietta. Justice of the Peace Jacob McLaughlin officiated.
Reid	Stuart E.	BD, p3c2, 10/3/1879	Stuart E. Reid married Deett Barton on Sept. 25, 1879. Bride and groom from Hickory Grove. T. J. Jones, Esquire officiated at the ceremony in Hickory Grove.
Reid	W. W.	BD, p3c4, 12/13/1878	Lost an arm from an accident on the Jacob Baumgartner farm where he was threshing clover.
Reid	W. W.	BD, p3c1, 8/1/1879	Taken from Hickory Grove to the Asylum in Madison for treatment. Became demented after losing an arm last fall.
Reid	Wallace W.	BD, p2c4, 10/7/1881	A notice was published that the guardian of Wallace W. Reid was selling Reid's real estate in Hickory Grove. Reid was an insane person.

Genealogical Events from Newspapers for Crawford, Vernon and Grant Counties, Wisconsin, 1870-1901

LAST NAME	FIRST NAME	NEWSPAPER, PAGE/COLUMN MONTH/DAY/YEAR	GENEALOGICAL DATA
Reilley	Frank	RH, p4c2, 1/20/1898	Lived in the Town of Lima near Platteville. Committed suicide by hanging himself last Saturday.
Reinhold	Charles	BD, p2c1, 6/18/1880	Charles Reinhold's 2-year-old son was badly scalded after upsetting a kettle of hot lard at his home in Prairie du Chien.
Reisel	Henry	BD, p2c4, 4/19/1878	Katharina Schmahlenberger died Aug. 21, 1877. Died intestate. Henry Reisel petitioned to administer estate. Edward and Gustave Meyer, of Grant Co., were creditors of the estate.
Reiter	C. D.	DC, p3c3, 6/26/1886	Sold his restaurant in De Soto to Oliver Tuttle.
Reiter	C. E.	DC, p4c3, 5/17/1889	Accepted a traveling sales position for a wholesale liquor house.
Reiter	C. F.	DC, p2c2, 5/14/1887	The De Soto Village Board approved licenses to C. F. Reiter and John McCormick to sell liquor at their saloons. The license bond of George Alcorn was approved.
Reiter	Charles	DC, p3c5, 6/12/1886	Sold wine, liquors, beer and cigars at a pool hall in De Soto.
Reiter	Charles	DC, p3c2, 12/3/1887	Traded his saloon for the William Bates farm.
Reiter	Charles E.	DR, p3c2, 1/4/1872	Charles E. Reiter married Cora A. Green on Jan. 1, 1872 at the residence of William Green in the Town of Freeman. Bride and groom were from the Town of Freeman. The Rev. D. L. Hubbard officiated.
Reiter	Charley	DC, p3c6, 6/12/1886	Proprietor of the Main Street Restaurant in De Soto.
Reiter	Mary, Mrs.	DC, p4c2, 5/24/1889	Left De Soto for Jackson, MN to spend the summer with relatives.
Remalis	Geo. W.	BD, p2c3, 12/8/1882	He was a celebrated violinist touring with the Burnett Musical Novelty Co. in Kentucky and Ohio. Resided in Richland County.
Republican Ticket		DC, p2c1, 10/9/1888	The Vernon County Republican ticket consisted of: Marcus C. Bergh, Sheriff; John R. Casson, Co. Clerk; Peres J. Layne, Clerk of Court; John C. Johnson, Co. Treasurer; John J. McCarty, Register of Deeds; Walter S. Field, Dist. Attorney; Daniel O. Mahoney, Co. Superintendent; William H. Knower, Co. Surveyor; and Stanley Stout, Coroner.
Republican Ticket		DC, p2c1, 10/9/1888	The Crawford County Republican ticket consisted of: John Stackland, Sheriff; C. E. Alder, Co. Clerk; R. F. Haskins, Treasurer; J. A. Curran, Clerk of Courts; Jos. D. Stuart, Register of Deeds; T. B. Ward, District Attorney; A. J. McDowell, Superintendent of Schools; J. J. Hurlbut, Surveyor; and Chancy Blancher, Coroner.
Retreat School Exercises		DC, p2c2, 3/19/1887	Combined graduation exercises were held for Retreat School members Maud V. Davis, Ella Cooley and Minnie Sallander, under the supervision of Miss May Hinkst, and adjoining District 12 School members Willie Newton, John Thayer, Hiram Miner, Delmar Morton, Albert Bates and Frank Lombard, under the supervision of Miss Myra Stephens. Students read their own essays as part of the program.
Retreat W.C.T.U		DC, p2c2, 5/28/1887	The Retreat W.C.T.U. held a program May 20, 1887. Essays were read by Miss Hattie R. Lowrie, Miss Achsah Morgan and Mrs. Mary J. Jordan. The recitation was by Miss Hattie Mellen. The declamation was by Miss Alice Hinds. Mrs. S. J. Dustan read scripture.
Retreat W.C.T.U. Officers		DC, p2c2, 7/16/1887	The officers of the Retreat Women's Christian Temperance Union were Mrs. S. J. Dustin, Mrs. A. D. Bean, Mrs. M. J. Jordan, Mrs. L. A. Sterling, Miss Hattie Mellen and Miss Maud Davis.
Reynolds	D. P.	BD, p3c1, 4/4/1879	Recently died of consumption in Marietta, Crawford Co. He was 41 years old and the son of W. H. Reynolds, Esquire.
Reynolds	Winnie	DC, p3c3, 8/21/1888	Died at her home in Lansing, IA on Aug. 19, 1888.
Rhein	Anna	BD, p3c1, 9/7/1879	Died a few hours after being burned by a broken kerosene lamp. She was the wife of Charles Rhein of Wauzeka.
Rhein	John	BD, p3c3, 8/26/1881	Died Aug. 17, 1881 in Boscobel of chronic diarrhea. Born Dec. 23, 1820 in Gannon, Prussia. Moved to American in 1856 and settled in Lancaster, Grant Co. where he worked as a bricklayer. Enlisted in 12th WI Infantry. Served 3 years and reenlisted. Contracted the disease from which he died in the war. Government gave him a pension.
Rice	Anson	BD, p3c2, 7/31/1883	Fell on a pitch fork tine that pierced his lung. A great deal of clotted blood came up. He was the son of Oliver Rice who lived 3 miles south of Boscobel.
Rice	Clarissa, Mrs.	BD, p3c1, 10/30/1883	Recently died of congestion in Boscobel. She was 75 years old and had a large family of children. She was the widow of M. M. Rice.
Rice	George M.	BD, p3c3, 4/19/1878	Recently died in Boscobel. The Temple of Honor passed a resolution to recognize his memory. It was published in the newspaper.
Rice	Mame	BD, p3c3, 12/14/1877	Charles L. Kellogg married Mame Rice on Dec. 12, 1877 at the home of the bride's uncle, J. H. Sarles, in Boscobel. Planned to live in Oconomowoc. The Rev. W. M. Stoddart officiated.

Genealogical Events from Newspapers for Crawford, Vernon and Grant Counties, Wisconsin, 1870-1901

LAST NAME	FIRST NAME	NEWSPAPER, PAGE/COLUMN MONTH/DAY/YEAR	GENEALOGICAL DATA
Rice	Moors	BD, p3c2, 11/14/1879	Died Nov. 6, 1879 in Boscobel. He was born Nov. 9, 1806 in Massachusetts and moved to Wisconsin in 1854. He was a Grant Co. resident for 25 years.
Rice	Moors, Mrs. [Morris?]	BD, p3c1, 11/6/1883	Her children published a card of thanks for kindness extended to their mother.
Rice	O. A.	BD, p3c1, 4/6/1883	Rice's farmhouse located 3 miles south of Boscobel was destroyed by fire.
Rice	R. B.	BD, p2c1, 7/6/1883	Named editor and agent for the *Boscobel Dial*.
Rice	R. B., Mrs.	BD, p3c2, 3/31/1882	Lived on Fremont Street in Boscobel. Advertised the sale of homegrown houseplants.
Rice	R. B., Mrs.	BD, p3c2, 9/1/1882	Mrs. Rice and her daughter, Kittie, returned to Boscobel area after visiting relatives in Menomonie, WI.
Rice	R. H.	DC, p3c3, 6/12/1886	Planned to open a restaurant and ice cream parlor in De Soto.
Rice	R. H.	DC, p3c2, 10/9/1888	Carried the mail.
Rice	R. H.	DC, p2c2, 2/26/1889	Operated a restaurant and kept boarders by day and week at his establishment in De Soto.
Rice	Rebecca Brooks	BD, p3c2, 11/6/1883	Rebecca Brooks Rice, wife of William S. Rice, died of apoplexy at the home of her daughter, Mrs. J. H. Sarles. She was 70 years old. Born in Lundy's Lane, Canada on Dec. 25, 1813. Married W. S. Rice on Sept. 5, 1831. Two of her seven children survive, Mrs. J. H. Sarles and R. B. Rice. Her husband is an invalid.
Rice	Robert	DR, p3c2, 12/29/1870	Ran a harness shop on Houghton Street in De Soto.
Rice	W. S.	BD, p3c3, 7/16/1880	Maddie, granddaughter of Mr. and Mrs. W. S. Rice of Boscobel, visited her mother in Milwaukee.
Rice	W. S.	BD, p3c2, 7/29/1881	Suffered his third stroke Friday night at his home in Boscobel.
Rice	W. S., Mrs.	BD, p3c3, 7/1/1881	Mrs. Rice's cousin, Mrs. J. H. Merriam of Conneaut, OH, arrived for a visit in Boscobel.
Richards	Joseph	BD, p3c1, 3/28/1879	Joseph Richards married Flora Ranney on Mar. 18, 1879 at the residence of the bride's father. Bride from Wauzeka. Groom from Cresco, IA. The Rev. William Stoddart officiated.
Richardson	Hattie E.	DC, p2c2, 5/21/1887	Hattie E. Richardson married James Warren on May 16, 1887 at the residence of the bride's parents in West Prairie. Groom from Mt. Sterling. The Rev. Thomas Couch officiated.
Richardson	J. C.	BD, p3c1, 3/26/1880	Planned to close his business.
Richardson	J. C.	BD, p3c1, 11/3/1882	Resided in Boscobel. He was issued several patents for labelling machinery.
Richardson	J. C.	BD, p3c1, 11/25/1881	Resigned his position as city justice in Boscobel. Replaced by S. H. [or J. H.?] Winn.
Richardson	James	BD, p3c1, 6/9/1882	Returned to Boscobel area after an extensive eastern trip.
Richardson	Levi	BD, p3c1, 4/28/1882	Former resident of Port Andrew. Killed 3 years ago in Dodge City, KS by Frank Loving [a gambler].
Richardson	Mary Eliza	DR, p2c2, 8/24/1871	Died August 19, 1871 at the age of 10 months and 25 days in the Town of Wheatland. She was the daughter of William and Caroline L. Richardson.
Richardson	T.	DC, p3c2, 7/16/1887	Left Liberty with 3 wagons. Crossed the river at De Soto. Headed for southwestern Kansas. Elias Martin went with him.
Richmann	Delia	BD, p3c1, 8/25/1882	John Kazda married Delia Richmann on Aug. 17, 1882 in Boscobel at the Wisconsin Hotel. Bride and groom from Wauzeka. J. McLaughlin, J.P. officiated.
Richter	Nelson	BD, p2c3, 2/2/1883	Fell in a hole in the ice while crossing the Mississippi River. He was saved by Joseph Pugmyre and Thomas Willoughby.
Ricks	Charles	BD, p3c2, 3/3/1882	Appeared in Boscobel after escaping from a Madison insane asylum. He was clad in light clothing, socks and slippers.
Ricks	Charles	BD, p3c1, 4/6/1883	Ricks was returned to a Madison asylum. He suffered from hallucinations.

Genealogical Events from Newspapers for Crawford, Vernon and Grant Counties, Wisconsin, 1870-1901

LAST NAME	FIRST NAME	NEWSPAPER, PAGE/COLUMN MONTH/DAY/YEAR	GENEALOGICAL DATA
Ricks	Isaac	BD, p3c2, 5/30/1879	Mr. and Mrs. John Ricks of Boscobel entertained Mr. Rick's parents at a dinner last Thursday. Soon after eating, everyone got sick. Isaac Ricks, age 91, died Thursday. Jane Ricks, 65, died Friday. Mr. and Mrs. John Ricks moved in with Mrs. Rick's father, Mr. B. Fear, during their recuperation. They are now out of danger. They were attended to by Dr. Armstrong. Isaac Ricks may have been the only surviving soldier who took part in the Battle of Waterloo [under Wellington] when he was 28 years old. Ricks born in England in 1788. Emigrated to America in 1836 and settled in Boscobel in 1852. Fathered 14 children, 10 of whom survive him. Mrs. Jane Ricks was his second wife. He married her in England.
Ricks	James	BD, p3c1, 3/3/1882	Lived in Boscobel. Ribs were kicked and broken by a horse while cleaning horses' legs.
Ricks	Minerva	BD, p3c1, 7/16/1880	William Hammond of Grant Co. recently married Minerva Ricks of Grant Co. at the residence of John Ricks in Boscobel. The Rev. W. W. Hurd officiated.
Rieger	Eddie	RH, p5c2, 7/15/1897	Bitten by a rattlesnake. Received treatment from Dr. Perrin. He was expected to live. He was the 12-year-old son of Mike Rieger and lived 6 miles NE of Readstown.
Rieter	Martin	DR, p3c2, 10/26/1871	Planned to hold a public sale of live stock and farm implements in the De Soto area.
Rieth & Boechk		DR, p2c6, 12/15/1870	Proprietors of the Lansing Foundary and Machine Shop.
Riley	Ella	DC, p3c4, 11/27/1886	Ben Gussetti recently married Ella Riley per the Genoa news column.
Riley	Frank, Mrs.	DC, p2c3, 5/1/1888	Returned to Lansing after visiting her ill mother, Mrs. Laylan in Genoa.
Riley	H.	RH, p4c4, 2/23/1899	Sold meat market in De Soto to Harry Gibbs.
Riley	John	DC, p2c1, 6/18/1887	Lived in the western part of the Town of Franklin. Had a mine of crystalized quartz-amethysts and garnets. Found in geodes.
Riley	Margaret	DR, p3c1, 9/7/1871	Hiram Caswell married Margaret Riley on Aug. 26, 1871. Bride and groom were from Genoa. Thomas D. Wallar, Esq. officiated.
Rindlaub	M. P.	BD, p3c2, 5/28/1880	Appointed to be a census enumerator in Platteville, Grant Co.
Ringinbaugh	boy	RH, p4c3, 5/16/1901	A son was born on May 13, 1901 to Henry Ringinbaugh of De Soto.
Ringinbaugh	Mammie	RH, p4c3, 5/2/1901	Resided in De Soto. Swallowed a pin a few days ago. She coughed it up and drew it into her lungs. Taken to La Crosse for an operation to remove it. She was in critical condition.
Ripley	A. C.	DR, p3c2, 7/20/1871	Planned to reopen the Mt. Sterling Academy. He was from Ohio.
Rippe	Henry, Mrs.	DC, p2c3, 5/29/1888	Resided in New Albin. Visited her sister, Mrs. Carrey [Cary?] of Genoa.
Risen	T. D.	RH, p5c4, 10/20/1898	T. D. Risen married Addie Hocking on Oct. 16, 1898 at the residence of, and by, George Wise, Justice of the Peace. Bride and groom from Mound Park.
Ritchie	Wallace	BD, p2c4, 11/26/1880	Grant County paid him a bounty for scalps turned into the county.
Ritter	Augusta	DR, p3c4, 2/9/1871	Fred Selle married Augusta Ritter on Feb. 4, 1871 in De Soto. Bride and groom were from Lansing. J. H. Hinds, J.P., officiated.
Ritter & Hubbell		BD, p2c4, 10/22/1880	Firm organized in Woodman in 1865. Moved the business to Boscobel 5 years ago. "Shelf and heavy hardware, farm machinery of every description, extras and repairs, tools, cutlery, builders and carriage-makers' hardware, cook and heating stoves, tin, sheet-iron and copperware, wooden ware, barb wire, etc. make up a stock ..."
Ritter & Hubbell		BD, p2c7, 1/5/1877	Sold hardware in Boscobel.
Rix	H. R.	DC, p3c2, 1/8/1889	Martha Rutter married H. T. Rix on Dec. 22, 1888 at the home of the bride's parents in the Town of Freeman. Bride taught school in Crawford Co. and in Nebraska. Planned to live in Lyons, NB.
Roach	Miles, Mrs.	DC, p3c4, 10/9/1888	From Winona, MN. Visited mother, Mrs. Gillett of Genoa.
Roach & Perkins		BD, p3c1, 5/7/1880	Messrs. Roach and Perkin's have finished a new building in Fennimore for their hardware and stove store.
Robb	Jennie, Miss	DC, p2c1, 9/18/1887	Resided in Gays Mills. Displayed several of her original oil paintings at the Crawford Co. Fair.
Roberg	A. S.	DC, p2c2, 5/28/1887	Worked as a shoemaker in Ferryville. [Robery?]

Genealogical Events from Newspapers for Crawford, Vernon and Grant Counties, Wisconsin, 1870-1901

LAST NAME	FIRST NAME	NEWSPAPER, PAGE/COLUMN MONTH/DAY/YEAR	GENEALOGICAL DATA
Roberts		BD, p2c4, 4/7/1882	The 60 year old father of George Roberts died in the woods after a tree fell on him near his home in the Town of Willow, Richland Co.
Roberts	C. A.	DC, p3c2, 2/25/1888	Received pension for military service. Resided in Viroqua.
Roberts	C. A., Mrs.	DC, p2c3 8/6/1887	Arrived in the Cooley Valley to visit her parents, Mr. and Mrs. S. T. Arnold. She resided in Viroqua.
Roberts	H. B., Mrs.	DC, p2c2, 7/3/1886	Arrived in the Cooley Valley from Organ, IL to visit her brother, W. F. Rose.
Robertson	E. H., Mrs.	DC, p2c1, 1/28/1888	Dr. C. V. Porter recently married Mrs. E. H. Robertson. The bride was a "lady farmer" from Viroqua.
Robertson	E. S., Mrs.	DC, p3c3, 7/16/1887	Departed Viroqua for a visit in New Bedford, MA, her old home. "This will furnish her much needed rest from the active duties of the farm and dairy she so well manages."
Robertson	Mrs.	DC, p3c3, 2/11/1888	Died Jan. 30, 1888 at West Prairie at the age of 86. She was the mother of Mrs. Martin Loftus.
Robertson	W. T.	DC, p1c1, 7/12/1889	W. T. Robertson married Minnie E. Adams on June 30, 1889. Bride and groom from Ferryville. The Rev. C. B. Gordon of Freeman officiated.
Robery	A. S.	DC, p1c3, 4/12/1889	Raised a house and built a cellar and stone foundation in Ferryville.
Robins	H.	RH, p4c2, 5/25/1899	Wife died last year. Now lives with son in Hebron, WI. He was 74. Visited nephew, L. D. Kellogg of Readstown.
Robinson	George	DC, p2c2, 4/2/1887	Miss Bird Thompson recently married George Robinson in Victory at the residence of Peter Wadynxkee. Bride from La Crosse. Groom from Bergen.
Robinson	girl	RH, p4c2, 10/24/1901	A daughter was recently born to Grant Robinson of the Readstown area.
Robinson	James	BD, p3c2, 9/26/1879	Sheriff Streeter took him to Waupon to serve a 1-year sentence for bigamy.
Robinson	John	BD, p3c5, 3/24/1882	First permanent settler in Fennimore. Moved in Legett's Grove, on section 35, in 1838. His daughter, Deborah, now Mrs. Peter Finegan, was the first child born in that territory.
Robinson	Mary M.	BD, p3c3, 9/20/1878	John Baker married Mary M. Robinson on Sept. 11, 1878 in Boscobel. Groom from Pleasant Hill, Richland Co. The Rev. Dr. Stoddart officiated.
Robson	Merti I.	DC, p2c3, 3/20/1888	Christian Weber married Merti I. Robson on Mar. 14, 1888 at De Soto at the residence of Willis Owens. Bride from Franklin. Groom from Sterling.
Robson	Paulina	DC, p2c3, 3/20/1888	Henry Weber married Paulina Robson on Mar. 13, 1888 at De Soto. Bride from Franklin. Groom from Sterling.
Rodolf	C. G.	BD, p3c2, 7/6/1877	Rodolf was rebuilding his flouring mill in the Town of Eagle.
Roe	Richard, Mrs.	BD, p2c2, 3/7/1879	Mrs. Richard Roe's home in Yankeetown was destroyed by fire. Fire blamed on a faulty chimney.
Roenish	C.	DC, p3c2, 1/21/1888	Kept saloon on the island opposite of Lansing. Brought before Judge Loftus for selling liquor without a license.
Roenish	Charles F.	DC, p3c4, 2/25/1888	Paid a fine for his barkeeper, Gottleib Smith. Kept bar on an island across from Lansing.
Roenish	Charles F.	DC, p3c3, 7/31/1888	Operated a blacksmith shop and later a saloon. Resided in Lansing. Taken to insane asylum.
Rogers	A. H.	BD, p2c1, 11/20/1883	A. H. Rogers married May Donaldson on Nov. 11, 1883 at the residence of the bride's parents in DeSmet, Kingsbury Co., Dakota. Groom from Dakota, but formerly from Boscobel.
Rogers	C.	DC, p2c2, 4/2/1887	Resided in Rising Sun. Daughter died March 17, 1887 in Minnesota.
Rogers	Ed, Mrs.	RH, p4c3, 5/16/1901	Granted a pension. Resided in De Soto.
Rogers	Edward, Mrs.	DC, p3c4, 7/2/1887	Resided in De Soto. Received a legacy from a relative.
Rogers	Effie	RH, p4c3, 11/23/1899	Hired to teach in Readstown. Lived in Towerville.
Rogers	Effie	RH, p4c2, 12/13/1900	Frank E. Salmon married Effie Rogers on Dec. 6, 1900 at the home of the bride's mother, Mrs. Ole Gunderson. Rev. Holm of Folsom Lutheran Church officiated.
Rogers	F. H.	RH, p4c2, 2/7/1901	An auction has been scheduled at the F. H. Rogers farm near Readstown. The farm was previously sold to R. L. Banty.
Rogers	F. H.	RH, p4c2, 2/21/1901	Moved from Readstown to Viroqua.
Rogers	Henry	DC, p3c2, 7/31/1886	Recenlty failed as a merchant in Rising Sun.

Genealogical Events from Newspapers for Crawford, Vernon and Grant Counties, Wisconsin, 1870-1901

LAST NAME	FIRST NAME	NEWSPAPER, PAGE/COLUMN MONTH/DAY/YEAR	GENEALOGICAL DATA
Rogers	Henry	DC, p3c4, 8/28/1886	His effects were recently sold at Rising Sun.
Rogers	J. H.	DR, p3c4, 12/29/1870	Served as postmaster in De Soto.
Rogers	J. H.	DC, p3c3, 8/28/1886	Roger's store safe was robbed of $200.
Rogers	James H.	DR, p4c5, 12/15/1870	Sold dry goods and groceries in De Soto.
Rogers	James H.	DC, p3c2, 7/24/1886	He was De Soto's postmaster for the last 21 years.
Rogers	James H.	DC, p3c5, 9/18/1886	"I will sell my building, known as the old post office block, corner of Main and Church Streets, on very reasonable terms. Call on or address James H. Rogers, De Soto, Wis."
Rogers	James H.	DC, p3c2, 10/8/1887	Lived in De Soto. The government doubled his pension [for military service].
Rogers	James H.	DC, p2c2, 2/19/1889	Started his merchant business in De Soto in 1866. He has been the postmaster for 21 years. Deals in general merchandise and buys wood each winter. Ships out large quanties of local butter and eggs.
Rogers	Joseph G.	BD, p3c2, 2/16/1877	Died last Sunday in the home of his son-in-law, E. S. Morse, in the Town of Lancaster. Aged 82 years. He had been married over 62 years. Resident of Grant Co. since 1842. Served in the War of 1812.
Rogers	Leota	RH, p4c2, 4/12/1900	Herman Aikins of Brookville married Leota Rogers on April 4, 1900. Groom from Brookville. Bride from Readstown. Rev. Peckham of Springville officiated.
Rogers	Lizzie	DC, p3c4, 12/4/1886	Taught school in the McCarten District per Liberty Pole news column.
Rogers	Minnie	RH, p4c4, 12/29/1898	Minnie Rogers and her brother, Charles, were among the first people this year to cross the Mississippi River by ice to go to Lansing from De Soto.
Rogers	Nettie	DC, p4c1, 5/3/1889	Recently died. She was the "little" daughter of J. H. Rogers of De Soto.
Rogers	Nettie	DC, p4c2, 5/10/1889	Died May 2, 1889 of inflamatory rheumatism at the age of 4 years, 10 months and 14 days. She was the daughter of J. H. Rogers of De Soto. Buried in De Soto Cemetery.
Rogers	Oppie	RH, p5c3, 10/13/1898	Resided in De Soto. Accepted a traveling position as a collector with A. B. Carson & Co., wholesale druggists of Chicago.
Rogers	S. W.	BD, p3c2, 4/22/1881	Recently left Boscobel for new homes in Watertown, Dakota: S. W. Rogers and wife, August Cress and, Thomas and William Heathcoat and wives. Nat. Burchard and wife and children will leave for Watertown next week.
Rogers	Salma	BD, p2c3, 2/2/1883	The Odd Fellows dedicated a new hall in Soldiers Grove. Deputy Grand Master Salma Rogers of Viola conducted the ceremonies. He was assisted by N. G., J. O. Davidson; Guide, T.N. Sime; Grand Marshall, A. Peterson; and Grand Heralds, Dr. Dinsdale, F. Whittemore, William Henry Smith, B. Moore. C. M. Poff was Grand Chaplain.
Rogers	Salma, Mr. and Mrs.	RH, p5c4, 4/27/1899	Celebrated their 50th wedding anniversary on April 22, 1899 in Viola.
Rollin	C. S.	DR, p3c1, 1/5/1871	Recently died in Decorah, IA. He was a Mason.
Rosch	John	BD, p2c4, 11/26/1880	Grant County paid him a bounty for scalps turned into the county.
Rose	Bell	BD, p3c1, 9/22/1882	Bell Rose, daughter of William and Hattie Rose, died Sept. 11, 1882 at the age of 2 months in Boscobel. She was buried in Ithaca, Richland Co. where a sibling was buried.
Rose	Carrie I.	DC, p3c3, 4/24/1888	Carrie I. Rose married Henry Conklin on April 18, 1888 at the home of the bride's father, W. R. Rose of Cooley Valley. Rev. Houghton officiated.
Rose	Carrie, Miss	DC, p3c5, 6/26/1886	Resided in Cooley Valley. Taught school in De Soto.
Rose	Cora	DC, p2c2, 6/18/1887	Cora Rose married Eli Mills on June 19, 1887. Bride of Cooley Valley, formerly of Village Creek, IA. Groom from Viroqua. The Rev. William Haughton officiated.
Rose	I. A.	BD, p3c2, 12/22/1882	I. A. Rose recently married Addie Wilton. Bride from Dane Co. Groom from Grant Co. Planned to live in Winona. Judge Jacob Story officiated.
Rose	J.	BD, p3c1, 11/05/1880	The only child of Mr. and Mrs. J. Rose of Boscobel area died on Monday.
Rose	J. M.	DC, p3c3, 11/6/1886	Lived in Chatauqua, KS. New subscriber to the *De Soto Chronicle*.
Rose	Jeremiah C.	BD, P3c2, 4/23/1880	Three-year-old son of Isaac A. and Eliza A. Rose of Boscobel. Recently drowned in the creek. Found by James Grant.

Genealogical Events from Newspapers for Crawford, Vernon and Grant Counties, Wisconsin, 1870-1901

LAST NAME	FIRST NAME	NEWSPAPER, PAGE/COLUMN MONTH/DAY/YEAR	GENEALOGICAL DATA
Rose	Mrs.	BD, p3c3, 2/22/1878	Received Boscobel city funds for boarding Mrs. Shippley.
Roselip	Gus E., Mr. and Mrs.	DC, p8c2, 6/7/1889	Started for a new farm near McGregor, IA. Mrs. Roselip was the former Kate Clawater. Recently married. Well-known in De Soto.
Roselip	Mrs.	DC, p1c1, 7/19/1889	Nee Kate Clawater. Visited parents in Liberty Pole.
Rosemeyer	Ona L.	BD, p3c2, 2/3/1882	Died Jan. 4, 1882 of consumption in Postville, Alamakee Co., IA. She was the wife of Horace Rosemeyer and daughter of Thomas Kirkpatrick. Aged 34 years. Former resident of Boscobel.
Rothe	Delphine	BD, p3c2, 9/10/1880	Charles Hinn married Delphine Rothe on September 9, 1880 in Whitewater, WI. Groom from Boscobel. Bride from Whitewater.
Rounds	Annetta J.	BD, p3c2, 5/31/1878	Theo Allen recently married Annetta J. Rounds in Gays Mills. The Rev. George Nuzum officiated.
Rounds	J. P.	BD, p3c2, 9/14/1877	Died Wednesday in Belle Center. He will be buried with Masonic honors.
Rounds	Mel	BD, p3c1, 8/18/1882	Lived near Bell Center. Lightning destroyed barn, and 8 tons of hay. Stock removed to safety.
Rounds	R. S., Mrs.	BD, p3c1, 3/3/1882	Died Feb. 18, 1882 of consumption in the Town of Haney, Crawford Co. Aged 26 years. Survived by husband and a 3-year-old child.
Roundtree	John H.	BD, p3c4, 5/26/1882	President of the Old Settlers Association for Grant Co. Announced a meeting in Lancaster.
Roundtree	John H.	BD, p2c1, 6/15/1877	John H. Roundtree, President, and William McGonical, Secretary, published a notice for a reunion of the Old Settlers Association of Grant Co.
Roundtree	Lydia, Mrs.	BD, p3c1, 7/1/1881	Died June 16, 1881. She was the wife of Major J. H. Roundtree and an early settler of Platteville, WI.
Rowe	Frank	BD, p3c1, 5/14/1880	Departed Boscobel to visit mother in Quebec.
Rowe	Frank	RH, p4c2, 9/14/1899	He was ready to move into his new saloon building in Readstown.
Rowe	Michael	BD, p2c3, 2/24/1882	Struck by a falling tree. Fractured his shinbone. Dr. Dinsdale attended him.
Rowe	Orville	BD, p3c2, 8/1/1879	Drowned in the Kickapoo River on July 20, 1879 while bathing with Henry Stuckey. Orville was the 17-year-old son of J. W. Rowe. The Rowe family lived 4 miles north of Wauzeka.
Ruby	Gabriel	DC, p2c3, 7/24/1888	Worked for Robert F. Lemon [of the De Soto area] when the Civil War started. Ruby may have been related to Lemon. Ruby volunteered when the first call was made for troops. He became a member of the 6th Wisconsin [Iron Brigade]. Ruby showed himself to be one of the "bravest of the brave." Lost a finger during second battle of Fredericksburg and was placed in the hospital. When he heard his regiment was going back to battle, he insisted on joining their ranks and died during battle.
Ruchtie	Mary Ann Catherine	BD, p3c2, 11/3/1882	Mary Ann Catherine Ruchtie married Henry Tetter on Tuesday. Bride from Boscobel. Groom from Marion. The Rev. R. Ramie officiated.
Ruck	Christian	BD, p3c5, 10/13/1882	Christian Ruck was the executor of the estate of Peter Schmahlenberger, late of Hickory Grove. He petitioned the Grant County Court to admit the will.
Ruka		BD, p3c3, 10/25/1878	The daughter of Louis Ruka and the son of F. G. Eisfelder [both of Boscobel] were taken to the deaf and dumb asylum in Milwaukee.
Ruka	boy	BD, p3c2, 11/22/1878	A son was born to Louis Ruka of Boscobel on Sunday.
Ruka	Charles	BD, p3c2, 11/11/1881	Died Nov. 4, 1881 from consumption. He was the eldest son of Lewis Ruka of Boscobel. Aged 19 years and 2 months. Funeral was held at German Lutheran Church.
Ruka	John	BD, P3c2, 4/23/1880	Sworn in as an alderman of Boscobel.
Ruka	John	BD, p3c3, 1/6/1882	John Ruka married Margaret Martin on Jan. 1, 1857. They recently celebrated their 25th wedding anniversary. Went to Muscoda for the ceremony. Traveled there by horse and cutter. Overturned 6 or 7 times in the deep snow. Father of Lou B. Ruka and 3 other children. Extensive coverage of guests and gifts at anniversary party.
Ruka	John	BD, p3c1, 9/25/1883	Ruka received a patent for an improved wagon brake.
Ruka	John and Louis	BD, p3c3, 2/27/1880	John and Louis Ruka expanded their hardware and agriculture machinery business in Boscobel 10 months ago when they decided to manufacture wagons. They purchased a building from John Benoy on Oak Street. The business has been very successful. Article describes plans for additional expansion.
Ruka	John, Mr. and Mrs.	BD, p3c1, 12/30/1881	Will celebrate their 25th wedding anniversary on Jan. 1st.

Genealogical Events from Newspapers for Crawford, Vernon and Grant Counties, Wisconsin, 1870-1901

LAST NAME	FIRST NAME	NEWSPAPER, PAGE/COLUMN MONTH/DAY/YEAR	GENEALOGICAL DATA
Ruka	Kate	BD, p3c3, 8/28/1883	Kate Ruka married Frank Steckwest [Stecknest?] on Aug. 22, 1883 at the home of the bride's parents. Bride was daughter of Louis Ruka of Boscobel. Groom was a businessman and former Grant County resident who lived in Peterson, IA. A gift list was published.
Ruka	Louis, Jr.	BD, p3c2, 5/28/1880	Ruka and his wife returned to Boscobel after an extended wedding trip in Milwaukee, Chicago, Dubuque and McGregor.
Ruka	Louis, Mr. and Mrs.	BD, p3c2, 9/17/1880	Louis Ruka married Eliza Wege on Sept. 11, 1855 in Hazelton, PA. Rev. Mr. Koenig officiated. Started west for Boscobel in Dec. 1855. Celebrated their 25th wedding anniversary. Guest list was published.
Ruka	Louis, Sr.	BD, p3c4, 2/10/1882	Returned to Boscobel after visiting western Iowa. While there he saw Mr. [a merchant] and Mrs. A. A. Funk [Ruka's daughter] of Peterson, Clay Co., IA; O. R. Olmstead of Cherokee who ran a boot and shoe business; Olmstead's son, R. S. Olmstead, who ran a lumber business in Cherokee; M. F. Crouch of Lemars and Mr. Duncan of Lemars. All were former residents of Boscobel.
Ruka	Mary	BD, p3c3, 12/24/1880	Andrew A. Funk married Mary Ruka at home of bride's father on Tuesday. Groom from Aurora, NB. Bride from Boscobel. The Rev. Frederick Mutschmann officiated at the German Lutheran Church. Kate and Charles Ruka were bride's siblings. Groom was previously employed in Boscobel as a salesman. The couple will live in Nebraska.
Ruka	Settie	BD, p3c3, 6/23/1882	Settie Ruka, Ella Harris and John Ruka, Jr. were the 1882 graduates of the Boscobel High School Class of 1882.
Ruka Bros.		BD, p3c2, 1/5/1883	They have sold over 100 pairs of bobsleds so far this season.
Ruka Bros.		BD, p3c2, 1/19/1883	Detailed business activities described.
Ruka Bros.		BD, p3c3, 7/13/1883	A history of this manufacturing company was printed.
Ruka Bros.		BD, p2c3, 10/22/1880	Louis and John Ruka represented several business interests. John Ruka and W. W. Field established the business in Boscobel 16 years ago under the name Ruka & Field. It was reorganized as Ruka Bros. about a year later. Now one of the largest hardware stores in the state. Owned 9 or 10 buildings on Main Street in addition to other valuable property. John was a practical mechanic and ran the industrial department comprised of the wagon and carriage shops, blacksmith shops, foundry and machine shop. Prepared to do job castings, wood and iron turning, and machine repair. Manufacture sulky horse rake, road scrapers, winepresses and cider presses. Ran a brickyard. Ran a public hall capable of seating 1000-1200 people.
Ruka Bros.		BD, p2c7, 1/5/1877	Sold hardware in Boscobel.
Runice	Caroline	DC, p3c5, 10/30/1886	Caroline Runice married Rev. Hanson on Oct. 20, 1886 at the home of the bride's parents. Bride from West Prairie. Groom from St. Paul.
Rusk	Ada M., Mrs.	DC, p3c4, 1/1/1889	Died Tuesday at her home in Chippewa Falls, per De Soto local news column. She was the wife of L. J. Rusk.
Rusk	Jeremiah M.	DC, Supp, 10/16/1886	Governor of Wisconsin. Resident of Vernon Co. Born in Morgan Co., OH in 1836. Biography printed in the newspaper.
Russ	John	DC, p3c3, 11/27/1886	Released from the county jail after serving 6 months. Returned to jail for 30 days for drunkeness and fighting.
Russell	I.	BD, P3c2, 4/23/1880	Sworn in as an alderman of Boscobel.
Russell	R. A.	DC, p3c2, 7/24/1886	Opened a hotel in Viroqua. Called it the Farmer's Exchange.
Russell	R. A.	DC, p3c3, 7/23/1887	Quit the hotel business in Viroqua.
Rutter		DC, p3c2, 3/19/1887	The four-year-old child of James R. Rutter died Sunday of diphtheria in the Town of Freeman.
Rutter	H.	DC, p3c3, 8/27/1887	The H. Rutter and I. Latimore families of Rush Creek, Town of Freeman were ill with diphtheria.
Rutter	Henry, Mrs.	DC, p2c2, 12/11/1886	Died last evening in Rush Creek per the Retreat news column.
Rutter	J. R.	DC, p2c2, 5/28/1887	J. R. Rutter and J. C. Newton will move on the Kickapoo with their sawmill soon, per Freeman news column.
Rutter	Martha	DC, p2c2, 5/28/1887	Taught school at Oak Ridge, per Freeman news column.
Rutter	Martha	DC, p3c2, 1/8/1889	Martha Rutter married H. T. Rix on Dec. 22, 1888 at the home of the bride's parents in the Town of Freeman. Bride taught school in Crawford Co. and in Nebraska. Planned to live in Lyons, NB.

Genealogical Events from Newspapers for Crawford, Vernon and Grant Counties, Wisconsin, 1870-1901

LAST NAME	FIRST NAME	NEWSPAPER, PAGE/COLUMN MONTH/DAY/YEAR	GENEALOGICAL DATA
Rutter	Mary	DC, p3c4, 12/4/1886	Native of Rush Creek. Taught school at Ferryville per Liberty Pole news column.
Rutter	Mary	DC, p2c2, 5/28/1887	Taught school at Rush Creek, per Freeman news column.
Rutter	Mary	DC, p3c2, 10/1/1887	Mary Rutter and John Barr, both of De Soto, were hired to teach near Merrill, WI.
Ryan	John	DC, p3c2, 8/14/1886	Drowned while bathing at Warner's Landing. Employed by North American Telegraph Co.
Ryan	Pat	BD, p3c1, 12/9/1881	Held on three warrants in a Prairie du Chien jail.
Ryan	Pat	BD, p3c3, 6/8/1877	Pat Ryan, Homer Nelson Taft [found guilty of a murder attempt on James Harris on Wauzeka], Mr. Nichols and 2 Lawyers escaped from jail in Prairie du Chien.
Ryan	Pat	BD, p3c2, 6/22/1877	Escaped from jail in Prairie du Chien. Caught in De Soto.
Ryan	Susie I., Mrs	DC, p3c3, 9/4/1886	Visited with her father, Mr. Ingersoll of De Soto.
Sabin	George	BD, p3c1, 11/10/1882	Plead guilty to a charge of lewd and lascivious conduct on the street and in saloons in Boscobel. Fined $23.
Sablotzky	Himan	BD, p3c2, 6/30/1882	Drowned below the gristmill in Boscobel last Thursday. Aged 11 years. He was the son of J. Sablotzky. The body was taken to Madison for burial with Jewish rites.
Sala	E. M., Dr.	BD, p3c1, 12/3/1880	Lived in West Grant. Died at Beetown on Nov. 15, 1880 at age 65.
Sallander		DC, p3c2, 8/21/1886	A child of M. J. Sallander died at Retreat on Tuesday.
Sallander	A.	DC, p4c1, 5/3/1889	Pension approved for military service. Resided in De Soto.
Sallander	boy	DC, p3c4, 7/24/1886	A son was born on July 13, 1886 to M. J. Sallander of Retreat.
Sallander	boy	DC, p3c3, 7/24/1888	A son was born on Wednesday to M. J. Sallander of Retreat.
Sallander	Fred	DC, p2c1, 7/2/1887	Lost a finger while at work on his self-binder in Retreat.
Sallander	Fred	DC, p2c1, 9/17/1887	Lived in Retreat. Hand crushed in his cane mill. One finger was amputated.
Sallander	John	DC, p3c2, 10/29/1887	John Sallander and Mr. Tilden left De Soto for Shell Lake, WI to seek new homes.
Sallander	M. J.	DC, p3c3, 5/21/1887	Granted a pension. Resided in Retreat.
Sallander	M. J., Mrs.	DC, p3c3, 6/19/1888	Resided in Retreat. Visited sister, Mrs. J. Warne of De Soto.
Sallander	Minnie	DC, p3c3, 11/20/1886	Minnie Sallander, Ella Cooley and Maud Davis attended a Teacher's Association meeting according to the Retreat news column.
Sallender	Minnie	DC, p2c2, 4/2/1887	Native of Retreat. Hired to teach school at Sag City.
Salmon	Ben	RH, p5c4, 7/29/1897	Resigned as treasurer of the Readstown school. Replaced by Mrs. E. E. Patterson.
Salmon	Ben	RH, p5c2, 4/21/1898	Erected a tobacco shed on his farm.
Salmon	Ben, Mrs.	RH, p4c3, 10/11/1900	Celebrated her 50th birthday on Oct. 8, 1900 in Readstown. Her children and friends held a surprise party for her.
Salmon	Benjamin	RH, p4c3, 10/19/1899	A resolution of respect was published by Joseph Groyer of the Philip Davenport Post of the GAR for Benjamin Salmon.
Salmon	Benjamin Frank	RH, p4c2, 10/5/1899	Died Oct. 1, 1899 of heart trouble at his home in Readstown. Born in Grant Co. on Jan. 22, 1844. Served in the Civil War for 3 years. He was a member of the GAR Married Remembrance Balzell on Sept. 23, 1869. They had 1 son and 3 daughters. Lived on a farm near Folsom until about 1887 when poor health compeled him to leave. He moved to Readstown. Loved music. Rev. Bell officiated at the funeral at the Methodist Episcopal Church. Buried in Readstown Cemetery.
Salmon	Benjamin, Mrs.	RH, p4c1, 7/11/1901	Resided in Readstown. Granted a widow's pension of $12 per month.
Salmon	boy	RH, p4c1, 3/7/1901	A son was born Mar. 31 to Frank Salmon of Readstown. [This must have been a typo in the newspaper. Did the author mean Feb. 21st?]

Genealogical Events from Newspapers for Crawford, Vernon and Grant Counties, Wisconsin, 1870-1901

LAST NAME	FIRST NAME	NEWSPAPER, PAGE/COLUMN MONTH/DAY/YEAR	GENEALOGICAL DATA
Salmon	Charles	RH, xxxx, 4/6/1899	Charles Salmon married Martha Wallace on April 2, 1899 at the home of the bride's parents near Readstown. Groom was a farmer from Soldiers Grove. C. H. Davenport officiated at the ceremony.
Salmon	Frank E.	RH, p4c2, 12/13/1900	Frank E. Salmon married Effie Rogers on Dec. 6, 1900 at the home of the bride's mother, Mrs. Ole Gunderson. Rev. Holm of Folsom Lutheran Church officiated.
Salmon	Joe	RH, p4c2, 3/2/1899	Returned from Plum Valley, NB to make his home in Soldiers Grove. He was the brother of Ben and William Salmon of Readstown.
Salmon	Lou	RH, p4c1, 8/31/1899	Found work on a wheat farm in Crookston, MN, per Readstown news.
Salmon	Luther	RH, p4c2, 9/28/1899	Returned to Readstown after spending the last few months working in the western fields.
Salmon	Luther	RH, p4c3, 12/7/1899	Luther Salmon married Leona Hale on Dec. 4, 1899 at the home of the bride's parents in Readstown. Groom from Soldiers Grove. Planned to live in Soldiers Grove.
Salmon	Lydia	RH, p5c2, 1/27/1898	Lydia Salmon married Earnest Sloanamaker on Jan. 16, 1898. Bride from Readstown. Groom from LaValle.
Salzman	Mr.	BD, p3c3, 8/10/1877	Mr. Salzman, a German, died last Sunday near Dickeyville.
Sanderson	Ada	BD, p3c3, 3/23/1883	Ada Sanderson married Elton L. Sanderson on March 13, 1883 in Marietta. Bride was the daughter of Mr. and Mrs. D. Sanderson of Marietta. Groom was from Michigan.
Sanderson	Elton L.	BD, p3c3, 3/23/1883	Ada Sanderson married Elton L. Sanderson on March 13, 1883 in Marietta. Bride was the daughter of Mr. and Mrs. D. Sanderson of Marietta. Groom was from Michigan.
Sandlin	J.	DC, p2c2, 10/22/1887	Lizzie Geese married J. Sandlin on Thursday, per the Victory news column.
Sandon	R.	DC, p2c2, 3/12/1887	Operated a merchantile business in Ontario, WI.
Sands	Jim	RH, p5c3, 11/30/1899	Worked as a stock buyer in Soldiers Grove.
Sands	John	RH, p4c1, 10/24/1901	Visited with brother, Jim Sands of Soldiers Grove. Took the stage home to Sparta.
Sanford	Mrs.	RH, p5c4, 9/16/1897	Mrs. Sanford's sister, Mrs. Dow, arrived from Perth, Scotland for a visit. Mrs. Sanford lived in Viola.
Sanger		BD, p3c2, 3/31/1882	Sanger Brothers bought property on Oak St. in Boscobel from John Benoy on which they plan to open a wagon factory.
Sanger	George	BD, p3c3, 2/27/1880	Employed as foreman of the iron works at the Ruka Bros' Wagon Manufactory in Boscobel.
Sargent	Cyrus	BD, p3c2, 11/6/1883	Died Monday after his team threw him to the ground while taking straw to his barn. Dislocated his neck. He was working with his tenant, Mr. Kinney. Born in New England about 70 years ago. Moved to the Bloomington area in 1847 and moved to California in 1854 where he amassed considerable wealth. Upon his death, he was the largest landowner in southern Wisconsin. He owned over 100 farms. He never married. Survived by one brother [Rodney Sargent of Westport, NY], two sisters and a niece, Miss Waits. [Some of above from 11/20/1883 issue.]
Sargent	Will	DC, p3c1, 11/26/1887	Will Sargent, George Voysey, Elmer Davis and Stacy Davis, all of the De Soto area, went to the pineries [Black River Falls].
Sargent	Will	DC, p4c2, 3/12/1889	Will Sargent married Cora Davis on Mar. 7, 1889 in La Crosse. Bride and groom grew up in De Soto.
Sarles	Daniel	BD, p3c1, 1/12/1883	Arrived in Boscobel to visit relatives. Resided in Butte, MT where he was the editor of the *Montana Miner*. He was a "49", having left Wisconsin in 1849 for the California gold fields. He has been back in "the states" but once since, that was 15 years ago.
Sarles	J. H.	BD, p3c1, 2/27/1880	Departed for the lumbering towns of northern Wisconsin to secure a stock of lumber.
Sarles	J. H.	BD, p3c1, 11/11/1881	Received 2 large rafts of lumber from the Upper Wisconsin River last week. It was tied up in the slough.
Sarles	J. H.	BD, p3c3, 9/18/1883	In the case J. H. Sarles vs Thomas Trollop, there was a verdict in favor of the plaintiff in Grant County Circuit Court. The case involved building materials.
Sarles	J. H.	BD, p3c1, 1/5/1877	President of the First National Bank of Boscobel.
Sarles	J. H., Mrs.	BD, p3c2, 7/9/1880	Mrs. Sarles and her children returned to Boscobel after an extended visit in the East. She was accompanied by Miss Minnie Cleveland of Conneaut, OH, who will be a guest for some weeks.
Sarles	J. H., Mrs. and Mrs.	BD, p3c2, 12/16/1881	Celebrated their 27th wedding anniversary last Monday.

Genealogical Events from Newspapers for Crawford, Vernon and Grant Counties, Wisconsin, 1870-1901

LAST NAME	FIRST NAME	NEWSPAPER, PAGE/COLUMN MONTH/DAY/YEAR	GENEALOGICAL DATA
Sarles	Jesse D.	BD, p3c2, 10/22/1880	Died Oct. 13, 1880 at Fennimore from Bright's disease. Aged 77 years. Abandoned farming in 1876 because of his illness and moved to Boscobel. Later moved to Muscoda and then Fennimore. Employed by Weston & Miner & Co., lumber dealers. Rev. T. M. Evans conducted the funeral at the Methodist Episcople Church in Boscobel. Born in Westchester Co., NY on Sept. 28, 1803. Married Phoebe Halleck, then of Washington, Dutchess Co., NY, on May 19, 1825. Fathered 14 children. Six sons and six daughters survive. Two sons died in infancy. In May 1842 he moved family [10 children] to Racine Co., WI from Washington, Dutchess Co., NY. Two daughters were born in Racine Co. Nine of his children attended the funeral.
Sarles	Jesse D.	BD, p3c1, 10/15/1880	Died Oct. 13, 1880 at Fennimore. Aged 77 years.
Sarles	Jesse D., Rev.	BD, p2c2, 3/17/1882	Letter he wrote from Central City, Dakota published in newspaper. He had been in Dakota for a year. Decided to return to Wisconsin. Will live in Sparta.
Sarles	John H.	BD, p3c2, 5/12/1882	"Mr. John H. Sarles [of Boscobel] returned home on Saturday evening from his Dakota trip and has much to tell of the immense immigration pouring into that famous territory. New towns are springing up as if by magic. Whole counties, yet unorganized, are being "squatted" upon, and the cry seems to be that there is not land enough for all. Business is also on the rushing order and everything denotes a tremendous settlement there this season."
Sarles	John H.	BD, p3c4, 4/13/1877	In the case John H. Sarles et al vs. R. F. See and wife, judgement was found for the plaintiff at the Iowa term of the Circuit Court held in Dodgeville. This was a case from Grant Co.
Sarles	John H.	BD, p3c2, 6/1/1877	Managed the Boscobel stave factory.
Sarles	Kate M.	BD, p3c2, 12/27/1878	Lee B. Durstine married Kate M. Sarles on Wednesday, Dec. 25, 1878 at the home of Mayor Sarles in Boscobel. Bride only daughter of John H. and M. B. Sarles of Boscobel. Groom resided in Wooster, OH. Their future home will be in Conneaut, OH. Elder J. D. Sarles officiated.
Sarles	Lill	BD, p3c3, 8/30/1878	Lill Sarles was the daughter of Rev. J. D. Sarles. Arrived in Boscobel from Iowa for a visit before departing for home in Sparta.
Sarles	Orley	BD, p3c2, 5/4/1877	Arrived from St. Paul to visit relatives in Boscobel.
Sarles	Roy	BD, p3c2, 8/25/1882	Died of cholera on April 15, 1882 at 4 years of age in Jamestown, Dakota during a 3-week visit. He was the son of J. H. Sarles and brother of Jesse.
Sarles	Roy K.	BD, p3c3, 9/1/1882	Recently died. Born April 15, 1878. His parents, sister [Kate] and brothers [Frank and Jesse] were with him when he died.
Sarles	S. E., Mr. and Mrs.	BD, p3c1, 3/7/1879	Arrived in Boscobel from Monticello, IA to visit relatives.
Sarles	W. R.	BD, p3c4, 8/19/1881	Notice published by J. H. Sarles. "Time given" to his son, W. R. Sarles.
Sarles	Wilbur T.	BD, p3c2, 4/13/1877	Son of Rev. J. D. Sarles. Visited relatives in Boscobel. Planned to assist his uncle in the lumber business. His uncle was S. E. Sarles of Montecello, IA.
Sarles	Will	BD, p3c1, 9/10/1880	Left Boscobel for school at Conneaut, Ohio.
Sarles	Will	BD, p3c1, 11/05/1880	Attending school in Ohio. Hit by a train. Convalesing in Conneaut.
Satterlee	R.	DC, p2c1, 4/16/1887	Came from Sparta to visit relatives in Ontario.
Sauer	Frank	DC, p3c3, 10/9/1886	Moved to De Soto from Brownsville.
Sauers	Frank	DC, p3c3 7/30/1887	Decided to move to Shell Lake, WI. Wrote his family in De Soto to join him.
Sauger	Mary	BD, p3c1, 6/6/1879	William L. Scott married Mary Sauger on May 29, 1879. Bride from Woodman. Groom from Mt. Ida. R. Buggins, Esquire officiated.
Saunders	Mary D., Miss	DC, p3c2, 7/16/1887	Died July 4, 1887 at home in Ontario. She and her sister taught school in St. Paul and came home for vacation.
Savage	John	BD, p3c2, 9/27/1878	Tramp. Raped the daughter of Leonard Ranson. Taken to Waupon for a 1-year sentence.
Sawyer & Favor		BD, p2c7, 10/22/1880	Dealers in drugs, groceries, books, stationary, wallpaper, tobacco, cigars, paints, oils, window shades and fixtures in Boscobel. Opened the mercantile in 1870, though both partners have been part of the town for the last 15 years.
Sawyer & Favor		BD, P3c6, 1/5/1877	Advertised a drug store in Boscobel.
Scanlon	C. M.	BD, p3c2, 6/15/1883	Former lawyer in Boscobel. Wrote a letter about his new home in Janesville. Letter was published in the *Boscobel Dial*.

Genealogical Events from Newspapers for Crawford, Vernon and Grant Counties, Wisconsin, 1870-1901

LAST NAME	FIRST NAME	NEWSPAPER, PAGE/COLUMN MONTH/DAY/YEAR	GENEALOGICAL DATA
Scanlon	John	BD, p2c4, 10/7/1881	Published notice that he had taken up a stray pig in Mt. Hope.
Scanlon	Johnnie	BD, p3c2, 10/30/1883	Supervised the mason work for a new Catholic Church on Irish Ridge in Grant Co.
Scanlon	M. J.	BD, p3c2, 11/20/1883	Taught school in Blue River.
Scheinpflug	F.	BD, p2c5, 10/22/1880	Ran a furniture business in Boscobel. It was established 13 years ago. Occupied a large, two-story building that was 82' long and 26' wide. He also ran an undertaking and picture framing business.
Scheinpflug	Fred	BD, P3c2, 4/23/1880	Sworn in as an alderman of Boscobel.
Scheinpflug	Fritz	BD, p3c1, 1/5/1877	Furniture dealer in Boscobel.
Schesiur	Henry	BD, p3c2, 9/26/1879	Sheriff Streeter took him to Waupon to serve a 5 year sentence for horse stealing.
Schlong	Henry	DC, p3c4, 8/7/1886	Tried to use the railroad bridge north of Genoa for the highway, but it resulted in the loss of the horse that belonged to Meister of La Crosse. Schlong lived in Bergen.
Schlong	Henry	DC, p3c5, 8/21/1886	Past chairman of the Town of Bergen. Recently judged to be insane in La Crosse.
Schlong	Henry	DC, p3c3, 6/18/1887	Died last week in La Crosse. Former resident of the Town of Bergen. Became a mail carrier in La Crosse.
Schmahlenberger	Calvin	BD, p3c1, 7/5/1878	Calvin Schmahlenberger married Anna Nauert on June 27, 1878 at the Henry Furderer residence in Boscobel. Bride from Fennimore. Groom from Hickory Grove. J. McLaughlin, Esquire officiated.
Schmidt	Anton	BD, p3c3, 12/15/1882	Published a notice that his wife left him without just cause or provocation. No one should trust her on his account. [Place of residence not mentioned.]
Schmidt	Anton	BD, p2c4, 2/2/1883	A summons was published by the Circuit Court of Grant Co. in the case, Anton Schmidt, plaintiff, vs. Catherine Schmidt, defendant.
Schmidt	F., Mrs.	DC, p3c2, 7/24/1886	Mrs. F. Schmidt and two children returned to De Soto by the steamer, *Ruby*, after a several week visit in Chicago.
Schmidt	Fred	DC, p2c4, 6/12/1886	Pharmacist in De Soto.
Schmidt & Collins		DC, p3c6, 6/12/1886	Sold farm equipment in De Soto.
Schmith	Anton	BD, p3c1, 8/25/1882	From Lancaster. Candidate for Sheriff.
Schmitt	Fred	BD, p3c1, 8/27/1880	Fred Schmitt and H. F. McNally of Muscoda passed through Boscobel in a prairie schooner. They were on their way to Colorado. They brought an Irish setter, Hancock, and a greyhound, Garfield, with them. Their motto is, "In God we trust, but where will we bust."
Schmitt	Peter	BD, p3c3, 11/21/1879	Funeral held last Wednesday in Muscoda. The Masons conducted the service.
Schneider	Regina, Mrs.	BD, p2c3, 12/30/1881	Died Dec. 17, 1881 at the residence of her son, Henry Schneider of Prairie du Chien. Born April 6, 1800 at Euskirchen, Province of the Rhine, Prussia. Married H. B. Schneider, Royal Postmaster, at Remengen on Sept. 26, 1826. Moved to America in 1856. Moved to Prairie du Chien in 1866. Husband is buried in Prairie du Chien. All children survive her. She was the mother of Mrs. A. H. Reitemeyer, Supervisor Henry Schneider of Prairie du Chien and two other sons. Died of nervous congestion. Funeral held at St. Gabriel's Catholic Church.
School Report		BD, p3c2, 9/4/1883	The Town of Marietta school district 2 released the average scores for its summer term students: Myrtie Barkley, 90; Emma Shockley, 90; Allen Taylor, 96; Belle Shockley, 92; Johney Shockley, 97; Mary Ann Foust, 96; Almira Foust, 90; Mattie Hanks, 96; Sammie Shockley, 91; Melvin Hanks, 97; Jimmie Foust, 98. Alice Pratt was the teacher.
Schovill	Harvey	RH, p4c1, 5/9/1901	Harvey Schovill[e] married Martha Kast on May 5, 1901 at the home of the bride's parents, Mr. and Mrs. George Kast of Readstown. Groom from Crawford Co.
Schraudenbach	Charles, Rev.	BD, p3c2, 8/14/1883	Died August 10, 1883 in Boscobel. Born May 25, 1819 in Achaffenbug, Bavaria. He was ordained a missionary priest for the Diocese of Milwaukee. Came to America in 1845. Left money to the Church and to his niece, Miss Mary Schraudenbach. His niece lived with him and attended to his wants in his declining years.
Schraudenbach	Mary, Miss	BD, p3c1, 8/21/1883	She thanked the community for its kindness during the illness of her uncle, the late Rev. Chas. Schraudenbach.
Schraudenbach	Mary, Miss	BD, p3c1, 10/23/1883	After spending 7 years in Boscobel, she returned to Baltimore.

Genealogical Events from Newspapers for Crawford, Vernon and Grant Counties, Wisconsin, 1870-1901

LAST NAME	FIRST NAME	NEWSPAPER, PAGE/COLUMN MONTH/DAY/YEAR	GENEALOGICAL DATA
Schroeder	Englehardt	DC, p2c2, 1/1/1887	Englehardt Schroeder married Marguette Wunder on Dec. 22, 1886 at the Bay State House in De Soto. Groom from Lansing, IA. Bride from Center, Township, IA. D. A. Steele, J.P., officiated.
Schubert	Henry	BD, p1c8, 5/3/1878	Arrested for forging pension papers. He was a Bohemian that lived in Muscoda. Seriously wounded in the Civil War. He was unable to get a pension. Through ignorance of the law he filled out blank application papers for himself.
Schumacher	C.	BD, p3c1, 11/27/1883	New baker in Boscobel. Former resident of Chicago and Prairie du Chien.
Schurbert	Amelia	DC, p2c2, 5/7/1887	Henry Lamprict married Amelia Schurbert on May 3, 1887. Groom partner in the firm Barnetsburger and Lamprict. Bride was the daughter of Edward Schurbert of the Town of Genoa. Bride was a former teacher.
Schurbert	Anna	DC, p2c2, 6/11/1887	May Devorce, Anna Schubert and Lizzie Gould graduated from Mound Ridge school this spring and passed the teacher examination.
Schweizer	John George	BD, p2c3, 5/19/1882	Died May 11, 1882 in Prairie du Chien. Born April 23, 1827 in Grossbetthngen, Germany. Came to America in 1851 and to Prairie du Chien in 1855. He was in the hotel business for 26 years. Proprietor of the Commercial House in Prairie du Chien.
Schweizer	Mr.	BD, p3c2, 12/6/1878	Died Wednesday in Town of Eastman, Crawford Co. He left his son's house to visit daughter, Mrs. Timothy Donahue, who lived a half mile away and fell off a cliff in the dark. Found 2 days later.
Scott	child	BD, p3c2, 4/27/1883	The 6-month-old child of Jacob Scott was buried on April 18, 1883. Scott lived east of Boscobel.
Scott	Frank and Perry	DC, p2c2, 3/12/1887	Departed Seneca for Dakota.
Scott	Jacob	BD, p2c1, 10/11/1878	Scott's Boscobel area barn was destroyed by fire. His loss was valued at $700. Barn insured for $300.
Scott	Jennie	BD, p2c5, 4/29/1881	Summons notice for Grant Co. Courts published. Jennie Scott, plaintiff, vs. William Scott, defendant.
Scott	John	BD, p3c2, 2/1/1878	John Scott married Emogine Lee on Jan. 29, 1878 at the home of the bride's father in Blue River Station. The Rev. Z. S. Hurd officiated.
Scott	John C.	BD, p3c2, 5/28/1880	Appointed to be a census enumerator in Patch Grove, Grant Co.
Scott	Luther	BD, p3c4, 2/20/1880	Son of Jacob Scott of Watterstown. Fell from a train platform in Blue River station. Injured. Has to quit his teaching position.
Scott	Thomas	BD, p2c4, 11/26/1880	Grant County paid him a bounty for scalps turned into the county.
Scott	W. L.	BD, p3c2, 4/16/1880	W. L. Scott of Boscobel deserted his wife, Mary. Mrs. Scott claimed he was unable to support himself and went west, but got homesick and returned.
Scott	William	BD, p3c3, 1/2/1880	From Blue River. A murder charge against him was dropped. Was charged for murder of the Hoskins family of Washington, IA.
Scott	William	BD, p3c1, 8/26/1881	Shipped a load of watermelons to market.
Scott	William	BD, p3c3, 8/30/1878	Departed Boscobel for Chicago and Milwaukee to sell his watermelon crop.
Scott	William L.	BD, p3c1, 6/6/1879	William L. Scott married Mary Sauger on May 29, 1879. Bride from Woodman. Groom from Mt. Ida. R. Buggins, Esquire officiated.
Scriven	Richard	DC, p3c2, 12/10/1887	Returned to Retreat after a visit in Dakota.
Scriven	Samuel	DC, p3c2, 12/10/1887	Returned to Retreat after a visit in Missouri.
Seaman	Amelia	DR, p3c1, 11/30/1871	F. Barker married Amelia Seaman on Nov. 21, 1871 by D. A. Steele, J.P., of De Soto. Bride and groom were from Lansing, IA.
Searles	A. N.	DC, p1c1, 8/9/1889	A. N. Searles and George Pease operated a farm machinery business in Lynxville.
Searles	Annie C.	BD, p3c1, 2/20/1880	Benjamin Bloyer married Annie C. Searles on Jan. 15, 1880 at Watterstown. Bride, daughter of Gideon Searles, Esq., from Watterstown. Groom from Muscoda. The Rev. J. Allison officiated.
Searles	Elder	BD, p3c2, 8/3/1877	Baptized S. D. Curry, Mrs. Porter, Mrs. McCord, Miss Wisdom and Miss Davey last Saturday afternoon.
Searles	Jesse D., Rev.	BD, p3c2, 1/26/1877	Presiding elder of the Methodist Episcopal Church. Scheduled to preach in Boscobel.
Searls	A. N.	DC, p3c4, 8/21/1886	Operated a general store in Lynxville.

Genealogical Events from Newspapers for Crawford, Vernon and Grant Counties, Wisconsin, 1870-1901

LAST NAME	FIRST NAME	NEWSPAPER, PAGE/COLUMN MONTH/DAY/YEAR	GENEALOGICAL DATA
Sears	Genevra	DC, p3c5, 8/21/1886	C. W. Nichols married Genevra Sears on Aug. 15, 1886 at the Bay State House in De Soto. Bride and groom from Mt. Sterling. The Rev. J. T. Morgans officiated.
Seaton	James, Mrs.	BD, p3c3, 5/6/1881	Mrs. James Seaton of Potosi, mother of Mr. T. R. Seaton of Boscobel, died Wednesday.
Seaton	Jennie	BD, p3c2, 5/11/1883	Daniel Green married Jennie Seaton on May 8, 1883 at the residence of Mrs. Beebee in Boscobel. Bride from Boscobel. Groom from Potosi. The Rev. James Havens officiated.
Seaton	T. R.	BD, p3c1, 11/4/1881	T. R. Seaton married Mrs. Mary Taft on Oct. 22, 1881 in Boscobel. The Rev. T. M. Evans officiated.
Seaton	T. R.	BD, p3c1, 10/6/1882	Decided not to move west. Bought more millinery goods to sell.
Seaton	Thomas R.	BD, p3c1, 1/12/1883	Creditors took possession of his store in Boscobel.
Seaton	Thomas R.	BD, p2c4, 1/5/1877	Foreclosure action was taken in Grant Co. Circuit Court held in Richland Center for mortgaged property in Boscobel. Land to be auctioned. Samuel H. Smithers, plaintiff vs. Thomas R. Seaton; Mary A. Seaton; Joseph Walker; William Livingston; F. G. Russell, an assignee of William Livingston estate; William Livingston, Jr. and George H. Moore; in Bankruptcy Court for District Court of the United States for eastern District of Michigan, defendants.
Seaton	Thomas, Mrs.	BD, p3c1, 8/8/1879	Attacked by paralysis, leaving her speechless. Lived in Boscobel.
Seaton	Winefred, Miss	BD, p3c3, 10/27/1882	Died Oct. 20, 1882 in Boscobel from spinal fever. She was 18 years old.
Secret Organizations and Societies		DC, p2c3, 2/19/1889	De Soto had several secret organizations and societies, namely: The Odd Fellow's, United Workmen, Good Templars, GAR Post, W. R. C. Corps, W. C. T. U. and the Literary Society. The *Chronicle* offices housed the Literary Societies' collection of 200 books.
See	George	BD, p3c4, 6/14/1878	Former resident of Boscobel. Now of Harvard, Clay Co., NB. Father, mother and siblings recently joined him. They traveled by prairie schooner train. The trip from Boscobel to Harvard took 24 days.
See	R. F.	BD, p3c1, 4/4/1879	Former resident of Boscobel. Purchased the Revere House at Harvard, NB on April 1 to become a hotelkeeper.
Seeds	L. E., Mrs.	BD, p4c4, 5/25/1883	Ran a millinery shop in Boscobel.
Seeds	L. E., Mrs.	BD, p3c2, 6/29/1883	Mr. and Mrs. Henry Hamilton of Concord, NH were guests of Mrs. L. E. Seeds in Boscobel.
Sees	Louisa, Miss	DC, p3c3, 6/26/1886	Resided in La Crosse. Visited her sister, Mrs. L. Stenseng of De Soto.
Sees	Mrs.	DC, p3c2, 12/11/1886	Arrived from La Crosse to visit her daughter, Mrs. Stenseng of De Soto.
Selle	Fred	DR, p3c4, 2/9/1871	Fred Selle married Augusta Ritter on Feb. 4, 1871 in De Soto. Bride and groom were from Lansing. J. H. Hinds, J.P., officiated.
Selton	Martin	RH, p4c2, 7/5/1900	Attempted suicide by hanging at his home near Folsom. He was cut down before the act was accomplished. Judged insane and taken to Mendota.
Severson	John O.	DC, p3c4, 3/10/1888	Picked up in De Soto by Sheriff Sime and sent to the Mendota Asylum.
Seymour	C. A., Mrs.	DC, p2c2, 7/9/1887	Left Retreat to visit daughter, Mrs. Winters of Minneapolis.
Seymour	G. F.	DC, p2c3, 9/17/1887	Hired to teach school in the Cooley Valley.
Seymour	G. F., Mrs.	DC, p1c2, 4/26/1889	Mrs. Seymour of Retreat visited her mother, Mrs. Marks of Viroqua.
Seymour	Mary	DC, p3c3, 11/13/1886	Mr. Wintees married Mary Seymour on Nov. 5, 1886 at the home of the bride's parents. Bride from Retreat. Groom from Horicon. The Rev. William Haughton officiated.
Shaffer	Mr.	BD, p3c4, 9/8/1882	Resided in Excelsior. He "slapped an axe into the top of his foot severing the leader and two or three bones."
Shambaugh	Dr.	DR, p3c1, 2/23/1871	A bed of coal was found on property owned by Shambaugh outside Viola.
Shaper	Albert	RH, p5c4, 11/4/1897	Viola Eckleberry recently married Albert Shaper at Bloom City.
Sharman [Sherman?]	Will	DC, p2c2, 5/7/1887	Former resident of Seneca. Arranged to have the remains of his father, mother and brother removed to a cemetery north of Seneca.
Sharp	Guy	RH, p5c3, 12/13/1900	Grace Lowrie recently married Guy Sharp. Bride from De Soto. Groom from Dakota.

Genealogical Events from Newspapers for Crawford, Vernon and Grant Counties, Wisconsin, 1870-1901

LAST NAME	FIRST NAME	NEWSPAPER, PAGE/COLUMN MONTH/DAY/YEAR	GENEALOGICAL DATA
Shattnck		BD, p2c3, 1/6/1882	A youth by the name of Shattnck from Sylvan was taken to Richland Center last Friday to serve a 30 day sentence for stealing a revolver from a store in Sylvan.
Shaughnessy	William	BD, p3c2, 5/19/1882	William Shaughnessy and John F. Peare were arrested and fined $5 each for fighting in Tom Crinklaw's blacksmith shop in Boscobel.
Shaw	Daniel	BD, p3c1, 12/1/1882	Daniel Shaw married Mrs. Diantha Steele on Nov.19, 1882. Groom was 81 and lived in Monroe Co., WI. Bride was 70 and lived in Marietta, Crawford Co.
Shaw	Fannie	BD, p3c2, 3/22/1878	George McGraw married Fannie Shaw on Mar. 7, 1878. Bride from Mt. Ida. Groom from Boscobel. The Rev. G. W. Nuzum officiated.
Shaw	J. T.	DR, p3c2, 12/7/1871	Took up a calf at his farm in the Town of Wheatland.
Shaw	Joel T.	DC, p3c2 8/27/1887	Mr. and Mrs. Joel T. Shaw of Red Mound celebrated their 39th wedding anniversary last week.
Shaw	Joel T.	DC, p3c3, 7/3/1888	Resided in Red Mound. He was one of Wheatland's earliest settlers. Subscribed to the *De Soto Chronicle*.
Shaw	Mr.	BD, p3c1, 6/3/1881	Lived in Crawford Co. His horse was stolen. Marshal Harrington of Prairie du Chien arrested the thieves who tried to sell the horse in Wauzeka.
Shay	John	DC, p3c4, 7/24/1886	Resided in Freeman. Suffered from dropsy caused by heart disease.
Shay	Maris	DC, p2c2, 5/28/1887	Died May 13, 1887 at Sugar Creek. She was 70.
Shearer	Ben	BD, p3c1, 1/5/1877	Attorney in Boscobel.
Sheets	Isaac	DR, p3c4, 11/30/1871	Published a notice that he took up a heifer in De Soto.
Sheldon	Ellery	DC, p3c3, 2/5/1887	Recently married. Killed last Friday by a falling tree. Resided in Ontario.
Shepard	William	DC, p3c3, 6/4/1887	William Shepard, of Wheatland, was sentenced to two years of prison a year ago by Judge Newman. He stole a horse. The Governor pardoned him after receiving a petition from "nearly everybody in the wet part of the county."
Sheppard & Son		BD, p2c7, 1/5/1877	Moved their Boscobel barbershop to rooms formerly occupied by William Kanne as a harness shop.
Shepperd	Andrew	RH, p5c5, 10/28/1897	Did contracting and construction work in Readstown.
Sherman	Henry	BD, p3c4, 1/5/1877	Killed last Wednesday at Sherman & Co. flouring mill in Sextonville. Arm drawn into the gears. About 23 years old. Married about 6 weeks ago.
Sherrard	[Perry?]	BD, p3c3, 6/14/1878	Former barber in Boscobel. Now lives in Harvard, Clay Co., NB.
Sherrard	Alice A.	BD, p3c1, 1/16/1880	Married Orin Case on Dec. 31, 1879 at home of bride's father in Boscobel. Groom from Crawford Co. The Rev. William Stoddart officiated.
Sherrard	David	BD, p3c3, 3/23/1883	Died Saturday in Boscobel from a disease he contracted while serving as a private in Co. G, 1st Iowa Calvary during the Civil War. Sherrard drew a pension because he had chronic diarrhea. A wife and several children survived him. Aged 50 years.
Sherwood		BD, p3c2, 3/26/1880	Mr. Sherwood's barn burned. Located 1/2 mile from Mt. Sterling on Black River Road. Also lost 6 head of horses, cows and calves, harnesses, farm implements, grain and hay. While people in the town came to help, the post office was robbed. Warren Merchant was arrested and later confessed. He implicated two Schafers. Merchant was turned over to George Thompson, deputy sheriff of Crawford County by Deputy Sheriff Bailey of Boscobel.
Sherwood	Herbert and Edwin	DC, p3c4, 10/23/1886	Taught school in Soldiers Grove.
Sherwood	Isaac, Mrs.	DC, p3c2, 12/31/1887	Died Dec. 26, 1887 at Mt. Sterling. Lived in Mt. Sterling for 30 years.
Sherwood	William A.	DC, p3c4, 7/24/1886	Replaced A. C. B. Vaughn as postmaster in Mt. Sterling.
Sheslar	Nancy	RH, p5c4, 3/16/1899	James Welsh married Nancy Sheslar on Feb. 22, 1899 per De Soto news column.
Shiek	Fred	DR, p4c4, 12/15/1870	Wholesale and retail dealer of wines and liquors in Lansing, IA.
Shilling	Purdy	RH, p4c2, 12/6/1900	Resided in Kickapoo. Lost his left hand in a corn shredder. His arm was amputated below the elbow by Dr. Burns of Viola. Shilling was a "prosperous farmer and well digger."
Shilling	W. P.	RH, p4c1, 7/20/1899	Fire destroyed his house in Kickapoo.

Genealogical Events from Newspapers for Crawford, Vernon and Grant Counties, Wisconsin, 1870-1901

LAST NAME	FIRST NAME	NEWSPAPER, PAGE/COLUMN MONTH/DAY/YEAR	GENEALOGICAL DATA
Shisler	Jacob and Fanny	DC, p2c2, 12/4/1886	Jacob and Fanny [Hayden] Shisler celebrated their 5th wedding anniversary on Thanksgiving. Over 100 people were present. Gift list and donors names were published. Some of the attendees were John Hayden, Willie Hayden, C. Clark, C. Griffin, Louis and Lawrence Brennan, W. H. Shisler, H. Shisler and Jennie Shisler.
Shisler	Louisa	DC, p2c3, 7/10/1888	Fred Wareham married Louisa [a.k.a. Jennie] J. Shisler on July 3, 1888 at the residence of Charles McDowell. Bride and groom from De Soto. The Rev. Thomas Crouch officiated.
Shock	Fred	DC, p3c3, 8/21/1886	Died Aug. 11, 1886 in Harmony after he was kicked in the head by a horse.
Showalter	C. R., Prof.	BD, p3c3, 1/13/1882	Prof. C. R. Showalter married Ida McDonald at the home of the bride's mother on Jan. 10, 1882. Groom taught at the Fennimore High School. Bride from Fennimore.
Showalter	Mr.	BD, p2c3, 6/22/1883	Mr. Showalter, Bertie Filbric and Emma Ferris were teachers at Fennimore High School.
Shrader	Emma	BD, p3c2, 1/3/1879	Emma Shrader married LeRoy Kilbourn Thursday. Bride from Lancaster. Groom from Cassville.
Shroeder	Herman	DC, p3c2, 3/19/1887	Resident of Harmony. Committed to the Hospital for the Insane by County Judge Butt.
Shultz	William	BD, p3c3, 4/27/1877	Resided in Wauzeka. While fighting a fire, his vest burst into flames. Fifty dollars in his pocket was burned. The remaining pieces were sent to the Treasury Department to be replaced.
Shumway	Mac	DC, p3c4, 11/27/1886	"Mac Shumway is the possessor of a lovable bride."
Shumway	Mack	DC, p2c2, 7/16/1887	Mack Shumway and Dody Morrelli of Genoa went to St. Croix Falls to work on the railroad.
Shumway	Mack	DC, p2c2, 2/25/1888	Departed Genoa with horses to sell in Dakota.
Shuttleworth	C.	BD, p3c2, 7/5/1878	Wrote a letter published in newspaper that described his European travels.
Shuttleworth	Craven	BD, p3c3, 5/3/1878	Lived in Fennimore. Planned to leave soon to go to his homeland. Wanted to visit his 90-year-old mother in Coniston Cold, England.
Shuttleworth	Ferrin	BD, p2c3, 6/22/1883	Ferrin Shuttleworth and Tressie Byerly were the first graduates of the Fennimore High School.
Sicko	Joseph	BD, p2c4, 11/26/1880	Grant County paid him a bounty for scalps turned into the county.
Silbaugh	Charley	RH, p4c3, 8/30/1900	Fatally injured when thrown from a running horse in Viroqua. He was the ony son of Abner S. Silbaugh.
Sime	boy	RH, p4c1, 8/2/1900	A son was born on Friday to E. H. Sime of Readstown.
Sime	Elmer	RH, p5c6, 9/9/1897	Advertised barber services at his shop over Peterson's Hardware in Readstown.
Sime	Elmer	RH, p5c2, 6/2/1898	Belonged to Co. A. Doing training drills in Viroqua. Expected to be called to the Front. Resided in Readstown.
Sime	Frank	DC, p2c1, 5/21/1887	He was an Indian. Well known in the De Soto area. Sent a letter from Chicago to N. F. French that was published in the newspaper. He worked for an Indian medicine company's advertising troupe.
Sime	Gerhart	RH, p4c3, 8/22/1901	Nearly died Thursday in Spring Valley. A cane mill being moved by Sime and his brother, John, fell and crushed Sime's skull. He was unconscious for several hours. He has greatly improved.
Sime	Mary	RH, p4c2, 10/10/1901	Died Oct. 3, 1901 of consumption at the home of her parents in Soldiers Grove.
Sime	Nettie	RH, p4c1, 8/1/1901	Peter Peterson married Nettie Sime on July 30, 1901 at the home of the bride's parents, Mr. and Mrs. H. H. Sime. The Sime's lived 4 miles southeast of Viroqua. Groom from Readstown. About 300 guests attended the wedding.
Sime	T. T.	DC, p3c4, 7/2/1887	Named game warden in Crawford County.
Sime	Thomas N.	BD, p3c2, 3/9/1883	Involved in the lawsuit, State of Wisconsin vs. Thomas N. Sime, John Severson and Perry Sissman [members of Town Board of Clayton] and William Barney [Assessor of Clayton]. The case claimed the town officers willfully neglected to assess and tax personal property and have equalized valuable real estate and productive property at ridiculously low figures. This policy favored large, wealthy taxpayors.
Simmons	Bertha	RH, p5c3, 8/26/1897	Allen Bliss married Bertha Simmons at the residence of the bride's brother, Dolph Simmons, last Sunday afternoon. Groom from South Dakota. Bride from Viola and was a former teacher in Readstown.
Simpkins	Frank P.	BD, p3c2, 1/24/1879	Frank P. Simkins married Mattie S. Bangs on Jan. 1, 1879. Bride from Woodman. Groom from Minnesota. The Rev. W. Stoddart officiated at the ceremony in Boscobel.

Genealogical Events from Newspapers for Crawford, Vernon and Grant Counties, Wisconsin, 1870-1901

LAST NAME	FIRST NAME	NEWSPAPER, PAGE/COLUMN MONTH/DAY/YEAR	GENEALOGICAL DATA
Simpkins	G. H., Mrs.	BD, p3c2, 9/10/1880	Mrs. G. H. Simpkins of Minnesota visited friends in Boscobel and then departed for Orangeville, Ohio.
Sinclair	Mr. and Mrs.	DC, p3c3 7/30/1887	Arrived from Springfield, MA. Visited Mrs. Sinclair's sister, Mrs. Heald of De Soto.
Sisley	Lewis	BD, p3c4, 6/23/1882	Married on Monday, June 12, 1882. Lived in Town of Lima, Grant Co. Arrested for murder of his bride who was found dead on Wednesday.
Skough	C. J.	DC, p2c2, 8/7/1886	Will probably run for Register of Deeds in Vernon Co. He is an incumbent.
Slabaych	Ole	BD, p3c1, 5/11/1883	S. Sickles of Platteville purchased the tobacco crops of John Severson and Ole Slabaych [Slayback?] of Crawford County for 7 cents a pound.
Slack	Charles S.	DC, p8c4, 7/19/1889	The Charles S. Slack & Co. advertised the sale of farm machinery. Samples could be seen at Viroqua, Westby, Seneca, Ash Ridge and Sugar Grove.
Slater	Anna, Miss	DC, p2c4, 1/14/1888	Came home to Retreat from La Crosse.
Slater	Augustus and Willie	DC, p3c4, 3/26/1887	Departed Retreat for Florida. The 4/16/1887 issue records their return to Retreat.
Slater	Henry	DC, p2c1, 12/18/1886	Resided in Retreat. Received a visit from his nephew, Mr. Slater of northern, New York [possibly Bug Hill, NY.]
Slater	Louise	DC, p1c2, 6/14/1889	Fred Bean married Louise Slater on June 5, 1889 at the residence of the bride's father in Retreat. Rev. Haughton officiated.
Sleightam	William E.	BD, p3c3, 2/22/1878	William E. Sleightam [Slightam?] married Elizabeth Miller on Feb. 13, 1878. Bride from Prairie du Chien. Groom from Madison. Rev. Mr. Samuels of the Episcopal Church officiated in a ceremony held at the home of the bride's mother in Prairie du Chien. Katie and Agnes Overton provided music with the assistance of Miss Taylor and Belle Beck of Madison and Charles and John Sleightam [brothers of the groom]. Groom was an engineer on Engine #104.
Slighton	boy	BD, p3c3, 10/25/1878	A son was born to William Slighton of Prairie du Chien on Sunday morning.
Sloanamaker	Earnest	RH, p5c2, 1/27/1898	Lydia Salmon married Earnest Sloanamaker on Jan. 16, 1898. Bride from Readstown. Groom from LaValle.
Sloanes	girl	DC, p2c2, 5/28/1887	A daughter was recently born to Mr. T. Sloanes of Ontario.
Sloggy	S., Hon.	DC, p3c2, 1/15/1887	Hon. S. Sloggy of Ontario was called home from the Legislature with the news of the death of his aged father.
Sloggy	Samuel	RH, p5c2, 8/12/1897	Appointed postmaster in Ontario.
Sloggy	T. A.	DC, p2c2, 3/12/1887	Conducted a hoop pole business in Ontario, WI.
Sloulin	E. O.	RH, p4c4, 3/29/1900	Advertised photography services. Based in Viola.
Slye	Will	DC, p4c2, 3/29/1889	Will Slye of Dakota visited his grandfather, Mr. Angell of Stoddard.
Smalley	James	BD, p3c1, 1/5/1877	Proprietor of the Smalley House in Muscoda.
Smethurst	D.	DC, p4c1, 5/3/1889	Storekeeper in Seneca. Robbed of nearly $3000. The safe was blown open. Most of the stolen money belonged to the town. He was Town Treasurer.
Smethurst	James	BD, p3c1, 5/4/1883	Offered a reward of $100 for the return of a pocketbook, papers and money [$500] lost on the road between Boscobel and Citron Valley, Crawford County.
Smethurst	Nellie	DC, p2c3, 1/22/1887	Suffered from inflammatory rheumatism, per Seneca news column.
Smith		DC, p2c2 8/27/1887	An infant child of Fred Smith was recently buried in the Retreat Cemetery. Died of diphtheria.
Smith		BD, p3c2, 6/13/1879	The 16-year-old son of Henry Smith died of a horse kick. Smith family lived in the northeast corner of the Town of Liberty.
Smith	A. J.	DC, p3c3, 1/7/1888	Wedding invitation were sent our for the Jan. 11, 1888 wedding of Emma Bevan and A. J. Smith.
Smith	A. J.	DC, p2c1, 3/10/1888	Brakeman A. J. Smith was found unconscious on the C. M. and St. P. freight train. He was about 25 years old. He was struck on the back of the head by a bridge beam. Son of Mr. and Mrs. G. Smith of De Soto area. Husband of Emma Bevan, whom he married in January.
Smith	A. K., Mrs.	DC, p8c2, 6/7/1889	Arrived from Mt. Pleasant, IA to visit her brother, H. T. Hare of De Soto. Mrs. Smith planned to meet her husband in Superior, WI, their new home. Mr. Smith worked as a surveyor.
Smith	A. N.	DR, p1c7, 12/14/1871	Proprietor of the Vernon House in Victory.

Genealogical Events from Newspapers for Crawford, Vernon and Grant Counties, Wisconsin, 1870-1901

LAST NAME	FIRST NAME	NEWSPAPER, PAGE/COLUMN MONTH/DAY/YEAR	GENEALOGICAL DATA
Smith	Benjamin N.	RH, p5c3, 3/14/1901	Died unexpectedly last Friday from heart trouble while sitting in his chair. He was the son of Capt. John R. Smith who served in the War of 1812 and Black Hawk War. Born Mar. 23, 1829 in Scuyler Co., IL. Died Mar. 1, 1901. Married Hannah Kershner on Nov. 5, 1850. Survived by his wife and 6 of his 8 children. Moved to Richland Co. in 1841, where he lived 40 years. He then moved to Vernon Co. for the last 20 years. He was the oldest Mason in Richland County, being a charter member of the Orion lodge and a member of the Viola lodge when he died. Enlisted in Co. K, 37th Wis. Reg. Vol. Inf. Funeral held at the Kickapoo Church. Buried in Kickapoo Cemetery. Originally published in the *Viola Intelligencer*. [There is more detail in this obituary.]
Smith	C. E.	BD, p3c1, 1/5/1877	Physician in Excelsior.
Smith	C. J.	DC, p3c3, 9/25/1886	Announced his candidacy for Vernon Co. Dist. Attorney.
Smith	C. J., Prof.	DC, p3c3, 7/24/1886	Recently graduated with honors at the Union law school at Albany. Passed the examination in Madison. Opened a practice in Viroqua.
Smith	Charles	DC, p2c2, 7/16/1887	His Newton home was burglarized while gone celebrating the 4th of July. Burglers broke open a trunk and took a gold watch and $12.
Smith	Charles	DC, p3c2, 11/12/1887	Died Nov. 5, 1887 in De Soto when he was 62 years and 9 months old. Born Feb. 5, 1825 in Tompkins Co., NY. Married Roxy Barden [Borden?] in 1857. She died Nov. 26, 1862. Married Eliza Ballard, the widow of Leroy Ballard, in 1865. Survived by his second wife and 1 son, Charles. Moved to Dodge Co. in 1866, to Liberty Pole in 1867 and to De Soto in 1868.
Smith	Charles	DC, p4c1, 4/12/1889	A Vernon County Probate Court notice was published "In the matter of the Guardianship of Charles E. Smith, minor heir of Charles Smith, deceased."
Smith	D. B.	RH, p4c2, 9/27/1900	Received a visit from his half-brother, Mr. Smith of Tennessee. He has lived in Tennssee for the last 18 years and would never like to live in Wisconsin again.
Smith	D. P.	DC, p2c3, 5/1/1888	Built a new barn for Frank Gross, per Retreat news column.
Smith	D. P.	DC, p1c1, 6/7/1889	Lived in Retreat. Granted a pension for military service.
Smith	D. P., Mrs.	DC, p2c2, 4/16/1887	Departed Retreat to visit her brother, Warren Davis of La Crosse.
Smith	Delia	BD, p3c1, 6/25/1880	Charles Brekke married Delia Smith on June 21, 1880 at Brekke's Hotel. Groom from Soldiers Grove. Bride from Viroqua. Prof. J. Allison of Boscobel officiated.
Smith	E. B.	BD, p2c5, 5/26/1882	Smith took up a stray horse in Marion, WI.
Smith	Ed	BD, p2c1, 10/5/1877	Taken to Waupon for a 2-year sentence by Sheriff Birchard. He was convicted of horse stealing.
Smith	Ethel	RH, p5c4, 11/17/1898	The funeral for Little Ethel Smith was held in Manning on Saturday.
Smith	Ethel	RH, p5c4, 11/24/1898	Died Nov. 11, 1898 at the age of 8. She was the daughter of Charles O. and Mary F. Smith of Kickapoo. Funeral held at Advent Church. Buried in Kickapoo Cemetery.
Smith	Frank	BD, p2c4, 11/26/1880	Grant County paid him a bounty for scalps turned into the county.
Smith	Frank	DC, p2c2, 9/24/1887	Hired to teach school in Seneca.
Smith	George	BD, p2c3, 10/1/1880	Resided in Boscobel. Published an announcement that no one should trust his wife, Susan Smith, on his account, as he would not pay debts contracted by her.
Smith	George	BD, p3c1, 7/4/1879	George Smith married Mrs. Margarett Barque on June 28, 1879 in Montfort. Bride and groom from Wingville. The Rev. D. L. Hubbard officiated.
Smith	George, Sr.	BD, p2c3, 10/11/1878	Published a notice that he was giving his son, George Smith, Jr. [aged 19 years], his time and that he would henceforth not be responsible for his son's debts. The Smiths lived in the Boscobel area.
Smith	girl	RH, p5c4, 1/12/1899	A daughter was recently born to Charley Smith of Kickapoo.
Smith	H. R., Prof.	BD, p3c4, 6/27/1879	Prof. H. R. Smith married the daughter of William Jameson on June 15, 1879. Groom was principal at Muscoda. His parents lived in Baraboo.
Smith	Harry Oliver	BD, p3c2, 12/25/1883	Died Dec. 13, 1883 from pneumonia at the age of 4 years, 1 month and 17 days. He was the only son of C. W. and Lucy Smith of Werley.
Smith	Jennie	RH, p4c1, 4/25/1901	Loyall Young married Jennie Smith on Tuesday at the home of the bride's parents. Bride and groom lived in Soldiers Grove. Groom employed by J. H. Stelzman. Bride was eldest daughter of R. L. Smith. The Rev. J. A. Neill officiated.

Genealogical Events from Newspapers for Crawford, Vernon and Grant Counties, Wisconsin, 1870-1901

LAST NAME	FIRST NAME	NEWSPAPER, PAGE/COLUMN MONTH/DAY/YEAR	GENEALOGICAL DATA
Smith	Jerry	BD, p3c2, 4/14/1882	Lived in Mt. Ida. Collected $75 in bounty for killing an old wolf and 7 pups. Has killed 16 wolves in the last 2 weeks.
Smith	John S.	DR, p3c2, 5/4/1871	John S. Smith married Julia Christian on May 1, 1871 in De Soto. Bride and groom were from Lansing. The Rev. D. L. Hubbard officiated.
Smith	Leb	BD, p3c1, 4/14/1882	Leb Smith, Pinkey McSpaden and Charley Smith were fined $3 in Boscobel for insulting language with Lillian Comstock, daughter of H. Comstock. In the 4/21/1882 issue, M. F. McSpaden denied the charge saying he was called as a witness to the incident.
Smith	Lee	RH, p4c2, 6/7/1900	Tumor removed from his body that proved to be cancer. A limb was amputated.
Smith	Lorey	DC, p3c3, 12/3/1887	Lorey Smith married Thomas Taylor on Nov. 24, 1887 in Seneca.
Smith	Lot P.	BD, p3c2, 4/26/1878	Worked as a railroad tie buyer. Spent the last 6 months in Boscobel. Departed for his home in Clinton, IA. His wife and family went ahead by rail. He went by raft on the Wisconsin River.
Smith	Mary	DC, p1c2, 8/2/1889	E. H. Dyer married Mary Smith on July 17, 1889 in Cassville at the Denniston House. Bride and groom from De Soto. The Rev. G. D. Stevens officiated.
Smith	Mrs.	BD, p3c2, 1/2/1880	Resident of Boscobel. Her funeral was held Dec. 23, 1879 at the Methodist Episcopal Church. Mr. Favor and Dr. Hurd directed the choir.
Smith	Mrs.	DC, p3c4, 10/9/1888	From Richland Co. Visited brother, Mr. Bailey. She was 81 years old and had not seen her brother for 40 years, per Victory news column.
Smith	Nehemiah Sleeper	BD, p3c2, 4/27/1883	Died April 17, 1883 in Mt. Ida from acute pneumonia. He was born in Grafton, NH in Dec. 2, 1821. Emigrated to Wisconsin in 1856 to what then was the Town of Fennimore where he farmed.
Smith	Nellie	BD, p3c1, 1/16/1880	Married Edward A. Austin on Dec. 25, 1879 in Boscobel. Bride and groom from Town of Marion. J. McLaughlin, Esq. officiated.
Smith	O. C.	BD, p3c2, 4/13/1877	New landlord of the Carrier House in Boscobel.
Smith	O. R.	BD, p3c2, 2/16/1877	The infant son of O. R. and L. M. Smith died Feb. 8, 1877 at the Muffley House in Boscobel. The child was 5 months and 23 days old.
Smith	Rosa	BD, p3c4, 11/11/1881	Summons published by Grant Co. Circuit Court in the case, Rosa Smith, plaintiff, vs. Charles E. Smith, defendant.
Smith	Ross L.	BD, p3c1, 9/9/1881	Ross L. Smith married Isabelle M. Dinsdale on Aug. 11, 1881 in Boscobel. Bride and groom from Soldiers Grove. The Rev. T. M. Evans officiated.
Smith	Ross L.	DC, p2c1, 8/21/1886	Appointed postmaster in Soldiers Grove.
Smith	Sarah, Mrs.	BD, p2c2, 12/9/1881	Mrs. Sarah Smith, wife of Benjamin Smith of Lima, was thrown from a wagon and died a few hours later. She had been in poor health and her husband took her to the city to consult with physicians. She was born 63 years ago in Pennsylvania.
Smith	Sarah, Mrs.	DC, p2c2, 12/11/1886	Hosted a meeting of the Women's Christian Temperance Union at her home in Retreat.
Smith	T. G.	DC, p2c2, 5/7/1887	Taught school in Seneca.
Smith	Vesta May	RH, p6c2, 2/8/1900	Died Feb. 1, 1900 of croup. She was the daughter of Charles and Mary Smith of Kickapoo. Aged 1 year and 25 days.
Smith	W. C.	DC, p3c3, 11/26/1887	Helped build the C. B. & N. Railroad. Left De Soto for his home in Bath, NY.
Smith	William	BD, p3c3, 10/26/1877	William Smith married Fannie Lesler Thursday. Groom from Mt. Sterling, IL. Bride from Boscobel.
Smith	Willie	BD, p3c3, 8/22/1879	Willie Smith, age 12; Charley Smith, age 14; Henry McSpaden, age 16; and Charley Brown, age 11 were sent to Reform School "for actions committed against Betsey Benson, aged 7, who was coaxed to prostitute herself to their base desires." All from Boscobel.
Smithson		RH, p5c2, 9/1/1898	A child of Mr. Smithson died this week in Readstown. Smithson was a brother-in-law of G. A. Ewers.
Sneclode	J. H. C.	BD, p3c2, 5/28/1880	Appointed to be a census enumerator in Cassville, Grant Co.
Snow		BD, p3c1, 7/15/1881	Stillborn son born Wednesday to Mr. W. C. Snow of Marion.
Snow	A. F.	BD, p3c2, 12/16/1881	Advertised the sale of his flouring mill in Boscobel.
Snow	A. F.	BD, p2c4, 4/13/1877	Advertised real estate services in Boscobel.

Genealogical Events from Newspapers for Crawford, Vernon and Grant Counties, Wisconsin, 1870-1901

LAST NAME	FIRST NAME	NEWSPAPER, PAGE/COLUMN MONTH/DAY/YEAR	GENEALOGICAL DATA
Snow	Emeline	BD, p3c5, 2/11/1881	Emeline Snow, wife of A. F. Snow, died Feb. 7, 1881 of a liver complaint in Boscobel. Born Nov. 15, 1833 in Ripley Co., IN. Joined the Methodist Episcople Church when she was 18 years old.
Snow	George W., Mrs.	BD, p3c3, 5/24/1878	Died Friday while giving birth to twin boys. One child lived. Mrs. Snow was buried in Yankton, Dakota [per the May 9, 1878 issue of the *Springfield Times* of Dakota]. The husband was the son of A. F. Snow of Marion Township, Grant County.
Snow	Will	BD, p3c2, 2/3/1882	Injured in the woods by a gun set for game while inspecting railroad ties near Green Bay.
Snow	Will	BD, p3c4, 4/13/1877	Will Snow, son of William Snow, was wounded by gun fire during a burglary attempt at his father's store in Richland City on Tuesday.
Snow	Willard	BD, p3c1, 4/30/1880	Snow's store in Richland City was destroyed by fire on April 21st. It was insured.
Snow	William	BD, p3c1, 5/7/1880	William Snow of Boscobel married Martha Lull of Boscobel on Monday afternoon at The Carrier House. Prof. John Allison officiated.
Snow	William	BD, p3c4, 8/9/1878	William Snow married Lell E. Chandler on Aug. 6, 1878 at the home of the bride's mother in Boscobel. Groom from Richland Center. Rev. Dr. Stoddart officiated. The wedding was attended by Mr. And Mrs. H. C. Snow of Milwaukee, Mrs. Williard Snow [mother of groom], Mr. and Mrs. N. H. Snow of Avoca and Miss Ida Snow of Worchester, MA.
Soderling	Swan [Sven?]	BD, p3c4, 9/11/1883	A foreclosure sale was announced in the case Martin O. Brekke [plaintiff] vs Swan M. Soderling and Christina Soderling his wife, Elijah Trollope and Hiram Comstock [defendants] for lots in Boscobel.
Soldiers of 1812 and 1861		DC, p3c4, 6/4/1887	The De Soto G.A.R and W.C.T.U. sponsored the De Soto Memorial Day exercises. The post decorated the graves of the following men from the War of 1812: Harvey Sterling, Alfred Moore and Richard Morgan. They decorated the graves of the following men from the Civil War: Harrison McAuley, Samuel Waller, Casper Fopper, Robert Campbell, Henry Chandler, John Ferguson, Soloman Newton, Benjamin King and Aaron Cooley.
Soldiers Reunion		DC, p3c4, 6/25/1887	Lynxville hosted a soldiers reunion. Speeches were made by Hon. O. B. Thomas, Wm. H. Evans, Capt. Hobbs, Hugh Porter, Walter Pease, Ed. Whaley, Wm. Witcraft, J. Evans, G. L. Miller and others. Music was provided by Chapek's band and Blanchards drum and fife corps. Drum Major Whaley of Prairie du Chien, a gentleman of 85 years and served in the Mexican War and Civil War, won first prize at a competitive drill. "Mr W[haley] and a brother enlisted in the U.S.A. when 8 and 10 years of age."
Soldiers Reunion		DC, p3c4, 6/25/1887	The following soldiers from the James Mason Post 106, G.A.R., De Soto, attended the Lynxville soldiers reunion: Com. C.F. Page, Wm. Witcraft, Wm. Green, Milo Whitney, R. G. Worman, Edward Rogers, C. Maxwell, Wm. Bates, J. M. Hill, C. S. Fourt, James Whitney, S. D. Taylor, W. S. Cushing, E. R. James, E. G. Lees, B. F. Roberts, B. I. Witcraft, LeGrand Hickok, Robert. Pennell, A. E. Blanchard, Wm. Davis, A. Sallander, Isaac Latimore and T. C. Rutter.
Soldiers Reunion		DC, p3c4, 6/25/1887	The following soldiers from the Phillip W. Plummer Post, No. 37, G.A.R., Prairie du Chien attended the Lynxville soldiers reunion: Capt. F. T. Hobbs, O. Stafford, Capt. O. B. Thomas, H. T. Rittenhouse, John Riser, William Whaley, D. H. Hadley, Maj. Ed. Whaley, A. M. Beach and W. H. Evans.
Soldiers Reunion		DC, p3c4, 6/25/1887	The following soldiers from the O. D. Chapman Post, No. 80, G.A.R., Mt. Sterling attended the Lynxville soldiers reunion: T. Harding, Gil Stewart, S. N. Brockaway, A. C. B. Vaughen, Lot Gay, Ed. Thomson, J. S. Dudley, Henry Moon and H. C. Newcomb.
Soldiers Reunion		DC, p3c4, 6/25/1887	The following soldiers from the Charles Green Post 216, G.A.R., Lynxville and Seneca attended the Lynxville soldiers reunion: S. C. Prince, E. Van Wormer, Hugh Porter, Bow Cron, James Waite, Peter Casey, Albert Randall and G. W. Pease. [p3c4, 6/25/1887] The following soldiers from this post were missing from the previous list: Isaac Baker, S. Armstrong, W. Elanuagah, W. H. Black, D. L. Heligar, Wm. Dickson, Thomas Dickson, Ed. Lawler, J. Vanderbilt, L. Gay, L. H. Noggle, James Falley, Geo. Newton. [p2c1, 7/2/1887] Others present but not members: W. Huard, 45 Reg.; A. E. Wolcot, 27 IA; and Elisaha Randell, C, 52 Reg. [p2c1, 7/2/1887]
Solomon	John	BD, p2c3, 9/9/1881	Arrested in Wauzeka and brought to Prairie du Chien to faces assault with intent to kill charges. Accused of assaulting J. E. Shaw. Solomon had approval to cut hoop poles from previous owner of land now owned by Shaw. Shaw did not know about the arrangement.
Sommars	Carrie Melva	RH, p5c5, 7/15/1897	Lemuel Rabbitt married Carrie Melva Sommars at the home of the bride's sister, Mrs. Fred Lepley, per Viola news column. Rev. Hitchcock of West Salem officiated.
Soniss	Ole O.	DC, p3c2, 10/8/1887	Home in Purdy was destroyed by fire after a lamp exploded. The building was insured for $250.
Sons of Temperance		BD, p3c2, 1/12/1877	The officers of the Boscobel Sons of Temperance were Dr. D. O. Pickard, Eleanor Duncan, Will Allen, Mrs. Desmond, Charles Cook, D. Walker, Mr. Bennis, Miss Benoy, James Ricks, Miss A. Allen, Nelson Farnham and S. R. Willoughby.

Genealogical Events from Newspapers for Crawford, Vernon and Grant Counties, Wisconsin, 1870-1901

LAST NAME	FIRST NAME	NEWSPAPER, PAGE/COLUMN MONTH/DAY/YEAR	GENEALOGICAL DATA
Sorenson	Pete	RH, p5c2, 4/21/1898	Landlord at the Park Hotel in Readstown.
Sovede	Elizabeth	RH, p4c3, 6/15/1899	J. T. Dregne recentlly married Elizabeth Sovede. Groom from Readstown. Bride from Town of Franklin.
Spangello	James	RH, p5c3, 2/14/1901	Traveled from Dakota to vist the Vold family in Spring Valley.
Spangler	C. D.	BD, p3c2, 4/20/1877	Mr. C. D. Spangler of Boscobel sold fresh fish that he kept in a submerged box at the upper ferry on the Wisconsin River.
Spangler	George	BD, p2c4, 2/13/1880	Lived in Richland County. Lost his right hand in a threshing machine accident.
Spangler	Jennie, Mrs.	DC, p3c4, 10/22/1887	Departed by train from De Soto for Hastings, NB. She was the daughter of Mrs. Carlyle.
Spangler	Jennie, Mrs.	DC, p3c3, 1/22/1889	Mrs. Spangler and her 2 children relocated to be with her husband who was going into business in La Crosse.
Spauling	Harry	DC, p3c3, 3/10/1888	Squire McMichael recently sentence 4 young men [aged 16-18] from Genoa for carrying concealed weapons. Abram Morr was sentenced to 30 days of hard labor. Harry Spauling sentenced to 20 days of hard labor. Eli Barrett sentenced to the Industrial School at Waukesha. Emil Gunderson paid a fine.
Spear	Ernest	RH, p4c2, 12/20/1900	Arrested for horse stealing by Viola Village Marshall Jacob Benn at the residence of Ed Kast [who was suspicious of Spear]. Spear [aged 18 years] and a man named Coleman were wanted in Tomah. Coleman was arrested in La Crosse.
Spear	G.	DC, p3c2, 2/19/1887	G. Spear of Geneva, NB visited his father, L. Spear of De Soto.
Spear	L.	RH, p5c4, 11/3/1898	Called from Pipin/Pipen to go to Viroqua to attend the funeral of his daughter, Mrs. Fred Eckhardt, per De Soto news column.
Spear	L., Mrs.	DC, p4c1, 3/12/1889	Returned to De Soto after a visit with her daughter in Pepin.
Spears	L.	DC, p3c3, 8/7/1886	Returned to De Soto from Nebraska.
Speery	Lou, Miss	DC, p3c2, 9/24/1887	Lou Speery married Walter Bock on Sept. 9, 1887 at her home in Bowville, MI. Groom was Chief Clerk of the Michigan Central Railroad. Bride was a steno for Detroit Stove Co. She was the sister of E. B. Speery of De Soto.
Speigelberg Bros. & Co.		BD, p2c3, 10/22/1880	Established in Boscobel about 4 years ago. Proprietors well-known in area for many years. Sold dry goods, boots, shoes, notions, hats, caps and clothing. Store was 80' by 24' with a basement. Sold exclusively by the cash system which means low prices.
Spencer	John L.	BD, p3c5, 4/14/1882	Lived near Hurlbut's Corner in Crawford Co. Recently drank arsenic and then told his younger brother who informed family. Restoratives were used. John L. left home the next day and hasn't been seen. It is believed he took poison with him and went into the woods.
Sperbeck	Aurora Belle	DR, p3c2, 12/7/1871	William S. Chambers married Aurora Belle Sperbeck on Dec. 3, 1871 by D. A. Steele, J.P., at the residence of the bride's father. Bride and groom were from Dec. 3, 1871.
Sperry	Dr.	DR, p3c2, 12/29/1870	Dr. Sperry was the only physician in De Soto. "He is kept going night and day, and cures more than he kills, which is something remarkable for physicians..."
Sperry	E. B.	DC, p2c3, 2/18/1888	R. P. Loftus hosted a farewell party for E. B. Sperry in De Soto.
Sperry	E. B.	DC, p3c3, 6/12/1888	E. B. Sperry married Mamie Chase Monday afternoon at the home of the bride's parents in Viroqua. Bride was daughter of Hon. H. A. Chase. Groom was an agent for the Chicago, Burlington and Northern R.R.
Sperry	E. B., Mr. and Mrs.	DC, p4c3, 5/10/1889	Visited their friends in De Soto while on their way to Viroqua to visit relatives, Dr. Chase and family. The Sperry family now lives in Chadwick, IL.
Sperry	G. S., Dr.	DR, p2c3, 12/15/1870	Physician in De Soto.
Sperry	George S., M.D.	DC, p2c1, 1/14/1888	Started a practice in De Soto in 1858. He came from St. Paul and wanted to slow down his practice. There is an extensive account of his personality. He died before 1888.
Spiegelberg	boy	BD, p3c3, 4/29/1881	A son was born to Richard Spiegelberg of Boscobel on April 15, 1881.
Spiegelberg	Richard	BD, p3c1, 9/1/1882	Purchased the Tillotson property in Boscobel for $1500.
Spofford	A. W., Rev.	BD, p3c2, 2/6/1880	Moved from Prairie du Chien. Accepted a call to preach at the Congregational Church at Darlington.
Spurier	Melvin	RH, p5c4, 3/2/1899	Melvin Spurier, Lester Smith and Monroe McDaniel left Sugar Grove for the Westto "seek their fortune."

Genealogical Events from Newspapers for Crawford, Vernon and Grant Counties, Wisconsin, 1870-1901

LAST NAME	FIRST NAME	NEWSPAPER, PAGE/COLUMN MONTH/DAY/YEAR	GENEALOGICAL DATA
Spurrier	George	RH, p4c2, 2/14/1901	Died yesterday [Wednesday] in Sugar Grove after a lingering illness.
Spurrier	Mr.	RH, p4c4, 12/29/1898	Celebrated his 73rd birthday on Nov. 3, 1898 at his home in Sugar Grove.
Squires	G. W.	BD, p3c1, 3/9/1883	G. W. Squires of Crawford Co. telegraphed his son in Iowa to come home as soon as possible as his sister was near death. A team met the son in Boscobel. The son brought with him his 16-year-old daughter's corpse to bury in Crawford County.
Stada	Frederick	DR, p3c5, 11/9/1871	The Vernon Co. Probate Court published an Order for Proof of Will for Frederick Stada, deceased, late of Vernon Co. Margaret Stada and Jacob Eckhard, Jr. applied to have the will sent to probate.
Stahel	Anna L.	BD, p3c1, 3/19/1880	Charles J. Dickerson married Anna L. Stahel on March. 11, 1880 in Muscoda. Bride and groom from Boscobel. The Rev. George Haigh officiated.
Stahel	Jacob	BD, p3c3, 10/1/1880	Lived in Lexington, KY. Visited his brother, Capt. John Stahel of Boscobel.
Stahel	John, Capt.	BD, p3c4, 6/25/1880	Resident of Boscobel. Placed in command of the Second Wisconsin Regiment at the Soldiers Reunion in Milwaukee. Fought at Antietam.
Stahl	John, Capt.	BD, p3c2, 2/24/1882	Stumbled in the dark, fell and later found unconscious by Myron DeLap and Gottleib Christ.
Stamp	T. W.	RH, p7c1, 7/1/1897	Pastor of the Methodist Episcopal Church in Readstown.
Stamp	T. W., Rev.	RH, p5c4, 10/21/1897	Resigned from the ministry in Wisconsin to be with his wife in Chicago. She is being treated there by physicians. He had a new job in the pastorate at Oak Park, Union Church.
Stamp	Tom A.	RH, p5c4, 7/22/1897	Graduated from Platteville last June. He will be the principal of the Wauzeka schools. He was the son of Rev. Stamp of this circuit.
Standiford		RH, p5c5, 7/15/1897	A baby was recently born to Frank Standiford of the Otter Vale area.
Standiford	John	RH, p5c5, 7/15/1897	John Standiford recently married Nellie Melvin in the Otter Vale area.
Standiford	Mrs.	RH, p5c4, 7/29/1897	Recently died at Viola. She was an old resident of the Ross area.
Stanley	Charles E.	DR, p3c2, 6/15/1871	Resided in Vernon Co. Received a visit from his brother of Lowell, MA.
Stanley	Fred	DC, p3c3, 6/12/1886	Returned to De Soto after spending the last 2 years in Montana.
Stanley	Mrs.	DC, p2c3, 3/19/1887	Ill with pneumonia in De Soto. Her son, Fred of Minneapolis, was called home.
Stannard	Chris	BD, p3c5, 3/8/1878	Chris Stannard, Gus Cole and George Lee dug on land of James Ashmore, about 4 miles northeast of Platteville. The ground caved in 35 feet underground. Stannard was buried 26 hours. Rescued under the leadership of William S. Waters.
Stanton	Luella Angeline	BD, p3c1, 3/9/1883	Francis B. Owens married Luella Angeline Stanton on Mar. 4, 1883 at the residence of Calvin C. K_____ in the Town of Scott. Bride and groom were from Richland Co. E. A. Brown, J.P., officiated.
Stark	Maggie	BD, p3c2, 8/17/1877	Anthony Beckwar married Maggie Stark on Aug. 10, 1877 in Boscobel. Groom from Crawford Co. Bride from Moscoda.
Stattuck	G., Col.	DC, p3c2, 5/1/1888	Married a lady in New York a number of years ago. They divorced. He moved to Vernon Co. and now lives in the Town of Stark. He remarried. His first wife recently died, leaving her entire fortune [over $40,000] to the Colonel.
Statzer	Frank A.	BD, p3c1, 1/2/1880	Married Annie Drinkwater on Dec. 24, 1879 in Fennimore at the residence of John Smith. Bride from Lancaster. Groom from Mt. Ida. Otho Shrader, Esq. officiated.
Steamboats		DC, p2c1, 8/7/1888	In the 1850s, "hardly an hour in the day would pass during the season of navigation when the black smoke of steamer would not be discernable either in one direction or the other." The Minnesota Packet Company of Galena, IL had a monopoly on the transportation. Their best boat was the *War Eagle*, commanded by Capt. Smith Harris. They also operated *Golden Era*; *Northern Light* [now in the bottom of Coon Slough], commanded by Capt. Preston Lodewick; *Itasca*, commanded by Capt. Worden; *Milwaukee*, commanded by Capt. Webb; *Gray Eagle* [damaged/sunk? at Rock Island Bridge], commanded by Capt. Smith Harris. The *Henry Clay* was operated by the St. Louis Line. Capt. Pate Davidson ran the *Jacob Traber* which broke its shaft below De Soto late one fall and lay there all winter.

Genealogical Events from Newspapers for Crawford, Vernon and Grant Counties, Wisconsin, 1870-1901

LAST NAME	FIRST NAME	NEWSPAPER, PAGE/COLUMN MONTH/DAY/YEAR	GENEALOGICAL DATA
Steamboats		DC, p2c1, 8/7/1888	The Diamond Jo Line was organized about 1862 or 1863. Its first boat was the Lansing, commanded by Capt. William Fleming. Shifting sand made landing at De Soto impossible one season, so Carr & Whiting employed Henry K. Miller to sleep in a shanty they erected on an island where goods and mail were received. During the steamboat period, De Soto furnished a lot of the wood burned for fuel.
Stearns & Co.		DC, p2c2, 2/26/1889	Commercial fishermen company in De Soto.
Steckwest	Frank	BD, p3c3, 8/28/1883	Kate Ruka married Frank Steckwest [Stecknest?] on Aug. 22, 1883 at the home of the bride's parents. Bride was daughter of Louis Ruka of Boscobel. Groom was a businessman and former Grant County resident who lived in Peterson, IA. A gift list was published.
Steele	A. M.	BD, p3c2, 5/28/1880	Appointed to be a census enumerator in Lima, Grant Co.
Steele	Bert, Mrs.	DC, p4c3, 4/5/1889	Miss Ivy Tuttle of Pepin visited her sister, Mrs. Bert Steele of the De Soto area.
Steele	Chauncey	BD, p3c1, 2/6/1880	Resident of Crawford Co. Attended the funeral of his sister, Mrs. Noah Hutchins, in Platteville.
Steele	Chauncey	BD, p3c2, 2/6/1880	Resident of Crawford Co. Employed Willard Moon of Boscobel to run a level to carry water from a well to his stock.
Steele	D. A.	DR, p1c1, 12/15/1870	Insurance agent and notary public in De Soto, WI.
Steele	D. A.	DR, p3c2, 12/29/1870	Sold insurance from his office on Houghton Street in De Soto.
Steele	D. A.	DR, p3c1, 6/29/1871	He was building a new house for Joseph Baker, next to the Congregational Church in De Soto.
Steele	D. A.	DR, p3c2, 8/17/1871	Bought the De Soto wagon manufactory from H. A. Jacobus.
Steele	D. A.	DC, p2c4, 6/12/1886	Proprietor of the Bay State House in De Soto.
Steele	D. A.	DC, p3c4, 7/16/1887	Celebrated his 55th birthday on July 11, 1887 at the Bay State Hotel in De Soto.
Steele	D. A.	DC, p2c3, 8/28/1888	Planned to leave De Soto the latter part of the week for Milledgeville, IL where he has rented a large hotel. Steele was one of De Soto's first settlers.
Steele	Diantha	BD, p3c1, 12/1/1882	Daniel Shaw married Mrs. Diantha Steele on Nov. 19, 1882. Groom was 81 and lived in Monroe Co., WI. Bride was 70 and lived in Marietta, Crawford Co.
Steele	girl	DC, p2c3, 8/28/1888	A daughter was born Aug. 26, 1888 to A. A. Steele of De Soto.
Steele	John S. R.	BD, p2c2, 1/26/1883	Former resident of Black Earth. Convicted 9 years ago on circumstantial evidence for a murder in Boulder, CO. He was sentenced to hang. The sentence was commuted to life in prison. New evidence came forth and he has now been exonerated.
Steele	Myrtie	DC, p8c2, 6/21/1889	Jacob Trumbower married Myrtie Steele on Saturday in Milledgeville, IL. Groom was the station agent in Milledgeville. Bride was daughter of D. A. Steele, formerly of De Soto.
Steele	Rena	BD, p3c1, 8/26/1881	Lintner W. Green married Rena Steele on Aug. 24, 1881 in Boscobel. Bride and groom from Scott, Crawford Co. The Rev. T. W. Evans officiated.
Stenseng	J., Mr.and Mrs.	DC, p3c2, 12/17/1887	Left De Soto for La Crosse to attend the funeral of Robert Mummy, her brother-in-law, who was injured on the Eagle Point wreck.
Stenseng	L.	DC, p3c1, 6/12/1886	Dealer in boots and shoes in De Soto.
Steolinson	D.	DC, p1c3, 4/12/1889	Left Ferryville for Spokane Falls, Washington Territory.
Stephens	Horatio George	BD, p2c3, 10/11/1878	Died in Boscobel on Sept. 30, 1878 at the age of 7 months, 2 weeks and 5 days. Son of R.C. and J. Stephens.
Stephens	Joel	BD, p3c3, 11/24/1882	Died Oct. 18, 1882 from heart disease at Rockville, Grant Co. Born in St. Ives [Cornwall?], England in 1806. Emigrated in 1845 to Rockville where he mined and farmed. Survived by daughter, Mrs. Ned Nicholas, and son, Joel H. His wife died 13 years ago.
Stephenson	Lizzie	DC, p3c4, 7/24/1886	Returned to De Soto. Taught school in Dakota for the last year.
Stephenson	Nettie	RH, p5c2, 7/8/1897	Died last Friday after being bitten by a rattlesnake while picking strawberries. Resided in Steuben.
Sterling	C. M.	DC, p2c2, 4/24/1888	C. M. Sterling of Victory sued Dennis and William Ryans for $1400. It was a boarding bill contracted while the railroad was being constructed in the area. Sterling won in the Wisconsin Supreme Court.

Genealogical Events from Newspapers for Crawford, Vernon and Grant Counties, Wisconsin, 1870-1901

LAST NAME	FIRST NAME	NEWSPAPER, PAGE/COLUMN MONTH/DAY/YEAR	GENEALOGICAL DATA
Sterling	C. M.	DC, p3c2, 11/13/1886	Planned to teach school in Victory.
Sterling	C. M.	DC, p3c4, 11/27/1886	Taught school in the Buchanan District per Victory news column.
Sterling	Cy	RH, p5c4, 12/1/1898	Resided in Victory. Hired by private parties to do surveying work in De Soto.
Sterling	Emma J., Miss	DC, p3c3, 10/29/1887	Resided in Ferryville. Visited her sister, Mrs. Vina Sterling of Retreat.
Sterling	Le Grand	DC, p2c1, 2/5/1887	Le Grand Sterling was interviewed by C. V. Porter for a series of articles on the Black Hawk War. In the article Mr. Porter wrote that "Le Grand Sterling informs me that a soldier, Leach, told him that at this pond, on Hyde's farm the whites over the first Indians who had given out. Mr. Sterling found a handful of silver brooches at the pond where those six Indians were killed, hence he concludes they were squaws."
Sterling	T. W.	RH, p4c2, 6/8/1899	He was 88. Found lying beside a road by Martin Robison of Manning near Robison's home. Sterling was drenched, full of mud and nearly dead from cold, hunger and exhaustion. Robison gave him dry clothes, fed him and put him to bed. Sterling told him the next day that he was from Mt. Sterling and that he had gotten lost while walking over to a neighbor's house. Robison claimed Sterling was not insane, but he was "childish." Sterling sent back to Gays Mills by train. Sterling was the founder of Mt. Sterling and was a pioneer of Crawford County. Sterling would have died "had it not been for the kindness of Mr. Robison."
Sterling	William T.	DC, p2c2, 1/29/1887	C. V. Porter interviewed William T. Sterling for his articles on the Black Hawk War. Sterling recalled that Black Hawk crossed the Pine River in Richland Co., just below the natural bridge.
Sterling	William T.	DC, p2c2, 2/5/1887	During the Black Hawk War, the American troops slaughtered the Indians at the Battle of Bad Axe. "Mr. Sterling says that [Capt.] Lindsay told him that during the fight the river was full of Indian ponies with women and children clinging to them. Lindsay saw six persons hanging to one pony. Many children were supposed to have drowned. Mr. James Fisher of Eastman, the oldest settler of American descent living in Crawford Co. says that the soldiers he conversed with 50 years ago informed him that Gen. Atkinson sounded the call and tried to stop the slaughter of women and children. But Col. Zachery Taylor told the Regulars not to mind it but go ahead. All the aged pioneers with whom I have conversed speak of this so called Battle of Bad Axe as a cruel butchery of women and children."
Stevens	B. A.	DC, p2c2, 11/26/1887	In 1857 the B. A. Stevens family moved to a ridge near De Soto. They were of New England extraction.
Stevens	B. A. and B. W.	DR, p3c2, 3/30/1871	Departed De Soto for new homes in Charles City, IA.
Stevens	boy	DR, p3c3, 12/14/1871	A son was born last Monday afternoon to Charles Stevens of De Soto.
Stevens	C. B.	DR, p3c1, 12/29/1870	The I.O.G.T. De Soto Lodge planned to meet at Steven's home on Houghton St. in De Soto until an appropriate hall can be secured.
Stevens	C. B.	DR, p3c2, 12/29/1870	The store of C. B. Stevens & Sons opened for business in De Soto in 1857. They sell dry goods, groceries, hardware, farming implements, stoves and tinware.
Stevens	C. B.	DC, p2c1, 12/31/1887	C. B. Stevens and Cyrus Worth of De Soto played violin for dancing [e.g. the Virginia Reel] at the Bay State Hotel housewarming party in 1856 or 1857. The town was founded on abstinence principals. The host, Seth Crowell, was horrified to find a whiskey jug had been sneaked into the festivities by Dr. Hyde and that most of attendees were intoxicated.
Stevens	C. B.	DC, p2c2, 2/3/1888	The De Soto House was abandoned as a hotel about 1859 and made into a store. C. B. Stevens united with John C. Kurtz to form C. B. Stevens & Co. and occupied the building.
Stevens	C. B.	DC, p3c2, 5/22/1888	Elected mayor in Ashton, Dakota. He was a former De Soto businessman.
Stevens	C. B. & Sons	DR, p2c4, 12/15/1870	Dealors in dry goods, groceries, plows, paint, etc. Established in 1857 in De Soto.
Stevens	Charles	DC, p2c2, 4/17/1888	Joined the Good Templar Lodge in De Soto [somewhere between 1856 and 1865]. While on a trip on the Great Lakes to visit friends in the east, he drank cider. The Good Templars brought him up on charges, which were not proven.
Stevens	Charley	DR, p3c1, 8/31/1871	He was the new telegraph operator in De Soto.
Stevens	Claud	RH, p5c3, 12/16/1897	Resided in Viroqua. He was a guest of Herman Davenport last weekend. Stevens will go to Boscobel to work on the new schoolhouse.
Stevens	Elsie	RH, p4c4, 2/16/1899	Left De Soto last week for Northville, SD.
Stevens	Fred	DC, p3c2, 12/10/1887	Fred Stevens and M. O. Woodhouse of Bloomington, WI are in charge of the newly opened St. Louis Store in De Soto.

Genealogical Events from Newspapers for Crawford, Vernon and Grant Counties, Wisconsin, 1870-1901

LAST NAME	FIRST NAME	NEWSPAPER, PAGE/COLUMN MONTH/DAY/YEAR	GENEALOGICAL DATA
Stevens	Ira H.	BD, p3c5, 7/27/1877	Ira H. Stevens married Julia Evans on July 13, 1877 at Jamestown. Groom from Liberty. Bride from Jamestown.
Stevens	Ira, Mrs.	DC, p3c5, 8/21/1886	Traveled from home in Victory to visit daughter in La Crosse.
Stevens	Ira, Mrs.	DC, p2c2, 9/17/1887	Left Victory for La Crosse to care for her daugher, Mrs. Ida Emberson, who was ill with diphtheria.
Stevens	M., Miss	DC, p3c4, 11/27/1886	Taught school at the Bishop neighborhood according to the Retreat news column.
Stevens	Mr. and Mrs.	DC, p3c4, 5/21/1887	Visited their daughter, Mrs. John Patterson of Genoa.
Stevens	Myra	DC, p2c2, 3/19/1887	Native of Lynxville. Taught school in Retreat.
Stevens	Myra	DC, p1c2, 4/19/1889	Resident of Lynxville. Taught school in Ferryville.
Stevenson	A. M., Mrs.	RH, p5c4, 2/16/1899	Came from Denver, CO to visit father, Samuel Abby of Viroqua.
Stevenson	Ellen	DC, p3c2, 3/12/1887	Departed De Soto for a teaching job in Martinsburg, NB.
Stevenson	James William	DR, p3c1, 8/10/1871	Died August 4, 1871. He was the only son of Hugh and Jennetta Stevenson of the Town of Genoa. The baby was 11 months old.
Stevenson	Lizzie	DC, p3c3, 7/9/1887	Returned to De Soto from Henry, Dakota where she had been engaged as principal of the Henry schools.
Stewart	R. B.	RH, p4c2, 6/15/1899	Arrived in Readstown from Sheridan, OR to visit with relatives.
Stewart	Sadie	DC, Supp, 10/23/1886	E. A. Craine married Sadie Stewart on Sept. 7, 1886 in La Grace, Dakota Territory.
Stickels	E. C., Rev.	BD, p3c1, 4/16/1880	New pastor in Boscobel.
Stillwell	Will	BD, p3c2, 8/29/1879	Will Stillwell married Carrie Rae on Tuesday evening at the residence of the bride's father. They took a train for Rushford, MN after the wedding. The Rev. John Allison officiated.
Stockert	Joseph, Mrs.	BD, p3c2, 1/10/1879	Died Thursday during childbirth in Little Green.
Stoda	Frank	DC, p3c3, 6/19/1888	Killed in a saw mill accident in Chippewa Falls.
Stoda	Frederick	DR, p3c2, 9/21/1871	Died Sept. 16, 1871 in the Town of Wheatland at 42 years of age.
Stoddart	Dr.	BD, p3c2, 3/9/1877	Tendered his resignation as pastor of the Congregational Church in Boscobel effective 15 May 1877, ending a 10-year term.
Stoddart	Emma	BD, p3c2, 9/19/1879	Brainard S. Burdick planned to marry Emma Stoddart next Wednesday at the Congregational Church in Boscobel.
Stoddart	Emma	BD, p2c2, 10/3/1879	Brainard S. Burdick married Emma Stoddart on Sept. 24, 1879 at the Congregational Church in Boscobel. There was extensive coverage of the guests.
Stoddart	John S.	BD, p3c4, 1/11/1878	John S. Stoddart married Sarah C. Carson on Jan. 8, 1878 at the home of the bride's mother. Groom from Boscobel. Bride from Richwood, Richland Co. The Rev. William Stoddart officiated.
Stoddart	W.	BD, p2c1, 10/2/1883	Newspaper published a letter written by W. Stoddart explaining his desire to separate himself from Bain Burdick. At the request of Burdick's second wife and evidence that Burdick thought the divorce from Stoddart's daughter had been completed, Stoddart decided not to travel to Memphis to help in the prosecution of Burdick.
Stoddart	William, Dr., Jr.	BD, p3c3, 2/20/1880	Accepted a position as district agent for the New York Life Insurance Co.
Stoddart	William, Jr.	BD, p3c3, 5/24/1878	Served as Treasurer of the Congregational Church in Boscobel.
Stoddart	Wm., Rev.	BD, p3c2, 6/3/1881	Moved to Black Earth to preside over at Congregational Church.
Stodke	Henry	DC, p2c2, 7/16/1887	Pluma Frazier married Henry Stodke on July 4, 1887. Bride and groom resided in Chaseburgh. The Rev. E. Trimin [Trumin?] officiated.
Stodsvold	N. H.	DC, p2c3, 7/3/1886	Opened a jewelry store opposite the Bay State House in De Soto.
Stoll	John	RH, p5c5, 7/15/1897	Served as postmaster in Ross.

Genealogical Events from Newspapers for Crawford, Vernon and Grant Counties, Wisconsin, 1870-1901

LAST NAME	FIRST NAME	NEWSPAPER, PAGE/COLUMN MONTH/DAY/YEAR	GENEALOGICAL DATA
Stolp	Bessie, Miss	DC, p2c4, 1/14/1888	Called on her many friends in Seneca. Spent the last few months of last year in Iowa and returned a short time ago to attend the wedding of her brother that took place Christmas at Mt. Sterling.
Stolp	Edwin	DC, p2c5, 1/14/1888	Edwin Stolp married Della McCrillis on Dec. 26, 1887 in Mt. Sterling at the home of the bride. Rev. Wm. Haughton officiated.
Stone	C. T.	BD, p3c1, 5/26/1882	Editor of a new publication, *Monfort Monitor*.
Stone	Charles T.	BD, p3c2, 3/16, 1877	Former resident of Boscobel. Now lives in Independence, IA. Makes background scenery for photographers for a living.
Stone	George	BD, p3c3, 5/11/1877	George Stone and LeRoy Rogers of Boscobel were charged with robbery.
Stone	W. C.	BD, p3c1, 3/25/1881	Formerly of Scranton, PA. The Las Vegas, New Mexico *Gazette* reported Stone made arrangements to operate the Hot Springs hotel.
Stone	W. C., Prof.	BD, p3c1, 6/25/1880	Formerly of Boscobel. Stone was spending the summer at his home in Waverly, Lackwanna Co., PA.
Stone	Winn C.	BD, p3c2, 3/18/1881	Formerly of Avoca. Now living in Las Vegas, New Mexico.
Stone	Winn C.	BD, p3c1, 3/7/1879	Played organ for the Congregational and Methodist Episcopal churches in Boscobel.
Storkson	Josephine	BD, p3c2, 2/13/1880	George E. Gates married Josephine Storkson on Feb. 4, 1880. Bride and groom were from Fennimore. Otho Shrader, Esq. officiated.
Storm	W. B.	DC, p2c3, 9/11/1888	Miss L. L. Clark married W. B. Storm on Aug. 22, 1888 at the home of G. C. Clark in Victory. Groom from Hector, MN. Took the train to Minneapolis to visit the bride's sister, Mrs. _. D. Forey. Planned to live in Hector where Storm was a druggist and grocer.
Stout	Frank	RH, p5c5, 7/15/1897	Departed the Ross area for a home in Minnesota. His sister's health is improving.
Stout	Minnie	RH, p5c3, 6/16/1898	William Bowling married Minnie Stout at home of the bride in Ross on June 1, 1898. They were both graduates of the deaf and dumb schools in Delavan.
Stowell	Cecil H.	BD, p3c1, 8/8/1879	Cecil H. Stowell married Anna Davenport on August 3, 1879. Bride and groom from Clayton, Crawford Co. Justice J. McLaughlin officiated.
Strait	Alva	RH, p4c2, 6/13/1901	Resided in La Farge. Opened a photograph gallery in Readstown.
Strait	Alva	RH, p4c3, 10/17/1901	Alva Strait married Daisy B. Huston on Oct. 9, 1901. Groom was a photographer in Readstown and the son of S. D. Strait of Otter Creek. Justice of the Peace W. J. Roberts officiated.
Stratton	H. K., Mrs.	RH, p4c2, 1/12/1899	Committed suicide on Wednesday with a revolver. She was despondent. Wife of the proprietor of the Viola House in Viola, WI. Moved to Viola about a month ago. Former resident of McGregor, IA. She was about 45 years old. Buried in Joliet, IL.
Strawn	David	DR, p1c3, 12/7/1871	Vernon Co. Board of Supervisors allowed payment to David Strawn, S. Steveson and J. E. Newell for services as commissioners of the poor.
Street	John	BD, p3c2, 5/27/1881	John Street recently married Dele Phelps. Street moved to Lancaster about a year ago and is connected with the woolen mill. Bride is daughter of Fred Phelps. Bride is niece of John Pepper of Boscobel.
Stroh	Millie	BD, p3c2, 12/25/1883	Antone Heine married Millie Stroh on Dec. 18, 1883 at the home of the bride's parents in Boscobel. Groom also from Boscobel. The Rev. T. W. Cole officiated.
Strong		BD, p3c1, 3/2/1883	Triplets were born last Saturday to William Strong of near Excelsior.
Strong		BD, p3c1, 7/20/1883	A second trial was ordered in the case, Strong vs. Philamalee, in Grant Co.
Strong	Giles	DC, p2c1, 5/29/1888	Resided in De Soto in the 1850s. He was the father of John Strong and Mrs. Darius Loper. "Giles was aged when he came to us, and although a little weak in the eyes and quite shaky in the legs, yet was very substantial after all." The Lopers lived in Brownsville at the time. [Interesting story about Giles is recorded here.]
Strong	Harry	RH, p5c4, 12/1/1898	Nearly drowned in the Winnesheik slough. Lived south of De Soto.
Strong	Jesse	DC, p2c2, 1/8/1887	Jesse Strong married Ada May Swan on Jan. 24, 1887. [Was date a typo?] Bride and groom from Lansing, IA. The Rev. Thomas Couch officiated at the ceremony in De Soto.
Strong	Jesse	DC, p2c2, 1/29/1887	Jesse Strong married Ada May Swan on Jan. 24, 1887. Bride and groom from Lansing, IA. The Rev. Thomas Couch officiated at the ceremony in De Soto.
Strum	Emma	RH, p5c4, 1/4/1900	Eugene Turnmire married Emma Strum on Jan. 1, 1900 at the home of F. H. Drake in Sugar Grove. Justice Ward officiated.
Stuka	Valentine	BD, p3c3, 4/16/1880	Valentine Stuka recently married Amelia Baumgartner at the Jacob Baumgartner residence in Fennimore. Planned to live in Plainville, Rock Co., KS.

Genealogical Events from Newspapers for Crawford, Vernon and Grant Counties, Wisconsin, 1870-1901

LAST NAME	FIRST NAME	NEWSPAPER, PAGE/COLUMN MONTH/DAY/YEAR	GENEALOGICAL DATA
Stunkard	Mr.	DR, p2c4, 8/24/1871	Operated a general store and flouring mill in Towerville.
Stussy	Jacob	DC, p3c2, 1/14/1888	Mary S. Ames married Jacob Stussy on Dec. 29, 1887. Bride from Freeman. Groom from Seneca.
Sullivan	George J.	RH, p5c5, 7/22/1897	In the case State vs. George J. Sullivan, the defendant was found guilty of murder in the second degree. Motion made for a new trial. Claimed the State failed to call Mrs. Gorman, wife of the deceased and an eye witness to the shooting. Motion denied.
Sumner	James and August	BD, p3c2, 9/26/1879	Sheriff Streeter took them to Waupon to serve a 1-year sentence for burglary.
Sunday School Institute		DR, p3c2, 8/31/1871	The Union Sunday School Institute was held at Morgan School House. The officers were E. T. Bishop, Henry Morgan, R. W. Jordan and J. C. Davis. The Executive Committee was comprised of E. B. Hyde, C. S. Fourt, Sister T. E. Engle, Spear and Rodgers. The Visiting Committee was comprised of Sister Battles, Victory; Bro. George Pullum, Asbury; Bro. Rodgers, West Prairie; Herman Delap, Munion; Sister Clara Lees, Rush Creek; Bro. C. S. Fourt, Gravel School; Bro. C. H. Tilden, Sunny Side; Bro. George Benedict, Cooley Valley; and Sister R. W. Jordon, Bishop School.
Sutherland	boy	RH, p4c4, 2/2/1899	A boy was recently born to Otis and Eva Sutherland of Sugar Grove.
Sutherland	boy	RH, p4c1, 6/22/1899	A son was recently born to George Sutherland of Readstown.
Sutherland	G. W.	RH, p4c1, 7/11/1901	Moved his family to Victory to fish for clams and hunt for pearls.
Sutherland	George	RH, p4c2, 12/28/1899	George's parents left on a trip to the south last May. They plan to spend the winter in Maryville, MO.
Sutherland	girl	RH, p5c4, 10/13/1898	A daughter was born on Tuesday to Dick Sutherland of Mound Park.
Sutherland	Henry	RH, p4c2, 12/29/1898	Henry Sutherland, W. B. Lossin, Clyde Danforth, John Loveless and Isaac Ewers of Co. M, 4th Wisconsin Volunteers came home for the holidays. They will be sent to Cuba for service in the Spanish American War..
Sutherland	Henry	RH, p4c2, 11/16/1899	Isaac Ewers and Henry Sutherland worked as detectives in Illinois, per a reprint of a news item published by a Springfield, IL newspaper.
Sutherland	Henry	RH, p4c2, 1/17/1901	Henry Sutherland married Julia O'Leary on Sunday at the residence of Vol Wilkinson in Readstown. Justice Davenport officiated.
Sutherland	Jeff	RH, p4c2, 1/19/1899	Jeff Sutherland and Jerry O'Lary returned to Readstown after spending the summer and fall working in Iowa.
Sutherland	Jefferson	RH, p4c3, 4/13/1899	Jefferson Sutherland married Rose O'Leary on April 8, 1899 at the residence of C. H. Davenport, Justice of the Peace. Bride and groom from Readstown.
Sutherland	John W.	RH, p4c2, 10/4/1900	Returned to Readstown after spending several months clamming for pearls on the Mississippi River near Victory. Found several fine pearls.
Sutherland	Lafe	RH, p7c2, 7/1/1897	Bought a new bicycle.
Sutherland	Lafe	RH, p4c2, 9/28/1899	Returned to Readstown after working in Tomah for the summer.
Sutherland	Ray	RH, p5c3, 7/27/1899	Resided in Kickapoo. Departed for Portland, OR.
Sutton		DC, p2c2, 5/21/1887	The youngest child of George Sutton died last week.
Swain	Blanche	RH, p4c2, 6/6/1901	George Townsend married Blanche Swain on June 3, 1901 at the home of the bride's parents, Mr. and Mrs. L. W. Swain of Readstown. Groom from Shortville, Clark Co., WI. Planned to move to Townsend's farm in Clark Co. The Rev. J. A. Neill officiated.
Swain	L. W.	RH, p2c1, 7/1/1897	Advertised services as a blacksmith in Readstown.
Swain	L. W.	RH, p5c2, 12/1/1898	Elected to fill the vacancy of Charles Aikins as Readstown Village Trustee.
Swain	L. W.	RH, p4c2, 2/14/1901	Returned to Readstown from Fond du Lac where he attended a High Court for the Foresters. He was a delegate from the Court Kickapoo.
Swan	Ada May	DC, p2c2, 1/8/1887	Jesse Strong married Ada May Swan on Jan. 24, 1887. [Was this a typo?] Bride and groom from Lansing, IA. The Rev. Thomas Couch officiated at the ceremony in De Soto.
Swan	Ada May	DC, p2c2, 1/29/1887	Jesse Strong married Ada May Swan on Jan. 24, 1887. Bride and groom from Lansing, IA. The Rev. Thomas Couch officiated at the ceremony in De Soto.
Swan	E. E.	DC, p4c1, 3/12/1889	E. E. Swan, Mart Low and Joe Adams of Ferryville attended Friday night's dance in De Soto.

Genealogical Events from Newspapers for Crawford, Vernon and Grant Counties, Wisconsin, 1870-1901

LAST NAME	FIRST NAME	NEWSPAPER, PAGE/COLUMN MONTH/DAY/YEAR	GENEALOGICAL DATA
Swan	Georgetta	DC, p2c2, 6/18/1887	Georgetta Swan married Uriah Nelson on June 19, 1887 at the Bay State parlors in De Soto. Bride and groom from Village Creek, IA. D. A. Steele, Esquire officiated.
Sweeney	Edward	DR, p1c1, 12/15/1870	Proprietor of the Sweeney House in De Soto.
Sweeny	Edward	DC, p2c1, 3/3/1888	He was a "linguist of the highest order. He was not only fluent in all known English words, but could, at a moment's notice, produce a coinage of unique phrases and expressive syllables that would lay out the most expert philologist in the whole country." Sweeny was a farmer outside De Soto. His sister and brother-in-law lived in Milwaukee. Extensive article on Sweeny.
Sweeny	Edward	DC, p2c2, 4/3/1888	Spoke Italian with a block of voters from Bad Axe City who were brought to Victory to help elect the opposition ticket in the Town of Wheatland in 1860.
Sweitzer	John	BD, p3c5, 3/24/1882	Second permanent settler in Fennimore. Moved to section 8 in 1838.
Swiber	Tena	BD, p3c1, 2/25/1881	Orange Gould married Tena Swiber on Tuesday in Boscobel. The Rev. T. M. Evans officiated.
Swiggum	J. C.	DC, p3c3, 8/14/1886	Resided in Town of Freeman. Sold Singer sewing machines.
Swigum	Anna	RH, p4c4, 6/27/1901	Resided in Viroqua. Taught school in Spring Valley.
Swingle	Edward	BD, p3c1, 10/30/1883	Edward Swingle married Mary Birk on Oct. 23, 1883 at Muscoda. The Rev. John Schoeberle officiated.
Sylvester	C. H.	BD, p3c2, 7/9/1880	Returned to Boscobel to study law. Spent the last two years in Arkansas City, KS where he was in charge of the schools.
Sylvester	C. Herb	BD, p3c2, 2/10/1882	Admitted to the bar in Grant Co. after reading the law in the offices of Hazelton and Provis in Boscobel.
Sylvester	D. R.	BD, p3c2, 9/8/1882	Lived in Lone Rock. Published a notice that he was declining an invitation to run for the Wisconsin Assembly.
Sylvester	D. R.	BD, p3c2, 5/28/1880	Appointed to be a census enumerator in Castle Rock, Grant Co.
Sylvestor	Asa B.	BD, XXXX, 1/25/1878	Died Jan. 20, 1878 in Yankton, Dakota of heart disease at the age of 24. He was the son of Hon. Daniel Sylvestor of Castle Rock, WI.
Syverson	Martha	BD, p3c3, 5/24/1878	Ole B. Forseth married Martha Syverson on Tuesday. Groom from Boscobel. They departed for Minneapolis. The Rev. O. Nuess officiated.
Syverson	O.	BD, p2c4, 10/22/1880	Has 15 years of experience as a shoemaker. Opened a boot and shoe trade in Boscobel 4 years ago.
Tabor	Eunice	BD, p3c3, 9/20/1878	Eunice Tabor will marry John Barnett at the home of the bride's parents in Independence, IA on Sept. 25, 1878. Bride daughter of Mr. and Mrs. S. J. W. Tabor. Groom from Independence, IA.
Tadder	Germain	BD, p2c4, 11/25/1881	Died yesterday in Richland Center, per the Nov. 18, 1881 issue of the *Richland Rustic*. Born in 1817 in Vermont. Resided in New York for some years and moved to Richland Co. 25 or 30 years ago. Served in the 25th Regiment WI Vol.
Taft	Daniel Oscar	BD, p3c1, 5/13/1881	Daniel Oscar Taft married Lena Lambert on May 4, 1881 in Boscobel. J. McLaughlin, J.P. officiated.
Taft	Homer Nelson	BD, p3c3, 6/8/1877	Pat Ryan, Homer Nelson Taft [found guilty of a murder attempt on James Harris on Wauzeka], Mr. Nichols and 2 Lawyers escaped from jail in Prairie du Chien.
Taft	J. Milton	BD, p3c1, 7/1/1881	Died May 1, 1881 in Boscobel of diabetes. Came to Boscobel for treatment. He was the 17-year-old son of Mrs. Mary Taft.
Taft	Mary, Mrs.	BD, p3c1, 11/4/1881	T. R. Seaton married Mrs. Mary Taft on Oct. 22, 1881 in Boscobel. The Rev. T. M. Evans officiated.
Taft	Olive L.	BD, p3c2, 9/27/1878	John Harris married Olive L. Taft on Sept. 22, 1878 at the Muffley House in Boscobel. Bride and groom from Crawford Co. Dr. William Stoddart officiated.
Talcott	Francis	RH, p5c4, 11/4/1897	Wright Hasking married Francis Talcott on Oct. 24, 1897 at the home of the groom's parents in Soldiers Grove. H. Gardner officiated.
Tate	George H.	RH, p5c3, 12/1/1898	Recently died in Viola. Suffered from Bright's Disease.
Tate	Lee	RH, p5c2, 10/27/1898	Planned to move from Readstown to Minnesota.
Tate	Mary, Mrs.	BD, p3c1, 9/1/1882	Lived in Bell Center. Purchased the Seaton place for $1500.
Tate	Rob.	RH, p5c3, 11/25/1897	Lived on Buckeye Ridge. He was an old settler who came to Readstown when it consisted of 3 houses.
Tate	W. W.	BD, p3c1, 8/7/1883	W. W. Tate and Nolan & Co. suffered severe loses when high water in the Kickapoo River washed out wood, ties and timber.

Genealogical Events from Newspapers for Crawford, Vernon and Grant Counties, Wisconsin, 1870-1901

LAST NAME	FIRST NAME	NEWSPAPER, PAGE/COLUMN MONTH/DAY/YEAR	GENEALOGICAL DATA
Tate	W. W.	RH, p4c2, 9/6/1900	W. W. Tate and wife left Bell Center for the Klondike to seek their fortune.
Tate	W. W., Mr.	RH, p4c1, 8/31/1899	Lived in Bell Center. Visited son, C. A. Huffman of Readstown.
Tate	William	BD, p3c2, 6/15/1883	Resided in Bell Center. Returned from Madison where he was a defendant in a U.S. District Court case brought by Northwestern University.
Tate	William	BD, p3c5, 9/27/1878	Resided in Belle Center. His barn was hit by lightening, killing 1 horse, 2 mares and 8 hogs. There were 4 men sleeping in the barn at the time. One man badly burned.
Tate	William, Mrs.	BD, p3c1, 2/4/1881	The body of Mrs. William Tate's sister was taken off the train in Boscobel. Mrs. Tate lived in Bell Center.
Taylor	Daniel	BD, p3c1, 3/12/1880	Planned to leave his home in Mt. Hope for Dakota. Taking 3 wagons. Wanted to put in a crop of spring wheat.
Taylor	David, Mrs.	BD, p3c3, 8/11/1882	Mrs. David Taylor of Cross Plains visited her mother-in-law, Mrs. J. L. Taylor of Boscobel.
Taylor	Ella	BD, p3c2, 7/7/1882	Died Monday evening [per 6/29/1882 issue of paper]. She was the 18-year-old daughter of Mr. and Mrs. H. M. Taylor of Richland Center.
Taylor	Ella, Miss	DC, p3c2, 10/15/1887	Lived in Buffalo, Wyoming Territory. Visited her brother, S. D. Taylor of near De Soto for the first time in 18 years.
Taylor	John	BD, p3c2, 5/28/1880	Appointed to be a census enumerator in Watterstown, Grant Co.
Taylor	John	BD, p2c2, 3/22/1878	John Taylor and Clarinda Russell were paupers chargeable to the Town of Fennimore.
Taylor	Leslie, Mr.	BD, p3c3, 8/1/1879	Arrived in Boscobel from Madison to visit with parents.
Taylor	Loyd	RH, p4c3, 7/18/1901	Maude Ewers married Loyd Taylor on July 4, 1901. Bride was daughter of G. A. Ewers of Readstown. Groom lived in Shortville, Clark Co., WI, the couple's future home. Justice C. H. Davenport officiated.
Taylor	Mary P.	BD, p3c2, 8/26/1881	Died Aug. 7, 1881 in Boscobel from cholera infantum. Aged 10 months and 14 days. Daughter of C. F. and M. S. Taylor.
Taylor	Miles	BD, p3c1, 12/1/1882	Taylor's wagon shop in Mt. Hope caught on fire. It was extinguished before severe damage was done.
Taylor	Thomas	DC, p3c3, 12/3/1887	Lorey Smith married Thomas Taylor on Nov. 24, 1887 in Seneca.
Teacher Examinations		DR, p3c3, 5/4/1871	The following persons passed an examination to teach school: Third Grade -- Misses Louisa Bartholomew, Eliza Kline, Fannie Caldwell; Third Grade 6 Months -- Missess Hannah Bishop, Huldah Davis, Emma Ankeny, Lavina Merrell, Lucinda Curtis, Messrs. James Heal, John Barr, George F. Seymour. At Mt. Sterling the following are entitled to certificates: Third Grade -- Misses Belle McCrillis, Ella Gay, Elizabeth Ingham, Rozella McAuley, Mr. W. S. Richardson; Third Grade 6 Months -- Misses Emma Bellows, Ellen Scott, Viola Wilcox, Bridget Haggarty. At Batavia the following are entitled to certificates: Third Grade -- Misses Lottie M. Jones, Emma Bonney, Mary Gear; Third Grade 6 Months -- Agnes Bray, Messrs. Eugene Alder, Albert Briggs.
Teacher's Institute		DR, p1c5, 9/28/1871	The semi-annual meeting of the Crawford Co. Teacher's Institute was held in Mt. Sterling. The officers were M. E. Mumford of Wauzeka, John Lovewell of Prairie du Chien, F. J. Tenney of De Soto, Peter Nolan of Prairie du Chien, A. C Ripley of Mt. Sterling and H. P. Kendall of De Soto. The instructors were M. E. Mumford, J. Lovewell, A. C. Ripley, H. P. Kendall, A. C. Wallin [of Prairie du Chien], Peter Nolan, F. J. Tenney, Miss Hattie Browne, Mr. Webster [of Prairie du Chien] and Martin Murphy. Prayer was offered by Rev. J. McKay. Music was provided by Ella V. Gay, Laura Miller, Belle McKendree, A. C. Ripley, Martin Murphy and J. C. Newcomb. Forty-five teachers attended the Institute.
Teacher's Institute		DR, p3c2, 4/20/1871	M. E. Mumford, Superintendent, organized a Teacher's Institute in De Soto. Instruction was provided by: F. J. Tenney of Mt.Sterling, George F. Seymore of Retreat, J. Malcomson of Prairie du Chien, Henry P. Kendall of De Soto, Hartwell Allen of Newton, Maggie Miller of Mt. Sterling, Mr. Hyde of Retreat, T. C. Ankeny of De Soto, Charles Tenney of De Soto, H. P. Kendall of XXX, Mr. Mitchell of XXX, and Miss Louisa Barthelomew of Victory. Lottie Rightmire and Laura Miller, in addition to several of the above teachers served on the Teacher's Institute Committee.

Genealogical Events from Newspapers for Crawford, Vernon and Grant Counties, Wisconsin, 1870-1901

LAST NAME	FIRST NAME	NEWSPAPER, PAGE/COLUMN MONTH/DAY/YEAR	GENEALOGICAL DATA
Teacher's Institute		DR, p3c2, 4/20/1871	The following attended the De Soto Teacher's Institute: from De Soto -- T. C. Ankeny, Emma Ankeny, Fannie Caldwell, Lucinda Curtis, Miss Haines, Henry P. Kendall, Mary Kendall, James Heal, Eliza Kline, Lavina Merrill, Charles Tenney, Anna Young; from Mt. Sterling -- Ella V. Gay, Belle McKendree, Maggie Miller, Laura Miller, Lottie Rightmire, Franklin J. Tenney; from Retreat -- Hannah M. Bishop, John Barr, Mr. Hyde, Robert McKay, George F. Seymore; from Freeman -- Hudson B. Engle, Mattie E. Engle; from Viroqua -- Louisa Barthelomew, Estella Ferguson; from Prairie du Chien -- J. Malcomson and from Newton -- Hartwell Allen.
Tedrtch	George	DC, p3c4, 5/14/1887	Resident of Ontario. Buried one of his children last week.
Teiuce	Christian	BD, p3c1, 12/3/1880	Purchased the Clark Linsay farm and will become a Grant Co. resident.
Telatko	Wencl	BD, p2c1, 6/10/1881	Bohemian man from Prairie du Chien area. Recently found hanging from a tree on the Black River Road. Committed suicide. Unmarried. Relatives lived in Philadelphia, PA.
Telfair	Bran [Brian?]	BD, p3c3, 2/15/1878	Bran [Brian?] Telfair married Miss Underwood about Feb. 4, 1878. [Marriage may have taken place in Lone Rock.]
Temple of Honor		BD, p3c2, 2/23/1877	The new officers in the Boscobel Temple of Honor are John H. Sarles; O. E. Miller; D. T. Parker, Jr.; Chad Barnett; William A. Muffley; B. S. Burdick; Henry Walters; Frank Parker; J. P. Miller; S. B. Willoughby; Rev. George Nuzum and Alexander Provis.
Temple of Honor		BD, p3c4, 3/1/1878	R. B. Rice, R. C. Stephens, A. B. Alden and O. B. Forseth of Boscobel instituted Crawford County's first Temple of Honor in Soldiers Grove on Feb. 21, 1878. The officers were F. Whittemore, George Baker, E. Williams, A. D. Smith, Charles Brekke, J. O. Davidson, Frank Smith, T. E. Hutchins, H. M. Knutson, Thomas Murphy and C. W. Baker.
Temple of Honor		BD, p3c3, 8/9/1878	The officers of the Richland Center Temple of Honor were W. M. Fogo, F. W. Burnham, R. Lybrand, M. Healy, Charles Spidel, D. O. Chandler, M. D. Hankins, D. G. Pease, W. Waters, O. F. Gibbs and George Jarvis.
Tennant	Elizabeth J.	BD, p3c2, 5/31/1878	John C. Bryson married Elizabeth J. Tennant in Mt. Ida on May 7, 1878. R. Buggins, Esquire officiated.
Tenney	Charles A.	DC, p3c4, 10/15/1887	Lived in De Soto. The government gave him a pension [for military service].
Tenney	Cora	DC, p3c4, 2/18/1888	Recently married Cora Tenney in Taylor Co. Bride from De Soto. Groom from Genoa.
Tenney	Lyman	DC, p3c2, 2/26/1887	Resided in Sioux Falls, Dakota. Visited his brother, Charles of De Soto.
Tenney	Martha	RH, p5c2, 10/20/1898	Taught school in Readstown. She was from Retreat.
Tennison	Odmund Allen	BD, p3c2, 4/4/1879	Died March 17, 1879 near Ashland, Saunders Co., NB of lung fever. He was the only child of William F. and Violetta Tennison and was 1 year, 2 months and 12 days old. He was the grandson of S. A. and M. A. Quincy.
Tenny	Franklin J.	DR, p1c4, 12/22/1870	Principal at the Mt. Sterling Academy.
Tenny/Tenney	Franklin J.	DR, p2c3, 12/29/1870	Principal at the Mt. Sterling Academy. Offered special instruction for teachers in the fall and spring terms. The 12-week term tuition was $5 for Common English Branches, $6 for Higher English Branches and $7 for Latin, Greek and Geometry. Board was $2.50 per week.
Terhune	W. F.	DC, p2c4, 6/12/1886	Advertised services as attorney-at-law and court commissioner in De Soto.
Tetter	Henry	BD, p3c2, 11/3/1882	Mary Ann Catherine Ruchtie married Henry Tetter on Tuesday. Bride from Boscobel. Groom from Marion. The Rev. R. Ramie officiated.
Tewalt		DC, p3c4, 9/11/1888	An infant child of Mr. Tewalt of Bad Axe was buried in the Retreat Cemetery on Sunday.
Tewalt	Freddy C.	DR, p3c1, 2/9/1871	Died Feb. 7, 1871 in Sterling. Aged 3 years, 6 months. He was the son of S. W. and Josephine Tewalt.
Thayer	John	DC, p3c4, 7/30/1887	John Thayer, Abram Bates and brother Bert, Frank Slater and Delmer Marton, all of Retreat, have gone to Dakota.
Thayer	Lewis	DC, p3c4, 12/4/1886	Taught school at Liberty Pole per Liberty Pole news column.
Thill	John	RH, p4c4, 1/26/1899	Worked as a barber in De Soto.
Thomas	A.	DC, p3c4, 6/11/1887	Died Monday night. He was an old resident. Lived about 3 miles from Lynxville.
Thomas	Charles	BD, p2c4, 5/10/1878	Formerly of Oregon. Ran the Grange Store in Bloomington.

Genealogical Events from Newspapers for Crawford, Vernon and Grant Counties, Wisconsin, 1870-1901

LAST NAME	FIRST NAME	NEWSPAPER, PAGE/COLUMN MONTH/DAY/YEAR	GENEALOGICAL DATA
Thomas	David, Mrs.	BD, p3c2, 9/7/1879	Arrived from Dane Co. to visit daughter, Mrs. J. P. Willis in Boscobel. Mrs. Thomas was 79.
Thomas	Frank W.	DC, p3c3, 6/19/1886	Accidently drowned while bathing in Lansing. He was the brother of Mr. Thomas of the *Lansing Mirror*.
Thomas	Fred	DC, p3c4, 6/18/1887	Resided in Hanover, IL. Visited friends in De Soto.
Thomas	George	BD, p3c3, 3/28/1879	Thomas was the foreman at the William McWilliams & Co. Stave Factory. V. Petty was in charge of the machinery. The factory was located in Crawford Co. across the Wisconsin River from Boscobel. Factories' history given.
Thomas	John I.	RH, p4c3, 10/31/1901	Resided in Prairie du Chien. Traveled to Soldiers Grove, went into the offices of the *Soldiers Grove Advance*, pulled out the racks of type and dumped them in the mud in front of the office. He was unhappy with a "scathing write-up in the previous issue of the paper."
Thomas	Morgan	BD, p2c3, 5/9/1879	The creditors of Morgan Thomas requested distribution of the estate.
Thomas	O.	BD, p2c4, 11/26/1880	Grant County paid him a bounty for scalps turned into the county.
Thomas	O. B., Captain	DC, p3c3, 9/18/1888	Renominated to be Representative to Congress for the 7th District. This will be his third term. He is known for fighting the monopolies and trusts.
Thomas	Ormsby B.	DC, p2c1, 10/9/1886	Candidate for Member of Congress, 7th District. Native of Prairie du Chien.
Thompson	A. P.	BD, p3c1, 1/5/1877	Attorney in Lancaster.
Thompson	Andrew	DR, p3c3, 5/11/1871	Sentenced to life in prison for the murder of the Haggarty family.
Thompson	Bird, Miss	DC, p2c2, 4/2/1887	Miss Bird Thompson recently married George Robinson in Victory at the residence of Peter Wadynxkee. Bride from La Crosse. Groom from Bergen.
Thompson	Charles R.	DC, p3c4, 6/12/1888	Resided in Ranton, NM. Subscribed to the *De Soto Chronicle*.
Thompson	Edith	BD, p2c2, 1/26/1883	The sleigh he was driving was destroyed in a run away accident. Resided in Mt. Sterling.
Thompson	Elman, Mrs.	BD, p3c1, 5/20/1881	She was formerly Amanda Maupin of the Boscobel area. Divorced her first husband on Mar. 1, 18__. One year later she married T. B. Wootton at Wa__Keeney, KS and now lives at Groton, KS. First husband was called a worthless, neglectful drunk.
Thompson	Frank	BD, p3c3, 11/15/1878	Came into town to attend his mother's funeral.
Thompson	G. S.	BD, p3c4, 5/3/1878	Recently died in Boscobel. A resolution of condolence was published by the I.O.O.F.
Thompson	girl	DC, p2c2, 3/19/1887	Daughter recently born to T. T. Thompson per the Ferryville news column.
Thompson	Gracie	DC, p2c3 8/13/1887	Died Aug. 8, 1887 at the age of 9 months. She was the daughter of Mr. and Mrs. James Thompson. The body was buried in Lawrence Cemetery.
Thompson	Hattie, Miss	DC, p3c4, 1/15/1887	Arrived from Nebraska to visit relatives in Seneca. Moved away 8 years ago.
Thompson	Helen	BD, p3c1, 1/26/1883	Bert B. Larson married Helen Thompson on Jan. 18, 1883 in Boscobel. Groom from Dakota. Bride from Marion, WI.
Thompson	J. L., Mrs.	BD, p3c2, 8/21/1883	Mrs. Miller and two children arrived from Waterloo, WI to visit her cousin, Mrs. N. B. Miller of Boscobel.
Thompson	Jo	DC, p3c3, 11/20/1886	Started up his feed mil for the season in Liberty Pole.
Thompson	John	BD, p3c1, 1/13/1882	John Thompson married Dell Wood in Mt. Ida on Jan. 1, 1882. Bride and groom were from the Town of Marion.
Thompson	Josiah, Mrs.	BD, p3c2, 11/15/1878	Died last Thursday in Boscobel. Her 12-year-old granddaughter tried to help. Word sent to husband who was in Iowa.
Thompson	Mrs.	BD, p3c4, 1/20/1882	The Boscobel City Council approved a motion to bind out Mrs. Thompson's two girls and send Mrs. Thompson to the county house for her support.
Thompson	Nancy, Mrs.	DC, p3c3, 2/18/1888	A. K. Bort recently married Mrs. Nancy Thompson at Viroqua, per De Soto news column.
Thompson	Sorren	RH, p4c2, 10/31/1901	Examined by the court in Prairie du Chien and found insane. Resided in Soldiers Grove. Sent to hospital for insane in Mendota. He was well known in Readstown. Served as clerk of the village for a year and was a clerk in William Crook's store for about 2 years.
Thompson	T. T.	DC, p3c5, 8/14/1886	Operated the Ferryville House in Ferryville.

Genealogical Events from Newspapers for Crawford, Vernon and Grant Counties, Wisconsin, 1870-1901

LAST NAME	FIRST NAME	NEWSPAPER, PAGE/COLUMN MONTH/DAY/YEAR	GENEALOGICAL DATA
Thompson	T. T.	DC, p3c5, 8/14/1886	Proprietor of the stage route between Ferryville and De Soto.
Thompson	Thomas	DC, p2c2, 12/11/1886	Kept a boarding house in Ferryville.
Thompson	W. F.	BD, p2c5, 10/22/1880	Manufactured the Wisconsin Valley Middlings Purifier in Boscobel. Product used by millers. Thompson was a millwright and inventor of the device.
Thompson	William	BD, P3c2, 4/23/1880	Sworn in as an alderman of Boscobel.
Thompson	William	BD, p3c1, 11/19/1880	A son was born Thursday to William Thompson of Boscobel.
Thompson	William, Mrs.	BD, p3c3, 8/23/1878	Survived a buggy accident with her mother, Mrs. Chandler.
Thompson Bros.		BD, p2c6, 10/22/1880	Thompson Bros. commenced business in Boscobel 15 years ago. They are among the "heaviest operators of live stock, grain and farm machinery in Grant County." They also do business in Fennimore and Montfort. Operated one of the principal grain operations in Boscobel.
Thomson	John	DR, p3c2, 1/4/1872	Building a new ferryboat for Gardner & Wareham for use on the Mississippi River. It will be called the *John Thompson* in his honor.
Thomson	Mr.	DR, p3c1, 10/5/1871	Lived in Mt. Sterling. He was deputy sheriff of Crawford Co. and an agent for Springville nurseries.
Thorp	Elizabeth	DR, p3c6, 3/23/1871	Probate notice stated that Elizabeth Thorp of Vernon Co., daughter of Lydia Griffin, petitioned that Thomas D. Weller be named administrator of the Griffin estate.
Thorpe	I. M., Jr.	BD, p2c2, 5/10/1878	Recently died. A resolution of condolence was published by the I.O.O.F.
Thurber	L. H., Mrs.	BD, p3c3, 9/19/1879	Lived in Muscoda. Entertained her sister-in-law, Mrs. Mack of South Bend, and her cousin, Miss Jervis of Milwaukee.
Thurston	A. R., Mrs.	BD, p2c4, 12/16/1881	Resided in Waterstown, Dakota. Husband abandoned her in Viroqua. She had advanced consumption. Married Thurston 6 months ago in Austin, MN. He took her money when he abandoned her. Lawyers had advised her earlier not to give property to her husband. Supposedly had a sister living in the Town of Kickapoo.
Tice	Christian	BD, p3c1, 4/20/1883	Lived near Boscobel. Committed suicide on Wednesday with a revolver. Suffered with rheumatism. Lived in the area for the last 17 years. He bought the Clark Lindsay place about 2 years ago.
Tice	Frank	BD, p3c2, 5/30/1879	Escaped from Boscobel jail before being transferred to Lancaster. He was a "self-styled detective" that was recently arrested for stealing. He was a Grant Co. resident.
Tichenor	E. D.	BD, p2c2, 3/23/1883	Left Seneca last January when he eloped with his wife's sister. R. G. Mathews, city marshall of Prairie du Chien, arrested Tichenor in Cedar Rapids, IA where he relocated under an assumed name. The young lady returned to Seneca.
Tier	Harry	BD, p2c4, 2/2/1883	A fire destroyed Floaten's Grocery Store, Harry Tier's abstract office and A. H. Krouskop's brick buildings in Richland Center. W. Herpel, "the bakery man," discovered the fire.
Tierney	Timothy, Mrs.	DC, p3c4, 4/16/1887	Died Good Friday at the age of 91. Buried on Easter at the Catholic Church. She was the grandmother of J. C. DeLacy of De Soto.
Tilden		DC, p2c2, 11/26/1887	The Tilden family arrived in De Soto in 1857.
Tilden	Charles H.	DC, p3c2, 10/22/1887	Subscribed to the *De Soto Chronicle*. Resided in Worchester, MA.
Tillotson		BD, p3c1, 3/24/1882	Involved with failure of the Exchange Bank in Boscobel. Creditors settled for 30% on the dollar and a note for return of the balance in 7 years.
Tillotson	M. D.	BD, p3c3, 3/10/1882	Opened the Exchange Bank in Boscobel in 1878 after the failure of the First National Bank of Boscobel. A. J. Pipkin ran a competing bank that was considered the successor to the First National Bank. Tillotson had been the cashier at the First National Bank. Speculation in wheat futures brought matters to a crisis for Tillotson, the depositors and creditors. The bank was closed on Mar. 3rd. The following is a partial list of the bank's creditors: L. A. Rounds, Belle Center; Lyman Brown, Belle Center; Krammer & Hanner, Chicago; Merchants Exchange Bank, Milwaukee; J. P. Willis; T. Carrier; Wm. Scott; Leroy Booher; J. Call; Thos. Keating; A. Palmer; P. Kelts; Mrs. Joseph Jackson; C. A. Steele; F. Mortimer; L. G. Armstrong; J. H. Sarles; Wm. McWilliams; T J. Brooks; L. P. Lesler; F. Flynn; Pittman & McWilliams; M. B. Pittman; Th. Kronshage; John Parker; Geo. C. Hazelton and M. Zwicky.
Tillotson	M. D., Mr. and Mrs.	BD, p3c3, 7/22/1881	Left Boscobel for Michigan to attend the funeral of Mr. Tillotson's father.
Timermans	boy	DC, p3c3, 1/7/1888	A son was recently born to H. Timermans of Ontario, WI.

Genealogical Events from Newspapers for Crawford, Vernon and Grant Counties, Wisconsin, 1870-1901

LAST NAME	FIRST NAME	NEWSPAPER, PAGE/COLUMN MONTH/DAY/YEAR	GENEALOGICAL DATA
Timmerman	D.	DC, p2c2, 3/12/1887	Operated a general store in place of O. H. Millards in Ontario. [Millards may have gone to San Diego, CA.]
Tippets	William	DC, p3c2, 7/31/1886	The skiffs owned by William Tipplets and William Kish of Victory were recently stolen.
Tippett	William	DC, p3c3, 1/28/1888	Lost 5 head of cattle at his Victory farm when a train hit them on the track.
Tippitts	Carrie	DC, p2c2, 4/9/1887	P. Reese recently married Carrie Tippitts. Groom from Lansing, IA. Bride from Victory.
Tobler	David H.	BD, p3c2, 8/10/1877	Died in Lancaster on July 27, 1877 at the age of 66.
Todd	Joseph	BD, p3c3, 10/27/1882	Killed by a falling tree limb that was cut to get at honey in a tree. He was 40 years old. Survived by wife and several children. Lived near West Lima, Richland Co.
Tohsh [or Tolish]	Sophia	BD, p3c2, 2/2/1883	Francis Kot married Sophia Tohsh [or Tolish] on Jan. 13, 1883. Bride and groom were from Hickory Grove. The Rev. Charles Schroudenback officiated.
Tompson	F. G.	BD, p3c2, 5/28/1880	Appointed to be a census enumerator in Hazel Green, Grant Co.
Tompson	girl	DC, p2c3, 3/12/1887	Daughter born last week to T. T. Tompson of Ferryville.
Tompson	Hattie	DC, p3c4, 3/5/1887	May Langdon and Hattie Tompson, both of Seneca, intend to start for Nebraska in a few days.
Toney	William	BD, p3c2, 9/16/1881	Resided on the old Enyart farm in Rolling Ground, Crawford Co. Recently found a notice fastened to his gate that threatened to kill him if he didn't leave the farm. Note said, "No man shall never work this farm."
Tongue	L. L.	DC, p2c2, 8/7/1886	Will probably run for Sheriff in Vernon Co.
Tongue	L. L.	DC, p3c5, 9/18/1886	Announced himself to be a Republican candidate for Sheriff of Vernon Co. He resided in Hillsboro, Wisconsin.
Tongue	L. N.	DC, p2c2, 7/2/1887	Died June 25, 1887 at his residence in the village of Hillsborough. Buried by G.A.R.
Tormey	Anna	BD, p3c1, 4/6/1883	Resided in Fennimore. Taught at the Highland school.
Tormey	Nicholas	BD, p3c1, 4/13/1883	Nicholas Tormey married Johanna Carmody on April 3, 1883 at Mt. Hope. Bride from Mt. Hope. Groom from Fennimore.
Tower		RH, p5c4, 1/27/1898	The Tower family was quarantined by Henry Maiben, Health Officer of Readstown. They had measles. This was the fourth time the home was quarantined in the last six months.
Tower	James	RH, p5c2, 7/22/1897	Family had diphtheria. His home near Readstown was quarantined.
Tower	L., Mrs.	DC, p3c2, 9/10/1887	Arrived in De Soto from Eau Claire. Planned to visiter her sister, Mrs. Tewalt.
Tower	Nora	RH, p5c3, 9/15/1898	Nora Tower married Richard Henry Osborn on August 21, 1898 at the home of the bride's parents near Readstown. C. H. Davenport, Justice of the Peace, officiated.
Tower	T. W.	DR, p2c4, 8/24/1871	Operated a woolen factory iand general store in Towerville
Towers	James	RH, xxxx, 8/12/1897	One of James Towers' children died of diphtheria.
Townsend	Byron	DC, p2c1, 10/29/1887	In 1856 Townsend drew the attention of C. B. Whiting, author of an article on De Soto's early history, because of Townsend's his immaculate linen, fashionable clothes and "the sort of proprietary interest he seemed to have in the place." Townsend later retired from his partnership with Ankeny and drove a team "in the costume of the country -- cowhide boots and blue jean overalls."
Townsend	Frances E.	RH, p5c4, 1/20/1898	I. A. Vernon recently married Frances E. Townsend, per Sugar Grove news column. J. H. Ward officiated.
Townsend	George	RH, p4c2, 6/6/1901	George Townsend married Blanche Swain on June 3, 1901 at the home of the bride's parents, Mr. and Mrs. L. W. Swain of Readstown. Groom from Shortville, Clark Co., WI. Planned to move to Townsend's farm in Clark Co. The Rev. J. A. Neill officiated.
Townsend	Hon.	RH, p5c4, 7/21/1898	Hon. Townsend of Illinois, a survivor of the Black Hawk War, will speak at the Old Settlers picnic at Battle Hollow near Victory, the site of the Black Hawk battleground.
Townsend	Sol	RH, p4c4, 3/30/1899	Injured while logging for Gladney Ewers. Tree fell and crushed his ankle.
Towsley	George	BD, p2c4, 7/22/1881	Received a telegram that he was to capture/arrest a passenger a train stopping in Lone Rock.

Genealogical Events from Newspapers for Crawford, Vernon and Grant Counties, Wisconsin, 1870-1901

LAST NAME	FIRST NAME	NEWSPAPER, PAGE/COLUMN MONTH/DAY/YEAR	GENEALOGICAL DATA
Trager	John	BD, p3c2, 5/28/1880	Appointed to be a census enumerator in Waterloo, Grant Co.
Tramp		BD, p3c3, 9/13/1878	A tramp fell under the train in Boscobel. His feet were amputated. Refused to give his name. His uncle was Patrick Carroll of Chenoa, Bloomington Co, IL. His sister was Annie of Bloomington. His mother was Kate Clock of 208 Broadway, Westminster, London.
Trayer	John	DR, p3c1, 12/21/1871	Resided in Lansing. Badly injured by a falling tree whle chopping on the island.
Treadwell	Charles T., Capt.	DC, p2c1, 11/26/1887	Capt. Charles T. Treadwell and Frederick Carr bought the De Soto sawmill property of A. B. Clapp in 1856 or 1857. Treadwell was an old friend of Capt. Washington Plummer. When Plummer's barrel enterprise failed, Treadwell let the sawmill revert to Clapp and returned to Boston, having lost considerable money. Treadwell took command of another sailing vessel and died some years later on shipboard.
Treseder	James	RH, p4c2, 9/19/1901	Sold his 372-acre farm at Viola to William Henthorn of Richland County for $4500.
Treseder	Mable	RH, p4c2, 12/29/1898	Mable Treseder of Viola, Allie Richards of Viroqua and Nettie Goyer of Readstown came up the railroad line from Platteville Normal School to spend the holidays.
Trott	B.	DR, p1c1, 12/15/1870	Proprietor of the Bay State House [a hotel] in De Soto. Also operated a billiard saloon.
Trott	B., Mrs.	DC, p3c4, 3/10/1888	Advertised the sale of the Bay State House in De Soto. Consisted of a hotel and barn.
Trott	Benjamin, Mrs.	DC, p2c3, 8/28/1888	Rented the Bay State House in De Soto to Mrs. A. N. Miller.
Trott	Hannah, Mrs.	DC, p3c3, 12/25/1888	Mrs. Hannah Trott married George Coffin on Dec. 20, 1888 at the residence of J. H. Rogers in De Soto. Bride from De Soto. Groom from Ashton, Dakota.
Trowbeidge	M. M., Dr.	RH, p5c4, 11/4/1897	Dr. M. M. Trowbeidge planned to marry Regna Linderman on Nov. 7, 1897 at the home of the bride's parents in Viroqua.
Truax	Dr.	RH, p4c2, 6/28/1900	Died Monday night of paralysis in Muscoda. He was the father of Mrs. Minnie Clark of Readstown. Funeral was held at Orion by Rev. McClasky of Muscoda.
Trumbower	Jacob	DC, p8c2, 6/21/1889	Jacob Trumbower married Myrtie Steele on Saturday in Milledgeville, IL. Groom was the station agent in Milledgeville. Bride was daughter of D. A. Steele, formerly of De Soto.
Trycle	Mr.	RH, p4c3, 12/16/1897	Erected a cigar factory near Spring Valley. Former resident of Viroqua.
Tryon	Mrs.	BD, p3c2, 11/9/1877	Mrs. Tryon and daughter, Mable, of Prairie du Chien, passed through Boscobel on their way to a new home in Richland Center.
Tucker		DC, p4c3, 4/26/1889	A little girl of Mr. and Mrs. F. W. Tucker unexpectedly died.
Tucker	F. W.	DC, p3c3, 7/31/1888	Belle White married F. W. Tucker on July 27, 1888 at the residence of the bride's parents. Bride was the daughter of H. H. White, the founder of Stoddard. Groom was an agent for the Burlington Railroad.
Tucker	F. W.	DC, p2c3, 2/19/1889	Agent in De Soto for the C. B. and N. Railroad.
Tucker	F. W.	DC, p4c1, 5/3/1889	He was the De Soto agent for the C. B. & N. Railroad.
Tucker	girl	DC, p4c4, 3/29/1889	A daughter was born on Wednesday to W. F. Tucker of the De Soto area.
Tuffley	George	BD, p2c2, 8/28/1883	Published a notice that he had taken up a stray mare in the Town of Marion.
Tuffley	George	BD, p3c2, 5/28/1880	Appointed to be a census enumerator in Marion, Grant Co.
Tuffley	George	BD, p3c2, 10/18/1878	Tuffley home in the Town of Marion was destroyed by fire. Loss valued at $800. It was partially insured.
Tuffley	Thomas	BD, p2c2, 12/25/1883	Thomas Tuffley was a private in Co. K, 12th WI Regt. during the Civil War. An article was publishing detailing his courage during the Battle of Atlanta. Though sick, he volunteered to replace a fellow soldier who was labeled a "coward" during a charge. Tuffley was a farmer in Grant County in 1883. Other soldiers mentioned in the article were: Lieut. Mike J. Cantwell, Col. Bryant Proudfit, Levi Bresee and Lieut. Nelson Chandler. Chandler was a native of Crawford County. "Chandler, brave to a fault, [he was afterward killed in the front of battle,] took the men out of position and began the perilous march."
Tulley	Minnie	RH, p5c2, 9/15/1898	Taught school in Readstown. She was from Rising Sun.
Tulley	Minnie	RH, p4c1, 5/25/1899	Returned to Boma from Readstown after completing the school year.

Genealogical Events from Newspapers for Crawford, Vernon and Grant Counties, Wisconsin, 1870-1901

LAST NAME	FIRST NAME	NEWSPAPER, PAGE/COLUMN MONTH/DAY/YEAR	GENEALOGICAL DATA
Tulloch	Alex	DC, p2c2, 6/4/1887	Clara Collins married Alex Tulloch on May 25, 1887 at the home of the bride. Bride from Purdy. The Rev. William Haughton officiated.
Turben	Lena	RH, p5c3, 11/24/1898	Miss Lena Turben of Soldiers Grove visited her sister, Mrs. Dick Sutherland of Mound Park.
Turner		RH, p5c4, 4/28/1898	A son was recently born to Henry Turner of Sugar Grove.
Turner	Charles	RH, p5c3, 3/30/1899	Charles Turner recently married Daisy Higinbotham per Sugar Grove news.
Turner	George	BD, p2c4, 11/26/1880	Grant County paid him a bounty for scalps turned into the county.
Turner	R. C.	DC, p3c5, 10/2/1886	Left home in Towerville to work on railroad bridges in Washington Territory.
Turnmire	Eugene	RH, p5c4, 1/4/1900	Eugene Turnmire married Emma Strum on Jan. 1, 1900 at the home of F. H. Drake in Sugar Grove. Justice Ward officiated.
Turnmire	Gean	RH, p5c4, 11/23/1899	Returned to Sugar Grove from the west where he worked last summer. He fell on corn stubble, "pushing an eye out."
Turnmire	girl	RH, p4c1, 8/2/1900	A daughter was recently born to Will Turnmire of Readstown.
Turnmire	Jim	RH, p5c4, 1/27/1898	Planned to work on the farm of Purdy Shilling of Kickapoo Center next season.
Tuttle	Ella, Mrs.	DC, p3c1, 12/31/1887	Visited her mother, Mrs. John Babcock of De Soto.
Tuttle	William E.	BD, p3c2, 2/21/1879	William E. Tuttle married Lizzie A. Palmer on Feb. 19, 1879. Bride from Fennimore. Elder Shears performed the ceremony at the Shears residence.
Twaites	R. S.	RH, p5c3, 8/4/1898	Spoke on the Black Hawk War in Soldiers Grove.
Twining	Jacob	BD, p3c4, 3/9/1883	Hiram W. Favor applied to the Grant County Court to admit to probate the will of Jacob Twining, late of Boscobel.
Tyler	Dr.	BD, p3c4, 8/29/1879	Died Aug. 24, 1879. He was an old resident of Muscoda and was buried with Masonic honors.
Tyler	Nathan	BD, p3c1, 2/14/1879	Found guilty of battery against Prof. Smith, Principle of schools in Muscoda.
Tyler	Nellie Estelle Alice	BD, p3c4, 2/23/1877	Died of diptheria on Feb. 5, 1877. Aged 1 year 9 months. Mary Ella Tyler died Feb. 14, 1877. She was 8 years 5 months old. They were the daughters of E. A. and A. R. Tyler, MD, of Muscoda.
Tyler	William	BD, p2c1, 10/5/1877	Died last Friday on the farm he lived on for the last 25 years in Wattertown.
Tyron	Cyrus	BD, p3c2, 5/7/1880	Received a letter from his two sons in Dakota. Their new home, barns, and farm equipment were destroyed by a prairie fire, per the *Richland Observer*.
Umback	Rosa	RH, p4c2, 1/4/1900	Oscar Marten married Rosa Umback last Monday at the home of George Sutherland. C. H. Davenport officiated.
Unclaimed Letters		BD, p3c3, 9/16/1881	Unclaimed letters in Boscobel for Mrs. Ella Brown, Nate Barto, Alva Bullock, Thomas Broadbent, George W. Cass, Joseph Fritz, Robert Gillett, Mrs. Betsy Taylor, John Mathias and Olive Mitchell.
Unclaimed Letters		RH, p4c3, 12/9/1897	Isaac Johnson, W. J. Maddox, Mrs. Geo. McPheters and Roy Skinner had unclaimed letters at the Readstown post office.
Unclaimed Letters		RH, p5c2, 12/8/1898	Mrs. Catherine Bankas, Mrs. Ramsey, Miss Kate Ward and Mrs. Clara Vance had unclaimed letters at the Readstown Post Office.
Underwood	Miss	BD, p3c3, 2/15/1878	Bran [Brian?] Telfair married Miss Underwood about Feb. 4, 1878. [Marriage may have taken place in Lone Rock.]
Unger	Fred	BD, p3c5, 10/12/1877	Died in Prairie du Chien last Saturday from suicide. He was a 45-year-old wagon maker.
Upham	boy	DC, p3c3, 7/31/1886	A son was born on July 24, 1886 to Clayton Upham of De Soto.
Upham	boy	DC, p3c4, 5/29/1888	A son was born May 15, 1888 to Clayton B. Upham of De Soto.
Upham	C. B.	DC, p3c4, 11/13/1888	Left De Soto for Great Barron, MS to bring back his grandmother. The grandmother planned to live with her daughter, Mrs. Thomas Minor of Retreat.
Upham	Charles H.	DC, p2c3, 2/19/1889	Built his store in De Soto in 1887 to sell general merchandise. Deals and ships all kinds of farm produce.
Upham	Lizzie, Mrs.	DC, p3c3, 7/30/1887	Mrs. Lizzie Upham and children of the De Soto area visited her mother, Mrs. Duffy of Fort Atkinson, IA.

Genealogical Events from Newspapers for Crawford, Vernon and Grant Counties, Wisconsin, 1870-1901

LAST NAME	FIRST NAME	NEWSPAPER, PAGE/COLUMN MONTH/DAY/YEAR	GENEALOGICAL DATA
Valentine	Grandma	DC, p2c2, 7/2/1887	Arrived from Greenwood, NB to visit old friends in Lynxville.
Valentine	J. C.	DR, p3c5, 1/12/1871	He was an early resident of De Soto who now lived in East Saginaw, MI. His friend, Henry Gardner of De Soto, sent him a copy of the new newspaper.
Valentine	J. C.	DC, p2c1, 2/3/1888	In 1857 J. C. Valentine became weary and the firm of Whiting & Valentine was dissolved in De Soto. Valentine ran a wood boat one season and then he went away for good.
Vallant	Richard	DC, p2c2, 4/2/1887	Richard Vallant recently married Minnie Hollinger at the residence of J. Hollinger.
Vallee	Anthony	DC, p2c1, 6/26/1886	"Forty years ago the place where De Soto now stands was a French trading post where Poor Lo traded his furs for beads, blankets, powder and firewater. About thirty years ago Anthony Vallee and Dr. E. K. Houghton came to De Soto and through their efforts others were induced to come to the place . . ."
Vallee	Anthony	DC, p2c2, 10/29/1887	Owned a house and workshop near the present site of the Bay State Hotel in De Soto in 1856.
Valley	Mr.	BD, p1c8, 11/23/1877	Mr. Valley of Crawford County passed his 100th birthday celebration. He was hale and hearty. He milked 5 cows everyday.
Van Allen	Charles	BD, p3c2, 7/16/1880	Aged about 19 years. Former resident of North Star, Crawford Co. Recently arrest for murder in Minnesota. Local friends are confident this is a mistake.
Van Alstine	Blanche	RH, p5c3, 8/30/1900	Died August 29, 1900 at the age of 3. Daughter of E. A. Van Alstine. Funeral held at Viroqua.
Van Alstine	E.	RH, p4c2, 6/13/1901	Lightening struck a telephone pole causing a blaze at the telephone company central office. Van Alstine put out the fire and saved Miss Iscia Reeve, the telephone girl.
Van Alstine	Irvin	RH, p4c2, 1/19/1899	Lived in Viroqua. Visited his brother-in-law, C. H. Davenport of Readstown.
Van Antwerp	Ed, Mr.	BD, p3c3, 7/1/1881	Resided in Yankton. Visited sister, Mrs. George Hazelton of Boscobel.
Van Buren	Nettie	BD, p3c1, 12/29/1882	W. E. Bell married Nettie Van Buren on Sunday at the residence of Mrs. Beebe. Bride was a teacher and native of Boscobel. Groom was a member of the Grant Co. Bar and resided in Montfort.
Van Dusen		BD, p3c2, 3/12/1880	A passerby stopped at the Van Dusen home near West Lima, Vernon Co. Wife was found dead in her bed. Husband was lying next to her. He was too sick and weak to get up. He died soon after he was found.
Van Fleet	Chloe	RH, p5c3, 1/10/1901	Chloe Van Fleet married Walter Elder on Christmas Day. Justice Ward of Sugar Grove officiated.
Van Horn	Wilan	BD, p3c5, 6/23/1882	A dissolution of partnership was published by James Gunklan and Wilan VanHorn of the Town of Scott.
Van Velzer	B.	DR, p2c6, 12/15/1870	Proprietor of the Mondell House in Prairie du Chien.
Van Wagner	F. K.	DC, p2c3 8/27/1887	Resided in Franklin. Mrs. Etta Brooks of Davenport, IA, a daughter, arrived for a visit.
Van Wagner	George C.	DC, p2c2, 10/29/1887	Owned a fanning mill shop in De Soto in 1856.
Van Wagner & Worth		DR, p3c3, 9/21/1871	Made fanning mills in De Soto in 1856.
Van Winter	E. T.	RH, p4c2, 9/6/1900	Minnie Aikins married E. T. Van Winter on Sept. 2, 1900. Bride was the daughter of W. H. Aikins of Kickapoo. Rev. Bell officiated.
Van Winter	E. Tenney	RH, p4c2, 6/21/1900	Named his leading cigar the "Readstown Belle." Van Winter was a cigar maker.
Van Winter	Ed.	RH, p4c2, 11/22/1900	Owned the Central Store in Readstown. He is "probably the only deaf storekeeper in Wisconsin" per *Deaf World* of Columbus, OH.
Van Winter	Tenny	RH, p4c2, 5/31/1900	Opened a cigar factory in the W. H. Aikins building in Readstown.
Van Winters	Walter	RH, p4c2, 6/8/1899	C. H. Davenport was teaching him the tinner trade.
Van Zant	Capt.	DC, p3c2, 8/28/1888	Ran the Steamboat, *Musser*.
VanBuren	Nettie	BD, p3c1, 3/17/1882	Taught school at Hickory Grove.
Vance	John M., Mrs.	DC, p3c3, 2/19/1887	Mrs. John M. Vance died Tuesday night in West Prairie.
Vance	Julia	BD, p3c4, 11/13/1883	A foreclosure sale was published for property owned in Boscobel in the case Julia Vance, plaintiff, vs Sylvester and Catherine [wife] Keyes defendants.

Genealogical Events from Newspapers for Crawford, Vernon and Grant Counties, Wisconsin, 1870-1901

LAST NAME	FIRST NAME	NEWSPAPER, PAGE/COLUMN MONTH/DAY/YEAR	GENEALOGICAL DATA
Vanderbilt	John	DC, p3c3, 11/13/1886	Planned to hold a dance in his hall in Lynxville on Nov. 25, 1886. Gardner's Quadrille [Quadville?] Band will furnish the music.
Vanderbilt & Coffin		DC, p3c4, 8/21/1886	Operated a saloon in Lynxville.
Vanderpool	A. C.	BD, p3c3, 7/1/1881	A. C. Vanderpool recently married Mary McWilliams. Bride daughter of Thomas McWilliams of Boscobel. Groom from Eagle, WI. Guest list printed.
VanPhillips		BD, p3c2, 7/15/1881	The 16-month-old daughter of Mr. and Mrs. VanPhillips of the Boscobel area recently drowned in a tub of water. Mrs. VanPhillips was visiting with her father who resides at Cannon's Mills, Crawford Co.
Vanvalkenburg	Miss	BD, p3c1, 2/27/1880	Resided in Millville. Jolted off her wagon and broke her leg in two places.
VanValkenburg	S. J.	DR, p3c2, 9/21/1871	Died Sept. 10, 1871 in Decorah, IA of intermittent fever. He was also known as "Big Auctioneer."
Varrell	Hiram	BD, p3c4, 7/1/1881	Died Friday evening. Born Sept. 9, 1824 in New Market, New Hampshire. Moved to Fennimore in 1872. He and brother, John, built the hotel in Fennimore. Married Elyra Perkins in Aug. 1847 at Manchester, NH. She was from Montpelier, VT. Father of one boy and one girl.
Varrell	John	BD, p2c1, 9/18/1883	Managed the Boscobel Agricultural & Driving Park Association grounds.
Vaughn	W. A.	BD, p3c4, 9/14/1877	Made a living buying grain in Wauzeka.
Vernon	I.	RH, p5c2, 1/13/1898	Moved to Sugar Grove from Readstown.
Vernon	I. A.	RH, p5c4, 1/20/1898	I. A. Vernon recently married Frances E. Townsend, per Sugar Grove news column. J. H. Ward officiated.
Vernon Co. Board		DC, p3c4, 4/10/1888	The following men were elected to the 1888 Vernon County Board: E. B. Homestead, Christiana; Helga Larson, Coon; Ole H. Netwick, Jefferson; Christ Didrickson, Webster; Chris Ellefson, Franklin; C. E. Morley, Kickapoo; T. J. Spear, Hillsborough; Peter Jerman, Sterling; R. T. Bentson, Viroqua; L. A. Aiken, Harmony; William L. Riley, Genoa; Alex Hill, Jr., Stark; R. H. Buchanan, Liberty; H. D. Williams, H. P. Proctor, Peter Nelson, all of Viroqua City; and D. Wilt, Wheatland.
Vernon Co. Mutual Protection Soc.		DC, p3c3, 6/4/1887	The meeting of the Vernon Co. Mutual Protection Society was held at Morgan School. Officers for the coming year are Thomas Lawrence, Peter Jerman, S. A. Mellen, Joel T. Shaw, J. L. Miller, H. H. Hinds and P. McIntyre. The society was formed to protect its members from "horse thieves, etc." and has about $800 in the Treasury.
Vernon County Democrats		DC, p3c4, 10/9/1886	The Vernon County Democratic ticket was: Sheriff, S. R. Pollard; Register of Deeds, M. Rentz; Treasurer, Ole Johnson; County Clerk, Matt Monti; District Attorney, Olav Skaar; Co. Supt. Schools, Mrs. E. F. Tollefson; Clerk of Court, Bernard O'Connell; Surveyor, I. F. Thorp; Coroner, W. F. Riley; Assembly, First District-John M. Vance, Second District-Col. C. M. Butt.
Vernon County Prohibitionists		DC, p3c4, 10/9/1886	The Vernon County Prohibition ticket was: Sheriff, S. R. Pollard; Recorder of Deeds, W. T. McConnell; Clerk of Court, C. S. Daniels; Courty Clerk, W. T. Markee; Supt. Schools, A. B. Miller; Assembly, First District-C. L. Wood, Second District-E. W. Sandon.
Vine	Charles D.	BD, p3c1, 1/7/1881	Charles D. Vine married Fannie Filkins on Dec. 30, 1880 at the home of Charles Cook of Boscobel. Bride and groom from Marquette, WI.
Viroqua Teachers		DC, p2c2, 7/31/1888	The following teachers have been hired by Viroqua: J. A. Aylward, Principal; Miss Farnsworth of Sheboygan Falls, Assistant Principal; Miss Woodward of Platteville; Hattie Terrill, Second Grammer; Mrs. Emma F. Tollefson, First Grammer; Edith Blume, Second Intermediate; Helen Neff, First Intermediate; Grace Morley, Second Primary; and Helen Walloe, First Primary.
Viroqua Village Officers		DR, p3c2, 3/30/1871	The Viroqua Village officers were William Nelson, President; John Dawson, Clerk; J. E. Newell, Police Justice; R. S. McMichael, Supervisor; and A. L. Russell, Calvin Morely, William A. Gott, Trustees.
Voegelin	Herman	RH, p5c6, 7/22/1897	Farmer in the Bad Axe Valley. Died last week in a run-a-way accident. His wife broke her arm. Born in Germany and came to America when he was about 6 years old. Aged 35 years. Survived by wife, 2 sons and 1 daughter. Buried in Buchanan Cemetery.
Vollmer	Daniel	BD, p3c3, 6/30/1882	Agent for Champion reapers and mowers at Bridgeport. Almost drowned when his wagon fell into high water. Saved by W. H. Washburn, general agent, who accompanied him on a trip to Prairie du Chien.
Voss	Mr.	BD, p3c3, 5/4/1877	Mr. Voss of the Town of Harrison in Grant Co. was charged with the murder of his neighbor, Mr. Cahrl. Cahrl had assaulted Mrs. Voss, his former wife.
Vought	Nick	DC, p3c4, 3/10/1888	Uncle Nick Vought, one of Viroqua's earliest settlers, died at the home of his brother in Fillmore Co., MN on Mar. 1, 1888.

Genealogical Events from Newspapers for Crawford, Vernon and Grant Counties, Wisconsin, 1870-1901

LAST NAME	FIRST NAME	NEWSPAPER, PAGE/COLUMN MONTH/DAY/YEAR	GENEALOGICAL DATA
Wachter	George	BD, p2c3, 8/26/1881	Owned the Palace Billard Hall in Prairie du Chien. The hall was robbed of $30 - $40.
Wadsworth		BD, p3c2, 4/14/1882	Station agent Wadsworth departed Boscobel for his farm in Iowa. Took stock, equipment, tree cuttings, etc.
Wadsworth	T. D.	BD, p3c1, 3/30/1883	Left Boscobel for a new home in Wauwatosa, WI.
Wadsworth	T. D., Mr. and Mrs.	BD, p3c1, 6/30/1882	Left Boscobel to visit their farm near Emmetsburg, IA.
Waggoner	George W.	RH, p7c4, 7/1/1897	Returned to Viola from Colorado to help father in his mercantile establishment.
Wagner	Henry	BD, p3c3, 6/1/1877	Committed suicide on Monday in the Town of Lima. He was "German by birth." Mrs. Wagner filed for divorce last fall. They reconciled.
Wait	S. G.	DR, p3c1, 3/9/1871	Resided in De Soto. Selling his farm.
Wait	S. G.	DR, p3c2, 4/6/1871	Advertised the sale of his home on lot One in Cheeney's Addition to De Soto, and known as the Osgood Homestead.
Wait	William S.	BD, p3c2, 8/3/1877	Hotelkeeper in Belle Center. He was swindled out of board by N. R. Gaylord.
Waite	W. S.	BD, p2c2, 3/7/1879	Served as Justice of the Peace in Belle Center.
Wakefield		DC, p2c3, 6/12/1888	"Old lady Wakefield" used to bring in woolen stockings to trade off for sugar in De Soto in the 1850s.
Wakefield	Mertie	RH, p4c3, 11/23/1899	Resided in De Soto. Attended school in Readstown.
Wakefield	Mr.	RH, p5c3, 12/13/1900	Died Monday. He was an old settler and lived 5 miles from De Soto.
Wakefield	Nathan	DC, p4c3, 3/29/1889	Died at Retreat on March 25, 1889. [It was later reported that this death did not occur. Wakefield had an epileptic fit while at the home of his daughter, Mrs. Loux on May Ridge. He has now recovered and is at the home of another daughter, Mrs. Griffin who lived near Victory. p1c2, 4/5/1889]
Wakeman	William	RH, p4c4, 11/11/1897	Mr. and Mrs. William Wakeman of the Clinton area visited their son-in-law, Austin Wilson, who was ill with typhoid fever.
Waldron	Samuel	DC, p1c6 7/30/1887	Granted a pension [for military service]. Lived in Ontario.
Waldron	W. M.	DC, p4c2, 5/10/1889	Operated a sidewheeled steamer between De Soto and Lansing.
Waldron	William	DR, p3c3, 12/22/1870	Resided in De Soto. Placed an advertisement in newspaper. Seeking woodchoppers.
Waldron	William	DR, p3c1, 4/13/1871	Caught an otter measuring 7' above De Soto.
Waldron	William	DC, p2c2, 1/1/1887	The residence and store of William Waldron were destoyed by fire in De Soto. Few of Mr. Waldron's possessions were saved. Nearly all the contents of Schmidt's drug store and apartment were saved. Ladies got water from the river to help save R. H. Rice's building. Waldron had a $500 insurance policy on the building. The Waldrons were at Ashton, IL when the fire erupted. The loss is estimated at $3000. The building was constructed in 1856 by C. B. Whiting and John Valentine. C. B. Whiting is now President of the Orient Insurance Co. of Hartford, CT.
Waldron	William	DC, p3c3, 1/15/1887	Received from the German American Insurance Co. the insurance on his building in full. Lived in De Soto.
Waldron	William	DC, p3c3, 5/28/1887	William Waldron and wife arrived in De Soto from New Hampshire. "Bill says he can't stand a country where he can't get a beer, has to go to church and can't go hunting on Sunday."
Waldron	William	DC, p2c2, 2/26/1889	Caught fish to sell for a living in De Soto.
Walker	Charles	BD, p3c4, 8/13/1880	Charles Walker of Boscobel published a notice that he had given his son, Elmer Walker, his time and that he is now empowered to make his own contracts.
Walker	child	BD, p3c3, 4/29/1881	A baby was born to George Walker of Boscobel on April 23, 1881.
Walker	George	BD, p3c1, 7/11/1879	George Walker married Olive DeLap on July 4, 1879 in Boscobel. The Rev. G. W. Nuzum of Viroqua officiated.
Walker	J.	BD, p2c5, 1/17/1879	Published a notice that he was giving his sons, Joseph J. Walker and Lester Walker, their time and that he will no longer be responsible for their debts. Walker lived in Fennimore.

Genealogical Events from Newspapers for Crawford, Vernon and Grant Counties, Wisconsin, 1870-1901

LAST NAME	FIRST NAME	NEWSPAPER, PAGE/COLUMN MONTH/DAY/YEAR	GENEALOGICAL DATA
Walker	Jerome	BD, p3c1, 5/21/1880	Jerome Walker's 3-year-old son drowned in a spring at his home 5 miles southeast of Boscobel.
Walker	Jonathon	BD, p3c1, 12/22/1882	Walker's home near Fennimore was destroyed by fire.
Walker	Joseph	BD, p3c1, 11/05/1880	Died Oct. 2, 1880 in Boscobel. Born in Bristol Co., MA on Jan. 2, 1800. Married Emerancy Rounds of North Rehoboth, Bristol Co., MA in July 1822. Fathered 5 sons and 2 daughters. Daughters now deceased. Youngest son died in Civil War at age 19. Moved to Alleganey Co., NY in 1822. Moved to Livingston Co., MI in 1837. Moved to Grant Co., WI in Dec. 1848. Died at home of son, Charles, of Boscobel. Organizer of the First National Bank of Boscobel in 1871. Survived by wife and 4 children, all of who live in Grant Co.
Walker	Judson P.	BD, p3c2, 7/13/1883	Laura B. Pepper married Judson P. Walker on Wednesday in Boscobel. Bride was daughter of Mr. and Mrs. John Pepper of Boscobel. Groom was a bookkeeper at Parker, Hildebrand & Co. in Boscobel. Bride was a Boscobel teacher for the last 5 years.
Walker	Justus A.	BD, p2c5, 5/5/1882	Resided in Hickory Grove. Published a notice that his wife, Jane B. Walker, had left his home with their 2 children without just cause or provocation. The public should not trust her on his account.
Walker	Linda	BD, p3c2, 9/13/1878	Henry Knutson married Linda Walker on Sept. 3, 1878 in Boscobel. Bride and groom from Hickory Grove. The Rev. Z. S. Hurd officiated.
Walker	Louisa	BD, p3c4, 2/16/1877	Recently died. The Fennimore Center Grange published a resolution of condolence and honored her life.
Walker	Nora, Miss	DC, p3c3, 1/7/1888	Former resident of Ontario. Recently married at Shell Lake, WI.
Walker	Perry	DC, p1c5, 11/26/1887	Granted a pension for his military service. Resided in Ontario.
Walker	W. A., Mrs.	BD, p3c2, 5/12/1882	Mrs. W. A. Walker and her 3 children came from Manitowoc to visit her sister-in-law, Mrs. T. J. Brooks of Boscobel.
Wallace	David	BD, p2c3, 11/25/1881	Died last Sunday in Lone Rock, per a reprint from the *Republican and Observer* of Nov. 17, 1881. Born June 10, 1800 in Iroquah, Matilda Co., Canada. Married Lydia Hitchcock in 1821. All children, 10 boys and 2 girls, survive him. Moved to Ohio in 1849. Moved to Richland Co., WI in 1853. Wife died in 1865, at which time he moved to the home of his son, John Wallace of Lone Rock.
Wallace	Lennie	RH, p5c3, 3/22/1900	Frank Holcomb married Lennie Wallace on March 19, 1900 at the home of the bride's parents, 2 miles east of Readstown.
Wallace	Mack	DC, p3c2, 5/29/1888	Resided in Ontario. Now employed as a barkeeper at the Winship House in Sparta.
Wallace	Martha	RH, xxxx, 4/6/1899	Charles Salmon married Martha Wallace on April 2, 1899 at the home of the bride's parents near Readstown. Groom was a farmer from Soldiers Grove. C. H. Davenport officiated at the ceremony.
Waller	David	DC, p3c2, 12/17/1887	While C. B. Whiting, the author of an article on De Soto history lived in the area [1856-1865] there was considerable rivalry between De Soto and Victory. The people in De Soto drew attention to prospective settlers that Victory had no church services and that they worked on Sundays. David Waller, who was of the Christian persuasion, "or as was known among us he was a Campbellite." He lived in West Prairie. He decided to respond to these criticisms and notified Victory that he would hold services at the schoolhouse. The whole village attended. He started speaking at 10:00 a.m. and continued until 3:00 p.m., with only a 15-minute break.
Waller	George	DC, p3c4, 2/25/1888	Won a lawsuit against the Champion Machine Co., per De Soto news column.
Waller	L.	DC, p3c4, 1/22/1887	L. Waller and family moved back to Victory after living in Nebraska for the last 7 years.
Walter	Henry	BD, p3c2, 5/27/1881	Henry Walter recently married Clara Meyer. Bride youngest daughter of Gustav Meyer of Boscobel and sister of Mrs. Lou P. Lesler [p3c2]. Groom was a teller at the bank of A. J. Pipkin of Boscobel [p3c3].
Walters	Earl	RH, p4c1, 6/1/1899	Worked as a clerk in Burgors Drug Store, Readstown. Planned to move to the south on account of his poor health.
Walters	Henry	BD, p3c3, 7/27/1877	Clerk at Meyers Bro's in Boscobel. Visited his brother in Chicago.
Walters	Jessie	RH, p5c4, 11/4/1897	Frank Musgrove married Jessie Walters on Oct. 24, 1897 at Wauzeka. Bride and groom from La Farge.
Walton	Mr.	BD, p3c1, 2/2/1883	To date, has sold over 5000 railroad ties this winter. Lived in Woodman.

Genealogical Events from Newspapers for Crawford, Vernon and Grant Counties, Wisconsin, 1870-1901

LAST NAME	FIRST NAME	NEWSPAPER, PAGE/COLUMN MONTH/DAY/YEAR	GENEALOGICAL DATA
Walton	William F.	BD, p3c2, 6/23/1882	Died Sunday while bathing in the Wisconsin River at Bridgeport. Father lived in Wheatville. Recently married the adopted daughter of Mr. J. G. Richardson of Bell Center and moved to a farm near Bridgeport.
Walworth	Della G.	BD, p3c2, 8/10/1877	Joseph Cover married Della G. Walworth on July 29, 1877. Bride from Richland Center. Groom from Lancaster. Rev. J. Walworth of Richland Center officiated.
Walworth	Frank	BD, p3c1, 5/25/1883	Resided in Boscobel. Arrested by Sheriff Lane of Richland County for misappropriating $150.
Walworth	J., Rev.	BD, p2c3, 12/2/1881	Rev. J. Walworth's horse tripped last week while being ridden by Frank Walworth. The horse, Dolly, was well known. She broke her neck. Horse was 3 years old when purchased over 25 years ago.
Walworth	Miss	BD, p3c2, 7/6/1877	Joe Cover married Miss Walworth on Thursday at the home of the bride in Richland Center. Groom from Lancaster.
Wamberg	H. J.	RH, p7c1, 7/1/1897	Proprietor of the Park Hotel in Readstown.
Wamberg	H. J.	RH, p5c2, 7/8/1897	Recently moved into his new hotel in Readstown.
Wamburg	John	RH, p5c2, 12/9/1897	Returned from his home in North Dakota to visit his brother, H. J. Wamburg of Readstown.
Wannamaker	Ella	BD, p3c1, 12/4/1883	Wore a dress made of newspapers to the masquerade ball. Becca Carson of Richland Center did, too.
Wannamaker	S.	BD, p3c1, 2/3/1882	From Crawford Co. Injured his kneecap when he fell into Duetch canal.
Wannemaker	S. L.	BD, p3c2, 7/26/1878	Wannemaker's horse recently stolen. Found lose in the woods 2 miles north of Orion.
Ward	C. C.	BD, p3c1, 4/30/1880	C. C. Ward, plaintiff vs. W. G. Moshier of Excelsior. Cash was awarded plaintiff. Moshier failed to pay for services training and caring for horses.
Ward	J. W.	RH, p2c1, 7/1/1897	Advertised services as a contractor and builder in Readstown.
Ward	J. W.	RH, p4c2, 10/3/1901	Awarded a contract to build the new school for Readstown. His bid was $6149.
Ward	John	BD, p2c1, 10/5/1877	Taken to Waupon for a 1-year sentence by Sheriff Birchard. His crime was forgery.
Ward	T. B.	BD, p2c3, 12/8/1882	Recently cut off his toes while chopping wood. Resided in Soldiers Grove.
Ward	W.	BD, p2c4, 11/26/1880	Grant County paid him a bounty for scalps turned into the county.
Wareham	Fred	DC, p2c3, 7/10/1888	Fred Wareham married Louisa [a.k.a. Jennie] J. Shisler on July 3, 1888 at the residence of Charles McDowell. Bride and groom from De Soto. The Rev. Thomas Crouch officiated.
Wareham	Mary J.	DC, p2c3 9/10/1887	A probate notice for the Mary J. Wareham estate was published by the Vernon Co. Courts. Alexander McDowell applied to be named Administrator.
Wareham	Richard	DC, p3c3, 9/25/1888	He was an old time resident of De Soto. Visited his sister, Mrs. Shep Cushing.
Warner	Helen	DC, p2c1, 5/7/1887	Died April 28, 1887 at her home 2 miles below Newton. She was the wife of Elisha Warner. Survived by 6 children.
Warner	Jared	BD, p3c3, 2/13/1880	Died of heart disease on Feb. 4, 1880 at his home in Patch Grove. Found in the barn when he did not return from tending the stock. Represented his district in the Wisconsin Legislature in 1861. Elected County Supervisor in nine times between 1849 and 1872. Served as chairman of Grant Co. Board of Supervisors in 1857.
Warner	Jesse	DR, p3c4, 6/29/1871	Died on June 26, 1871 at his home in Harmony. He was 55 years old. Committed suicide with a revolver.
Warren	James	DC, p2c2, 5/21/1887	Hattie E. Richardson married James Warren on May 16, 1887 at the residence of the bride's parents in West Prairie. Groom from Mt. Sterling. The Rev. Thomas Couch officiated.
Washburn	F. B.	BD, p3c1, 2/16/1883	F. B. Washburn of Excelsior sold his dry goods and grocery stock to Messrs. Dosh and Noble. He retained his hardware business.
Washington	Plummer	DR, p3c3, 9/21/1871	Managed a barrel making and lime works establishment in De Soto in 1856.
Wasson	Rosa, Mrs.	DC, p3c4, 4/9/1887	Arrived from Black River Falls to visit relatives in Hillsborough.
Waters	Charley	DR, p3c1, 10/19/1871	Owner of the Springville Nursery in Springville, Vernon Co.

Genealogical Events from Newspapers for Crawford, Vernon and Grant Counties, Wisconsin, 1870-1901

LAST NAME	FIRST NAME	NEWSPAPER, PAGE/COLUMN MONTH/DAY/YEAR	GENEALOGICAL DATA
Watkins	Isabell, Mrs.	BD, p3c3, 11/16/1877	Dies Tuesday at the age 75 years, 3 months and 27 days. She was the mother of Steven Watkins in Boscobel. She was the oldest settler in Boscobel. Resided there 23 years. Gave birth to 8 boys and 2 girls, all of whom lived more than 21 years. Survived by 4 children.
Watkins	S. F., Major	BD, p3c4, 6/14/1878	Resident of Boscobel. He was a friend of G. W. Limbocker, who recently bought a farm in Clay Co., NB. Watkins went to Clay Co., too. May buy land there.
Watkins	Steve F.	BD, p3c2, 7/19/1878	Returned to Boscobel after a visit to Nebraska. Planned to relocate there.
Watson	Joshua W.	BD, p3c2, 8/19/1881	Died Aug. 15, 1881 in Boscobel at age 46. Born 1835 in Philadelphia. Married Ellen Twining on July 29, 1853. Moved to Boscobel in 1870 and worked as a painter for G. W. Cowan. Most recently employed as a wagon maker for Ruka Brothers. Died from aggravated inflamation of the bowels.
Watson	Thomas	BD, p3c2, 5/28/1880	Appointed to be a census enumerator in Clifton, Grant Co.
Waukon	John	DC, p3c4, 6/11/1887	John Waukon and family, Indians, returned to their summer residence in the Cooley Valley.
Waukon	John	DC, p3c3, 10/22/1887	Recently robbed of $240 outside La Crosse. He received the money from the government 7 weeks ago.
Waukon	Lizzie	DC, p3c3, 9/25/1886	She was the wife of John Waukon, a former chief of the Winnebago Indians. Mrs. Waukon is 100 years old. She was baptized in the Catholic Church about 1840. Visited with Mrs. Lyttle in De Soto.
Waukon	Lizzie	DC, p3c2, 2/5/1887	J. M. Dunley took a portrait of Lizzie Waukon, aged 103, widow of Chief Waukon. Sold copies of it for 25 cents to the public.
Wayne	James N.	BD, p3c2, 7/21/1882	Died Monday morning from excessive fat on the heart. Resident of Woodman. Autopsy conducted by Dr. Halsted of Wauzeka and Dr. Bailou of Woodman. He was a Crawford Co. resident for about 50 years. Lived 57 years.
Webb	girl	BD, p3c2, 5/25/1883	Kidnapped from her parents in Potosi about 5 years ago. She was found in Carroll, IA and will be returned to her parents. She was legally adopted under the name Mabel Gilley by a farm family in Carroll.
Weber	Christian	DC, p2c3, 3/20/1888	Christian Weber married Merti I. Robson on Mar. 14, 1888 at De Soto at the residence of Willis Owens. Bride from Franklin. Groom from Sterling.
Weber	Henry	DC, p2c3, 3/20/1888	Henry Weber married Paulina Robson on Mar. 13, 1888 at De Soto. Bride from Franklin. Groom from Sterling.
Webster	John, Mr. and Mrs.	BD, p3c4, 7/28/1882	The Websters and a niece arrived from Lincoln, NB to visit with Mr. and Mrs. J. Flint of Boscobel. Mr. Flint was Mrs. Webster's father. This was their first visit in 27 years.
Wegdahl	Andrew Olson	RH, p5c2, 7/8/1897	Died last Wednesday after being tramped on by a colt. He was a very old man who moved to the Readstown area from Norway several years ago.
Weggins	George	BD, p3c3, 12/10/1880	George Weggins married Mary Murphy on Dec. 3, 1880 in Boscobel. Bride and groom were from Postville, IA.
Weidman	Dorthia, Mrs.	BD, p3c2, 4/25/1879	Died April 18, 1879 of consumption in Wauzeka at the age of 25 years, 11 months and 18 days. She was the wife of John G. Weidman.
Welch		DR, p3c2, 8/31/1871	"There is an old man named Welch, living three miles from De Soto, who will be, if he lives until next Christmas, one hundred years old. The old gentleman is in very fair health, his sight is good and he appears as though he might live several more years yet."
Welch		DC, p3c2, 7/9/1887	Mesdames Welch, Howarth and Wyburn were elected school district officers after the resignations of the men in the Howarth District.
Welch	Father	DR, p3c1, 9/7/1871	Mentioned in last week's newspaper. Died last Monday night at the age of 99.
Welch	girl	DC, p3c2, 5/28/1887	A daughter was recently born to John Welch of De Soto.
Welch	James	BD, p3c1, 11/20/1883	Resided in Rolling Ground, Crawford Co. Kicked in the jaw by a horse. Taken to Boscobel where Dr. W. R. Hurd removed a section of the alveolar process and with 3 attached teeth. An additional 3 teeth were also removed.
Welcher	Miss	DC, p3c3, 12/17/1887	Arrived from Concord, Jefferson Co. to spend the winter with her father in Ontario.
Weldon	Mr. and Mrs.	RH, p4c1, 8/3/1899	Arrived in Readstown from Lebanon, KS. Came to see their daughter, Mrs. L. W. Swain, who is very sick.
Weldon	Mr. and Mrs.	RH, p4c1, 6/21/1900	Arrived in Readstown from Lebanon, KS to visit with L. W. Swain of Readstown.
Wellman	Scott	BD, p3c1, 1/13/1882	The officers of the Boscobel Hook and Ladder Company were L. B. Ruka, Scott Wellman, Nels Ellingson, A. Bobel and Max Nobis.
Wells	Fanny	BD, p2c2, 6/29/1877	Milton Kitch married Fanny Wells two weeks ago in Fennimore. The bride was from the Town of Wingville.

Genealogical Events from Newspapers for Crawford, Vernon and Grant Counties, Wisconsin, 1870-1901

LAST NAME	FIRST NAME	NEWSPAPER, PAGE/COLUMN MONTH/DAY/YEAR	GENEALOGICAL DATA
Wells	Morris, Mrs.	BD, p3c3, 10/25/1878	Mrs. Morris Wells of Boscobel area taken to the Insane Asylum in Madison for treatment.
Wells	Mr.	BD, p3c3, 11/22/1878	After visiting his son, Morris Wells of Boscobel, he left for his home in Milwaukee.
Wells	T. M.	BD, p3c1, 1/9/1880	Served as Chief Engineer for the Boscobel Fire Department.
Welsh		RH, p5c3, 3/7/1901	An infant of James Welsh died last week of lung fever at his home in the De Soto area. Buried at Rising Sun.
Welsh	James	RH, p5c4, 3/16/1899	James Welsh married Nancy Sheslar on Feb. 22, 1899 per De Soto news column.
Welsh	Peter	BD, p2c1, 6/10/1881	Recently died of cancer of blood poisoning at Horse Creek. He was the brother of John Welsh. Item originally printed in the *Richland Farmer*.
Wentworth	Mr.	BD, p3c3, 1/5/1883	A bucket brigade saved his home from fire in Boscobel.
Wentzel	H. C.	BD, p3c4, 5/12/1882	Found dead in East Dubuque. May have been robbed of $600-$1000. He was on his way to visit his father in Stitzer. Wentzel ran the Central House and saloon in Fennimore. His brother, August, and a stepson, John Wilcox, went to East Dubuque to identify the body. Buried in East Dubuque because of decomposition.
Wepking	Charles	BD, p3c1, 12/3/1880	Charles Wepking married Sarah Keys on Nov. 28, 1880. Bride and groom from Fennimore.
Werner	C., Mrs.	BD, p3c3, 7/25/1879	Mr. and Mrs. M. J. Schierchswitz of Portage City visited their daughter, Mrs. C. Werner of Boscobel.
Wernick	E. V.	DC, p3c4, 7/2/1887	E. V. Wernick married Mrs. Josephine Quinn on June 16, 1887. Groom was the principal of Hillsboro High School.
Wernick	Emil V.	DC, p2c2, 7/2/1887	Returned to Hillsborough after a wedding tour.
West	E. B., Mrs.	DR, p2c6, 12/15/1870	Milliner in De Soto.
West	Maud, Mrs.	DC, p3c3, 6/12/1886	Arrived in De Soto from Chicago. Returned with her sister, Mrs. Fred Schmidt.
West	William	DC, p3c2, 6/19/1886	Former resident of De Soto. Current resident of Caledonia, MN.
West	William	DC, p2c2, 10/29/1887	Ran a blacksmith shop in De Soto in 1856.
West	William N.	DR, p2c5, 12/15/1870	Proprietor of the U.S. Stage Line between Lansing, IA, De Soto, and La Crosse.
West	William N.	DC, p3c4, 12/4/1888	Died Nov. 28, 1888 in Caledonia, MN. Former resident of De Soto. Mr. Woodbury and daughter, Mamie, went to Caledonia when they heard the sad news.
West	William N., Mrs.	DC, p3c2, 7/30/1887	Traveled from Caledonia, MN to visit her brother, Mr. Woodbury of De Soto.
West and Williams		DR, p1c1, 12/15/1870	Owners of a blacksmith shop in De Soto, WI.
Wetmore	Elizabeth	BD, p3c2, 12/23/1881	John W. Hale married Elizabeth Wetmore at the Betts House in Boscobel on Dec. 21, 1881. Bride and groom from Little Grant. The Rev. E. L. Morse officiated.
Wheeler	boy	RH, p4c2, 4/5/1900	The 7-year-old son of George Wheeler died in tonsillitis last Saturday in Sylvan.
Wheeler	G. B.	BD, p3c2, 5/28/1880	Appointed to be a census enumerator in Beetown, Grant Co.
Wheeler	Jane, Mrs.	RH, p4c2, 6/22/1899	Arrived in Liberty Pole and Readstown from Oklahoma to visit relatives. She was the daughter of Orrin Wizle, one of the first settlers of Readstown. Mrs. Wheeler left the area nearly 40 years ago, when she was a young girl. Of those she knew, only 5 or 6 people are still living in the area. She knows Uncle Daniel Hale, N. D. Hale, Mrs. Phillips, Mrs. Fox and Mrs. E. M. Bliss. Mrs. Wheeler's mother is buried in Readstown Cemetery. She is arranging to have a monument erected on the grave. Father died in Oklahoma. One brother died in Wyoming, one brother died in South Africa and another brother died in Missouri. Two remaining brothers live in Oklahoma. She is the mother of 3 sons and 1 daughter. Her cousin, Sidney Higgins of Liberty Pole, drove her to Readstown.
Wheeler	Norman	RH, p4c2, 3/14/1901	Resided in Sylvan. Bought a baritone trombone.
Whitaker	Tilly	BD, p2c2, 4/4/1879	Read an essay at a Good Templars meeting in Belle Center.

Genealogical Events from Newspapers for Crawford, Vernon and Grant Counties, Wisconsin, 1870-1901

LAST NAME	FIRST NAME	NEWSPAPER, PAGE/COLUMN MONTH/DAY/YEAR	GENEALOGICAL DATA
White	Alice C.	DR, p1c4, 12/22/1870	From De Soto. She was a student [or teacher?] at the Mt. Sterling Academy. Died in Nov. 1870.
White	Belle	DC, p3c3, 7/31/1888	Belle White married F. W. Tucker on July 27, 1888 at the residence of the bride's parents. Bride was the daughter of H. H. White, the founder of Stoddard. Groom was an agent for the Burlington Railroad.
White	Charles P.	DC, p2c2, 10/2/1888	Vinnie Godfrey married Charles P. White Wednesday evening. Bride daughter of Mr. and Mrs. M. Godfrey of S. Lansing. Groom from Stoddard. Rev. Hutchenson officiated.
White	Clifton	DC, p2c2, 11/19/1887	Returned from Dakota to spend the winter in Retreat.
White	Clifton	DC, p1c2, 4/12/1889	Resided in Retreat. He "has taken him a wife, but has not brought her home yet."
White	Didreck O.	DR, p3c6, 9/28/1871	Published a notice regarding a lost colt. He lived in Sugar Creek in the Town of Freeman, Crawford County [had a Rising Sun post office].
White	E. J.	DR, p3c1, 12/22/1870	City Marshall in Lansing, IA. He and his son, Ed, were the first people of the season to cross the river by ice to De Soto.
White	E., Mrs.	DC, p3c2, 12/10/1887	Left Retreat to live with her son, M. Davis of Viroqua.
White	French B.	DC, p3c3, 8/13/1887	Mrs. E. R. Dodge recently married French B. White. Bride, a teacher, was the daugher of Mrs. Marshall of Red Mound, WI. Groom was a farmer in Sterling. The Rev. Thomas Crouch officiated.
White	H. H.	DC, p2c2, 12/11/1886	Early settler in the area. Had a good trade at his store in Stoddard.
White	H. H., Mrs.	DC, p4c3, 4/26/1889	Mrs. White of Stoddard visited her daughter, Mrs. F. W. Tucker of De Soto.
White	J. W.	DC, p3c3, 8/28/1886	White's blacksmith shop safe was broken into by thieves who took $25.
White	John M.	DC, p2c2, 2/26/1889	Operated a blacksmith shop on Main Street in De Soto.
White	John W.	DC, p3c4, 1/15/1887	Died Jan. 7, 1887 in De Soto. Born Sept. 9, 1822 at Acusnet, near New Bedford, MA. Traces his family to Peregeue White, the child born on the Mayflower. Moved to De Soto on May 1, 1855. Served in Co. I, 6th WI Volunteers [part of the Iron Brigade]. He verbally willed his property to his widow and $100 to each to his sons, John M. and Ed I. and $10 each to his grandchildren, Arthur and Eugene.
White	John W.	DC, p3c3, 1/15/1887	Died Jan. 7, 1887. He had been the Quartermaster of the James Mason Post 106, GAR, De Soto.
White	John W.	DC, p2c4, 2/12/1887	Died about Jan. 7, 1887 in Vernon Co. Catherine White petitioned to have John M. White's estate administered.
White	John, Mrs.	DC, p3c4, 7/17/1888	Mrs. White is at the bedside of her mother, Mrs. Hannah Pulver, who is seriously ill.
White	Josie B.	DC, p3c2, 9/18/1888	Frank H. Pulver married Josie B. White on Sept. 4, 1888 at the home of Rev. J. K. Eckman in Osborne, KS. Bride from Bloomington.
White	Martin A.	DC, p2c1, 1/21/1888	Died Jan. 8, 1888 at Retreat. He was the 29-year-old son of F. B. White.
White	O. P.	DC, p2c2, 3/12/1887	Operated a butcher shop in Ontario, WI.
White	O. P.	DC, p2c2, 7/9/1887	Carried the mail between Ontario and Viola.
White	Thomas	DC, p3c3, 12/11/1888	Died Dec. 4, 1888 of dropsy at the residence of J. M. Hill. He was one of the first settlers in the county. Cared for by his daughter since last spring. Services were held at the Christian Church, per Retreat news column.
Whiteaker	H. E.	RH, p4c2, 7/5/1900	Resided in Bell Center. Arrived in Readstown to start up a lodge of the Mystic Workers.
Whiteaker	Mrs.	RH, p4c1, 5/2/1901	Died last Saturday at 6:00 p.m. at the home of her son, Scott Coleman of Readstown. She died of heart failure at the age of about 70 years. She lived with her son for the last few years. Funeral conducted by Rev. Gander in the Methodist Episcopal Church. Buried in Readstown Cemetery.
Whiting	C[harles] B.	DC, p2c2, 10/15/1887	Wrote a series of articles on early De Soto history. Several years ago he sent a collection of papers pertaining to De Soto history to the Honorable George D. McDill, now of Osceola Falls. Mr. McDill planned to write a DeSoto history, but did not do so, nor did he return the papers to Whiting. Whiting had to write from memory. The *De Soto Chronicle* published the series. The first in the series was published on p2c2, 10/15/1887 and continued approximately every two weeks.

Genealogical Events from Newspapers for Crawford, Vernon and Grant Counties, Wisconsin, 1870-1901

LAST NAME	FIRST NAME	NEWSPAPER, PAGE/COLUMN MONTH/DAY/YEAR	GENEALOGICAL DATA
Whiting	C. B.	DC, p3c4, 10/30/1886	Lived in Hartford, CT. New subscriber to the *De Soto Chronicle*.
Whiting	James	BD, p3c2, 3/31/1882	Railroad engineer. Promoted to breakman on a passenger train.
Whiting & Carr		DC, p2c2, 2/3/1888	About 1859, purchased the warehouse on the levee in De Soto from A. B. Clapp and subsequently the saw mill at the upper end of De Soto.
Whiting & Carr		DC, p2c2, 2/3/1888	Moved into Woodbury's De Soto store building about 1859. Andrew Glodery became tired of farming and took over the space vacated by Whiting in De Soto and opened a store. Whiting & Carr became steamboat agents and express agents and sold railroad tickets and lumber of the "steamboat variety."
Whiting and Valentine		DC, p2c1, 11/12/1887	In 1856 after satisfying Mr. S. D. Powers and Dr. Houghton, two of the town proprietors, of their character, C. B. Whiting and his new partner, J. C. Valentine, were sold a lot just below the present site of the Bay State Hotel in De Soto. Whiting and Valentine felt fortunate because they were from New York and New Jersey and the proprietors wanted De Soto to be a "New England town." Whiting and Valentine wanted to grow up with the country. Whiting stayed in De Soto for 9 years. Dr. Houghton mentioned "Victory as being a place where there was a laxity in this direction and consequently persons had been admitted whom they would not care to have settle in De Soto."
Whiting and Valentine		DC, p2c2, 11/12/1887	On June 4, 1856 they started to dig a cellar for their new store in De Soto. Hired Mr. Holms to do the carpentry work. After stocking the store, they waited for the farm teams to come in to town once the crops were harvested. The farmers didn't come.
Whitmarsh	Dora, Mrs.	DC, p3c2, 6/4/1887	Nee Coffin. Resided in Pepin. Visited mother, Mrs. L. Spears of De Soto.
Whitney		BD, p3c2, 2/20/1880	Messrs. Whitney, Sr., Ed Whitney and Frank Robinson hosted a successful masquerade party in Mazomanie.
Whitney	boy	BD, p3c2, 5/4/1877	A son was born to Ed Whitney of the Boscobel area on April 24, 1877.
Whitney	C. E.	DC, p3c3, 2/25/1888	Relocated his barbershop from Viroqua to Tomahawk, WI.
Whitney	D., Mrs.	DC, p2c2, 6/18/1887	Mrs. D. Whitney of Bad Axe visited her sister, Mrs. Barber [Barker?] of Freeman.
Whitney	E. J., Mrs.	BD, p3c1, 12/31/1880	Died Dec. 25, 1880. Resided in Mazomanie. Husband was a train conductor. She was daughter of Mr. and Mrs. J. C. Whitney of Boscobel.
Whitney	James	DR, p3c3, 11/9/1871	A summons for relief from the Vernon Co. Circuit Court was published in the case, James B. Turck and William N. West, assignees of A. Carlyle, D. A. Steele and Jahiel Baker, bankrupts, plaintiffs, vs. James Whitney and Abigail Whitney, his wife, and Ellen Morgan, defendants.
Whitney	James, Mrs.	DR, p3c1, 9/28/1871	Found a large black bear drinking water out of a spring near her farm on the ridge outside De Soto.
Whitney	Parley	DC, p3c3, 6/19/1888	Lived in De Soto. Adjudged insane by Judge Butt. Whitney sent to Mendota Asylum. He has been "affected" since he left the army. Enlisted in Co. B. 18th WI Infantry on Dec. 19, 1861. He was a prisoner at Newburg, Indiana and discharded Jan. 20, 1863 to join the Marine Brigade. His insanity is mild and his family hopes for a speedy recovery.
Whitts	M., Miss	BD, p3c1, 1/2/1880	Married Robert Bloyer on Dec. 28, 1879 in Boscobel. Bride from Watterstown. Groom from Muscoda. Prof. J. Allison officiated.
Wicken	George	BD, p3c1, 2/16/1883	George Wicken married Minnie Brown on Feb. 6, 1883 in Excelsior.
Wicks	Ida Virginia	BD, p3c1, 3/16/1883	Daniel Barnett married Ida Virginia Wicks on Mar. 12, 1883 in Boscobel. Bride from Boscobel. Groom from Wauzeka.
Widmeier	Aug.	DC, p2c3, 10/9/1888	Fined $700 in Lansing for selling beer.
Wiederaendrs	Ed	BD, p3c2, 10/25/1878	Ill health forced Wiederanendrs to sell his Boscobel meat market business.
Wier	Clark	DR, p3c2, 12/15/1870	Proprietor of the Excelsior Drug Store in Lansing, IA.
Wightman	Marcia	DC, p2c3 8/20/1887	James Jordan recently married Marcia Wightman of Oregon.
Wightman	Marcie	DC, p2c2 8/20/1887	Arrived from Oregon [the state?, the town?] to visit her cousin, Mrs. W. W. Butler of Retreat.
Wikinson [Wilkinson?]	John	RH, p5c2, 8/26/1897	John Wikinson and Ob. Sutherland of the Readstown area attended the soldiers reunion in Star.
Wilcox	Ira	DC, p2c2, 2/5/1889	Purchased an organ for his home in Victory.

Genealogical Events from Newspapers for Crawford, Vernon and Grant Counties, Wisconsin, 1870-1901

LAST NAME	FIRST NAME	NEWSPAPER, PAGE/COLUMN MONTH/DAY/YEAR	GENEALOGICAL DATA
Wilcox	Ira, Mr. and Mrs.	DC, p2c2 7/23/1887	Mrs. Stephen Cass and Mrs. Frank Cooley of Sumner, IA visited their parents, Mr.and Mrs. Ira Wilcox of Victory.
Wilcox	Ira, Mr. and Mrs.	DC, p2c2, 11/19/1887	Hosted a family reunion at their home in Victory. Their children attended. Mrs. Stephen Cass of Sumner, IA, Mrs. C. Coleman and husband and Dr. Mary Lambert and husband of Chicago came for the reunion.
Wilcox	J. B.	DR, p2c3, 12/29/1870	Advertised the Farmer's Warehouse in Victory, WI. Wilcox bought wheat, stored grain. Sold cement, coal and salt.
Wilcox	J. B.	DR, p2c2, 2/23/1871	Published a notice that his son, Fred, left his home in De Soto without the father's permission. The father asserted he no longer had control over his son and would not be responsible for the son's debts and would not recognize him as in any way related to him.
Wilcox	J. B., Capt.	DR, p3c2, 12/29/1870	Built the first house in De Soto in 1854. S. Wait now lives in this house. A log cabin was built in the area by French trader at an earlier date. The cabin was called Winnesheik Hotel and was used for shelter by the early pioneers.
Wilder		DC, p2c1, 2/5/1887	C. V. Porter wrote a series of articles on the Black Hawk War. In it he says, the Black Hawk trail ". . . crossed the Black River Road about eight rods south of the old Wilder house and some 15 rods north of the cluster of houses at Rising Sun. A few rods north of Wilder's house is a spring where in 1852 the bones of two men were found."
Wilder	Eugene	RH, p4c4, 3/24/1898	Named new janitor at the church in Kickapoo Center, replacing Jim Wilder.
Wilder	George, Mrs.	RH, p4c2, 5/3/1900	Died last week from consumption in Kickapoo.
Wilder	J. P.	DC, p4c2, 3/29/1889	Shipped his stock and household goods from Ferryville to Estherville, IA.
Wilder	Mrs.	RH, p5c4, 10/28/1897	Died this morning at her home a few miles north of Readstown.
Wilford	Nettie	RH, p4c2, 9/8/1898	Nettie Wilford married Charles Joseph at the home of the bride's parents on August 2, 1898, per De Soto news column.
Wilkins	Jesse, Mrs.	DC, p3c2, 10/9/1888	From Dubuque. Visited grandparents, Mr. and Mrs. C. G. Caldwell of the De Soto area.
Wilkinson	Eda, Mrs.	RH, p4c3, 6/14/1900	Mrs. Eda Wilkinson and her sister, Mrs. Ella Pond, took a train for Mauton, MI to visit their father, Mathew Harris, whom they have not seen for several years.
Wilkinson	Elbert	RH, p5c2, 5/19/1898	Elbert Wilkinson and Ob Sutherland returned to Readstown from Iowa.
Wilkinson	J. C.	RH, p3c2, 2/15/1900	Died last Wednesday evening in one of his outbuildings, probably from paralysis. Born in 1832 in Ohio. Moved to Wisconsin when he was a young man. Enlisted in Co. C., 19th Regt. WI Vol. in Feb. 1862. Discharged a few months later with a disability. In May 1862 he entered Co. K., 9th IL Cavalry. Mustered out in 1865. Survived by wife and 4 children. Funeral held at Methodist Episcopal Church. Buried in Readstown Cemetery.
Wilkinson	John C.	RH, p4c3, 2/8/1900	Died last evening in Readstown.
Wilkinson	Nelson	BD, p2c4, 11/26/1880	Grant County paid him a bounty for scalps turned into the county.
Wilkinson	Vol	RH, p5c4, 3/24/1898	Vol Wilkinson married Norah O'Leary last week. C. W. Reeve officiated at the ceremony.
Wilkinson	Vol	RH, p4c4, 4/28/1898	Departed for Iowa.
Wilkison	Elbert	RH, p5c4, 3/24/1898	Departed Readstown for a new home in Iowa.
Willard	George	BD, p2c2, 1/12/1883	Injured in a train accident in Madison. Resided in Lowertown [Prairie du Chien].
Williams	B. F., Mrs.	BD, p3c1, 8/22/1879	Arrived in Boscobel from Sterling, IL to visit parents for the first time in 13 years. She was the daughter of Com. Rogers.
Williams	Belle, Mrs.	BD, p3c3, 8/11/1882	Arrived from Washington to visit with her sister, Mrs. George W. Parker of Boscobel.
Williams	boy	RH, p4c3, 11/23/1899	A son was born on Nov. 10, 1899 to G. W. Williams of Readstown. He weighed 11 ½ pounds.
Williams	C. D.	DR, p3c3, 6/29/1871	C. D. Williams married S. Virginia Jewell on June 24, 1871 at the home of the bride's father. Groom from Liberty Pole. Bride from Town of Freeman.
Williams	Crystal	RH, p5c2, 12/15/1898	Crystal Williams, the little child of G. W. Williams of Readstown, died of heart failure on Dec. 10, 1898. The funeral was held at the Methodist Episcopal Church by Rev. Bell. She was buried in the Manning Cemetery.

Genealogical Events from Newspapers for Crawford, Vernon and Grant Counties, Wisconsin, 1870-1901

LAST NAME	FIRST NAME	NEWSPAPER, PAGE/COLUMN MONTH/DAY/YEAR	GENEALOGICAL DATA
Williams	D. R.	BD, p3c5, 3/24/1882	Starting in 1874, Williams lobbied his neighbors in Fennimore for the development of a railroad line through Fennimore. After several defeats, the railroad opened in 1878.
Williams	Edward G.	BD, p3c1, 4/8/1881	Edward G. Williams married Lucinda Lee on Mar. 3, 1881 at the residence of Joseph Lee in Watterstown. Bride and groom from Watterstown.
Williams	George	RH, p5c3, 3/7/1901	He is erecting a third, large barn on his new property in Sugar Grove. "This fact will surely make some of our supposed well-to-do farmers blush as his are the only painted barns that Sugar Grove can boast of."
Williams	Grant, Mrs.	RH, p4c3, 4/13/1899	Sick with malarial fever at her home in Readstown.
Williams	Mrs.	DC, p2c2, 6/18/1887	Resided in St. Paul. Visited parents, Mr. and Mrs. Lawrence of Victory.
Williams	Mrs.	RH, p4c3, 2/14/1901	Traveled from La Crescent, MN to visit sister, Mrs. LeGrand Hickok of De Soto.
Williams	R. S.	BD, p3c2, 7/18/1879	Died in a railroad accident in Minneapolis lat Friday. Remains taken to Whitewater for burial. He was the son-in-law of the late Dr. Cannon.
Willis	Ada, Miss	BD, p3c2, 7/9/1880	Left Boscobel to visit relatives and friends in Dane and Iowa counties.
Willis	Addie	BD, p3c3, 12/10/1880	John Brindley, Jr. married Addie Willis on Thursday at t he Congregational Church in Boscobel. Mrs. Stickel played the organ. The bride and groom were from Boscobel. Their new home will be in La Crosse. An extensive guest list was published.
Willis	J. P.	BD, p3c2, 2/24/1882	Bought the Betts House [a hotel] on Thursday.
Willis	J. P.	BD, p3c1, 2/9/1883	Retired from Betts House in Boscobel. Succeeded by D. B. Richardson.
Willis	J. P.	BD, p3c2, 5/28/1880	Appointed to be a census enumerator in Boscobel, Grant Co.
Willis	J. P.	BD, p2c7, 10/22/1880	Opened a restaurant and confectionary in Boscobel about 2 years ago. The confectionary department is well stocked with candies, fruits, canned goods, fancy groceries, cigars, tobacco, etc. The oyster trade during the winter season is a special feature. Oysters arrive direct from Baltimore.
Willis	J. P.	BD, p3c2, 1/12/1877	Appointed deputy sheriff in Boscobel.
Willis	J. P.	BD, p3c2, 12/13/1878	Opened a restaurant in the restaurant formerly run by J. L. Dean in Boscobel.
Willison	Eli	RH, p4c4, 2/2/1899	Eli Willison married Mrs. May Boss on Jan. 22, 1899, per Sugar Grove news column. Justice Benson officiated at the ceremony.
Willoughby	Bliss	BD, p3c2, 5/25/1883	Presided over a school in Harvard, NB.
Wilsey	Abraham	BD, P3c4, 4/23/1880	From Hall's Valley, Town of Jefferson. Missing. Worked on a bridge for a neighbor. Not seen since end of the working day.
Wilson	Edna Agnes	BD, p2c3, 8/8/1879	Died Aug. 4, 1879 at the age of 3 months, 3 weeks and 3 days. Daughter of John D. and Hattie Wilson of the Boscobel area.
Wilson	Elma	RH, p5c4, 1/13/1898	Taught school in Kickapoo Center.
Wilson	Frank	RH, p5c3, 10/4/1900	Frank Wilson and G. W. Wilson of Kickapoo went to La Crosse last Tuesday to hear William Jennings Bryan speak. [Bryan was a candidate for President.]
Wilson	G. W.	RH, p4c4, 12/9/1897	Recently celebrated his 50th birthday at his home in Kickapoo Center. The party was attended by Grandmother Wilson, A. G. Grace & Oris Wilson, Mr. and Mrs. Frank Baldwin, J. Kellogg, Mr. and Mrs. Kellogg, Fred Baldwin and Mr. and Mrs. D. Cannable. He was given an easy chair and a pet white owl as gifts.
Wilson	girl	BD, p3c1, 3/30/1883	A daughter was born to John D. Wilson on Easter Sunday. Wilson was the mayor of Boscobel.
Wilson	Grace, Miss	RH, p4c1, 10/18/1900	Lived in Readstown. Planned to visit her sister, Mrs. J. S. Konkee, of West Superior for the winter.
Wilson	Isabel	BD, p3c1, 1/16/1880	Married E. D. Langford on Dec. 25, 1879 at residence of bride's parents. Groom from Kentucky. Bride from Town of Marion. J. McLaughlin, Esq. officiated.
Wilson	John D.	BD, p3c2, 7/9/1880	Featured speaker at the Independence Day celebration in Excelsior.
Wilson	John D.	BD, p3c1, 7/30/1880	Went to Minneapolis to defend Charles Van Allen who was arrested for murder. Van Allen was found not guilty.
Wilson	John D.	BD, p3c4, 12/21/1877	John D. Wilson married Hattie L. Meyer last Tuesday at the home of the bride's father in Boscobel. Bride was daughter of Gustave Meyer. Groom was an attorney in Boscobel.

Genealogical Events from Newspapers for Crawford, Vernon and Grant Counties, Wisconsin, 1870-1901

LAST NAME	FIRST NAME	NEWSPAPER, PAGE/COLUMN MONTH/DAY/YEAR	GENEALOGICAL DATA
Wilson	John N.	BD, p3c1, 1/5/1877	Attorney in Boscobel.
Wilson	Minnie	RH, p5c3, 1/13/1898	The Rev. John Ellis married Minnie Wilson at the residence of the bride's parents near Webster. Rev. Ellis is pastor of the Kickapoo Congregational churches.
Wilson	Mrs.	RH, p4c2, 3/17/1898	Arrived from Bloomingdale to visit her sick daughter, Mrs. Clease [Lillie] Holcomb of Kickapoo Center.
Wilson	Otis	RH, p4c2, 11/22/1900	Resigned from Readstown band where he played tuba. Planned to most to West Superior. Stanley Morris took his place in the band.
Wilt		DC, p2c1, 1/29/1887	During the Black Hawk War, it is said that Gen. Henry's command encountered the Sac warriors about half a mile below Wilt's house [present day] in Vernon Co.
Wilt		DC, p2c1, 2/5/1887	The main part of the Black Hawk War in Vernon Co. took place about a half mile below Mr. Wilt's house in Battle Hollow.
Wilt	Vincent	DC, p3c4, 11/13/1886	Published a notice that he had taken up a heifer at his farm at De Soto, Town of Wheatland.
Wing	Emily, Mrs.	DC, p2c2, 8/13/1887	Returned to Lynxville after an extended visit in Brimfield, OH.
Winkler	Andrew	BD, p2c4, 11/26/1880	Grant County paid him a bounty for scalps turned into the county.
Winn	J. H., Mrs.	BD, p3c3, 8/11/1882	Lived in Boscobel. Visited her children in Crawford Co.
Winn	John	BD, p3c4, 2/22/1878	Winn's barn in North Clayton was burned to the ground last Friday. Arson suspected.
Winn	L. D.	RH, p4c1, 8/31/1899	Lived in Soldiers Grove. Received the contract to build a new Methodist Episcopal Church in Readstown.
Winn [Wynne]	John Henry	BD, p3c1, 8/25/1882	John Henry Winn [Wynne] married Matilda Pommey on Tuesday at the Betts House in Boscobel. Bride was from Montello, WI. The Rev. E. L. Morse officiated.
Winnebago John		BD, p3c2, 3/16/1883	The body of Winnebago John was brought to Boscobel on Saturday by railroad section men working west of the depot, about a mile this side of Woodman. He was 86, according to his nephew, Mike Cloud [also an Indian], and one of the "oldest of the tribe in this section." He was well known in the area for over 40 years. A coroner's jury viewed the body. The jury consisted of Justice McLaughlin, J. W. Varrell, J. P. Willis, John N. Comstock, F. G. Eisfelder, James Bailey and Frank Lewis. Mr. Scheinpflug prepared a coffin. Mike Cloud and his followers from Blue River and George Goodvillage and his band from the Kickapoo were at the burial held Sunday in the Potter's Field section of the cemetery. He was buried in "regular Indian fashion." [Cont.]
Winnebago John		BD, p3c2, 3/16/1883	Part 2. At the inquest, railroad workers stated that they were unable to stop soon enough after seeing a person lying across the track. Winnebago John's leg was severed and his body thrown below a bridge. The witnesses believed that Winnebago John and his companion, Lewis Johnson, or Black Hawk, were so drunk they did not recognize the impending danger and could not help themselves. The death occured on March 10, 1883 about 3:00 p.m. in the Town of Marion, Grant County.
Winneshiek Landing		DR, p3c2, 12/29/1870	Winneshiek Landing was the former name of De Soto, Vernon Co. Named in honor of an Indian chief. Chief Winneshiek's body was placed on an adjacent bluff after his death.
Winney	William James	BD, p2c3, 7/8/1881	Died June 20, 1881 in Glen Haven. Born June 11, 1817 in Cherry Valley, NY. Moved to Wisconsin in 1842. Married Annie Eliza Blessing on Oct. 11, 1844. Farmed in Blake's Prairie in 1843.
Winsor	J. C.	DC, p3c3, 5/14/1887	Viroqua resident. Received a patent for an extension ladder.
Wintees	Mr.	DC, p3c3, 11/13/1886	Mr. Wintees married Mary Seymour on Nov. 5, 1886 at the home of the bride's parents. Bride from Retreat. Groom from Horicon. The Rev. William Haughton officiated.
Wirts	John	BD, p3c2, 6/11/1880	Recently died of heart disease. Aged 50 years. Survived by wife and 8 children. Worked as a blacksmith in Richland Center.
Wisdom	Amelia	DC, p2c3, 1/22/1887	Badly scalded her hands, per Seneca news column.
Wisdom	F. M.	BD, p2c4, 11/26/1880	Grant County paid him a bounty for scalps turned into the county.
Wisdom	Frank	BD, p3c2, 2/18/1881	Killed two wolves that were ravaging sheep and hogs in Hickory Grove.

Genealogical Events from Newspapers for Crawford, Vernon and Grant Counties, Wisconsin, 1870-1901

LAST NAME	FIRST NAME	NEWSPAPER, PAGE/COLUMN MONTH/DAY/YEAR	GENEALOGICAL DATA
Wise	E.	DC, p3c3, 12/25/1886	Struck with a club and robbed after closing his store in Victory. Robber got cash and the pension checks of H. E. Blanchard, R. M. Ferguson and George Ammund. Claude Griffin of Victory was arrested for the robbery. Per the 1/1/1887 newspaper, Griffin stated he could account for his time and the money found on him during his arrest. "... heretofore he has been considered an exemplary young man."
Wise	E., Mrs.	DC, p3c3, 12/25/1886	Resided in Victory. Traveled to La Crosse to visit her sister, Mrs. Emberson.
Wise	Ella	DC, p3c4, 4/30/1887	Hired to teach at the Newton School this summer per the Victory news column.
Wise	George, Mr. and Mrs.	RH, p5c4, 10/20/1898	Visited daugher, Mrs. Pott of Ross. The Wise family lived in Mound Park.
Wise	William O., Hon.	BD, p3c1, 11/27/1883	Served in the Colorado legislature. Former resident of Marietta, Crawford Co. Visited friends in Boscobel.
Witcraft	Emma, Miss	DC, p3c3, 12/18/1886	Recently died of consumption at her home in Newton.
Witcraft	William	DC, p3c3, 1/7/1888	Pension application for military service was approved. Lived in Romance.
Witcraft	William	DC, p3c3, 2/3/1888	Resided in Romance. Received a $600 pension for military service. Applied for the pension 9 years ago.
Witcraft	Willie	DC, p3c4, 11/27/1888	Recently died from an injury to his back. Funeral preached at the Methodist Episcopal Churchin Retreat. Resident of Bad Axe.
Withe	George	DC, p2c2, 4/2/1887	Departed Seneca for Dakota. If he likes the area he will send for his family.
Withee	A. B.	BD, p3c1, 7/29/1881	Secretary for the Crawford Co. Fair held in Seneca.
Withington	Emma, Mrs.	BD, p3c3, 3/9/1877	Arrested for drunkeness in Boscobel.
Withrow	Capt.	DC, p3c3, 7/9/1887	Lived in Lansing. Ran the ferry while Capt. Furman was at Prairie du Chien.
Wolcott	Miss	DR, p3c4, 1/12/1871	Served as assisstant in the primary department at the De Soto school.
Wolfing	Eugene	BD, p3c3, 2/15/1878	Eugene Wolfing married Katie Downs on Feb. 4, 1878. Bride and groom from Richland Center. Rev. Sturges of Richland Center officiated. Bride's parents recently died.
Women's Sufferage		DC, p2c1, 4/9/1887	Twenty-four ladies in the Town of Wheatland decided to take advantage of the school suffrage law and demanded the ballot at the polls. Adam Carlyle served as spokesman and "made a plea so strong, and at the same time so touching, that everyone began to think themselves pretty small for not allowing women the ballot years ago, but the inspectors were hard hearted and invincible ..." [p2c1] Sixteen women in Lynxville "took advantage of the privilege, went to Seneca and cast their votes for such officers as they were allowed to vote for." [p2c2]
Wonzor	Lou P.	BD, p3c3, 11/25/1881	Mrs. Wonzor of Boscobel received a dispatch Monday announcing death of her husband that morning in La Crosse. He staggered and fell, striking his head on a stove at the Minnesota House. Death caused by the fall and liquor. "Despite his love for liquor, Lou was well liked by his fellow citizens." Per issue dated 12/2/1881, Wonzer was 41 years old and buried in Forest Hill Cemetery, Madison on Nov. 24, 1881.
Wonzor	Mary, Mrs.	BD, p3c1, 6/8/1883	Took Will Revel as a partner at her barbershop in Boscobel.
Wood	A.	BD, p3c1, 8/21/1883	Lived in Boscobel area. Thanked his friends and neighbors for the attention given to his late wife during her illness.
Wood	Abe	BD, p3c2, 7/29/1881	Lived in the Boscobel area. Killed a 6-foot-long water snake.
Wood	Dell	BD, p3c1, 1/13/1882	John Thompson married Dell Wood in Mt. Ida on Jan. 1, 1882. Bride and groom were from the Town of Marion.
Wood	Hiram O.	BD, p3c3, 12/20/1878	Planned to marry Flora MacDonald of Milwaukee on Jan. 1st.
Wood	J. P.	BD, p3c3, 8/30/1878	Published a notice in the newspaper announcing that his 19-year-old son, George Wood, was emancipated. J. P. would no longer be accountable for the son's debts.
Wood	Julia, Mrs.	RH, p4c1, 5/23/1901	Mrs. Wood's funeral was held in Bell Center on Thursday. She was an aunt of H. H. Lewis and wife of Readstown.
Wood	Martha, Mrs.	BD, p3c2, 8/21/1883	Died Aug. 17, 1883 at the age of 58 years and 13 days. She moved to Boscobel in 1860 with her husband, A. Wood. She was a member of the Baptist Church.
Wood	Richard	BD, p3c4, 3/24/1882	First postmaster in Fennimore. Postoffice was located in the grove on D. T. Parker's land.

Genealogical Events from Newspapers for Crawford, Vernon and Grant Counties, Wisconsin, 1870-1901

LAST NAME	FIRST NAME	NEWSPAPER, PAGE/COLUMN MONTH/DAY/YEAR	GENEALOGICAL DATA
Woodard	A. E.	DR, p3c4, 3/16/1871	Resided in Harmony. Wrote a poem on the death of Lydia Griffin.
Woodard	Ameda, Miss	BD, p3c1, 2/18/1881	From the Boscobel area. Buried Sunday.
Woodard	Eli	BD, p3c2, 5/23/1879	Joe Jenkins was arrested for injuring Eli Woodard in a knife fight in Boscobel. Woodard may lose his arm.
Woodard	I.	BD, p3c1, 5/11/1883	Resigned his post as Boscobel town constable. Replaced by D. R. Lawrence.
Woodard	Ike	BD, p2c5, 1/5/1877	Worked as an auctioneer in Boscobel.
Woodard	Isaac	BD, p3c1, 3/17/1882	Named to replace John Kelty as Boscobel's marshall. Kelty resigned.
Woodard	Isaac	BD, p3c1, 5/30/1879	Bought the well-known running horse, Burglar, of Madison. Resident of Boscobel.
Woodard	Joseph	BD, p3c2, 4/1/1881	Foot recently amputated. He was accidently shot in the heel 24 years ago. It never fully healed. Resided in Boscobel.
Woodard	Nathaniel	BD, p3c3, 4/27/1877	Resided in Town of Clayton. He was robbed on April 9, 1877. Lost $27.50, a gold watch and an overcoat.
Woodburn	John	DC, p2c1, 2/5/1887	C. V. Porter wrote a series of articles on the Black Hawk War. In it he says, "The Black Hawk trail passed from the latter place a little north of Pine Knob, Sec. 27, T. 11, R. 4, struck the Towerville Creek at the old John Woodburn farm Sec. 19, and then kept the ridge to Rising Sun."
Woodbury	"Deacon"	DR, p3c1, 6/29/1871	Resided in De Soto. He was "now a full blossomed citizen of the U.S., having been admitted at the last term of court."
Woodbury	C. E.	DR, p3c2, 11/2/1871	Resided in De Soto. Lost a stable and hay on an island owned by him above the village.
Woodbury	C. L.	DC, p3c2, 7/31/1886	The post office was moved to his store in De Soto.
Woodbury	C. L.	DC, p2c3, 2/19/1889	Sold general merchandise in De Soto. Current postmaster.
Woodbury	Charles E.	DC, p2c1, 2/3/1888	Arrived in De Soto in 1859 to visit his sisters. He was probably from Nova Scotia. He intended to only stay for a visit, but remained and erected a store that was afterwards occupied by Whiting and Carr.
Woodbury	Frank	DC, p2c3, 2/18/1888	Frank Woodbury and Ernest Dyer returned to De Soto from Guttenburg and Turkey River, IA.
Woodbury	G. L.	DC, p2c3, 7/10/1886	Advertised the goods in his general store in De Soto.
Woodcock	F. D.	RH, p4c3, 12/16/1897	Lydia Green married F. D. Woodcock at the residence of the bride's family. The marriage took place about 3 miles north of Readstown. C. W. Reeve officiated at the ceremony.
Woodhouse	George E.	DC, p2c2, 3/10/1888	Emma M. Geesa married George E. Woodhouse on Feb. 28, 1888 at the home of the bride's father, Frederic Geesa of Wheatland. Groom from Genoa.
Woodman	C. J.	BD, p2c4, 11/26/1880	Grant County paid him a bounty for scalps turned into the county.
Woodman Election Results		BD, p2c1, 4/4/1879	The Woodman election results were: Supervisors - George Brown, Orlin Garvin, Patrick Glynn; Treasurer - James Ellis; Clerk - H. F. Walton; Assessor - James A. Faris; Justice of the Peace - D. H. Ballou, John Quinn, J. H. Horsefall and Constables - Leander Knox, Patrick Morgan John Harrower.
Woodruff	Charles	DC, p3c4, 12/4/1886	"Charles Woodruff and wife of Minneapolis, Abe Woodruff and brother, Ike, of Canada, spent Thanksgiving with their parents. This was the first time the whole family has been together for several years." [From the Lansing news column.]
Woods	Dode	BD, p3c2, 8/30/1878	Right eye injured by gunpowder grains. Treated by Dr. Pickard. Probably won't lose the eye.
Woolcut	V.	DR, p1c3, 12/7/1871	Vernon Co. Board of Supervisors allowed payment to V. Woolcut for services rendered in the arrest of J. Hoover and A. Davis.
Wooley	Lew, Rev.	BD, p3c2, 6/24/1881	From Wonewoc. Visited his parents in Boscobel.
Woolley	L. J.	BD, p3c1, 1/5/1877	Attorney in Boscobel.
Woolley	Lutie	BD, p3c1, 10/13/1882	Died Oct. 3, 1882 in Viola, Richland Co. He was 2 years, 4 months and 10 days old. His parents were the Rev. Louis N. and Estella S. Woolley.

Genealogical Events from Newspapers for Crawford, Vernon and Grant Counties, Wisconsin, 1870-1901

LAST NAME	FIRST NAME	NEWSPAPER, PAGE/COLUMN MONTH/DAY/YEAR	GENEALOGICAL DATA
Worden	James H.	DC, p2c2, 12/31/1887	Head sawyer at Treadwell & Carr's Mill in De Soto in 1857/8. "He was of pure New England extraction, and therefore belonged to the inner circle. Worden was not handsome, but he made up for the lack of beauty in his cheerfulness." Warden wrote poetry and parodies. Some of his lines were published.
Worth		DC, p2c1, 2/3/1888	The Worth boys established a wagon shop in De Soto in 1857.
Worth	A. R.	DR, p3c3, 7/27/1871	Returned to De Soto after breaking 90 acres of his 100-acre farm near Charles City, IA. He will probably move there soon. Seymore Wait returned with him.
Worth	A. R.	DR, p3c1, 4/27/1871	A. R. Worth, I. W. Blake and S. G. Wait left De Soto for a tour of northern Iowa. They were seeking a more suitable place to live.
Worth	Addison	DR, p3c3, 4/6/1871	Advertised the sale of a milk cow.
Worth	C. B.	DR, p2c6, 12/15/1870	Proprietor of a grocery and restaurant in De Soto.
Worth	C. B.	DR, p3c2, 12/29/1870	Dr. E. B. Houghton, J. Osgood, S. D. Powers and C. B. Worth, were among the "First Families" who settled in De Soto in 1854. In 1870, C. B. Worth was the only pioneer from this group still in De Soto. Captain Worth opened the second store in the village. " . . . the venerable mariner, Captain C. B. Worth, who although in his 70th year, is hale and hearty."
Worth	C. M.	DR, p3c1, 3/9/1871	Resided in De Soto. Worked as an agent of the Beaver Dam Nursery.
Worth	C. M. & A. R.	DR, p2c4, 12/29/1870	Operated a saw and planing mill in De Soto.
Worth	C.M. & A.R.	DR, p3c2, 5/25/1871	A notice of dissolution was published for the partnership of C. M. Worth and A. R. Worth. C. M. will run the business by himself in De Soto.
Worth	Capt.	DR, p3c3, 9/21/1871	Ran a brickyard in De Soto in 1856.
Worth	Cyrus B., Capt.	DC, p2c2, 10/15/1887	Early resident of De Soto. Worth was born on Martha's Vineyard and hailed from Edgartown. When he was old enough, he went to sea and rose to the rank of Captain. He made frequent trips on whalers. After tiring of the sea, he went to Port Washington, WI where he met Dr. S. D. Powers. Power soon moved to De Soto, bringing a large following with him, including Capt. Worth. The party stopped at the West Prairie home of Lewis Sterling, where Worth met T. C. Ankeney, who was also heading for De Soto.
Worth	Cyrus B., Captain	DC, p2c1, 11/26/1887	Owned a brickyard in De Soto in the 1850s. After the market became saturated with bricks, he sold the horse used in the brick operation to Giles Hayden. Worth went into the restaurant business. Hayden took the horse to his home in the Cooley Valley. During the first night in its new home, the horse managed to break into a grain pen, gorged itself and died. Hayden skinned the horse and gave it to Capt. Worth, asking him to take it on what he owed Worth for the horse. Worth accepted the deal.
Worth	S. A., Mrs.	DC, p3c3, 7/24/1886	Died June 27, 1886. She was the wife of Dr. Worth of Hesper, IA. Born Dec. 9, 1832 at Cardington, OH. Educated at Antioch College during the presidency of Horace Mann. She was an earnest Christian and temperance worker. Resided in De Soto 12 years ago.
Wright	boy	BD, p3c3, 10/25/1878	A son was born to George Wright [car repairman] of Prairie du Chien on Sunday morning.
Wright	Eldora, Mrs.	BD, p3c1, 11/6/1883	Andrew Harris married Mrs. Eldora Wright on Oct. 30, 1883 at Blue River Station. Bride and groom were from Blue River Station. The Rev. Q. R. Wright officiated.
Wright	J. N.	DR, p3c3, 4/27/1871	Served as Superintendent of Schools in Vernon Co. Complained about the qualifications of teachers.
Wright	J. N.	DR, p3c2, 9/7/1871	Resigned as Vernon Co. School of Superintendent. He was replaced by O. B. Wyman of Hillsborough. Wyman was a teacher.
Wright	Owen	BD, p3c2, 4/5/1878	Died Friday at his home in Belmont. He was one of the old settlers of Lafayette Co. and widely known in southwestern Wisconsin. Aged about 60 years. Buried nearby.
Wright	Sarah, Mrs.	BD, p2c3, 2/17/1882	Aged 95 years and 7 days. Died Feb. 4, 1882 at the residence of her daughter, Mrs. Joseph Prew [Drew?] of Wauzeka. She was a Revolutionary War pensioner. Her father was a soldier under Washington's command. Funeral held at St. Gabriel's Church in Prairie du Chien.
Wunder	Marguette	DC, p2c2, 1/1/1887	Englehardt Schroeder married Marguette Wunder on Dec. 22, 1886 at the Bay State House in De Soto. Groom from Lansing, IA. Bride from Center, Township, IA. D. A. Steele, J.P., officiated.
Wunterle	Frank	BD, p3c1, 9/18/1883	Planned to move to Boscobel from Milwaukee. He leased the brewery.
Wyman	O. B.	BD, p3c1, 7/29/1881	Secretary for the Vernon Co. Fair.

Genealogical Events from Newspapers for Crawford, Vernon and Grant Counties, Wisconsin, 1870-1901

LAST NAME	FIRST NAME	NEWSPAPER, PAGE/COLUMN MONTH/DAY/YEAR	GENEALOGICAL DATA
Wyman	Orvis P., Judge	RH, p4c1, 12/6/1900	Died on Dec. 2, 1900 at a private hospital in Buffalo, NY. He was 55 and resided in Viroqua. Survived by wife, 1 son and 1 daughter.
York	H. D.	BD, p3c2, 2/15/1878	H. D. York of Hazel Green was admitted to the bar at Grant Co. Circuit Court.
York	William	RH, p4c1, 3/7/1901	Traveled from home in Wauzeka to visit with parents, Mr. and Mrs. Robert York of Readstown.
Young	C. L.	BD, p3c4, 6/21/1878	C. L. Young married Hattie Day on June 18, 1878 in Boscobel. Bride from Cresco, IA. Groom from Chicago. The Rev. George W. Nuzum officiated.
Young	Henry W.	BD, p3c2, 6/7/1878	Henry W. Young married Lena Potter on June 3, 1878 at the home of the bride's mother. Bride from Boscobel. Groom from Cresco, IA. They departed for a home in Iowa. The Rev. G. W. Nuzum officiated.
Young	John	BD, p1c4, 3/8/1878	Died last week in Reedsburg. At 88, he was the oldest member of the Masonic Order in Wisconsin.
Young	Loyall	RH, p4c1, 4/25/1901	Loyall Young married Jennie Smith on Tuesday at the home of the bride's parents. Bride and groom lived in Soldiers Grove. Groom employed by J. H. Stelzman. Bride was eldest daughter of R. L. Smith. The Rev. J. A. Neill officiated.
Young	T. C.	BD, p3c3, 2/9/1877	The son of T. C. Young of Millville lost his team and sleigh when the ice on the Wisconsin River cracked open. The son survived.
Zabolia	A., Sr.	DC, p2c1, 4/30/1887	A. Zabolia, Sr. and his daughter, Angeline, [both of Genoa] planned to visit Italy in June.
Zeigelmaire	George, Jr.	BD, p3c1, 9/1/1882	George Zeigelmaire [Zeigelmeyer?], Jr.; Will Palmer and Olof Nelson were each fined $3 for disturbing the peace in Boscobel.
Zeigelmaire	George, Jr.	BD, p3c2, 4/20/1883	A warrant was issued for his arrest for a series of robberies in the Boscobel area. Zeigelmaire admitted to James Bailey, Constable of Neilsville, Clark County, that he and his brother were guilty of multiple robberies. George Zeigelmaire, Sr. found some of the stolen items on his farm and advised the sheriff. Henry Zeigelmaire, age 15, was missing and last seen in Woodman heading west. The father was not implicated.
Zeigelmaire	George, Jr. and Henry	BD, p3c2, 5/4/1883	George Zeigelmaire, Jr. and his brother, Henry, of Lancaster, escaped from jail in Lancaster. They were later captured. George was 18 years old, 5' 10" tall, weighed 140 pounds, dark brown hair, smooth face and black eyes. Henry was 25 years old, 5' 7" tall, weighed 138 pounds, brown hair, blue eyes and had a left hand crippled with palsy.
Zeigelmaire	Henry	BD, p3c3, 4/27/1883	Captured at the home of his uncle, about 20 miles southeast of Elkader, IA. He claimed his father did not know he was involved in robbery, but that his mother helped to hide the plunder.
Zeigelmeyer	George	BD, p3c1, 9/12/1879	Plead guilty to selling beer on Sunday to minors in Boscobel.
Zillinger	Emma M.	BD, p3c1, 4/7/1882	Cortland Main married Emma M. Zillinger on April 2, 1882 in Boscobel. The bride and groom were from Crawford County. J. McLaughlin, J.P. officiated.
Zollar	girl	DC, p2c3, 7/3/1886	Daughter recently born to T. Zollar of Victory.
Zollar	T.	DC, p3c5, 9/25/1886	Resided in Retreat. Went to Minneapolis to arrange for the construction of a house [in that city].

NEWSPAPER ARTICLES OF GENEALOGICAL AND HISTORICAL INTEREST

This section consists of several articles that were copied in whole or in part from the original newspaper article. These articles provide a context to researchers who may be able to discover kinship and other relationships between colleagues, neighbors, peers, etc. who are mentioned in the same article. The articles also place our ancestors in the social history of the region and the country.

Organization of a Voluntary Military Company in Boscobel, WI

On reading and filing the petition of H. D. Farquharson and sixty-four others, residents of the County of Grant, Wisconsin, representing that said petitioners are residents of Boscobel, Grant County, Wisconsin, are all over 18 years of age, and under the age of 45 years, and praying that some suitable person be appointed to superintend the organization of said petitioners and others into a Volunteer Military Company of Light Infantry pursuant to the laws of the State of Wisconsin, it is here ordered that Ben. M. Coates, of Boscobel, in the County of Grant, be and he is hereby appointed to superintend the organization of a Volunteer Light Infantry Company at Boscobel, in said County of Grant, as prayed for in said petition.

Witness my hand and the seal of the County Court of said County of Grant, at Lancaster, in said County, this 16th day of August, A. D. 1877.

W.M. McGonigal, County Judge

We, the undersigned residents of Boscobel, Grant County, Wisconsin, being over 18 and under 45 years of age, do hereby agree to become members of an organization for the purpose of forming ourselves into a Company of Light Infantry under the Militia Laws of this State.

Muster Roll

Name	Residence	Height	Name	Residence	Height
H. D. Farquharson	Boscobel, WI	5' 9"	G. W. Limbocker	Boscobel, WI	6'
John D. Wilson	do.	5' 8"	T. M. Wells	do.	5' 10"
Henry Walter	do.	5' 6"	E. A. Brookins	do.	5' 4"
Olof G. Brekke	do.	5' 10"	Robt. J. Arthur	do.	5' 6"
Charles DeWitt	do.	5' 9'	C. R. Garrett	do.	5' 8"
Robert Anderson	do.	6' 1"	R. B. Lesler	do.	5' 10"
O. B. Forseth	do.	6'	Mike Gannon	do.	5' 7"
Fred N. Mortimer	do.	5' 9"	Valentine Stucky	do.	5' 5"
H. W. Hubbell	do.	5' 11"	John Bowers	do.	5' 6"
F. N. Rowe	do.	5' 9"	O. E. Comstock	do.	5' 8"
D. T. Parker, Jr.	do.	5' 7"	C. S. Jencks	do.	5' 6"
B. Kronshage	do.	5' 9"	J. H. Clark, Jr.	do.	5' 11"
Arthur Nixon	do.	5' 7"	F. M. Keltenbech	do.	6' 2"
W. T. Hurd	do.	5' 8"	Cornelius O Brekke	do.	6'
D. G. Bliss	do.	5' 11"	A. B. Alden	do.	5' 5"
J. O. Davidson	do.	5' 6"	Harry G. Hawley	do.	5' 7"
Will Gordecke	do.	6' 1"	Matth. Dilger	do.	5' 6"
_ C. Christopherson	do.	5' 10"	D. Bartels	do.	5' 6"
B. S. Burdick	do.	5' 10"	J. Bohl	do.	5' 7"
A. Kimball	do.	5' 3"	H. Hobus	do.	5' 7"
Louis Ruka, Jr.	do.	5' 10"	E. G. Thompson	do.	5' 5"
Louis Neil	do.	5' 10"	Frank J. Muffley	do.	5' 8"
W. A. Muffley	do.	5' 9"	Mike Heller	do.	5' 7"
John Brindley, Jr.	do.	6' 2"	A. A. Clark	do.	5' 6"
Frank C. Muffley	do.	5' 7"	P. H. Sherrard	do.	5' 5"
M. McSpaden	do.	5' 5"	W. Wagner	do.	5' 11"

Genealogical Events from Newspapers for Crawford, Vernon and Grant Counties, Wisconsin, 1870-1901

Name	Residence	Height	Name	Residence	Height
John Keity	do.	5' 9"	John S. Stoddart	do.	5' 8"
A. Hurlburt	do.	5' 9"	Max Nobis	do.	5' 5"
Will E. DeLap	do.	5' 8"	G. A. Christ	do.	5' 8"
Chas. P. Hinn	do.	5' 9"	Lou P. Lesler	do.	5' 9"
Syver Anderson	do.	5' 5"	A. G. Meyer	do.	5' 8"
W. A. Partridge	do.	5' 9"	William Cook	do.	5' 10"
M. A. Sawyer	do.	5' 9"			

From the *Boscobel Dial*, August 24, 1877, Page 3, Column 4

Genealogical Events from Newspapers for Crawford, Vernon and Grant Counties, Wisconsin, 1870-1901

Civil War Soldiers Residing in the Boscobel Area

The Roster

The following is the roster, so far as made up by the town committee, of ex-soldiers in the city of Boscobel. Should there be any ex-soldier whose name is omitted, he will report the same to Mr. J. McLaughlin:

Last Name	First Name	Unit	Company	Post Office
Cook	Charles	1st WI Infantry	D	Boscobel
Dean	C. K., Adjutant	2nd WI Infantry		Boscobel
Stahiel	John, Capt.	2nd WI Infantry	K	Boscobel
Bartholomew	Samuel, Sargeant	3rd WI Infantry	F	Boscobel
Dolme	F. W.	3rd WI Infantry	F	Boscobel
Armstrong	L. G., Surgeon	6th WI Infantry		Boscobel
Osborn	J. N.	6th WI Infantry		Boscobel
Lesler	R. B.	7th WI Infantry	G	Boscobel
Cowan	G. W.	7th WI Infantry	F	Boscobel
Taylor	J. L.	7th WI Infantry	F	Boscobel
Coates	Isaac	7th WI Infantry	H	Boscobel
Grant	James	7th WI Infantry	H	Boscobel
Cook	William	10th WI Infantry	F	Boscobel
Kimball	R. E.	11th WI Infantry	D	Boscobel
Enright	P. H.	11th WI Infantry	A	Boscobel
Rogers	Commodore	12th WI Infantry	K	Boscobel
Rein	John, Capt.	12th WI Infantry	K	Boscobel
Ricks	J. B.	12th WI Infantry	K	Boscobel
Scofield	Henry	12th WI Infantry	K	Boscobel
Kumarine	Frank	17th WI Infantry	I	Boscobel
McLaughlin	J., Lieutenant	20th WI Infantry	C	Boscobel
Francisco	N. J.	20th WI Infantry	C	Boscobel
McKinney	A. M.	20th WI Infantry	C	Boscobel
France	J. V. B.	20th WI Infantry	C	Boscobel
Clark	H.	20th WI Infantry	C	Boscobel
Huff	W. L.	20th WI Infantry	F	Boscobel
May	J. W.	20th WI Infantry	F	Boscobel
Oleson	A. F.	22nd WI Infantry	D	Boscobel
Farquarharson	H. C., Captain	25th WI Infantry	C	Boscobel
Nice	J. W.	25th WI Infantry	C	Boscobel
Muffley	F. C.	25th WI Infantry	I	Boscobel
Carley	D. W., Surgeon	33rd WI Infantry		Boscobel
Burdick	F. B., Captain	33rd WI Infantry	G	Boscobel
Cheever	A.	33rd WI Infantry	G	Boscobel
Ableiter	M.	33rd WI Infantry	G	Boscobel
Wurster	G.	33rd WI Infantry	G	Boscobel
Reichel	L.	33rd WI Infantry	G	Boscobel
Kelty	John	33rd WI Infantry	B	Boscobel
Scott	W. T.	33rd WI Infantry	B	Boscobel
Robinson	A. W.	36th WI Infantry	D	Boscobel
Renshaw	A. J.	42nd WI Infantry	D	Boscobel

Genealogical Events from Newspapers for Crawford, Vernon and Grant Counties, Wisconsin, 1870-1901

Last Name	First Name	Unit	Company	Post Office
Kellogg	Charles	43rd WI Infantry	C	Boscobel
Ricks	John	47th WI Infantry	E	Boscobel
Barbeau	John	49th WI Infantry	A	Boscobel
Devoe	Amos	50th WI Infantry	H	Boscobel
Rose	W. H.	2nd WI Calvary	C	Boscobel
Woodard	Isaac	3rd WI Calvary	M	Boscobel
Pittgener	John	3rd WI Calvary	M	Boscobel
Smith	F. A.	3rd WI Calvary	M	Boscobel
Sherrard	D.	1st IA Calvary	G	Boscobel
Alden	A. B.	6th US Calvary	G	Boscobel
Rice	R. B.	8th IL Calvary	H	Boscobel
Bolster	G. W.	1st VT Calvary		Boscobel
Willis	J. P.	92nd IL Mounted Infantry	I	Boscobel
Hayman	L. H.	174th OH Infantry	F	Boscobel
Sawyer	M. A., Hosp. Steward	3rd NH Infantry		Boscobel
Cole	S. C.	38th IA Infantry	I	Boscobel
Meyers	E. C.	154th NY Infantry	D	Boscobel
Anderson	C. D.	83rd IL Infantry	A	Boscobel
Flora	H. R.	116th IN Infantry	F	Boscobel
Pike	Ed	Regiment Unknown		Boscobel
Knaub	L.	Regiment Unknown		
Wagner	Henry	Regiment Unknown		

From the *Boscobel Dial*, September 10, 1880, Page 3, Column 3

Genealogical Events from Newspapers for Crawford, Vernon and Grant Counties, Wisconsin, 1870-1901

The Reunion
What Boscobel Did to Entertain the Soldier Visitors

(The following was paraphrased from an extensive article in the Boscobel Dial of June 16, 1882, pages 2 and 3. The full texts of many of the speeches offered at the reunion were printed.)

The third annual meeting of the Grant County Soldiers and Sailors was held June 7 and 8, 1882 in Boscobel, WI. Veterans from Grant, La Fayette, Crawford, Richland, Sauk, Dane and Iowa Counties attended the reunion. The newspaper praised the decorations. "The decorations were of a high and artistic order. Buildings were draped with colors, bunting was flying from every house, and across Wisconsin Avenue were stretched three large flags, on the center one of which, erected by the DeLap brothers was "Welcome Comrades" on one side while on the reverse was "We welcome the heroes that saved our country." The work of the reunion committees was lauded and the reunion called a success.

Veterans started coming in Tuesday, the day before the reunion. They came by train, wagon, horseback and foot. Most brought blankets and stayed in newly built barracks. The visitors were enthusiastically met at the Boscobel train depot by bands of music and then escorted to the grounds. Special trains arrived with soldiers from Richland Center and Platteville. "The campgrounds were covered over with people; the streets, on either side were lined with visitors and they felt that their pleasure was the whole object of the citizens whom they had come to spend a couple of days among." The soldiers embraced each other, recounted their brave deeds, fun of camp life, long marches, sufferings endured and the misery of rebel prisons. The old regimental flags were greeted with cheers, tears and hugs.

On Wednesday the Boscobel soldiers elected Samuel Bartholomew their Captain. A company of soldiers formed to escort the arriving soldiers and citizens. The day was spent receiving guests and organizing into companies. At 5:00 p.m. a dress parade was held. More than 13,000 people were estimated to be in the city during the reunion.

Thursday morning the soldiers fell in for the grand parade. The column was reviewed by the Governor of Wisconsin, Jerry Rusk. Loud huzzahs went up from the multitude as the boys marched the streets. After the parade, the soldiers returned to the Fair grounds where the oral exercises took place. The speeches were highly inspirational and commemorated the bravery, sacrifice and patriotism of the soldiers. Capt. Charles H. Baxter, of Lancaster, President of the Association provided the opening remarks, some of which follow, " . . . nearly a quarter of a century has passed and gone since those eventful days of hardship and peril endured for a common cause–days of marching in the rain, through the mud, under an almost tropical sun, along the banks of the Yazoo, through the swamp and under the pine wood of Georgia with 'Sherman to the sea,' on with Grant through the Wilderness to victory at Appomattox. But I do not believe there is one of our number here today that can forget or would ignore the friendship for that comrade who shared with him the last of the contents of his haversack or his canteen. Nor do I believe that you regret having done what you could to preserve the Union, to maintain the supremacy of the old flag and the liberties and institutions which it represents. ...It is unnecessary for me to remind you of the fact that the civil and religious liberties you enjoy today in this land has been purchased at the price of blood."

Following a prayer by the Rev. S. W. Eaton of Lancaster, John D. Wilson, Mayor of Boscobel, delivered the welcoming address. He said, "The citizens of Boscobel feel that they cannot do enough for you, to reward you for what you have done for them and your country. Your deeds stand out above the deeds of all other soldiers of the world for bravery and daring." Next came the singing of "America," in old army fashion.

Capt. A. R. Bushnell of Lancaster responded to the welcome. He told the audience "I well remember that twenty-one years ago this summer, when Co. C of the 7th regiment came up across the country from Platteville on our way to rendezvous at camp Randall, no commissary's billet was necessary to find us house room and rations here in Boscobel. You then took us into your families, as you have again done now, fed and lodged us, bade us God Speed, as you again do all of the old soldiers here now, and all will leave you, as Co. C did then, with a warm corner in their hearts for Boscobel. ....We remember the soldiers' aid societies in every neighborhood, where the women made clothing, scraped lint, prepared hospital stores, and put up and sent boxes of good thing to the boys in the dreary winter quarters; boxes that cheered many a homesick soldier lad when the dismal dead march, drumming some poor fellow out of camp to his last resting place, was often more frequent than reveille or tattoo." This speech was followed by the words of the Hon. W. B. Clark, orator of the day.

Clark said, "The war in which you so dearly earned your title as Veterans was one of the most memorable in history. A war notable for the vast territory over which it was waged; its enormous cost in treasure, and in human life, and for the high character of its soldiery. A war pregnant with brilliant exploit, heroic daring, patient suffering. A war significant in the conflict of great principles which led to it–principles which neither the war's compromise nor legislation of past centuries could settle. A war most notable for the results it accomplished, the issues it forever settled, and the impress it made upon man's political destiny for all the future. ...Great was the valor, costly the sacrifice through which in many a brilliant exploit --by steadiness under decimating fire, by patient heroism, unrivalled in the story of war, by voluntary surrender to every form of danger and death, before masked batteries on bloody fields, in crowded hospitals, and the untold horrors of southern prisons, the Second, Sixth and Seventh, Wisconsin Regiments won that title full of grand significance, the 'Iron Brigade of the West.'" Some of the "Old Iron Brigade" requested a speech from Gen. John Gibbon. The soldiers then yelled for some words from Gov. Rusk and Gen. Thomas Reynolds. After the speeches, the soldiers reformed into columns and marched back to the campgrounds where 2,100 to 2,300 people were fed.

Visiting continued as the soldiers broke camp in the evening. Cornet bands from Boscobel, Richland Center, Platteville, Excelsior and Sand Prairie serenaded the departing veterans and visitors.

Soldiers at the 1882 Boscobel, Wisconsin Reunion

Last Name	First	Rank	Co.	Inf./Other	Address	Last Name	First	Rank	Co.	Inf./Other	Address
Ableiter	M.	Pr.	G	33 WI	Boscobel	Bartholomew	A. J.	Pr.		4 CO	Boscobel
Adams	M.	Pr.	G	23 WI	Boscobel	Bartley	P.	Pr.	G	5 MO CAV	Bloomington
Adkins	W.	Cor.	D	21 IN	Platteville	Baxter	C. H.	Capt.	K	47 WI	Lancaster
Aikens	E.	Pr.	B	31 WI	Spafford	Beebe	W.	Pr.	I	10 WI	Excelsior
Alcorn	H.	Pr.	A	41 WI	Lancaster	Beebe	W. H.	Capt.	K	44 WI	Platteville
Alcorn	J. W.	Pr.	A	18 WI	Lancaster	Beer	J. M.	Cor.	B	33 WI	Wyalusing
Alderson	H.	Pr.	I	15 WI	Eagle	Beilter	E.	Pr.	I	20 WI	Millville
Alexander	C. D.	Pr.	I	19 WI	Montfort	Bell	A. W.	Lt.	K	44 WI	Platteville
Allen	H.	Pr.	F	3 WI	Lone Rock	Benner	G.	Sgt.	K	47 WI	Wauzeka
Anderson	T. B.	Sgt.	C	41 WI	Millville	Benshon	A. J.	Cor.	D	42 WI	Boscobel
Anderson	H.	Pr.	I	15 WI	(Basiord?)	Bentley	E. J.	Capt.	F	3 WI	Platteville
Anderson	H.	Pr.	G	1 MN ART	Montivdeo, MN	Bidgood	B.	Pr.		1 WI ART	Lancaster
Andrew	G.	Pr.	B	33 WI	Fennimore	Bigler	L. A.	Pr.	C	50 WI	Darlington
Armstrong	S. W.	Pr.	A	1 WI		Bilckie	Wm.	Pr.		79 NY	Port Andrew
Atkinson	J.	Pr.	H	11 WI	Port Andrew	Birchard	N.	Capt.	B	33 WI	Fennimore
Bagley	M.	Pr.	A	44 WI	Hurlbuts Cor.	Bishop	W. H.	Pr.	G	12 WI	Platteville
Bailey	J.	Pr.	H	38 WI	Cobb	Bishop	M. E.	Pr.	B	24 WI	Platteville
Baker	J.	Pr.	C	9 WI	Platteville	Blair	L.	Pr.	M	1 WI CAV	Ida Grove
Baker	W. H.	Pr.	B	30 WI	Linden	Blanchard	E.	Pr.	E	25 WI	Fennimore
Balister	G. D.	Pr.	H	Mer. Horse	Lone Rock	Blanding	L.	Pr.	K	12 WI	Boscobel
Banmot	G. H.	Pr.	C	31 WI	Ridgeway	Bliss	A. K.	Pr.	C	20 WI	Mt. Ida
Barber	L.	Pr.	I	15 WI	Bell Center	Bliss	D.	Dr.	C	20 WI	Fennimore
Barber	J. A.	Lt.	C	25 WI	Lancaster	Bolster	G. W.	Pr.		1 VT Batt.	
Barker	J.	Pr.	H	36 WI	Ellenboro, Dak.	Border	J.	Pr.	K	1 IA CAV	McGregor
Barker	B.	Pr.	G	5 WI	Darlington	Bowen	E. A.	Pr.	A	17 WI	Boscobel
Barker	John	Pr.	C	12 IL CAV	Platteville	Brackett	J. W.	Pr.	H	7 WI	Bloomington
Barnett	John	Pr.	C	25 WI	Inde., IA	Bradburry	N.	Sgt.	F	7 WI	Platteville
Barnum	Dr.	A. Sr.		49 WI	Fennimore	Bradley	L. S.	Pr.	R	43 WI	Ellenboro, Dak.
Bartholomew	W. A.	Pr.	A	25 WI	Boscobel	Bradley	J. C.	Pr.	F	7 WI	Ellenboro, Dak.
Bartholomew	S.	Pr.	F	3 WI	Boscobel	Brand	T. H.	Sgt.	I	3 WI	Shullsburg
Bartholomew	E. G.	Pr.	H	2 WI CAV	Excelsior	Brands	H.	Pr.	I	20 WI	Mt. Hope

Genealogical Events from Newspapers for Crawford, Vernon and Grant Counties, Wisconsin, 1870-1901

Last Name	First	Rank	Co.	Inf./Other	Address	Last Name	First	Rank	Co.	Inf./Other	Address
Brazell	J. W.	Cor.	E	11 WI	Rowey	Clark	J. J.	Pr.	H	7WI	Boscobel
Breckner	W.	Pr.	F	49 WI	Haney	Clark	Harvey	Pr.	C	20 WI	Boscobel
Brehmen	A.	Pr.	L	3 WI	Pt. Andrew	Clark	S. W.	Pr.	B	33 WI	Blue River
Bremmer	J. S.	Pr.	K	12 WI	Fennimore	Clark	H. W.	Pr.	M	3 WI CAV	Fennimore
Briggs	W. T.	Sailor			Eagle Corners	Clawson	C.	Pr.	G	33 WI	Excelsior
Brighthaupt	L. A.	Pr.	C	25 WI	Lancaster	Clayton	A. P.	Pr.		6 WI ART	Richland Center
Brindley	W.	Capt.	D	33 WI	Boscobel	Cleary	J.	Pr.	D	53 NY	Eagle
Brinkman	H.	Pr.	F	7 WI	Lancaster	Clemmons	J.	Sgt.	C	21 IA	Boscobel
Brookins	Jas.	Pr.	D	33 WI	Bloomington	Closson	B.	Pr.	G	33 WI	Boscobel
Brother	P.	Pr.	F	7 WI	Bloomingtonl	Coates	C. C.	Pr.	C	25 WI	Montfort
Brownell	D. H.	Pr.	K	12 WI	Wauzeka	Coates	J. T.	Pr.		2 Sharp Sht	
Brownell	H. S.	Pr.	H	11 WI	Pt. Andrew	Cobb	L.	Sgt.	B	33 WI	Viroqua
Brumumer	A.	Cor.	F	49 WI	Leclede, MO	Colburn	C.	Cor.	G	47 WI	Hurlbuts Cor.
Brunson	M. B.	Pr.		7 WI	Prairie du Chien	Cole	T. M.	Pr.	B	33 WI	Wauzeka
Bryant	J.	Cor. ?	E	11 WI	Belmont	Coleman	H.	Pr.	H	3 WI	Bell Center
Budworth	B. F.	Pr.	I	20 WI	Bloomington	Collins	J. A.	Pr.	K	6 WI	Excelsior
Bugbee	H.	Pr.	C	3 WI	Fennimore	Comerine	F.	Pr.	C	17 WI	Boscobel
Burchard	N. E.	Cor.	I	171 O. N. G.	Boscobel	Coney	A. A.	Pr.	C	80 IL	Port Andrew
Burkholder	D.	Pr.	C	7 WI	Hurlbuts Cor.	Cook	Sol	Pr.	H	50 WI	Pt. Andrew
Burnham	O. J.	Bugl.		6 WI ART	Richland Center	Cook	Wm.	Pr.	F	10 WI	Boscobel
Burrington	L.	Pr.	E	1 WI	Orion	Cook	A.	Pr.	I	47 WI	Clifton
Burris	O.	Pr.	C	1 WI	Platteville	Cook	L.	Pr.	K	31 WI	North Star
Burris	J.	Cor.	M	3 WI CAV	Boscobel	Cook	C. E.	Pr.	C	3 WI	Boscobel
Burton	J. R.	Pr.	D	30 WI	Glen Haven	Cook	W.	Pr.	A	33 WI	Belmont
Burton	J.	Pr.	A	33 WI	Annaton	Cook	V. T.	Pr.	K	1 US INF	North Star
Bushnell	A. R.	Capt.	C	7 WI	Lancaster	Cooley	R.	Pr.	D	31 WI	Mt. Hope
Butcher	B.	Pr.	G	33 WI	Boscobel	Cooper	J.	Cor.	I	15 WI	Port Andrew
Butler	Dan	Pr.	D	25 WI	Rockville	Cowan	G. W.	Sgt.	F	7 WI	Boscobel
Butler	S.	Pr.	G	11 WI	Richland Center	Cox	J. P.	Sgt.	H	25 WI	Lancaster
Butler	L.	Pr.	C	2 WI	Mt. Hope	Craig	J.	Pr.	F	2 WI CAV	Port Andrew
Byers	J.	Pr.	E	6 WI	Boscobel	Craig	P. P.	Pr.	K	92 OH	Excelsior
Callis	J. B.	B. G.		7 WI	Lancaster	Craige	L.	Pr.	B	25 WI	Port Andrew
Camp	M. T.	Pr.	C	7 WI	Platteville	Crane	W. M.	Cor.	F	2 WI CAV	Woodman
Carlan	P.	Pr.	G	47 WI	Boscobel	Cranes	J. P.	Pr.	G	141 OH	Boscobel
Carrell	C.	Pr.	E	5 WI	Soldiers Grove	Craven	W.	Pr.	F	102 OH	Platteville
Carson	P.	Pr.	D	7 WI	Eastman	Croft	C.	Pr.	C	25 WI	Werley
Carter	T.	Pr.	I	10 WI	Richland Center	Crouch	T.	Cor.	A	50 WI	Wauzeka
Casson	J. R.	Capt.	A	25 WI	Viroqua	Crow	J. T.	Pr.	A	14 IN	Mt. Hope
Cast	J. N.	Cor.	D	31 WI	Bell Center	Cull	John	Pr.	I	20 WI	Mt. Hope
Cast	W.	Pr.	K	12 WI	Hurlbuts Cor.	Cullins	C. M.	Cor.	A	37 WI	Basswood
Catlin	J.	Pr.	H	5 WI	Excelsior	Culner	L. D.	Pr.	F	7 WI	Ellenboro, Dak.
Caughey	L. C.	Pr.	K	22 WI	Belmont	Cummin	A. R.	Pr.		2 OH Lt Art.	Boscobel
Chadwick	A. D.	Cor.	I	113 IL	Boscobel	Cummins	D.	Pr.	K	3 WI	Spring Green
Chandler	C. P.	H. S.		5 WI	Madison	Curley	T.	Brig Gen		15 A.C.	Bell Center
Chapman	W.	Pr.		10 MO CAV.	Platteville	Curran	J. W.	Capt.	G	5 WI	Madison
Chapman	E. W.	Cor.	K	62 OH	Boscobel	Curtis	S. G.	Pr.	D	45 WI	Orion
Chena	C.	Pr.	C	28 WI	Wauzeka	Daughertee	J. W.	Pr.	E	35 WI	Boscobel
Chesemore	D.	Pr.	D	11 WI	Rockbridge	Daugherty	E.	Pr.	G	69 PA	Boscobel
Chisholm	J.	Pr.	I	20 WI	Mt. Hope	Dave	E.	Pr.	H	10 NY CAV	Richland Center
Chisholm	J.	Pr.	G	20 WI	Mt. Hope	Davenport	Philip	Pr.	K	12 WI	Pine Grove
Chismore	D.	Pr.	D	11 WI	Rockbridge	Daves	T.	Pr.	G	33 WI	Excelsior
Christ	J.	Pr.	G	33 WI	Boscobel	Davis	W. W.	Pr.	O	7 WI	Platteville
Churchill	G. W.	Sgt.	C	12 WI	Hurlbuts Cor.	Davis	D.	Pr.	K	33 WI	Helena
Clark	Steve	Pr.	C	25 WI	Boscobel	Davis	J. M.	Sgt.	G	33 WI	Excelsior

Genealogical Events from Newspapers for Crawford, Vernon and Grant Counties, Wisconsin, 1870-1901

Last Name	First	Rank	Co.	Inf./Other	Address	Last Name	First	Rank	Co.	Inf./Other	Address
Day	R. M.	Pr.	L	20 WI	Mt. Hope	Former	W.	Pr.	B	23 WI	Homer
Day	G. W.	Sgt.	I	20 WI	Mt. Hope	Forsyth	E. W.	Pr.	G	31 WI	Gratiot
Dean	C. F.	Pr.	F	7 WI	Ellenboro, Dak.	Foster	G. H.	Pr.	C	25 WI	Millville
Dean	O.	Pr.	K	31 WI	Seneca	Foust	M. V.	Pr.	A	147 IN	Woodman
Decker	D.	Pr.	C	35 WI	Lancaster	Fox	F.	Lt.		7 WI ART	Chilton
Decker	Abe	Pr.	C	25 WI	Lancaster	France	G. B.	Pr.	C	20 WI	Boscobel
Deidrick	A.	Cor.	G	33 WI	Cassville	Francisco	N. J.	Pr.	C	20 WI	Boscobel
Dempsey	S. H.	Pr.	B	38 WI	Fennimore	Frank	G. R.	Mj.		33 WI	Muscoda
Denuy	O. C.	Lt.	A	33 WI	Muscoda	Franklin	B.	Pr.	K	33 WI	Fennimore
Devoe	E. J.	Pr.	I	20 WI	Blue River	Freed	J. S.	Pr.	D	42 IN	Richland Center
DeVoe	A.	Lt.	H	50 WI	Boscobel	French	J.	Mus.	I	36 WI	Wauzeka
DeWitt	L. A.	Pr.		4 WI ART	Avoca	Fry	John	Pr.	A	33 WI	Ellenboro, Dak.
Dillon	John	Pr.	H	7 WI	Fennimore	Fuller	C.	Cor.	A	110 NY	Woodman
Dillon	J.	Cor.	I	47 WI	Blue River	Gardner	O. P.	Pr.	H	25 WI	Lancaster
Dingman	A.	Pr.	H	33 WI	Port Andrew	Garner	J. W.	1 Lt.	G	57 WI	Port Andrew
Dobler	S.	Pr.	B	27 IA	Excelsior	Garner	D.	Pr.	H	25 WI	Lancaster
Dodds	J. J.	Pr.	D	42 WI	Woodman	Garner	W. R.	Pr.	G	57 IN	Port Andrew
Dohme	F. W.	Pr.	F	3 WI	Boscobel	Garner	S.	Pr.	A	130 IN	Port Andrew
Donahue	T.	Pr.	H	43 WI	Eastman	Garner	J. W.	Sgt.		57 IN	Port Andrew
Dosch	Ed.	Pr.	B	25 WI	Eagle	Garner	A. J.	Pr.	A	130 IN	Port Andrew
Driver	J.	Pr.	H	3 WI	Darlington	Garthwait	W. E.	Sgt.	H	43 WI	Bloomington
Dudley	J. L.	Pr.	A	31 WI	Mt. Sterling	Garthwait	J. G.	Pr.	C	2 WI CAV	Bloomington
Duey	Jashel	Pr.	B	1 WI CAV	Hurlbuts Cor.	Garthwaite	B.	Pr.	H	43 WI	Lancaster
Duncan	E.	Pr.	G	47 WI	Boscobel	Garthwaite	I.	Pr.	H	43 WI	Lancaster
Dunstan	E.	Pr.	I	19 WI	Richland Center	Garvey	T.	Pr.	F	7 WI	Werley
Durley	W. P.	Capt.	C	7 WI	Lancaster	Garvin	M. P.	Pr.	B	25 WI	Blue River
Dustan	A.	Pr.	A	33 WI	Boscobel	Gates	W.	Lt.	H	10 WI	Reedstown
Dyer	W. J.	Pr.	K	47 WI	Lancaster	Gates	J.	Pr.	G	33 WI	Boscobel
Eastman	D.	Pr.	I	10 WI	Montfort	Gay	T. W.	Cor.	A	31 WI	Mt. Sterling
Edgecomb	R.	Pr.	E	27 WI	Boscobel	Geyer	Ed	Pr.	C	12 WI	Spring Green
Ellis	G. H.	Pr.	A	11 WI	Mazomanie	Gibbon	J. H.	Cor.	H	43 WI	Millville
Ellis	T.	Pr.	A	54 IL	Boscobel	Gibbon	John	Brig Gen		U. S. V.	St. Paul, MN
Ellsworth	T. J.	Cor.	A	44 WI	Excelsior	Gibbons	R.	Pr.	E	73 IN	Sextonville
Emmons	E.	Cor.	G	47 WI	Boscobel	Gibbs	A. V.	Pr.	E	35 OH	Boscobel
Enright	D.	Pr.	A	11 WI	Seneca	Gilbert	W.	Pr.	A	17 WI	Boscobel
Esman	J. W.	Pr.	A	111 PA	Spring Green	Gilbert	S. A.	Pr.	G	47 WI	Lancaster
Eversoll	R.	Pr.	G	33 WI	Beetown	Gillian	J. G.	Sgt.	A	41 WI	Platteville
Ewing	T.	Pr.	K	44 WI	Richland Center	Gillingham	W.	Pr.	D	11 WI	Gillingham
Ewing	J.	Pr.	F	44 WI	Eagle	Gillingham	W.	Pr.	D	11 WI	Gillingham
Ewing	J.	Pr.	F	44 WI	Muscoda	Gillman	B.	Cor.	C	20 WI	Fennimore
Fant	J. T.	Pr.	H	44 WI	Woodman	Girdler	T. B.	Pr.	H	12 WI	Mt. Sterling
Farrell	J. L.	Sgt.	K	12 WI	Marietta	Goan	S.	Pr.	F	3 WI	Millville
Farris	D. J.	Pr.	D	5 IL CAV	Boscobel	Goodwin	D. A.	Sgt.		6 WI ART	Spring Green
Farth	A.	Pr.	H	44 WI	Excelsior	Gould	H. A.	Pr.	I	20 WI	Millville
Faulkner	J.	Pr.	C	43 WI	Mt. Hope	Graves	A.	Sgt.	K	31 WI	North Star
Ferrel	S. S.	Cor.	K	12 WI	Boscobel	Graves	R.	Pr.	C	2 WI	Beetown
Ferrel	J. M.	Cor.	G	47 WI	Boscobel	Gray	Henry	Pr.		4 WI ART	Port Andrew
Field	C. F.	Pr.	K	20 WI	Aetna	Green	G. N.	Pr.	E	14 WI	Wauzeka
Finnegan	W.	Pr.	G	47 WI	Westfield	Green	I.	Pr.	G	47 WI	Boscobel
Finnel	W. F.	Pr.	A	3 WI CAV	Muscoda	Greenfield	A. D.	Pr.	G	47 WI	Boscobel
Fitzgerald	C.	Pr.	K	47 WI	Lancaster	Gribbel	W.	Pr.	A	16 WI	Boscobel
Fleck	M.	Pr.	F	37 WI	Towerville	Gribile	J.	Pr.	I	16 WI	Boscobel
Flora	H. R.	Cor.	F	116 IN	Boscobel	Grindell	W. F.	Pr.	A	44 WI	Platteville
Ford	S.	Pr.	H	46 WI	Orion	Groom	E.	Pr.	C	25 WI	Boscobel

Genealogical Events from Newspapers for Crawford, Vernon and Grant Counties, Wisconsin, 1870-1901

Last Name	First	Rank	Co.	Inf./Other	Address	Last Name	First	Rank	Co.	Inf./Other	Address
Grunn	C.	Pr.		1 WI ART	Castle Rock	Hopkins	C. B.	Pr.	F	3 WI	Homer
Guilford	W.	Cor.	C	20 WI	Excelsior	Horsfall	J. W.	Pr.	C	25 WI	Millville
Gurpsey	C. W.	Sgt.	H	11 WI	Mt. Hope	Houghton	C. R.	Pr.	I	83 PA	Hazelton
Hadley	W.	Pr.	A	2 Col. Cav.	Bloomington	Hoyt	H. H.	Pr.	H	5 WI	Boaz
Haggerty	D. B.	Pr.	I	17 WI	Hurlbuts Cor.	Hoyt	A.	Pr.	B	25 WI	Eagle
Haggman	J. G.	Pr.	K	2 WI	Arena	Hoyt	H. H.	Pr.	B	5 WI	West Branch
Hake	Geo.	Pr.	H	37 WI	Sextonville	Hubbard	P. A.	Pr.	C	31 WI	Hyde's Mills
Hale	C.	Pr.		79 IN	Richland Center	Hudson	S.	Pr.	O	25 OH Bat.	Excelsior
Hall	A.	Pr.	I	25 WI	Georgetown	Huff	W. L.	Pr.	F	20 WI	Boscobel
Hall	M.	Pr.	C	7 WI	Mimia (Mifflin?)	Hughbanks	T.	Pr.	K	44 WI	Excelsior
Hallen	B. C.	Pr.	A	36 WI	Richland Center	Hull	M.	Pr.	C	36 WI	Boaz
Halstead	L. C.	Pr.	B	1 WI	Wauzeka	Hunson	J.	Pr.	K	1 WI CAV	Eagle
Hamilton	P.	Pr.	E	6 WI	Richland Center	Hunting	W. J.	Pr.	B	31 WI	Shullsburg
Hamilton	Wm.	Pr.	G	47 WI	Boscobel	Hurlbut	J. W.	Pr.	C	87 IN	Muscoda
Hamilton	H.	Pr.	D	1 WI CAV	Seneca	Hutson	J. C.	Cor.	E	30 WI	Spring Green
Hammond	J. S.	Mus.	F	3 WI	Platteville	Huugerford	U. M.	Pr.		6 WI ART	Blue River
Hammond	S. S.	Cor.	K	21 WI	Boscobel	Hynes	P.	Pr.		22 WI	Excelsior
Hammond	R. A.	Pr.		6 WI ART	Sextonville	Irving	G. B.	Pr.	C	6 WI	Mt. Sterling
Haney	P.	Pr.	H	43 WI	Wauzeka	Ishmel	A.	Pr.		1 WI ART	Beetown
Hapgood	F.	Pr.	B	10 MI	Sextonville	Jackson	G.	Capt.	D	43 WI	Boscobel
Harding	T.	Pr.	K	38 WI	Mt. Sterling	Jacobs	M.	Pr.	A	31 WI	Hazelton
Harkins	T.	Pr.	C	44 WI	Muscoda	Jacoby	P.	Pr.	E	67 PA	Bridgeport
Harner	H.	Pr.	I	19 IL	Gratiot	James	D. G.	Pr.	C	16 WI	Richland Center
Harrows	R.	Sgt.	D	42 WI	Millville	James	W. G.	Pr.		6 WI ART	Richland Center
Harsberger	J. G.	Pr.	F	3 WI	Montfort	Jeide	J.	Bugl.	C	2 WI CAV	Bloomington
Hart	T. F.	Pr.	C	18 WI	Mt. Hope	Jeredoe	P.	Lt.	C	31 WI	Platteville
Harvey	H.	Pr.	F	39 IL	Fennimore	Joby	J. M.	Pr.	G	47 WI	Boscobel
Haskins	R. F.	Cor.	K	31 WI	North Star	Johnson	C. B.	Pr.	H	44 WI	Basswood
Haskins	E.	Pr.	A	9 MO	Excelsior	Johnson	N.	Pr.	H	7 WI	Boscobel
Haston	G. H.	Pr.	K	47 WI	Fennimore	Johnson	H. W.	Pr.	E	25 WI	Platteville
Hayden	J. M.	Dr.	L	25 WI	Bloomington	Johnson	J.	Pr.	D	31 WI	Excelsior
Hayes	S. D.	Pr.	C	43 WI	Preston	Johnson	A.	Pr.	H	43 WI	Boscobel
Hayes	John	Midship.		Kearsarge	Eagle	Johnson	J.	Pr.	B	25 WI	Port Andrew
Hefner	J. M.	Pr.	D	36 WI	Muscoda	Johnson	J.	Pr.	A	31 WI	Wauzeka
Helm	C. B.	Cor.	E	31 WI	Darlington	Jones	R. K.	Pr.	I	7 WI	Boscobel
Henderson	A. T.	Pr.	D	12 WI	Annaton	Jones	F. R.	Pr.		6 WI ART	Richland City
Henderson	J.	Pr.	A	50 WI	Platteville	Jones	Oscar	Sgt.	D	96 NY	Excelsior
Henderson	C. D.	Pr.	A	83 IL	Boscobel	Joslyn	W. H.	Mj.		25 WI	Richland Center
Henry	L.	Pr.	I	38 WI	Richland Center	Julien	S.	Cor.	A	142 IN	Boscobel
Henry	D.	Pr.	I	38 WI	Richland City	Kane	C.	Pr.	C	50 WI	Seneca
Herold	J.	Cor.	A	31 WI	Bridgeport	Kanouse	T.	Pr.	F	2 WI CAV	Port Andrew
Hewitt	Byron	Capt.	H	31 WI	Prairie du Chien	Kast	H. C. C	Pr.	K	12 WI	Steuben
Hickok	G.	Cor.	F	7 WI	Bloomington	Keene	H. S.	Q.M.S.		6 WI ART	Lancaster
Hines	F.	Cor.	G	33 WI	Wheatville	Kellogg	L.	Pr.	N	188 NY	Boscobel
Hoke	G. M.	Pr.	M	1 WI CAV	Sextonville	Kelly	L.	Pr.	K	12 WI	Bell Center
Holbrook	D.	Pr.		12 WI ART	Woodstock	Kelly	J.	Pr.	I	3 WI	Boscobel
Holcomb	J.	Lt.	C	7 WI	Platteville	Kelly	John	Pr.	C	15 TN	Wheatville
Holcomb	D.	Pr.	G	11 WI	Arena	Kendall	S.	Cor.	D	38 WI	Montfort
Holford	C. H.	Pr.	D	53 WI	Bloomington	Kendall	S.	Cor.	D	38 WI	Montfort
Holford	S. D.	Pr.	C	6 WI	Bloomington	Kendrick	J. C.	Pr.	F	20 WI	Montfort
Holliday	D.	Pr.	H	35 IA	Boscobel	Ketelinger	J. N.	Pr.	B	5 WI	Lancaster
Hood	A. J.	Sgt.		6 WI ART	Muscoda	Ketlinger	T.	Pr.	A	12 WI	Fennimore
Hood	Geo.	Cor.	I	58 IL	Platteville	Keyes	S.	Pr.	D	42 WI	Woodman
Hoper	G. W.	Dr.	A	9 IA	Maquoketa, IA	Keyes	E.	Pr.	C	7 WI	Fennimore

Genealogical Events from Newspapers for Crawford, Vernon and Grant Counties, Wisconsin, 1870-1901

Last Name	First	Rank	Co.	Inf./Other	Address	Last Name	First	Rank	Co.	Inf./Other	Address
Keyes	R. W.	Sgt.	C	1 WI CAV	Mt. Sterling	Mayhew	P. F.	Pr.	B	42 WI	Mt. Hope
Kilpatrick	J.	Pr.	E	11 WI	Belmont	Mayo	Wm.	Pr.	D	42 WI	Boscobel
Kincannon	C.	Pr.	B	49 WI	Port Andrew	Mayo	J.	Pr.	H	49 WI	Boscobel
Kincannon	M. A.	Pr.	B	46 WI	Boscobel	McCarthy	T. M.	Pr.	H	46 WI	Richland Center
Kinder	G. B.	Pr.	D	31 OH	Boscobel	McCleary	J.	Cor.	D	65 NY	Avoca
Kindig	J.	Pr.	E	73 IN	Spring Green	McClintock	A.	Pr.	D	11 WI	McClintock
King	T.	Pr.	A	16 IL	Platteville	McCoy	J. B.	Capt.	E	25 WI	Platteville
King	T.	Pr.	A	16 IN	Platteville	McDaniels	J.	Pr.	G	47 WI	Boscobel
Kinney	A. J.	Pr.	D	11 WI	Richland Center	McDonald	J. H.	Pr.	D	11 WI	Eastman
Kirby	W. F.	Pr.	K	33 WI	Boscobel	McDougal	J. W.	Pr.	A	33 WI	Boscobel
Kirkham	J. O.	Pr.	K	4 IN CAV.		McFarland	J. C.	Pr.	F	2 WI CAV	Richland Center
Kissock	T.	Pr.	H	158 IL	North Clayton	McKinfrey	J. P.	Pr.	F	44 WI	Boscobel
Kite	Geo.	Pr.	B	36 WI	Eagle	McKinney	A. M.	Pr.	C	20 WI	Boscobel
Knapp	A.	Cor.	D	25 WI	Bloomington	McKnight	T.	Pr.	G	47 WI	Lancaster
Knapp	W. G.	Chap.		19 WI	Richland City	McLain	J.	Pr.	B	6 WI	Wauzeka
Knapp	C. C.	Pr.	K	31 WI	North Star	McLaughlin	J.	Lt.	C	20 WI	Boscobel
Knapp	W.	Chap.		19 WI	Richland City	McLyman	J.	Pr.	H	7 WI	Boscobel
Krans	J.	Pr.	C	31 WI	Excelsior	McMillion	J.	Pr.	B	49 WI	Orion
Kyzer	H. C.	Pr.	H	5 WI	Knapps Creek	McWilliams	J.	Pr.	B	44 WI	Orion
Lacy	T. W.	Dr. M.		8 WI	Prairie du Chien	Menert	W. C.	Pr.	H	3 WI	Arena
Lance	G. A.	Pr.	D	42 WI	Wheeler	Meredith	L.	Drmr	K	101 PA	Chicago
Larimer	J.	Pr.	I	44 WI	Boscobel	Meyers	J. L.	Pr.	B	33 WI	Boscobel
Larson	A.	Pr.	A	3 WI	Soldiers Grove	Meyers	G. L.	Pr.	D	49 WI	Boscobel
Lathrop	P. A.	Pr.	B	112 NY	Boscobel	Meyers	W. W.	Pr.	C	48 WI	North Star
Lemont	S. W.	Sgt.	M	4 WI CAV	Gratiot	Meyers	E. C.	Pr.	D	154 NY	Boscobel
Lennox	W.	Sgt.	B	31 WI	Yankeetown	Meyers	J.	Pr.	H	57 OH	Boscobel
Lesser	P.	Pr.	C	25 WI	Fennimore	Miles	John	Pr.	B	25 WI	Orion
Lewis	B. G.	Pr.	D	33 WI	Mt. Hope	Miller	Geo.	Pr.	H	5 WI	Richland Center
Lewis	J. M.	Pr.	B	25 WI	Eagle	Miller	A.	Pr.	B	25 WI	Richland Center
Lewis	G. H.	Pr.	A	41 WI	Potosi	Miller	Geo.	Pr.	B	25 WI	Eagle
Lewis	Ike	Pr.	G	2 IL ART	Boscobel	Miller	L.	Pr.	B	4 WI	Livingston
Linsendorf	C.	Pr.	F	9 WI	Lancaster	Miller	C. A.	Pr.	C	45 WI	North Star
Linton	I. C.	Pr.	F	3 WI	Mt. Hope	Miller	M.	Pr.	K	7 WI	Bloomington
Locke	J. C.	Pr.	H	100 PA	Boscobel	Miller	C. B.	Pr.	G	47 WI	Boscobel
Logue	J. M.	Pr.	B	25 WI	Orion	Miller	O. E.	Pr.	A	31 WI	Bridgeport
Loomis	O. M.	Pr.	C	43 WI	Werley	Miller	Peter	Pr.	M	3 WI CAV	Boscobel
Lowe	J.	Pr.	I	1st NY Eng.	Bell Center	Miller	M. P.	Pr.		2 WI ART	Eagle
Loy	W.	A. Sr.		6 WI	Annaton	Miller	M.	Pr.	C	92 OH	Hurlbuts Cor.
Lykes	J.	Pr.	C	6 WI	Patch Grove	Miner	O. E.	Sgt.	D	30 WI	Belmont
Lyon	E. L.	1 Lt.	H	43 WI	Marshalltown	Mitchell	Z.	Pr.	F	53 IN	Boscobel
Lyons	F.	Cor.	F	3 WI	Fennimore	Monnahan	W.	Sailor			Boscobel
Mabbatt	G. R.	Pr.	C	31 WI	Helena	Monroe	I.	Pr.	B	19 WI	Richland Center
Madden	O.	Pr.	D	43 WI	Castle Rock	Monson	A.	Pr.	B	50 WI	Excelsior
Mahan	P. P.	Pr.	B	42 WI	Mt. Hope	Monteith	J.	Sgt.	H	7 WI	Fennimore
Manchester	A.	Pr.	G	40 WI	Muscoda	Moody	S. F.	Pr.	I	25 WI	Annaton
Mannel	E.	Pr.	I	19 WI	Richland Center	Moon	P. H.	Pr.	D	31 WI	Mt. Sterling
Mark	Wm.	Pr.	K	12 WI	Boscobel	Moore	E. H.	Pr.	E	25 WI	Fennimore
Marsh	F. G.	Lt.	B	23 WI	Darlington	Moore	A. G.	Pr.	F	2 WI CAV	Montfort
Mart	J.	Pr.	C	43 WI	Woodman	Moore	A.	Pr.		6 WI ART	Soldiers Grove
Martin	B. T.	Pr.	K	12 WI	Woodman	Moore	G.	Pr.	A	56 NY	Mazomanie
Mather	W.	Pr.	A	9 WI	Blue River	Morey	H. M.	Pr.		6 WI ART	Avoca
Mathews	H.	Sgt.	F	49 WI	Boscobel	Morey	H. W.	Pr.		6 WI ART	Avoca
May	D. B.	Pr.	F	3 WI	Boscobel	Morgan	P.	Pr.	I	20 WI	Werley
May	Wm.	Pr.	F	20 WI	Boscobel	Morris	C.	Pr.	G	1 WI	Platteville

Genealogical Events from Newspapers for Crawford, Vernon and Grant Counties, Wisconsin, 1870-1901

Last Name	First	Rank	Co.	Inf./Other	Address	Last Name	First	Rank	Co.	Inf./Other	Address
Morris	T. S.	Or.	I	105 OH	Hurlbuts Cor.	Phillips	D. C.	Cor.	A	33 WI	Rockville
Morrison	J.	Pr.	C	25 WI	Fennimore	Pickard	D. O.	Hos. Sr.		USS D	Fennimore
Morrow	J.	Pr.	O	33 WI	Bloomington	Pier	M.	Pr.	C	43 WI	Boscobel
Morse	R. S.	Pr.	I	20 WI	Beetown	Pierce	L. K.	Pr.	G	33 WI	Pine Grove
Moses	M.	Pr.	E	25 WI	Platteville	Pierson	J.	Pr.	D	42 WI	Woodman
Moyar	J. H.	Pr.	D	25 WI	Bloomington	Pike	E.	Pr.	B	33 WI	Boscobel
Muffley	F. C.	Pr.	I	25 WI	Boscobel	Pine	W. B.	Pr.	C		Helena
Mulford	C. M.	Sgt.	M	3 WI CAV	Wauzeka	Pittinger	L.	Pr.	C	20 WI	Lancaster
Muller	J.	Pr.	H	50 WI	Boscobel	Pittinger	John	Cor.	N	3 WI CAV	Boscobel
Munns	G.	Pr.	K	12 WI	Boscobel	Plait	J.	Pr.	H	47 WI	Lancaster
Murphy	J. B.	Sgt.	H	7 WI	Boscobel	Platt	P. B.	Maj.		11 WI	Mazomanie
Murphy	J. R.	Pr.	I	20 WI	Woodman	Polander	L.	Pr.	H	25 WI	Rockville
Murphy	W. A.	Pr.	A	11 WI	Wauzeka	Posey	J.	Pr.	B	43 WI	Wauzeka
Murwin	D. G.	Pr.	B	44 WI	Boscobel	Posy	D. C.	Pr.	C	40 WI	Steuben
Myers	J.	Cor.	H	6 WI	Wauzeka	Potts	J. C.	Pr.	K	36 IA	Montfort
Nebans	B. W.	Pr.	K	47 WI	Fennimore	Powers	S.	Pr.	B	44 WI	Port Andrew
Neely	S.	Pr.	D	42 WI	Wheeler	Powers	S.	Pr.	B	44 WI	Port Andrew
Nice	J. W.	Pr.	C	25 WI	Boscobel	Prater	J.	Pr.	H	50 WI	Muscoda
Nichols	B.	Pr.	C	43 WI	Soldiers Grove	Pratt	C. R.	Pr.	F	3 WI	Wauzeka
Nichols	D. P.	Pr.	I	19 WI	Richland City	Prideaux	L.	Pr.	A	33 WI	Bloomington
Nickerson	M. F.	Pr.	D	1 WI	Seneca	Prouty	A.	Pr.	D	25 MI	Sylvan Corners
Nickerson	W.	Pr.	C	43 WI	Excelsior	Pruitt	E. E.	Sgt.	B	44 WI	Sextonville
Noble	R.	Pr.	H	33 WI	Gratiot	Purell	P.	Pr.	B	25 WI	Port Andrew
Nolan	J.	Pr.	I	19 WI	Sextonville	Purington	A. B.	Lt.	K	30 IA	Bell Center
Northus	F.	Pr.	G	1 WI	Muscoda	Putnam	J.	Capt.	F	53 IL	Boscobel
Oates	E. H.	Cor.	C	33 WI	Shullsburg	Pyzer	A.	Pr.	G	2 CA	Fennimore
Oates	Ed	Pr.	G	53 WI	Lancaster	Quigley	W.	A. Sr.	B	33 WI	Mt. Hope
O'Daniel	J.	Pr.	C	7 WI	Georgetown	Quincy	S. A.	Pr.	I	12 WI	Ashland N.
Ogden	W.	Cor.	L	12 WI	Sylvan	Ransom	L.	Cor.	C	20 WI	Mt. Ida
Okey	L. W.	Pr.		1 WI ART	Casville	Rector	Fred	Pr.	G	92 IL	Fennimore
Olson	Ole	Pr.	I	20 WI	Port Andrew	Reichel	L.	Pr.	O	33 WI	Boscobel
Olson	E.	Pr.	B	34 WI	Castle Rock	Resaer	P. J.	Pr.	H	43 WI	Avoca
Osborn	J.	Cor.	I	43 WI	Port Andrew	Rew	John	Pr.	I	19 WI	Orion
Osborn	H.	Pr.	I	5 WI	Boscobel	Rew	C. W.	Pr.	B	45 IL	Orion
Ostrander	H.	Pr.	B	33 WI	Boscobel	Reynolds	S.	Pr.	D	20 WI	Boscobel
Oswald	M.	Mus.		3 WI	Fennimore	Reynolds	Wm.	Pr.	I	50 WI	Boscobel
Owaley	M. B.	Pr.	I	20 WI	Decorah, IA	Reynolds	G. W.	Pr.	M	3 WI CAV	Boscobel
Owens	W. J.	Pr.	H	44 WI	Excelsior	Rice	O. A.	Pr.	B	33 WI	Boscobel
Owens	J. R.	Pr.	H	7 WI	Boscobel	Rice	Ben	Pr.	H	7 WI	Boscobel
Oyden	C.	Pr.	G	33 WI	Soldiers Grove	Rice	R. B.	Pr.	H	8 IL CAV	Boscobel
Packer	A.	Pr.	C	10 IN	Port Andrew	Richardson	G. W.	Pr.	D	42 WI	Werley
Pake	E. M.	Pr.	C	3 WI CAV	North Star	Richardson	J. G.	Pr.	G	47 WI	Bell Center
Parker	D. A.	Pr.	I	20 WI	Mt. Hope	Ricks	J. B.	Pr.	K	42 WI	Boscobel
Parker	C. W.	Pr.	G	1 WI	Soldiers Grove	Ricks	R.	Cor.	K	12 WI	Boscobel
Parker	J. J.	Sgt.		U.S. Mar.	Wauzeka	Ricks	J.	Pr.	E	47 WI	Boscobel
Parks	J.	Pr.	I	14 WI	Lancaster	Riggs	J. M.	Pr.	B	33 WI	Boscobel
Parks	J.	Pr.	I	14 WI	Lancaster	Ripley	A. S.	Lt.	A	36 WI	Boaz
Parr	W. L.	Cor.	A	33 WI	Wyoming	Roberts	A.	Pr.	F	49 WI	Lancaster
Pate	John	Pr.	A	1 WI CAV	Hurlbuts Cor.	Robinson	A.	Pr.	D	36 WI	Richland Center
Pearson	E. W.	Pr.	B	25 WI	Excelsior	Robinson	A. W.	Pr.	D	36 WI	Richland Center
Pendleton	W. J.	Pr.	F	10 WI	Bloomington	Rogers	A.	Sgt.	B	33 WI	Boscobel
Peterson	Isaac	Pr.	K	15 IL CAV	Boscobel	Rogers	C.	Cor.	K	12 WI	Boscobel
Pettis	W.	Pr.	B	43 WI	Montfort	Rogers	J. S.	Pr.	B	50 WI	Towerville
Phillamalee	M.	Pr.	A	20 WI	Boscobel	Rogers	J.	Pr.	C	47 WI	Boscobel

Genealogical Events from Newspapers for Crawford, Vernon and Grant Counties, Wisconsin, 1870-1901

Last Name	First	Rank	Co.	Inf./Other	Address	Last Name	First	Rank	Co.	Inf./Other	Address
Roice	T.	Pr.	C	25 WI	Lancaster	Spencer	S. B.	Sgt.	G	33 WI	Platteville
Ross	J. R.	Dr.	K	23 WI	Goodwin Dak.	Sprague	G. B.	Pr.	C	25 WI	Bloomington
Rounds	L. A.	Pr.		1 WI ART	Mt. Sterling	Sprague	H. L.	Lt.	C	6 WI	Beetown
Rowan	M. W.	Pr.	A	49 NY	Hurlbuts Cor.	Squires	G. W.	Lt.	K	12 WI	Wheatville
Rowley	J. W.	Pr.	K	33 WI	Muscoda	Stahel	J.	Capt.	K	2 WI	Boscobel
Rusk	J. M.	Col.		25 WI	Madison	Stant	A.	Pr.	E	25 WI	Sylvan Corners
Russel	Geo.	Pr.	H	15 NY CAV		Stantorf	P. G.	Pr.	I	1 WI	Cobb
Ryder	G.	Pr.	H	43 WI	Wauzeka	Steele	C. A.	Pr.	G	33 WI	Boscobel
Sala	O. P.	Pr.	A	1 IA CAV	Bloomington	Steele	C. H.	Sgt.	G	47 WI	Boscobel
Salisbury	J. J.	Pr.	D	7 VA (VT?)	Soldiers Grove	Stehl	C. E.	Cor.	D	12 WI	Washburn
Salmon	B.	Pr.	I	19 WI	Reedstown	Sterling	G. H.	Pr.	F	8 WI	Mt. Sterling
Sampson	G. W.	Pr.		2 US BAT	Middleton	Stetler	C.	Pr.	H	36 WI	Eagle
Sanderson	D.	Pr.	K	51 WI	Boscobel	Stevenson	J.	Capt.	B	171 OH	Bell Center
Sandleback	C. R.	Pr.	I	20 WI	Mt. Ida	Stewart	S. F.	Lt.	H	184 PA	Darlington
Sanger	J.	Pr.	G	33 WI	Woodman	Stoll	B.	Cor.	H	25 WI	Lancaster
Sawyer	M. A.	Hos Stw		3 NY	Boscobel	Stratton	A. L.	Pr.	C	2 WI	Mt. Hope
Schararer	J. H.	Pr.	K	51 IN	Richland City	Stratton	A. N.	Pr.	K	50 WI	Excelsior
Scheble	A. C.	Pr.	C	36 WI	Lime Ridge	Streeter	H. H.	Pr.	E	30 WI	Fennimore
Schilds	H.	Capt.	F	6 WI	Mazomanie	Streeter	G. D.	Capt.	B	31 IA	Lancaster
Schreiner	D.	Pr.	C	25 WI	Lancaster	Strong	M. J.	Sgt.	A	31 WI	Seneca
Scofield	F.	Pr.	K	12 WI	Boscobel	Sweeney	Ed	Pr.	K	158 NY	Excelsior
Scofield	H.	Pr.	K	12 WI	Boscobel	Sylvester	D. R.	Capt.	K	12 WI	Castle Rock
Scott	M. D.	Pr.	B	23 WI	Boscobel	Tabor	L.	Pr.	C	2 WI CAV	Darlington
Scovill	L.	Pr.	H	37 WI	Boscobel	Talcott	M. M.	Dt.	A	92 NY	Woodman
Selleck	W. W.	Lt.	M	4 MO CAV	Wauzeka	Talkuer	John	Pr.	L	1 WI CAV	Excelsior
Shaffer	G. P.	Pr.	H	33 WI	Aetna	Tallman	A. A.	Pr.	A	31 WI	Mt. Sterling
Shannon	A. B.	Pr.	E	30 WI	Port Andrew	Taylor	J.	Pr.	A	33 WI	Excelsior
Shappell	C.	Pr.	C	7 KS	Lancaster	Taylor	J. L.	Pr.	F	7 WI	Boscobel
Shaw	J. S.	Pr.		IN Battery	Boscobel	Taylor	C. F.	Sgt.	H	7 WI	Boscobel
Sheffield	J.	Pr.	G	48 WI	Woodman	Taylor	W. L.	Sg. St.		USS St. GA	Mt. Hope
Sheiver	Th.	O. S.	G	33 WI	Mt. Sterling	Tenant	Wm.	Pr.	C	25 WI	Werley
Sherrard	D.	Pr.	G	1 IA CAV.	Boscobel	Thomas	O. B.	Capt.	D	31 WI	Praire du Chien
Shields	T.	Pr.	K	12 WI	Boscobel	Thomas	O.	Sgt.	F	3 WI	Montfort
Sidler	J. A.	Cor.	F	48 WI	Boscobel	Thomas	J. A.	Pr.	C	31 WI	Montfort
Siebert	F.	Pr.	E	25 WI	Platteville	Thompson	C.	Sgt.	K	31 WI	Mt. Sterling
Simons	A.	Pr.	G	47 WI	Boscobel	Thompson	J. M.	Pr.	H	44 WI	Eagle
Slaugh	M.	Pr.	K	40 WI	Lone Rock	Thompson	G.	Pr.	B	33 WI	Tunnel City
Sloan	Wm.	Pr.	D	31 WI	Wauzeka	Thompson	I. M.	Pr.	H	44 WI	Orion
Slosson	P.	Cor.	F	7 WI	Bloomington	Thompson	John	Pr.	I	16 WI	Shullsburg
Smethurst	J.	Sgt.	C	43 WI	Seneca	Tipp	Henry	Pr.	I	5 WI	Gratiot
Smith	E. B.	Sgt.	C	20 WI	Fennimore	Traber	H. J.	Lt.	H	33 WI	Platteville
Smith	T. J.	Pr.	B	25 WI	Sextonville	Traber	S. W.	Pr.	G	1 WI	Platteville
Smith	J. W.	Sgt.	I	44 WI	Richland Center	Trague	T.	Pr.	C	33 WI	Shullsburg
Smith	J.	Pr.	D	38 WI	Eagle	Trollopp	E.	Pr.	I	20 WI	Lancaster
Smith	G. A.	Pr.	I	17 WI	Muscoda	Tropp	J. W.	Pr.	C	20 WI	Mt. Hope
Smith	J.	Pr.	H	5 WI	Lancaster	Truman	D.	Pr.	C	40 WI	Woodman
Smith	E.	Pr.	F		Excelsior	Trunkill	L.	Pr.	I	19 WI	Woodman
Smith	M.	Pr.	H	7 WI	Madison	Tuffley	Geo.	Cor.	K	12 WI	Boscobel
Smith	T. J.	Pr.	B	25 WI	Sextonville	Tuffley	T.	Pr.	K	12 WI	Boscobel
Smythman	W. E.	Pr.	I	42 WI	Castle Rock	Turk	J.	Pr.	F	29 WI	Wheatville
Solmon	C.	Pr.	B	25 WI	Reedstown	Twining	D. M.	Pr.	D	31 WI	Mt. Sterling
Southwick	H. H.	Pr.	I	3 WI	Darlington	Twining	W. A.	Pr.	I	6 WI	Knapp Creek
Sparkmiller	M.	Pr.		2 WI ART	Muscoda	Utt	G. D.	Pr.	H	25 WI	Lancaster
Spencer	L.	Pr.	G	37 WI	Platteville	Van Horn	W.	Sgt.	A	46 WI	Boscobel

Genealogical Events from Newspapers for Crawford, Vernon and Grant Counties, Wisconsin, 1870-1901

Last Name	First	Rank	Co.	Inf./Other	Address	Last Name	First	Rank	Co.	Inf./Other	Address
Van Warner	E.	Sgt.	A	20 WI	Lynxville	Whittaker	Wm.	Pr.	H	44 WI	Wheatville
Vance	H.	Pr.	H	5 WI	Excelsior	Whittleton	R. J.	Capt.	G	25 WI	Harvard, IL
Vaughan	W. A.	Cor.	A	11 WI	Wauzeka	Wiley	Geo.	Pr.	B	25 WI	Muscoda
Vaughan	O.. P.	Pr.	H	49 WI	Wauzeka	Wilkinson	G.	Sgt.	I	2 WI	Mifflin
Vaughn	H. H.	Lt. C.		33 WI	Platteville	Wilkinson	E.	Pr.	C	33 WI	Lancaster
Vickers	C.	Sgt.	C	33 WI	Darlington	Wilkinson	J. T.	Cor.	C	25 WI	Ellenboro, Dak.
Waddell	W.	Pr.	B	25 WI	Richland City	Williams	L.	Pr.	H	31 WI	Orion
Walker	T.	Pr.	H	7 WI	Annaton	Williams	L. R.	Pr.	H	31 WI	Orion
Walker	J.	Pr.	H	33 WI	Fennimore	Williamson	J. H.	Pr.	I	16 WI	Boscobel
Walker	E. S.	Pr.	C	2 WI CAV	Lancaster	Willis	John	Pr.	H	44 WI	Boscobel
Wallace	F. C.	Sgt.	G	27 WI	Port Andrew	Willoughby	W. G.	Pr.	B	25 WI	Montfort
Wallace	H.	Pr.		6 WI ART	Boscobel	Wilson	G. C.	Pr.	H	44 WI	Orion
Walsh	F.	Pr.	H	3 WI	Darlington	Winn	N. A.	Pr.	K	12 WI	Boscobel
Ward	Edgar	Pr.	B	33 WI	Sylvan	Winn	M. J.	Pr.	A	12 WI	Boscobel
Ward	Edwin	Pr.	F	37 WI	Sylvan	Winn	J. H.	Pr.	H	1 WI CAV	Boscobel
Ward	A.	Pr.	E	47 WI	Boscobel	Wisdom	W.	Pr.	B	33 WI	Boscobel
Ward	R.	Sgt.	I	3 ME	Lancaster	Wiseman	E.	Q. M.	C	2 WI CAV	Patch Grove
Warnu	C.	Pr.	I	47 WI	Livingston	Witherow	P. W.	Pr.	B	22 WI	Richland Center
Washburn	W. H.	Cor.	G	28 WI	Pewaukee	Witsic	F.	Pr.	C	41 WI	Annaton
Washburn	B. F.	Pr.	I	17 WI	Excelsior	Wizner	Sam	Pr.	D	33 WI	North Andover
Waters	B. T.	Pr.	I	10 WI	Excelsior	Wood	Ed	Pr.	K	12 WI	Ridgeway
Waters	John	Pr.	D	42 WI	Wheeler	Wood	D. C.	Pr.	B	25 WI	Werley
Wayne	M. H.	Pr.	A	20 WI	Fennimore	Woodard	I.	Pr.	K	12 WI	Boscobel
Wayne	S. P.	Pr.	K	12 WI	Boscobel	Woodbury	A. M.	Pr.	A	33 WI	Lone Rock
Wayne	Frank	Pr.	K	12 WI	Boscobel	Woods	P.	Pr.	C	2 WI CAV	Mt. Hope
Wayne	F.	Pr.	K	12 WI	Boscobel	Wooster	G.	Pr.	G	33 WI	Boscobel
Weaver	W.	Dr.	F	33 WI	Fennimore	Worden	David	Pr.	D	42 WI	Mt. Hope
Welch	D.	Pr.	F	3 WI	Bell Center	Wright	J. M.	Pr.	C	2 WI	Boscobel
West	J. J.	Pr.	F	63 OH	Soldiers Grove	Wright	R.	Pr.	M	5 IA CAV	Fenimore
Wey	W. M.	Pr.	E	50 WI	Excelsior	Yager	S.	Pr.	D	11 WI	Excelsior
Wheaton	Thom.	Pr.	D	92 OH	Eagle	Yates	Wm.	Pr.	H	124 IN	Woodman
Wheeler	H. H.	Pr.	K	12 WI	Boscobel	Young	H. F.	Capt.	G	7 WI	Patch Grove
Wheeler	E. B.	Fife	B	42 WI	Lone Rock	Young	J.	Pr.	D	7 WI	Muscoda
Wheeler	A. W.	Pr.	K	12 WI	Boscobel	Young	W. H.	Pr.	H	7 WI	Boscobel
White	J. G.	Cor.	I	20 WI	Mt. Hope	Young	John	Pr.		44 WI	Muscoda
White	Wm.	Pr.	I	20 WI	Mt. Hope	Young	W. W.	Pr.	H	12 IL CAV	Boscobel
Whitesides	M. J.	Pr.	I	20 WI	Mt. Hope	Youngs	F.	Pr.	C	153 IL	Hurlbuts Cor.
Whitesides	G.	Pr.	I	20 WI	Mt. Hope						

Genealogical Events from Newspapers for Crawford, Vernon and Grant Counties, Wisconsin, 1870-1901

Boscobel Area Civil War Pensioners

(Copied from the *Boscobel Dial*, Page 2, Column 1, Oct. 30, 1883)

"The following is a list of pensioners whose post office address is at Boscobel. In the first column appears the pensioner's name. In the second, cause of disability, and in the third, the amount of pension allowed per month."

Aldrich, Mary	Widow	$8.00
Cowan, Geo. W.	Chronic diarrhea and injured right knee	14.00
Scott, Wm. T.	Injury of breast, result in disease of stomach	
Shaw, James S.	Disease of eyes	12.00
Scoville, Levi	Loss of part of right thumb	4.00
Stahel, John	Disease of heart	20.00
Sherrard, David	Chronic diarrhea	8.00
Clark, Harvey	Chronic diarrhea	4.00
Christ, Jacob	Disease of eyes	8.00
Young, Wallace W.	Heart disease	8.00
Dixon, James	Chronic diarrhea	8.00
Dougherty, Jacob	Disease of spine, result injury	8.00
Devoe, Amos	Chronic pleurisy	8.00
Taylor, James L.	Loss of leg	18.00
Tuffley, George	Rheumatism	12.00
Woodard, Isaac	G. A. W. right knee	4.00
Wheeler, Hiram H.	Wound right arm	8.00
Ricks, Reuben	Sunstroke	8.00
Rice, Oliver A.	Varicose veins left leg	6.00
Reichel, Louis	Disease of lungs	18.00
Williamson, James H.	G. A. W. left forearm	4.00
Wayne, Nathaniel L.	Disease of lungs and chronic diarrhea result disease of rectum	4.00
Allen, Eleanor L.	Widow	8.00
Kellogg, Minerva	Mother	8.00
Kimball, Solomon	Father	8.00
Kellogg, Betsey	Mother	15.00
Classon, Mary	Mother	8.00
Wood, Louisana	Widow	8.00
Ruchti, Benedichti	Chronic diarrhea	12.00
Rice, Benjamin E.	G. A. W. left arm and shoulder	14.00
Bolster, Geo. W.	Chronic diarrhea	4.00
Byers, Robert	(Disability?) from bil. Fever	4.00
Barkley, Daniel F. S.	G. A. W. left leg	18.00
Pettinger, Matilda	Mother	8.00
Classen, Bezabel	G. A. W. right eye	4.00
Cheever, Albertus B.	(???) right leg with (???)	6.00
Clark, Samuel W.	Partial deafness right ear and shell wound right arm	4.00
McClymen, Jane	Mother	8.00
McMaster, Susan C.	Mother	8.00
Miller, Charles R.	Chronic diarrhea	4.00
Clements, John	Injury to abdomen	8.00
Blandin, Walter	Father	8.00

Genealogical Events from Newspapers for Crawford, Vernon and Grant Counties, Wisconsin, 1870-1901

Barton (Marton?), Elizabeth	Mother	8.00
Pike, Edwin	Chronic diarrhea	$6.00
Pake, Edmund M.	G. A. W. both thighs	8.00
Peterson, Hiram	Injury thumb	2.00
Havens, Henry B.	Frost bite feet and (???)	8.00
Myers, Joseph	Chronic diarrhea and disease of spine	4.00
Clark, Joseph J.	G. A. W. left hand	6.00
Osborne, John H.	G. A. W. right forearm	8.00
Wayne, William G.	Minor	14.00
Whitt, Meredith	Father	17.00
Huey, Rachel	Widow	8.00
Jacobs, Maryett	Widow	10.00
Brimmer, George	Disease of heart and liver	4.00
Bowen, Ethan A.	Chronic diarrhea and disease of (???)	6.00
Burkholder, David	Dysp. and ch. (???) spleen with res. venal calculi	12.00
Houn, Charity	Mother	8.00
Sanborn, Malissa	Widow	8.00
Parce, Sarah	Widow	8.00
Lathrop, Piatt A.	Disease of liver	4.00
Allan, George	Amputated index finger right hand	3.00
Kellogg, Charles	Chronic diarrhea, res. disease and (???)	8.00
Kincannon, M. A.	Chronic (rh????) res., heart disease	12.00
Bartholomew, S.	Loss (???) and (???) foot	4.00
Kimball, Renel R.	Chronic diarrhea	6.00
Kost, William F. N.	Injury knee	12.00
Kelty, James	Wound left thigh	8.00
Burris, John H.	Disease of eyes	2.00
Jones, Robert K.	Wound right ankle	6.00
Johnson, Nathaniel	Chronic diarrhea and disease of abd. vis.	6.00
McDougal, James W.	Varicose veins left leg, chronic diarrhea and dis. abd. vis. part deaf	8.00
McCord, James K.	Injury to abdomen	6.00
McDaniel, James	Disease of lungs and eyes	6.00
McLaughlin, Jacob	Injury left knee	10.00
Mathew, Hugh	Disease of heart and liver	8.00
May, David R.	Wound of head	8.00
Merwin, Daniel G.	Loss of right leg	18.00
Bevier, William M.	Wound of right arm	6.00
Ferrel, Stephen S.	Disease of lungs	4.00
Francisco, N. J.	Chronic rheum.	4.00
Lawrence, Daniel R.	Injury to chest, resp. dis. lung	6.00
Brown, Lucius	Chronic diarrhea	2.00
Grant, James	Wound right hand	4.00
Gotz, James	Sunstroke and chronic diarrhea	8.00
Gribble, Joseph	Chronic diarrhea	4.00
Jackson, George	Chronic pleurisy	10.00
Green, Tompkins	Injury to abdomen	8.00
Myers, John S.	Chronic rheumatism and disease of eyes	10.00
Nice, John W.	Chronic diarrhea	6.00
Adams, Martin	Sunstroke, res. paralysis and disease of heart	12.00

Genealogical Events from Newspapers for Crawford, Vernon and Grant Counties, Wisconsin, 1870-1901

Arms, John R.	Wound left shoulder	3.00
Miller, Martin	Disease of heart	$8.00
Hayman, Lucius H.	Wound right hand	4.00
Miller, Ebenezer C.	Minor of (???)	6.00

Genealogical Events from Newspapers for Crawford, Vernon and Grant Counties, Wisconsin, 1870-1901

List of Members Belonging to James Mason Post No. 106, G. A. R., De Soto, Wisconsin

(Copied from the *De Soto Chronicle*, July 30, 1887, Page 2)

De Soto

Orlando Ewers	M. N. Whitney	W. W. Miller
Peter Bartholomew	C. A. Tenney	John W. White
J. H. Rogers	W. Stevenson	James Whitney
W. F. Rose	J. H. Stephens	S. D. Taylor
A. E. Fosdick	Peter Campbell	M. B. Balch
W. S. Cushing	William Bates	P. Whitney
Ed. Rogers	Z. T. Clark	James Voysey
G. W. Furman	R. Pennel	T. Crouch
L. G. Hickok	C. F. Page	E. G. Lees
C. S. Fourt	W. M. Green	

Retreat

Thomas De Lacy	G. F. Seymour	P. Jacobus
J. S. Gibbs	A. A. Richardson	C. Shied
Jesse Adams	J. T. Bates	F. B. White
C. A. Newton	F. Sallander	V. E. Aiken
J. M. Hill	S. A. Mellen	E. H. Ames

Victory

R. L. Ferguson	L. B. Waller	W. A. Hodge
F. M. Crofoot	J. Billard	A. Keheun

Red Mound

E. R. James	J. W. Rineheart	C. Brown

Ferryville

W. J. Hutson	W. Davis	I. Lattimore

Freeman

John Campbell	C. P. Tower	T. C. Rutter
T. Peterson	J. Devenport	

Romance

B. I. Witcraft	W. B. Witcraft

Lansing

C. M. Maxwell

Genealogical Events from Newspapers for Crawford, Vernon and Grant Counties, Wisconsin, 1870-1901

Vernon County Teachers

(Copied from the *De Soto Chronicle*, January 15, 1887, Page 7)

The following is a list of persons who are now holding CERTIFICATES and entitled to teach in Vernon County.

J. A. Aylward, Prin. of High School, Viroqua
Millie C. Forsythe, Assistant, Viroqua
Hattie E. Terrill, Grammer Department, Viroqua
Emma F. Tollefson, 1st, Intermediate, Viroqua
Dora B. Pollard, 2nd, Intermediate, Viroqua
Eda Blume, 1st, Primary, Viroqua
Jessie Richards, 2nd, Primary, Viroqua
Lucy M. Nuzum, 3rd, Primary, Viroqua
E. V. Wernick, Prin. of High School, Hillsboro
Agnes Wernick, Grammar, Hillsboro
Elia A. Madden, Intermediate, Hillsboro

Mary McKenzie, Primary, Hillsboro
Joseph Freehoff, Prin. Graded School, De Soto
Ellen Lawrence, Intermediate, De Soto
Florence M. Gott, Primary, De Soto
J. L. Hefferman, Prin. Graded School, Ontario
Nellie Tuttle, Primary, Ontario
Anna McDermott, Prin. of Graded School, Westby
Ida Gullford, Primary, Westby
Alex Hill, Prin. of Graded School, Rockton
Sarah Shattuck, Primary, Rockton

VIROQUA

Flora Meacham
M. O. Hill
Eliza Smith
Rowena Stout
Wilmetta Davis
Idella De Garmo
Jennie McGarry
Paul Steenson
Hattie Hazen
Caroline Pierce
Lizzie M. Weeden
Anna Steenson
Samuel Morgan
Patience McDermott
Theresa Finkle
Katie Haughton
W. H. Norris
Clara Groves
C. E. Powell
Malena Stevens
Carrie A. Bennett
Sadie Bold
Nettie Jenness
Carrie Rhodes
Ola McGarry
Rose White
Susie Lamma
Mary Nuzum
Theodore Running

LIBERTY POLE

Lewis Thayer
Henry Gardner
Catherine McManamy
Malina Skildum
May Hinkst
Belle Morton
William Hornby
Vina Keir
Patrick McManamy
James O'Murphy
Carrie B. Slack
Jennie Hinkst
Mame Connor
M. L. Hornby

HILLSBOROUGH

Nancy Riley
Mamie Madden
Eliza Madden
Huldah Ludewig
Jessie Collins
Henry Linke
P. J. King
Maggie King
Nettie Cole
Anna Shear
Katie Costello
Ella Healey

Katie Madden
Fremont Johns
Sylvia Hansberron
Libbie Linke
W. A. Hedding
Eliza King
Anna KelleyMartha King
Anna Brandon

DE SOTO

Ara E. Bartholomew
Mary Loftus
Mary E. Cushing
Frank Pulver
F. Z. Alexander
Hattie A. Conklin
Ellen Stevenson
Cora B. Tenney

ONTARIO

Ida McFee
Annie O'Connell
Patrick Shaughnessy
Frank Keyes
E. R. Daniels
Jennie De Lap
Katie O'Connell
John Donahue
Newton M. Boldon

Genealogical Events from Newspapers for Crawford, Vernon and Grant Counties, Wisconsin, 1870-1901

ROCKTON

Susanna Kline
Flora Marshall
Charles Coler
Judith Shattuck
Jennie Shelbach

READSTOWN

Hartwell Allen
Elva J. Aikins
Ole S. Thompson
Mary E. McCarty
Torger Berge
Nellie Flanagan
Electa Wilkinson
Rosalpha Smith
Marcella McCarty

NEWTON

Mary Horton
Adelia J. Grant
Carrie Parsons
Cora Patterson
Nellie Horton
Alice C. Jackson
Hattie Bemis

CHASEBURG

Hattie M. Stevenson
J. L. Clawson
Pluma Frazier

WEST LIMA

Eliza Morrison
B. F. Poorman
A. W. Telfer
May Poorman
Cyril Jansky
W. H. Poorman
J. H. Potts
Anna Bean
Ida M. Mathews

ESOFEA

Charles R. Frazier
William Frazier

VALLEY

J. J. Butcher
Davis R. Wood
John Marshall
Hattie Cancutt

DELL

J. A. Norris
Olive A. Lewis
Sumner Smith

COON VALLEY

Fred P. Rough
Matilda Jacobson
Christina Johnson
Martha M. Brye
Caroline Jacobson
Bertha Johnson
Elizabeth Brye

REST

Hattie L. Dudley
B. C. Gallaher
Alice Quackenbush

SPRINGVILLE

Estella Mills
Amy Officer
Nettie Goldrick
Ella Hunter
W. C. Miller
Mary Doerr

BLOOMINGDALE

E. J. Older
Romanzo Adams
J. M. Bold

WEST PRAIRIE

Jennie Finney
Frank Davis

VICTORY

C. M. Sterling

Lola Clark
F. J. Brown
H. E. Bean
Ella M. Wise
Johanna Mueller

RETREAT

George F. Seymour
W. H. Morgan
E. J. Lees
Edna Broadhead
Myra Stevens

MT. TABOR

A. T. Bolden
W. H. Sterling

YUBA

Prudie Heckendorn
George L. Moody

AVALANCHE

Carrie Oliver
Jennie Oliver

CASHTON

Rose Bartlett
N. J. Thayer

RISING SUN

Lizzie Rogers
Nellie Rogers

HUB CITY

Mary E. Grinsell
Hattie Kennedy
B. E. Kennedy

WESTBY

Elizabeth Thompson
Ida Gullord
Ellen M. Thompson
Matilda M. Unseth

BURR - W. F. Bingman

Genealogical Events from Newspapers for Crawford, Vernon and Grant Counties, Wisconsin, 1870-1901

RED MOUND – Fred P. Bean	LA FARGE - E. P. Southworth	GENOA - Amelia Schubert
SOLDIERS GROVE - Ida Hanson	SUGAR GROVE - Dora Crumrine	PURDY - Christena Otteson

Total number of teachers in list 200, of which number 167 are required to teach the schools.

The remainder, 33 is employed as followed: 14 are attending school, 5 teaching in adjoining counties, and 5 engaged in other pursuits, leaving 9 unemployed. D. O. Mahoney, Co. Sup't. Viroqua, Wis., Dec. 14, 1886

Genealogical Events from Newspapers for Crawford, Vernon and Grant Counties, Wisconsin, 1870-1901

THE LIVE TEACHERS

(Copied from the *De Soto Chronicle*, March 12, 1887, Page 3)

The largest and most successful Teacher's Institute ever held in Vernon county was conducted by Prof. Hutton and Supt. Mahoney at Viroqua this week. About 180 workers were enrolled. It is to be regretted that De Soto did not send a good delegation. No district board should hire a teacher unless they attend these Normal Institutes or can give a satisfactory reason for not so doing. Below is a list of

INSTITUTE WORKERS.

VIROQUA: Rosella De Garmo, May Parker, Florence Williams, Ellen C. Natwick, Lester Tilton, Clara M. Groves, Blanche R. Stevens, W. H. Morris, F. J. Bold, Nell C. Stricker, Carrie E. Rhodes, Hattie Hazen, Eva E. Dunlap, Ettie L. Taylor, Rosa Silbaugh, Ella M. Fridell, John R. Hall, Albon Meacham, Clare E. Tongue, Flora Meacham, Viola Meacham, Maud Baldwin, Cora Goraline, Arba Morrison, John E. Silbaugh, James May, Carlos Buchanan, Carson Powell, William E. Nuzum, Albert Broadhead, C. E. Powell, Thomas A. Henry, Sadie M. Bold, Susie Lamma, Lillie Lake, Charles H. Minshall, Anna Henry, Daisy Nuzum, Belle M. Honaker, W. W. Powell, Mamie E. Chase, Carrie Pierce, Grace Morley, Rose E. White, Lucie Nuzum, Eliza Smith, Ellen Minshall, W. E. Butt, Mary E. Heal, Eda Blume, Mrs. Emma Tollefson, John G. Bliss, W. O. Nuzum, Grant Robinson, Luella Silbough, Bertha Hauge, Wilmetta Davis

LIBERTY POLE: Imogene Munyon, Jannie Chamber, George Hornby, Sarah J. McCoey, L. L. Thayer, Martin Hornby, William Hornby, Josie Hopp, Mary J. McGill, Mame Conner, Minnie A. Hornby, Belle Morton, Stephen Kier, Malina Skildum

SPRINGVILLE: Autie Groves, Alton Mills, Cora Hunter, Ella Hunter, Myrtie Smith, Estella Mills, Stephen Mills, Mattie Hamilton, Wilmettie Wade, Sarah Goldrick

WESTBY: Oliver Unseth, Elizabeth Thompson, Ida Gullord, Thresa Finkle, Annie Steenson, Sena Nestingen, Josie Davidson, Clara J. Moen, Ellen Thompson, Matilda Unseth, Anna McDermott, Nordal Unseth

NEWTON: Carrie Parsons, Mettie A. Buswell, Cora Patterson, L. A. Buswell, Nellie Horton, May Horton, Alice C. Jackson

ONTARIO: J. L. Hefferman, Ursula Holcomb, Ida McFee, Annie O'Connell, Luie Steadman, Annie Donohoe, Mildred M. White, Flora Rothschild

ESOFEA: Dora H. Frazier, Mary B. Frazier, C. A. Saxton, William Frazier

LA FARGE: Eva Paul, George E. Southworth, J. E. Southworth, Altie Paul, Jennie Thayer

WEST PRAIRIE: Leora M. McClurg, Matilda Finney, Stella Cade, Jennie Finney, Maggie Finney

READSTOWN: Kiva J. Aikins, Ole S. Tompson, Mary McCarty, Marcella McCarty, Nellie Flanagan

COON VALLEY: Caroline Jacobus, Christina Johnson, F. P. Rough, Martha M. Brye, Bertha Johnson

RISING SUN: Nellie Rogers, Mary Melvin, D. E. Desmond, Dennis Leahy, Delia Broderick, Lizzie Rogers

BLOOMINGTON: Rosetta R. Bold, R. C. Adams, J. M. Bold, Myra A. Dickson, Clara Yakey, Luna Yakey

WEST LIMA: Lydia P. Griffin, Ida A. Carpenter, Ira S. Griffin

AVALANCHE: Carrie Oliver, Jennie Oliver, Ninna Potter

SOLDIERS GROVE: Susanna Fortney, Ida S. Hansen, Helen Severson

STAR: Alex Hill; VICTORY, Ella Wise; GENOA, Lizzie M. Gould; RETREAT, W. P. Morgan; REST, Alice Quackenbush; ROCKTON, Jennie Selblach; CASHTON, Nellie Quinn, Allie Quinn; PURDY, Otto Otteson, George Brunck; HILLSBOROUGH, Fremont C. Johnson; DE SOTO, Cora B. Tenney, Ella J. Tenney; SUGAR GROVE, Henry Russell, Rose Kellogg

Genealogical Events from Newspapers for Crawford, Vernon and Grant Counties, Wisconsin, 1870-1901

List of Voters of the Town of Wheatland, Vernon County

(Copied from the *De Soto Republican*, October 26, 1871, Page 3)

Arnold, Samuel S.
Ankeny, T. C.
Anderson, Magnus
Baker, Johiel
Benedict, Egbert C.
Bartholomew, Peter
Bailey, James M.
Brayman, William
Brannan, Michael
Bartholmew, William
Brannan, Thomas
Bailey, William
Battles, George H.
Beck, Alexander
Bartholomew, Robert
Bates, William
Benedict, George L.
Baker, James
Coffins, Seth
Clark, Z. T.
Coppernoll, Elias H.
Cilley, Erastus,
Corbett, Isaac
Caldwell, C. G.
Coe, Lloyd (Floyd?)
Conaway, J. D.
Clark, William P.
Carpenter, Timothy
Carpenter, Hiram
Corey, James
Covey, William
Cushing, W. S.
Chase, Arvin
Connor, A. B.
Conaway, Ezra
Cole, William
Chapman, George
Coleman, C.
Davis, J. C.
Dyer, Woodbridge
Dailey, William P.
Davis, Ed. E.
Dolan, Thomas
Eckhart, Jacob, Jr.
Fosdick, Williard

Foster, George
Freeman, Joseph
French, N. E.
Ferguson, William
Ferguson, H. H.
Ferguson, James
Glodery, Andrew
Green, L. W.
Hinds, J. H.
Huntington, J. F.
Heal, Stephen
Houghton, Edmund
Hodge, William A.
Hayden, Giles
Hale, O. E.
Huntington, Samuel
Hickok, LeGrand
Henderson, J. H.
Hickok, David H.
Heald, William E.
Haverly, William
Hollander, Jacob
Hurlburt Thaddeus
Ingersoll, C. J.
Joseph, D. W.
Joseph, William
Kane, Henry
Krumm, George
Kendall, Daniel B.
Kendall, William
Kendall, Henry P.
King, Robert
Kahler, Michael
Loftus, James
Lawrence, W. C.
Latshaw, Alex
Lemen, Robert
Loftus, Martin
Latshaw, James
Latshaw, Albert
Lewis, George
Larson, Chris
Luth, John
Loftus, James, Jr.
Moore, Michael

Miller, Joseph
Miller, Henry K.
Miller, Lester P.
Morgan, Richard
Morgan, Henry H.
Muller, August
McDill, George D.
Miller, L. J.
McDonald, Ensign
McAuley, R. R.
McDowell, Alex
McShane, Thomas
Marshal, Walker
Marshal, Shirley
Miller, Henry
Moore, William
Mitchel, J. M.
Melton, B. F.
Mossholder, D.
Miller, S. C.
McDowell, Albert
Orr, Thomas G.
Porter, Henry G.
Price, Nathan
Proctor, Alfred
Pulver, John
Pearsons, Charles
Rogers, James H.
Richardson, William
Riter, Martin
Roberts, B. F.
Roberts, Ezra
Rice, Robert H.
Russ, John
Stevens, Charles B.
Sperry, G. S.
Stevens, Correll B.
Shaw, Joel T.
Stanley, Charles E.
Shisler, William
Shisler, John
Sweeney, Ed.
Steele, D. A.
Stevens, Ira
Smith, C. W.

Smith, B. C.
Sargeant, A. E.
Sperback, Martin
Stevens, John M.
Shocko, William
Stanley, Fred
Trott, Benjamin
Tenney, J. J.
Tenney, Charles A.
Tenney, Lyman
Tilden, C. J.

Tharp, E.
Van Zant, W. J.
Voicey, James
Whitney, James
Worth, Cyrus B.
Worth, Addison R.
Worth, Cyrus M.
Woodbury, C. E.
White, J. W.
Whitney, Parley
Williams, Benjamin

West, William W.
Warne, Edward
Whitney, Milo
Wareham, A. H.
Wilson, O. D.
Wilt, David
Wilt, Vint
Wilcox, Jos. B.
Whitney, L. A.
Zillig, George
Zillig, Nick

Genealogical Events from Newspapers for Crawford, Vernon and Grant Counties, Wisconsin, 1870-1901

People's County Convention

(Copied from the *De Soto Chronicle*, Sept. 25, 1886, Page 3)

We, citizens of Crawford county, irrespective of political party hereby resolve to call a Mass Convention for the purpose of nominating County Officers to be voted for at the coming election. Said convention to be held on the fair grounds at Seneca on Friday, October 1st at ten o'clock a.m.

Ambrose Thompson
J. P. Mitchell
O. M. De La Mater
P. A. Lathrop
John Low
J. S. Ingraham
A. F. West
J. F. Haskins
N. A. Tallman
Morris Joy
B. H. Biederman
C. V. Porter
A. P. Anderson
S. L. Brown
R. S. De La Mater
C. R. Barker
C. W. Lathrop
B. Oppreicht
T. Druen
Elmer Thomson
A. C. B. Vaughan
D. W. Kenneflick
O. P. Sampson
T. A. McDowell
Thos. Dickson

John Vanderbilt
Chas. Welch
O. G. Barker
Wm. McAuley
Gilbert Stuart
C. E. Peck
James Smith
I. Itgham (Ingham?)
E. A. Caswill (Caswell?)
Ole Oleson
M. G. Mitchell
A. G. Peterson
Henry Hamilton
Ralph Barker
Wm. H. Langdon
L. Hammerly
A. B. Withee
B. D. Bellows
J. L. Turner
F. F. Bell
A. Sears
Martin Loftus
F. McCarty
Robert Stuart
And twenty-five others (unlisted)

Genealogical Events from Newspapers for Crawford, Vernon and Grant Counties, Wisconsin, 1870-1901

De Soto Plum History

(Copied from the *De Soto Chronicle*, Nov. 19, 1887, Page 2)

The De Soto Plum orchard is about a mile south of the County line and consists of 59 trees, a part set regularly and a part without much regularity.

The origin of the plum is not known. Some have supposed it to be a variety brought from the St. Lawrence region by the French. The Indians have stated that it came from the west. The prevailing opinion however among the oldest settlers is that this Trayer or De Soto plum is simply a wild plum of the superior quality.

It is not however the only wild plum of excellent quality found in the locality. Mr. Edmund Houghton, the oldest resident of De Soto informs me that in a ravine two miles north of the village he dug up and planted in his garden, plum trees which bear equally as good as the De Soto plum, and Major Pike when at Turkey River in 1805 refers to the "excellent plums" give him by the Indians.

The De Soto plum is known to nurserymen as one of the hardiest and very best varieties. It is grown from Massachusetts to Oregon.

The present grove of trees was set out by Mr. Quirin Trayer, now of Lansing, about the year 1857. Mr. says: "With my brother I went to De Soto and bought the lot now occupied by the plum orchard, in 1856. Next year we removed to that spot. There was a log house there built by an old man, Elisha Tupper, a sot, who had no wife. At that time the plum trees occupied a space about 10 feet square and were 2 feet high. I took them and set out about 200 trees. I think it to be a wild plum. There was no trace of trading post there in 1857. Have plowed up many Indian bones buried there."

Mr. James Fisher of Eastman who visited this spot fifty years ago (1837) states that at the lower trading post half a mile below the present town, was a plum orchard. At the post he with a friend bough a bottle of "miserable whiskey which puked both of us." – Rambler in the Union

Genealogical Events from Newspapers for Crawford, Vernon and Grant Counties, Wisconsin, 1870-1901

Christian Temperance Union

"With Malice Towards None, and Charity for All"

"I, the undersigned, do pledge my word and honor, (God helping me,) to abstain from all Intoxicating Liquors, as a beverage, and that I will, by all honorable means, encourage others to abstain."

Armstrong, L. C.
Anderson, Mr.
Allen, Anna
Anderson, Anna
Austin, Lizzie
Armstrong, Chas. A.
Anderson, Otto
Anderson, Martin
Abrams, F.
Anderson, George
Alden, Mrs. A. B.
Allen, Eleanor L.
Arnold, Albert
Alden, A. B.
Anderson, C. D.
Allen, Eva
Allen, Viola A.
Arnold, S.
Armstrong, George
Anderson, Jessie
Anderson, Mabel
Anderson, Maria
Anderson, Cora
Arnold, Agnes

Barnett, John
Bailey, Inez
Brekke, Lawrence O.
Brekke, C. O.
Barnett, Chas.
Bartholomew, W. L.
Bartholomew, Sam
Bird, Lizzie
Brookins, Eugene
Bartholomew, Ara
Beach, Mary
Bailey, Ella
Bohl, Sarah
Boynton, I.
Barnett, Willie
Benoy, Willie
Bower, Nellie
Brown, Eugene
Brown, Charlie
Barnett, Mattie
Bailey, Emma
Barnett, Mrs. James
Bailey, Cora
Brindley, John
Barnett, Nellie
Barnett, Mrs. Mary
Brainerd, N.
Brainerd, S. N.
Barnhart, Rebecca
Brainerd, Alvin
Bennis, Henry
Beinborn, Charlie
Bailey, James
Bliss, D. G.
Bell, A.
Barnett, Bal. P.
Butler, Cora
Bailey, May

Carley, D. W.
Colby, Nettie
Conners, Georgia
Childs, DeLap
Chandler, Mary J.
Coates, Melissa
Clark, J. H.
Collins, Minnie
Curry, Frank
Chandler, Mattie
Comstock, Cora
Comstock, Mrs. H.
Carroll, Lizzie
Carroll, Mary
Carroll, Maggie
Carroll, Johanie
Cook, Walter
Contoit, J. B.
Casselson, Emily
Cannon, Geo.
Christ, G. A.
Christ, Lot
Crouch, M. F.
Crouch, J. M.
Cobb, F. M.
Clark, A. A.
Curry, Mrs. S. D.
Campbell, Will
Curry, Seth D.
Craemer, Joel
Clark, Harvey
Conit, Harry
Chievor, A. V.
Carley, Edd
Cook, Chas.
Cobb, Lewis
Crouch, Willie
Curry, Libbie
Creager, Mrs. Sophia
Cramer, Frank
Cullins, Maggie
Curry, Ella
Carroll, Morris
Cramer, Ara
Cobb, Willie
Crouch, Etta
Creager, Harry
Creager, Katie

Clark, Frank
Coleman, Mike
Coomes, Willard
Clark, Nettie
Crouch, L. M.
Cramer, Henry
Coates, Harriet
Carrier, Alice
Clark, Vera
Chandler, Emma
Chandler, Bell
Cramer, Ruth
Clark, Mrs. Harvey
Creager, Elle S.

Duncan, H. J.
DeWitt, Mrs. M.
Deame, Mary
Davy, Mamie
DeWitt, M.
Duncan, John E.
Duncan, Mrs. J. E.
Devoe, Josie
Dennis, Clara
Duncan, Mollie
Duncan, Cora E.
DeLap, Olive M.
Dexter, H. M.
Dunston, A. L.
Dix, Mary
Devoe, George
Devoe, A.
Dennis, G. F.
Davy, N.
Dickerson, Albert
Duncan, M. G.
Dexter, Austin
Duncan, Joseph
Duncan, Emma
DeLap, W. E.
Dickerson, Geo.
DeLap, M. W.
Dunston, Mattie
Davy, Wm.
Devoe, Gussie
Dexter, Nellie
DeWitt, Charles A.
DeLap, Amelia

Ellingson, Matilda
Enright, Katie
Ellingson, Huge
Evans, W. R.
Enright, John

Francisco, Hattie
Flinn, Eliza
Farnham, Nettie
Flint, Althea
Forseth, O. B.
Flint, O. E.
Francisco, Roneldo
Flint, John
Francisco, Geo.
Feare, F.
Farnham, Bell
Ford, Ella

Garrett, C. R.
Garrett, Mrs. C. R.
Gray, S.
Gratz, Minnie
Gray, James
Guentzel, Ada
Guentzel, Bertha
Gibbs, Albert
Guentzel, Emil
Gross, Jacob
Guentzel, G.
Gross, John
Green, Mrs.

Henderson, A.
Hummel, Henry
Hummel, Henry, Jr.
Hummel, Bertie
Hof, Sammie
Haven, Joe
Harris, Ella
Huff, Altie F.
Huff, Mary E.
Hart, Rosie
Hurd, Mary
Hurd, F. N.
Huff, Willie
Hickey, Patrick
Hogel, Andrew
Hogel, Hannah
Hummel, Helen
Hall, W. W.
Howley, Hal
Hughbanks, Maggie
Hurd, Willis W.
Hart, W. W.
Hurd, Z. S.
Hummel, Ida
Hubbell, H. W.
Hof, Sarah
Hof, Lizzie
Hurd, W. T.
Hurd, Emma
Hurd, Etta

*Genealogical Events from Newspapers for Crawford, Vernon and Grant Counties,
Wisconsin, 1870-1901*

Hamilton, Nellie
Hof, Phillip

Jacobs, Lansil
Jewett, Abbie
Jencks, Cora
Jackson, Bennett
Jackson, Geo.
Johnson, O. E.
Johnson, Ella
James, Frank
Jaquette, ___ac
Kellogg, H.
Keity, John
Kaltenbach, F. M.
Kratochwill, V. A.
Kratochwill, Lizzie
Kelley, Frank E.
Keiren, Theo.
Kratochwill, Gustav
Kramer, F.
Kistler, Kattie

Lindsey, Olive
Lathrop, Willie
Low, Rebecca
Limbocker, Lillie
Lathrop, Walter
Lincoln, Stanton
Lipska, John
Loberg, Christa
Lathrop, Flora
Lenoretz, Catherine
Lincoln, Samuel

McLoughlin, W.
McCord, Willie
Muffley, Frank
Mathews, Geo.
McKey, Bertie
McReynolds, W. T.
McReynolds, T. L.
Molle, W.
Miles, John A.
McGraw, Chas.
Muffley, Chas.
Miller, Estella
McSpaden, Henry
Miller, Belle
Mortimer, M. J.
Muffley, Albert
McLaia, A. E.
McCord, Mrs. E.
McCord, Gertrude
Menkhausen, Anna
McReynolds, Alice
McWilliams, Mrs. C.
Miller, O. E.
Miller, Mrs. O. E.
Meyer, O. G.
McGraw, Sylvia
May, Mrs.

May, D. R.
McGraw, Ransom
Meyer, Clara
McSpaden, F.
Murley, Julia
Miller, J. P.
McCord, Jas. K.
McGraw, Mr. M.
McKinney, Eugene
McKinney, H.
McCord, Mary
Muffley, W. A.
Miller Eddie
Miller, Robbie
May S. W.
McFall, Andrew
Manchester, T. A.
McKinney, E.
McSpaden, Mattie
McFall, Mrs. Andrew
Motle, Nellie
McKinney, Elisa
Markham, E. F.
McFall, J. H.
McMillan, Alma
Metzger, H.
Merwin, J. S.

Nuzum, G. W.
Nuzum, Richard
Nell, Louis
Nixon, Arthur
Nobis, Max
Nobis, Mrs.
Nuzum, Mattie
Nuzum, Willard
Nelson, Olof

O'Leary, Florence
Olmstead, Minnie
Olmstead, O. R.
Ostrander, Sarah
Osborn, J. H.

Popejoy, Alice J.
Pittman, Frank
Partridge, H. L.
Prouty, E.
Proudfit, Juliet
Parce, A.
Parce, Freemont A.
Parce, E. T.
Parce, James
Parce, Marion
Popejoy, Stella
Parnell, W. H.
Pike, Bessie
Pittman, Will II
Pattee, M. E.
Pike, Richard
Parce, Eliza
Pike, M. J.

Potter, Charles
Peterson, Minnie
Parker, Chas.
Proudfit, Annie
Porter, Emily A.
Pittinger, Leander
Phillips, W. B.
Perrigo, James
Pickard, D. O.
Peacock, Mrs. Susan
Prosty, Demie
Prouty, Nena
Petty, Gussie
Petty, Bruce
Palmer, W.
Potter, Lena
Pepper, Mrs. L. B.

Ruka, John
Ruka, Johnnie
Ruka, Charlie
Ruka, May
Rue, Harry
Rein, W. W.
Rein, Ervin
Ricks, J. B.
Ricks, A.
Rogers, H. A.
Reichel, L.
Reichel, Daniel
Richards, M. E.
Reichel, Kate
Ricks, Gloria
Ricks, Minerva
Ruka, Settie
Rae, Frank
Reichel, Louis
Rogers, Helen
Ryan, Thos.
Ricks, Wm.
Ricks, John
Ruka, Freddie
Russell, L. S.
Reichel, Elizabeth
Rose, James
Rose, Wm.
Rose, Hannah
Richards, Will G.
Ricks, Delos
Rice, H. L.
Rice, Mrs. R. B.
Rice, Mattie
Rice, Kittie
Rice, Walter

Sarles, J. H.
Sarles, Mrs. J. H.
Searles, Jessie D.
Searles, Mrs. Jessie
Sarles, Mrs. Phebe H.
Sarles, Kate M.
Sarles, Willie R.

Sarles, Frank B.
Sarles, Jesse E.
Shockley, James
Smith, Charley
Smith, Willie
Scheinpflug, John
Scott, Luther
Sanborn, Levi
Sidler, Cecilia
Shipley, Frank
Sidler, Albert
Sanderson, Dexter
Sanderson, Almira M.
Smith, Adam
Stephens, F. W.
Simpkins, Harriet
Snow, W. C.
See, R. F.
See, Almma
See, Nellie
Stephens, Janie
Stephens, R. C.
Stahel, Ferdinand
Sherrard, W.
Swartz, Mary
Sherrard, P. H.
Stephens, C. H.
See, Clark
Stoddart, S. A.
Stephens, Annia
Schriber, Christen
Stoddart, Wm.
Stoddart, H. P.
Simpkins, Alice
Schriber, George
Stahel, Louisa
Smith, Agnes
Stroh, Christina
Stone, Frank
Sylvester, ___
Stephens, Bessie
Stone, W. C.
Shipley, Sherman
Sherrard, Hope
Stroh, Anna
Swartz, Thos.
Schuer, Frances

Taylor, Ed. B.
Thompson, Mettie
Thompson, Mrs. Wm.
Thompson, W. F.
Taylor, James
Thompson, C. A.
Thompson, Sarah
Trehey, Maggie
Thomas, Ellen
Taylor, K. E.

Waney, R. T.
Willis, Mrs. J. P.
Wheeler, George

Genealogical Events from Newspapers for Crawford, Vernon and Grant Counties, Wisconsin, 1870-1901

Wisdom, F. M.	Willoughby, S. R.	Winters, Frances A.	Venest, Albert
Wisdom, James	Wonzor, L. P.	Walstrum, S.	
Willoughby, B. P.	Watson, Jacob		Young, F.
Wells, T. M.	Wonzor, Mrs. Mary	Van Buren, M.	York, Wm.
Willis, Frank	Woodard, Nettie	Van Buren, Fred	
Walker, Henry	Watson, Isaac	Van Buren, Claude	Zallman, Leon
Walker, Ella	Wagner, Mary	Van Buren, Nettie	
Watrous, T.	Walker, J. P.	Van Buren, Anna	

[This list was published in the *Boscobel Dial*, November 9, 1877, on page 3, column 4. Newspaper accounts indicate that many temperance meetings were held in the region at the time. It was a popular movement and found fertile ground in the Boscobel area.]

Genealogical Events from Newspapers for Crawford, Vernon and Grant Counties, Wisconsin, 1870-1901

National Christian Temperance Union Activity in the Boscobel, Wisconsin Area

(This list was published in the *Boscobel Dial*, March 22, 1878, page 3, column 3.)

"Besides the 113 that took the pledge in December 1877 and January 1878, the following Catholics have bound themselves to observe the following pledge of temperance.

                        Respectfully Yours

                        Rev. Charles Shroudenback

"I promise with God's aid and in honor of the sacred thirst and agony of our Savior Jesus Christ, to abstain from all intoxicating drinks, to prevent as much as possible, by advice and example, the sin of intemperance in others, and to discountenance the treating and other drinking customs of society."

Johanna O'Shaughnessy	Cath. Murphy	Sarah Bartley
Bridget Carmody	Mary Cull	Mrs. Elizabaeth Trainor
Lizzie O'Brien	Ann Carmody	Mary Cull
Ellie Mulrooney	Ann Cull, Jr.	Ellen Quinn
M. A. Mulrooney	Alice Cull	John Quinn
Mary O'Shaughnessy	Liza Collins	Annie Morgan
Ellie O'Brien	Liza Roseman	Bessie Frier
Patrick Mulrooney	Magie Mooney	Mrs. Ellen Loynett
Mary Keating	Ellen Hanley	Thomas Culkin
C. A. Scanlan	Bridget Brennan	Mrs. Bridget Glynn
P. W. Scanlan	Mary Garvey	Harmon Smyth
Katy Lynett	Alias Garvey	Any Quinn
Katy Corcoran	Margaret Corcoran	Rosa Mulrooney
Rose Woods	Mary Carmody	Mary A. Mulrooney
Mrs. James Trainor, Jr.	Hanna O'Brien	Ellen Cull
Mary Corcoran	Mary Frier	Cassy Quinn
Mary F. Hanley	Mrs. Hannora Mulrooney	Honora Keating
John Scanlan, Sen.	Peter Morgan	Patrick Phelon
Thomas Corcoran, Sen.	Laur Keating	Thomas Carmody
Thomas O'Brien	Mr. Honora Scanlon	Mrs. Johanna Carmody
Celia M. Collins	Bridget Carmody	Mrs. Ellen Hanly
John Scanlan, Jr.	Annie Culkin	Michael Frier
Peter Garvey	Mary Mooney	Mrs. Mary Collins
Thomas Hanley	Norah Mooney	Daniel Roseman
Rosey Mulrooney	Lula Mooney	Michael James
Bridget Brennan	Mrs. B. Corcoran	John Mulhair
Ann Cull, Sen.	Mrs. Mooney	Geo. W. Dyer
Mary Murphy	Richard Connelly	Catharine Riordan

APPENDIX

Genealogical Events from Newspapers for Crawford, Vernon and Grant Counties, Wisconsin, 1870-1901

Appendix 1

MAPS

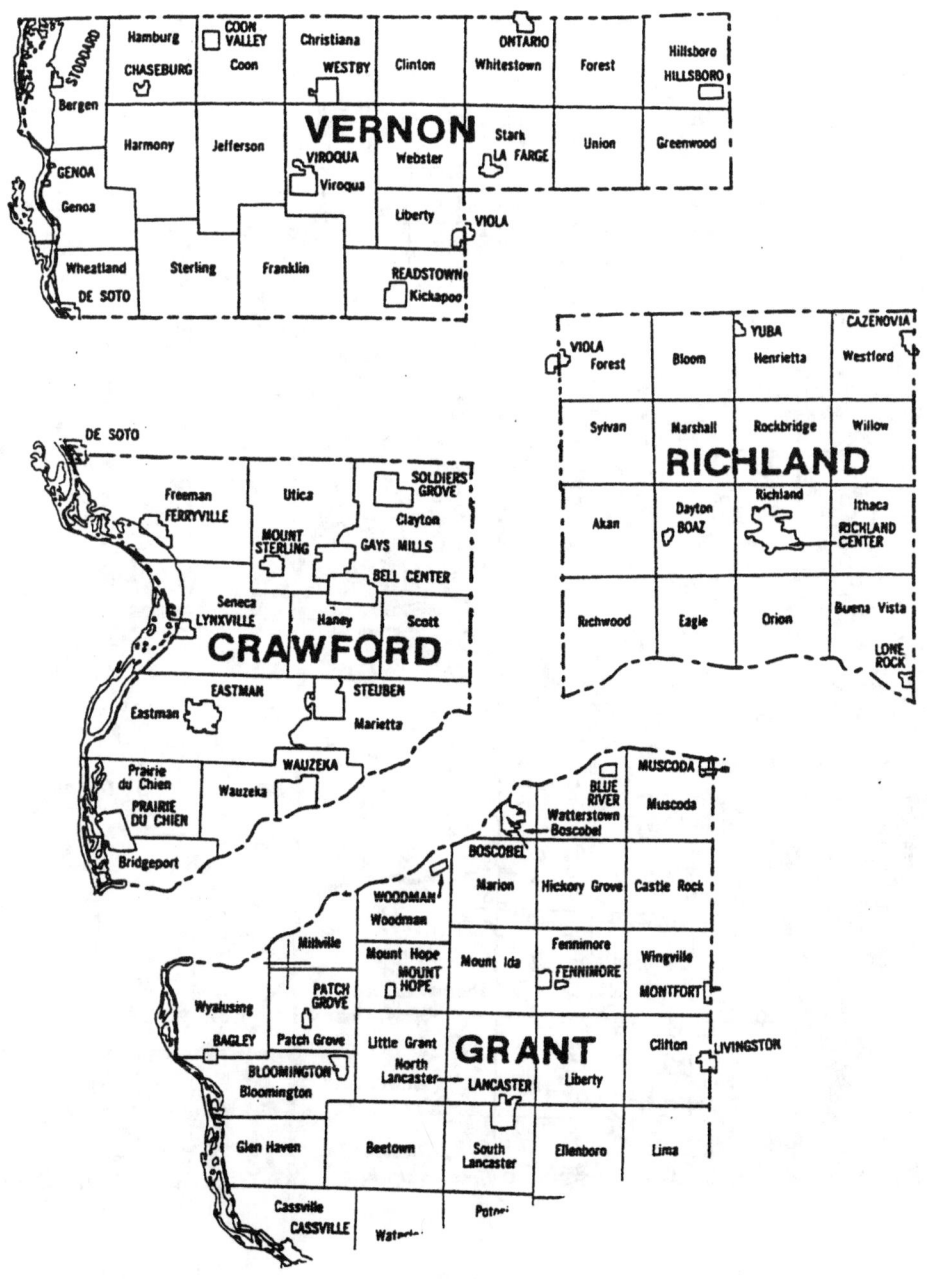

Townships in Crawford, Vernon, Richland and Grant Counties

Genealogical Events from Newspapers for Crawford, Vernon and Grant Counties, Wisconsin, 1870-1901

Southwestern Wisconsin

Appendix 2

GAZETTEER

Adney	Post office in the eastern part of the Town of Clayton, Crawford County.
Akan	Township in Richland County. Sometimes spelled Aiken.
Ash Ridge	Village in Town of Bloom, Richland County.
Avalanche	Village on West Branch of Kickapoo River in Town of Webster, Vernon County.
Barnum	Village in Town of Haney, Crawford County.
Battle Island	Site of the Battle of Bad Axe during the Black Hawk War. Near Victory, Vernon County.
Bear Creek	Creek in Town of Clayton, Crawford County.
Belle Center	Village in Town of Clayton, Crawford County. Sometimes spelled Bell Center.
Bergen	Township in Vernon County.
Bloom	Township in Richland County.
Bloom City	Village in Town of Bloom, Richland County.
Bloomingdale	Post office in Town of Clinton, Vernon County.
Bloomington	Village in Town of Bloomington, Grant County.
Blue River	Village in Town of Watterstown, Grant County. Also called Blue River Station.
Boma	Neighborhood in Town of Utica, Crawford County.
Boscobel	Village in Town of Boscobel, Grant County.
Brady	Post office in western part of the Town of Akan, Richland County.
Bridgeport	Township in Crawford County.
Burr	Post office in Town of Forest, Vernon County.
Cadott	Village in Chippwa County. Center of lumber industry in late 19th century and early 20th century.
Chaseburg	Village in Town of Hamburg, Vernon County.
Chippewa Falls	City in Chippewa County. Center of lumber industry in late 19th century and early 20th century.
Christiana	Township in Vernon County.
Citron Valley	Valley in Town of Haney, Crawford County.
Clayton	Township in Crawford County.
Clinton	Township in Vernon County.
Coon Valley	Village in Town of Coon, Vernon County.
Crawford	County in southwest Wisconsin. Bounded by Vernon County to the north, Richland County to east, Grant County to the south and the Mississippi River to the west.
De Soto	Village in Town of Wheatland, Vernon County and Town of Freeman, Crawford County.
Dell	Post office in Town of Clinton, Vernon County.
Eagle	Township in Richland County.
Eagle Corners	Village in Town of Eagle, Richland County.
Eastman	Township in Crawford County. Village in Town of Eastman, Crawford County.
English Ridge	Ridge in eastern part of the Town of Clayton, Crawford County.
English Run	Tributary of Knapps Creek in the eastern part of the Town of Clayton, Crawford County.
Esofea	Post office in Town of Jefferson, Vernon County.
Excelsior	Village in Town of Richwood, Richland County.
Fennimore	Township in Grant County. Village in Town of Fennimore, Grant County.
Ferryville	Village in Town of Freeman, Crawford County.
Five Points	Village in Town of Akan, Richland County.
Folsom	Village in Town of Franklin, Vernon County.
Forest	Township in Richland County.
Franklin	Township in Vernon County.
Freeman	Township in Crawford County.
French Town	A section of Prairie du Chien, Crawford County.

Genealogical Events from Newspapers for Crawford, Vernon and Grant Counties, Wisconsin, 1870-1901

Gays Mill	Village on Kickapoo River in Town of Clayton, Crawford County. Also called Gays Mills.
Genoa	Village on Mississippi River in Town of Genoa, Vernon County.
Georgetown	Village in Town of Smelser, Grant County.
Georgetown	Neighborhood in Town of Scott, Crawford County.
Grant County	County in southwest Wisconsin. Bounded by Crawford County to the north, Iowa and Lafayette Counties to the west, Illinois to the south and the Mississippi River to the west.
Greenwood	Township in Vernon County.
Halls Valley	Valley in Town of Seneca, Crawford County.
Hamburg	Township in Vernon County.
Haney	Township in Crawford County.
Harmony	Township in Vernon County.
Henrietta	Township in Richland County.
Hickory Grove	Township in Grant County.
Highland	Township in Iowa County.
Hillsboro	Village and Township in eastern Vernon County.
Hub City	Village in Rockbridge Township, Richland County.
Hurlbuts	Village in Town of Scott, Crawford County.
Hustler Ridge	Neighborhood near Sugar Grove, Vernon County.
Irish Ridge	Neighborhood in Town of Scott, Crawford County. Neighborhood in Town of Prairie du Chien, Crawford County.
Jefferson	Township in Vernon County.
Jimtown	Neighborhood in the western part of the Town of Akan, Richland County.
Johnstown	Neighborhood on Tainter's Creek in Section 9 of the Town of Utica, Crawford County.
Kickapoo	Township in Vernon County.
Kickapoo Center	Village on East Branch of the Kickapoo River in Town of Kickapoo, Vernon County.
Kickapoo River	River which flows through eastern Vernon County and eastern Crawford County before it discharges into the Wisconsin River.
Knapps Creek	Creek which drains eastern Crawford County and western Richland County before it discharges into the Wisconsin River.
LaFarge	Village on Kickapoo River in Town of Stark, Vernon County.
Lancaster	City in Grant County.
Lansing	Town on Mississippi River in Allamakee County, Iowa.
Liberty Pole	Village in Town of Franklin, Vernon County.
Lower Town	A section of Prairie du Chien, Crawford County.
Lynxville	Village in Town of Seneca, Crawford County.
Manning	Village in Town of Kickapoo, Vernon County.
Marietta	Township in Crawford County.
Mendota	Town in Dane County. Site of the State Hospital for the Insane.
Mill Creek	Village in Town of Marshall, Richland County.
Missouri	An early name for the part of De Soto located in Crawford County.
Mt. Hope	Village in Town of Mt. Hope, Grant County.
Mt. Ida	Township in Grant County.
Mt. Sterling	Village in Town of Utica, Crawford County.
Mt. Tabor	Post office in Town of Forest, Vernon County.
Mt. Zion	Village in Town of Scott, Crawford County.
Newton	Post office in Town of Harmony, Vernon County.
North Clayton	Village in northern Town of Clayton, Crawford County.
North Star	Village on Kickapoo River in Town of Haney, Crawford County.
Ontario	Village on Kickapoo River in Town of Whitestown, Vernon County.
Orion	Township in Richland County.
Ottervale	Village on West Kickapoo River in Town of Webster, Vernon County.
Patch Grove	Village in Patch Grove Township, Grant County.

Genealogical Events from Newspapers for Crawford, Vernon and Grant Counties, Wisconsin, 1870-1901

Petersburg	Village on Kickapoo River in Town of Haney, Crawford County.
Pine Grove	Early name for Soldiers Grove, Crawford County.
Pine Knob	Village in Town of Utica, Crawford County.
Port Andrew	Village in Town or Richwood, Richland County.
Poplar Ridge	A neighborhood between Lynxville and Eastman in Crawford County.
Prairie du Chien	County seat of Crawford County. Located on Mississippi River in Town of Prairie du Chien.
Purdy	Village in southwest Vernon County.
Readstown	Village on Kickapoo River in town of Kickapoo, Vernon County.
Red Mound	Post office in Town of Wheatland, Vernon County.
Rest	Post office in Town of Bergen, Vernon County.
Retreat	Village in Town of Sterling, Vernon County.
Richland	County in southwest Wisconsin. Bounded by Vernon County to the north, Crawford County to the west, Grant County and Iowa County to the south and Sauk County to the east.
Richland Center	County seat of Richland County. Located in Town of Richland.
Richwood	Township in Richland County.
Rising Sun	Village in Town of Freeman, Crawford County.
Rockton	Post office in Town of Whitestown, Vernon County.
Rolling Ground	Neighborhood in southern Town of Clayton, Crawford County.
Romance	Village in Genoa Township, Vernon County.
Ross	Post office in Town of Liberty, Vernon County.
Rush Creek	Village in Town of Freeman, Crawford County and creek in Town of Freeman which empties into the Mississippi River.
Sabin	Village in Town of Sylvan, Richland County.
Scott	Township in Crawford County.
Seneca	Township in Crawford County. Village in Town of Seneca, Crawford County.
Soldiers Grove	Village on Kickapoo River in Town of Clayton, Crawford County.
Springville	Village in Jefferson Township, Vernon County.
St. Philips	Neighborhood around St. Philips Catholic Church in southern Town of Clayton, Crawford County.
Star	Village on Kickapoo River in Stark Township, Vernon County.
Stark	Township in Vernon County.
Sterling	Township in Vernon County.
Steuben	Village on Kickapoo River in Town of Marietta, Crawford County.
Stoddard	Village in Town of Bergen, Vernon County.
Sugar Grove	Village in Town of Kickapoo, Vernon County.
Sylvan	Township in Richland County.
Tainter Creek	Creek which flows through the Town of Franklin, Vernon County and the Town of Utica, Crawford County.
Tavera	Village in Town of Richwood, Richland County.
Towerville	Village in Town of Utica, Crawford County.
Trout Creek	Creek east of Soldiers Grove in Town of Clayton, Crawford County.
Union	Township in Vernon County.
Utica	Township in Crawford County.
Valley	Post office in Town of Forest, Vernon County.
Vernon County	County in southwest Wisconsin. Bounded by La Crosse County and Monroe County to the north, Richland County to the east, Crawford County to the south and the Mississippi River to the west.
Victory	Village on the Mississippi River in Town of Wheatland, Vernon County.
Viola	Village in Town of Forest, Richland County and Town of Liberty, Vernon County.
Viroqua	County seat of Vernon County in Town of Viroqua.

Warner's Landing	River landing in Town of Bergen, Vernon County.
Waupon	Town in northcentral Wisconsin. Site of a state prison.
Wauzeka	Village in Town of Wauzeka, Crawford County.
Webster	Township in Vernon County.
Werley	Village in Mt. Ida Township, Grant County.
West Lima	Post office in Bloom Township, Richland County.
West Prairie	Village in Town of Sterling, Vernon County.
Westby	Village in Town of Christiana, Vernon County.
Wheatland	Township in Vernon County.
Wheatville	Post office in the northern part (Section 5) of the Town of Scott, Crawford County.
Woodman	Village in Town of Woodman, Grant County.
Wooster	Village on Kickapoo River in Town of Clayton, Crawford County.
Yankeetown	Neighborhood west of Soldiers Grove in Town of Clayton, Crawford County.
Yuba	Village in Henrietta Township, Richland County.

Appendix 3

NEWSPAPERS RESEARCHED FOR THIS PROJECT

Newspaper - Where Published	Code	Years	Call Numbers
Boscobel Dial - Boscobel, WI	BD	1877 – 1879	P43420
Boscobel Dial - Boscobel, WI	BD	1880 – 1883	P43421
De Soto Republican - De Soto, WI	DR	1870 – 1872	P90-4610
De Soto Chronicle - De Soto, WI	DC	1886 – 1889	P74-6316
Readstown Herald - Readstown, WI	RH	1897 – 1898	P46118
Readstown Herald - Readstown, WI	RH	1899 – 1900	P46119
Readstown Herald - Readstown, WI	RH	1900 – 1901	P46120
Kickapoo Chief - Wauzeka, WI	KC	1900 – 1902*	P76-5668

The State Historical Society of Wisconsin Library in Madison, Wisconsin has an outstanding collection of microfilmed newspapers. I have provided the call numbers used at the State Historical Society of Wisconsin for researchers who wish to consult the original sources for the citations contained in this book. The Lower Wisconsin River Genealogical and Historical Research Center also has copies of early Wauzeka, Wisconsin newspapers (*Kickapoo Chief, Kickapoo Papoose, Wauzeka Chief* and *Wauzeka Kickapoo Chief*). This genealogical society can be contacted at P.O. Box 202, Wauzeka, WI 53826.

* Denotes partial coverage in this book. These newspapers are extensively abstracted in *Genealogical Gleanings from Early Newspapers for Residents In and Near Crawford County, Wisconsin, 1897–1902*, compiled by Vernon D. Erickson.

Appendix 4

Southwestern Wisconsin Ministers Mentioned in Local Newspapers
1870 – 1910

Minister	Church Affiliation	Residence/s	Book **	Book**	Book**
Aasheim, Rev.		Utica	1		
Adrian, Isaac N., Rev.	Methodist Episcopal				3
Allaback, F. C., Rev.	Methodist Episcopal	Mt. Zion (Town of Scott)	1		
Allison, John, Rev.	Methodist Episcopal	Boscobel			3
Artman, H. J., Rev. Father	Catholic (St. Philip's and Gays Mills)	Soldiers Grove area, Gays Mills area	1		
Aspinwall, J. C., Rev.		Boscobel*	1		
Atkinson, Rev.		De Soto*	1		
Ausime, Rev.	Lutheran	West Fork	1		
Austin, N. S., Rev.	Methodist Episcopal	Beetown			3
Avery, J. H., Rev.	Methodist Episcopal	Viroqua	1	2	3
Balch, M. B., Rev.	Methodist Episcopal	De Soto, Madison, Minneapolis		2	3
Bell, David, Rev.	Methodist Episcopal	Mt. Sterling, Excelsior		2	
Bell, Frank, Rev.	Methodist Episcopal	Readstown, Montfort, Mt. Sterling, Soldiers Grove	1	2	3
Bell, Rev.	Methodist Episcopal				3
Bell, Rev.		Sylvan*			3
Bichford, I. B., Rev.	Methodist Episcopal	Reedsburg			3
Blanchard, Rev. Dr.		Hickory Grove*	1		
Bond, W. J. C., Rev.	Congregational	Boscobel	1	2	
Bradley, A. C., Rev.		Readstown	1		
Bradley, N. C., Rev.	Methodist Episcopal	West Branch, Excelsior	1	2	3
Breed, Rev.	Seventh Day Adventist				3
Brothers, J. D., Rev.	Methodist Episcopal	Patch Grove			3
Brown, Rev.		Bergen			3
Brown, W. L., Rev.					3
Brunson, Alfred, Rev.	Methodist Episcopal	Prairie du Chien	1		3
Burnett, O., Rev.	Methodist Episcopal	Bell Center			3
Buroker, M., Rev.	Methodist Episcopal	Sylvan	1		
Cameron, J. A., Rev.	Congregational	Gays Mills, Prairie du Chien	1		
Cameron, M. J., Rev.	Congregational	Gays Mills		2	
Case, Elder			1		
Casper, Rev.	Methodist Episcopal	Bell Center*, Readstown *	1	2	3
Chapel, Elmer Octavius, Rev.	Congregational	Readstown			3
Chase, George W., Rev.	Methodist Episcopal				3
Cheney, Rev.	Congregational	Janesville		2	
Chynoweth, W. H., Rev.		Boscobel	1		
Clack, William, Rev.	Baptist	Prairie du Chien, Milwaukee		2	

Genealogical Events from Newspapers for Crawford, Vernon and Grant Counties, Wisconsin, 1870-1901

Minister	Church Affiliation	Residence/s	Book**	Book**	Book**
Clifton, J. J., Rev.	Methodist Episcopal	Arion			3
Clingman, D., Rev.	Methodist Episcopal	Fairchild			3
Cole, T. W., Rev.	Congregational	Boscobel, Gays Mills	1		3
Conley, Rev. Father	St. Phillips Church, Catholic	Clayton			3
Cook, Rev.	Congregational	Maple Ridge		2	
Cooper, F. M., Rev.			1		
Cough, E. E., Rev.	Methodist Episcopal	Platteville			3
Crouch, Thomas J., Rev.	Methodist Episcopal	De Soto, Boscobel	1	2	3
Custer, J. W., Rev.	Methodist Episcopal	Gays Mills, Mt. Sterling, Marietta, Barnum		2	
Davenport, Arthur, Rev.	Reorganized Church of Jesus Christ of Latter Day Saints	Montgomeryville and Soldiers Grove area	1		
Day, John, Rev.			1		
DeLap, W. Fletcher, Rev.	Methodist Episcopal	Viroqua, Elroy			3
DeLap, John, Rev.	Methodist Episcopal	Boscobel, Ontario			3
Dinsdale, M., Rev.			1		
Dixon, Rev.			1		
Drake, Rev.			1		
Duffey, Rev.	St. James Church, Catholic	Rising Sun			3
Duffy, H. F., Rev. Father	Catholic (St. Philip's)	Soldiers Grove area	1	2	
Earl, H. H., Rev.	Methodist Episcopal	Fennimore			3
Eaton, S. W., Rev.			1		
Elder, W. A., Rev.	Christian Church	Pleasant Ridge	1		
Ellis, John, Rev.	Congregational	Kickapoo			3
Epp, G. E., Rev.			1		
Evans, T. M., Rev.	Methodist Episcopal	Boscobel			3
Ewers, M. H., Rev.	Methodist Episcopal	Readstown			3
Fardy, Rev. Father	Catholic	West Superior	1		
Finstad, Martin, Rev.	Lutheran	Soldiers Grove	1		
Flett, Rev.	Congregational	Eastman		2	
Ford, James, Rev.		Town of Scott*, De Soto*	1		
Frisk, L. L., Rev.		Waukon, IA*			3
Gander, David, Rev.			1		
Gander, Rev.	Methodist Episcopal	Readstown			3
Garner, Henry, Rev.		Kickapoo	1		3
Gordon, C. B., Rev.		Freeman			3
Gordon, Rev.		Rush Creek			3
Grimsby, Henry, Rev.		Soldiers Grove, Viroqua	1		
Gruber, G. F., Rev.	German Lutheran	Boscobel	1	2	
Guldbrand, Rev.		Westby	1		
Hackner, Rev. Father	Catholic	Alma			3
Hackney, H. J., Rev.	Methodist Episcopal	Boscobel			3
Hadden, J. W., Rev.		Steuben		2	
Haigh, George, Rev.	Methodist Episcopal and Congregational	Boscobel, Avoca, Muscoda			3
Halvorson, Rev.		Westby	1		
Hanson, Rev.		St. Paul, MN			3
Harris, John, Rev.	Methodist Episcopal	Fayette		2	

Genealogical Events from Newspapers for Crawford, Vernon and Grant Counties, Wisconsin, 1870-1901

Minister	Church Affiliation	Residence/s	Book**	Book**	Book**
Harrison, John, Rev.	Methodist Episcopal	Fayette		2	
Haughton, William, Rev.	Congregational	Retreat, Cooley Valley	1		3
Havens, James, Rev.		Boscobel*			3
Helbig, Rev.	German Lutheran	Boscobel			3
Hendricks, Rev.	Lutheran	Soldiers Grove	1		
Hill, Rev.	Methodist Episcopal	De Soto			3
Hillman, W. J., Rev.				2	
Hitchcock, Rev.		West Salem			3
Hof, Philip J., Rev.		Boscobel			3
Hogan, Harding, Rev.		Steuben		2	
Hogenfrost, Rev. Father	Catholic	Wauzeka		2	
Holberg, J., Rev.		Lansing, IA			3
Holm, Rev.	Norwegian Lutheran	Folsom	1		3
Hood, Alex., Rev.		Boscobel	1		
Horton, G. W., Rev.	Methodist Episcopal	Richland Center	1		
Houghton, William, Rev.	Christian Church	Retreat*	1		3
Hubbard, Delos L., Rev.	Methodist Episcopal	De Soto			3
Hurd, T. Z., Rev.			1		
Hurd, W. W., Rev.	Methodist Episcopal	Boscobel, Prescott			3
Hurd, Willis	Methodist Episcopal	Boscobel			3
Hurd, Z. S., Rev.	Methodist Episcopal	Boscobel			3
Hurlbut, A. L., Rev.	Methodist Episcopal	Mt. Zion	1		
Hutchenson, Rev.					3
Irish, J. E., Rev.	Methodist Episcopal				3
Irish, W. R., Rev.	Methodist Episcopal	Sextonville			3
Jackson, B. L., Rev.	Methodist Episcopal	Mount Hope			3
Jameson, Rev.		Muscoda*	1		
Jansen, J. E., Rev.	Congregational		1		
Jefferson, James, Rev.		De Soto	1		3
Jencks, H. D., Rev.	Methodist Episcopal	New Lisbon			3
Jenney, E. W., Rev.		Boscobel*	1		
Johnson, O. M., Rev.			1		3
Jones, Rev.	Church of Christ	Readstown			3
Keeley, J. M., Rev. Father	Catholic	Seneca	1	2	
Kermott, J. C., Rev.	Baptist	Boscobel			3
Kiefner, Rev. Father	Catholic	Prairie du Chien	1	2	
Knapp, William, Rev.		Richland City			3
Knight, James C., Rev.	Methodist Episcopal		1		
La Baron, Ira, Rev.		Prairie du Chien	1	2	
Laird, A. M., Rev.		Lynxville		2	
Leavitt, I. S., Rev.	Methodist Episcopal	Prairie du Chien			3
Lench, Rev. Bishop		Avoca			3
Lewis, Rev.	Church of Christ	Viroqua			3
Loomis, A. A., Rev.		Fennimore*	1		
MacMurray, Thomas, Rev.			1		
Maes, Rev.		Lancaster		2	
Martin, J. W., Rev.		De Soto			3
Martin, M. M., Rev.		Black Earth	1		

Genealogical Events from Newspapers for Crawford, Vernon and Grant Counties, Wisconsin, 1870-1901

Minister	Church Affiliation	Residence/s	Book**	Book**	Book**
McClasky, Rev.		Muscoda			3
McClung, T. M., Rev.		Readstown*			3
McDermout, Rev.	Christian Church	Tavera	1		
McGinley, E., Rev.			1		
McKay, W. John, Rev.	Methodist Episcopal	Mt. Sterling, Madison			3
McMaster, Rev. A.					3
McMillan, W., Rev.	Methodist Episcopal	Bloomingdale			3
McMillin, Rev.		Readstown			3
McNeese, H., Rev.	Methodist Episcopal	Richland Center	1		
McNuse, J. H., Rev.		Richland Center	1		
McReynolds, Franklin L., Rev.		Grant County			3
Medd, J., Rev.	Methodist Episcopal	Springville			3
Miller, E. K., Rev.	Congregational				3
Miller, Rev. Father		Eastman*		2	
Mitchell, James M., Rev.	Congregational	De Soto			3
Mocket, Rev. Father			1		
Momo, Gabriel, Rev. Father	Catholic	Rising Sun	1		
Morgans, J. T., Rev.	Methodist Episcopal	De Soto, Onalaska			3
Morse, E. L., Rev.	Congregational	Boscobel			3
Mulhern, Dennis, Rev.	Baptist	De Soto			3
Mundt, F. A., Rev.		Wauzeka		2	
Mutschmann, Frederick, Rev. (also Mutchman)	German Lutheran	Boscobel		2	3
Naese, O., Rev. (also Naes, Naase and Nuess)	Norwegian Lutheran	Boscobel	1	2	3
Neill, J. A., Rev.	Methodist Episcopal	Readstown, Tunnel City, Soldiers Grove	1		3
Nelson, J. G., Rev.		West Prairie	1		
Nordgaard, Rev.		Westby	1		
Nuzum, George W., Rev.	Methodist Episcopal	Viroqua, Boscobel, Springville	1	2	3
Nuzum, I. F., Rev.	Methodist Episcopal	Mauston			3
O'Connors, Rev. Father	Catholic (St. Philip's)	Soldiers Grove area	1		
O'Reilley, Rev. Father	Catholic	Rising Sun	1		
O'Riley, Rev. Father	Catholic	Rising Sun	1		
O'Toole, Rev. Father	Catholic	Mondovi		2	
Pally, Rev.	Christian Church			2	
Pearce, Rev.		Richland Center			3
Peckham, L. E., Rev.	Methodist Episcopal	Soldiers Grove	1		
Peckham, Rev.		Springville			3
Pengilley, R., Rev.			1		
Perry, Rev.	United Brethren	Sylvan			3
Porter, T. A., Rev.	Congregational	Lynxville, Seneca		2	
Potts, S. A., Rev.		Woodman			3
Pratt, Arthur, Rev.				2	
Pronty, E., Rev.			1		
Pulley, Rev.	Christian Church				3
Pulley, Rev.		Town of Clayton*	1		

Genealogical Events from Newspapers for Crawford, Vernon and Grant Counties, Wisconsin, 1870-1901

Minister	Church Affiliation	Residence/s	Book**	Book**	Book**
Rabehl, Rev.		Wauzeka		2	
Radcliff, Rev.	Congregational	De Soto, Prairie du Chien			3
Rami, R., Rev.		Boscobel			3
Reichert, G. W., Rev.		Prairie du Chien		2	
Rice, Albert, Rev.		Boscobel, Chicago		2	
Rowell, J., Rev.		Mt. Sterling	1	2	
Sackett, E. H., Rev.	Methodist Episcopal	Wauzeka			3
Samuels, Rev. Mr.	Episcopal				3
Sarles, Jesse D., Rev.	Methodist Episcopal	Boscobel			3
Schoeberle, John, Rev.		Muscoda*			3
Schoenfeld, F. W., Rev.	Congregational	Prairie du Chien	1		
Schraudenbach, Charles, Rev. Father	Catholic	Boscobel			3
Scoville, A. B., Rev.	Methodist Episcopal	Mt. Sterling			3
Searles, Jesse D., Rev.	Methodist Episcopal	Boscobel			3
Shears, Rev.		Fennimore*			3
Shephard, William, Rev.	Methodist Episcopal	Boscobel, Soldiers Grove	1	2	
Sime, Rev.		Mt. Sterling	1		
Smeby, H. E., Rev.		Viroqua	1		
Smelzer, Rev.		Boaz	1		
Smith, A. E., Rev.		Wheatland/Town of Scott	1		
Smith, John, Rev.		Gillingham	1		
Smith, Rev. Mr.		Orion	1		
Snodgrass, T. J., Rev.	Methodist Episcopal	Merrimac			3
Snow, Walter C., Rev.		Soldiers Grove	1		
Spofford, A. W., Rev.	Congregational	Prairie du Chien			3
Stamp, Thomas W., Rev.	Methodist Episcopal	Viola*, Readstown	1		3
Steble, James, Rev. Father	Catholic	Boscobel	1		
Stehle, James, Rev. Father	Catholic	Boscobel	1		
Stevens, G. D., Rev.		De Soto*			3
Stickels, E. C., Rev.		Boscobel			3
Stoddart, William, Rev. Dr.	Congregational	Boscobel	1		3
Straw, F. W., Rev.		Liberty Pole*	1		
Streeter, D., Rev.	Methodist Episcopal	Mt. Sterling	1		
Sturges, Rev.		Richland Center			3
Tresidder, John, Rev.	Methodist Episcopal			2	
Trimm, E., Rev.	Methodist Episcopal	Necedah	1		3
Trimm, E., Rev.			1		
Vaughan, A. C., Rev.					3
Walker, H. J., Rev.	Methodist Episcopal	Spring Green			3
Walworth, J., Rev.		Richland Center			3
Webster, J. E., Rev.		Town of Clayton*	1		
Webster, Rev.	Methodist Episcopal	Boscobel		2	
Wells, Milton, Rev.		Greene, IA	1		
Wells, Rev.					3
Wells, Rev.	Christian Church	Sugar Grove	1		
Westphal, Rev.		Viroqua	1		
Wheaton, W. W., Rev.	Methodist Episcopal	Avoca			3
Whitelaw, Rev.	Congregational	Portage	1		

Genealogical Events from Newspapers for Crawford, Vernon and Grant Counties, Wisconsin, 1870-1901

Minister	Church Affiliation	Residence/s	Book**	Book**	Book**
Willan, John, Rev.		Viola	1		
Wirtz, Rev. Father	Catholic	Genoa			3
Woolley, Lewis N., Rev.	Methodist Episcopal	Wonewoc, Viola, Melrose			3
Wright, I. J. (or J. J.), Rev.		Boscobel*			3
Wright, J. P., Rev.		Readstown	1		
Wright, Q. R., Rev.		Blue River*			3

Book 1 refers to *Births, Deaths, Marriages and Other Genealogical Gleanings from Newspapers for Crawford, Vernon and Richland Counties, Wisconsin, 1873-1910*, Compiled by Vernon D. Erickson, Published by Heritage Books, Inc., 1997.

Book 2 refers to *Genealogical Gleanings From Early Newspapers for Residents In and Near Crawford County, Wisconsin, 1897-1902*, Compiled by Vernon D. Erickson, Published by Heritage Books, Inc., 1999.

Book 3 refers to *Genealogical Events from Newspapers for Crawford, Vernon and Grant Counties, Wisconsin, 1870-1901*, Compiled by Vernon D. Erickson, Published by Heritage Books, Inc., 2001.

Note: In many cases a minister's residence was not mentioned in the newspapers. If a minister performed several marriages or funerals in a location, this site is highlighted with an * and should be considered to be his likely residence, subject to additional research. Keep in mind that ministers frequently moved, especially Methodist Episcopal ministers.

INDEX

A

Aasheim, 241
Abbey, 60
Abby, 172
Ableiter, 1, 12, 21, 43, 119, 203, 206
Ables, 68
Abolition, 22
Abrams, 1, 23
Ackelberry, 2
Adams, 1, 2, 5, 19, 22, 42, 44, 51, 60, 69, 73, 115, 133, 134, 147, 148, 152, 174, 206, 215, 217, 219, 221
Adkins, 2, 63, 120, 206
Adopted, 6, 82, 101, 121, 141, 187, 188
Adrian, 130, 241
Adson, 2
Aduddell, 2
Aikans, 147
Aiken, 2, 50, 184, 217
Aikens, 2, 44, 65, 70, 206
Aikins, 2, 3, 33, 120, 143, 148, 153, 174, 183, 219, 221
Akey, 3, 25, 118
Albee, 3
Alcheon, 3
Alcorn, 3, 118, 149, 206
Alden, 3, 14, 57, 71, 116, 177, 201, 204, 227
Alder, 43, 149, 176
Alderman, 3, 42, 141
Alderson, 206
Aldrich, 101, 214
Alexander, 3, 4, 42, 84, 99, 111, 118, 120, 138, 140, 143, 206, 218
Alford, 4, 76
Allaback, 241
Allan, 215
Allen, 4, 5, 14, 19, 46, 54, 64, 76, 102, 148, 167, 176, 177, 206, 214, 219
Allingson, 111
Allison, 5, 18, 21, 33, 113, 117, 146, 160, 165, 167, 172, 191, 241
Alsop, 5
Altizer, 5
Amaun, 1, 5
Ames, 5, 8, 13, 70, 76, 174, 217
Ammund, 195
Amos, 1, 5
Amphlett, 5
Amundson, 5
Ancheutz, 5
Ancient Order of United Workmen, 5
Anderson, 5, 6, 9, 10, 15, 19, 42, 48, 56, 109, 124, 137, 139, 147, 201, 202, 204, 206, 223, 225, 227
Andrew, 6, 108, 206
Andrews, 2, 6, 7, 27, 38, 43, 46, 76, 85, 106, 114, 147
Angell, 7, 8, 23, 39, 40, 50, 67, 83, 99, 142, 143, 164
Ankeney, 197
Ankeny, 8, 10, 29, 42, 44, 59, 83, 89, 119, 176, 177, 180, 223
Anschuetz, 8
Anthwerp, 8
Appleby, 8
Arenndo, 8
Arms, 8, 216
Armstrong, 5, 8, 37, 67, 87, 113, 115, 119, 120, 133, 151, 167, 179, 203, 206, 227
Arneson, 8, 74, 113
Arnold, 8, 13, 39, 87, 109, 152, 223
Arthur, 5, 8, 41, 201
Artman, 241
Asbury, 9, 29, 47, 135, 145
Asheley, 11
Ashley, 143
Ashmore, 9, 169
Aspinwall, 241
Atkinson, 10, 37, 45, 60, 91, 109, 171, 182, 206, 241
Auel, 9
Ausime, 241
Austin, 9, 25, 30, 126, 166, 241
Avery, 9, 111, 124, 134, 241
Ayer, 142
Aylward, 184, 218

B

Babcock, 9, 10, 148, 182
Babel, 25
Bachman, 9
Backus, 71
Bacon, 8, 95
Bagley, 9, 206
Bailey, 9, 10, 17, 19, 22, 56, 59, 67, 74, 102, 115, 124, 162, 166, 194, 198, 206, 223, 227
Bailie, 64
Bailou, 188
Baily, 124
Baker, 6, 10, 152, 167, 170, 177, 191, 206, 223
Balch, 10, 70, 81, 111, 124, 217, 241
Baldrick, 10, 88
Baldwin, 10, 78, 103, 193, 221
Balister, 206
Ball, 10, 84
Ballard, 53, 165
Ballon, 10
Ballou, 196
Balzell, 156
Bancroft, 10
Bangs, 10, 37, 163
Bankas, 182
Banker, 10
Banks, 10, 11, 26, 120
Bankus, 33
Banmot, 206
Bannon, 11
Banta, 60
Banty, 152
Barabeaux, 11
Baraboo, 11
Barbeau, 204
Barbeaux, 119
Barber, 11, 57, 191, 206
Barden, 165
Barham, 11
Barker, 11, 160, 191, 206, 225
Barkley, 159, 214
Barlett, 11
Barnard, 9, 11
Barnes, 11, 42, 48
Barnetsburger, 105, 160
Barnett, 6, 11, 19, 36, 52, 53, 113, 175, 177, 191, 206, 227
Barney, 11, 12, 58, 60, 74, 163
Barnum, 17, 90, 206
Barque, 12, 165
Barr, 12, 19, 89, 156, 176, 177
Barrett, 12, 78, 128, 168
Barrie, 12, 54, 78
Barron, 12
Bartells, 53
Bartels, 12, 201
Barth, 12
Barthelomew, 111, 176, 177
Bartholemew, 12, 50
Bartholomew, 12, 13, 26, 43, 58, 70, 76, 111, 176, 203, 205, 206, 215, 217, 218, 223, 227
Bartlett, 11, 12, 79
Bartley, 19, 206, 230
Barto, 130, 182
Barton, 12, 129, 148, 215
Bartow, 12
Bash, 12
Bass, 12
Bassett, 12
Baswortz, 13
Batchelor, 108
Bates, 13, 32, 46, 63, 71, 76, 86, 95, 112, 139, 149, 167, 177, 217, 223
Battle of Bad Axe, 117, 171
Battle of the Bad Axe, 4
Battle of Waterloo, 151
Battles, 13, 14, 59, 60, 174, 223
Baty, 13, 142
Baumgartner, 13, 33, 148, 173
Baxter, 13, 205, 206
Baxton, 75
Bayse, 13
Beabel, 13
Beach, 13, 76, 167
Beals, 13, 19
Beam, 12, 13, 52, 69

Bean, 4, 13, 14, 39, 52, 58, 69, 83, 89, 105, 149, 164, 219, 220
Beardsley, 14
Beaumont, 14, 113
Beck, 14, 89, 125, 164
Beckler, 104
Beckwar, 14, 169
Beckwith, 14, 30, 54
Becwith, 54
Beebe, 14, 15, 183, 206
Beekman, 56
Beeley, 14
Beer, 206
Beffa, 14
Beiderman, 72
Beilter, 206
Beinborn, 72
Bell, 3, 4, 14, 15, 45, 84, 110, 140, 148, 156, 183, 192, 206, 225, 241
Belling, 64
Bellows, 176, 225
Belt, 94
Bembrick, 15
Bemis, 15, 219
Bender, 15, 81, 148
Benedict, 15, 36, 89, 91, 174, 223
Benhart, 60
Benn, 15, 65, 88, 100, 146, 168
Benner, 206
Bennett, 15, 21, 25, 26, 34, 43, 47, 61, 66, 76, 77, 80, 110, 115, 116, 140, 144, 218, 228
Bennington, 11
Bennis, 41, 167
Bennish, 15
Benoy, 15, 16, 19, 37, 154, 157, 167
Benshon, 206
Benson, 1, 16, 19, 51, 73, 74, 166, 193
Bentley, 206
Benton, 16, 26
Bentson, 184
Bequith, 54
Berg, 16, 60, 80
Berge, 219
Bergh, 16, 149
Bernier, 16
Berry, 16
Betts, 16, 30, 31, 33, 53, 193
Bevan, 16, 89, 111, 164
Bevans, 89
Bever, 16
Bevier, 215
Bichford, 124, 241
Bidgood, 206
Biederman, 225
Big Canoe, 51
Bigelow, 16
Bigler, 206
Bilckie, 206
Billard, 185, 217
Billiard, 16, 71
Bills, 16
Bingman, 219

Birchard, 1, 46, 131, 132, 165, 187, 206
Bircherd, 119
Bird, 16, 42, 48, 152
Birk, 16, 175
Bisbee, 64
Bishop, 9, 16, 17, 25, 36, 39, 46, 76, 83, 87, 90, 99, 102, 105, 172, 174, 176, 177, 206
Bixton, 75
Black, 9, 17, 71, 167
Black Hawk War, 4, 10, 13, 14, 17, 32, 37, 54, 64, 91, 103, 109, 111, 117, 165, 171, 180, 182, 192, 194, 196
Blackburn, 17
Blackwell, 72
Blair, 17, 59, 60, 206
Blake, 17, 34, 105, 194, 197
Blakely, 17
Blanchard, 17, 19, 20, 36, 96, 145, 148, 167, 195, 206, 241
Blancher, 43, 149
Blandin, 214
Blanding, 41, 206
Blessing, 194
Bliss, 6, 17, 18, 48, 62, 65, 73, 85, 93, 117, 127, 135, 163, 189, 193, 201, 206, 221, 227
Block, 58
Blood, 87
Bloss, 18
Blossingham, 18
Bloyer, 18, 160, 191
Blue Cloud, 72
Blume, 184, 218, 221
Bobel, 18, 131, 188
Bobst, 60
Bock, 18, 133, 168
Bodendine, 18
Boebrer, 139
Boechk, 151
Boenner, 18
Bohl, 201, 227
Bohland, 18
Boise, 145
Bold, 218, 219, 221
Bolden, 18, 219
Boldon, 218
Boldt, 116
Bolster, 18, 39, 204, 206, 214
Bond, 241
Bonney, 176
Booher, 64, 179
Booth, 18
Boothby, 18
Borah, 54
Borden, 165
Border, 206
Borgen, 18
Borst, 18
Bort, 19, 178
Boscobel Agricultural & Driving Park Association, 184
Boscobel Baseball Team, 19

Boscobel Congregational Church, 19
Boscobel Fire Department, 19, 189
Boscobel High School, 9, 19, 139, 155
Boscobel Light Guard Band, 64
Boscobel Mills, 19
Boscobel Pauper Fund, 19
Boscobel Protection Fire Co., 19
Boscobel Teachers, 19
Bose, 19
Bosh, 19
Boss, 19, 193
Bosworth, 19
Bottom, 19, 70
Bouley, 29
Bovee, 19, 142
Bowe, 76
Bowell, 19, 42
Bowen, 19, 206, 215
Bower, 19, 139, 148
Bowers, 5, 20, 34, 201
Bowles, 20, 63
Bowling, 20, 173
Bowman, 20
Bown, 20
Boyce, 70
Boyd, 20
Boylan, 20
Boyle, 20
Bracken, 54
Brackett, 206
Bradburry, 206
Bradley, 20, 75, 126, 206, 241
Brady, 56, 110
Bragg, 23
Brainard, 20, 60
Brainerd, 19, 20, 25, 52, 125
Brake, 20
Braley, 93
Brally, 93
Brand, 206
Brandenburg, 20
Brandes, 20
Brandon, 20, 37, 121, 218
Brands, 206
Brandt, 20
Brannan, 223
Brannon, 21, 127
Brar, 21
Bratlie, 60
Bray, 133, 176
Brayman, 223
Brazell, 207
Brechler, 1, 21
Breckler, 21
Breckner, 207
Breed, 21, 241
Brehmen, 207
Brekke, 9, 15, 21, 36, 43, 130, 165, 167, 177, 201, 227
Brekler, 21
Bremmer, 21, 76, 207
Brennan, 21, 163, 230
Brenneman, 21
Bresee, 181

Genealogical Events from Newspapers for Crawford, Vernon and Grant Counties, Wisconsin, 1870-1901

Brewer, 21, 144
Brice, 21
Brickler, 21, 77
Brickner, 21, 100
Bridger, 56
Brienig, 21
Briggs, 21, 60, 76, 93, 125, 147, 176, 207
Briggson, 21, 94
Brigham, 22
Bright, 22, 76, 113
Brighthaupt, 207
Brightman, 22, 60
Brimmer, 215
Brindler, 22, 114
Brindley, 6, 19, 22, 65, 193, 201, 207, 227
Brinkman, 207
Brisbane, 22
Brisbois, 125
Broadbent, 182
Broadhead, 22, 219, 221
Brockaway, 167
Broderick, 221
Brookins, 201, 207, 227
Brooks, 22, 30, 32, 80, 83, 150, 179, 183, 186
Brother, 207
Brothers, 15, 41, 53, 64, 85, 124, 126, 188, 241
Brott, 147
Brown, 16, 22, 23, 24, 26, 34, 35, 40, 42, 61, 64, 70, 76, 81, 90, 92, 94, 102, 108, 112, 115, 121, 137, 138, 166, 169, 179, 182, 191, 196, 215, 217, 219, 225, 241
Browne, 176
Brownell, 207
Brudas, 24
Bruhn, 24
Bruland, 24
Brumumer, 207
Brunck, 222
Brunk, 115
Brunson, 24, 35, 126, 207, 241
Bryant, 181, 207
Brye, 219, 221
Bryson, 24, 177
Buchanan, 24, 104, 133, 171, 184, 221
Buckmaster, 24
Budworth, 207
Buffa, 14, 68
Bugbee, 24, 207
Buggins, 24, 158, 160, 177
Bull, 24, 43, 118
Bullock, 24, 92, 182
Bunnell, 24
Burchard, 24, 153, 207
Burchardt, 25
Burchill, 25
Burdick, 25, 41, 69, 172, 177, 201, 203
Burgbur, 25
Burgen, 10, 88
Burger, 25

Burgess, 25, 43
Burgh, 25
Burgor, 3, 25, 118, 186
Burke, 26
Burkholder, 207, 215
Burlin, 79
Burlock, 29
Burn, 26
Burnard, 26
Burnett, 125, 126, 149, 241
Burnham, 177, 207
Burnn, 26
Burns, 26, 54, 60, 64, 162
Buroker, 26, 146, 241
Burr, 26
Burrell, 59, 76
Burrington, 207
Burris, 207, 215
Burrison, 26
Burrows, 15, 26
Burton, 26, 207
Busby, 26
Buschhausen, 26
Bush, 26
Bushnell, 205, 207
Buss, 73
Buswell, 60, 221
Butcher, 26, 207, 219
Butler, 6, 26, 27, 32, 102, 191, 207
Butt, 27, 163, 184, 191, 221
Button, 16, 43
Buxton, 27, 147
Byer, 27
Byerley, 139
Byerly, 27, 163
Byers, 76, 207, 214

C

C. M. A. Lodge of Kickapoo, 27
Cabinas, 27
Cade, 7, 27, 46, 59, 221
Cahrl, 184
Cain, 27
Caitlin, 27
Calbert, 27
Caldwell, 27, 50, 59, 60, 89, 137, 176, 177, 192, 223
Calkins, 27
Call, 179
Callahan, 27
Callis, 11, 207
Calloway, 27, 28, 56
Caloway, 28
Cameron, 241
Camp, 28, 70, 71, 207
Campbell, 23, 28, 42, 71, 76, 167, 217, 227
Cancutt, 219
Candidates, 29
Canfield, 28, 86
Cannable, 193
Cannon, 1, 28, 98, 130, 193

Cantwell, 181
Capron, 28, 38
Carey, 58
Carlan, 207
Carley, 19, 28, 105, 110, 119, 203, 227
Carlin, 28, 122
Carlson, 28
Carlyl, 28
Carlyle, 8, 28, 29, 39, 48, 50, 60, 90, 94, 105, 108, 111, 168, 191, 195
Carmody, 29, 180, 230
Carpenter, 29, 128, 221, 223
Carr, 23, 29, 50, 99, 105, 170, 181, 191, 196, 197
Carrell, 30, 51, 207
Carrier, 16, 19, 30, 49, 68, 90, 98, 113, 121, 129, 166, 167, 179
Carrigan, 30, 123
Carroll, 30, 51, 181
Carry, 30
Carson, 30, 76, 153, 172, 187, 207
Carswell, 30
Carter, 5, 30, 31, 62, 86, 131, 140, 147, 148, 207
Carver, 31
Cary, 31, 58, 151
Caryle, 29, 70, 81
Case, 31, 143, 162, 241
Casey, 167
Casler, 31
Casper, 22, 94, 241
Caspers, 31
Cass, 3, 31, 108, 119, 182, 192
Casseboom, 31, 92
Casson, 31, 39, 149, 207
Cast, 207
Castle, 31, 34, 137
Castley, 31
Caswell, 31, 32, 79, 151, 225
Caswill, 225
Cate, 29, 32, 48
Catlin, 207
Caughey, 207
Cawley, 32
Chadeayne, 32, 64
Chadwick, 168, 207
Chamber, 221
Chamberlain, 32, 42, 48, 64
Chambers, 22, 32, 49, 51, 168
Chandler, 19, 32, 38, 43, 167, 177, 179, 181, 207, 227
Chapek, 167
Chapel, 32, 110, 241
Chapman, 32, 50, 167, 207, 223
Chase, 16, 32, 33, 39, 55, 61, 63, 75, 76, 124, 137, 139, 141, 146, 168, 221, 223, 241
Cheaver, 19
Cheever, 96, 203, 214
Chena, 207
Cheney, 39, 50, 241
Chenoweth, 33
Chenvert, 33
Cherrier, 33

Genealogical Events from Newspapers for Crawford, Vernon and Grant Counties, Wisconsin, 1870-1901

Chesebro, 33
Chesemore, 207
Chester, 33
Chilson, 76
Chippewa, 24
Chisholm, 207
Chismore, 207
Chitwood, 33, 83, 122, 147
Chizek, 33
Cholerton, 33, 68
Christ, 13, 19, 33, 59, 72, 76, 96, 98, 146, 169, 202, 207, 214
Christian, 166
Christianson, 33, 60
Christie, 33, 60
Christopherson, 131, 135, 201
Church, 127
Churchill, 4, 33, 34, 43, 61, 80, 207
Chynoweth, 34, 241
Cilley, 34, 223
Civil War, 9, 14, 15, 31, 36, 37, 40, 45, 54, 63, 80, 82, 83, 86, 87, 89, 93, 106, 110, 111, 112, 121, 154, 156, 160, 162, 167, 181, 186
Clack, 241
Clancy, 34, 93
Clapp, 34, 181, 191
Clark, 12, 17, 19, 34, 35, 36, 39, 40, 50, 67, 70, 71, 83, 94, 96, 101, 116, 119, 122, 124, 125, 130, 138, 163, 173, 181, 201, 203, 206, 207, 214, 215, 217, 219, 223
Clary, 60
Classen, 214
Classon, 214
Claus, 36
Clawater, 36, 69, 154
Clawfot, 36
Clawson, 207, 219
Clayton, 36, 207
Cleary, 207
Clement, 36, 76
Clements, 214
Clementson, 36
Clemmons, 207
Cleveland, 157
Cliff, 30, 36
Cliffton, 36, 89
Clifton, 126, 242
Clingman, 124, 242
Clise, 36
Clock, 181
Clossen, 36
Closson, 19, 207
Cloud, 72, 97, 194
Clyde, 36
Co. I, 6th WI Regt, 36
Coalburn, 36, 37
Coards, 71
Coates, 37, 111, 138, 201, 203, 207, 227
Coats, 130
Cobb, 19, 36, 69, 207, 227
Coe, 84, 108, 223

Coffin, 37, 59, 89, 119, 133, 181, 184, 191
Coffins, 223
Coher, 37
Coker, 37
Colburn, 37, 98, 207
Cole, 37, 43, 50, 75, 80, 84, 112, 124, 169, 173, 204, 207, 218, 223, 242
Coleman, 37, 38, 56, 105, 130, 138, 141, 168, 190, 192, 207, 223, 227
Coler, 219
Collard, 38
Collens, 38
Collier, 23
Collins, 32, 38, 60, 65, 70, 83, 93, 102, 113, 159, 182, 207, 218, 227, 230
Colwell, 50
Combe, 38, 116
Combes, 38
Comerine, 207
Compton, 38
Comstock, 4, 22, 23, 28, 38, 39, 57, 60, 131, 132, 166, 167, 194, 201, 227
Conaway, 223
Cone, 27
Coney, 39, 207
Congregational Church Sunday School, 39
Congregational Convention, 39, 83
Conklin, 39, 60, 70, 94, 118, 129, 142, 153, 218
Conley, 39, 40, 59, 66, 82, 108, 118, 119, 138, 242
Connelly, 39, 66, 230
Conner, 221
Connor, 39, 133, 218, 223
Conrad, 39
Conti, 39
Contoit, 40, 43
Conway, 29, 109
Cook, 2, 3, 19, 23, 40, 65, 119, 167, 184, 202, 203, 207
Cooley, 39, 40, 60, 76, 89, 108, 149, 156, 167, 192, 207
Cooley Valley School Board, 40
Cooly, 40
Coomes, 40
Coon, 41
Cooper, 16, 41, 42, 43, 50, 74, 76, 94, 106, 111, 120, 207, 242
Copper, 60, 79
Coppernoll, 223
Copsey, 41, 76
Corbet, 42
Corbett, 223
Corcoran, 41, 230
Cordry, 41, 43
Corell, 41
Corey, 223
Cornet Band Assoc., 41
Cornet Band Association, 41
Cornwall, 41, 170
Correll, 30, 41
Cory, 41

Costello, 218
Cothren, 38, 41, 66
Cottrell, 41, 83
Couch, 96, 150, 173, 174, 187
Cough, 242
Couillard, 41
Coult, 41, 42, 73, 113, 116
Coumbe, 112
County Board, 2, 42, 43, 184
Court Cases, 42
Cover, 42, 187
Covey, 223
Cowan, 42, 43, 78, 119, 132, 188, 203, 207, 214
Cowden, 42, 147
Cowdon, 147
Cowdrey, 42, 43
Cowdry, 42
Cowell, 19, 42
Cowen, 40, 42, 60
Cox, 34, 42, 70, 106, 107, 207
Coy, 41, 42, 43
Coyne, 43
Cragan, 43
Crago, 135
Craig, 96, 207
Craige, 207
Craigo, 10, 43, 147
Craine, 43, 172
Cramer, 43
Crane, 43, 207
Cranes, 207
Craven, 64, 163, 207
Crawford, 39, 43
Crawford County Agricultural Society, 143
Crawford County Election Results, 43
Crawford County Republicans, 43
Crawley, 43
Creager, 19, 43
Cress, 153
Crinklaw, 40, 41, 43, 44, 162
Crofoot, 217
Croft, 207
Crolmbeck, 8
Cron, 43, 44, 60, 167
Crook, 5, 7, 44, 45, 46, 47, 66, 94, 147, 148, 178
Crooks, 147
Cropsey, 24
Crouch, 29, 36, 44, 54, 69, 79, 85, 87, 88, 99, 106, 112, 124, 128, 145, 155, 163, 187, 190, 207, 217, 227, 242
Crow, 37, 44, 88, 207
Crowell, 44, 143, 171
Crowfoot, 44
Crowley, 44, 76, 96, 133, 134
Crum, 42, 44
Crumerine, 44
Crumrine, 220
Culkin, 230
Cull, 44, 120, 207, 230
Cullins, 207, 227
Culner, 207

Culver, 16, 44, 45
Cumerine, 45
Cumings, 45
Cummens, 45
Cummin, 207
Cummings, 45
Cummins, 66, 207
Curley, 45, 207
Curran, 149, 207
Currie, 45
Curry, 45, 124, 131, 160
Curtis, 45, 64, 78, 94, 176, 177, 207
Cushing, 2, 16, 36, 45, 51, 167, 187, 217, 218, 223
Cushman, 45
Custer, 242
Custin, 45
Cutts, 111

D

Dagget, 144
Daggett, 39, 52, 121
Dailey, 45, 59, 126, 223
Dalton, 46, 57
Daly, 50, 89, 137
Danforth, 174
Daniels, 184, 218
Danils, 46
Dankleff, 139
Darnell, 46, 87
Darret, 39
Dasen, 75
Daughertee, 207
Daugherty, 207
Dave, 207
Davenport, 2, 7, 9, 23, 35, 43, 46, 47, 50, 59, 63, 79, 88, 91, 100, 102, 106, 116, 120, 132, 134, 136, 138, 147, 148, 156, 157, 171, 173, 174, 176, 180, 182, 183, 186, 207, 242
Daves, 207
Davey, 47, 160
David, 47, 66, 133, 141
Davidson, 10, 18, 21, 24, 47, 48, 50, 76, 80, 85, 108, 111, 114, 153, 169, 177, 201, 221
Davis, 1, 11, 16, 48, 49, 51, 59, 60, 71, 72, 75, 76, 84, 105, 112, 121, 123, 138, 149, 156, 157, 165, 167, 174, 176, 190, 196, 207, 217, 218, 219, 221, 223
Davisson, 49
Davy, 36, 51
Dawson, 184
Day, 32, 42, 49, 50, 82, 167, 198, 208, 242
De Garmo, 221
De Hart, 50, 114
De La Mater, 225
De Lacy, 33, 50, 70, 76
De Lap, 50, 218
De Rhine, 50
De Soto, 50

De Soto Baseball, 50
De Soto Cemetery Assoc., 50
De Soto Chronicle Subscribers, 50
De Soto Coronet Band, 71
De Soto History, 57, 186, 190
De Soto Literary and Library Association, 10
De Soto Lumber Co, 50
De Soto M. E. Church, 50
De Soto Officers, 50
De Soto Plum, 50
De Soto Settlers, 50
De Soto Teachers, 50, 177
De Soto Union School, 3, 51, 69, 75, 89
De Witt, 60
Dean, 30, 51, 193, 203, 208
Dearman, 51, 74, 117, 118, 147
Deaver, 51
Decker, 51, 208
Decorah, 51
Dederick, 1, 51
Deertz, 51
DeGrote, 51
DeHart, 51
DeHaven, 51
DeHeus, 52
Deidrick, 208
DeJean, 80
Delacy, 39
DeLacy, 52, 179
Delany, 6
Delap, 124, 126, 174
DeLap, 19, 47, 52, 101, 133, 169, 185, 202, 205, 227, 242
DeLapp, 41, 52
Delvin, 52
Dempsey, 52, 54, 208
Dennis, 20, 52
Dennison, 13, 52
Densmore, 52
Denson, 52
Dent, 52
Denuy, 208
Deringsfeld, 19
Dermody, 52, 135
Desmond, 167, 221
Devaney, 52
Devenport, 52, 217
Devlin, 50, 52, 53, 66, 93, 118, 144
Devoe, 53, 119, 204, 208, 214, 227
DeVoe, 53, 208
Devol, 146
Devorce, 53, 75, 160
Dewey, 53, 57
DeWitt, 14, 16, 21, 53, 60, 100, 201, 208, 227
Dexter, 11, 53
Diamond Jo Line, 170
Dickerson, 53, 169
Dickinson, 53, 122
Dickson, 8, 167, 221, 225
Didrickson, 184
Dike, 53
Diley, 53

Dilger, 53, 201
Dilley, 70
Dillon, 54, 208
Dingman, 208
Dinsdale, 18, 54, 134, 153, 154, 166, 242
Dixon, 54, 214, 242
Doan, 64
Dobler, 208
Dobson, 138
Dodds, 208
Dodge, 54, 66, 190
Doe, 54
Doerr, 219
Dohme, 86, 119, 208
Dolan, 19, 54, 223
Dolly, 54, 76
Dolme, 203
Dolphin, 54
Don, 54
Donahue, 54, 110, 160, 208, 218
Donaldson, 54, 152
Donavan, 54
Donohoe, 221
Doose, 55
Dosch, 55, 208
Dosh, 187
Dougherty, 214
Douse, 7, 8, 29, 55
Dousman, 50, 55
Dow, 157
Dowd, 111
Dowlen, 55
Dowling, 55, 76
Downey, 26, 55, 77, 100, 101, 120, 146
Downs, 10, 55, 195
Dowse, 7, 29, 48
Doyle, 55
Drake, 11, 51, 55, 76, 79, 118, 124, 173, 182, 242
Drecne, 56
Dregne, 24, 34, 56, 67, 147, 168
Drew, 56
Drinkwater, 56, 169
Driscoll, 56
Driskill, 51
Driver, 208
Druen, 225
Druier, 90
Druver, 90
Dubois, 56
DuChess, 84
Dudley, 70, 167, 208, 219
Duey, 208
Duffey, 242
Duffy, 242
Duke, 56
Dull, 28, 56, 147
Duncan, 56, 57, 88, 155, 167, 208
Dunlap, 38, 46, 57, 221
Dunlevy, 50, 57, 74
Dunn, 57
Dunstan, 208
Dunston, 57, 84

Durand, 11, 57
Durant, 35
Durley, 208
Durrie, 57
Durstin, 57
Durstine, 57, 158
Durtz, 51
Dustan, 75, 149, 208
Dustin, 149
Duston, 37, 57, 105
Dutcher, 57
Dyer, 12, 29, 50, 57, 58, 60, 71, 94, 99, 101, 126, 140, 147, 166, 196, 208, 223, 230

E

Eales, 15
Earl, 58, 110, 242
Eastman, 58, 76, 147, 208
Eaton, 30, 58, 205, 242
Eberly, 58, 123
Eck, 30, 58
Eckhard, 9, 58, 169
Eckhardt, 14, 34, 50, 58, 60, 168
Eckhart, 17, 58, 59, 223
Eckleberry, 59, 161
Eddy, 24, 70
Edgcomb, 125
Edgecomb, 125, 208
Edson, 22, 59
Eerickson, 75
Eggleston, 19, 59
Eike, 59
Eisfelder, 59, 154, 194
Eisfelter, 59
Eitzert, 47, 59
Elanuagah, 167
Elder, 59, 138, 183, 242
Eldon, 33, 59
Election Results, 59, 60, 196
Elger, 33, 60
Ellefson, 42, 59, 60, 184
Ellifson, 60
Ellingson, 188
Elliott, 60
Ellis, 7, 60, 143, 194, 196, 208, 242
Ellsworth, 208
Elmandorf, 61
Elston, 61
Elton, 137
Ely, 15, 39, 61, 72
Emberson, 61, 172, 195
Emendorf, 61
Emery, 61, 132
Emmons, 208
Endfield, 61
Eng, 61
Engle, 61, 174, 177
English, 2, 13, 33, 110
Enos, 51
Enright, 61, 71, 141, 203, 208, 227
Enyart, 61, 180

Epp, 242
Epsworth League, 148
Erickson, 61, 147
Erricson, 61
Esler, 60
Esman, 208
Estes, 61
Evans, 11, 14, 19, 48, 54, 61, 62, 66, 75, 77, 104, 109, 113, 133, 148, 158, 161, 166, 167, 170, 172, 175, 242
Eversoll, 208
Everson, 60, 62, 89
Ewers, 22, 38, 50, 60, 62, 63, 65, 69, 70, 84, 116, 117, 147, 166, 174, 176, 180, 217, 242
Ewing, 208
Eyers, 63

F

Fairchild, 63
Falley, 167
Fanny, 63
Fant, 208
Fardy, 242
Farewell, 131
Faris, 2, 63, 196
Farmer, 63, 102
Farnham, 64, 167
Farnsworth, 184
Farquarharson, 203
Farquharson, 63, 110, 201
Farr, 60, 133
Farrell, 64, 125, 208
Farrin, 64
Farris, 121, 208
Farth, 208
Faulkner, 208
Faust, 64
Favor, 5, 10, 19, 64, 71, 84, 124, 158, 166, 182
Fawcett, 64
Fay, 64
Fayant, 128
Fear, 151
Felde, 76
Felton, 32, 64
Felty, 64
Fennimore, 64
Fennimore Businessmen, 64
Fennimore High School, 27
Fennimore's Forefathers, 139
Ferguson, 29, 58, 60, 64, 77, 89, 167, 177, 195, 217, 223
Ferrel, 31, 208, 215
Ferrell, 64
Ferris, 64, 163
Ferryboat, 125, 179
Fetterhoff, 64
Fettie, 65
Fetty, 65
Field, 65, 139, 149, 155, 208
Filkins, 65, 184

Finegan, 152
Finkle, 65, 218, 221
Finley, 76
Finn, 13
Finnegan, 208
Finnel, 208
Finney, 65, 133, 219, 221
Finstad, 242
Fish, 20, 27, 62, 65, 89, 147
Fishel, 15, 65
Fisher, 37, 64, 65, 147, 171, 226
Fitch, 66, 75
Fitzgerald, 208
Fitzgibbons, 66
Flagg, 66
Flanagan, 35, 44, 66, 123, 148, 219, 221
Flannagon, 66
Flannigan, 66
Fleck, 208
Fleming, 53, 66, 170
Flett, 242
Flinn, 66
Flint, 66, 143, 188
Floaten, 179
Flora, 204, 208
Flugstad, 60
Flynn, 45, 66, 76, 128, 179
Fogo, 177
Foley, 66
Folie, 15, 66, 77
Folks, 66
Folsom, 66, 124
Folson, 111
Folyer, 9, 67
Foner, 52, 67
Fonrt, 70
Fopper, 60, 67, 167
Ford, 19, 23, 67, 208, 227, 242
Foreman, 67, 83
Forest City Cornet Band, 90
Forey, 34, 35, 67, 173
Former, 208
Forseth, 67, 175, 177, 201, 227
Forsyth, 208
Forsythe, 218
Fort Crawford, 37
Fortney, 67, 144, 222
Fortune, 112
Fosdick, 36, 65, 70, 217, 223
Foshay, 67
Foster, 7, 50, 58, 59, 67, 83, 208, 223
Fourt, 67, 71, 80, 116, 167, 174, 217
Foust, 159, 208
Fowel, 67
Fowell, 2, 62, 67, 68, 91
Fowler, 5, 52, 68, 70
Fox, 16, 19, 68, 128, 189, 208
Fralick, 68
France, 68, 119, 203, 208
Francisco, 5, 33, 68, 119, 203, 208, 215, 227
Francois, 68
Frank, 68, 119, 121, 208

Franklin, 4, 14, 28, 31, 38, 42, 56, 59, 60, 66, 75, 81, 122, 151, 152, 168, 177, 183, 184, 188, 208
Franzeni, 14, 68
Franzini, 79
Frater, 68
Frazier, 1, 68, 69, 148, 172, 219, 221
Free, 36, 69
Freed, 208
Freehoff, 10, 69, 218
Freeman, 42, 59, 69, 223
Freis, 69
French, 50, 51, 59, 69, 85, 90, 102, 145, 163, 192, 208, 223
French trader, 90
French trading post, 183
Freymiller, 25
Friar, 69, 134
Fridell, 221
Frie, 69
Frier, 69, 230
Frisk, 132, 135
Fritz, 18, 69, 72, 182
Frohawk, 135
Fry, 69, 70, 208
Frye, 70
Fuka, 70
Fuller, 18, 208
Fulton, 25, 39
Funk, 70, 115, 155
Furderer, 70, 131, 159
Furguson, 89
Furman, 2, 70, 71, 74, 81, 89, 94, 195, 217
Fursch, 121

G

Gadola, 14, 71, 74
Gage, 64, 71
Gaithwait, 71
Gale, 101
Gallaher, 219
Gander, 38, 50, 76, 190, 242
Gannon, 149, 201
GAR, 24, 70, 71, 96, 118, 156, 161, 167, 180
Gardner, 24, 71, 81, 82, 92, 111, 175, 179, 183, 184, 208, 218
Garlick, 71
Garmo, 218
Garner, 71, 208, 242
Garratt, 71
Garret, 71, 72
Garrett, 71, 72, 121, 201, 227
Garthwait, 208
Garthwaite, 100, 208
Garvey, 72, 76, 208, 230
Garvin, 196, 208
Gates, 72, 115, 173, 208
Gault, 29
Gay, 60, 61, 72, 167, 176, 177, 208
Gaylord, 185
Gear, 176

Geddes, 79
Geesa, 72, 196
Geese, 72, 157
Genola, 72
George, 72
German Lutheran Church, 1, 21, 33, 70, 72, 116, 154, 155
Gese, 72
Getter, 72
Geurnsey, 72
Geyer, 53, 208
Ghory, 72
Gibb, 26
Gibbert, 20
Gibbon, 206, 208
Gibbons, 72, 208
Gibbs, 54, 60, 70, 72, 73, 151, 177, 208, 217, 227
Gibson, 94
Gienk, 73
Gilbert, 57, 71, 73, 208
Gilbertson, 73, 90
Gill, 73
Gillas, 73
Gillett, 25, 73, 151, 182
Gillette, 60, 73
Gilley, 188
Gilliam, 73
Gillian, 208
Gillingham, 208
Gillman, 208
Gilman, 73, 113
Gilmore, 73
Girdler, 208
Glaiser, 73
Glass, 1, 73, 147
Gleason, 43
Glenn, 73
Glick, 73
Glodery, 42, 59, 74, 89, 191, 223
Glynn, 74, 196, 230
Goan, 208
Gobin, 74
Goble, 64
Gochenauer, 74
Gochenaur, 142
Gochnour, 74
Godfrey, 50, 74, 190
Godola, 74
Goehde, 74
Gohring, 111
Gokey, 74
Golden, 8, 74
Goldrick, 219, 221
Goman, 74
Good Templar, 74, 171
Good Templars, 41, 143, 148, 161, 171, 189
Goode, 51, 74, 102
Goodenow, 19
Goodrich, 84
Goodridge, 74
Goodvillage, 74, 97, 194
Goodwin, 208

Goraline, 221
Gordecke, 201
Gorden, 74
Gorder, 74
Gordon, 1, 74, 152, 242
Gorman, 49, 74, 174
Gornan, 74
Gorrell, 100
Gorsline, 75, 142
Gosling, 75, 97
Gott, 54, 75, 110, 147, 184, 218
Gotting, 75
Gotz, 215
Gould, 53, 69, 75, 87, 104, 160, 175, 208, 222
Govier, 64, 75
Goyer, 20, 41, 75, 147, 181
Grace, 193
Graduates, 76
Graham, 4, 64, 76, 97, 115, 130
Graiser, 76
Grandstaff, 76, 136
Grant, 76, 119, 153, 203, 215, 219
Grass, 41, 76
Graves, 13, 35, 64, 76, 208
Gray, 3, 51, 77, 145, 169, 208, 227
Grazer, 21, 77
Green, 9, 39, 40, 60, 63, 64, 66, 70, 71, 74, 77, 83, 111, 161, 167, 170, 196, 208, 215, 217, 223
Greene, 76, 77
Greenfield, 208
Greenman, 42, 77
Grenum, 71
Gribbel, 208
Gribble, 77, 100, 119, 215
Gribile, 208
Griesbach, 76
Griest, 77, 115
Griffin, 35, 42, 55, 64, 77, 89, 163, 179, 185, 195, 196, 221
Griffis, 77
Griffith, 64
Grimm, 78
Grimsby, 242
Grindell, 40, 208
Grinsell, 219
Griswold, 78
Groom, 78, 208
Grosbeck, 73
Gross, 10, 51, 78, 133, 165
Grote, 78
Groves, 33, 51, 78, 100, 218, 221
Groyer, 156
Gruber, 78, 242
Grunn, 209
Gudhertz, 78
Guentzel, 78, 87
Guilford, 209
Guilfuss, 129
Guist, 12, 78
Guldbrand, 242
Gullford, 218
Gulliford, 101

Gullord, 78, 219, 221
Gunderson, 12, 56, 60, 78, 124, 128, 152, 157, 168
Gunerus, 78
Guntzel, 78
Gupth, 42, 78
Guptill, 42, 78
Gurnsey, 78
Gurpsey, 209
Gussetti, 14, 75, 78, 151
Gustison, 78

H

Hackett, 79
Hackner, 70, 115, 242
Hackney, 79, 126, 242
Hadden, 242
Hadley, 79, 167, 209
Haggarty, 176
Haggerty, 68, 209
Haggman, 209
Haigh, 23, 53, 79, 115, 169, 242
Haines, 11, 18, 78, 79, 177
Hainsworth, 79
Hake, 209
Halderson, 32, 79
Haldorson, 60
Hale, 30, 62, 65, 79, 104, 105, 117, 144, 147, 148, 157, 189, 209, 223
Hall, 17, 43, 60, 66, 79, 92, 106, 209, 221
Halleck, 158
Hallen, 209
Halpin, 32
Halstead, 209
Halsted, 188
Halverson, 16, 80
Halvorson, 242
Hambleton, 99
Hamblin, 80
Hamilton, 80, 87, 111, 161, 209, 221, 225
Hammer, 67, 80
Hammerly, 80, 225
Hammond, 80, 151, 209
Hancock, 80
Hand, 68, 76
Haney, 209
Hankins, 80, 177
Hanks, 80, 146, 159
Hanley, 230
Hanly, 230
Hansen, 222
Hanson, 16, 40, 80, 81, 88, 97, 135, 155, 220, 242
Hapgood, 209
Hardin, 135
Harding, 167, 209
Hare, 50, 60, 70, 71, 81, 164
Harkins, 209
Harlocker, 111
Harn, 81
Harner, 209

Harper, 81, 144
Harrington, 74, 81, 94, 133, 162
Harris, 34, 42, 49, 51, 81, 82, 97, 106, 108, 133, 143, 155, 156, 169, 175, 192, 197, 242
Harrison, 24, 82, 107, 121, 138, 243
Harrower, 82, 134, 196
Harrows, 209
Harsberger, 209
Hart, 117, 146, 209, 227
Hartman, 57
Hartwell, 82, 137
Harvey, 82, 209
Haskell, 82, 113, 133, 134
Hasking, 82, 175
Haskins, 82, 149, 209, 225
Hastings, 82
Haston, 209
Hatch, 82
Hauge, 82, 221
Haughton, 1, 4, 7, 13, 14, 18, 38, 39, 41, 42, 43, 48, 50, 74, 76, 82, 83, 99, 101, 118, 120, 126, 131, 153, 161, 164, 173, 182, 194, 218, 243
Hauxshurst, 41, 83
Havens, 77, 83, 136, 161, 215, 243
Haverley, 7, 67, 83
Haverly, 13, 83, 223
Hawes, 83
Hawkins, 83
Hawley, 64, 83, 201
Hayden, 34, 60, 83, 163, 197, 209, 223
Haydon, 83
Hayes, 83, 111, 209
Hayman, 204, 216
Haynes, 83
Hazeltine, 4, 83, 84
Hazelton, 8, 84, 175, 179, 183
Hazen, 50, 76, 84, 96, 218, 221
Heal, 23, 27, 84, 108, 176, 177, 221, 223
Heald, 41, 42, 84, 164, 223
Healey, 218
Healy, 177
Heart, 144
Heathcoat, 153
Hebard, 65, 84, 102, 129, 147
Hebbard, 15, 30, 39, 61, 84
Heberlin, 72, 84
Heberling, 57, 84
Heckendorn, 219
Hedding, 218
Heffard, 84
Hefferman, 218, 221
Hefner, 209
Heil, 84
Heine, 84, 173
Heiss, 42
Helbig, 72, 243
Helgerson, 20, 60, 84
Heligar, 167
Heligas, 113
Heller, 85, 91, 145, 201
Hellmand, 85

Hellmund, 85, 147
Helm, 209
Helmond, 85
Helmund, 85, 89, 93, 147
Helpman, 34, 85, 133
Hemenway, 50, 85, 146
Hemingway, 89
Henderson, 5, 13, 15, 26, 52, 76, 81, 85, 112, 119, 131, 139, 209, 223, 227
Hendrick, 85
Hendricks, 243
Henerson, 12, 13
Henika, 56, 85, 147
Henkle, 96
Henrich, 85
Henry, 59, 85, 147, 209, 221
Henthorn, 85, 86, 147, 181
Herbst, 39
Hermanson, 60
Herold, 209
Herpel, 179
Herrick, 86
Hershey, 35
Hesler, 86
Hess, 86
Hetland, 147
Heupel, 86
Hewey, 86
Hewitt, 51, 86, 209
Hibbard, 146
Hibberd, 131
Hickey, 86
Hickling, 91
Hickok, 4, 28, 70, 71, 74, 77, 86, 167, 193, 209, 217, 223
Higgins, 189
Higinbotham, 86, 182
Hildebrand, 19, 87, 122, 124, 138, 139, 186
Hildebrant, 134
Hill, 1, 42, 69, 86, 87, 111, 167, 184, 190, 217, 218, 222, 243
Hillman, 243
Hinders, 46, 87
Hinds, 18, 50, 51, 59, 87, 133, 149, 151, 161, 184, 223
Hine, 87, 96
Hiner, 87
Hines, 209
Hinks, 87
Hinkst, 13, 87, 149, 218
Hinn, 64, 72, 87, 105, 137, 154, 202
Hire, 87, 120
Hitchcock, 146, 167, 186, 243
Hoadley, 70, 81, 87
Hobbs, 167
Hobis, 88
Hobus, 201
Hockenbury, 88
Hocking, 81, 88, 151
Hodge, 50, 88, 217, 223
Hodges, 88
Hodgins, 88, 135

Hof, 88, 101, 243
Hoff, 88
Hoffland, 76
Hoffman, 88
Hogan, 243
Hogenfrost, 243
Hogle, 88
Hoke, 209
Holberg, 88, 243
Holbrook, 209
Holcomb, 46, 88, 127, 186, 194, 209, 221
Holford, 209
Holin, 30
Hollander, 223
Holliday, 209
Hollinger, 15, 88, 183
Holm, 152, 157
Holmes, 50
Holms, 191
Holton, 88
Holverson, 43
Homer, 10, 88
Homestead, 184
Homsted, 133
Honaker, 221
Honn, 141
Honor Roll, 51, 89
Hood, 209, 243
Hook, 89
Hoover, 89, 196
Hooverson, 89
Hoper, 209
Hopkins, 7, 19, 27, 31, 32, 65, 77, 89, 125, 209
Hopp, 221
Hoppin, 36, 89
Hopwood, 89
Hornby, 218, 221
Horsefall, 196
Horsfall, 89, 209
Horstman, 13, 33
Horton, 89, 105, 219, 221, 243
Hoskins, 160
Hosmer, 89
Host, 50, 89, 90
Houghton, 39, 59, 90, 101, 103, 106, 130, 136, 144, 150, 153, 170, 171, 183, 191, 197, 209, 223, 226, 243
Houn, 215
How, 73, 90
Howard, 39
Howarth, 77, 90, 188
Howe, 30, 90, 110, 147
Howell, 64
Howerth, 90
Hoyt, 42, 90, 106, 147, 209
Huard, 90, 113, 167
Hubbard, 12, 15, 17, 58, 59, 65, 70, 73, 77, 82, 89, 90, 110, 115, 121, 126, 134, 149, 165, 166, 209, 243
Hubbell, 2, 19, 30, 41, 72, 90, 116, 151, 201, 227
Hudson, 90, 177, 209

Huey, 215
Huff, 90, 119, 203, 209, 227
Huffman, 56, 90, 91, 176
Hufschmidt, 91
Hughbanks, 75
Hughes, 91, 141
Hughey, 19
Hull, 209
Hulls, 91
Hummel, 91
Hummell, 91
Humphrey, 91
Hunson, 209
Hunt, 91
Hunter, 219, 221
Hunting, 209
Huntington, 91, 92, 223
Hurd, 19, 24, 31, 80, 92, 96, 104, 109, 112, 122, 124, 138, 139, 146, 151, 160, 166, 186, 188, 201, 227, 243
Hurlbert, 92
Hurlburt, 92, 202, 223
Hurlbut, 2, 36, 43, 49, 61, 92, 141, 147, 148, 149, 168, 209, 243
Hurlbutt, 94
Hurley, 50, 92, 93, 112
Hurrd, 41
Huschka, 139
Huse, 93
Hushka, 93
Huston, 93, 173
Hutchenson, 74, 190, 243
Hutchins, 170, 177
Hutchison, 44, 65, 93, 94, 102, 147
Hutson, 76, 94, 209, 217
Hutton, 221
Huugerford, 209
Hyde, 90, 94, 120, 171, 174, 176, 177
Hynes, 209

I

I.O.G.T., 36, 106, 148, 171
I.O.O.F., 19, 44, 50, 178, 179
Ibach, 106
Independent Foresters, 147
Indian, 16, 24, 37, 50, 53, 72, 91, 97, 109, 163, 171, 194, 226
Indian Relics, 53
Indians, 24, 37, 50, 97, 109, 171, 188
Infield, 92, 94
Ingebretson, 94
Ingebrigtin, 94
Ingersol, 39, 94
Ingersoll, 13, 36, 38, 42, 50, 57, 59, 60, 69, 94, 142, 156, 223
Ingham, 35, 94, 176, 225
Ingle, 91
Ingraham, 225
Inman, 94
International Order of Odd Fellows, 12
Irish, 126, 130, 243
Iron Brigade, 23, 70, 154, 190
Irving, 209

Ishmel, 209
Itgham, 225
Iverson, 76
Ivey, 95

J

Jackson, 14, 95, 105, 126, 179, 209, 215, 219, 221, 243
Jacobs, 95, 209, 215, 228
Jacobson, 95, 132, 219
Jacobus, 87, 95, 170, 217, 221
Jacoby, 209
Jaeger, 42
James, 50, 70, 95, 96, 117, 143, 167, 209, 217, 230
Jameson, 96, 165, 243
Jansen, 243
Jansky, 219
Jarvis, 133, 177
Jefferson, 1, 5, 96, 99, 131, 243
Jeffries, 96
Jeide, 96, 209
Jelinek, 70
Jencks, 96, 124, 201, 228, 243
Jenkins, 61, 76, 96, 196
Jenness, 218
Jenney, 39, 243
Jennings, 76, 96, 109
Jeredoe, 209
Jerman, 60, 184
Jervis, 179
Jesuit Missionary, 24
Jetter, 33, 96
Jewell, 42, 96, 192
Joby, 209
John, 97
Johns, 218
Johnson, 17, 31, 60, 70, 73, 76, 80, 81, 85, 97, 98, 137, 140, 149, 182, 184, 194, 209, 215, 219, 221, 243
Johnsroot, 98
Johnston, 59
Johnstone, 62, 98, 147
Jones, 12, 37, 43, 83, 98, 110, 111, 147, 148, 176, 209, 215, 243
Jope, 98
Joran, 75
Jordan, 42, 60, 98, 99, 149, 174, 191
Jordon, 99, 174
Joseph, 7, 8, 42, 59, 79, 99, 131, 192, 223
Josephson, 65
Joslyn, 209
Joy, 76
Jrmbois, 99
Judge, 99
Judkins, 99
Juelson, 99
Julien, 209
Juston, 60

K

Kahlar, 17, 89
Kahler, 89, 223
Kaitenbach, 99, 101
Kalenbach, 99
Kalhar, 10, 51, 60, 74, 92, 99, 100, 118
Kalish, 100
Kaltenbach, 99, 101
Kaltenback, 100
Kalvestran, 100
Kanable, 15, 100
Kane, 100, 130, 134, 209, 223
Kanouse, 209
Karrigan, 100
Kast, 21, 35, 43, 100, 133, 159, 168, 209
Kau, 100
Kavanaugh, 100
Kayo, 100
Kazda, 100, 150
Keating, 179, 230
Keeley, 243
Keene, 39, 100, 209
Keheun, 217
Keily, 100
Keir, 218
Keiren, 51, 100
Keirin, 100
Keity, 202, 228
Kellar, 100
Keller, 33, 69
Kelley, 100
Kellicut, 100
Kellogg, 10, 19, 27, 67, 100, 101, 114, 122, 134, 145, 147, 149, 152, 193, 204, 209, 214, 215, 222, 228
Kelly, 48, 209
Kelsey, 35, 101
Keltenbech, 201
Kelts, 24, 92, 101, 179
Kelty, 21, 60, 96, 101, 196, 203, 215
Kemper, 101
Kendall, 61, 99, 101, 146, 176, 177, 209, 223
Kendrick, 209
Kenefic, 55, 101, 106
Kenefick, 106, 111
Kennedy, 219
Kenneflick, 225
Kent, 101
Kenyon, 101
Keop, 102
Kermott, 3, 102, 243
Kerndt, 102
Kerr, 38, 102
Kershner, 165
Ketch, 102
Ketchum, 102, 105
Ketelinger, 209
Ketlinger, 209
Keyes, 23, 102, 183, 209, 210, 218
Keys, 102, 189
Kickapoo Athletic Club, 102
Kid, 102
Kidd, 63
Kiefner, 243
Kier, 221
Kieren, 1, 5, 102
Kilpatrick, 210
Kimball, 4, 102, 201, 203, 214, 215
Kimberlin, 67, 102
Kimgry, 102, 132
Kincannon, 102, 210, 215
Kinder, 102, 210
Kindig, 210
King, 102, 167, 210, 218, 223
Kingsland, 39, 102
Kingston, 102, 103
Kinney, 103, 157, 210
Kintzinger, 80
Kinzie, 103
Kipp, 103
Kirby, 103, 145, 210
Kirkham, 210
Kirkpatrick, 103, 154
Kish, 103, 180
Kissack, 103
Kissock, 210
Kistler, 19, 103
Kitch, 103, 188
Kite, 210
Klanskey, 103
Klansky, 103
Klausky, 103
Klegg, 103
Kline, 103, 176, 177, 219
Kloak, 40, 103
Klok, 103
Klook, 103
Knapp, 35, 103, 210, 243
Knaub, 103, 204
Knight, 103, 243
Knower, 103, 104, 149
Knowlton, 19, 42, 104
Knox, 196
Knutson, 104, 133, 177, 186
Koenig, 155
Koepet, 104
Kohn, 104
Kolb, 104
Konkee, 193
Korber, 104
Kost, 215
Kot, 104, 180
Kraemer, 104
Krans, 210
Kratchwell, 104
Kratochwill, 104
Krauss, 51
Kretsch, 104
Kreul, 21, 72, 104
Kronschage, 104
Kronshage, 60, 104, 179, 201
Krouse, 104
Krouskop, 179
Krumm, 223
Kumarine, 203
Kumreen, 36
Kumrein, 119
Kurtz, 29, 104, 105, 108, 171
Kussel, 105
Kyes, 105
Kyser, 89, 105
Kyzer, 210

L

La Baron, 243
La Flash, 105
Lacy, 105, 210, 217
Ladd, 51
Ladies Aid Society, 46
Ladies Mite Society, 105
Laheurty, 105
Laird, 105, 243
Lake, 105, 221
Lamb, 37, 105, 127, 145
Lambert, 105, 115, 128, 175, 192
Lamma, 218, 221
Lamphire, 105
Lamprict, 105, 160
Lanam, 105
Lance, 76, 105, 131, 210
Lane, 11, 16, 19, 51, 70, 79, 89, 96, 101, 102, 105, 106, 110, 111, 187
Lang, 106
Langdon, 48, 106, 180, 225
Lange, 7, 27, 106
Langford, 106, 193
Langlais, 106
Lankford, 42, 106
Larimer, 130, 210
LaRoque, 106
Larson, 11, 20, 79, 81, 106, 131, 178, 184, 210, 223
Latamore, 106
Lathrop, 20, 44, 103, 106, 210, 215, 225, 228
Latimer, 8, 106, 107, 133, 139
Latimore, 71, 107, 155, 167
Latshaw, 34, 35, 50, 59, 60, 64, 67, 77, 83, 107, 223
Lattie, 107
Lattimore, 106, 217
Laughlin, 137
Lavis, 107
Law, 14, 107
Lawler, 6, 167
Lawrence, 2, 12, 36, 39, 40, 42, 50, 51, 60, 70, 74, 76, 84, 89, 96, 107, 108, 111, 119, 178, 184, 193, 196, 215, 218, 223
Lawson, 60, 108
Lawton, 51, 108
Lawver, 108, 133, 175
Laydan, 108
Layer, 31, 108
Laylan, 108, 151
Laylans, 108
Layne, 108, 149
Layton, 109

Lazenby, 109
Leach, 171
Leahy, 221
Leamere, 109
Leasle, 76
Leasman, 109, 131
Leatherberry, 109
Leavitt, 34, 64, 126, 243
Lee, 109, 160, 193
Leech, 109
Lees, 70, 109, 167, 174, 217, 219
Leiving, 109
Lemen, 59, 109, 223
Lemon, 109, 154
Lemont, 210
Lemy, 109
Lenahan, 76, 109, 148
Lench, 36, 89, 243
Lenehan, 109, 130
Lengele, 106
Lennox, 210
Leoby, 6, 109
Lepley, 146, 167
Lesler, 5, 63, 90, 109, 110, 124, 131, 166, 179, 186, 201, 202, 203
Lesser, 210
Levergreen, 32, 110
Levings, 110
Lewis, 3, 11, 50, 56, 58, 62, 74, 100, 110, 118, 134, 194, 195, 210, 219, 223, 243
Lewison, 110, 111
Lien, 111
Limbocker, 19, 60, 111, 188, 201, 228
Lincoln, 111
Lind, 50, 60, 111
Lindemann, 50
Linderlin, 23
Linderman, 111, 181
Lindsay, 171, 179
Linke, 218
Linn, 111
Linsay, 177
Linsendorf, 210
Linton, 64, 210
Liscum, 111
Liseum, 111
Literary Society, 18, 73, 111, 161
Livingston, 161
Locke, 210
Lockwood, 111
Lodewick, 169
Loftus, 8, 13, 26, 42, 50, 60, 74, 89, 108, 109, 111, 112, 139, 152, 168, 218, 223, 225
Logan, 7, 112
Logue, 210
Lombard, 76, 87, 112, 128, 149
Lombart, 112
Lonahans, 91
Loney, 54, 112
Long, 20, 23, 110, 112
Longbottom, 112
Longcore, 35

Longmire, 112
Loomis, 72, 112, 124, 210, 243
Looney, 64
Loper, 29, 89, 112, 173
Lord, 112, 139
Lorimer, 112
Lossin, 174
Lough, 85, 112
Loux, 185
Love, 112, 113, 131
Loveless, 174
Lovewell, 176
Loving, 150
Low, 143, 225
Lowe, 210
Lowell, 120
Lowers, 113
Lowrie, 40, 60, 74, 89, 113, 149, 161
Lowry, 93
Loy, 210
Lubke, 113
Lucas, 113
Lucis, 14, 113
Luckey, 11, 113
Ludewig, 218
Lull, 113, 167
Lund, 8, 60, 113, 144
Lunde, 113
Luth, 113, 117, 223
Luxom, 113
Lybrand, 177
Lykes, 210
Lyman, 113
Lynch, 60
Lynett, 230
Lynxville, 113
Lyon, 59, 60, 210
Lyons, 81, 112, 113, 151, 155, 210
Lysne, 60
Lyster, 113
Lytle, 38, 113
Lytlle, 111
Lyttle, 50, 55, 86, 113, 114, 133, 134, 188

M

Mabbatt, 210
MacDonald, 195
Mack, 179
Mackie, 7, 114
MacMurray, 243
Madden, 210, 218
Maddox, 182
Maeby, 114
Maeliotka, 22, 114
Maes, 243
Mahan, 210
Mahoney, 4, 50, 114, 149, 220, 221
Mahony, 76
Maiben, 2, 47, 114, 147, 180
Main, 59, 76, 114, 198
Maine, 114

Malcomson, 176, 177
Malin, 114
Mallalley, 114
Maltrasia, 114
Manchester, 210
Manger, 114
Manhart, 42
Mankey, 146
Manley, 115
Manlon, 115
Mann, 10, 70, 115, 121, 197
Mannel, 210
Manning, 115
Mansfield, 50, 76, 115
Mara, 115
Marin, 15, 115
Mark, 210
Markee, 184
Marker, 41, 50, 94, 115, 120
Markham, 115
Markle, 115
Marks, 115, 161
Markt, 115
Markum, 115
Marsen, 139
Marsh, 115, 210
Marshal, 223
Marshall, 54, 219
Marshell, 115, 126
Marsten, 77
Marston, 77, 115, 116
Mart, 210
Marten, 116, 182
Martin, 116, 150, 154, 210, 243
Martner, 76
Marton, 177
Mason, 42, 70, 71, 96, 116, 153, 167
Masonic Lodge, 3, 116
Masonic Order, 198
Massiker, 116
Mather, 210
Mathew, 215
Mathews, 76, 106, 116, 179, 210, 219, 228
Mathias, 182
Maupin, 178
Maxum, 116
Maxwell, 71, 116, 167, 217
May, 61, 101, 116, 203, 210, 215, 221
Mayhan, 51, 117
Mayhew, 210
Mayo, 210
McAfee, 117
McAllister, 117
McAuley, 2, 28, 29, 60, 69, 109, 113, 117, 167, 176, 223, 225
McBergh, 117
McCabe, 43
McCarthy, 18, 117, 210
McCarty, 63, 117, 146, 149, 219, 221, 225
McCaskey, 117
McClaran, 110, 117, 118
McClary, 118

Genealogical Events from Newspapers for Crawford, Vernon and Grant Counties, Wisconsin, 1870-1901

McClasky, 181, 244
McClay, 29
McCleary, 210
McClimans, 141
McClintock, 210
McClung, 120, 133, 244
McClurg, 76, 90, 99, 118, 221
McClury, 118
McClymen, 214
McCoey, 221
McCollum, 3, 25, 118
McConnell, 115, 184
McCord, 118, 160, 215, 228
McCormick, 29, 45, 66, 76, 94, 118, 119, 121, 149
McCouey, 118
McCoy, 24, 210
McCracken, 147
McCrillis, 74, 118, 173, 176
McDaniel, 1, 64, 76, 118, 140, 168, 215
McDaniels, 210
McDermont, 56
McDermott, 118, 119, 141, 218, 221
McDermout, 244
McDill, 8, 29, 36, 42, 105, 119, 190, 223
McDonald, 76, 118, 119, 129, 163, 210, 223
McDougal, 210, 215
McDowel, 38
McDowell, 2, 50, 60, 89, 117, 119, 120, 132, 147, 149, 163, 187, 223, 225
McEathron, 4, 118, 120, 133
McEathrun, 120
McEvoy, 26, 120
McFadden, 120
McFall, 30
McFarland, 120, 210
McFee, 218, 221
McGarry, 218
McGill, 221
McGinley, 244
McGinnis, 41, 51, 120
McGonical, 154
McGonigal, 120, 134, 201
McGowan, 120
McGranahan, 120
McGraw, 53, 120, 162
McGrew, 120
McGuigan, 44, 120
McGuinness, 120
McGuinnis, 120, 131
McHarg, 87, 120
McHugh, 121
McIntyre, 121, 184
McKay, 49, 50, 121, 124, 126, 176, 177, 244
McKee, 121
McKendree, 176, 177
McKenzie, 218
McKinfrey, 210
McKinney, 4, 19, 76, 80, 119, 121, 203, 210, 228
McKitrick, 121

McKittrick, 68, 121
McKnight, 210
McLain, 210
McLaine, 121
McLamans, 121
McLaughlin, 4, 9, 16, 19, 23, 30, 35, 46, 48, 51, 55, 61, 76, 100, 101, 104, 105, 106, 112, 114, 119, 131, 132, 148, 150, 159, 166, 173, 175, 193, 194, 198, 203, 210, 215
McLean, 121, 141
McLiman, 20, 121
McLimans, 115, 121
McLyman, 210
McMahan, 110
McMahon, 121
McManamy, 122, 218
McMaster, 13, 24, 76, 214, 244
McMasters, 80, 97
McMichael, 12, 78, 128, 168, 184
McMillan, 122, 124, 244
McMillen, 33, 122
McMillin, 122, 244
McMillion, 210
McMullen, 122
McMurray, 122
McNair, 54, 119, 122
McNamara, 60, 76
McNamee, 122
McNeely, 122
McNeese, 244
McNelly, 53, 122
McNuse, 244
McPherson, 122
McPheters, 111, 182
McQueen, 122
McRenolds, 122
McReynolds, 18, 47, 122, 146, 244
McShane, 223
McShore, 122
McSpaden, 30, 102, 104, 122, 123, 166, 201, 228
McSweeney, 28, 122, 123
McVay, 123
McVey, 66, 123
McWilliams, 123, 142, 178, 179, 184, 210, 228
Meacham, 123, 218, 221
Meachem, 18
Meade, 34
Meagher, 76
Medary, 123
Medd, 126, 244
Meechan, 123
Meeker, 123
Meger, 15
Meister, 159
Mellen, 50, 60, 70, 75, 94, 123, 149, 184, 217
Mellum, 31, 108
Melton, 123, 223
Melvin, 73, 76, 123, 221
Menert, 210
Menges, 43

Menkhausen, 9, 123
Menkhauser, 58, 123
Mepesmith, 54
Merchant, 123, 162
Meredith, 210
Merrell, 176
Merriam, 150
Merrick, 123
Merrill, 12, 13, 14, 21, 89, 177
Mertz, 72
Merwin, 215, 228
Messersmith, 53, 124
Messmore, 27
Metcalf, 124
Methodist Ministers, 124
Metic, 124
Metric, 124
Mettic, 124
Mettick, 16
Metz, 124
Mexican War, 39, 54, 70, 116, 167
Meyer, 11, 33, 34, 35, 59, 110, 112, 124, 149, 186, 193, 202, 228
Meyers, 9, 130, 204, 210
Michaels, 124
Michaelsohn, 50
Michelet, 42
Middleton, 26, 124, 147
Midthum, 55, 124, 131
Miles, 24, 28, 42, 96, 125, 151, 176, 210, 228
Milham, 125
Millard, 125
Millards, 180
Miller, 14, 16, 29, 36, 42, 43, 59, 60, 64, 70, 71, 76, 83, 89, 105, 108, 113, 115, 119, 125, 126, 128, 142, 164, 167, 170, 176, 177, 178, 181, 184, 210, 214, 216, 217, 219, 223, 244
Millett, 126
Milliken, 50, 70, 81, 126
Mills, 53, 75, 126, 143, 153, 219, 221
Mindham, 49, 61
Miner, 66, 83, 95, 99, 126, 149, 158, 210
Ministerial Appointments, 126
Minkhausen, 58, 123
Minnesota Packet Company, 169
Minor, 13, 126, 127, 128, 182
Minshall, 16, 221
Mitchel, 127, 223
Mitchell, 8, 25, 48, 76, 101, 117, 119, 127, 133, 145, 176, 182, 210, 225, 244
Mithum, 127
Mitscher, 127
Mobley, 90
Mocket, 244
Moe, 127
Moen, 60, 221
Moffit, 127
Molie, 127
Molland, 60

Mollie, 127
Molly, 127
Momo, 244
Monnahan, 210
Monroe, 10, 64, 127, 210
Monson, 76, 210
Montague, 127
Monteith, 210
Monti, 9, 21, 60, 77, 86, 127, 145, 184
Montieth, 127
Montson, 127
Montz, 64
Moody, 64, 117, 127, 210, 219
Mookrie, 127
Moon, 67, 70, 127, 167, 170, 210
Mooney, 230
Moore, 29, 64, 68, 118, 127, 128, 133, 147, 153, 161, 167, 210, 223
Moran, 66, 128
Moreland, 128
Morelli, 71, 128
Morely, 184
Morevitch, 47
Morey, 210
Morgan, 22, 29, 76, 101, 128, 136, 149, 167, 174, 178, 184, 191, 196, 210, 218, 219, 222, 223, 230
Morgans, 27, 44, 111, 124, 128, 133, 161, 244
Mork, 128
Morley, 7, 93, 128, 143, 147, 184, 221
Morr, 12, 78, 128, 168
Morrelli, 71, 163
Morris, 12, 13, 19, 27, 28, 52, 102, 129, 137, 139, 150, 189, 194, 210, 211, 221, 225, 227
Morrison, 129, 211, 219, 221
Morrow, 118, 129, 211
Morse, 16, 24, 33, 39, 42, 79, 129, 133, 142, 143, 153, 189, 194, 211, 244
Mortimer, 30, 124, 129, 179, 201
Morton, 50, 129, 149, 218, 221
Moses, 129, 147, 211
Mosher, 84, 129
Moshier, 129, 187
Mosholder, 19, 129
Mosier, 129
Moss, 130
Mossholder, 130, 223
Moulton, 36, 124, 130
Moyar, 211
Mt. Sterling Academy, 22, 40, 45, 109, 130, 151, 177, 190
Mt. Zion M.E. Church, 130
Mt. Zion Methodist, 14
Mueller, 130, 219
Muffley, 9, 11, 17, 18, 19, 36, 56, 79, 82, 117, 130, 141, 166, 175, 177, 201, 203, 211, 228
Muhr, 130
Mulford, 211
Mulhair, 130, 134, 230
Mulhern, 105, 130, 244

Mulick, 42
Mullany, 76
Muller, 125, 211, 223
Mullikin, 76
Mulrooney, 230
Mumford, 131, 176
Mummy, 170
Mundt, 244
Munns, 54, 211
Munson, 131
Munyon, 93, 131, 221
Murley, 131
Murphy, 85, 119, 131, 176, 177, 188, 211, 218, 230
Murray, 131
Murry, 131
Murwin, 211
Musgrove, 131, 186
Mutchman, 21, 104, 244
Mutschman, 33
Mutschmann, 70, 155, 244
Myer, 131
Myers, 120, 129, 131, 211, 215
Mystic Workers, 190

N

Naase, 244
Naes, 244
Naese, 244
Naler, 131
Names, 131
Nash, 42, 86, 131
Natwick, 124, 131, 221
Nauert, 54, 131, 159
Nebans, 211
Neeley, 99, 131, 132
Neely, 105, 131, 211
Neff, 184
Neil, 131, 201
Neill, 14, 165, 174, 180, 198, 244
Nell, 132
Nelson, 19, 42, 64, 98, 104, 108, 111, 112, 113, 122, 132, 133, 135, 140, 175, 184, 198, 244
Nelvin, 132
Nemmick, 132
Nestingen, 221
Netwick, 184
Nevill, 132
Newberry, 102, 132
Newbury, 38, 132
Newcomb, 71, 167, 176
Newcome, 103
Newell, 53, 132, 135, 173, 184
Newick, 132
Newlin, 61, 132
Newman, 132, 162
Newspaper Subscribers, 133
Newton, 2, 4, 29, 53, 81, 114, 126, 127, 133, 149, 155, 165, 167, 176, 177, 187, 195, 217
Nice, 40, 41, 119, 141, 203, 211, 215
Nicholas, 170

Nichols, 39, 54, 108, 115, 133, 156, 161, 175, 211
Nicholson, 133
Nickerson, 71, 133, 211
Niehause, 64
Nihil, 133
Nikil, 133
Niland, 76
Nilson, 18, 104, 133
Nims, 113
Nixon, 6, 41, 120, 133, 201
Nobel, 24, 133
Nobis, 133, 188, 202, 228
Noble, 47, 133, 187, 211
Noggle, 76, 108, 113, 133, 167
Nolan, 175, 176, 211
Noon, 133, 134
Nordgaard, 244
Norris, 43, 134, 218, 219
Northus, 211
Norton, 134
Nottingham, 134
Nowotny, 134
Nuess, 67, 175, 244
Nugent, 43
Nutt, 134
Nuzum, 4, 5, 6, 14, 19, 23, 44, 49, 52, 55, 63, 77, 79, 83, 84, 106, 108, 117, 120, 124, 127, 138, 139, 144, 145, 154, 162, 177, 185, 198, 218, 221, 228, 244
Nye, 82, 134

O

O'Brien, 230
O'Connell, 218, 221
O'Shaughnessy, 230
Oakfield, 133
Oates, 211
Obereder, 134
Obreight, 134
O'Brien, 69, 134
Ochiltre, 29
Ochsenberger, 134
O'Connell, 184
O'Connors, 244
O'Daniel, 211
Odd Fellow Lodge, 134
Odd Fellows, 12, 70, 102, 116, 121, 125, 153
Officer, 134, 219
Ogden, 134, 211
Oine, 134
Okey, 211
O'Lary, 174
Old Settlers Association, 120, 134, 154
Oldenberg, 60
Older, 219
Olds, 134
O'Leary, 66, 101, 134, 135, 148, 174, 192
Oleson, 19, 60, 80, 132, 135, 203, 225
Oliason, 135

Oliver, 135, 219, 221
Olliver, 135
Olmstead, 23, 155
Olmsted, 88, 135
Olsen, 135
Olson, 97, 135, 188, 211
One-eyed Decorah, 51
O'Neil, 135
O'Neill, 135
Ophtodahl, 135
Oppreicht, 135, 225
Oram, 135, 138
O'Reilley, 244
O'Riley, 52, 135, 244
Orr, 132, 135, 223
Orrison, 135, 136, 146, 147
Orth, 112, 136
Ortscheid, 136
Orvis, 136
Osborn, 64, 136, 180, 203, 211, 228
Osborne, 136, 145, 190, 215
Osgood, 103, 130, 136, 144, 185, 197
Ostinan, 40
Ostman, 50
Ostrander, 83, 136, 140, 211, 228
Ostranders, 6
Oswald, 64, 72, 87, 105, 136, 137, 211
O'Toole, 244
Ott, 136, 137
Otteson, 97, 137, 220, 222
Otto, 43
Ottoson, 60
Overton, 125, 164
Owaley, 211
Owen, 64, 112, 133, 137
Owens, 50, 60, 137, 152, 169, 188, 211
Owsley, 137
Oyden, 211

P

Packer, 211
Page, 36, 51, 70, 71, 96, 127, 137, 167, 217
Paine, 58
Pake, 137, 211, 215
Pally, 244
Palmer, 6, 31, 82, 121, 137, 141, 179, 182, 198
Panders, 76
Pape, 29
Parce, 60, 137, 215, 228
Parfrey, 95, 137
Parish, 65, 137
Parker, 5, 17, 29, 34, 42, 45, 49, 50, 51, 57, 80, 87, 107, 110, 116, 122, 135, 137, 138, 139, 177, 179, 186, 192, 195, 201, 211, 221, 228
Parkinson, 54
Parks, 37, 211
Parnell, 44, 82, 138
Parr, 37, 138, 211
Parsons, 219, 221

Partridge, 19, 23, 75, 138, 202, 228
Pate, 169, 211
Patrick, 4, 138
Patridge, 119, 138
Patten, 43, 54, 102, 138
Patterson, 17, 60, 138, 147, 156, 172, 219, 221
Paul, 221
Paulson, 111, 138
Payne, 37, 138
Peacock, 59, 61, 72, 74, 138
Pearce, 3, 25, 118, 244
Peare, 162
Pearson, 92, 138, 211
Pearsons, 223
Pease, 71, 113, 139, 160, 167, 177
Peaslee, 60
Peck, 60, 76
Peckham, 3, 139, 153, 244
Peddicorn, 64
Peer, 112, 139
Peir, 69
Pendleton, 9, 17, 211
Pengilley, 244
Pennel, 217
Pennell, 13, 70, 139, 167
Pepper, 11, 19, 60, 139, 140, 173, 186
Peppers, 19
Perham, 6, 93, 139, 141, 143, 147, 148
Perkins, 64, 139, 151, 184
Perrigo, 1, 116
Perrin, 151
Perry, 64, 120, 244
Persing, 53
Persinger, 134
Pester, 140
Peterson, 18, 43, 54, 60, 63, 70, 76, 89, 97, 119, 132, 140, 147, 153, 155, 163, 170, 211, 215, 217, 225, 228
Petitt, 140
Pettey, 140
Pettinger, 214
Pettis, 211
Pettit, 4, 81, 118, 136, 140
Petty, 123, 140, 141, 178
Pettygrove, 135, 140
Peugh, 140
Phelon, 230
Phelps, 16, 140, 141, 173
Philamalee, 173
Philips, 37, 141
Phillamalee, 141, 211
Phillips, 59, 64, 70, 91, 92, 116, 131, 139, 141, 189, 211
Pickard, 64, 121, 133, 141, 167, 196, 211, 228
Pidcock, 141
Pier, 109, 211
Pierce, 117, 128, 139, 141, 211, 218, 221
Pierson, 211
Pigg, 141
Pike, 141, 204, 211, 215, 226

Pilz, 141
Pine, 211
Pion, 141
Pipkin, 124, 141, 142, 179, 186
Pitcher, 142
Pittenger, 142
Pittgener, 204
Pittinger, 142, 211, 228
Pittman, 19, 51, 116, 123, 124, 142, 179
Place, 42
Plait, 211
Plato, 142
Platt, 211
Plum, 142
Plummer, 142, 167, 181
Podewetz, 142
Poehler, 13, 142
Poff, 142, 153
Polander, 211
Pollard, 75, 142, 184, 218
Pollock, 142
Pomery, 142
Pommey, 142, 194
Pond, 25, 92, 128, 141, 142, 143, 147, 192
Pool, 143
Poole, 31, 143
Poorman, 219
Pope, 29
Popejoy, 64, 102
Porter, 17, 37, 43, 54, 71, 76, 89, 91, 103, 109, 133, 143, 144, 152, 160, 167, 171, 192, 196, 223, 225, 244
Posey, 144, 211
Post, 144
Postle, 144
Posy, 211
Pott, 195
Potter, 5, 144, 198, 221
Potts, 94, 144, 211, 219, 244
Powel, 52
Powell, 95, 118, 144, 218, 221
Powers, 7, 130, 136, 144, 191, 197, 211
Prater, 144, 211
Pratt, 39, 70, 144, 159, 211, 244
Preiner, 144
Prentice, 144
Prentis, 144
Prescott, 144
Prestgard, 144
Preston, 144
Price, 3, 16, 131, 132, 144, 223
Prideaux, 211
Prince, 71, 144, 167
Prindle, 144
Pritchard, 145
Privott, 145
Proctor, 145, 184, 223
Pronty, 244
Protsman, 4
Proudfit, 19, 127, 145, 181
Prouty, 211, 228

Genealogical Events from Newspapers for Crawford, Vernon and Grant Counties, Wisconsin, 1870-1901

Provin, 77, 145
Provis, 103, 145, 175, 177
Pruitt, 211
Puckett, 56, 145
Puff, 86
Pugh, 145
Pugmyre, 150
Pulham, 145
Pulley, 145, 244
Pullman, 145
Pullum, 174
Pulmann, 85, 145
Puls, 145
Pulver, 32, 42, 63, 89, 145, 146, 190, 218, 223
Punnell, 146
Purell, 211
Purington, 211
Putman, 146
Putnam, 211
Pyzer, 211

Q

Quackenbush, 146, 219, 222
Quamme, 146
Quick, 61
Quigley, 211
Quincey, 122
Quincy, 122, 146, 177, 211
Quinn, 107, 108, 123, 146, 189, 196, 222, 230
Quinnett, 146

R

Rabbitt, 146, 167
Rabehl, 245
Radcliff, 29, 105, 245
Rae, 20, 57, 84, 121, 146, 172
Rami, 85, 145, 245
Ramie, 154, 177
Ramsey, 182
Randall, 5, 26, 76, 86, 117, 129, 146, 147, 167
Randell, 167
Randolph, 32, 110
Rands, 76
Rannetsberger, 90, 147
Ranney, 147, 150
Ranny, 67
Ransom, 7, 67, 76, 120, 147, 211, 228
Ranson, 158
Rapalee, 35
Rastall, 147
Ray, 147
Readstown, 147
Readstown Ball Team, 147
Readstown Band, 128, 147
Readstown School Board, 147
Readstown Teachers, 147
Readstown Village officers, 147
Readtown I.O.G.T. Officers, 148

Rector, 211
Redmain, 148
Redmayne, 148
Reed, 68, 148
Reep, 148
Reese, 148, 180
Reeve, 51, 77, 84, 117, 129, 134, 147, 148, 183, 192, 196
Reeves, 147
Register of Deeds, 148
Regly, 82
Reichel, 119, 148, 203, 211, 214, 228
Reichert, 245
Reichman, 19, 148
Reid, 12, 80, 135, 148
Reilley, 149
Rein, 203, 228
Reinhold, 149
Reisel, 149
Reitemeyer, 159
Reiter, 50, 77, 149
Remalis, 149
Renshaw, 119, 203
Rentz, 184
Republican Ticket, 149
Resaer, 211
Rese, 19
Retreat School Exercises, 149
Retreat W.C.T.U, 149
Retreat W.C.T.U., 86, 121, 149
Revel, 195
Revolutionary War, 22, 74, 197
Rew, 211
Rewey, 110, 122
Reynolds, 90, 149, 206, 211
Rhein, 149
Rhodes, 218, 221
Rice, 19, 51, 59, 100, 119, 149, 150, 177, 185, 204, 211, 214, 223, 228, 245
Richards, 64, 147, 150, 181, 218, 228
Richardson, 119, 150, 176, 187, 193, 211, 217, 223
Richmann, 100, 150
Richter, 150
Ricks, 19, 80, 119, 150, 151, 167, 203, 204, 211, 214, 228
Rieger, 151
Rieter, 151
Rieth, 151
Riggs, 13, 52, 211
Rightmire, 176, 177
Riley, 9, 31, 54, 60, 71, 78, 128, 144, 151, 184, 218
Rily, 135
Rindlaub, 151
Rinehart, 70
Rineheart, 217
Ringinbaugh, 151
Riordan, 230
Ripley, 151, 167, 176, 211
Rippe, 151
Risen, 88, 151
Riser, 167

Ritchie, 151
Riter, 223
Rittenhouse, 167
Ritter, 30, 72, 151, 161
Rix, 151, 155
Roach, 64, 151
Robb, 151
Roberg, 151
Roberts, 71, 93, 152, 167, 173, 211, 223
Robertson, 1, 143, 152
Robery, 151, 152
Robins, 152
Robinson, 10, 23, 152, 178, 191, 203, 211, 221
Robison, 171
Robson, 35, 152, 188
Rodgers, 174
Rodolf, 118, 152
Roe, 152
Roenish, 152
Rogan, 69
Rogers, 3, 19, 24, 36, 37, 42, 50, 51, 54, 59, 60, 70, 71, 74, 78, 80, 130, 147, 148, 152, 153, 157, 167, 173, 181, 192, 203, 211, 217, 219, 221, 223, 228
Roice, 212
Rollin, 153
Rosch, 153
Roscinp, 61
Rose, 19, 36, 39, 67, 70, 85, 116, 126, 129, 133, 152, 153, 154, 174, 204, 217, 228
Roselip, 154
Roseman, 230
Rosemeyer, 154
Rosencrans, 126
Ross, 212
Rossin, 62
Roth, 73
Rothe, 87, 154
Rothschild, 221
Rough, 36, 219, 221
Rounds, 5, 76, 154, 179, 186, 212
Roundtree, 154
Rowan, 212
Rowe, 7, 19, 41, 54, 65, 154, 201
Rowell, 245
Rowen, 66
Rowley, 212
Rozencranz, 126
Ruby, 154
Ruchti, 214
Ruchtie, 154, 177
Ruck, 154
Ruka, 15, 19, 41, 51, 59, 68, 70, 72, 102, 116, 124, 154, 155, 157, 170, 188, 201, 228
Runice, 60, 81, 155
Runnigen, 60
Running, 119, 140, 218
Rusk, 4, 42, 43, 55, 96, 155, 205, 206, 212

Russ, 155, 223
Russel, 212
Russell, 2, 155, 161, 184, 222
Rutter, 42, 76, 151, 155, 156, 167, 217
Ryan, 52, 53, 94, 108, 133, 156, 175
Ryans, 170
Ryder, 212

S

Sabin, 156
Sablotzky, 35, 156
Sac, 194
Sackett, 126, 245
Sacs, 51
Sala, 156, 212
Salie, 75
Salisbury, 212
Sallander, 13, 149, 156, 167, 217
Sallender, 70, 156
Salmon, 2, 79, 110, 147, 152, 156, 157, 164, 186, 212
Salyer, 4, 138
Salzman, 157
Sampson, 76, 212, 225
Samuels, 19, 125, 164, 245
Sanborn, 215, 228
Sanderson, 157, 212, 228
Sandleback, 212
Sandlin, 72, 157
Sandmire, 6
Sandon, 157, 184
Sands, 27, 157
Sandy, 60
Sanford, 54, 157
Sanger, 116, 157, 212
Sargeant, 224
Sargent, 48, 125, 139, 157
Sarles, 19, 51, 57, 64, 100, 101, 112, 124, 140, 149, 150, 157, 158, 177, 179, 245
Satterlee, 158
Sauer, 158
Sauers, 158
Sauger, 158, 160
Saunders, 158
Savage, 145, 158
Sawyer, 23, 116, 119, 158, 202, 204, 212
Saxe, 89
Saxton, 221
Scanlan, 64, 230
Scanlon, 158, 159, 230
Schararer, 212
Schaumacher, 100
Scheble, 212
Scheinpflug, 72, 116, 159, 194
Schesiur, 159
Schidee, 86
Schierchswitz, 189
Schilds, 212
Schlong, 52, 159
Schmahlenberger, 131, 149, 154, 159
Schmidt, 159, 185, 189

Schmith, 159
Schmitt, 159
Schneider, 21, 159
Schneller, 39
Schoeberle, 16, 175, 245
Schoenfeld, 245
Schofield, 51
School Report, 159
Schovill, 100, 159
Schraudenbach, 44, 99, 101, 120, 159, 245
Schreiber, 75
Schreiner, 212
Schroeder, 160, 197
Schroudenback, 6, 104, 109, 180
Schubert, 53, 75, 133, 160
Schuchart, 138
Schumacher, 160
Schurbert, 105, 160
Schwab, 72
Schwauber, 19
Schweizer, 160
Scofield, 203, 212
Scott, 14, 80, 109, 119, 158, 160, 176, 179, 203, 212, 214
Scott Cornet Band, 28
Scovill, 212
Scoville, 76, 124, 214, 245
Scraudenbach, 130, 134
Scriffin, 75
Scriven, 160
Seaman, 11, 160
Searle, 113
Searles, 18, 92, 106, 118, 160, 245
Searls, 160
Sears, 36, 133, 161, 225
Seaton, 31, 72, 77, 78, 100, 161, 175
Secret Organizations and Societies, 161
See, 161
Seeds, 47, 91, 161
Seely, 98
Seeman, 72, 116
Sees, 161
Selblach, 222
Selle, 151, 161
Selleck, 212
Selton, 75, 161
Seventh Day Adventists Church, 21
Severson, 60, 161, 163, 164, 222
Seymore, 176, 177
Seymour, 70, 76, 105, 161, 176, 194, 217, 219
Shaffer, 161, 212
Shambaugh, 161
Shannon, 42, 212
Shaper, 59, 161
Shappell, 212
Sharman, 161
Sharp, 113, 161
Shattnck, 162
Shattuck, 218, 219
Shaughnessy, 162, 218
Shaw, 39, 50, 59, 120, 162, 167, 170, 184, 212, 214, 223

Shay, 162
Shear, 218
Shearer, 43, 54, 162
Shears, 137, 245
Sheets, 4, 162
Sheffield, 212
Sheiver, 212
Shelbach, 219
Sheldon, 162
Shepard, 162
Shephard, 245
Sheppard, 162
Shepperd, 162
Sherman, 40, 82, 161, 162, 205
Sherrard, 31, 133, 162, 201, 204, 212, 214, 228
Sherwood, 123, 162
Sheslar, 162, 189
Shesler, 41
Shied, 217
Shiek, 162
Shields, 133, 134, 212
Shilling, 162, 182
Shipley, 19, 36
Shippley, 19, 154
Shisler, 20, 137, 163, 187, 223
Shock, 163
Shockley, 159
Shocko, 224
Shorey, 42
Shorty, 19, 24
Showalter, 119, 163
Shrader, 2, 56, 63, 64, 72, 136, 139, 140, 163, 169, 173
Shroeder, 163
Shroudenback, 230
Shultz, 163
Shumway, 29, 163
Shuttleworth, 27, 64, 121, 136, 148, 163
Sickles, 164
Sicko, 163
Sidler, 212, 228
Siebert, 212
Silbaugh, 147, 163, 221
Sime, 18, 43, 62, 140, 147, 153, 161, 163, 245
Simkins, 10, 163
Simmons, 17, 163
Simons, 212
Simpkins, 19, 163, 164
Sinclair, 164
Sioux, 24
Sisley, 164
Sissman, 163
Sjerve, 60
Skaar, 184
Skildum, 218, 221
Skinner, 182
Skough, 164
Slabaych, 164
Slack, 164, 218
Slade, 50
Slater, 14, 86, 164, 177

Slaugh, 212
Slayback, 164
Sleightam, 125, 164
Slightam, 125, 164
Slighton, 164
Sloan, 212
Sloanamaker, 157, 164
Sloanes, 164
Sloggy, 164
Slosson, 212
Sloulin, 164
Slye, 164
Smalley, 164
Smeby, 245
Smelzer, 245
Smethurst, 60, 164, 212
Smiley, 20
Smith, 9, 12, 16, 21, 27, 36, 38, 43, 47, 49, 54, 55, 56, 57, 64, 70, 73, 74, 75, 96, 100, 106, 109, 118, 119, 131, 152, 153, 164, 165, 166, 168, 169, 176, 177, 182, 198, 204, 212, 218, 219, 221, 223, 224, 225, 228, 245
Smithers, 161
Smithson, 166
Smyth, 230
Smythman, 212
Sneclode, 166
Snodgrass, 124, 245
Snow, 32, 96, 113, 166, 167, 245
Snyder, 137
Soderling, 167
Soldiers of 1812 and 1861, 167
Soldiers Reunion, 167, 169
Solmon, 212
Solomon, 167
Sommars, 146, 167
Sonard, 111
Soniss, 167
Sons of Temperance, 167
Sorenson, 95, 168
Southwick, 75, 212
Southworth, 220, 221
Sovede, 56, 168
Spangello, 168
Spangler, 2, 29, 38, 168
Spanish American War, 46, 62, 174
Sparkmiller, 212
Spauling, 12, 78, 128, 168
Spear, 42, 50, 168, 174, 184
Spears, 168, 191
Speery, 18, 168
Speigelberg, 100, 168
Spencer, 4, 14, 19, 60, 115, 138, 168, 212
Sperback, 224
Sperbeck, 32, 168
Sperry, 17, 42, 48, 59, 74, 105, 168, 223
Spidel, 177
Spiegelberg, 69, 168
Spofford, 168, 245
Sprague, 145, 212

Spurier, 168
Spurrier, 169
Squires, 169, 212
Stacey, 94
Stada, 169
Stafford, 167
Stahel, 19, 53, 119, 169, 212, 214, 228
Stahiel, 203
Stahl, 169
Stamp, 169, 245
Standiford, 123, 169
Stanley, 87, 89, 107, 169, 223
Stannard, 169
Stant, 212
Stanton, 137, 169
Stantorf, 212
Staples, 35
Stark, 14, 169
Starr, 9
Stattuck, 169
Statzer, 56, 169
Steadman, 221
Steamboat, 7, 8, 28, 29, 35, 37, 58, 70, 74, 91, 107, 125, 128, 170, 183, 191
Steamboats, 71, 169, 170
Stearns, 170
Steble, 245
Steckwest, 155, 170
Steel, 12
Steele, 6, 10, 11, 29, 32, 39, 40, 59, 73, 76, 77, 89, 97, 105, 113, 132, 138, 160, 162, 168, 170, 175, 179, 181, 191, 197, 212, 223
Steenson, 60, 218, 221
Stehl, 212
Stehle, 245
Steinback, 76
Stelting, 42
Stelzman, 165, 198
Stenseng, 161, 170
Steolinson, 170
Stephens, 36, 64, 71, 104, 141, 149, 170, 177, 217, 228
Stephenson, 115, 170
Sterling, 37, 76, 90, 109, 167, 170, 171, 197, 212, 219
Sterns, 76
Stetler, 212
Steuert, 54
Stevens, 17, 45, 57, 61, 62, 71, 92, 95, 105, 126, 140, 166, 171, 172, 218, 219, 221, 223, 224, 245
Stevenson, 9, 12, 60, 172, 212, 217, 218, 219
Stewart, 43, 71, 87, 167, 172, 212
Stickel, 22, 193
Stickels, 172, 245
Stillwell, 146, 172
Stockert, 172
Stoda, 39, 172
Stoddart, 9, 10, 11, 15, 17, 19, 21, 23, 25, 28, 30, 31, 32, 33, 36, 37, 40, 42, 43, 45, 56, 59, 68, 77, 78, 82,
85, 87, 90, 92, 98, 100, 102, 105, 120, 121, 129, 131, 138, 141, 147, 149, 150, 152, 162, 163, 167, 172, 175, 202, 228, 245
Stodke, 69, 172
Stodsvold, 172
Stogdill, 70, 81, 94
Stoll, 172, 212
Stolp, 118, 173
Stone, 173
Storkson, 72, 173
Storm, 35, 173
Story, 153
Stout, 20, 35, 149, 173, 218
Stowel, 60
Stowell, 46, 173
Strait, 93, 173
Stratton, 173, 212
Straw, 245
Strawn, 173
Street, 140, 173
Streeter, 12, 25, 152, 159, 174, 212, 245
Stricker, 221
Stroh, 84, 173
Strong, 173, 174, 212
Strother, 129
Strum, 173, 182
Stuart, 12, 43, 149, 225
Stuckey, 43, 154
Stucky, 201
Stuka, 13, 173
Stunkard, 174
Sturges, 55, 195, 245
Stussy, 5, 174
Sullivan, 174
Sumner, 174, 192
Sunday School Institute, 174
Sutherland, 47, 62, 100, 116, 134, 140, 147, 174, 182, 191, 192
Sutton, 113, 174
Swain, 174, 180, 188
Swan, 132, 167, 173, 174, 175
Sweeney, 42, 123, 175, 212, 223
Sweeny, 175
Sweitzer, 175
Swiber, 75, 175
Swiggum, 175
Swigum, 175
Swingle, 16, 175
Sylvester, 19, 28, 104, 111, 175, 212
Sylvestor, 102, 175
Syverson, 67, 175

T

Tabor, 11, 175, 212
Tadder, 175
Taft, 82, 105, 108, 133, 156, 161, 175
Talcott, 82, 175, 212
Talkuer, 212
Tallman, 212, 225
Tate, 12, 34, 48, 66, 78, 147, 175, 176

Genealogical Events from Newspapers for Crawford, Vernon and Grant Counties, Wisconsin, 1870-1901

Taylor, 28, 40, 63, 68, 70, 71, 119, 125, 137, 159, 164, 166, 167, 171, 176, 177, 182, 203, 212, 214, 217, 221, 228
Teacher Examinations, 176
Teachers Institute, 176, 177
Tedrtch, 177
Teiuce, 177
Telatko, 177
Telfair, 177, 182
Telfer, 219
Temperance Saloon, 51
Temple of Honor, 17, 149, 177
Tenant, 212
Tennant, 24, 177
Tenney, 42, 59, 60, 70, 103, 133, 176, 177, 183, 217, 218, 222, 224
Tennison, 177
Tenny, 177, 183
Terhune, 87, 93, 97, 177
Terrill, 184, 218
Tetter, 154, 177
Tewalt, 35, 60, 177, 180
Tharp, 224
Thayer, 18, 60, 149, 177, 218, 219, 221
Thill, 177
Thoma, 50
Thomas, 25, 43, 60, 71, 167, 177, 178, 212
Thompson, 19, 21, 29, 43, 50, 53, 64, 71, 74, 76, 93, 98, 106, 139, 147, 152, 162, 178, 179, 195, 201, 212, 219, 221, 225
Thomson, 167, 179, 225
Thorp, 12, 13, 179, 184
Thorpe, 52, 179
Thurber, 179
Thurston, 179
Tice, 22, 179
Tichenor, 179
Tier, 179
Tierney, 179
Tilden, 105, 156, 174, 179, 224
Tilford, 29
Till, 58
Tillotson, 24, 112, 168, 179
Tilton, 221
Timermans, 179
Timmerman, 125, 180
Tinker, 75
Tipp, 212
Tippets, 180
Tippett, 180
Tippitts, 148, 180
Tipplets, 103, 180
Tobler, 180
Todd, 180
Tohsh, 104, 180
Tokkleson, 75
Tolish, 104, 180
Tollefson, 147, 184, 218, 221
Tompson, 76, 106, 180, 221
Toms, 137

Toney, 61, 180
Tongue, 71, 93, 180, 221
Tonkfort, 76
Torger, 60, 97
Tormey, 29, 65, 139, 180
Torrey, 71
Tower, 71, 136, 180, 217
Towers, 180
Townsend, 8, 31, 44, 137, 174, 180, 184
Towsley, 82, 180
Traber, 169, 212
Trager, 181
Trague, 212
Trainor, 230
Trainor,, 230
Tramp, 181
Trayer, 146, 181, 226
Treadwell, 181, 197
Treseder, 181
Tresidder, 245
Treuax, 31
Trimin, 68, 69, 148, 172
Trimm, 124, 245
Trollop, 157
Trollope, 167
Trollopp, 212
Troop, 42
Tropp, 212
Trott, 37, 44, 89, 181, 224
Trotts, 71
Trowbeidge, 111, 181
Trowbridge, 39, 94
Truax, 31, 181
Trum, 25
Truman, 212
Trumbower, 170, 181
Trumin, 68, 69, 148, 172
Trunkill, 212
Trycle, 181
Tryon, 181
Tucker, 181, 190
Tuffley, 119, 181, 212, 214
Tull, 32, 38
Tulley, 147, 181
Tulloch, 38, 182
Tupper, 226
Turben, 182
Turk, 212
Turner, 50, 58, 60, 86, 111, 182, 225
Turnmire, 173, 182
Tuttle, 82, 100, 137, 149, 170, 182, 218
Twaites, 182
Twining, 143, 182, 188, 212
Tyler, 19, 182
Tyron, 182

U

Umback, 116, 182
Unclaimed Letters, 182
Underwood, 177, 182

Unger, 182
Unseth, 219, 221
Updike, 139
Upham, 9, 28, 50, 60, 182
Uphan, 60
Utt, 212

V

Vaghlan, 60
Valentine, 67, 80, 143, 183, 185, 191
Vallant, 88, 183
Vallee, 105, 183
Valley, 40, 105, 183
Van Allen, 183, 193
Van Alstine, 183
Van Antwerp, 183
Van Buren, 9, 15, 121, 183, 229
Van Dusen, 183
Van Emberg, 71
Van Fleet, 59, 183
Van Horn, 183, 212
Van Velzer, 183
Van Wagner, 3, 59, 90, 183
Van Wagoner, 16, 29, 42, 105
Van Warner, 213
Van Winter, 3, 147, 183
Van Winters, 148, 183
Van Wormer, 71, 167
Van Wyck, 101
Van Zant, 12, 137, 183, 224
VanBuren, 183
Vance, 60, 182, 183, 184, 213
Vanderbilt, 113, 167, 184, 225
Vanderpool, 123, 184
Vanhorn, 76
VanPhillips, 184
Vanvalkenburg, 184
VanZant, 60
Varnell, 64
Varrell, 64, 139, 184, 194
Vaughan, 15, 65, 213, 225, 245
Vaughen, 167
Vaughn, 2, 162, 184, 213
Veighland, 142
Venest, 229
Venner, 68, 128
Vernon, 147, 184
Vernon Co. Board, 22, 32, 173, 184, 196
Vernon Co. Mutual Protection Soc., 184
Vernon County Democrats, 184
Vernon County Prohibitionists, 184
Verson, 97
Vickers, 213
Viele, 33, 96
Vine, 65, 184
Viroqua Teachers, 184
Viroqua Village Officers, 184
Voegelin, 184
Voicey, 224
Vold, 107, 168
Vollmer, 184

Voss, 184
Vought, 184
Voysey, 50, 70, 157, 217

W

W.C.T.U, 51, 68, 94, 167
W.C.T.U., 51, 68, 86, 121, 149, 167
Wachter, 185
Waddell, 213
Wade, 221
Wadsworth, 25, 185
Wadynxkee, 152, 178
Waggoner, 185
Wagner, 109, 133, 185, 201, 204, 229
Wait, 89, 185, 192, 197
Waite, 167, 185
Waits, 157
Wakefield, 185
Wakeman, 185
Walbridge, 27, 63
Waldron, 42, 50, 74, 185
Walker, 9, 11, 43, 52, 57, 89, 104, 118, 126, 137, 139, 161, 167, 185, 186, 213, 229, 245
Wall, 142
Wallace, 34, 88, 91, 157, 186, 213
Wallar, 31, 151
Waller, 29, 36, 42, 77, 167, 186, 217
Wallin, 76, 176
Walloe, 184
Walsh, 147, 213
Walstrum, 229
Walter, 124, 186, 201
Walters, 5, 131, 177, 186
Walton, 130, 186, 187, 196
Walts, 28
Walworth, 42, 111, 187, 245
Wamberg, 38, 80, 147, 187
Wamburg, 147, 187
Waney, 228
Wannamaker, 64, 187
Wannemaker, 187
War of 1812, 6, 30, 34, 73, 74, 153, 165, 167
Ward, 5, 19, 46, 59, 60, 118, 140, 147, 149, 173, 180, 182, 183, 184, 187, 213
Wareham, 36, 71, 163, 179, 187, 224
Warne, 51, 156, 224
Warner, 109, 112, 156, 187
Warnu, 213
Warren, 23, 89, 150, 187
Washburn, 36, 89, 112, 134, 184, 187, 213
Washington, 187
Wasson, 187
Waters, 169, 177, 187, 213
Watkins, 19, 188
Watrous, 229
Watson, 96, 121, 126, 188, 229
Watts, 28
Waukon, 50, 57, 188
Wayne, 118, 188, 213, 214, 215

Weaver, 64, 213
Webb, 169, 188
Weber, 152, 188
Webster, 39, 176, 188, 245
Weeden, 218
Wegdahl, 188
Wege, 155
Weggins, 131, 188
Wehrley, 139
Weidman, 188
Welch, 113, 188, 213, 225
Welcher, 188
Weldon, 188
Weller, 179
Wellman, 188
Wells, 19, 42, 103, 118, 188, 189, 201, 229, 245
Welsh, 50, 162, 189
Wendle, 63
Wentworth, 189
Wentzel, 64, 189
Wenzel, 47, 64
Wepking, 102, 189
Werner, 189
Wernick, 146, 189, 218
West, 108, 189, 191, 213, 224, 225
Weston, 57, 66, 158
Westphal, 245
Wetmore, 79, 189
Wettie, 147
Wey, 213
Whaley, 119, 167
Wheaton, 126, 213, 245
Wheeler, 19, 35, 189, 213, 214, 228
Whitaker, 189
Whitcomb, 102
White, 29, 36, 42, 46, 51, 54, 59, 70, 74, 86, 115, 145, 181, 190, 213, 217, 218, 221, 224
Whiteaker, 76, 190
Whitelaw, 245
Whitesides, 213
Whiting, 23, 48, 57, 105, 108, 143, 170, 180, 183, 185, 186, 190, 191, 196
Whitmarsh, 191
Whitney, 42, 50, 51, 70, 71, 89, 96, 133, 167, 191, 217, 224
Whitt, 215
Whittaker, 213
Whittemore, 153, 177
Whitting, 8
Whittleton, 11, 213
Whitts, 18, 191
Whitworth, 81
Wiard, 42
Wicken, 21, 23, 191
Wicks, 11, 191
Widmeier, 191
Wiederaendrs, 191
Wiefel, 139
Wier, 191
Wightman, 98, 191
Wigley, 117

Wikinson, 191
Wilcox, 37, 59, 176, 189, 191, 192, 224
Wilder, 136, 192
Wiley, 213
Wilford, 99, 192
Wilharbor, 147
Wilkie, 31
Wilkin, 31
Wilkins, 192
Wilkinson, 78, 134, 147, 174, 191, 192, 213, 219
Wilkison, 192
Willan, 246
Willard, 192
Williams, 11, 59, 73, 96, 108, 109, 111, 129, 133, 177, 184, 189, 192, 193, 213, 221, 224
Williamson, 213, 214
Willis, 19, 22, 60, 178, 179, 193, 194, 204, 213, 228
Willison, 19, 193
Willoughby, 19, 150, 167, 177, 193, 213, 229
Wilmarth, 22
Wilsey, 193
Wilson, 5, 22, 35, 46, 59, 60, 65, 106, 120, 124, 147, 148, 185, 193, 194, 201, 205, 213, 224
Wilt, 70, 184, 194, 224
Wilton, 153
Winayack, 111
Wing, 194
Winkler, 194
Winn, 119, 128, 142, 143, 150, 173, 194, 213
Winnebago, 37, 97, 188, 194
Winnebagos, 51, 72
Winnesheik, 50
Winneshiek Landing, 194
Winney, 194
Winsor, 194
Wintees, 161, 194
Winters, 161, 229
Wirts, 194
Wirtz, 52, 112, 135, 246
Wisdom, 160, 194, 213, 229
Wise, 50, 80, 88, 151, 195, 219, 222
Wiseman, 213
Witcraft, 71, 96, 167, 195, 217
Withe, 195
Withee, 83, 195, 225
Witherow, 213
Withey, 60
Withington, 195
Withrow, 195
Witsic, 213
Wizle, 189
Wizner, 213
Wolcot, 167
Wolcott, 113, 195
Wolf, 64
Wolfe, 139
Wolfing, 55, 195
Wolford, 4

Womens Christian Temperance Union, 51
Women's Christian Temperance Union, 13, 75, 149, 166
Women's Relief Corps, 96
Women's Sufferage, 195
Wonsor, 133
Wonzor, 133, 195, 229
Wood, 43, 76, 146, 147, 178, 184, 195, 213, 214, 219
Woodard, 60, 96, 110, 119, 122, 127, 196, 204, 213, 214, 229
Woodburn, 196
Woodbury, 15, 26, 46, 50, 59, 66, 77, 89, 108, 111, 136, 189, 191, 196, 213, 224
Woodcock, 77, 196
Woodhouse, 72, 171, 196
Woodman, 196
Woodruff, 196
Woods, 138, 196, 213, 230
Woodward, 14, 47, 184
Woolcut, 196
Wooley, 124, 196
Woollery, 60

Woolley, 130, 196, 246
Woolstenholme, 113
Wooster, 213
Wootton, 178
Worden, 64, 141, 169, 197, 213
Worman, 167
Worth, 29, 83, 90, 105, 136, 144, 171, 183, 197, 224
Wright, 38, 54, 81, 102, 175, 197, 213, 246
Wunder, 160, 197
Wunterle, 197
Wurster, 203
Wurstur, 119
Wurtz, 55, 101
Wyant, 80
Wyman, 197, 198
Wynne, 142, 194

Y

Yager, 213
Yakey, 221
Yates, 125, 213

Yeager, 122, 123
Yocum, 72
York, 198, 229
Young, 19, 49, 119, 144, 165, 177, 198, 213, 214, 229
Youngs, 213

Z

Zabolia, 198
Zallman, 229
Zeigelmaire, 198
Zeigelmeyer, 198
Zeiprecht, 42
Zeirfuss, 129
Zens, 3
Zillig, 224
Zillinger, 114, 198
Zitzner, 50
Zobolla, 60
Zollar, 198
Zwicky, 179